The LABRADORIANS

Voices from the Land of Cain

LYNNE D. FITZHUGH

BREAKWATER
100 Water Street
P.O. Box 2188
St. John's, NF
A1C 6E6

Canadian Cataloguing in Publication Data

Fitzhugh, Lynne D.

The Labradorians

Includes bibliographical references and index.

ISBN 1-55081-148-7

1. Labrador (Nfld.) — History.   I. Title.

FC 2193.4 F57 1999   971.8'2   C99-950184-4
F1137.F57 1999

The Canada Council | Le Conseil des Arts
for the Arts | du Canada

We acknowledge the financial support of
The Canada Council for the Arts for our publishing activities.

The publisher gratefully acknowledges the financial support of the Government of Newfoundland and Labrador that has helped to make this publication possible.

We acknowledge the financial support of the Government of Canada through the Book Publishing Industry Development Program (BPIDP) for our publishing activities.

We also wish to thank the Jeanne and King Cummings Charitable Trust, and the Anne Abraham Memorial Fund for supporting this project.

Printed in Canada.

TO ANNE

CONTENTS

PREFACE

WHEN I BEGAN SIFTING THROUGH sixty-odd issues of *Them Days* magazine in 1989 it was with the idea of selecting for a wider readership some of the most colourful stories published in this regional quarterly of oral histories. I found that what I had instead of a simple anthology was the raw material for a social epic, a history of Labrador as it was experienced by the people who have lived there—some of them for thousands of years.

They took control of the project early on, these Labradorians, filling my head with stories until my ears rang with voices. A persistent dream image formed in my mind of the darkly silent Labrador landscape spread out below me, a vast and seemingly uninhabited wilderness. People began to emerge, just a few at first, then more, gathering by cabin doors at the edge of the forest, pulling boats above the tide, leaning axes against woodpiles, drying hands on aprons, talking to me. By nature taciturn, by accident of geography estranged from a world most knew little of, the people of Labrador were telling their story with a sense of urgency I had not heard in my original readings of *Them Days*. The task they had assigned to me, it seemed, was to impose some order on the din and see that this story found the place it deserved in the collective record of human experience on this planet.

The material more or less arranged itself according to places where the people gathered on the landscape: Innu (Montagnais-Naskapi Indians) mainly in the interior; the Anglo-Celtic "liveyers" on the southern coasts, Inuit (Canadian Eskimo) and Moravian Settlers along the north coast, and the great mixed-race trapping clans around Sandwich Bay and Lake Melville. This arrangment became the format for the chapters in the book.

Zooming in closer, it was possible to identify communities on the landscape that shared a section of fishing and trapping grounds, a gene pool, and a common set of memories and yarns. Zooming closer yet, to cove or clearing, the gatherings were of families, generations of them reunited around ancestral homesteads where now only the persistent rhubarb patch on a hummocked bawn signals this was once a place where people lived. Lived by the grace of God in the jaws of a formidable wilderness, and died, most often taking with them to oblivion the stories of the ordeals they survived, the secrets of their own personal courage and pleasure in life, and a piece out of the collective memory of a remarkable race. Were it not for the few voices captured on tape and the memories passed on to grandchildren, there would be nothing but silence, for the modern world has finally reached this country, and the last of her frontiersmen and women are passing away.

My first criteria in selecting narratives for this collection were story, style, and character, especially the narrators'. If it was palpable Labrador talking, it made the cut. Most written articles were omitted, as well as how-to accounts, some excellent but historically superfluous local legends, and stories of the post-Goose Bay generations, since construction of the air base in 1941 and Confederation with Canada in 1949 effectively brought about the end of 'them days'. Within these omitted categories, and indeed all the narratives excluded from this book, is wonderful material for other books.[1]

The narratives have been arranged in regional and family groups to create a profile of the history, lifeways, beliefs, values, and character of the region. As these accounts were never recorded with any such purpose in mind, they make a patchy mosaic. In time, you will begin to sense its shape and coherence and, ultimately, to feel at home among the people.

Labrador dialects are rich with the soft percussiveness of German-laced Inuktitut, of melodic Innuemun,[2] and the lilting patter of old maritime brogues from the British Isles. The vocabulary reflects these influences, so you may find the glossary of local terms and usage at the back of this book helpful. It is not necessary to understand every word, but names are worth noting because they are often the threads that weave stories together. The population of Labrador has always been small and isolated. With careful research one could conceivably reconstruct the whole woodlot of family trees, Aboriginal and Settler, their roots and branches elaborately entwined. These family trees probably would not exceed three hundred in number.

Genealogical recitations with which many Settler accounts begin are important both because of the significance narrators ascribe to origins and the historical information they contain. Unfortunately, these are usually absent from the narratives of families whose European progenitors came before 1835, perhaps because these men perished too soon, or changed their names, or their children were raised by Inuit mothers who spoke little if any English. Or maybe they did not wish to acknowledge or remember their origins. In these cases the name alone survived, indifferently spelled, providing a single imprecise clue for genealogists to track in merchant logs, shipping manifests, and British church registries. There is almost no written genealogical information about Aboriginal families, although José Mailhot has done some excellent research on the Innu, many of whom have retained their traditional histories orally. The Christianization of Aboriginal names during the conversion period effectively eradicated the traces of Aboriginal families in early written records, and the tendency of some Settlers to refer to less Europeanized Inuit by ethnic type rather than personal name has had a corresponding effect in the oral narratives. However, these families have equally rich and venerable histories which, for all their invisibility in the accounts available for this book, remain strong threads in the social fabric of mixed-race Labrador.

Many of the accounts in this book describe life during the first half of the twentieth century. These narrators (most born between 1890 and 1920) had known the early generations of Settlers and historic-period Natives. They also knew one another. Geographic groupings allow you to encounter them as characters moving through each other's stories, since generations that never met in life mingle as freely as neighbors in the multi-dimensional, temporal and spatial environment of isolated communities.

As the pattern of existence in every Labrador community, and indeed, most every family, has the same basic components, a certain redundancy is inevitable in the narratives. I have tried to minimize it by elaborating on different components in each chapter. For example, most Settler families fished in the spring and summer, trapped and hunted in the fall and winter, and experienced the Spanish Influenza of 1918-19, but to degrees varying by community. While there are allusions to these topics in every chapter, the fishery is developed fully in the chapters on the south coast, trapping in that on Lake Melville, and the great Influenza in the Torngat region, where it was most devastating.

With few exceptions, the narratives in this book are transcribed exactly as published in *Them Days*. No alterations have been made in the dialect or wording of sentences,[3] although some adjustments were made in punctuation and spelling of transcriptions. A very few accounts have been shortened, and some by the same narrator excerpted and combined. Occasional citations from the historical record provide what I hope is an interesting counterpoint to the personal stories. Many of these have also appeared in *Them Days Magazine*.

The story of *Them Days* is worth a chapter in itself. Started in 1975 by members of the Labrador Heritage Society concerned that a unique way of life was slipping away undocumented, it has done more than anything else to give the region a sense of pride in its own history and unique character. And it has given us outsiders a more profound understanding of the inhabitants of this "marvelous terrible place"[4] than we could possibly derive from books or artifacts or even years among the people.

Them Days came into being at a time when Labrador's cultural integrity and pride appeared to be disintegrating. Old-timers were disillusioned or bewildered by the changes in their lives. Their children and grandchildren seemed adrift between a culture with no future and a future in which they seemed to have no part. When television reached the country in the late 1970s, the Labradorians could no longer escape the realization that, relative to the world they saw on screen, their beloved country and the lives which they had proudly made with their bare hands, generation by generation, were not only impoverished but irrelevant.

The founding editor of *Them Days*, Doris Saunders, is a Martin from Cartwright whose family belatedly joined the great exodus to Goose Bay in the 1960s. Her mother, Harriet Pardy, was the infant Spanish Flu survivor from Mountaineer Cove of whom you will read in Chapter 4. For nearly twenty-five years, Doris and a handful of dedicated volunteers have collected most of the narratives, manned the office, provided reference services for students of Labrador history, welcomed visiting tourists, transcribed tapes, developed photographs, typeset and laid out issues, serviced subscriptions, raised funds to cover remaining publication and administrative expenses, and created a valuable archive of written and photographic records on Labrador history. Doris's capable daughter Gillian has taken over the administrative and fundraising duties. But the vagaries of public grant funding and below-cost subscription rates have kept the magazine from attaining the kind of financial security a now venerable enterprise should have, especially one which is celebrated across Canada and has contributed so greatly to Labrador's sense of identity.

While the economic dilemma of a people with little control over use of their country's natural resources persists, it can no longer be said that they lack a sense of cultural identity and pride. Much of the credit goes to the resilient spirit of the Labradorians, but some must go to *Them Days*. In recognition of her achievements, Doris Saunders received the prestigious Order of Canada in 1986. She has also earned the affection of her fellow Labradorians from L'anse Eau Claire to Nain.

In 1994 Memorial University awarded Doris an honorary doctor of letters for her contributions to the cultural life of the province. In her convocation address she said:

> *Them Days* came into being because Labrador and its people were not often portrayed honestly in books written about Labrador. I was given an article some years ago written by John Moss, a writer and critic teaching at the University of Ottawa. He wrote, 'For people native to the North—native to any place—landscape is the extension of personal being, as intimate and far-reaching as genealogy. Inuit and Northern Indians have lived within the landscape…as an existential fact.' He went on to explain that for writers from outside, the experience of a place—such as the North—becomes a world made of words, and again I quote, 'almost all those words are devoted to the articulation of alien imperatives and dreams.' Moss said, 'Anyone who features himself in his own narrative, whether implicitly like Mowat, explic-

itly like Peary, or surreptitiously like Stefansson, will inevitably document the landscape and its people as extensions of his own experience.'

Joe Goudie, Mike Martin and others responsible for setting up the Labrador Heritage Society never read John Moss's article, but they knew that so many books written about Labrador went from being quite good to absolute rubbish. And thus an idea for a Labrador book by Labradorians was born. The idea was to let the rest of the world and, in particular, the island portion of our province understand the real Labrador as experienced by the people of Labrador.

Labrador's association with Newfoundland goes back a long way. Before Europeans came, aboriginal people lived in Labrador and on the island of Newfoundland. The aboriginal people on the island were wiped out in one way or another, which meant that Newfoundland started over again, as far as human population was concerned, as an extension of the Old World.

The Natives of Labrador, by that time, were—according to explorers and colonists—Indians and Eskimos. However, their own names for themselves were Innu and Inuit, both meaning 'The People.'

The Labrador Natives went from being people in their own eyes to being ignorant savages in the eyes of the newcomers. Many were killed and others were taken as curiosities to the homelands of their tormentors. When the Labrador Natives tried to defend themselves they were called murderers and thieves.

When the first white men came to Labrador they had to marry native women in order to survive. First they gave their wives Christian names because they looked on Native names as 'heathen' names. Then they forced them to give up whatever they—the white men—considered heathen customs. They could, however, do whatever was necessary to provide comfort for their husbands, such as chewing skins to make clothing. My own great-great-great-grandmother, renamed Susan, was beaten by her husband when he caught her eating raw meat or doing anything else that he considered heathen acts. The children were raised to think of themselves as white and were encouraged to marry whites.

So you see, people who were secure in their identity and who were self-sufficient, were made to feel inferior by the intruders. Women who married white men lost their names.... They were forced to speak a foreign language, and their children were raised to ignore the heritage of their mothers. As a result, many of the descendants of those mixed marriages grew up being ashamed of their Native roots, some totally denying they even had Native roots. Fortunately some—like my great-great-grandmother Lydia

Brooks, then Blake, then Campbell—passed stories on to her children and grandchildren, who passed it on to theirs and so on, until today, and I am now passing those stories on to my grandchildren. . . .

Since the start of Native land claims negotiations, people in Labrador have become very interested in their roots and are accepting the fact that they do indeed have aboriginal roots—and that is good. They are accepting their true identities and will once more become people with pride in their heritage, proud to be The People. . . .

John Moss's indictment of authors whose descriptions of alien cultures are more self-descriptive than perceptive is glaringly, and embarrassingly, evident in the work of virtually all the outsiders who have written about Labrador, however eloquently. I knew from the start that it would be true of any introductions I wrote about these narratives. There is no way around it. Not only did I bring to Labrador a most un-Labradorian optic, I was bringing to this project two decades of my own emotionally charged experiences there. However, my husband and friends convinced me that introductions were necessary to make the narratives in this book accessible to readers from outside the region. Since that was my goal, I agreed to give it a try. Having accepted the responsibility, I have attempted to make the introductions as accurate, concise, and useful as possible and to let my inevitable subjectivity show. I hope these words help set the stage for the real authors of this history, the people of Labrador telling their own story in their own words, just as Doris Saunders and the co-founders of *Them Days* envisioned.

ACKNOWLEDGEMENTS

IT GOES WITHOUT SAYING THAT this book would not exist but for the hundreds of Labradorians willing to share their stories with the readers of *Them Days Magazine*. Nor would it exist without *Them Days* staff, volunteers, and donors for whom this has always been a labour of love. Doris Saunders above all deserves special thanks not only for publishing such an important historical record come hell or high water, but also for her unstinting support of this project. Her generosity in allowing me to use copyrighted material, and her assistance in finding historical information, compiling maps, producing photographs, and proofing drafts has been humbling. She has shared her home with me, made me an honorary member of her family, and extended a friendship I consider among my most treasured possessions.

In addition to providing photographs, Doris also contributed to the illustrations by locating place names in the narratives that are not found on published maps. Her informants included Roland Baikie, Ruby and Pat Cabot, Robert Davis, Stella Fowler, Joe and Horace Goudie, Tom and Pearl Holwell, Chesley Lethbridge, Lawrence O'Brien, Ray Oliver, Janice Penton, and Calvin Poole. Thanks also to Gilbert Hay and Bill Ritchie for supplementing published works by Tony Williamson (1997) and Carol Brice-Bennett et all (1977) identifying Inuit place names on the north coast (see also E. P. Wheeler, "List of Labrador Eskimo Place Names," *National Museum of Canada Bulletin 131,* Ottawa, 1953.).

I would like also to acknowledge some of the people who provided the encouragement and resources necessary for an amateur historian with a demanding full-time job in an unrelated field to complete a project like this. First, of course, there is my archaeologist husband Bill, who has always taken me more seriously than I take myself. He gave me the courage to try to produce historical introductions of academic caliber, shared his Labrador library, read and edited sections on archaeology, and encouraged me when the going got rough. His colleague and our friend Stephen Loring joined in urging me on and gave me access to his private book collection and extensive archive on Labrador history. Tony Williamson reviewed an early draft of the lengthy manuscript and, in addition to providing valuable suggestions for the final draft, became a tireless promoter of the book to potential publishers in Canada. Lynn Noel was also supportive and helpful. Wally McLean, who will someday write the ultimate multi-volume history of Labrador, never hesitated to answer my inquiries. Had we corresponded earlier than the weeks just before this manuscript went to the publisher, it would have been a better book. My son Josh, bless him, is to be thanked for patiently solving my endless computer problems and letting me turn his now-vacated childhood bedroom into 'Labrador South.'

I wish to thank my employers, colleagues, and staff at the Folger Shakespeare Library for their extraordinary indulgence during the four years it took to complete the manuscript. In awarding me a part-time sabbatical (probably the only one in history ever awarded to a fundraiser) and another six months in various leaves of absence, they added considerably to their own workloads and inconvenience. To Werner Gundersheimer and Jane Kolson, thank you for approving these leaves, and Jane for taking on the extra burden of responsibility it entailed. To Jeff Cronin, Matt Hoenck, and Bianca Beckham, thank you for keeping the Corporate and Foundation Relations Office running so smoothly when I was away and for indulging my Labrador enthusiasms when I was present.

Finally, the publisher and I wish to join in thanking the King and Jean Cummings Charitable Trust of the Maine Community Foundation for helping support the publication of this book. Thanks also to the Arctic Studies Center of the Smithsonian Institution for supplementing this contribution with funds collected many years ago in memory of Anne Abraham, whose spirit remains my inspiration and a part of the magic of Labrador.

THE LAND GOD
GAVE TO CAIN

"...it should not be named the Newland, but the land of stones and rocks, frightful and ill-shaped. –Except at Blanc Sablon there is nothing but moss and stunted wood; in short, I dream rather than otherwise that it is the land God gave to Cain."

— Jacques Cartier, 1534

THIS IS A BOOK ABOUT the hard, wild country at the northeastern extremity of the North American mainland called by early European mapmakers *Baccalaos*—motherland of the cod, or *Terre des Esquimaux*, or simply Labrador—"labourer" in Portuguese. No one is certain why or how it got this name. Some say it was that of the seaman who sighted land, or the prospect of harvesting Native slaves. Either way, it was oddly portentous.

This was one of the first-found regions of the New World, but European adventurers thought it so austere that most moved on to more hospitable environments, letting Labrador drift into a forgotten backwater of history under the shadow of Jacques Cartier's unflattering epithet. The few white people who stayed—petty entrepreneurs, hopeful émigrés, loyal tradesmen, fishermen, seekers of solitude or adventure, outcasts and castoffs, the sons of Cain, and the merely destitute—were left to fend for themselves armed with little more than hope for better lives than they had known abroad and a dogged determination to survive from one day to the next. Unable to negotiate a truce with the natural and institutional forces arrayed against them, they faced the same struggle day after day, generation after generation. Unimaginable hardship became normal. So did an unaccountable buoyancy of soul. Perhaps it was introduced by Aboriginal mates, or imported from abroad like the seed of flowers that thrive in poor soil. Perhaps the awesome beauty of this stark land proved more nourishing for the human spirit than Cartier could possibly have imagined from the railing of his ship. Whatever the reason, the Labrador described by its people often resembles Eden more than exile.

Labrador is not a country in the political sense. In 1927 when the governments of Britain and Canada finally troubled to establish a boundary between the Quebec and Labrador sectors of the great Labrador Peninsula, Labrador was assigned to the British colony of Newfoundland, since independence was not an option. But Labrador is a very different country from the island to its south, and in the minds of Labradorians the union has never been consentual. Many consider Newfoundland's relentless exploitation of their resources as tantamount to rape. Some of the Innu feel the same about Euro-Canadians in general, including the métis Settlers who have for so long shared both the landscape and their bloodlines.[1]

As defined by the Boundary Settlement, Labrador is approximately 112,000 square miles of nearly virgin wilderness, an area larger by far than all the British Isles, inhabited by a population that would fit comfortably in a single English fishing town. Them days, before construction of Goose Bay air base in 1941, even before the coming of Europeans and their diseases, the head count is thought not to have exceeded five thousand. Today it is barely thirty thousand, much of it concentrated in the sandy town of Happy Valley-Goose Bay under the shrieking wings of NATO jets, and in the iron-mining towns of Labrador City-Wabush on the Quebec border.

Labrador is a far more arctic land than its almost temperate latitude (51-60°N) would suggest. Its climate is governed by exposure to winds sweeping down from the polar ice fields and by the notorious Labrador Current, which drains the Arctic Ocean. Winter temperatures can drop to minus 60°F, snowfall reach ten feet or more. From January to June a collar of storm-buckled sea ice up to a hundred miles wide hugs the coast, scouring the shoreline bare and consuming whatever mankind has left within reach of its rafting slabs as it tears itself loose in the spring. The sea ice breaks up in May or June, choking fishing grounds and shipping lanes with migratory packs that in a bad year can pin the fishermen in their harbours until August. Once clear, the Current becomes highway for a procession of majestic icebergs on route to their dissolution in the Gulf Stream off the Grand Banks of Newfoundland. It was one of these that took the Titanic.

Summers can be quite warm in the interior and inner bays but cool enough on the coast to render wool caps, gloves, and parkas indispensable. August snow showers and freezing nights are not uncommon on the north coast. The occasional 'T-shirt days' are plagued with hoards of mosquitoes and black flies fierce enough to drive most sentient creatures to the mountain tops, the edge of the sea, or mad. But even on the north coast, some days—maybe two or three a season, maybe a whole week— are so glorious that the insects themselves take a holiday. Then children from the villages flock to favorite swimming ponds, families pack their small boats with plastic buckets and head for the berry islands, and expedition members wander from work sites to find the perfect bathing pool or abandon themselves to the lure of distant hills. These are the days of innumerable solitary epiphanies, days when journals and sketchbooks are pulled from backpacks, thoughts take the shape of poems, and humming tunes rise from the syncopated rhythm of a trapboat engine or weave like a water skier through the harmonics of a 20 hp. outboard.

Labrador's is among the most lethal climates on the continent not because it is the most harsh, but because it is so utterly disarming. The balmy southwest breeze that glorifies a summer morning can slam around in a heartbeat—dark shadows racing across the limpid sea like chills, stripping the skin from the flattened water and hurling it against the land so hard it makes the ledges flute and scream. Within minutes waves are leaping and foaming like a pack of mad wolves on the deepening swells. In October 1885, one of many gales to hit "the Labrador" that fall claimed sixty-four vessels and three hundred souls in about an hour. Even now, people hear the spirits of drowned mariners cry from the shore on stormy nights, and every headland, they say, has its ghost ships, phantom lights on the dark void.

Weather in Labrador is dramatic, capricious, and omnipotent, ruling the lives of residents like a band of outlaw gods. Temperatures in a single day can span sixty degrees, winds spin a full 360, and weather switch in minutes from thickest fog to brilliant sun to driving rain. But there is a terrible beauty in such unfettered wildness—and the sky shows are spectacular: lenticular clouds that drift in from the great bergs like a fleet of space ships; white ice fog that rolls over islands and hills like a heavy blanket, keeping the shapes of the land beneath; evening landscapes chiming with larks and stagelit by the lingering golden dusks of northern summer; double rainbows radiant against the dark back of a retreating storm; burnished sunsets in four acts; northern lights that begin as gently flowing neon curtains and end in storms of pulsating energy fierce as the trumpets of the apocalypse.

From a hilltop surrounded from horizon to horizon by unbroken, unbounded wilderness, the Labrador sky is the biggest, most transparent, wide-open sky imaginable, dwarfing even the Torngat Mountains beneath the fathomless blue of midday. If you let it, it will absorb you, stripping you of perspective and subjectivity until you become whatever you can see, to the farthest humming atoms of the zenith. In a terrain devoid of human frames of reference, you are one moment a giant astride Lilliputian forests of moss and evergreen, the next a micro-speck on a speck of a planet adrift in a dizzying void. In the brief deep blue nights of summer, stars hang in a three-dimensional space like tiny crystals, so close you want to reach among them with both hands and set them tinkling.

Sound travels like light in the thin clear air of a northern country without noise, and you begin to hear whatever you can see—like fog and auroras—and feel what you cannot see or hear, like tension building in a distant berg about to calve. The poof! of a lazy whale blowing as he rolls far out in the bay ricochets across the water, sharp and immediate as the rock beside you. The scrabbling traffic of insects in the understories of the tundra, the hum of mosquitoes outside a cabin, become discernible elements of silence on a windless afternoon. These qualities of atmosphere and space—clarity, purity, majesty—are perhaps what pass as beauty here. It is so seductive many visitors find it difficult to shake off, and the people who have made this their home can rarely be induced to leave. It has become part of their souls, whether Aboriginal or Settler, and of the culture that binds them together, willingly or not.

Cartier can be forgiven his hasty judgment because there is probably little on this earth less seductive than the coastline Labrador presents to the sea. Rocky and barren from one end to the other, much of it is aggressively mountainous, rising in elephantine promontories from a snarling surf. Island clusters near the bays and capes are guarded by myriad razor-backed shoals. Even today there are few navigational markers, and one threads these archipelagos with a sharp eye on the water. Arctic seas are much like the sky, even to the nocturnal galaxies of phosphorescent plankton that sparkle in the wake of a passing boat. Although dense with cold, the bottle-green water is clear enough by day to reflect light off a sinking penny at six fathoms. But when the visibility is poor, the best mariners in Labrador have run afoul of her submerged rocks. Ships large enough to take the full brunt of the North Atlantic keep well outside the islands between their ports of call.

For smaller boats, the archipelago provides an infinite number of excellent harbours and access both to the ice edge where marine mammals congregate in winter and to what was once among the most abundant sources of marketable protein known to man—the great tide of Atlantic codfish that came to feed along the coasts of Labrador each summer. Inuit seal hunters frequented the islands long before white men arrived. Later they became staging grounds for a codfishery that attracted fleets from England, France, Portugal, Spain, America, Quebec, Nova Scotia and, most of all, Newfoundland to the Labrador Banks each summer. Today they are all but deserted.

Anyone fortunate enough to visit the archipelagos of Labrador will find an array of landscapes and adventures worthy of Odysseus. One island has a cove that winks with multicolored eyes of iridescent Labradorite.[2] Another yields a yawning shaman's cave near a bald hilltop where three human stick figures sketched in lichen-crusted stones stare into space with large round eyes. Yet another has a lush hidden valley ringing with birdsong, and a sun-warmed rain pool atop a cliff where one can bathe within arms reach of breaching whales. Another has an arctic hare that holds its ground, big and bony as a goat, its eye too certain for a beast. Tolkien himself could not have invented a more enchanted universe.

Island and coastal hills alike were sculpted in the conflict between the continent's upwelling crust and seaward-moving glaciers. On summits and promontories rubbed smooth as the backs of ancient pachyderms by the elements, rain pools mirror sky from ice-carved pits and cracks, and the hills are littered with the glacier's cargo of boulders spalled from inland bluffs. Hillsides today weep all summer with melting permafrost, and eternal snowbanks in high, sunless clefts feed rivulets that nourish bank-side thickets of fern and willow. In the coastal valleys, streams tumble from pond to boggy pond, pure as moss-filtered arctic rain can be and variable in flavour as fine wines.

Inland far as the frigid breath of the Labrador Current holds sway—at least several miles in most places—the land is mantled in tundra. During its brief summer, this nappy coat is as lush as a Persian carpet, an infinitely variable tapestry of colour and texture in elegant combinations, busy with insects, spicy as Christmas air, springy-firm underfoot—a joy to the walker. By September it has intensified to blazing reds and orange, palest sage and darkest green, everywhere imbedded with colourful berries that make a pre-winter feast for bird and beast and wonderfully savory pies.

This exquisitely minimalist vegetation is also useful. Radiant tufts of cottongrass that nod in the marshes once served as wicks for Inuit lamps; sphagnum moss and rotten stump wood became diapers, menstrual pads, and chinking or insulation for log cabins. Labrador tea, dwarf juniper, larch, birch, alder, willow, spruce, and fir provided Labradorians with the active ingredients for infusions and antiseptic salves. Tundra sods made thick, cold-proof walls and roofing for Inuit huts. Scurvy grass, rich in vitamin C, revived sailors after a long voyage. The local beach or sweet grass (*Elymus arenarius*) was dried, dyed, and fashioned into delicate baskets and warm insoles for skin boots. Edible plants like Scotch lovage, sweet cecily, dock, fireweed, roseroot, angelica, puffballs, and delicious boletus mushrooms grow near shore—as do the poisonous amanitas and deadly hemlock. Berries have always been an important winter staple for Labradorians, and the mats of crowberry (*Empetrum nigrum*)—roots, soil, and all—are what impart to Labrador-smoked fish a flavor unrivaled by any commercially available product. In fact, like much of Labrador's gourmet fare—among which I count above all else the common red-fleshed arctic trout, wild Atlantic salmon and salmon roe, bakeapples (cloudberries), redberries (lingonberries), the tiny ground-hugging blueberries, mussels, soft-shell clams, and the liver of the bedlamer seal—it is hard to find outside the region.[3]

The shoreline itself is incised with bays fed by rivers off the high inland plains. The longer ones cut deep into the forest zone, but others too have been colonized by thickets of spruce, birch, and larch that spill down the river valleys toward the sea. In sheltered places one can still find hoary old-growth trees over thirty inches in diameter and a hundred feet tall. These watersheds were home bases to the Innu bands that travelled seasonally between hunting grounds at the headwaters and summer fishing camps at the river mouths. They became the main resource areas for Settler families, who wintered at the mouths while their men trapped the upstream valleys and highlands.

Behind its rim of hills, the interior of the Labrador Peninsula is a rolling plateau nearly two thousand feet above sea-level, a vast wilderness strung with lakes, rivers, beavered ponds, and emerald bogs set amid legions of shoulder-to-shoulder spruce, erect as bayonets against the sky, their branches knit together stiff and unyielding as barbed wire. This is *Nitassinan*, the Innu's homeland and hunting ground. Over much of this land, the forest parts only for fire, rock, or water, but the network of waterways is so extensive that one can traverse the entire Peninsula in almost any direction without a portage longer than five miles.

On the hilltops and northward, where the country begins to point towards the Arctic Circle, the forest is overpowered by the elements and breaks rank, fanning out across pale carpets of caribou moss, backing to the wind, crouching in sheltered crannies and, finally, prostrating itself altogether in the warp and weft of the tundra. In the desolation of far northern Labrador, nothing remains of the mighty spruce but pale green rings of wind-blown pollen around the rain pools. Over six thousand years have passed since the continent's mile-thick mother glacier retreated from this, its final stronghold, plowing long U-shaped fjords into the sea through an Archaean bulwark five thousand feet high. In all that time, the threadbare veil of moss and lichen has barely begun to cover her tracks across bedrock that is among the oldest on the planet. This is the land of Torngak and Te-pe-nam-we-su, the deer god of Inuit and Innu. From its mountain fastness a great flood of caribou—called "deer" by all Labradorians—is said to have spilled each year across the high barrens and into Nitassinan.[4] The George River caribou herd, recovered at last from two centuries of over-hunting and massive loss of feeding areas to forest fires, is now the largest in the world.

Mountainous northern Labrador is a terrifying, fanged, decaying land, abode of the Inuit's dark spirits and seemingly every other malign god banished from the world of modern man. Yet even here, the guileless pink faces of the river beauty nod beside crumbling boulders, and nesting phalaropes spin giddily in the high ponds, coralling a meal of water bugs. Even here, ancient tent rings mark the places where people found some narrow purchase for their families, places where stories were told and love was made under the radiant aurora.

Europe's earliest armchair explorers reflected high expectations for Labrador in their maps, but most storm-weary mariners gave her comfortless shores a wide berth. In point of fact, for all its subtle charms and seeming abundance of forest, fish, and wildlife, the country is no more generous than her initial visage suggests. She exacts a high price for her resources, which took many thousands of years to accumulate and are not readily renewable. The history of human settlement, whether by Aboriginals from the West or Europeans from the East, must be read with that in mind, and with enormous admiration.

Since 1968 my husband has led a team of archaeologists in search of information about the aboriginal peoples of Labrador. He and his colleagues now believe that occupation began about nine thousand years ago on the heels of the last ice age. The first inhabitants appear to have been a vigorous branch of seafaring North American Indians who painted themselves in red ochre and buried their dead in headland mounds with spectacular ceremonial tool kits and panoramic views. The Maritime Archaic Indians had Labrador to themselves for over four thousand years, a longer residency than any single culture since. Evidence suggests it was warmer then than now.

The Maritime Archaic vanished from Labrador when the climate chilled and foreigners appeared—a new Indian culture from the southwest, and the first small bands of proto-Eskimo from the north. Archaeologists call the paleoeskimo culture Pre-Dorset. Like the Innu and Inuit after them and the Maritime Archaic before, they may have called themselves "the People." They hunted sea mammals on the edge of the winter ice as well as deer in the interior. Their houses, soapstone lamps, and tools are small and refined, their dwelling places few and far between. They left little behind.

About the time of Christ, the Dorset Eskimo, named for the Baffin Island cape where their culture was first identified, began moving into Labrador along the same route. Reputedly large and peaceable, giants some say, their feats of strength may survive in the tales of the Tunit that Inuit still tell their grandchildren. Among other things, we know they hunted sea mammals, carved exquisite figurines in soapstone, and lived in skin tents and semi-subterranean sod huts with well-made stone foundations. Dorset culture vanished around 1500 AD, replaced by the aggressive, whale-hunting Thule Eskimos, named for an archaeological site in Greenland. With their skin boats, dogsleds, and advanced maritime technologies, the Thule were well equipped for life in the eastern Arctic. As they spread down the coasts of Labrador and Greenland, they encountered and possibly exterminated the last of the Vikings and watched with apprehension as European sails again began to approach the New World two centuries later. The present-day Inuit of both continents are their cultural descendants.

In southern and interior Labrador, the Maritime Archaic Indians were succeeded by other proto-Algonquian cultures, some of which shared interior and coastal regions with their Pre-Dorset and Dorset contemporaries. The present-day Innu seem to have emerged from the last of these Indian groups concurrently with the arrival of the Thule Eskimo from the north. By this time the Innu lived almost exclusively in the interior, while the Thule and their Inuit successors kept mainly to the sea-coast. In spite of having had economic and spiritual ties with Europeans since the sixteenth century, the Montagnais Innu of southern and western Labrador, like their Naskapi (Mushuau, or barren-ground, Innu) cousins to the north, managed to retain many of their traditional lifeways well into the third quarter of the twentieth century.

The last of North America's aboriginal people to leave the bush, the Innu of Labrador are still finding the transition painful and disorienting.

Until the arrival of Europeans, Labrador's human populations were kept in check less by inadequate food resources than by temporary vagaries of game populations and climate, a dangerous terrain, and the limitations of their technology. It is not even clear that the Inuit's reputed propensity for bloodshed, and Innu-Inuit conflicts over access to coastal resources predated European contact. Infectious diseases were virtually unknown, and neither Aboriginal group had the means or inclination to exterminate even vulnerable game species like the Great Auk so quickly dispatched by Europeans. As a result, white explorers found fish as thick as black flies near the shore, bears by the dozens feeding on the spawning salmon, and hillsides alive with deer. Labrador was a veritable garden in this respect, and our species remained an integral part of its ecology as long as our harvests did not exceed what the land and sea could annually renew.

Norsemen cruising the coasts of Labrador in 1000 AD would have encountered the precursors of the Innu whose culture has been named "Point Revenge" by archaeologists. They may also have met Beothuks, Late Dorset or, by 1400 AD, Thule Eskimos and Innu. It is difficult to say precisely which groups peopled the Sagas, as they were all indiscriminately called *skraelings*, a term roughly equivalent to 'savages.' Although there was some trade and perhaps even linguistic influence as suggested (at least to a non-linguist) by Inuit place names like -vik, the meetings were often unfriendly, and atrocities were committed on both sides. The most illustrious victim on record, Leif Eriksson's brother Thorvald, has long taunted would-be discoverers from a hidden coastal grave near a "west-flowing river" supposedly on the coast of Labrador, which was called Markland by the Norse. When John Cabot and his son Sebastian re-discovered Newfoundland and Labrador (and thereby North America) in 1497, the last of the Vikings were but recently gone from the western Atlantic.[5]

Neither the Cabot voyages in 1497 and 1498, nor the Natives they brought home as potential slaves, nor the tales of codfish so thick they hindered navigation, inspired King Henry VII to pursue England's claim to the Newlands. For the next two centuries official England remained obsessed only with locating a northern passage to the riches of Cathay. In 1586 explorer John Davis poked his bow into Tasiujatsuak Bay, later known as Voisey's Bay (Emish by the Mushuau Innu), describing the "very fayre woods on both sides" and the abundance of fish and game. Several days later he discovered the Labrador Banks, to which he escorted a fleet of British fishing ships the following year. But Davis was disappointed by his failure to reach a Northwest Passage and never appreciated that the annual harvest of cod from the Labrador and Grand Banks would ultimately have an economic impact far greater than the China trade, for it sustained the working classes on whose backs the empires of Europe were built. George Weymouth and John Knight followed Davis in 1602 and 1606 respectively. Knight was slain by Inuit upon landing to repair his ship near Nain. Like Frobisher, Hudson, Button, and Gibbons, Britain's finest invariably headed for Hudson's Straits, paying scant attention to the ragged land off their portside rail. The seamen of Bristol who followed Davis to the Labrador Banks seem to have been less shortsighted.

Sixteenth-century references to English fishing ships on the Labrador are sparse and off-hand, but it is more than likely that the captains engaged in this profitable enterprise, preferring wealth to glory, simply cloaked their trans-Atlantic ventures in secrecy. The probability of inscription in England's endless wars with France and Spain would have offered further incentives for silence, as even before Shakespeare's time the Crown considered the fisheries, particularly the small English fleet sponsored by Bristol merchants that began working the banks off Newfoundland in the early sixteenth century (if not before), to be the principal source of experienced mariners and ships for the English Navy. Conscription was seldom voluntary.

Azorian-Portuguese brothers Gaspar and Miguel Corte-Real sailed the Labrador and Newfoundland coasts in 1500, 1501, and 1502, followed soon after by Portuguese, Basque, and Breton fishing vessels. Basques and Bretons immediately established shore stations on the Labrador side of the Strait of Belle Isle. The port of Brest, erected at Old Fort Bay around 1504, reportedly served a large volume of traffic to the New World throughout the sixteenth century, although the absence of building remains suggests that it was little more than a garrisoned harbour.

While Portugal and France took an early lead in the Newfoundland and Labrador fishery, most nations regarded the Newlands as England's by right of discovery, and the minority British fleet held sway in any harbour on the coast in which it had a presence. While France planted its flags along the Gulf of St. Lawrence, Britain established stations on the island of Newfoundland, which Sir Humphrey Gilbert officially accessioned for the Crown in 1583 to reinforce Cabot's ambiguous and by then suspect claim. The port of St. John's rapidly eclipsed Brest as the principal staging ground for the multinational North American fishery. Later, the island of Fogo and the old Basque port of Carpunt (now Quirpon) off the northeast tip of Newfoundland joined St. John's as bases for English trade in Labrador. While Newfoundland served as a bargaining chip in the duels between England and France for two centuries, the Avalon Peninsula and Conception Bay around St. John's remained definitively British by occupation and usage. Settlement began in that area as early as 1610.

Within decades of discovery, the Newfoundland and Labrador fisheries had made both Portugal and the Norman city of Rouen wealthy. It was also taking such a high toll in boats and lives (including both Corte-Real brothers) that in 1541 the King of Portugal withdrew his financial support for these voyages. Portuguese captains who continued to cross the Atlantic did so at their own considerable risk and expense. As the number of Portuguese voyages declined, those from other European countries increased, and with them the skill of the seamen and boatbuilders engaged in this demanding enterprise. The North Atlantic fisheries did, in fact, play a significant role in the development of the great European navies. Notwithstanding Britain's low profile in the annual migration to the American Banks, her victory over the Spanish Armada in 1588 was no coincidence.

Basque mariners pursuing the whales that ran through the Strait of Belle Isle established shore posts for rendering blubber in "Buttes" (Red Bay), Pinware, Pleasure Harbour, Cape Charles, and Henley Harbour.[6] Skilled seamen though they were, the Basques went down with Portugal and Spain in the Armada and their trans-Atlantic fisheries declined. Red-roofed storehouses, galleons, iron vats, tankards, pipes, plates, and even fellow countrymen were abandoned. A century later, when European shore posts of any substance were again attempted in the eastern Straits, the only visible traces of the Basque outposts were sea-worn roof tiles among the beach stones and the thick tufts of grass and fireweed that luxuriate in the footprints of ancient dwellings. Recent evidence suggests that a few vessels continued to harvest Labrador's whales until around 1640, and others returned to the French shores of the Gulf in the eighteenth century, but the era of the Basques in North America had ended. This venerable nation-less people had lost the opportunity to establish a country of their own in the New World.

The Dutch also took Labrador whales and were probably the first to engage in a floating trade with the Inuit in the seventeenth century. They garnered little in the way of useful products, as Inuit were not in the practice of spontaneously stockpiling goods marketable in Europe. However, Dutch descriptions of the native people and rough charts of the coast made valuable contributions to Labrador's ethnography and cartography. As navigational charts improved and became more widely available, ships from virtually every maritime nation in Europe gave at least an arms-length glance at this strange, forbidding territory.

It was the one-time Breton fisherman from St. Malo, Jacques Cartier, who, on entering the St. Lawrence River as captain of his own boat in 1532, first claimed the wild Canadian mainland for a European country, a claim the English did not immediately trouble to dispute. By 1600, French ships accounted for some two hundred of the 350 European vessels reported on the Newfoundland-Labrador fishing grounds each summer. Unlike England, which was ambivalent about settlement in her Canadian colonies, France actively promoted it. The first French families began clearing land near what is now Quebec City around 1620 . By the end of the century, small French farmsteads clustered around all the King's Posts west of Mingan on the Gulf, and there were sealing stations as far as the St. Augustine River near the entrance to the Strait of Belle Isle.

Management of the King's Posts and eastern seigneuries alternated between government representatives and private lessees operating under government contract. All were subject to the King's policies regarding fair and respectful treatment of the

Innu, who were viewed as potentially equal citizens of France. Stewards of the posts were instructed to encourage the work of missionaries among their affiliated Innu bands, outlaw or discourage the distribution of alcoholic beverages, trade fairly, and allow distribution of goods on credit. At the same time that France was developing the fur trade and exploiting marine resources, it promoted agricultural colonization as a way to solidify French claims to the territory and create a self-sufficient local economy.

It was during a period when the King's Posts were leased to well-connected private entrepreneurs that development spread into Labrador. In 1702 the King granted a seigneurial holding of all lands between Bradore and Hamilton Inlet to Augustin Legardeur, Sieur de Courtemanche. His station at Bradore—Fort Pontchartrain— served as the base for the first French trading operations into Labrador and a southern destination for Inuit seeking opportunities to obtain European goods by trade or theft. We know from historical accounts that the post was fortified, and archaeologists have uncovered foundations of over two hundred buildings. Courtemanche's stepson Brouague tried to promote goodwill between his people and the Inuit, but there was little one man could do to stop what had by then become a full-blown ethnic war.

For 250 years the Inuit of Labrador had witnessed the annual parade of sails on the horizon and spars in outer island harbours from a wary distance. They had learned early that whites could not be trusted, and sporadic European attempts to amend the transgressions of their predecessors had little effect. By the eighteenth century, ship captains on official missions usually forbore insults to the native people, but the fishermen, whose vulnerability to attack was great and whose qualms about killing 'heathen savages' were minimal, are said to have shot Inuit on sight. In open warfare with fishermen, Inuit cunning gave them the advantage, even over firearms. Raiding parties allegedly made a sport of ambushing the shore posts at night or under the cover of fog, terrifying the fishermen with their war cries and making off with abandoned boats and iron implements. Anyone who remained to defend them was killed. So fearsome did the Inuit's reputation for violence become that it effectively inhibited development of shore stations north of the Straits until the 1740s, by which time the Inuit's preference for European iron and boats too dearly acquired in raids had begun to erode their independence.[7]

As long as Canada's more hospitable regions rewarded the burgeoning population of entrepreneurs and fishing fleets, there was little incentive for them to challenge determined aboriginal defenders for a land as "worthless" as Labrador. No one even bothered to draw boundary lines on the evolving map of Canada until the 1660s, when proprietors of Nouvelle France, on finally reaching Hudson's Bay from the south, discovered that the newly chartered British "Company of Adventurers" was already established in the Bay. But even when the nasty war over "Rupert's Land" ended in 1713 with the Company firmly in control of its territory to the west, jurisdiction over Labrador remained not only unresolved but essentially uncontested. In 1752, a group of English merchants petitioned for a grant of the country called Labrador "not at this time possessed by any of His Majesty's subjects or the subjects of any Christian Prince."[8] The Hudson's Bay Company (HBC), fearing that bases there would be used to poach on its territory, tossed off a perfunctory objection on the grounds that its original charter included most of the peninsula, an assumption eventually dispelled by the Lords of Trade. In any case, none of these British parties seemed aware that the traders and sealers of Nouvelle France had by then been active in the Terre des Esquimaux for decades.

Permanent French settlement of the Gulf Coast reached the Strait of Belle Isle around 1715, when Sieur la Vallee Constantin, active in concessions on both sides of the Straits for nearly two decades, established outposts at what is now West St. Modeste and Pinware, and at L'anse au Loup several years later. Sieur Antoine Marsal's concession at Charles River, established in the early 1730s, was the end of the line. Beyond it lay the forbidding 'Land of the Esquimaux.' For nearly two centuries after the Inuit threat subsided, Cape Charles remained the boundary between the Labrador Straits, with its Old World/Newfoundland orientation, and the wilder lands beyond, where the mixed-race culture that evolved was unique, the orientation internal, and the outside world little more than a rumor.

While fur trade with the Innu was conducted at many of the French posts in the Straits, most were headquarters for fishing, whaling, and especially sealing operations, employing men and women who would begin to settle not only the shores of what is now eastern Quebec, but also the southernmost harbours of Labrador. New Englanders quickly dominated the whaling industry, taking seals and walrus as well, and there were always vessels from Nova Scotia among the offshore fishers. During the Napoleonic Wars, they infiltrated some of Labrador's prime salmon streams. But as settled residents of the coast, the French were able to specialize in the seal fishery, which is best conducted in the spring and fall from stationary posts. The French period in Labrador (1702-1763) is therefore characterized by year-round rather than seasonal establishments.[9]

In 1734 Sieur Jean-Louis Fornel of Quebec, already sealing in southern Labrador, asked the French Crown for rights to operate in Baie des Esquimaux—Hamilton Inlet. His petition again refers to Marsal's post as the frontier beyond which "no one, previously, had ventured near shore" for fear of the Inuit. Fornel leased Louis Bazil's post at Chateau in 1736 and, in 1742, finally obtained a concession for the Baie.

Primarily hoping to capitalize on the abundance of seals in Hamilton Inlet and on the access Lake Melville offered to the hunting grounds of the northern Innu, Fornel also hoped to initiate trade with the Inuit.[10] In 1743 he sailed to Ivuktoke, their southernmost homeland in the narrows of Hamilton Inlet, claimed the Baie des

Esquimaux for Nouvelle France, and left a small crew with Innu guides on shore to establish stations.[11] Within the next few years Fornel erected what are probably the first outposts at all Lake Melville's principal salmon and trapping rivers, including North West River and Rigolet. After his death in 1745, Fornel's widow, Marie-Anne Barbel, assumed management of the Esquimaux Bay concessions. These endured, if not thrived, for another decade, evidently spared the barrage of Inuit raids to which the coastal outposts were subjected at this time.

In 1756 the European conflict known on this side of the Atlantic as the French and Indian War allegedly brought commercial activity in Labrador to a halt. For the next seven years the reportedly peaceable Innu, deputized by the French, used guns to further the territorial aims of their allies while dominating old rivals—the Iroquois to the west (allies of Britain) and the Inuit of Labrador, whose access to firearms was still limited. The Labrador coast as far north as Nain is peppered with "Battle Harbours" and "Massacre Islands" dating from this period. In their conflicts with the Innu, the fearsome Inuit were more often victims than aggressors. Scattered skulls with bullet holes confirmed survivors' tales of genocide on an Ivuktoke island around 1760, just a few years after a legendary slaughter at Battle Harbour and others near Nain. These assaults conspired with European diseases to hasten the demise of the southern Inuit during the eighteenth century. By the time the French and Indian War ended, only a few Inuit families remained near the outposts their people had established during the seventeenth century at Bradore, Cape Charles, and Sandwich Bay. They (and northern kin who gravitated toward the southern trading centers between 1780 and 1850) were gradually absorbed into the advancing Settler population.[12] Their influence is still discernible, however, in the features of families from Fox Harbour, Indian Tickle, and Sandwich Bay. Their technologies, transhumance lifestyle, and many characteristic social behavoirs and customs infused Settler culture south as far as St. Augustine, just as it did in northern Labrador.

With the Treaty of Paris in 1763, Canada officially became English—almost three centuries after John Cabot planted the British flag on her shores. Before the ink was dry on the treaty, a handful of gentlemen merchants, seeing profits and adventure in the long-disdained territory of Labrador, hastened to stake their claims on the land. Almost immediately, those bearing grants from the Crown would find themselves in fierce competition with aggressive firms already established in Newfoundland as well as with French Canadians holding long-standing title and grants to the same stations. Their legal suits would lead the governors of Quebec and Newfoundland in a forty-odd-year tug of war over jurisdiction of the Labrador coast. However, before resolving international disputes, the first priority must be to subdue what remained of the nettlesome "Esquimaux Indians." By happy coincidence, a band of Inuktitut-speaking Moravian brethren from the Greenland Missions were petitioning to establish stations among the Labrador Inuit. If these instruments of God could accomplish what guns and fortifications had not, the authorities reasoned, the temporary sacrifice of as yet unvalued "Crown lands" would surely prove a worthwhile investment.

The Moravian Church—or *Unitas Fratrum*—was part of the reformist tide that sprang from fifteenth-century Bohemia and, forced underground and westward, seeped across Europe nourishing the seeds of reformation. By the time Luther nailed his "ninety-five theses" to the church door, the sect had a quarter-million members. While fading into obscurity in the Old World, where it retained a tenuous footing in England and Germany, it became an important agent in the spread of Christianity to Protestant colonies during the eighteenth and nineteenth century, notably in Greenland, the Caribbean, Oceania, and Alaska. Work among the Inuit of Greenland had inspired Brother Jean Christian Erhardt to attempt a mission in unknown Labrador in 1752,[13] when Inuit hostility to whites was at a peak. Failure of this impulsive enterprise, in which Erhardt and seven of the shore party (none of whom spoke Inuktitut) were presumably martyred by Natives, only strengthened the resolve of other missionaries determined to execute a more carefully planned attempt, this time by men able to communicate with the subjects of their mission.

In 1764 a company of ships embarked from England carrying many of the principal players in the development of modern Labrador: Governor Hugh Palliser;[14] Moravian missionary Jens Haven; Captain James Cook; and possibly Lieutenant Francis Lucas, who would briefly join the first British merchant adventurers on the coast and play a seminal role in the northern Inuit's acceptance of the Moravians. The expedition was a stupendous success. The governor conceived his plans for development of the country as a British fishery from which would come the manpower and expertise for the Royal Navy; Captain James Cook and his associate Michael Lane began surveys of the coast which, when published in *The North American Pilot*, would remain the principal guide for navigation in these waters until the twentieth century; and Brother Haven befriended a group of Inuit travelling on the northern peninsula of Newfoundland who were delighted at his knowledge of their language and would not forget him.

The following year, Jens Haven returned to Labrador with brethren Christian Drachardt, John Hill, and Christian Schlozer to further the goal of establishing a mission. While Governor Palliser was impressing upon the British fishing fleets the consequences awaiting anyone who violated the civil rights of native peoples, Drachardt negotiated a treaty with the Inuit at Chateau Bay. Within three years these initiatives effectively brought the Euro-Inuit war in Labrador to a close. Britain could now proceed with exploitation of marine resources, and the Moravians could embark on their great social experiment with some hope of success.

Labrador's history as a colonial region begins at this moment and immediately split along divergent paths, one dedicated to exporting Labrador's resources for profit overseas, the other to importing European social values and structures. While central and southern Labradorians would develop a society in the absence of external institutions, law, or government, the Inuit of northern Labrador would be encompassed by the protective embrace of a totally alien religious community.

Within a decade of their arrival on the coast in 1771, the Moravians had established stations at Nain, Okak, and Hopedale and laid out the institutional foundations for a European social order—schools, a peer judicial system, churches, community rituals and seasonal festivals—all explicitly devoted to the spiritual, not the material, improvement of the Inuit. While the psychological and, ultimately, the economic price of membership in these paternalistic communities was high, their contributions to modern Labrador cannot be overstated. Among other things, they were responsible for the preservation of secular cultural attributes such as the Inuit language and material culture, and the fact that many Inuit who left the stations for an independent life among the early Settlers brought literacy (albeit Inuktitut) and Christian social values into the mixed population.

By contrast, southern and central Labrador developed entirely in relation to outside mercantile interests whose sole objective was the exploitation of marketable resources and, in time, of a captive resident population. In the almost complete absence of governmental stewardship, this would not change for over 150 years. Settlers and Natives alike lived in isolated locations with no access to education, justice, police protection, medical care, political representation, spiritual and religious instruction, financial assistance, or social life but what they brought with them and made, or what was offered by occasional itinerant missionaries and a few uncharacteristically supportive merchants.

The story of Labrador's early mercantile firms is dramatic and colourful enough for a book of its own. Because the origins of the first Settlers reflect the recruiting practices of these companies, the records of their operations hold the keys to the country's European genealogies, as well as references to some of the Native people who dealt with those firms. First to arrive after the Treaty of Paris were British gentlemen adventurers already active in Newfoundland, like Nicholas Darby (father of the famous English actress Perdita), who had a base in St. John's; the West Country firm of Noble & Pinson, also out of St. John's and Conche; John Slade & Company of Fogo and Twillingate; and Jeremiah Coghlan, whose base like Slade's was on Fogo Island. All four appear on the Labrador side of the Strait in 1765, sealing, furring, and fishing.

Coghlan began his Labrador sealing operation in Chateau Bay and within four years had established a settlement at Cape Charles. Darby took over the old Marsal post on the Charles River from the Quebec partnership of Bayne and Brymer. There he hoped to employ Inuit in a whaling operation—hopes which were dashed two years later when Inuit reportedly destroyed his establishment and killed three of his men in misdirected retaliation against a random attack by American whalers.[15] The youthful Lieutenant Lucas, under orders from Governor Palliser, responded to this breach of treaty by assaulting the camp of an Inuit band presumed to have perpetrated the raid, killing at least twenty and taking a young woman named Mikak, her seven-year-old son, and another youth captive to England in 1768. Mikak remained in England through the winter of 1768-9 as Lucas's charge and, some have speculated, his lover. In any case, they learned each other's languages. She was popular at court and often saw Brother Jens Haven of the *Unitas Fratrum*, whose kindness and knowledge of Inuktitut won her friendship. Lucas was lost on the Labrador sea in 1770 soon after joining Captain George Cartwright in a partnership with Jeremiah Coghlan. Some reports claim he died seeking Mikak, who had remarried. Lucas actually went down with his ship on its return to England the following fall.

In 1771, Mikak and her then-husband Tuglavina persuaded a large company of Inuit to welcome Jens Haven and his fellow Moravians to Nain on the north coast of Labrador, an area used mainly by the Nonynoke Inuit. The couple helped the missionaries found their first station but stopped short of accepting Christianity and its implicit denigration of Inuit values and pride. Like many of the Inuit, whose pragmatism is a defining attribute, Tuglavina was keenly interested in the material advantages to be gained from whites and assumed the Mission would play the role of merchant on the north coast. When this assumption proved false—the Moravians being at first adamantly opposed to trade—he himself took on the function of middleman between the northern Inuit and the southern merchants. Cartwright's journal for the year 1785 records the visits of Tuglavina and Mikak to his post in Sandwich Bay. Tuglavina returned to Nain and converted to Christianity before his death. His descendants soon became leaders of the Moravian congregation and still live in the town. Mikak remained in Ivuktoke until 1795, when she too returned to die unconverted in Nain. Her Ivuktoke descendants, named in honor of Newfoundland's first governor Hugh Palliser, who had sponsored the peace treaty, became prominent members of the small southern Inuit band and mixed-race population of Hamilton Inlet. The Palliser name survives in Rigolet and Happy Valley. Mikak's last husband (or young namesake), Pualo, later anglicized as Paulo, shows up on Slade & Company's Battle Harbour ledgers in 1795. His family became part of the Fox Harbour population in the nineteenth century. A 'Paulo' alleged to have murdered William Reed, one of the original Settlers of central Labrador, is said to have died near Hopedale in the 1850s. This tale is recounted in Chapter 7 by a descendant of Reed's contemporary Ambrose Brooks.

Noble & Pinson (Pinson & Hine after 1806) proved the most tenacious, and some say ruthless, of the original adventurers, remaining active on the south coast for over fifty years. They survived not only the last of the Inuit hostilities but the demolition of their Chateau headquarters by French men-of-war in 1797 and a half-century of predation by American privateers and whalers. In addition to Chateau, they operated posts at L'anse au Loup, St. Lewis Bay (Fox Harbour), and Sandwich Bay, employing over four hundred people a year from Bristol, Dartmouth, and Ireland. Some of these men remained to join the Settlers of Conception Bay in Newfoundland and outports in the Straits.

The most important of the coastal entrepreneurs in terms of the impact on settlement history were Monsieur De Quetteville of Jersey, who brought men from the Channel Islands; Slade & Company of Devonshire, who recruited in South Devon; Philip Beard & Company of Dartmouth; Joseph Bird & Son of Poole and Sturminster-Newton, who recruited in the Dorset hinterlands of the Blackmore Vale and Stour Valley; Hunt & Company of Liverpool, who brought men from Ireland; and George Cartwright, whose servants came from Bristol, Dartmouth, Cork, and Waterford.

After the dust of the first chaotic decade of British rule settled, three major players had emerged in southern Labrador. Noble & Pinson by then dominated the upper Straits, having moved its regional headquarters to Fornel's old Chateau post in 1774. Slade & Company had begun its long and amazingly stable tenure at Battle Harbour and the Atlantic Shore. And on the threshold of central Labrador, Jeremiah Coghlan and George Cartwright, having opened the formerly hostile coastline north of Cape Charles to European trade and settlement, were established in the northern bays of the Atlantic Shore and in Sandwich Bay. Unwilling or unable to maintain a coherent partnership like Noble & Pinson, Cartwright and Coghlan soon split up into separate enterprises with loosely affiliated outposts. Coghlan had his eye on Ivuktoke and Kaipokok, whence he sent a reconnaissance expedition under Captain Hellinss in 1777. By 1778, the year his men Phippard and Nooks became the first English crew to winter in Hamilton Inlet, Coghlan employed over a hundred sharemen in sealing and codfishing operations, and another forty in salmon and furring operations.[16] Within four years, he was bankrupt and had to leave Labrador, a victim of the pirates and de facto embargoes spawned by the Revolution in America. At the peak of his career, Cartwright too employed several hundred men and a few women at his Labrador posts. In 1786, after suffering repeated losses to New England pirates and Atlantic storms, he followed Coghlan into bankruptcy and returned to England, retaining some financial interests at Sandwich Bay until 1815.[17] His associate Robert Collingham remained in Labrador at least throughout the 1780s, reappearing in various alliances with Canadians Marcoux, Plante, and Dumontier at North West River and Kaipokok Bay. The Inuit of Hopedale called him "Kallingame," and his name endures on islands and coves in the vicinity of Groswater Bay, as does that of George Plante.

While coastal trade south of Moravian territory was dominated by merchant adventurers from the West Country of England and Channel Islands who were principally engaged in the export of fish and marine mammal products, rugged Canadian entrepreneurs joined independent planters previously affiliated with coastal firms in monopolizing the deep bays of Hamilton Inlet and Kaipokok—once Innu territory.

Although they too took seal and salmon, their main interest was fur. The Labrador Peninsula is home to virtually every major fur-bearing mammal found in North America. Their pelts are among the thickest and most luxuriant in the world, but their populations are thin, scattered, and ephemeral.[18] To harvest them cost-effectively, a merchant required a cohort of widely dispersed trappers capable of covering the lengthy river systems where the animals wintered. When European and American wars again disrupted trans-Atlantic commerce for much of the period between 1789 and 1815, Labrador's British-based companies—in spite of official exemption from embargoes—were hard pressed to sustain a viable presence in the northwestern Atlantic. To reduce costs, it seems companies like Slade's encouraged its servants to become independent planters. Apparently this appealed to the handful of men capable of surviving in Labrador and attached to their Native families, for whom the other options—military service or flight to America—were less attractive. The vacuum created by the downsizing of British firms was quickly filled by Newfoundland- and Canadian-based outfits with markets and suppliers on this side of the Atlantic. The new independent planters benefited from the need for local resource harvesters in both cases.

Although Fornel's old Esquimaux Bay posts were leased to Canadians related to the Quebec dynasties of Dumontier and Jacob Pozer after the Treaty of Paris, they were probably unoccupied from 1755 until 1778, when Phippard and Nooks were left on shore near English River to carve out the first British posts in Hamilton Inlet.[19] The misadventures of these English pioneers and their colleagues over the next decade flicker like ghosts through George Cartwright's extraordinary journals and the family legends of frontier-period Settlers: the drowning of Phippard's partner John Wrixson, abandonment and desperation in Ivuktoke, marriage to Inuit women, partner Nooks' murder by his Native brothers-in-law, and the death of Nooks' son, or sons. Phippard's own mixed-race son survived to perpetuate his bloodlines in the Settler population of Batteau on the Atlantic Shore, but the name has recently become extinct.

Nicholas Gabourite of the Quebec Fur Trading Company, John and Adam Lymburner, and William Grant, also of Quebec, had agents in Hamilton Inlet after 1784, the year that Pierre Marcoux and his then rival Baptiste Dumontier appear in central Labrador. Marcoux became a colourful figure in the Kaipokok area during the last fifteen years of the century, luring Inuit away from the Hopedale Mission with liquor, guns, European foods and papist ideas. The Moravians claim the traders of this era were a rough lot given to preying upon the innocence of the Natives. Indeed, Marcoux's associate Plante lodged a formal complaint against him for selling rum. The Inuit, however, held their "Makko" in high esteem, extolling his good character to the minister at Hopedale and perhaps bestowing his name on the place that would become Makkovik[20] and the Rigolet family of Muckos.

What little we know of life in Labrador during the late eighteenth century derives mainly from the Periodical Accounts written up each year at the Moravian stations or from George Cartwright's evocative journals.[21] Cartwright's descriptions of Native people and wildlife, marauding pirates, outpost life, rivalry and skullduggery among coastal entrepreneurs, and the passing traffic of poorly outfitted Canadian and English traders on their maiden trips into Hamilton Inlet provide the first slender threads of a historical record for Labrador. Some of these threads can be picked up again in the earliest accounts of Settlers included in this volume.

Like his competitors, Cartwright manned his stations with teams of artisans, fishermen, and labourers from the docks and prisons of mother England. They were a diverse lot, ranging from criminals to social idealists, beggars to borderline bourgeoisie, but nearly all were men. Some could read and even write—Protestants usually, for the promotion of popular literacy by the Protestant churches was the key to their ascendancy over Papism in the seventeenth century. Servants of the "lower orders" are said to have suffered involuntary indenture, extortion, and other forms of physical and economic abuse at the hands of the merchants in those early years. It was a system of bondage even then considered vicious. Governor Palliser himself issued legislation prohibiting the adventurers in his jurisdiction from holding servants against their will or charging them for everything they consumed while in service, but these unenforceable proclamations were nullified by less idealistic successors.[22] Cartwright himself entertained enlightened ideas about noble savages yet remained oblivious to the contradictions implicit in his behavior toward commoners of his own race.

From the outset, the Crown viewed Labrador, and to some extent Newfoundland, as a pantry to be raided by its mercantile companies for the benefit of the Motherland, not a place to be colonized. The civil and property rights of indigenous New World inhabitants, elsewhere protected by Royal decree, were systematically disregarded in Labrador. As shallow and duplicitous as were land acquisitions in other regions of North America, they at least bore the pretext of legality as defined by prevailing authorities. In Labrador, even that formality was ignored. No Labrador land was traded or purchased, none won in battle, none transferred by treaty. Labrador and its resources were simply appropriated, and the legitimacy of this process is only now being contested by her aboriginal people.

By suppressing colonization in Newfoundland and Labrador in the late eighteenth century, the government hoped to stimulate trans-Atlantic traffic and thereby expand the pool of potential recruits and ships for its Navy. Like the government, the British ship fishery and merchant adventurers hoped to prevent the diversion of revenue that would occur should a population of local middlemen or, worse yet, competitors develop. Perhaps, too, an element of "never again!" invaded British thinking as the expanding population of its American colonies became increasingly troublesome.

The Crown controlled access to the land and its resources by granting limited charters to certain companies with the understanding that they act as its surrogates and determine who lived where. For the first forty-plus years of British rule in Labrador, government encouraged merchants to keep only enough servants in winter residence to conduct furring and sealing operations, and to guard fishing stations and prepare equipment for the summer fishery. In his 1765 "Regulations for the Coast of Labrador," Governor Palliser ordered all British stations to leave crews of twelve men at the fishing posts to provide maintenance and protection during the winter. Lieutenant Roger Curtis reiterated the order in 1772, by which time 173 men and a few women wintered over. In 1773 there were 283, and the numbers continued to grow.

Sanctions notwithstanding, the irrepressible engines of colonization seem to have been moving in Labrador from the very beginning, fueled by human nature, the ambivalence of government and merchants to their own policies, and the difficulties of enforcement. Men in lonely winter huts will seek female companionship. Cartwright tells of the liaisons between his men and Inuit women and alludes to the child he himself fathered. Casual liaisons became permanent. Children were born and households established.

Transporting hundreds of workers and gear across the Atlantic every year, especially during a period of incessant naval conflicts and rampant piracy, was risky and expensive. Merchants quickly realized that, in permitting men to remain in the country after their terms of service expired, they were creating not only a cheap local labour force but another exploitable market. "Freemen" could be prevented from becoming competitors simply through lack of access to cash. In fact, they could be kept in perpetual bondage through a credit system controlled by the merchants. The Crown was too distant and too dependent on its share of the revenue to prevent abuse of such awful power and, for the most part, became a willing party to crimes committed in the name of profit. Officials who found it repugnant could do little more than complain on record. By the second quarter of the nineteenth century, most Settlers were burdened with crushing debts which bore no relation either to their labour and productivity, or to their meager purchases of equipment and provisions. After the War of Independence, only the most loyal or timid British citizens resisted the temptation to escape from the reach of creditors by slipping away with the American fishing fleets that came to Labrador every summer.

America won unlimited access to Labrador waters in the treaty ending the Revolutionary War and had a significant impact on residents of the south coast throughout the first half of the nineteenth century (some residents claim that American slaves-turned-pirates contributed a strain of African blood to the population). Although constrained from trading with the residents, they did so illegally, providing goods at cheaper prices than local merchants could and paying higher prices for fish. They also imported "offensive, insulting, democratic" ideas "fatal to the moral character of fishermen" and quickly led to "Disobedience and Insubordination," according to Newfoundland authorities and merchants. Although those who resisted the lure of America to stay in Labrador could easily be dismissed as wanting pluck, they probably earned Governor King's dubious accolade as "sober, hard-working, industrious men…entirely subject to the oppression of the merchants."[23]

Captain Cook counted thirteen Settlers on the Labrador in his inventory of the spoils of war in 1763, probably Canadian agents and planters at outposts in the Straits. By 1806 there were five hundred permanent residents in southern Labrador alone, including families. This undoubtedly represented a small minority of company servants, most of whom returned to England or headed for more temperate New World climes when their term of indenture ended. Curiously, some of the Englishmen who settled permanently in Labrador between 1815 and 1835 bear the same names as eighteenth-century planters and servants who vanish from Slade's ledgers during the early decades of the nineteenth century—caught up in the war, perhaps, or returning to a rapidly changing Motherland which ultimately failed to meet their expectations. If these are indeed the same people, they invariably returned to Labrador with a clean slate for their family stories begin after the wars, with no hint of an earlier stay in the region.

The few who remained as independent planters in Labrador before the 1830s seem to have had two options. They could try to make it on their own, eking a living from the wilderness and selling any surplus to the merchants in exchange for gear and flour, or they could maintain an official, quasi-independent relationship with the company. Firms like Slade's and Hunt's retained former servants as professional free-lance sharemen to open and manage the company's northern outposts. There these men gained the experience, contacts, and confidence they would eventually need to succeed as independent petty traders and planters while retaining a degree of security denied those who cut all formal ties with the company. Quite a few survived the dark ages of early settlement and are well represented in the present population.

Those who went off on their own seem to have fared less well, becoming more, rather than less obligated to the mercantile establishment. As the big firms claimed exclusive rights to areas in which they had manned operations, the unaffiliated planters had to find suitable places in remote, less economically valuable bays. Winter resources in these areas could support fewer people, so these families were even more isolated than others and, lacking any support system at all, were even more vulnerable to accident, illness, and starvation.

Settlement during the frontier period did not creep incrementally up the coast from the commercial centers at Blanc Sablon, Forteau, Battle Harbour, and Sandwich Bay. Instead it seems to have dispersed widely and, considering the intermittent wars, rather quickly as companies and planters leapfrogged over each other in a race for prime locations. The would-be Settlers of central Labrador, finding the prosperity they had hoped for elusive or the arrival of newcomers in their territory intolerable, moved from place to place in search of the ideal furring ground and salmon river. Those who found such places put down roots to the extent that their mandatory seasonal migrations permitted, building solid cabins at the sites where they would spend the winter, spring, and summer. In time the places assumed their names by association, names that in many cases have outlived the memory or tenure of the people who lent them. But for the most part, by the time the Hudson's Bay Company (HBC) arrived in the area, they were inhabited by established families, some of them already third-generation mixed-race Labradorians.

George Cartwright encountered mixed families at Cape Charles and St. Lewis Bay (Fox Harbour) as early as 1775. By 1835 most of the thirty-five European and Canadian Settlers in Ivuktoke had Inuit partners, and half of the 120 children were of mixed race, the rest presumably Inuit.[24] By 1850 Inuit blood ran in the veins of nearly all Labrador families from Hopedale to Cape Charles. In the absence of support from mercantile companies during the long winters, the pioneers depended on Native wives and tutors for their survival, adopting their warm seal-skin clothing, komatiks and dog-teams, snowshoes ('racquets'), igloos, sod huts, and hunting techniques. While many whites contributed little more than their language, guns, boats, and drinking habits, others brought Western values and religion into the household. In Hamilton Inlet, eighteenth-century Settler Ambrose Brooks and his Inuit wife Susan taught their daughters to read and love God. They in turn taught their children, and so on through the widening circle of generations. When Methodist missionaries finally came to bestow their favours on the forgotten people of the bay around 1900, they found to their astonishment that all could read, and most, in their estimation, lived more virtuous lives than members of their own congregations. Similar observations had been made in 1823 by Rev. U. Z. Rule at Battle Harbour, who wrote in his journal that he preferred to lodge with the mixed-race families, as opposed to the Newfoundlanders or Europeans. Their houses were cleaner and more comfortable, he said, and the men treated the women and children more kindly.[25]

The credit system established by the original merchants became the norm and, even when honestly employed, kept the Settlers in thrall if not in debt. Labradorians were inadvertently earning the name given to their land— 'labourers.' From the very beginning, they were obliged to harvest every marketable resource they could get their hands on in order to survive. This required arduous seasonal migrations among the resource areas accessible to each family. Most spent summer and early fall on the outer coast fishing for salmon, cod, and herring, gathering berries for the winter, and hunting seal for pelts, oil, and food for their sled dogs. Later in the fall they moved to the bays, cut their winter supply of firewood, and the men left for distant trapping grounds while women provided for the families at home. In spring they prepared for the fishing season, netted seals, and took salmon at the river mouths. Everyone hunted when they could, including women and children, who also helped process fish. During the winter when their husbands were gone, wives provided all the fresh meat and fish for the family, and many trapped fur animals near the homestead. By the age of ten most boys joined their fathers on the trap lines and fishing grounds.

In principal, a good yield of furs would guarantee a family adequate supplies for the fishing season. A good fishing season would supply a family with staples for the winter and an outfit for trapping. The merchant would advance credit to tide the family over a bad period—up to a point—and would carry any net profit on his books toward future debts, rather than hand it over to the Settler to invest in his own betterment. As long as the resident population remained illiterate and innumerate, as were the majority of Settlers in all but central Labrador, it had little chance of challenging the storekeepers; and until wage-labour opportunities and protective government policies emerged in the twentieth century, the people had no viable alternatives or judicial recourse. Not surprisingly, few early merchants welcomed government intervention or even visiting clergymen (until they were perceived as lures for the Innu), and only one, Donald Smith of the Hudson's Bay Company, is known to have made any attempt to encourage education. As a result, the subsistence lifestyle that characterized the population of Labrador during its frontier period would change very little before the 1940s.

A few individual Settlers able to negotiate a relationship with a supplier/marketer in Newfoundland, Quebec, America, or England, as some on the north coast did, could achieve a level of relative affluence and even inflict some damage on the big firms through competition. Aware of this danger, companies like Noble & Pinson and later the Hudson's Bay Company sought to eradicate economic rivals in their vicinity. When the HBC came to Labrador in 1835, it immediately bought out neighboring entrepreneurs, large and small, and made it almost impossible for former employees to engage in trade except as surrogates for the Company.

There were fair merchants. There were even times, such as the 1860s and 1930s, when merchants were ruined for having helped so many people stay afloat through prolonged periods of hardship. But abuses continued to occur, and many productive Settlers were kept in a state of perpetual insolvency by unscrupulous storekeepers. Far more were kept from advancement by exaggerated capitalistic policies that distributed windfall profits to overseas investors as compensation for the financial risk involved in these investments—without a thought for the people who daily put their very lives on the line to wrestle that wealth from an ungenerous wilderness. The Hudson's Bay Company, which dominated trade in Labrador from 1835 to 1942, is a good example.

The "Great Company of Adventurers," as the Hudson's Bay Company was called, first came to Labrador overland from its relatively new outposts in Ungava Bay. There they had succeeded in obstructing the westward expansion of Moravian stations,[26] but the Ungava posts were logistically difficult and unprofitable to maintain. They had also alerted the Company to a more immediate threat: traders in Hamilton Inlet who were diverting Innu from their customary trek between the Labrador hunting grounds and the King's Posts on the St. Lawrence River, by then also run by the HBC.

Within three years, the Company had obtained the main posts at Rigolet, North West River, and Kaipokok, and had opened smaller stations at Aillik and Tikkaratsuk. In 1857 it vied with A.B. Hunt & Co. for the Innu trade at Davis Inlet, finally ousting its rival in 1869. In 1873 they bought out Hunt & Henley's operations in Sandwich Bay as well. Determined to break the Moravians lucrative hold over the produce of the mission Inuit, HBC opened posts at Nachvak, Saglek, and Killinek in the 1860s and '70s. Only in Kaipokok did they utterly fail to overwhelm the local competition—an independent Canadian planter named Antoni Perrault, whose descendants still live in the bay (and whose ancestor may have been a prominent sealer on the Gulf Coast at the end of the French period).[27] Not until the powerful French fur company Revillon Freres established a post on the Innu side of North West River in 1901 were they obliged to offer competitive prices for fur.

In addition to her century-long monopoly over the Labrador fur trade, the HBC played an important role in the seal and salmon fisheries, and her posts became the nucleus for such community life as existed in the region—weddings, funerals, New Year and Easter celebrations, even Sunday services. She was the principal point of access and reference to the outside world, and the point of entry for a majority of Labrador's European Settlers after the pioneer period. Factor Donald Smith, who would later rise to the head of the company and win the title Lord Strathcona, introduced a more humanitarian approach to the role of merchant in Labrador by providing rudimentary medical assistance and encouraging the Settlers to supplement their subsistence base with handicrafts and short-season vegetables like potatoes and greens. His tenure was unfortunately marred by episodes of starvation among the Innu caused by Company policies carried out in his district. While he was never personally implicated (HBC Governor Simpson was tried and acquitted), it is difficult to imagine he had no role in the implementation of these policies.

As the Settler population increased, firms like HBC hired fewer fishermen and furriers from abroad; but the Company had always maintained a very small payroll compared to its rivals. They employed three classes of men. Gentlemen with a good basic education were hired as factors, traders and storekeepers. These men kept the accounts and journals at their posts and could advance through the hierarchy of Company management. To hone their incentives for profit, they were paid in full shares of the produce from their posts as well as wages. Most remained loyal employees of the Company until retirement but seldom settled in Labrador. Servants employed by the Company included skilled tradesmen needed for specialized work at the main stations—coopers, boat builders, tinsmiths, blacksmiths, storekeepers, and carpenters—who were paid in wages and half shares. Fishermen, furriers, and other labourers were paid wages held by the Company until employment ended, at which time they received their net earnings after deduction of expenses, purchases, and the return voyage. Employees who left the Company to settle in Labrador went on the credit system.

In recruiting men for skilled jobs, HBC specifically sought candidates of sound moral character and constitution, frequently from the Orkney Islands of Scotland. When their terms of service ended, quite a few of these men stayed in Labrador, where the terrain was not unlike their homeland, and the prospects for a decent life may have seemed, or even been, more promising. A few continued to serve as freelance artisans, receiving wages for the time worked. Some opened subsidiary trading and fishing operations on shares.

Except for the few Company servants who had brought Indian wives from posts on Hudson's Bay or the St. Lawrence River, HBC Settlers took sturdy Inuit or, increasingly, mixed-race girls to wife. Thanks to the Moravians, Inuit girls could read and write as well as trap, hunt, and outfit their families with the indispensable skin boots, parkas, and snowshoes. Mixed-race daughters of pioneer-period liaisons between literate whites and southern Inuit were equally capable and had the advantage of speaking English. By temperament as well as skills, local women made ideal partners for husbands relatively inexperienced in wilderness life. And HBC's carefully selected employees generally proved to be devout and caring family heads whose standards of conduct gradually spread throughout the population. Those who had received a rudimentary education abroad joined their Native partners in raising children who could both read the Bible and live off the land. Together they passed on the tenets of the Ten Commandments along with the Native code of unstinting generosity and hospitality to others. By the 1870s Labrador's core Settler population was distinguished not only by a mixed-race genealogical network but by a common basic culture and self-enforced system of social values.

During the last half of the nineteenth century, yet a third major influence began to infiltrate the genetic and cultural fusion along the Atlantic coast—the annual influx of Newfoundlanders engaged in the summer fishery. While the Hudson's Bay Company in the bays of central Labrador, Moravians in the north, and Hunt & Henley *et al* south of Hamilton Inlet dominated Labrador life from October until May, June brought most of the population to the outer islands for the codfishing season where, by then, the old West Country fishing firms had been replaced by Newfoundland-based companies with seasonal stations on the coastal archipelago. Like the fur companies, the fish merchants made all transactions in trade, and the storekeepers kept the ledgers.

Labradorians alone supplied the furs, but Newfoundlanders, with their superior boats and equipment, harvested most of Labrador's fish. They came in a flurry of sails each June, thousands of schooners racing through the drifting pack ice for favoured fishing berths among the islands. Deserted harbours sprang to life, and in a matter of days, the coastal population exploded into life. Until October the islands seethed with a level of activity unknown in Labrador during the rest of the year. Labrador's solitary and laconic liveyers, a West Country moniker for 'people who live here,' were engulfed by fast-paced Newfy banter and bravado, rum and scuffles, step dances and tin whistles, and with the visiting preachers, magistrates, and government officials who came in the wake of the schooners. When the codfishery ended, the entire littoral margin of Labrador packed up again and returned to the Island—storekeepers, preachers, magistrates and all. The liveyers were left to mind the empty buildings or withdraw to lonely winter quarters deep in the shelter of frozen bays.

The Newfoundland fishery on Labrador's coast has its own unique culture and nomenclature based on the extent of contact with land. Although this has evolved over time, there have always been two distinct classes of operation, the 'floaters' who lived and processed their fish on board the schooners that brought them; and the 'stationers' or 'Labradormen' who had summer rooms on shore much like the liveyers. The stationers came mainly from Conception Bay, where it is said a good two-thirds of the residents spent their summer's 'on the Labrador,' as had their fathers and grandfathers before them as far back as anyone could remember. Their sense of proprietorship over the islands and fishing berths was deeply ingrained, as well it might be if, as some claim, they were descendants of seventeenth-century immigrants to Newfoundland.

As Newfoundland stationers and liveyers increased in number, the tides of immigration and emigration, marriage in and marriage out considerably diluted the strains of Native blood in some of the Atlantic Shore and Moravian Coast families. But even those whose Aboriginal lines remained strong, or were renewed following resettlement of northern Inuit populations in the 1960s, became infected with patterns of speech and behavior more characteristic of Newfoundland than of Labrador proper, as one can discern from some of the narratives in Chapters 2, 5, and 8. The same is happening today in Labrador West and Happy Valley, where Newfoundlanders have flocked in pursuit of jobs at the mines, hydroelectric facilities, and air base.

Around the middle of the nineteenth century, Newfoundland fishing vessels began moving up the Moravian Coast in search of fresh territory. Here, it was the floaters whose influence was felt. From vessels anchored among the offshore islands, Newfoundlanders introduced the Inuit to jigs and Celtic revelry and conducted a black-market trade in goods the Mission would not sell, including liquor. As they did not stay on land or, as a rule, marry into the population, their role in the formation of the resident character was less profound than on the Atlantic Shore. They seem mainly to have given the Inuit an outlet for their lighter side and an alternative model for their relationships with whites.

This is not to suggest that the spirit of the Moravian Inuit had been repressed in the Missions. Inuit are largely irrepressible by nature. They have a survivor's ability to compartmentalize their soul, and seem to have invested only part of their spiritual capital in the Church. The "heathens" who welcomed Jens Haven and his first company of missionaries to Nain in 1771 were, it must be understood, confident of their superiority over other races, especially the ludicrously inept and naive Europeans. Moreover, they saw no virtue in replacing a value system based on sharing and group-reliance with one that espoused hoarding, not in an environment as fickle as this. But the Inuit social order, based as it was on robust pragmatism, was patently testos-terone-driven. Like the environment and its *torngat*, it rewarded the strong and penalized the weak. It was ultimately the women who led their people to Christ, rec-ognizing perhaps some potential advantages in the new social order offered by the Moravians. The men followed only when the missionaries had succeeded in discred-iting the powerful shamans through their better grasp of scientific phenomena and mechanics.

Initially, Inuit were attracted to the stations by the flattering (and in their view well-deserved) attentions of the Moravians and the hope of access to European goods. Bible stories appealed to their vivid imaginations, and they enjoyed theolog-ical debate. But their visits were necessarily short and infrequent as the station turned out to be far from Inuit hunting grounds, to the chagrin of the first Moravians, who had been under the mistaken impression that Nain Bay was Ivuktoke. To over-come this obstacle, the missionaries opened a northern station for the Keewedlock band at Okak in 1775, and a southern station near the village of Arvertok[28] in 1781. They called this Hopedale.

By then, however, the Inuit had grown impatient with the Moravians' refusal to trade and were already leaving the stations to try their luck with the merchant adven-turers and independent traders to the south.[29] Within ten years the prodigals had returned in pitiable condition, their numbers dramatically reduced by disease and misfortune. In response to the exodus, the Moravians had meanwhile relented on the issue of trade, convinced that it was an inevitable prerequisite to conversion of the Inuit. Thenceforth the chastened Inuit remained near the stations, and the process of salvation began in earnest.

So sudden and powerful was the onset of religious fervor among the Inuit during the first years of the nineteenth century that the episode has been called "the Great Awakening." The movement started with women at Okak and spread quickly to those at Nain and Hopedale. Within a decade, most of the northern bands had been bap-tized and were settled into the community life of the stations. They took readily to instruction in the schools, learned to read, sing hymns, and play Western musical instruments. Although the Inuit year was still circumscribed by seasonal migrations between hunting camps, Moravian festivals and rites now punctuated the calendar.

The first half of the nineteenth century was a "golden age" for the Labrador Mission. The Inuit seemed content and docile. Still, the missionaries always suspected that some part of their soul was being withheld. It was the apparent ease with which they reverted to 'heathen' practices when away from the stations, and the cheerful sincerity of their subsequent confessions. And it was the certainty with which, when faced with a choice between traditional and Christian practices—polygamy and monogamy for example—they could unabashedly defend their choice of pagan ways.

The "Northlanders" were another challenge altogether. The Inuit of the grim fjords and barrens of northernmost Labrador visited the stations only to trade, resolutely adhering to their age-old belief systems through much of the nineteenth century. Some never accepted Christianity. To reach them, the Moravians built stations at Hebron in 1829, Ramah Bay in 1871, and Killinek in 1904. Hebron immediately filled with converts from the over-crowded Okak station who had originally come from the north. Ramah attracted only the orphaned, elderly, and infirm cast-offs of the unconverted bands. While most of the northern family groups eventually joined the Moravian communities for economic and social reasons, their commitment to its teachings were seldom as deep as those of their cousins at the southern stations. With close affiliations in the Ungava region to the west, a number of Labrador's northernmost Inuit families ultimately came within the fold of Church of England missionaries who proselytized at Killinek in the twentieth century.

In the last half of the nineteenth century, periods of starvation and sickness grew more frequent and intense at the southern mission stations. At the same time, the Inuit's increasing exposure to Settlers and fishermen presented them with viable alternatives to mission life and its restrictive, if well-intentioned, trading practices. Some of the Mission Inuit left the stations, but the majority manifested their independence by demanding that the Brethren live up to their espoused principles and deal competitively in matters of trade. The Christianity of the leading Inuit of Okak, Nain, and Hopedale was by then sincere and profound, their loyalty unflagging, but it is typical that they never doubted their right to defend the Church even against its own imperfections.

Unfortunately, the missionaries were unresponsive both to the Inuit leadership and to their own governing board, which as early as 1861 warned that the aim of the Mission should be to render the need for its social protections obsolete by empowering its charges. The resident missionaries doggedly resisted pressure to improve the Inuit's material condition through proper medical care,[30] or by allowing them to learn English so they could compete economically with the Settlers. Infectious diseases carried from Europe by the annual Moravian supply ship swept through the Inuit population with increasing frequency toward the end of the nineteenth century. When the Spanish Influenza hit the stations in 1918, killing a third of the Moravian Inuit, the faith of the survivors was dealt a blow from which it never fully recovered. Without that, the Mission as envisioned by its founders was doomed. What remained of Moravian trading operations succumbed to the Depression. The rival Hudson's Bay Company took over the stores. By 1960 the Moravian Church was becoming a marginalized institution in an increasingly secular society.

For all its faults, the Moravian Mission in Labrador was a noble enterprise. It demanded extraordinary sacrifices from the missionaries and their families, and it made enormous contributions to the moral character of the region. Had it not been for Moravian protectionism, the language and material culture of the Labrador Inuit would have been irretrievably lost during the settlement period. Ultimately, the Mission declined because of its inability to let the Inuit grow and advance, to acknowledge their status as adults, to let them go. In the end, it was they who were dependent on the Inuit, not the Inuit on the Moravians. In some respects it was ever thus.

The impact of European settlement on Labrador's indigenous Indians is quite another story. Having long ago had their access to coastal areas inhibited by the Inuit, the Labrador Innu relied on inland fish and game, especially caribou, for sustenance. Their contact with whites was therefore minimal. Deer are notoriously prone to wild swings in number and location, and the Innu often burned more calories in pursuit than they could reclaim in the kill. Early Dutch explorers describe them as tall and gaunt compared to the short, stocky Inuit, whose diet of sea mammals was more nutritious and less exacting. Innu fared best when beaver and other more sedentary species were available as a back-up for the deer—more often the case in the Montagnais regions than in the barrens of Labrador—and when they had some way of obtaining the vitamin-rich oil from seals and iodine from ocean fish.[31]

By the middle of the nineteenth century, conditions favourable to the Innu had deteriorated to the point where the people began to experience an accelerating decline in health and numbers that would continue for at least a century. The problems originated with the policies of traders and missionaries in Hudson's Bay and the Gulf of St. Lawrence but reverberated across Labrador through the Innu's extensive wilderness networks. Relentless nomads even today, Innu regularly walked and paddled between Ungava and the St. Lawrence, Hudson's Bay and Lake Melville—a trek roughly equivalent to the distance between New York and Chicago—but even the remote bands from the barren grounds of northern Labrador, whose mobility was limited by a lack of open water and materials for canoes, were drawn into the stream of trade. In time, all Innu were compelled by their desire for European goods and spirits into trapping when they would otherwise have been hunting, and into killing more beaver and deer for pelts than they needed for food. To make matters worse, a series of forest fires large enough to blacken skies as far as Montreal—the legendary "dark days of Canada"—destroyed large tracts of Innu hunting grounds in 1785, 1814, and 1821. The effects would last for generations in this fragile, slow-growth environment. Within a century beaver and deer had almost disappeared from Nitassinan, and the Innu were increasingly dependent for their survival on semi-dormant fish deep in her ice-bound lakes.

At least one of the ensuing famines was further aggravated by the aggressive policies of the Hudson's Bay Company. In 1868, [32] for example, HBC agents intentionally withheld ammunition from the Innu so they would tend their traps instead of hunt for food. While starving families waited in the interior, men strong enough to travel made their way to the King's Posts on the St. Lawrence in search of help. There they were cut down by one of the worst smallpox epidemics of the century. A similar fate befell the Naskapi, whom the Gulf Coast missionaries had coaxed from the far reaches of northern Labrador and Ungava to be baptized, knowing they would inevitably succumb to exhaustion and disease on arrival at the missions.

And so the Labrador Innu, probably never very numerous, were reduced to a few destitute bands by the twentieth century. Eschewing the reservations to which their southern cousins had resorted in desperation, most withdrew again into Nitassinan. Only starvation, or the desire for flour, tobacco, ammunition, and the blessings of a priest could compel them to visit the trading posts.

The affinity between Innu and French, and later Canadian, administrations survived the shift to English rule even in Labrador. For all their mistakes, these governments had treated the Innu sympathetically, trying to protect them from the greed of unscrupulous merchants as well as disease and starvation. If they failed, it was because the inevitable pressures of expanding settlement on the Gulf coast were too great and their reach into Nitassinan too short. The Canadian government even provided welfare assistance and inoculations to the Labrador Innu during the nineteenth and early twentieth century. It was as though Canada had accepted eternal responsibility for the Innu; and Innu territory, by extension, was tacitly assumed to be Canadian. Thus it was that Quebec would challenge the rights of a Nova Scotian logging company permitted by the English Crown to harvest the forests of Lake Melville in 1903, precipitating the Labrador Boundary Dispute settled at last in 1927. It was the first time since Britain's offhand claim of ownership 430 years earlier that the region's political boundaries were defined.

For their part, the Montagnais Innu were devoted to their black-robed priests, who had followed them into the difficult wilderness for the sake of a few souls and had been their advocates in times of need. They never forgot their allegiance to the French who had pushed back the advances of the terrible Iroquois. French blood runs in the veins of most Innu today, for like all aboriginal peoples, those lacking European genes succumbed more readily to European diseases. The Gulf posts remained their

Meccas and the ultimate destination for major pilgrimages well into the twentieth century. Although more accessible to the northern bands, during much of the British Period the Lake Melville posts seem to have served merely as waystations in which to stock up for another leg of the journey, or as fallbacks in emergencies and off years.

While Montagnais Innu had been guides and companions for French traders in the Straits and Hamilton Inlet during the eighteenth century, most remained reserved and aloof in their dealings with Englishmen after the Treaty of Paris. Only a few worked for, or on "shares" with, the Hudson's Bay Company in Labrador. They rarely intermarried with Labrador's Settlers, and when adopted by Settler families as children, usually returned to the band as young adults.[33] In Labrador's isolation, the Golden Rule held sway over other considerations, even ancient animosities, so it was invariably the common crises of frontier life that brought Innu and whites together. In time, even the Inuit were able to lend a hand to their long-demonized rivals. But intermarriage between the two was virtually non-existent in all but the Ungava region, where they have been close and relatively amicable neighbors since the middle decades of the nineteenth century.

On the trapping grounds, Innu and Settler were at once confreres and competitors. Not until an expanding younger generation of trappers crowded into Nitassinan during the 1920s did the Innu's careful deference (or inscrutable silence) give way to open anger. And not until government policies and social services compelled them to leave Nitassinan for ghetto communities at Utshimassit (Davis Inlet) and Sheshashiu (North West River) did the pride abandon them which had sustained their culture for so long. Of all the First Nations of North America, few have been as severely demoralized by their incorporation into "the White society way" as the Labrador Innu. There is reason to hope their recovery may now have begun, but the odds against them are still formidable.

Probably the most striking characteristic of Settler life, one shared with the Innu, was self-reliance in the context not only of an extremely challenging wilderness environment but an almost total absence of external support or attention. It was not so much a matter of governmental neglect, or a point in time when the world abandoned and then forgot these children of Europe's acquisitive, oppressive, and bellicose monarchies. It was more a deliberate failure ever to acknowledge their existence.

Most of the immigrants reveled in their escape from social and legal authorities who had rarely made their lives easier, but they must have missed the support of churches, families, and the community safety nets that provided at least a first line of defense against disaster. Their mixed-race descendants thought nothing of it, however, oblivious as they were to the industrializing world beyond their endless forest and stormy sea. Later, when the government began its often-clumsy efforts to intervene on behalf of the general good, many rued their lost freedom. And it was freedom. In spite of the constraints of the environment and their bondage to the merchants, people were free to sink or swim, to enrich their souls or demean them, to create harmony or discord in their homes and communities. Most of them figured it out for themselves and made it work. In America and southern Canada, the frontier was so quickly overtaken by the nation-builders and the Industrial Revolution, our pioneers experienced that kind of liberty only briefly if at all. But the nation-builders never came to Labrador, and the people were suspended in a perpetual frontier for nearly four generations.

Politically, coastal Labrador (after 1927, interior Labrador as well) was a component of the British colony of Newfoundland until its Confederation with Canada in 1949. Newfoundland itself got little attention from the Motherland, and the cultural and economic stimulation she might have derived as a waystation for trans-Atlantic shipping did not even percolate to the Island's outport communities, let alone to Labrador. Nor was it in the nature of the Newfoundland establishment to make sure distant Labrador had a share in whatever incremental civilizing elements developed on the Island. In effect, as soon as Newfoundland itself became an operative entity, Labrador became its colony, a summer home for Conception Bay and its fishing fleets, a place from which to take things.

Capitulating to coastal merchants who objected to paying duties when they received no services in return, Newfoundland sent a magistrate to the Labrador coast once each summer from 1811 to 1824, and again between 1826 and 1834, and 1863 to 1874. Cases were heard at L'anse au Loup, Chateau, Cape Charles, Cape St. Francis, Venison Islands, Huntingdon Harbour at Sandwich Bay, and Rigolet or Indian Harbour in Groswater Bay. Most concerned fishing and property rights, a few assault and battery. The odd case of "bastardy" was prosecuted, presumably against the unfortunate mother, though it would be completely out of character for a Labradorian to press such charges. But in all, there were so few cases—rarely more than a dozen a year—that the government eventually discontinued the service until prodded again by the competing fish merchants.

Travellers to Labrador often noted the orderly conduct of its residents and the lack of criminal behavior and immorality. It seems remarkable, even incredible to our cynical minds, that a strong code of civil conduct would evolve in a frontier environment absent externally imposed laws and punishments, or even religious guidance. Yet diaries and narratives from the frontier and HBC periods support this contention. Whether it developed for pragmatic reasons or through the spread of Christian values by a few influential Settlers and Moravian Inuit wives, we will never know. We do know that it was not without exception. Crimes did occur, people went 'moon crazy,' a common attribution for violent behavior, and on at least one occasion advocates for government intervention complained that people known to have committed murder remained at large. Rape, abuse, and incest happened in certain isolated family homesteads, notwithstanding their conspicuous absence from written accounts, court records, and oral histories. The people never tell us—except perhaps with their silence—how they treated these injuries to the spirit and the social fabric. We can only speculate, and admire the resilience of survivors.

For most Labradorians between the Straits and the Moravian territories, religion was little more than an inherited affiliation with one or another denomination and a simple set of beliefs and observances passed down by forebears. Those who could read interpreted the Bible for their families, and almost every homestead had a copy brought over from the Old World or obtained from the Moravian Mission. This became the family record, the children's primer, the storybook which nurtured their imaginations, and the language and cadence of their poetry. Marriages and burials were sanctified whenever possible by anyone who could decipher the appropriate passages, though ship captains and store managers lent stature to the occasion when available.

Churchmen rarely visited the coast. Wesleyans who attempted to set up a mission in Ivuktoke in the 1820s left after several fruitless years because "of the opposition of the traders, and the excessive indulgence in spirits on the part of those who were the object of their labour."[34] The Moravians, who themselves bemoaned the "rough and ungodly" nature of that early cohort of Settler-traders, viewed the Wesleyans as spiritual competitors and withheld assistance. Although the Methodists did not return to establish a permanent ministry in Hamilton Inlet until the 1880s, they claimed the area from Sand Hill Cove to Cape Harrison as their territory on the basis of a handful of member families.

Between 1849 and 1860 the Church of England (called "C of E" by Labradorians) opened summer chapels for the Newfoundland stationers along the Atlantic Shore and year-round churches at Battle Harbour, Forteau, Henley Harbour (Chateau), and Francis Harbour. The Atlantic Shore and Straits were considered predominantly C of E territory. The Catholic Church served Irish and French-Canadian communities at West St. Modeste and Pinware in the Straits, and at Black Tickle on the Atlantic Shore. At the urging of the Hudson's Bay Company, which was then suffering from competition on the Gulf, the Catholic Church established a mission for the Innu at North West River in 1872.[35] Although the effect of these community churches and their little day schools was localized, the clergymen assigned to them often made calls on a large area. Whatever their impact, the travelling preachers were effectively the first outsiders to have as their sole objective the spiritual welfare of the resident population south of the Moravian stations.

For most Labradorians below Hopedale, and even for Settlers on the Moravian Coast, such formal education as existed before 1920 took the form of sporadic winter tutorials by itinerant teachers from the Wesleyan seminary in Newfoundland or basic instruction at C of E day schools at the main communities of the Straits and Atlantic Shore. The short home visits got a mixed reception from many Settler families and seldom rewarded the young teachers, but they did help some coastal Labradorians achieve basic literacy and a broader perspective on the world.

Professional medical care was essentially nonexistent before 1893. Families took care of themselves and their neighbors as best they could, employing a wide range of traditional cures and herbal remedies from the Old and New Worlds, many of them effective, most not. Maternal and infant mortality was extremely high, as was the death rate from infectious diseases and accidents. Tuberculosis dogged the population for over a hundred years, fueled like all Labrador's health problems by pervasive malnutrition. Sir Wilfred Grenfell first visited Labrador in 1892 as representative of the London-based Mission to Deep Sea Fishermen (MDSF), a charitable organization providing spiritual and medical services to the British fishing fleets in the North Atlantic. Stunned to find a resident population as profoundly neglected as Labrador's, this charismatic doctor-lawyer-preacher immediately devoted himself to improving their well being.[36] Eventually breaking off from the Deep Sea Mission, he founded the International Grenfell Association (IGA, or Grenfell Mission) in 1912 and launched a formidable one-man crusade in England, Canada, and America to raise awareness of the Labradorians' condition and funds for his projects on their behalf.

The MDSF opened its first Labrador hospitals at what were then the principal fishing stations on the coast: Battle Harbour in 1893, Indian Harbour the following summer, and soon after a large facility at St. Anthony on the north coast of Newfoundland. The Moravians followed suit in 1900 with a hospital for the Inuit at Okak. By 1914 there were four hospitals and six nursing stations in Labrador and northern Newfoundland (all now run by the IGA) treating over six thousand patients a year, mostly for TB and deficiency diseases like scurvy, rickets, and beriberi. In 1916 the first IGA hospital at North West River was built. The nursing station at Cartwright was expanded and a TB sanitarium added to the complex. By the time Grenfell retired, there was a Grenfell Mission hospital or nursing station within a two-day journey of all but the most remote settlements south of Hopedale. The IGA hospital ship *Strathcona* provided outpatient services at virtually all the summer stations as far north as Killinek, and Dr. Harry Paddon of the North West River Hospital visited northern communities by dogsled during the winter months. Grenfell himself was appointed magistrate for the coast of Labrador, and the *Strathcona* served as circuit court and distribution point for donated books and clothing. The Hudson's Bay Company fumed while Grenfell and his associates initiated cooperative stores, craft-producing "industrials," fishing enterprises and other ventures meant to promote economic independence for Labradorians. Grenfell built chapels where visiting clergymen of all denominations could hold services. And perhaps most importantly, he opened schools and orphanages.

While Dr. Grenfell personally favoured sending promising students to the United States and England for an education, his protégé, Rev. Henry Gordon, felt strongly that Labradorians should remain in Labrador. Gordon fervently believed that boarding schools were the only feasible solution for families as dispersed as these and, in 1920, opened the first one five miles west of Cartwright at Muddy Bay. Necessity demanded that the Muddy Bay School serve first as an orphanage for children of the Spanish Influenza. However, by the time a disgruntled student burned it down eight years later, it had become a model for subsequent schools at Cartwright, Red Bay, Mary's Harbour, Forteau, and North West River. In 1940 the Moravians opened a boarding school for Settlers at Makkovik. Collectively these institutions helped create the first generation of educated and socialized Labradorians, many of them the narrators of this volume.

As Grenfell's fundraising lecture-tours brought international attention to forgotten Labrador from scholars like W. G. Gosling and Väinö Tanner and adventurers like Dillon Wallace and Leonidas Hubbard, volunteers from England and America inundated IGA hospitals and schools. This provided Labradorians with their first not-always-favourable exposure to the more adventurous and charitably inclined young members of our privileged classes. And it presented Labrador to the outside world. Even today, what little Americans know of the region relates to the work of the Grenfell Mission.

Like the Moravian Church, Grenfell is given a great deal of credit by historians for his impact on the human condition of Labrador. While the praise is fully deserved—this was a campaign of monumental good will with extraordinary results—the Labradorians themselves are less apt to attribute their salvation to outsiders, even a man of Grenfell's stature and popularity. The reasons are complex but include the fact that they did not share his view that they led impoverished lives or required outside intervention. They had their own internal heroes and social safety nets, and they were proud of their homely medical accomplishments. More to the point, as long as the people were widely dispersed and seasonally migratory, IGA and other cursory external services would remain inaccessible to a majority of residents when assistance was most needed. In 1918, for example, the notorious Spanish Influenza hit Labrador like a tidal wave. Within days most of the adult Inuit of Okak and Hebron were dead. In Sandwich Bay, whole communities of Settlers succumbed in their cabins. It took only hours, or even minutes, to claim its victims. In many families, children alone survived. Even with treatable illness and injury, the Grenfell Mission was a distant and impractical recourse. Nevertheless, by providing Labradorians with a relatively non-judgmental, non-invasive, and benevolent exposure to the advancing modern world, Grenfell did much to prepare them for the inevitable changes ahead with their self-confidence more or less intact.

Most of the narratives in this book tell of Labrador life during the first decades of the twentieth century when the social landscape was undergoing the tectonic shifts that would eventually bring about the end of 'them days.' People began to have access not only to schools and health care but to alternative occupations and currency. In 1900 the Dickie Lumber Company of Nova Scotia opened a sawmill at Mud Lake which paid wages to its Labradorian employees, precipitating the final squabble with Quebec over Labrador's resources and borders. Settlement of the Boundary Dispute in 1927 resulted in the present outline of the country and necessitated the installation of customs officers at Blanc Sablon and Forteau. The Dispute itself occasioned an all-out effort to compile affidavits and documents relating to the history and settlement of the region. This collection of Privy Council Records, housed at the National Provincial Archives in St. John's, is now an indispensable resource for the small international community of scholars working in Labrador studies.

Wages paid at IGA hospitals and schools affected even more Labradorians than the lumber company. Women found employment as cooks, laundresses, and nurses' aides. Girls formerly sent to more affluent neighbors and relatives as boarded servants when their families could no longer afford to keep them could now actually enhance the family's means. The Grenfell Industrials made enormous contributions not only to family income but also to the economic advancement and independence of women. In 1933 the Labrador Development Corporation opened a logging operation in Alexis Bay. While it employed mainly Newfoundlanders, local people also found work here. Wherever there were schools, hospitals, and employment opportunities, formerly dispersed families began to gather into communities. By 1930 Cartwright, North West River, Makkovik, and Rigolet boasted clusters of frame houses where a decade before there had been only a log cabin or two.

While a few Labradorians were sampling employment at twenty-five cents an hour, or a day, others rode a swelling market for furs. For the first time it became possible for those with paths in the productive river systems of western Lake Melville and Sandwich Bay to accumulate wealth, albeit in credit. The burgeoning population of young trappers was, however, now obliged to trek over a hundred miles into the interior to reach unclaimed trapping grounds. These 'Height-of-Landers,' as they proudly called themselves, spent over half the year walking the snowbound highlands of Nitassinan, inadvertently competing with the Innu in their final refuge. The trapping way of life became a romantic Labrador subculture, something akin in memory to the *coureurs de bois* or the western cowboy—manly and free. For once the physical demands of Labrador life were rewarded economically. You can see it in the photographs of these vigorous young men, and you can hear it in the spirit of their narratives.

The Great Depression brought the boom in trapping to a precipitous end before tensions between the Innu and Settler came to a head. When a family's credit ran out, the Hudson's Bay Company—in charge of distributing government relief at that time—favoured productive trappers at the expense of Aboriginals and liveyers, for whom trapping was a peripheral activity. The plight of liveyers was further aggravated by an increase in salt prices that drove the cost of curing fish above its market value. Relief—welfare—was the only recourse. When merchants responsible for relief distribution refused to allocate food, desperation sometimes led to uncharacteristic aggressiveness. In 1934 the Newfoundland government assigned Rangers— the provincial police force—to Labrador communities, for the first time subjecting the proud and generally upright Labradorians to the singular arrogance of 'The Law.' Rangers took over relief distribution from the merchants as well, but there was not enough to go around, not enough in anyone's allotment to fend off hunger, and for the better part of a decade people who had never lived far from the edge of disaster teetered on its very brink. Not a few died of starvation or its handmaidens, illness, exposure, and preventable accidents.

In the spring of 1941, before the ice broke up, word spread along the coast that outsiders wanted all the strong Labrador men they could get to build an air base for Allied Forces on a broad, heavily forested alluvial terrace between Goose Bay and the mouth of the Grand River. They promised good wages. A few Labradorians had fought with distinction in World War I. It had been a coming out of sorts for the country. But the construction of Goose Air Base was more than another opportunity for communal patriotism; it was a lifeline from the prolonged Depression. The young men responded in droves. They came on dog teams, they walked on snowshoes. They came from the new town of Postville which the Pentecostal Church had just established on the old HBC site in Kaipokok Bay. They came from Island Harbour, Makkovik, and Aillik, from Jack Lane's Bay and Webbek Harbour, from Rigolet, and Sandwich Bay, from Mary's Harbour and Port Hope Simpson, North West River, Mulligan, Sebaskachu and Mud Lake.

These Labradorians who had never seen a car, let alone an airplane, built an air base, then a town. Once the base was operating it needed labourers. Those willing to give up the freedom of their traplines for the financial security of a regular workday stayed on. Families came and the village grew. Some lonely American servicemen who enjoyed the company of the women named it "Happy Valley," like so many other civilian villages near U.S. military bases. The name stuck and is now proudly defended by residents in spite of its derogatory connotations. Today Happy Valley-Goose Bay is an attractive and very active town of eight thousand.

Goose Air Base saved many a Labradorian from the long, slow Depression, and it got the Height-of-Landers out of the Innu's Nitassinan, but it had little impact on the Moravian Inuit. When the Hudson's Bay Company took over the Moravians trading operations in 1926, they also assumed distribution of charitable assistance. As they treated relief like they had credit—favouring potentially productive trappers—they consistently shortchanged the Inuit, whose terrain yielded fewer valuable furs. Fortunately, many Inuit were able to keep their families fed in the traditional ways, with game foods and fish, until Newfoundland's Confederation with Canada in 1949 at last brought Labrador under the protective wing of a responsible government.

Newfoundland and Labrador had been Britain's last North American colony, and in spite of the neglect and abuse she had suffered, many of her people remained blindly loyal to the Crown until the very end. The vote for Confederation was a close one. Almost immediately thereafter, Canada assumed responsibility for education, welfare, stores, and medical care. Canada's has been activist government at its best, or at least, its best intentioned. She has tried to take good care of the Labradorians. None was ever left totally destitute again; none was obliged to rely on an unpredictable land for survival. People could grow old in a warm place, the sick received care, and children had a chance to achieve their full potential. In spite of the limitations of federal authority over provincial jurisdiction in Canada, the safety net was broad and strong, and most of the people have never looked back. But for some, the freedom to sink or swim, to make or break their own rules was—they like to claim—too high a price to pay for security.

Within the next two decades, the provincial government vigorously encouraged all the people of Labrador to move into centralized communities where services could be rendered more efficiently. Willing or not, most eventually complied. Those who continued their age-old migrations from trapping grounds to salmon rivers to codfishing shacks and back again, as was common until well into the 1970s, did so from a tract house in the village. Old family homesteads gradually succumbed to the weight of winter snows. Their ruins now haunt the shores of deserted bays, moss and grass mounding over fallen timbers and rusted stove parts. Bright green patches of rhubarb and the silvery skeleton of a trapboat are often the only visible sign of a former residence.

Confederation transformed Labrador as dramatically as house lights transform a theatre at the end of a play. It was the end of "them days," a corner absolute as adolescence around which people would no longer be able to go or see except in memory, a place where precious things they thought would never change were left irretrievably behind. Although undoubtedly enhanced by isolation, the innocence of Labrador's old timers and their way of life—way of seeing life—is of course not wholly unique. It is to some extent as much a reflection of the times as of the place. Even in New York City, cynicism was still an intellectual affectation in the early years of this century, and trust was not yet fatal. In that respect, 'them days' is a place we all come from.

One generation cometh
and another passeth away,
but the land abideth forever.
           – *Ecclesiastes*

On a coastal barren north of Nain, the stone knife newly made lies balanced still upon the rock beside its maker, absent now some thousand years. Waste flakes from his knapping silhouette the shadows of his feet. He sat on a little boulder. I can almost guess his foot size. In another cove, down near the shoreline, stones in rough circles remain where they rolled when the hems of skin tents were tugged loose and lashed to komatiks that would never return. Now they are thinly carpeted with prostrate alder and willows, but not hidden. On an island near Aillik, a human skull gapes from a little tumble of stones piled against the rock I sat on while watching whales. Company, these omnipresent bones. There are many cairns in this land. At Ballybrack, below the ancient burial mound and the nest of an anxiously circling rough-legged hawk is an ancient cookfire barely covered by moss. A tiny bone, bleached white by the sun and dried by wind, lies on the lichen—the half-charred remains of a duck that last flew before the Pyramids were built. My archaeologist husband and his colleagues read from these meager clues a history of travels and migrations, conquest and annihilation, prosperity and austerity, but they will never know what made the people laugh or cry, or what they said in the evening when the last morsel of duck had been sucked from the bone and the oil lamp flicked long shadows on the tent walls.

Historians, sociologists, journalists have in their turn come to document the lives of more recent Labradorians. While their commentary is useful, it is unavoidably distorted and subjective, and it has very little to do with the history people actually live or how they understand the forces that shape them. Not that personal accounts are any more objective than observations, especially when recalling youthful years through the rosy glasses of nostalgia or history distorted by family lore. But their subjectivity is as much a part of a person's profile, or a group profile, as the events they chose to tell us about and the personality that emanates from the telling. Writers may be adept at painting clearer portraits of their subjects, but absence of artifice gives the narratives in the following chapters a degree of transparency no writer could duplicate.

Through their stories, as through the layers of ancestral bones they have left in this thin ground, the people too will abide forever, an integral part of their land, and of them. Who better, then, to guide a tour through their rich and adventurous chapter in the human epic, across this haunting country so little known beyond its borders. We will begin the journey not at the beginning, but from a point more readily accessible to most "Outsiders," in the Celtic South. Before turning you over to your guides, you may find a brief orientation to this part of Labrador helpful.

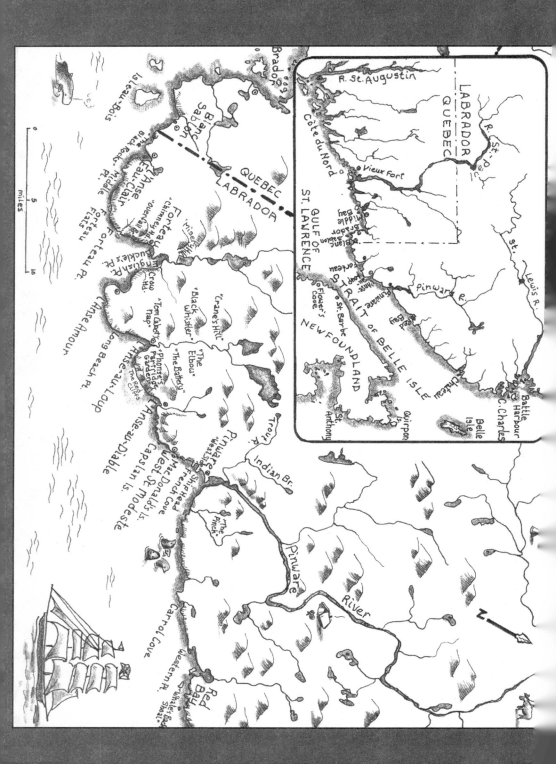

CHAPTER

Two

THE STRAITS

THE ISLAND OF NEWFOUNDLAND DANGLES from the eastern-most point of the North American Continent like a giant plug expelled from the mouth of the St. Lawrence River. Its long northern arm reaches up as though trying to grab hold of the mainland, a gesture some might find symbolic. For seventy miles the Great Northern Peninsula of Newfoundland and the southern coast of Labrador are severed only by a passage nine to eighteen miles wide—the Strait of Belle Isle—named for the cliff island that guards its Atlantic entrance.

On a clear day, a woman hanging her laundry in the Newfoundland outport of Sandy Cove can see the bluffs of Forteau on the Labrador shore, known simply as "The Straits." Her cousin in Forteau can only see the low arm of Newfoundland when it is not enveloped in fogs from the east or sea mists raised by westerly winds, but she can cross over on a Sunday for something to do—take the ferry from Blanc Sablon to St. Barbe and drive to Sandy Cove for tea. Or instead of crossing over, she can pack the kids in the car and drive "down north" along the coastal road to the Basque museum in Red Bay, where the road now ends (though not for long). Beyond that, the rest of Labrador and its six thousand miles of coastline is accessible only by sea, air, or ski-doo. For most of the people of the Straits, it might as well not be there at all. Liveyers to the core, they are united in their independent spirit and sense of moral superiority over those who caught their fish in Labrador waters then left for Newfoundland or England in the fall. But the presence at their back of the great Labrador Peninsula, indeed, of the whole wilderness landmass of arctic Canada, has almost always been more a validation of their self-image than a part of their reality.

Incidentally, visitors need to know that one goes "down" north and "up" south in this part of the world. Most of us find that a difficult concept to entertain for very long, so thoroughly does it up-end assumptions about the orientation of the planet essential to our sense of equilibrium. Yet there exists a subculture of maritime people as far south as Rhode Island for whom it seems either the poles or the meaning of "up" and "down" are reversed. The actual direction of prevailing winds and currents, here or in the British Isles, do not support common assumptions about the derivation of this puzzling custom. A more plausible explanation is suggested by Warrick Smith in his 1943 letter to Premier J. R. [Joey] Smallwood of Newfoundland.[1] This is that British sailors travelling to the New World during the seventeenth and eighteenth centuries universally relied on a published map of Newfoundland rendered in 1616 by Captain John Mason using the classical cartographic orientation in which south was at the top. Smith says this map and its orientation became so fixed in the minds of mariners frequenting these coasts that it dictated the terms of reference henceforth. Thus "down north," "down to Labrador" (from Newfoundland), and "up south" were chiseled forever into the language of the region. It is still prevalent, even among young Labradorians from Happy Valley who have never been to the coast.

The Strait of Belle Isle has its own contrary hydro-dynamics. Currents run in opposite directions along the facing shores. Contrasting water temperatures create frequent fogs, and there is almost twice as much precipitation here as in the rest of Labrador. While prevailing westerly winds regularly plow fog and heavy seas against the almost harbour-less Newfoundland side, the generally clear Labrador shore takes the brunt of big storms from the east and northeast. Licked by a spur of the Labrador Current, it is colder there, but its excellent harbours made it a prime location for the headquarters of early mercantile companies and a center of commerce not only for southern Labrador but at one time also for northwestern Newfoundland.

The Strait is a gateway for whales migrating between calving grounds in Davis and Hudson's Straits and the ice-free estuaries along the Gulf of St. Lawrence. In the sixteenth century when Basques first came to Red Bay the waters teemed with sea mammals—walrus, seals, orcas, beluga whales, minkes, grays, sperm, blues, humpbacks, and best of all, the lethargic, oil-rich bowheads. Southern Innu made annual springtime trips to the Gulf for seals and sometimes walrus, but only Inuit hunted whales before the white man came, and they took only what they needed for food. Early European merchants wanted everything but food. They hunted for oil, bone, baleen, and, in the case of seals, skins as well, and left the meat to rot on the carcass. Later, when settled planters had adopted the Inuit dogsled for winter transportation, the meat was used to feed the dogs.

Basques were the first to corner the market on whales from Labrador. They plied the waters of the Straits and Gulf from 1540 to around 1640 and again, at the sufferance of the French, from 1710 to 1755.[2] Traces of their rendering stations can still be found along the beaches. Dutch and Bretons joined them in the hunt until the eighteenth century, but it was Americans who dominated Labrador whaling during the eighteenth and nineteenth centuries. By 1830 walrus, belugas, and bowheads had all but vanished from southern Labrador, and other species were in decline.

Whales had never been of much interest to the British ship fishers in Labrador or to their Newfoundland successors. Messy whaling operations are incompatible with the codfishery. Since 1763 there have probably been fewer than six whaling stations on the Labrador coast, and none lasted more than a decade or so. Job Brothers station at Schooner Cove in L'anse au Loup lasted only four years. For all of that, the whalers made a big impression on local residents and have become part of their lore.

Sealing remained a primary occupation in the Gulf and Straits until the oil lost its value in the twentieth century, and environmental activists curtailed the trade in pelts. Along with caribou, the seal has probably always been the most versatile and vital subsistence resource in Labrador. Its flesh nourished families and sled dogs; its blubber fueled stone lamps and stoves; its skin covered feet, bodies, boats, and homes; and its organs made pouches, inflatable floats, and containers. Oil and pelts could be exchanged for store goods. It was the oil that had the greatest commercial value for Europeans, oil to illuminate the city streets and homes of a growing middle class, oil even to lubricate the engines of the Industrial Revolution that were driving dispossessed cottagers and artisans to the shores of Labrador. Until petroleum products became widely available after 1859, the rapidly urbanizing Western world depended on the oil of sea mammals for light and lubrication.

The fishery was important in the Straits, as in all of Newfoundland and Labrador, especially during the century after 1850 when Newfoundland firms controlled most of the commercial activity on the outer coasts of Labrador. But there are better fishing grounds than those of the Straits. Salmon rivers are few and short. And there are none of the succulent lobsters that reach their northern limit on the west coast of Newfoundland.

The land appears formidable enough, with its brow of high barrens and toothy shoreline, but sheltered coves at the foot of the mountains capture the warmth of long summer days. The sandy soil is arable. Patches of thick, glossy grass furl and stream in the wind, and abundant berries grow especially plump on the hillsides and marshes. When the sea failed the Settlers, as it often did, people of the Straits could count on a supply of hardy tubers and greens, eggs, and milk from their small farms. Without this edge, winters would have been grim indeed, for hunting on the highlands is poor and, with the exception of the Pinware system, the river valleys yield little in the way of furs.

Maritime Archaic Indians used the area as a link in their long coastal trading chain but the Innu seem to have avoided it, possibly due to the proximity of Inuit bands drawn to the Basque and Breton stations. During the nineteenth century Innu families from St. Augustine, just around the corner on the Gulf shore, would occasionally make a detour from their annual trek to hunting grounds near the Eagle and Grand rivers to descend the Pinware for seals, fish, trade, or later, a visit to the priest, but they never stayed long. The highland plain immediately behind the Straits and Atlantic

Shore is the only inland area in southern Labrador not identified as Innu hunting territory on ethnologist Frank Speck's 1939 map.[3]

By the seventeenth century, Inuit were hunting whales, walrus, and seals in the Straits, and terrorizing European fishing stations as far west as Sept Isles. From their villages near Battle Harbour and on Belle Isle, kayak flotillas regularly crossed to the east coast of Newfoundland for yew-wood from Fogo, which they used for bows, and for European trade goods from the old Carpunt station. In 1764 such a flotilla encountered the Moravian Jens Haven on his maiden voyage to North America. After pacification and throughout much of the nineteenth century, ever-dwindling Inuit bands continued to visit the Straits, but there is no indication that any married into the Settler population of these particular communities as they did on either side of them.

The first whites to settle here were French. Small communities clustered around the trading concessions at Blanc Sablon, L'anse Ste. Claire (L'anse Eau Claire), L'anse au Loup, St. Modet (St. Modeste), Riviere des Francois (Pinware), and Chateau during the eighteenth century. These were servants of prosperous mercantile dynasties in France and Quebec City whose intrepid frontier partners and agents, men like Louis Joliet, Courtemanche, and Pierre Constanin, explored the Labrador coast in the late 1600s and established the first permanent outposts in the Straits during the ensuing decades. After the British victory in 1763, there was a decade of confusion during which the French were initially expelled from their holdings in Labrador. From time to time this included the shores of eastern Gulf, known as Canadian Labrador, or the Lower North Shore. Those who remained in the area as citizens of now British Quebec appealed to the courts for restitution. Although these suits were occasionally or temporarily successful, and coastal Labrador periodically ended up under Canadian jurisdiction, the old French families of the Straits eventually disappeared from the area. Some would reappear by 1784 among the Canadian firms and Settlers in Hamilton Inlet and Kaipokok Bay.

When French names reappear in the western Straits and eastern Gulf after 1774, they were primarily former Bretons from the Channel Islands—English since the Norman Conquest. Most came as shoremen for the large firms of De Quetteville and Boutillier Brothers, some with smaller companies like Emery & Best. Many were artisans, some farmers, only a few were fishermen. De Quetteville was involved in the fishery but took most of his fishing crews home in the fall, leaving a small company of shoremen to trade, trap, and mind the stations. Among those who remained when their terms of service ended were progenitors of the Mesher, Dumaresque, Saulter, Linstead, and Cabot families. Best himself, like Mesher, may have ended up in Hamilton Inlet, where a venerable family by that name still exists. "Old" Robert Best is said to have lived with Ambrose Brooks at Mulligan when Lydia Campbell was a child.

The first merchant adventurers to establish successful operations on the eastern Straits after the Treaty of Paris were John Noble of Bristol and Andrew Pinson of Dartmouth. Noble & Pinson had been active in Newfoundland and Labrador since the late 1760s, operating from bases in St. John's and Conche. In 1772 they brought 150 men, most from Ireland, to their Labrador headquarters at Temple Bay, Chateau. They later established fishing and sealing outposts at L'anse au Loup, St. Lewis Bay (probably Fox Harbour), and Sandwich Bay. Smaller crews worked the unoccupied coves and river mouths of the coast, taking salmon and fur and trading with Innu and planters.

Just as the annual traffic of British ship fishers and merchant adventurers was beginning to rise, along with an infrastructure for trans-Atlantic commerce, the seas again became a battleground. From 1793 until 1815 England's successive wars with France rendered already risky crossings both dangerous and unprofitable. American privateers, French gunboats, and press gangs for the Royal Navy ruled the shipping lanes.

Merchants already committed to their Labrador enterprise responded by keeping more supplies and workers on this side of the Atlantic. Most found legitimate or illegitimate New World markets for their goods. Two companies took root in the Straits during that period, Lymburner and Grants' "Labrador Company" from Quebec, and the Birds of Sturminster-Newton in Dorset. Lymburner employed about a hundred men at sealing stations on the Lower North Shore from 1784 into the early nineteenth century. He also had a sizable operation at Pinware and is reported by Cartwright to have been active in Hamilton Inlet.

Joseph Bird and his partner Thomas Street established a base at Forteau in the 1790s, employing men from Blackmore Vale and the Stour River valley whose traditional occupations as artisans were becoming obsolete in the Industrial Revolution. From Forteau, Bird and company sent small crews north to Tub and Seal Harbours on the Atlantic Shore and to posts in Hamilton Inlet. Thomas Bird, perhaps a son, operated the northern outposts until 1835, when he sold them to the Hudson's Bay Company. He seems to have run the family business from 1824 until 1844, three years after Joseph's death, and may have been progenitor of the Birds of Sandwich Bay. Like Best, the name survives in Labrador, but the connection has been temporarily lost. The Birds were a wealthy Dorset family, and Thomas is known to have spent at least some time in Sturminster-Newton during the last decade of the company's Labrador operations.

During the wars, Noble & Pinson entrenched themselves at Temple Bay to protect their stations from pirates and rivals while eluding the attention of naval officers at St. John's who might have been tempted to commandeer the company's ships. For their precautions they were subjected instead to raiding and looting by privateers and a blistering attack by three French men-o-war in 1797. Known for its hardball competition with George Cartwright, Pinson's operations nevertheless survived in the Straits until 1830. American whalers and privateers harassed the defenseless planters of southern Labrador as well as the merchants, usurping their fishing berths and littering the coves with whale offal. But they also offered the planters an alternative market for their catch and, in many cases, escape to America.

With the end of the Napoleonic Wars in 1815, the seas opened once again just in time to carry to the New World a flood of British refugees from the Dickensonian stage of the Industrial Revolution. Displaced cottagers and farmers able to emigrate to the colonies embarked in droves for America, until she temporarily closed her doors in the 1840s, and then to Canada. A handful ended up in Labrador—not all of them runaways and stowaways as is so often claimed. Despite its relatively poor trapping and indifferent fishery, the Straits is one of the only areas in Labrador where a farmer could feel even marginally at home. Many of its Settlers were solid family men with useful skills and a household. They brought with them a ragtag blend of ancient rural dialects and cultural traditions that would be preserved in this area virtually unchanged until the mid-twentieth century, to the delight of ethnologists. This was also true of those who came to the Labrador Straits after living for two centuries in the time warp of a Newfoundland bay. The Newell, Butt, Pike, Parsons, Davis, Petten, and Hopkins families are among those who had lived in Conception and Trinity Bay since the seventeenth century, resisting efforts by both the Crown and French invaders to remove them.[4]

It was Joseph Bird who, in a letter to his agent at Forteau, said, "I think if you were to calculate on getting out 6 boats next year...employing about 26-28 hands it would do.... The extra provisions could then be sold [to Settlers] to produce fish, oil, fur, or salmon." And later, "What I wish is to have a few fixed planters.... *who look to us for supplies*,"[5] (my italics). As increasing numbers of merchants recognized that a small, dependent resident population was another potentially profitable resource, they established a system of exchange based on its exploitation. This was the context for settlement, for 150 years the cause of untold hardship and suffering, the reason for the population's economic retardation, and ultimately also the downfall of the mercantile companies. But at one time it may have been the only viable system for a land with no safety nets.

In the Straits as elsewhere the choicest areas were dominated from the outset by the large mercantile establishments and their employees. Settlement began on the margins, wherever a man could find a vacant salmon stream and large enough sealing territory to support himself and a growing family. Salmon streams were prize possessions, chartered, bought and sold like land. When the bays on the Labrador side of the Strait filled up, newcomers spilled over to the Newfoundland side. Some seasoned old-timers headed for less-crowded areas to the north. According to Patricia Thornton (1977), about seven families settled on the Straits between 1770 and 1830—the Frontier Period—primarily in and around Forteau. British settlement began in earnest after that.

At least twenty-five men, mostly from the British Isles, moved to the Straits between 1830 and 1850.[6] They were joined by five Newfoundland women in the company of their families. After 1850, when the summer codfishery became more important economically than sea mammal oil and furs, most of the newcomers were Newfoundland fishermen. Englishmen who arrived thereafter were more often from the Isle of Jersey. Several Frenchmen also came, possibly from the French Shore of Newfoundland or the Gaspe Peninsula where De Quetteville and other Jersey merchants had bases which may well have served as conduits for goods passing between Labrador and Canada during the wars.[7] When the Banque Union of Jersey crashed in 1873, all the Jersey firms in Labrador folded. Most sold their operations to Job Brothers of Newfoundland, which went on to dominate the shore fishery in the Straits until well into the twentieth century.

Initially, the Settlers of the Straits followed the pattern of seasonal migration typical of the Labrador frontier. By 1850, however, the growing emphasis on fishing and farming led to a more sedentary lifestyle. Families began to gather in year-round communities where they could tend their gardens, perhaps a cow and chickens, and from which they could base their fishing and residual sealing activities. During the winter they would make occasional brief trips into the country for game or a 'bit of fur' to top off their yearly income, but it was not a significant occupation for most. Their new communities had regular contact with Newfoundland and some access to church services and schooling. By mid-century the more prosperous Settlers had graduated from log cabins and huts to comfortable two-storey frame houses. By the twentieth century some were even sending their children to schools on the Island, where they could board with relatives.

Forteau was the largest British settlement in Labrador during the initial decade of the frontier period—1774 to 1785—when Philip De Quetteville had a fishery in the bay. After Governor Palliser instructed merchants to leave men at the shore stations over the winter, Devonshiremen began to winter at English Point on the east side. In time Guernsey fishermen with stations at Buckle's Point on the west side also began staying through the winter. William Buckle himself settled down in Forteau around 1795, as did Edward Cribb and William Bell of Portsmouth. Bell is said to have been a runaway, but Buckle and Cribb were evidently men of some means, independent planters, with servants. Both family names show up on Slade Company ledgers around the turn of the century, but only in passing. It was not uncommon during the first decades of settlement for independent planters to procure both goods and servants from the ship fishers. The servants would crew for the fishery during the summer and for the planters through the winter.

Joseph and Thomas Bird had their headquarters in Forteau from 1800 until 1844. By 1849 the community was large enough to support a C of E church—the first in Labrador. Reverend Algernon Gifford's parish extended across the Straits and attracted another wave of Settlers to Forteau. Newfoundlanders like the Trimms of Trinity Bay and the Pooles of Carbonear arrived in the 1850s and '60s. In 1909 the International Grenfell Association established a nursing station in the community and, in 1939, a boarding school. In 1940 the nursing station was expanded to a hospital. Today the village has a population of around five hundred.[8]

A colony of Irish Settlers, led by the large O'Dell family, began to form at Pinware around 1800. The O'Dells allegedly left Ireland for the New World when Protestants confiscated their lands in the seventeenth century. They went first to Nova Scotia, then Carbonear, and from there to Pinware several generations later. The Labrador progenitor and his wife may have been in Pinware before the nineteenth century, as their deaths occurred around 1805, according to extant headstones. Michael Moore of Bally Hale and Thomas McDonald of Killiewy came to Pinware directly from Ireland around the same time as the O'Dells came from Carbonear. By 1887 the population of the bay was large enough to compel the Bishop of Newfoundland to erect Labrador's first Roman Catholic church in the village. Innu came down the river for services.

Family histories published in *Them Days* provide much valuable information about early settlement, but as some families contributed more heavily than others to the magazine, and many of the very oldest have lost track of their origins, the history outlined by the narratives must be viewed as a starting point for more systematic research currently being done by some of the descendants.[9] They indicate that L'anse Eau Claire was settled around 1825 by Newfoundlanders and people from the south coast of England, L'anse Amour around 1840, when William Elworthy of Devonshire arrived. Labrador's first lighthouse was built on the point in 1854.

L'anse au Loup's original residents—John Cabot and Tom Linstead of Jersey, and John Barney of Cornwall—arrived around 1850. They were followed by Charles Ryland of Somersetshire in 1860; Thomas Belben in 1865; William Normore of Bell Island in 1868; John Barber, the farmer from Somerset, around 1870; Thomas O'Brien from St. John's in 1875; and "Old Phonse" (whose last name was apparently never used) around 1880. Job Brothers of St. John's opened a whale factory at nearby Schooner Cove in the first years of the twentieth century, employing some of the local residents. Today L'anse au Loup, with its population of around six hundred, is the largest community in the Straits.

In 1800 or thereabouts, Thomas Buckle—possibly William's son from Forteau—settled Capstan Island beneath the looming headland called "The Battery." The land there is said to be especially fertile and today supports a small community with several greenhouses. Newfoundlanders from Conception Bay settled Red Bay before

1850, according to Thornton. It was in this community that Dr. Grenfell opened the first IGA cooperative store in 1896, providing residents with an opportunity to share in the risks and gains of capitalism. In 1939 he established a school. West St. Modeste seems to have been settled around 1850 when William Fowler of Somersetshire arrived. In 1903 IGA opened its second cooperative store there.

Chateau, the easternmost community of the Straits, was so named by fifteenth-century Bretons because of the rectangular basalt crown that gives to an island in the bay the imposing appearance of a Norman keep. From earliest times it served as Labrador's main port of call as well as a principal landfall for ships en route to points south and north. It was Noble & Pinson headquarters from 1774 to 1830, and Pierre Marcoux is said to have run his Hamilton Inlet and Kaipokok operations from here in the last two decades of the eighteenth century. Since the departure of Pinson and his final partner, Hine, Chateau and neighboring Henley Harbour have primarily served as summer fishing stations for families from Newfoundland and Red Bay.

Perhaps the single most defining episode in the lives of this chapter's narrators was the designation of the boundary between Quebec and Labrador in 1927. After centuries of ambiguity and decades of fact-finding and debate, contesting parties in the dispute over possession of Labrador agreed to draw the line at the western extremity of the Strait of Belle Isle between Blanc Sablon and Forteau. The decision was made at the dawn of the great Depression. It would fall like an ax across the slender threads of commerce and economic activity that sustained the Settlers of the Straits, severing not only their economic networks but also dealing a blow to their centuries-old sense of self-determination and pride. Blanc Sablon, always an integral part of the Straits and the location of important merchants, was now in Canada, a nation away. Rules were imposed about crossing the border, duties added to the price of goods, and customs officers installed to enforce the rules and extract the duties. This was incomprehensible to the people of the Straits, especially those in Forteau, L'anse Eau Claire and L'anse au Loup who were obliged to trade in Blanc Sablon because there was no accessible store on their side of the border. By the time Newfoundland Rangers were assigned to Labrador's principal communities in 1935, the enmity between liveyers and officers of the law had become almost genetic.

Given the inevitable hardships of life on the edge of wilderness, the people of the Straits have led relatively comfortable lives. Having food on the table, maybe sugar and tinned milk for their Sunday tea, was a kind of prosperity any Labradorian could be proud of 'them days,' and they were. Their orientation until recently has been east and south, an outpost of the Old World clinging to the edge of the New. The relative sophistication of the Straits communities, their penchant for farming, and the purity of their European bloodstock and culture distinguish them from most other residents of Labrador and the Lower North Shore of Quebec. While this is a distinction few Labradorians would make, least of all they, it is useful to keep in mind as you venture into the narratives. The people of the Straits represent the British component of the Labrador equation, more or less as it was introduced two centuries ago. Later, when you have met the Aboriginal components, you may better appreciate the contributions each group has made to the singular character that today defines "the Labradorian."

1786
August
Wednesday 23
Wind fresh
N. Moderate

The land hereabouts looks well to the eye, being clear of wood; the hills rise gradually, but not high, exhibit great verdure, and an appearance of more fertility than I have ever seen on any other part of the coast. In the valley where Noble & Pinson's fishery is carried on is a garden in which every thing grows more luxuriantly than I ever saw before in this country; and I also observed great plenty of scarlet strawberries growing among the grass. Curlews are now abundant and fat; I killed one. The fishery has proved very indifferent here this season.
*   A very fine day throughout.*

• • • •

Monday 28
S.S.W. fresh

The boats being returned, and captain Packenham having finished his business at this place, we went to sea at eight this morning, and at one o'clock came to an anchor in Forteau Bay. I went on shore to Mr. Durrell's house, where I staid the night; he is an agent to a Jersey company. Several planters live here who, dividing their winter business between this place and the opposite part of Newfoundland, do tolerably well for themselves.

— Geo. Cartwright
Journals, Sixth Voyage

To His Excellency, the Governor
Blanc Sablon
27th July 1835

Sir:

I beg you will excuse my taking the liberty of addressing you on the following subject. Having been a Planter on this Coast for these Forty years and being at the head of a large Family who almost all depend on my fishing Post in Middle Bay [Quebec Labrador] I laid out my seal Frame this Spring on the hopes of doing the fishery when on the 9th of June last an American Schooner Commanded by Captain Sampia entered my Frame altho I entreated of him not to and at the same time weighed anchor when they hooked an broke our Nets and hawser whereby I lost my best anchor.

Two days afterwards the American Schooner the James Murrow, Captain Bodie, and the Admiral Captain Templeton entered my frame although I told them not to as they kept me from taking any seals. Still they stopt in many days which caused me a great lost.

I have therefore humbly to request you would take this in consideration and be kind enough to let me know whether those vessels had a right to do so and if not what I can do to recover the lost I have sustained.

I remain,
William Buckle

COMMANDER I. HOPE OF THE ROYAL Navy investigated William Buckle's complaint, and reported to H.B.M. Ambassador Extraordinary at Washington.

His report gives in some detail the damage caused by the American vessels (apparently these were not the only incident along the coast), and the harassment of the local people. When William Buckle's sons went to complain to the captain, some of the crew threatened to throw them overboard.

In his letter to the Ambassador, Commander Hope has this to say, "…William Buckle…has been a Settler on the coast fifty-one years [ca. 1785], forty-one of which he has resided at Forteau; he has brought up a large family of six sons and four daughters and been a most excellent character." He concludes, "These people complain that justice is so distant that it is beyond their means to seek it and beg that something may be done for their protection."

— Rev. Francis Buckle
[1.3:29]

THE FIRST MAN WHO EVER lived in Forteau, over on the Forteau side, was a Cribb. I don't know exactly where the first Cribbs come from, but I believe it was from England. The first old feller that lived on English Point, they tells me, was old Grandfather Bell who came from Portsmouth in England. I can't remember him of course. I suppose he was a runaway, 'cause most all who came here to this coast was runaways, deserted their country.

Mr. Barbour and Mr. Phonse was the first two ever lived in L'anse au Loup, so I been informed. There's a place they goes partridge hunting called Phonse's Partridge Garden.

Some of the first old people in Forteau was ol' Grandfather Hancock, ol' Mr. Cribb, ol' Skipper Joey Buckle and old great-grandfather Bell who came from Portsmouth. Now they had servant men. Ol' Mr. Buckle had a Frenchman and an Englishman and these two couldn't hold a candle with each other. In the spring of the year butter got scarce. Ol' Mrs. Buckle laid the table this day with just a little bit of butter on the dish. The Englishman reached over and took one piece of butter and put it on his bread then he reached over, before the Frenchman got a chance to get the rest, and he put it in his tea. He said he'd just as soon have cold water if he had to drink his tea without butter in it.

Finally, in the fall of the year, it come time to haul up the boats. Uncle Joey Buckle sent over for Mr. Cribb's men to come and help. Mr. Cribb told 'en he had some other fish to fry. That was an ol' sayin', you know, some other fish to fry. Very well! He got the boat hauled up wit' tackles. Then it come time when Mr. Cribb got in trouble wit' he's boat and he sent a man over to after Uncle Joey. The Frenchman was sot to the table, he hunched up his shoulders and said he had to cook some fish. [14.1:24]

MY PEOPLE COME FROM HANT'S Harbour, Trinity Bay, Newfoundland. He come down here fishin'. He said he'd eat his fish where he caught it. You ask Father how he come to come here. He said he come to look for what was left out in the Lord's Prayer, Give us this day our daily bread. They left that out in the Lord's Prayer in Newfoundland, he said.

I was born the 28th of December, 1911. I married a Barney girl from L'anse au Loup, Elsie Barney. [15.4:31] I fished with me father and me grandfather. We usen't catch much, the odd one like the feller catchin' trout. I used to go around to the trap then, we'll say, because the Newfoundland people used to be around with the traps. I used to have a hand gaff, up forward, and when they was throwin' up the fish I'd hook away until I'd get me pound full. I usen't ask no permission. We'd get about $2, $2.50 a quintal.

I remember when you could walk across Forteau Bay on schooner decks. Just the same as a big forest of woods in the bay, spars, stuck up everywhere. Fifty, sixty schooners to a time, perhaps more than that. They'd be all anchored up, lined up in the bay. The Twelfth of July[10] you'd hear 'um all blowin' their horns. They used to keep up the Twelfth of July then, firin' guns and blowin' fog horns. Nobody fishin' the Twelfth of July, they used to keep it up see, the old Newfoundland fishermen. There'd be ten dory bankers right down to the little small ones with two and three dories, accardin' to the size of the schooner.

We sold our fish to Mr. Organ and Mr. Pike, and the traders used to come, in schooners, buyin' fish. They'd anchor in the bay and you'd go aboard with so much fish, sell it and get something for it. But the main b'ys was ol' Uncle Matt Organ and ol' W.Y. Pike.

I can remember when the Diver Jack was lost. She had a load of fish aboard, just drove ashore over there to Forteau Flats. We was only bedlamers then.

Me Daddy's parents come from Newfoundland, Trinity Bay. That's where we sprung from, Trinity Bay, New Chelsea. A lot of people that used to come here in schooners got married, some stayed and some took their women back to Newfoundland with 'um.

— Stanley & Robert Trimm
[14.1:21]

WHEN THE PEOPLE COME TO L'anse au Loup they lived here all the time. Most of the old people come here as apprentices. Ol' Tom Linstead and ol' John Cabot come from the Isle of Jersey. My grandfather's father come from Ireland to Bonavista Bay in Newfoundland and that's where he pitched. After my grandfather got growed up and married, he shift to St. John's, Newfoundland. He had four children: Mike, Jack, Mary, and Jane. His wife was Margaret Hogan but she later died.

B'm'by grandfather come fishin' here. He come alone the first year, I think, and he stayed with his sister Jane. She was married to John Barber [or Barbour], another ol' Englishman, from Somerset, England. He was a farmer so he took half of L'anse au Loup when he come. Anyhow he was married to Grandfather's sister.

The next year Grandfather come back with the two girls and Mike. Jack stayed in Newfoundland with his grandmother. Grandfather had bought a little store the fall before so now he had a place to put his fish in. The second summer he lived with Aunt Jane again until he bought a house. The next year they all come down and then they stayed and, like everybody else, they got more b'm'by.

When my grandfather was sixty years old he married Elizabeth Ann Barney. Annie was twenty-eight years old. They had Thomas, Richard, Margaret, Bridget and Julie Ann. Richard died shortly after he was born. Three of 'um got married in L'anse au Diable. They were so fine a people as ever lived on the bloody coast. Fine women and men.

I can remember Grandfather well enough, and I can remember Annie. I was five or six when she died. I can mind when Grandfather come over to Father's ol' house. 'Twas in the winter, dirty day, boy, dirty. I seems I see 'en now, all muffled up.

He said, "Mike, come over. Annie is dyin'." And he went out again. Father jumped up and went on too. I can mind when I went over there and seen her in the coffin. She had TB.

Tom Linstead had a path cut right out through the woods. I seen the bloody path but I didn't know who owned it 'till Father told me. He was cut right out to the Battery.

The first of 'um comin' here wanted comfort. Labrador had a bad name then about bad weather, people gettin' lost and one thing and another. Those people when they came here was very timid. In where he was he couldn't get no salt water birds. They didn't want to be trampin' out over the barrens because of bad weather comin' on, so he cut a path. He could follie along be the shore and then b'm'by come to his path. He'd come in his path and get right home. 'Twas only he and his sons and they had all their families there.

There was more woods then than there is now. Cripes, I can mind when Uncle George used to cut all his wood down inside the Battery, a damn sight better than you can cut in to the Elbow now.

When I was a young feller, about nine or ten, I fished with poor ol' Phonse. I got eight quintals, eight barrels of fish. I was a big shot then! Anyhow I wouldn't fish with 'en no more because he was too contrary.

The next year I went with Uncle George Cabot. Uncle Ambrose Hogan used to fish with 'en but he died that winter, so I went with Uncle George that summer. We had five lines of trawl; I had two lines and Uncle George had three. Whatever I got on me own two lines I owned, and I owned whatever I jug, and what I killed I owned. When it was square-up time he never had too damn much more than I did. The next year was about the same, so the third year Uncle George said we'd share and share alike.

Fish makin' time, them times, you had to catch 'um, bring 'um in, clean 'um and salt 'um. Around the fifteenth of August you had to wash it out and fulled up your flakes dryin' 'um. The time would come then to make your first trip in the country and then you'd come out at your fish again. That's the way we got along.

We never had no cod traps. We had the trawl, hand-line and jigger. An odd man might have a trap, like up there to Schooner Cove or down around Pinware. But there's no fish now, they got it all hooked up, caught up or something or other. They caught all the big fish, the breedin' fish. Where the hell is the small ones goin' to come from when all the big fish are gone? All the mother fish? Poor ol' Jack Cabot, down to L'anse au Diable, and the crew he had, they used to come down with a big load of fish, and all the biggest kinds of fish. I haven't seen nare big fish for years, not what I call a big fish like you could catch in them times.

— Pat O'Brien
[15.4:10]

THE FIRST PERMANENT SETTLERS IN Pinware were the O'Dells, seven brothers of them. They were driven from Ireland during the Reformation and their land was confiscated. At first they settled at Carbonear and used to come to Labrador in schooner to fish for cod. Finally they heard of an abandoned French house on the west side of Ship Head, they took possession of it and made Pinware their home.

My great-grandfather, John O'Dell, was one of these seven brothers and he and his wife, Jane, were the first to be buried in the cemetery on the neck of land dividing Pinware Bay from French Cove. They have two large granite tombstones, which are both split down the middle with age and weather. Their names can easily be read but the dates of their deaths, 1803 and 1807, are nearly worn off.

John O'Dell's sons were Richard, William, Henry, Hugh, Mark, Luke, and John. These names followed the O'Dells even to this day. There is a Mark, a Luke, and a John, but to my knowledge there has never been a Matthew O'Dell. All the first O'Dells built their homes in Pinware, which was then on the western side of Ship Head.

In them days there were many shipwrecks, and there was always much timber to be picked up. One of these ships went ashore in Pinware Bay with a whole load of balk, so much that they dug a large hole near the bottom of the Head to store the balk. They built a pit-saw scaffold beside it and they then had plenty of pine lumber with which to build their houses. These houses were all two-apartment houses or, as they called them, double houses, built with cottage roofs. They also built a little church near the cemetery where my grandparents were buried. Their graves lie east and west, but the church was built north and south, so all the other graves lie parallel with the church. The bell that came out of this ship was placed in the belfry near the church and besides being used to call the people to prayer it was rung when boats went astray in the fog. Its clear sound could be heard far out to sea. The captain had put twenty pounds sterling worth of silver in this bell.

— Belle Butt
[5.4:20]

Pinware River
Jan. 7, 1888

My dear Mary Jane,

I am happy to have this opportunity of writing, hoping you are well and happy. How anxious I am to have a letter from you to know how you are getting on. It is now five months since I left you and only received one letter from you, that was in September. I received one from Mrs. Scully in October. I am writing in hopes to hear how you are.

We are all well home thank God, except Uncle Hughy. He was paralyzed in the right arm and leg in the fall, his leg is getting better and he can walk around. I don't think his arm will be any better.

Edith Lilly died the sixth of this month. Her mother and sister are very sorrowful about her. She got a cold last fall going to Lance-au-Mort.
We have lots of company here this month. There were seven or eight families of Mountaineer Indians come out here and the leader of them is brother to old Mitchell [Michel?] that lived seven or eight year with your father. They are always at our houses. They have lots of fur, beavers, otters, martens and all kinds. The people in the river are making all kinds of trade with them every day. They have over $300 worth of fur and no shop or place to buy food nearer than nine miles east or west. If I had brought some goods from St. John's when I was there I would have sold them. Your Uncle Mike, Steven and Uncle John are making trade. They are up there now preparing to go away. They are talking of buying a stock of all sorts.
Father MacCarthy was down here a fortnight ago for a while. He made the first mission. He stayed at our house. He had Mass every morning in the school-room. The place was crowded with people. The Mountaineers sang vespers Sunday evening and came next morning to Mass. They sing grand. Father MacCarthy was delighted with them, and with the river, too. He said he did not think there was any such place on the shore. He saw a wedding and funeral and Indians all the same time. He said it reminded him of the town.
I must not forget to tell you that Lottie O'Dell and James Bolger were married that morning after Mass. He looked down the river and saw Poor Edith's funeral going with a large attendance of mourners. It looked very sad.
Next morning he called out the names of the persons to lead the different crews to cut sticks to make the house in Pinware for the priest to live in. On the following Monday it was very frosty and rough, the men assembled nevertheless and each one trying to outdo the other. In two days they had it all lodged by our door on the river and two flags flying over it. Rich and Ned O'Dell went up yesterday to bring the priest down here to see it according to orders. These two days I could not get a chance to write, we were so busy. The mailman is expected here every moment I thought I would not get a chance to write, if the priest had come I would not. Ann Marie have not time to say her prayers. She has her letter waiting for a chance to send it. You must excuse all this news. Mark is the only one that has good times, when he sees the rest so busy he takes it easy. He joins me in sending love to you.

Your affectionate mother,
Catherine O'Dell

[9.1:48]

THE FIRST O'DELLS, I heard my father say, they come out from Ireland in the first of it. They come to Nova Scotia, from there to Newfoundland, and from that to Labrador, and that's where a lot of them stayed. I heard my father saying that they were the first that settled in Pinware, that's just below here. Them times, they says, fish was numerous, seals was numerous, everything was plentyful. I suppose that's why they settled in Labrador. They could make a good living then, everything was cheap.

I was a McDonald before I was married. That's an Irish name. My grandfather was Thomas McDonald [b.1791], he came from Cork. Grandmother was Catherine Cull, she came from Kilarney. 'Twas on the headstones down to Pinware, but when they had that blasting down there, they shook the ground, and the headstones got broke up, two great big stones. I can't remember the dates on them.

My father was Michael McDonald, and my mother was Annie Beals. I was born out on McDonald's Island. All the McDonalds lived on McDonald's Island in the summer time. In the fall, after the fishery was made, we'd move over on the mainland. There was ten of us altogether, in family. One little brother died when he was about three weeks old. I had another brother twenty-one years old, he got kicked in the lower part of his stomach when he was playin' football. He went down to the General Hospital in St. John's, Newfoundland. Them times, now, they couldn't do anything, but p'haps today, now, they might be able to. He suffered a lot. The only way he could get any rest was to put his legs up in slings. He died.

Mostly we had Newfoundland teachers in them days, because we was under Newfoundland. I went to school at Pinware, mostly. I remember a Mr. Brazil from St. John's and a Paddy Morrisey. I had a married sister down to Pinware, so I used to stay down there. Sometimes, we'd walk home for weekends, sometimes we'd come by boat.

The first gramophone that ever come here in West St. Modeste, my father brought it from a Captain Keatch, who came here in a fishin' vessel. I believe we had the first sewing machine. I was tryin' to sew on the machine, and I drove the needle down through my finger, I never forgot about that. I was about fourteen then.

The main religion in West St. Modeste, in them days, was Roman Catholic. We'd see a priest once a year until Confederation took over, and then there was a priest to Long Point. Father Tessier was here for years, sure. We used to see the bishop every four years, mostly, it was poor old Bishop March from Harbour Grace, and there was a Bishop O'Neil.

We had a good many more Holy days then than we do now. We always kept St. Patrick's Day, Annunciation Day, and we always kept Sundays. Seems like we had more then. Of course, there was Christmas. The Tuesday before Ash Wednesday, we called that Stroth Tuesday. I don't know if I'm pronouncing that right, but we always called it Stroth Tuesday. We'd have a big cooked feed then because the next day was a fast day. We'd have a big dinner of cabbage, peas, turnips, things like that...just like you'd cook on Sunday. The next morning everybody would fast 'till twelve o'clock. My father always fasted.

We had good times Christmas. I'll never forget once when I went to a time to Pinware with poor old Jack Lowe. He's my cousin, you know. When you're goin' over the neck there's a great big head that you got to lower the komatik down over.

Jack said, "I'll have a look now. You're all right? I won't be long."

The dogs gave a pluck, and I knowed nothing 'till I was face and eyes and all the clothes on me back down in the snow.

I heared Jack bawl, he was almost cryin', "You're killed,"

I couldn't get anything out, I was laughin' so much. After a bit, I said, "No, no, no. I'm all right. I'm not hurted at all."

Well, what a way he was in to. He thought I was killed. I fell in the soft snow so I wasn't hurted, but I'll tell you, I got some fright.

We had lots of dances them times. We mostly danced over home 'cause we had a great big kitchen, you know. Hardwood floor. Mostly we'd have times over there. We had accordion and violin music, those two. I love music. I can sit for hours and listen to music.

— Mary Ellen O'Dell
[3.2:17]

I SAW A GHOST ONE TIME. He wasn't a ghost, 'twas really, but people wouldn't believe me just the same, and up to this day they don't think 'tis right.

There was a feller here to Pinware then by the name of Rich Dooley. I left his place in the noonday to go in the river and when I got to Trout River (my father used to live there one time). 'Twas a lovely splendid day. I turned off to go over for the river and when I did this feller sung out to me.

He said, "Hold on."

When I slewed around, sure enough here he was comin' on behind me. I had me rackets on and he had a pair on too. When I seen 'en comin' I was sure 'twas Rich Dooley so I wasn't ascared, not a bit. He come up so far from me and he brought up and he slewed around. When he slewed around he had a pair of seal skin cuffs hung on his back. He had a pair of worsted mitts on and a pair of black boots with the strings hanging right on the snow. I looked at him a little while. I still thought 'twas him. He come on and when he come that close I knew 'twasn't Rich Dooley. I knowed I never seen him before.

That was all, I went home and when I got there and got in the house they asked me what was wrong and I couldn't speak, I was that far gone. After a spell I asked me mother fer a drink of water and she asked me what was the matter so I told her. First they said it was nonsense, they said 'twas me imagination. I said, "No Sir."

We got ready and went down to see his footin' 'cause he had rackets on, you know. Earlier, when he turned back, brother I watched 'en, he went up over a big cliff and he went fair up over, I watched 'en. He went up and over clear out of sight. We went down and there was no footin' only mine. They said again 'twas my imagination.

I said, "No, Sir, 'twas real."

Poor old Father History used to come here then, he was a preacher from Long Point. I said when he comes down I was gonna ask him about seein' ghosts, spirits. So when he come down I went to Confession and I asked him. I told him what I seen and asked him could it be true. He said that it could be a soul and if you had had the heart to speak to 'en he'd have answered back. He must have wanted me fer something, he said.

"P'haps," he said, "'twas your father."

Well, that's the kind of man me father was in looks. I never seen me father before, only I seen his picture all right.

I said, "Yes, Sir, p'haps it was."

"I'll tell you what to do," he said, "And you'll never see 'en again. You give me five dollars for a Mass fer 'en and you will never see 'en no more."

He told me also never be scared of ghosts but go on just the same.

I give 'en the five dollars and I never seen nothing after but I believed in that one all right.

— Edward O'Dell
[3.2:32]

IN CHRISTMAS TIME WE'D JANNY up. We'd make a hobby-horse, just as big as a real horse. You'd cut out a horse's head, saw the jaw and split the mouth. You'd have a big red flannel tongue or a piece of seal skin painted red. Use felt tins or something like that for his eyes. You'd put a stick in a hole bored in the head and put a sail on it. Two or three people would get under the sail and you'd form a horse. You'd haul on a line to work the horse's head, have the lines concealed.

The hobby-horse would go around with the jannies. You would knock on the doors and they'd let the hobby in, he wouldn't hurt nobody. A lot of children used to be frightened of the hobby, a lot of grown-ups used to be frightened too.

One night we went over with the hobby over to the old school. The C of EWA [Church of England Women's Auxiliary] was having a sale of work. Poor old Uncle Esau Roberts was the man looking after everything so we asked his permission to go in with the hobby. He claimed he never saw one. They had the tables lined right out with soup and all that. But we wasn't going to break anything. There was five or six of us with the hobby. We asked permission just to go in and come right out again, we wasn't going to tear nothing up. So he gave permission and Uncle Ray Flynn, poor old feller, he took the hobby by the reins, we'll say, and went on in through the door, went along between the table and the wall on one side and over around the other one. When we went up, everyone was seated and when we turned around for to come out, there wasn't a soul to nothing, everyone was gone. Poor old Uncle Joe Barney, he never stopped before he got home to Buckle's Point, frightened to death. When we got out, Uncle Esau started a big racket, after giving us permission to go in. Two or three women, not mentioning any names, fainted away.

Then we went over to poor George Hart's, over there where Reggie got his house now. Poor old Will was alive then. Poor George and Kels and Carrie was there. We knocked to the door and open he comes, and Carrie was going to boot the guts out of the horse. She give a big kick at the horse and hit his head and damn near broke her foot on this solid piece of wood.

We went on over the road then, we was getting real fun out of it. We went over to Maudie Poole's, Uncle Bill Poole's. We knocked on the door and out comes Maudie and she thought 'twas the jannies and she was going to get a kick out of them. When she opened the door here was this bloody horse. He shoved his head right in through the door and here goes Maudie bottom up. The United Church minister was boarding there then. Crocker was his name, he was over six feet tall.

On our way back over the road, we got in breast of Uncle Bob Hancock's and here we met Mr. Crocker, and he started to run. 'Twas hard as flint, the snow was. You'd haul on the ropes and the hobby's mouth would open and close, and his head was as big as any horse. We chased Crocker right to the door. Talk about sport.

The next evening we went over and went in every house in Forteau, with the hobby. We went in Uncle Phil Dumaresque's, he was the real hobby man in his day. He never had a house like we got today, sealed up over the beams. Uncle Phil got showing us how to use the hobby. He used to knock the lofting off the beams with his head up like a bloody old horse, you know. Aunt Sis, she was going for Uncle Phil but he didn't mind her a bit, what he smashed up. That was the kind of people they was for sport, yes sir.

We don't have any fun now, sure. Little youngsters can go to houses now and they don't let them in. Them days, forty-five and fifty years ago, Forteau people would come over and janny up with us and we'd get ready and go back with them. That was in our race. Every house you went to you'd have a piece of cake, syrup or lime juice. Everybody was happy. You'd take a hobby now and go to Forteau, you'd be in the penitentiary in St. John's the next day. [6.2:12]

I used to play the violin. I got the prize three times for playin' the violin. I used to play for dances up on the Quebec side. They had a concert over to Bessie Flynn's one time and I was there 'till daylight. The last thing I played that night was "Good night, Ladies, I'm going to leave you now." We had a wonderful time. Poor old Raymond was alive then. He was a wonderful man, wonderful man.

I have a violin that was made in 1704. Me great-grandfather owned it, over in England, and he gave it to me grandfather and Grandfather gave it to me when he was done usin' it. She was made by Antoine Stradivarius.

I learned to play when I was twelve or fourteen. I just learned from watchin' Grandfather and me father playin' One night Grandfather was playin' and I said to 'en, "Grandpa, I believe I could do that."

He said, "Here, go ahead and do it."

He handed me over the violin and I played "Pop goes the Weasel." I thought more about that than if someone had given me a fortune.

I been singin' songs all me life. I learned 'um from listenin' to other people sing and from books. I only had to hear a song once and then I had it. I never taught 'um to anyone, if they didn't learn 'um when I was singin' 'um that was it. I composed a lot of songs meself, wrote a lot of pieces. [15.4:31]

I figured I played the violin as good as any feller that ever played one, until a few years ago, when I had an accident with the skidoo and lost the top of me finger. I was the violinist around here for all the times, and there was Uncle Bill Dumaresque and Henry Letto from L'anse au Claire. I never seen a cross look or heard a cross word then, but what is it today? Why is it you don't enjoy yourself now...its a row now.

We got a licensed club now, but in them days you had no licensed club. If you ran off your moonshine, it seemed like everybody could keep it under their shirt collar, nobody kicked up a row with anybody. Today we got licensed clubs, government approved clubs. You go and sit down in any club and before you leaves there's a row on.

I made and distilled hundreds of gallons of moonshine. You can take molasses, yeast cake and water and distill moonshine after four days. More than once I filled up the kerosene lamp when we had no kerosene and burned the moonshine the same as kerosene oil. [6.2:12]

You had no laws then, no Mounties. Seemed like everybody did what they liked. There was plenty of game, plenty fish, plenty salmon, plenty trout, plenty caribou, plenty everything. You had what you had and what the eye didn't see the heart didn't feel.

You were free then now you're bound. You didn't need nare as much to live in them days as we do now. Them days me father just had the food bill. What he had he spent it on food. Today you got your light bill, your phone bill and your food bill. Them days you worked all summer, cleared $250, $280 in the fall of the year and you were a rich person. You could buy twelve months' of food out of that for yourself and your family. Raisins was $.06 a pound, $.27 a pound for butter, Canadian butter, $.85 for a gallon of molasses, $.65 for a pound of tea, $5 for a barrel of flour, $14 for a three hundred pound barrel of pork. Two hundred fifty dollars wouldn't go far now, sure that's not enough to go to the Snack Bar with now.

During the Depression anybody who worked made a livin'. If they didn't make it on the fish, they made it on the furs and everything like that. As far as I could see everybody was happy. You never went into a house here in Forteau but you could get your glass of syrup and a piece of cake at Christmas time. I don't say you'd get that now in most of the houses if you did go around Forteau on a Christmas. There's some would.

Yes, everybody was happy, girl. Everybody had a pair of barked sealskin boots and their binding on 'um. When you'd go to a dance they couldn't get lanterns enough to put in the Hall. Now it's reversed. I went to a dance last winter and when the dancin' started they put the lights out. I said, "Where in the hells am I?"

— Stanley Trimm
[14.1:23]

THEY USED TO MAKE SHEETS, pillow cases, table cloths, cup towels and bloomers, underskirts, or petticoats 'twas called then. Aprons, made beautiful aprons after 'twas washed a few times and embroidered, and lunch cloths, all from flour bags. They were good especially for quilts, make white patches, join the patches together and then embroider them.

In the old days, when we'd get ready for fishin' in the spring of the year, the first thing we would do is we'd get some calico and we'd cut out the dresses, the women always had dresses. They didn't wear oil pants in those days, but we'd get the calico and then we'd get some linseed oil and we'd oil the dresses. We'd put them out to dry on the clothes poles, probably for a couple of days. Then we'd take em down and we'd oil them over again—mostly give them three coats of linseed oil. Then they'd be all ready and waitin' for the fish to come. When the fish come the women would work in the stage at the fish and they'd always have their dresses on. They had long sleeves and high necks right up to their chin, buttoned up in the back, big skirts, that's how the dresses were made. Put that on over all their clothes so they'd be good and warm when they go down to the stage.

I was probably fourteen or fifteen when I started making oil clothes, I wasn't very old when I started with the dress and workin' at the fish. We'd make the oil pants for the little boys out of calico, the same thing, oil pants and oil jackets and we oiled them with linseed oil, two or three coats, let it dry. The men too, they'd make the same thing for them men. That's what we had in them days, there was no oil clothes to buy. When flour sacks come up they used to use those, used to find them better than calico because the flour sacks was heavier and they was thicker. Three or four coats of linseed oil on it used to make a good job. And Cape Anns too, used to make the Cape Anns and oil them with the linseed oil.

Every spring you'd see a man goin' around with his gallon jar to the store. We didn't have many stores then but we had one that used to supply all the needs like the linseed oil, tar, and the pitch, and the rosin for the boats and all that. The jars used to be the old earthenware jars, old fashioned jars what the old fellows brought with them, I suppose, from England or France or where ever they come from. Be no tin cans or plastic bottles in them days. Every feller had his jar and he had its purpose to put linseed oil into it, put nothing else into it, and he always had one for his kerosene and put his gallon of kerosene in.

That'd be a go every spring, gettin' oil clothes made, oiled and get it dried, men bein' at their boats, tarring their boats, tarrin' the roofs and stages and stores, barkin' their twine with the kootch tar. Them days it smelled some good walkin' along the road and smelling all this goin' on! Now it's nothing like that. Get a bit of tar now and it don't even smell like tar.

— Bessie Flynn
[10.2:58]

I SUPPOSE THE FIRST [MODERN] merchants that ever come on the Labrador coast was Baxter Gordon. He and Job Brothers came and set up the big whalin' factory over in Schooner Cove. They had thirty or forty men, planters, come there after they built it up down in Schooner Cove. Schooner Cove is about a mile and a half from L'anse au Loup. They had a big whalin' ship called the *MicMac*. They'd go out and harpoon the whales and moor them, then they'd go out and take them in tow, seven and eight, and tow 'um in to the whale factory.

There was a Mr. Brown had out seven cod traps. When Brown would get vex his lip used to almost hang down to his chin. One very foggy morning the *MicMac* was comin' in. No radar of course in them days. They never knew anything until they saw a trap. They went full speed astern but with the speed she was goin' she went right through the trap. Then wit' the head weight the whales had, seven whales, four of them went into the trap too and three others passed that trap and went into another one. Brown come down on the wharf, savage, and that was before the men was up, only one was up I think. He kicked the bunkhouse door and called, "Heave out, boys." There was never a man had such a haul as Brown had that morning in his cod traps. He had seven whales, he said, and the *MicMac*. That was back in the good ol' days.

We used to go out there and get on the whales' backs. Get on their heads and walk right back to their tails, a hundred and thirty or forty feet long. They have flags stuck up in their backs. It's around thirty years ago that the last whale was killed right here in Forteau.

I can remember back a long ways, girl. For my part I wish I was back where I came from. I lived a lot happier than I have under Confederation, a lot. Thank God I was never hungry, without I was outdoors or in the country, get hungry walkin' or something like that. We always had plenty of what we had, but I wasn't brought up with a silver spoon in me mouth, just the same, no more than anybody else. As far as I know everybody in Forteau had plenty to eat. They had the same privilege, certainly. They had plenty of flour, bread and molasses, anyway. No sugar, certainly. I never drank a pound of sugar in me life. Grandmother had two or three pound in the fall of the year for when the Minister [came]. When he came around we'd be glad, me and Rob, to see the sugar basin go on the table. We'd get the spoon into the sugar basin unknown to 'um. They'd have milk and the only time a can of milk was on the table was when the Minister'd come. We had a lamp stuffed with red flannel, a kerosene lamp, and that was only lit for the Minister.

They'd make the mission here once a month, from Red Bay to L'anse Eau Claire, that's the United Minister and the Church of England Minister. Of course there was Canon Richards. I seen one Canon Richards and I'll never see another like 'en. He was forty-four years in the ministry at Flower's Cove. Sure as you see an easterly wind and rain, in the spring of the year, that's the day he'd come across the Straits. He would spend about two weeks around here.

Dear ol' man, he'd have his sealskin boots on and ol' rubbers over them and a little suitcase in his hand. He walked proud. If 'twas civil weather someone would give 'en a lift along in boat, but if it happened to be stormy he'd walk from L'anse Eau Claire to Red Bay.

Canon Richards was a very educated man, very intelligent. I heard him say that Fred Goudie was the smartest man he ever met in his life. He never told nare lie there. Everyone can witness that for Fred. You tell Fred to estimate from the date you was born and the hour you was born—say I was born on a Thursday, eleven o'clock the nineteenth of such and such date. Now, how many minutes old is I in the world? Just as quick as you could ask 'en, he'd tell you how many minutes old you was. You say, "Fred, there was a ship left St. John's last year with 145,000 quintals of fish aboard, bound for across to Jamaica or Brazil. It takes seventy-five fish to make a quintal. How many fish did they have on board?" Just as quick as you could ask 'en, he'd tell ya.

I was helpin' me uncle in the woods up to L'anse Eau Claire this one particular day. Canon Richards walked up and come in. Poor Gertie had a barrel of redberries picked and a half another one. She had it covered wit' a cloth. Canon Richards was walkin' around the floor. We used to call Uncle Elijah, Uncle Lisha. "Elijah, how plentiful is these berries this year?" He had walked from Forteau, out around the shore to L'anse Eau Claire. "Elijah, I saw millions of these berries today comin' up."

He took a quick thought, "Elijah, that's a lot of berries for me to see, millions. Could be possible, Elijah, that I passed that many berries but I don't think I seen that many."

He went over to the cupboard and took down a pint jug. It was marked, you know, half pint and pint and ounces. He went out in the barrel and dipped up a pint of redberries. Aunt Minnie put a cloth down and he counted 'um. Well, of course, he knew how many berries was in a pint and how many pints was in a gallon, and he knew how many gallons was in the barrel, so he runned it up to see how much berries it was for a million. How many barrels do you think a million fulled? Twenty-seven gallon barrels and one quart over.

While we was talkin', he had it all cleared away and everything, he went over to Uncle Jim's, Canon Richards did. Fred [Goudie] come out of the woods and Canon Richards saw 'en come in to Uncle Lisha. Canon Richards come right back. When he come in Fred was washin' his hands with grease. Canon Richards hold out his right hand to shake hands. Fred looked down at his hands.

"Oh, don't mind that, Fred," he said. "I got one for ya this time."

"Yes," Fred said, "What's that."

He said, "In a pint of berries there's so many berries (he said the number). How many barrels would it take to hold a million?"

Fred turned his head a little bit. He looked at Canon Richards and he said, "Twenty-seven gallon barrels and you'd have enough left over for your supper, somewhere around a quart."

Canon Richards said, "That beats it all."

I can remember the first hospital was built in Forteau, I helped put the shingles on the roof. I can't remember the year it was built.

They was on repairs at the hospital in the spring, Uncle Will Jameison had it in charge. One day Uncle Will wanted Uncle Dan Bell to go over to he's place for dinner but Uncle Dan and Bob had their dinner wit' 'um and they boiled the kettle there. When they was finished their dinner, Uncle Dan was stood up alongside a little store there, cuttin' up a pipeful of tobacco. He said to Bob, "The Bible says, Bob, that two men shall be workin' in the field and one shall be taken and the other left," and he started to slide down by the side of the wall just as Uncle Will Jameison got there. Uncle Will ran and grabbed 'en in his arms. He carried 'en to the Grenfell Mission and he died there that night. Grandfather was over there the same time and that was his brother.

— Stanley Trimm
[14.1:29]

WHEN I WENT FISHIN' FIRST, there was no motor boats, no engines around. There would be two or three come around shortly after I got fishin'. I was about fourteen or fifteen years old fore I saw a engine, and they was called hot-heads. You'd take the damper off a them an' unscrew 'um and take 'um out an take a torch an' light 'en, an' put 'en in there an hottin' 'en fifteen minutes. Ten, twelve or fifteen minutes. While you was eatin' ya breakfast, she was warmin' up. You'd take the torch an' light 'en up, and you'd heave her up an' she'd catch, and she was goin' all day. They were known as gasoline boats then. The word motor wasn't used too much, gasoline boats, we used to call 'um, an' they had wonderful power, what they'd catch hold of, they could tow. They would deck those boats right over, something like Noah's ark. They'd take the fish an' they'd throw it down through the hatch-way down in the middle of her. You wouldn't be allowed aboard of her with a box of matches in your pocket, hardly even. If you took 'um out, you wouldn't be allowed aboard the next day. You'd smoke no pipes aboard a them, and it didn't pay ya if you laid a match down in the engine room. The engine room would catch fire, that was it, the gas was that strong, that powerful.

I was sixteen years old when I can mind about the first engine. I helped earn her, certainly. There was t'ree brothers of us and me father. Me older brother said we'd get an' engine and we bought her out of the fish. The Normores down there they took the second one. They had the two of 'um out on the water the same year. I think we launched ours eight or ten days 'fore they launched theirs. We bought a boat already made, and they had to build one. They didn't finish theirs, and ours came in the fall and theirs come down in the spring. That was the first two engines in L'anse au Loup, two four-[hp] Acadias. I wrote the order for both of 'um. My hand guided the pen. I knows what I'm talkin' about, 'cause I handled the business. Two of 'um went out floatin' an we went out on the fishin' grounds with those two engines when the rest was in.

With the wind off from the land, in them times, 'twas a bit rougher than it be's now. If a barge went out and she went up along shore, well, she couldn't come back, 'cause the tide was goin' up, she had to stay in, she had to beat in, but we could go up there and stim the tide and wind.

The next year they started in, and the next year there was three more added to the fleet. That was the first ones. Those engines was a hundred and sixty-eight dollars, an' a man had a job to pick up a hundred and sixty-eight dollars at that time to buy an engine. We managed it and those other boys managed it, too. They picked 'um up from one year to the other. They wasn't too fast comin' in because they didn't make 'um too fast then. The merchants wouldn't back ya up on a engine, the agents wasn't too fast on it either, but you could get one if you was able to pay down half on her. They'd get the other half over a year. If the merchant had the will, the good willing power to put the engines around, he would've sold his engines. He would have been paid fer every one of 'um, and people would've been a lot better off until the Depression struck. When Depression struck, anything could happen then, you could put 'um back.

Before Depression there was plenty of fish, and a man with the engine was much like a man with a ski-doo and a team a' dogs. The man with the ski-doo was always ahead of the man with the dogs, he was able to heave away the team a' dogs. The motor boat was what was wanted. There was nothing come in L'anse au Loup that played its part like the marine engines. They can bring in what they like now. These other ones don't keep up to their work. They're all right if there's a mechanic around. Engines was the lifesaver of the fishermen once they found out how to use 'um and how to get 'um and how to put 'um in those trawl boats. 'Twas the best thing that ever went into 'um.

I worked with the paddles, and I worked with the sail. I knows what it is to be under the double reef. I knows what it's like to be under the engine. The engine was made for the fisherman, not that it made 'en rich, but it got 'en where he couldn't go. He could go in the engine where he couldn't pull 'en back with the paddles. I knows what it is to pull her out long be Long Beach Point with a set of ash paddles across the boat, the wind blowin' out the bay. I knows what it is to have me hands galled with the paddles. I knows what it is to have me back-side chafed on the tho't. I knows what it is to see the gunnels under the water, too, with the sails on her, and I knows what it is to see the sea breakin' over her, and I wasn't in half so rough as some fellers round here. People made a livin', risin' from the bed at half past twelve, one o'clock. Two o'clock was ya hour. One o'clock out, two o'clock leave ya collar, go up in Forteau Bay waitin' fer dawn to break, after pullin' it with the oars. Well, when the engine come out, we took up trawlin' a lot. The trawl was a wonderful thing.

— Ellis Barney
[3.4:9]

I WELL REMEMBER THE YEAR 1918. The first two make-and-break motors were landed here at L'anse au Loup from the SS *Ethie*. At that time she was operating from Corner Brook, Newfoundland, to her destination at Battle Harbour, Labrador, carrying freight, mail, and passengers. She became a total wreck at a place called Sally's Cove on the Newfoundland Coast. I forget the exact day but it was the month of December, 1919.

These two engines were purchased from a man by the name of Brake Meadows, Bay of Islands. He acted as agent for the Acadia Gas Company, N.S.

The men that purchased these engines were William Normore and his two brothers, and Josiah Barney and sons. They were two 4 hp. Acadia engines. The next year, 1919, John Belbin and sons, Solomon Barney and his brother George purchased two 4 hp. Hubbards. In 1920, my father, with the help of my brothers and I, purchased a 4 hp. Acadia, William Cabot and sons purchased one and so did John Linstead and his sons. Every year after that there would be four or five engines purchased until every fisherman here had a motor boat. It was the same with fishermen all along the coast. It was very convenient for the fishermen to be moving through the water much faster than they could when they had to use oars in large boats, and eight foot paddles in our small boats which we called dinghies.

The year 1921, as we were preparing for our fish to be salted, someone looked out over the water and saw a large schooner drifting west with her sails hoisted. Her sails were as white as the snow. We knew there was something wrong, although it was calm. Thomas O'Brien and I jumped aboard our motor boat and went to her assistance. When we arrived to the side of the schooner the captain rushed along and caught our painter. He told us there was a part broken on their engine and asked if we would tow him in the bay and show him where to drop anchor.

I asked the captain his name and he answered, "Bob Bartlett.¹'"

When our boat was secured to the schooner's side, Tom and I got on board. Captain Bartlett told us to come and see what he had on board. While we were walking along he told us to be sure and keep our hands in our pockets. I wondered what he meant by saying those words, but I soon found out.

To my surprise I saw a large cage extended across the deck leaving just a small passage just large enough for a man to walk. The cage was made with one-by-six boards and in it was two young polar bears. The boards on top of the cage were one half inch apart. When we approached the bears were lying together at one end of the cage. I had a five-inch nail in my pocket, I drew it out and tapped it on the board. Immediately the two bears were over to us. They came so fast that neither of us saw them coming.

They had very short but large legs, and large bodies. I presume they were as large as a forty-five gallon barrel. Their heads were large and they had very large teeth which were as white as snow. I realized then why Captain Bartlett told us to keep our hands in our pockets. If we had put one finger through an open seam, a bear, moving as quickly as they did, could bite it off very quickly.

I asked Captain Bob where they got the bears and he told me they got them from Greenland. When I asked him how they caught them, he told me, "The cowboy threw a rope over their heads."

I never saw a full-grown polar bear but I saw the tracks many times. They drove through the Straits of Belle Isle on the arctic ice, then they would leave the ice and make for the land. If there was a lake they would swim across and go on land and ice again travelling northward. I often wondered if they ever got back to where they come from, because it would be the month of April when they would leave the ice. The snow would be very soft then and they had many miles to travel. Many times I saw where they crossed over brush wood, three to four feet high, they would leave a trench right through, but the bear was gone on. I often wondered what they got to eat on their way back home.

He then asked me did I think him and six other men would get a dinner cooked when they went ashore. I asked him what he would prefer and he said, "Green cabbage and fresh potatoes."

I told him he would get it, so the seven of them, Captain Bartlett and six million-aires from the States got aboard my boat and we made for land. I made my way as fast as I could and asked my mother if she would prepare the meal requested by Captain Bartlett. She said she would. She went to the garden and got the cabbage and I got the potatoes and soon the old boiler was letting off steam. My dear old mother dressed the table in our inside kitchen and the seven men sat around and enjoyed their dinner, Labrador cabbage and potatoes.

When they were finished, Captain Bartlett asked Mom what she was going to charge for their dinner. She answered that she wasn't going to charge anything. Then one of the millionaires pulled a ten-dollar gold piece from his pocket and the other five did the same thing, and Captain Bartlett pulled out a ten-dollar bank note. She had seventy dollars for that meal. She was some delighted and the seven men were delighted, too, with their delicious meal of salt beef, cabbage, and potatoes.

After the meal was finished and we were enjoying a good chat, I asked if either of them would sell me a rifle. One man spoke up and told me he would sell me his. I asked him how much money he would want for it and he told me twenty dollars, which was cheap for a rifle. I went and got the money and put it in my pocket. Then there was a very light wind come up from the east which was a fair wind through the Straits of Belle Isle, so Captain Bartlett ordered all men aboard the schooner. I jumped aboard our motor boat and soon they were on board their schooner again. Captain Bartlett began to shout, "Hoist the sails!" "Weigh anchor!" The man that was selling me the rifle rushed down to the cabin, grabbed the gun and came to give it to me.

He said, "You'll want some cartridges."

I said, "Yes, sir, but I didn't take any money to pay for them."

He turned around and passed me two hundred cartridges. So I made a wonderful bargain, a Winchester rifle and two hundred cartridges for only twenty dollars. Anyway, the schooner sailed out the bay with all on board and I never heard from any of them after.

— Leo O'Brien
[14.4:48]

The furring Business requires a thorough knowledge of the interior part of the country which, on account of the deep snows and the rigour of the furring season, is only to be acquired by slow degrees. The country furnishes no other subsistence to the furrier than what his traps provide him, and these require a wide extent of ground to have any tolerable success. In order to penetrate to any distance, each furrier (for they all separate and hunt singly) must, at short distances from one another, build himself huts to live in, proof against bad weather, so that he shall never be far from shelter in case of storms. Hence it is easy to conceive that, to fur that country properly, each adventurer should have an exclusive right; and otherwise that it never will be practised, except in a very insignificant manner just around the Sealing Posts, by way of something to do at idle times....

— A. P. Low, "Report on Exploration of the Labrador Peninsula," 1896

At the close of the fishery, the greater number of the planters leave their small houses on the coast, and proceeding to the heads of the various bays, go into their winter quarters in their small houses there. During the winter they are engaged in hunting fur-bearing animals. These also are not so plentiful as formerly owing, probably, to the large areas burnt over, either from fires accidentally made, or set on purpose by the owners of schooners, who often fire the country along the shore, so as to easily make dry firewood for future seasons. Each planter has a path or line of traps, often extending fifty miles or more inland, and as these paths cannot be covered in one day, he has small tilts, or log houses at convenient intervals along them, where he can pass the night with some degree of comfort. Some of the paths are so long they require a week to go over and attend to the traps on the way.

— Geo. Cartwright
[9.3:26]

ALL ME LIFE I TRAPPED in the country. No three-wheelers, airplanes or anything, we used to have to go on foot, near about twenty-five mile, walk in. Leave home Monday morning and come back Saturday night. Have a week home then go in for another week. Every fall like that for about a month.

We used to wear them ol' sealskin boots then. 'Twas all sealskin boots. More than once I had to take the pocket knife and shove 'en down through to let the water out. If 'twas pourin' down rain they'd full up with water and there was no way for it to get out, the only way was to shove your pocket knife down, cut a hole and the water would go in and come out, eh.

You take in the fall of the year now, wet snow and everything else, you knows how warm it was as long as you were walkin', but as soon as you'd stop you'd be froze to death. Now when we gets up in age you're goin' to be sayin', "What's wrong?" There'd be loads on your back with the blood almost comin' through the flesh. I've come in the ol' house, sat down and couldn't move. My wife would have to go to work and take the game bag, cut the strings, and let 'en fall. I'd almost fall to the floor when she'd let 'en go. In the morning me shoulders would be blood red with the blood peasin' through from where the straps was on me back. That's what's wrong when you get up in age.

I'll tell you a story about Uncle Lawrence O'Brien, what happened to 'en.

This was in the month of November, he trapped in there that fall. We were pickin' up our traps on the way home. The day before we had walked across the little pond and it was all black ice, you could see through it. We walked out on the pond and all of a sudden his feet went out from under 'en, he came back on the ice on his back and broke through with the pole of his head. He was there a long time.

"Boy," he said, "I seen stars that time."

I looked at 'en. I thought he was dead.

We used to carry these little bottles that Redway's Painkiller used to be in. They're flat. When we'd go in the country in the fall of the year we'd take two of them and fill 'um up with rum, for like if you got sick or anything. You'd take two and roll 'um up in cotton or something and then put 'um away in the shack.

Uncle Lawrence used to say to me, "Don't touch that unless you get sick."

Sometimes, in the night when we'd be together, it used to come in me mind about this rum.

I'd say, "Uncle Lawrence."

"What?"

"I got an awful feelin' in my stomach," I'd say.

He'd look at me and say, "You're not turnin' white. You're supposed to turn white when the pain gets so bad, turn white before you finishes."

I'd let out a big laugh.

The morning we was leavin' for home I said, "The best thing to do is have a drink of rum before we leaves."

"No," he said, "we might need that before we gets home."

So we come on, come on out and come down on this pond, the two of us.

I said, "Take the axe."

He took the axe and put it on his shoulder with his gun. We walked out on the pond, on the snow that had it covered over. I thought I could hear the ice crackin'. I told Uncle Lawrence I thought I heard it crack but he kept on goin'. I kept off from him a bit. Uncle Lawrence made a chop with the axe and he chopped through his boot. I turned and went for a big flat rock. I hold me breath, put me foot on the rock and stepped ashore. When Uncle Lawrence got to the rock and put his foot up, the ice must have been cracked. When I turned around the bag on his back was goin' under the water. I reached out and caught 'en by the fingers.

I said, "Don't haul. Don't haul."

I couldn't keep me balance yet, see. So I got back a little bit and gradually I got 'en on the rock.

He said, "I never touched no bottom."

The water was deep there. It was cleared right away and cold with little low drifts.

He had to haul off every bit of his clothes right there and that started to freeze. I grabbed the clothes and started to rub it to keep it from freezin'. I hauled off me boots and hauled off a pair of vamps and give 'en. I pulled off me overalls and give 'en that to haul on over the skin.

We left and come on, and after we got so far his legs got so bad he didn't know what to do.

He said, "I'm not goin' to make it."

We had another cabin outside so I told 'en we'd have to try and get out there. Not far from the cabin we had some muskrat traps.

He said, "Go in and pick up the traps."

"Leave 'um there, " I said.

"I wants to have 'um."

"You won't be able to have 'um," I said. "They'll have to stay there."

He said, "No, boy, we got to pick up the traps."

I went on in around for the traps. I always used to listen to 'en. I suppose if he told me to jump overboard I'd do it. 'Cause I was scared of 'en, eh.

When I was comin' out I was lookin' for the smoke from the cabin because he said he'd be there when I got out. I found his footin' and seen that he went to the cabin. I figured something was wrong because he should have had the fire in.

When I went inside there he was laid down on the bunk. That's where he would have died. He would never have moved no more.

We had these sticks from off the *Raleigh*, we'd have them shoved somewhere or buried somewhere for lightin' the fire. I got some, lit the fire and scravelled off to the pond for water, come back and boiled the kettle. I turned to and got his clothes off to dry it up.

No trouble to get a bit of rum now! The first thing he spoke about when he got a bit better was the rum. So when the kettle was boiled I put some rum in the water and sweetened it with a bit of sugar. That went right through his system, see.

I was dryin' his clothes until almost four o'clock that evening. I figured we'd stay there, after restin' up all night he'd be all right.

He said, "The best thing we can do is go on tonight because tomorrow morning I might not be able to make it. I thinks I can make it now."

I didn't mind waitin' but I said, "Boy, it's up to you." So we got ready and come out part ways. As 'cardin' as we started to come out over Crane's Hill the snow was gettin' deeper. There was twice as much snow now as there had been inside. So we come on with me walkin' ahead. I talked to 'en, you know, tryin' to keep 'en goin'.

B'n'by I missed 'en. I looked back and he was away behind me. I was kind of forgettin', tryin' to get as far as I could I suppose. I waited for 'en to come up longside of me, and I was only takin' me dead time.

B'n'by he said, "I can't do no more, boy."

"You go on ahead," I said. "I'll walk behind ya."

But he couldn't do nothing at all with that. When I was ahead, when I took my foot up he would put his down in my footin'. We come on out until we got to the Black Whistler and we stopped there and had a cold lunch.

"Do you think you're goin' to make it?" I asked 'en.

He said, "I don't know. I don't know what I'm goin' to do. We got to go on and we'll see."

That was his last trip. He was chilled with the cold and paralyzed from the waist down, all turned dark. He never got the better of it. The shock he got when he fell and hit his head didn't do him any good either. Fallin' in the water, that fixed 'en altogether.

— Michael Normore
[15.3:53]

MANY OF THE STORIES MY grandfather told, I don't think they were meant to be taken seriously. He just wanted to entertain, make the stories interesting. That's the way I always see them. I don't believe he really wanted to tell lies, or stretch the truth or whatever you call it. He even went as far one time to say, "Yes, it's true, just as true as I eat a axe handle." He was saying this with a serious look on his face, as if to say, "It's really, really true." But how can you eat an axe handle? Things like that gave me the clue that he meant no harm, but that he was trying to make his story interesting.

You go to him and say, "Grandfather, I heard this story today that you just wouldn't believe."

He'd say, "What was that."

"Well, so'n'so, up in Forteau, he says that he remembers one time, back in the thirties, when he was in ice trouting in to the pond and it got so foggy on the way out that he had to tie his ice chisel fast to the head of his komatik to cut the fog away."

"That's not a big story," he'd say, "I seen it a lot thicker than that. That's nothing, that's not. I was out trawlin' one time, out in boat, and I had me trawl all baited up and I was sittin' around, waitin' for the trawl to fish, and I lit up a cigarette and the fog got so thick I leaned up against it. I smoked away, and b'n'by I fell off to sleep. When I woke up I was in the water where the fog had cleared up when I was asleep. I fell head long in the water."

Another story that Grandfather told us, one time, that was very hard to believe, well, we all knew it just wasn't true. It leaves you with the impression that back in those days it got really cold. Not that it got so cold but they didn't have very much clothes to wear, and that's why they got so cold. He just wanted to make the point that it was very, very cold.

Someone came to him once and said, "'Twas some cold in the country last week when I was in there."

He said, "Yah, what happened."

He said, "I had the kettle boiling on the stove and when I went to take it off the stove it was so hot I had to put it outdoors to let it cold off. I forgot about the kettle and when I went back it was froze solid."

"What did you do, had to go and boil it over again?"

"No, no, took it and put it on the stove and melted the ice and the water inside was still hot." It froze so fast that the water inside didn't have time to cold off.

"That's not a bad one either," Grandfather said, "I was in there worst than that. Yes, I went in there with poor old Hughie O'dell one time, down to West St. Modeste. Old Hughie O'dell had one of them old sealskin whips, had it all braided up. On the end of the whip he had a small piece of string, smaller than a piece of sud line and on the end of that he had a little shot, pellet from a shot gun. He used to crack that whip in the morning at the dogs, and that used to crack right hard and the dogs used to take right off. If you hit a dog with one of those shots it'd really hurt. This day we was in there and Hughie Udell was coming right back on this dog with the whip, the dogs wasn't goin' fast enough. It was a really cold day, 'nough to freeze ya and the dogs wouldn't go, so all of a sudden Hughie got mad and let the head one have it with the whip. He took 'en right in the broad of the back and he split 'en right down the middle. Hughie didn't want to lose his dog, 'cause dogs was so precious you couldn't part with your dog, so he took off runnin' after the dog to save 'en before he died. He took 'en and slapped 'en together. It was so cold he just froze together like he was and he come to life again and started movin'. There was only one thing wrong, he had two legs up and two legs down."

— Lawrence Normore
[7.1:51]

'SLOW COME IS LONG LAST' and it will be still longer before th\. .iemory of that Christmas gale ceases to blow in our memories. The mail steamer was lost in it, violently blown out of the water on that evil coast. But these happenings are not strange in our world and we never got the story 'till the following year when one fine Sunday morning I happened to drop into young Harry Barney's home, a little wooden cottage on the glorious sandy beach at L'anse au Loup in Labrador. Harry was enjoying a morning pipe of peace. This was my reward for a Sunday visit. For it is as easy to catch a weasel asleep as Harry with time to burn from midnight Sunday 'till the next Day of Rest comes around. A big liner had run ashore close to us only a week before, and was now an abandoned wreck lying well out of the water on the north side of Burnt Island, so we fell to talking about wrecks, and the topic of the loss of the mail steamer came up. To my amazement he said, "Yes, I knows about her, Doctor, I was fireman aboard when she was cast away."

"You? What have you to do with steamers?"

"Oh, they shipped me and poor Cyril Manstock as they couldn't get men south. I'd acted runner before, but it was Cyril's first voyage, and he died after with consumption, as you know. They says it was the chill did it."

"Tell us about it, Harry. We heard that a dog saved all hands by carrying a line ashore. I've been crazy to get the facts from an eye-witness."

"I wasn't much of an eye-witness 'till we were high and dry, but I saw the dog do his bit, Doctor, and he certainly did it all right. Its a long story," he began, "but we knew below decks by six o'clock—that's just at dark—that it would be a fight for life. What was left of our coal was all dust, and we'd had trouble keeping steam with it even in smooth water. We were anchored then, right on the straight shore, landing some freight for the village at Cowhead, and the wind was already rising and the sea beginning to make. My watch was eight to twelve. But I was a new hand and wanted to give her every chance, so I went on at six to watch that the fires were kept clear and a good head of steam when we made a start. It did seem an awful time delaying and I wished a hundred times that we would throw the freight overboard. I guess I was a bit excited. But when at last the bell did go, we were already below. It was a hard fight, however, from the first. For the boat was small and we knew she couldn't do much in a dead hard sea. Her propeller comes out and she races, and it's no soft job trying to fire at the best of times. She wasn't so bad first out in the spring either. But like everything else, she had run down with hard usage, and at the end of the long season, she couldn't do her best by a long way. However, as I said, we had a full head of steam, when the gong rang at last, and for a time it looked as if we might make it by standing right out to sea.

"The fierce dust in the stokehole from the powdery coal, and the heavy and quick rolling soon made our eyes blind and our throats dry, and before my watch was out at midnight I just had to go up for water. I found the doors were all sealed up with ice, so I had to crawl out through a ventilator to get that drink. I hadn't been up two minutes, it seemed, before the chief sent for me to hurry down again, as the steam was going back. I was only second fireman really on my watch, but the first, a Frenchman, who had been at it seven years, was an oldish man and was getting all in. At midnight watches were called, but both of us stuck to it, for in spite of all our efforts we were losing steam again. Water was now washing up over the plates in the engine room, and we were wet and badly knocked about by the ship rolling us off our legs when we tried to shovel in coal. At two o'clock the old man gave in altogether and went up. I never saw him again until it was all over. Cyril was in as trimmer, and he came in to help me. Every time I opened the fire-box door Cyril would grab me by the waist, and hold on hard, but in spite of it I got thrown almost into the fire one time by the ship diving as I let go to throw the coal in. Harry showed me a big scar across his arm and one on his face. "I got these that time," he remarked, "just to remember her by."

"The water was rising then in the engine-room and the pumps had got blocked, so we couldn't pump it out. We didn't think she was leaking, but we heard after some portholes had been stove in, and she took water every time she rolled. We got the pumps to work again after a while. But the doors being frozen up above we had no way to get rid of our ashes, and they were washing all around in the engine-room, and it was impossible to keep the runways clear.

"The worst of it was that now the water was in the bunkers and mixed up with the coal, making it into a kind of porridge. It was just like black mud to handle, and you couldn't get it off the shovel until you banged the blade against the iron fire bars.

"So steam began to drop again, and went so low that our electrics nearly went out and we got repeated orders from the bridge for more steam and more steam. It appears we were making no headway at all with only eighty pounds pressure, and in fact we were slowly being driven sideways into the cliffs. We worked all we could, but things went from bad to worse, the water rose and splashed up against the fire-box making clouds of steam, so though the dust was laid, what with the steam and the darkness, and the long watch, we couldn't keep her going. Moreover, it seemed as if we would be drowned like rats below there, and I tell you we wouldn't have minded being on deck, cold as it was.

"We heard after that one of the stewards had been fishing on this part of the coast. He knew every nick and corner, and said there was a little Sandy Cove round St. Martin's Cape, where a small head of rock might break the seas enough to let us land, for they knew on deck now that the ship was doomed. For my part I knew nothing but that, work as we would, the steam gauge would not rise one pound. Beyond that, what happened didn't even interest us, we hadn't time to worry about danger. One sea did, however, make us madder than others. Something had been happening on deck. The heavy thumps like butting ice had reached us below. It turned out to be the lifeboat that had washed out of davits and went bumping all down the deck, clearing up things as it went. Anyhow something came open and as we were getting coal from the lee bunkers a barrel full of ice water came through the gratings and washed us well down, sweaty and grimy as we were. Somehow that seemed to set my teeth again, and we had the satisfaction of seeing the steam crawl once more up to one hundred pounds. The bridge must have got on to it at once and have noticed we were making headway again. The fact was we were now rounding the Cape called Martin's Head. We knew they knew, for they again called us for still more steam—thinking we had got the top hand. It so happened that a long shoal known as Whale's Back was now the only barrier we had to weather. But 'till this spurt all hope of doing it had almost gone. Well, all I know is that suddenly there was a scrape—a bumpety, bumpety, bump, and then a jump that made us think we were playing at being an aeroplane—and then we went on as before. She was making water more rapidly now, but beyond that we knew nothing more. It was rising now to our knees nearly, and any moment might flood the fires. We had actually been washed right over the tail end of the whale-backed reef, the tremendous ground sea having tipped us right over, almost without touching. They say it was only ten minutes or so more to the end—it seemed hours. The motion had changed and we knew we were before the sea. Then suddenly there was a heavy bump, that made us shiver from deck to keel on, then she seemed to stop, take another big jump, then do the whole thing once more. We were on the beach, and the water was flooding into the stokehole. Cyril had gone some time before, played out. I could see nothing for steam but waded towards the 'alloway' into the engine-room. There also everything was pitch dark but I knew by feeling which way to go. It seemed a long while, but at last I found the ladder, and made a jump to hustle out of the rising water. My head butted into something soft as I did so. It was our second engineer—he had been at his post 'till the end. There was only one chance now for escape. It was the ventilator. I was proud I had learnt that in the night. It did not take me long to shin up through it and drop on the companion clinging to the edge. The icy wind chilled me to the bone and sheets of spray were frozen over everything. A sea striking her at that moment washed right over me, but before the next came I was behind the funnel, hanging on for dear life to one of the stays. Another dive between seas landed me in the saloon and from there I dropped down, and climbing to the fo'c'sle got some dry clothes."

"That's all you know, I suppose?"

"About all," he answered, "except that I had to go some miles when I landed to get shelter, and got no food 'till next night."

"Did any one thank you for your work?"

"Not yet," he answered with a smile.

"What steam had she when you struck the last time?" I asked.

"A full hundred pounds," and a gleam of the joy that endures lit his eyes—that joy that assures us of the real significance of life.

"Well, you see, Doctor, about daylight the ladies' cabin got flooded out and they were all driven out of that, all the passengers that could crowd into the little saloon on deck. The baby did not seem to mind at all and as there was no use going on deck, even if we had been able, that's where I took it. After we struck, however, and the seas were washing partly over the ship, I went out to see if there were any chance for us. The captain, who had never left the bridge, was there. His cheeks were all frost bitten. He had already launched a boat and was trying to get some men landed. It was broad daylight, a little after mid-day, and we were right under a big cliff, so close that you could almost touch it. The projecting head of the cliff sheltered the fore-part of the ship fairly well, but a thundering surf was beating on the beach. The boat was soon glad to be hauled in again. She was smashed and filled, and the men had been nearly lost. So we all fell to it, and tried to get a line ashore. There were men there now from the shore who had seen us. They were watching us from above the breakers, and evidently understood what we were doing. For when at last we flung the line into the water, they rushed down and tried to get it. But the back wash carried it always beyond their reach. One of them ran up to a cottage near by and came back with a jigger, and as the seas washed the rope along, tried to fling it over, and hook the line. But they somehow couldn't do it. Then I suddenly saw there was a big dog with them, rushing up and down, and barking as they tried for the line. All of a sudden, after they seemed to have done their best and failed, the dog rushed down into the sea, held the rope in his teeth 'till the tide ran out, and then backed with it 'till the men grabbed it. They took the line up the cliff, and I helped rig a chair on it in which we tied the passengers, and so sent them every one ashore safely. No, I didn't get my feet wet myself. You see I had my rubbers on. The baby? Oh, I tied the baby up in a mail bag and sent him ashore by himself. They told me when they opened the bag to see what was in it, the baby just smiled at them, as if it had only been having a bit of a rock in the cradle of the deep. We were home for Christmas after all. And somehow, Doctor, I had my mind made up to how it would be about that when I said good-bye to them that morning at Wild Bight. The folks all got together and gave that dog a hundred-dollar collar but the poor owner had to sell the dog, the collar and all, a little later to get food."

— Wilfred Grenfell
Northern Neighbors, 1906
[13.3:8]

I WAS BORN MARCH 11, 1891, at L'anse au Loup. My mother was Keziah Sinnicks from St. Anthony and my father was from Somersetshire, England. My mother's father drowned at St. Anthony and she went to live with Grandma Barney here in L'anse au Loup. Father died when he was sixty-three years old, in 1906.

I was ten years old when I started fishin' with me father. One time Father was carried down the middle of the bay by a whale. The whale took the graplin' and, just as Father was goin' forward to cut the rope, the graplin' came out.

There was lots of fish around when I was a young man. Me two brothers, Charlie and Albert, took charge of a barge when they was old enough to go fishin'. They caught 250 quintals that summer on hook and line. 'Twas $2.50 to $3 a quintal then—not like it is today. Barges was all was here, 'em times, with long masts stuck up in 'em. There was a ballast box in the middle full with ballast. She had a fors'il and a mains'il.

Women certainly helped in 'em days. They spent days and nights puttin' away herring. There was t'ousants of herring. They used to haul 'em in like capelin, use a herring seine, you know. Mother had no one to mind her youngster, my oldest brother, so she'd take 'en down in the stage and have 'en in a puncheon tub. He'd stay there all night sometimes I think.

Back in them times we'd only get enough fish to pay off our bills. Udell used to be comin' here then. He was the dealer. He'd was sure to be here by the first of May with a load of salt and grub. He'd heave it out to us. Then in the fall he'd come back for our fish. If we never had enough to pay our bill in the fall, well, he'd let it go 'till next year.

Back in them days you'd go and get your molasses in a gallon can. If you could afford to get a cask, or a barrel, you would. That molasses had to stand us all winter.

I can remember when Solomon Tilley's boat tipped over by Crow Head. Hubert Tilley got up this morning and cried for his father to take 'en out in the barge. Mr. Tilley got the barge from Funston for the summer. There was three of 'em—Hubert, his father and Fraser Loder. They went out in a little punt that wasn't much bigger than those you go out to the collar in. That's what they went out in. They sailed along shore with the wind nar'west. A squall came up and tipped 'em over. If they'd stayed in the middle of the boat she mightn've turned over, see, but three of 'em got on one side of the boat. Poor Jack, he was in the gasher and he seen 'em just before he went around Jersey Point in his boat. Jack seen 'em and turned around. He was just about ten yards from 'em when they went down for the last time. They could swim like dogs but, I guess, it never come in their minds. That was Fraser Loder, Hubert Tilley and Solomon Tilley.

Some men went down in a cod seine skiff and, when they looked down, the three of 'em was arm in arm on the bottom. When they got 'em they laid 'em out in a big store. I see Granny Barney put six coppers on their eyes. I was on one side of 'em and me uncle was on the other side. I seen 'en when he picked up the six coppers and put 'em in his pocket—sure as God is over me that's what he done.

— William Ryland
[13.4:15]

THERE WAS NO SMUGGLIN' GOIN' on when Sam Grant was there with Blanc Sablon. That was still under Newfoundland. In 1927 they changed the border, shifted the marks down there on the Black Rocks.

I was born in 1916 and I got married in 1937. But we smuggled before I got married, not much though, because we didn't have much money to smuggle wit'.

There was no roads. If you wanted a box of matches, a gallon of kerosene or a drop of molasses, or anything, you had to hitch a ride in somebody's boat or walk up to Blanc Sablon. There was nothing here to get after Sam Grant give up is store, so there was a lot of smugglin' then. You'd walk up to Blanc Sablon and get a catalogue and have it come someone else's name, mostly the postmistress, then you'd walk up to get it. That was two days' work to walk up there to get your parcel and walk back home.

One time, shortly after I was married, I sent for a little milk jug and sugar basin set, two little pieces. I had to walk that far for that, two days' walk.

People had no money and, of course, there was nothing here then. People was poor. You had nothing to drink out of hardly. There was no sets of dishes around, no sets of tumblers and milk jugs. Its a job for people to believe that in this day and age.

If you got caught smugglin' you had to pay duty. If you paid duty you were okay. I don't know where the money went. I don't know if it ever went back to the Newfoundland government or whether the Customs Officer of the Newfoundland Ranger, or whoever, kept it. That was something no one ever knowed, where the money went.

Customs Officer Butt was an oldish man. He never went anywhere. He seen all the boats that come in daylight, but there was lots he never seen. They'd wait 'till about twelve or one o'clock and then they'd stop their engines out there around Chimney Head and row in, if they had very much on board. There was a lot of people would tell on you though.

If you was goin' to Blanc Sablon in boat there was always such and such a feller would ask if he could go wit' ya.

"Yes, Boy, come on if you wants to."

Be probably four or five go wit' you and there'd probably be one in the boat that would betray ya, like St. Peter when he betrayed the Lord. Yes, sir, every time you'd go you had worries.

My husband, Ray, and them went up one time, probably as many as five in the boat. They got a lot of stuff and they had a good bit hide away and the flour bags hauled over it. I know they had ten or twelve rolls of felt for a new store they built to put their dry fish in. There was a heavy duty on felt so they had it stored away with the stuff put on top of it.

When they come to the wharf old man Butt come down and looked into the boat. "What have you got, boys? Anything with duty on?"

"No, we haven't got anything with duty tonight."

"Okay, go on."

Next morning they got up, a beautiful morning, and they was puttin' the felt on their store. Around dinnertime they looked down and seen Butt walkin' up.

He said, "You never told me you brought felt in the boat last night."

They said, "No."

He said, "I don't want you tellin' me now. When I got up this morning there was a note on the step of me door, told me everything you had in the boat last night, even to the felt."

So they had a Judas Iscariot in the boat with them that night. They never found out who 'twas and I 'low 'twas a good thing they never. Although they had their suspicions I'm sure.

— Bessie Flynn
[15.4:57]

'TWAS HARD TIMES THEM DAYS. There was no cash, we'd say, it was all relief orders. We used to smuggle things from Blanc Sablon.

I know, one time, there was an old blind man over on the point and his son went to Blanc Sablon and bought a pound of cheese for 'en. The Customs took it from 'en when he come back. They took the cheese from 'en.

I was in trouble wit' the Rangers more than once.

I put a feller over the head of the outside room wharf one time. Robert was in the boat wit' me. That was in smugglin' days. I had a big boat. Me and me brother Bob and Ed Buckle went up to the Customs house. Certainly the Customs Officer Butt had it in for me. He couldn't hold a candle wit' ya. When He cometh to make up his jewels, Customs Officer Butt will never be a jewel. I may not be either. Because if there's a place called Hell that's where he's to 'cause for sure I never forgive 'en. I don't think Christ will.

Uncle Arthur Hancock was on the head of the wharf and he wouldn't let me make an entry, to tell 'en what was in the boat. We had a sack of sugar and a hundred sacks of flour, of course we had a lot of smuggled goods underneath the flour which I never intended to tell 'en about. But he wouldn't let me make an entry. He come down on board the boat and saw the sack of flour. The wind was up from the easterd and snowin' hard. He asked Arthur, in the King's name, for an axe. The Ranger, Glendenning, was on the wharf and he jumped down on board the boat and they were goin' to sink 'er. The water was goin' right over the head of the wharf out there to the Flats. I made a sign to Bob to start the engine. Bob started the engine and I give it to 'en [Glendenning] and he went right over the stern of the boat, sloughed into the water, and I jumped for the wharf. Here I was on the wharf—and Custom Butt he was jumpin' like an ol' rooster—and grabbed the gaff. Certainly I'd have been in Hell today because I would have killed Ranger Glendenning. Bob ran off a little ways and sung out to ask what would he do. I said carry 'er home and unload 'er. Glendenning went and got dry clothes on. He ran all around the shore and was goin' to take Jack Buckle's boat, over there to the Point. Jack wouldn't give 'en the boat to come across. The next morning he did come over. Of course they had the order from St. John's. That's where I lived for a good fourteen years in the Court House. I tell you that more than once he came after me and carried me to the Customs house for a law suit, for tryin' to live and keep somebody else alive.

I had to pay fifty dollars that time.

That fall when the government [dole] came to Labrador I had me boat out for landin' freight. The old Customs Officer wanted me to land freight to Forteau and English Point. He never asked me what I charged.

After it was all done he come and said, "What do you charge for your boat?"

I said, "Two hundred and fifty dollars."

He refused to pay me.

I said, "All right, I got about two thousand dollars worth of stuff belonged to ya in me stores. I'll take the money out of that."

I paid 'en fifty dollars. He paid me two hundred and fifty. Yes.

You'd see Custom Butt out watchin' people comin' down over Misery Hill from Blanc Sablon. The Rangers used to watch for 'um comin' down Misery Hill.

I remember Ed Hancock went up one time, he and his father, went to get supplies. I believe he had on a lot of supplies for the Ranger over here in Forteau. I was there [Blanc Sablon] at the same time. We got caught in a cruel storm and a cruel storm it was. The storm struck sudden. Poor Tom Cabot left English Point to get his relief order and the Ranger wouldn't give 'en a relief order. He was up there all day, poor ol' feller. When the Ranger seen his own time, in the evening, he give 'en his order. Dirty weather was on then. Half clad, [Cabot] left for home but he never reached home. The wind struck nort'west, freezin' ice and snow. We got caught in the same storm. When we got in L'anse Eau Claire we couldn't get the harnesses off the dogs. They had to cut the clothes off of me, iced up. Three of us got in there together, me and Ed and Arthur Hancock.

The place they found Tom Cabot is called Tom Cabot's Nap. There's a cross placed right where his body was found.

After Tom Cabot's funeral I went back to Blanc Sablon and who should come in the store but the Ranger. When dinnertime come I went over to Tom Letemplier's and in the evening I went back to the store again. The Ranger was still there.

"What time are you goin' back, Stan?"

"Boy," I said, "I'm not goin' to be too much longer I don't 'llow."

He said, "What about a trip down?"

"Yes," I said and I thought to meself, I won't be able to buy anything now. Certainly I wasn't goin' to buy much in any case, you didn't have the money to buy anything wit'. He picked up a few things and asked me if I would carry it for 'en. I picked up the few things I bought, $8, $10, $15 worth. I loaded me komatik and we left. When we come to L'anse Eau Claire he wanted to call to Sam Jones's. We left Sam's, dark. We was goin' to come down across Long Pond and when we come to up over the Nap to come down on the first pond, he said, "Stan, to save a lot of trouble to go down to the Custom house, I'll check over what you got in your box and you won't have to go down." Good enough.

So he checked over the stuff I had in me komatik box and he charged me five dollars duty. When we got to Forteau he said, "Are you goin' to pay me?"

I said, "What about the trip? I'll charge you $5.50 for bringin' you down."

He said, "Good enough."

So he gave me the fifty cents and I came on home. I made fifty cents that day.

— Stanley Trimm
[14.1:26]

DEPRESSION STRUCK AROUND 1929 AND some of those people who had a few dollars put up, spent it. With the hard times, depression, fish went down, credit went out and the man who had a thousand dollars in his keepin', five hundred or whatever he had, he had to be always pickin' at it and finally he went down, dried out—most of the people dried out. People seemed to be very well off when the Depression struck but it dried them out.

If you were to go back...if there was a way to picture it, and I don't know if you could or not, it's unbelievable...it's almost unbelievable to the man who sits down, the man who went through it...you can't study it out.

Depression brought on that great relief program they used to have. When you figure it out, you'd get six cents a day. That's about what they used to figure out. One five cents chocolate bar and a one cent candy. That was relief! They wanted to see that work out! I don't know what it was for, unless it was to cover up something. That was unreal. That was false. The people of that particular moment was treated like people who went down through their own fault. I would use the word laziness. That's what was shoved on the people, like it was lazy people. But there was nothing to earn. People worked hard! People didn't fall down because they were lazy, they fell down because they couldn't make it, there was no payment for it.

I never made a good summer after I was married. I got married when I was a young man. Fished with me father. Now you take two or three people into a house, fishin' together and all hands would get their store full of fish, you had to live. But I never got up to the point where I had as much fish as I did before I got married. The biggest voyage I ever knew, or ever can remember havin', I never got five cents leave alone a five-dollar bill, cash. Plenty to eat, yes, plenty to eat, such as we had. This is what happened...people were too poor to fish. I knew people who had cod-traps, reared up with them, they come down to where they couldn't buy a jigger. It's too sad to tell. I think you're the first man I told it to on a set. I always turned the rest down and said it wasn't fit to talk about, and I wouldn't tell you the names of the people that I remember. I knows what I'm talkin' about, I handled some of it. Good, stollard, upright, hard working people. I knows what it's like to see people cry for their breakfast…no breakfast in the house. That's too sad to tell. I wouldn't like to speak the names of them. Some man may go over this and hear you play it off and say, "I don't know when it is that Ellis Barney saw that?" But they've been here in this house with no breakfast. I could go and tell you the full story but perhaps it's better for me to keep it. They're gone…they got breakfast enough now.

We went through it, the hard times of Depression, I think the hardest times ever the Labrador could recognize. I'll be doubtful if there's not people gone to their graves. They mightn't have gone through starvation, but they went through the want of nutrition. I covered 'um up. Don't tell me I don't know about it. There's things that happened then that's too sad to tell. It's gone, and all the people it happened to, most of them is gone. 'Tis only some like me left. That's life, if you want to pass that to the children and children's children and children's children. If I was able to walk along by their headstones I could tell them the story, perhaps they'd sit down and shed tears over it. I can hardly tell it without shedding tears now, and I'm not a feller that breaks down very quick. But did we see bad times? Somebody may come along and say, "No we never seen 'um, I can't mind." But they never had no contact. The way I could get into contact was this, I had a little store, that's the why, not because I had any more than the other feller had, but I had a little stock, I was the one they had to come to. They'd tell their story and just go on, whether I helped 'um or not, that's up to them to tell. 'Tis hard to send someone away with no food. Good people…good people to return, yes! Don't think you'd help those people and they wouldn't return. Oh yes, they would return, you may have to wait a little while but they would return. Before the twelve month would be up, they'd be back, supposin' it was back to shake hands with you. If you helped 'um, if they were able to repay you, they'd be back, and always ready to heave a welcome hand to you some other way. I wasn't the only one they was comin' to. You'd go to your friend and the other feller'd go to his friend, that was the way. The beauty of it is that you can look at the offsprings of those people today. They can't remember it perhaps, see what they got around them…they're riding today in cars, and the grandchildren will go even further.

It wasn't because people weren't workin' hard. They were hard workin' people. They didn't want too much money, but you just imagine a man fishin' here and gettin' ten or twelve quintals or fifteen quintals of fish. I can remember one time havin' twenty-nine and a half quintals when I straightened up in the fall of the year. Just imagine! I can remember another time walkin' ashore from the merchant with only forty-five dollars to buy my winter's food. So if you think I wasn't into it to, think the second time. Have another thought. But now, why did I come out of it? O.K, O.K, I got out of it. I seen it with no fish, but I didn't have the heavy load the other feller had. He had seven children, perhaps, and I only with one. We had to do without a lot of stuff and we lived without it. You can live without lots you're going through today if you had to. You can and the people today can live without a lot they have and be just as fat and strong. Where we got so much today and wastes, we never had enough then and we paid the penalty.

— Ellis Barney
[5.1:57]

I FISHED HERE ON BUCKLE'S Point all my life. We used to use a dory all summer. The maximum amount of fish was a hundred quintals. We used to fish with trawl and jigger. We used to jig a lot. There were no motors or gill nets. We used to get fifty dollars a quintal. There was thousands of cod. I remember we put out the trawl one morning and got it full of dog fish. The next morning we hauled five lines and got a dory full of cod.

Most of my life I fished with Bobby Davis of L'anse Amour, that was before 1945. After that we would get anywhere from ten to twelve dollars a quintal. Now, my wife, who is from Henley Harbour, remembers when her father got two dollars a quintal. We would sell it all dried in the fall. Organ used to come to Forteau in the fall and we would straighten up our summer bills. By the time we got provisions for the winter there wasn't much money comin' to us. Now it's different, everything is changed. People got everything they need for fishing but now there's no fish, and Labrador was one of the best fishing grounds ever.

The fishing industry really started when the people came here from St. John's, Newfoundland. They would come here in June, in schooners, and stay until late in the fall, around October. They would take their catch back to St. John's to dry on the flakes before they sold it. Now, I don't know what company they sold it to, or how much they acquired for their catch.

I guess it was around 1950 when the schooners stopped coming. Then a few people along the coast started getting longliners and then most of them started giving it up altogether when Goose Bay and Churchill Falls opened up. Myself, I still fish sometimes, but not all that much—a few weeks in summer—except for that I don't fish at all.

I think the fishery will slowly become extinct. Times have changed and people are changing too so, I guess, that's something we will have to accept. But it's not easy to look out in the morning and see no boats. I think the fishery was ruined when the draggers came here. They own the fishery now, the draggers do.

— George Buckle
[10.4:47]

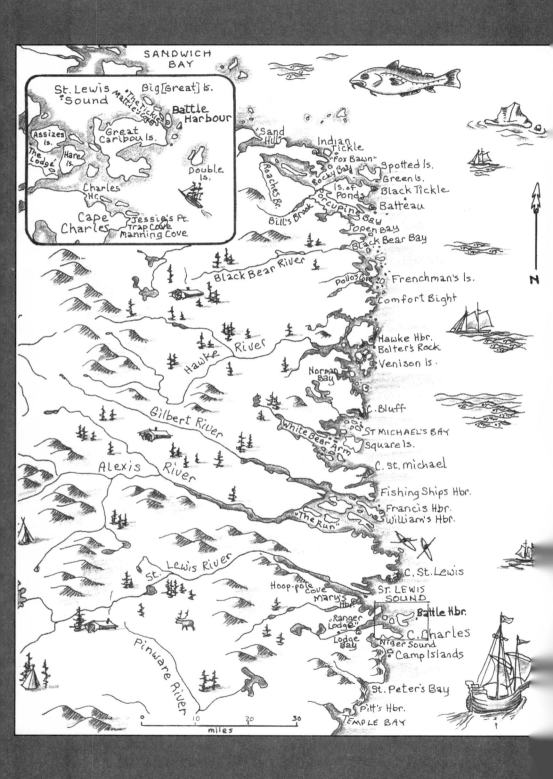

SANDWICH BAY

St. Lewis Sound
Big [Great] Is.
The Tickle
Mattie Is.
Battle Harbour
Assizes Is.
Great Caribou Is.
The Lodge
Hare Is.
Double Is.
Charles Hr.
Cape Charles
Jessie's Pt.
Trap Cove
Manning Cove

Sand Hill
Indian Tickle
"Fox Bawn"
Rocky Bay
Reaches Bk.
Bill's Brook
Is. of Ponds
Porcupine Bay
Spotted Is.
Green Is.
Black Tickle
Batteau
Open Bay
Black Bear Bay

Black Bear River
Pollos Cove
Frenchman's Is.
Comfort Bight

Hawke River
Hawke Hbr.
Bolter's Rock
Venison Is.
Norman Bay

Gilbert River
C. Bluff
White Bear Arm
St. Michael's Bay
Square Is.

Alexis River
C. St. Michael

Fishing Ships Hbr.
Francis Hbr.
William's Hbr.

"The Run"

St. Lewis River
C. St. Lewis

Hoop-pole Cove
Mary's
ST. LEWIS SOUND
Battle Hbr.
Ranger Lodge
C. Charles
Lodge Bay
Niger Sound
Camp Islands

Pinware River

St. Peter's Bay
Pitt's Hbr.
TEMPLE BAY

N

0   10   20   30
miles

Three

NORTH OF CHATEAU

1773, January 6

*To the Right Honorable Earl of Dartmouth, His Majesty's Secretary of State for the
American Department, First Lord of Trade and Plantations, &c, &c, &c.*

Sheweth

*That, in the Spring of the Year 1770, when no British Subject in Labrador would ven-
ture to reside farther northward than Chateau Bay and the islands immediately adjacent, your Lordships Memorialist, at great hazard and expense settled himself in the
River Charles on the said Coast, in order to establish Seal and Salmon Fisheries; to
fish for Cod; to carry on the Furring Business; to open a friendly and Commercial
intercourse with the Eskimaux Indians with whom we were then upon very bad
terms; and to commence, if possible, a Shore Whale-fishery....*

*Your Lordships most respectful
and most obliged Servant
Geo. Cartwright*

WHEN CAPTAIN GEORGE CARTWRIGHT REOCCUPIED the old Darby and Marsal stations on
the River Charles after the French were evicted from Labrador, Cape Charles was still
the boundary between a tenuous European frontier and the wild "Land of the
Esquimaux." Within a few years, Cartwright and the Moravians between them succeeded in opening the gates to Labrador once and for all, and the inevitable process of
colonization began.

Cartwright was a social renegade of sorts, an amateur naturalist, and a would-be
enlightened humanist. But for his unshakable loyalty to the Crown and his inbred
sense of class superiority, he might have been at home among America's lesser found-

ing fathers. He believed that if he treated the Inuit fairly and with respect they would respond in kind, and he was not disappointed. After several years in Labrador he wrote, "The Esquimaux…are the best tempered people I ever met with, and most docile; nor is there any nation under the sun, with which I would sooner trust my person and property; although, 'till within these few years, they were never known to have any intercourse with Europeans, without committing theft or murder, and generally both."[1]

At the time of Cartwright's arrival on the coast, bands of Inuit camped from time to time near Chateau Bay, Isle of Ponds, and on Huntingdon Island in Sandwich Bay. Some may still have resided on Belle Isle and near Battle Harbour, the former home of the Putlavamiut massacred by Innu around 1750. In October 1770, his first year in Labrador, Cartwright convinced chief Attuiock and eight members of his extended family to winter near him at Charles River.[2] The group stayed for several years as Cartwright's wilderness tutors and companions. Some of the women bore children for his employees.

In 1772 Cartwright took his adopted family to England, where they became overnight celebrities and favorites of the royal household and his own. No lesser artists than Angelica Kaufmann and Nathaniel Dance painted their portraits. But after the initial fascination with a land where all the woods and greens were shaped by man, the Inuit longed for home. As they were preparing to depart, the group contracted smallpox. Only Caubvick, wife of Attuiock's brother Tooklavinia, returned alive to her people in Ivuktoke, unwittingly carrying the infection in the locks of hair she had shed during the sickness and kept among her belongings. Judging from the untended corpses discovered by trader William Phippard on Eskimo Island several years later, there were few if any survivors.[3]

The early ledgers of Slade & Company at Battle Harbour record trade with Inuit, some of whose names also appear in journals of George Cartwright and the Moravian missionaries, or on the map Brother Leo Elsner made of his travels south of the Mission stations.[4] Shelmuck of Sandwich Bay, "Captain Jack" (a name that first appears in Fornel's account of his voyage to Baie des Esquimaux in 1743), "Young Jack," Eteweooke, Oglucock, Pompey (the legendary murderous recluse said to have lived on islands in Sandwich and Groswater bays that now bear his name), and Paulo Owettowey are among them. There is in 1798 also a Magaruse and a Mawcoo— names reminiscent of Marcoux/Marcuse/Mucko. As late as 1851 Bishop Feild of the Church of England reported that all but one of the resident women between Forteau and Dumplin Island in Sandwich Bay were either Inuit, Innu, or mixed. This would suggest that the wives of both first and second generation Atlantic Shore Settlers were Aboriginal.

For all its distinction as the easternmost extremity of the North American continent, the Atlantic Shore is physically unprepossessing. The five hundred foot high plateau that extends to within five miles of the Straits before stepping abruptly down to the water's edge here withdraws into the interior some twenty-five miles or more, as though driven back in disarray by the ferocity of the open sea. It was, however, seaward-moving glaciers that breached the plateau's rim, leaving a few isolated mountain clusters in their wake. Through these the land bumps gradually down to a broad, thickly wooded coastal apron drained by long, frothy rivers. This is broken country, heavily wooded, difficult to traverse. Like the rest of Labrador it presents a precipitous and menacing face to the sea, but terrain was not responsible for the extreme (even by Labrador standards) hardships her resident human population was enduring by the end of the nineteenth century, as described in some of the narratives. That seems to have had more to do with the kind of population that evolved and its reliance on the sea.

Europeans who moved into the bays of the Atlantic Shore early in the frontier period adopted the Aboriginal inhabitants' migratory lifestyle required for survival in Labrador, initially depending on seal, salmon, game, and fur for their livelihood. Cod was procured mainly for personal use, as the merchants then imported their fishing crews from abroad. As long as competition for the limited terrestrial resources remained light, people could get by, so there were seldom more than two or three families in a bay. Most had some kind of relationship with the dominant English trading company, Slade's of Poole.

John Slade came to Newfoundland in 1748 as a captain in the merchant marine. Upon acquiring his own vessel in 1753, he returned to try his hand in the fishery. Within a decade he had a fleet of four ships and maintained crews at Twillingate, Fogo, and Tilting Harbour and had begun operating along the Labrador coast. In 1772 he prevailed in a tussle with Noble & Pinson over a station on Seal Island, Chateau Bay, and within a few years was firmly established at Battle Harbour, just north of Cape Charles.[5] By 1775, when this became Slade's Labrador headquarters, the island community that formed around it had superseded Forteau as the most populous and commercially active in the region, a distinction it would retain through much of the nineteenth century. The firm itself remained intact until 1871.

During its tenure, Slade & Company employed a number of men who would ultimately settle in Labrador. Samuel Acreman; Charles and Mark Anstey; William Blake Sr. and Jr., and John Blake; William Reed; William and John Broomfield; George Dempster; William Brown; John Buckle; Robert Coombs; John and James Davis; William and Daniel Dicker; John, Joseph, Thomas & William Ford; John Lane; Samuel Luscombe (whose surname remains on a brook in Groswater Bay); John Martin; James Gready; Thomas Oliver; John and Joseph Painter; John Peyton; William Phippard; John Rumbolt; William & Jacob Thomas; John Tilsed; Joseph Whittle; and Samuel Wolfrey are but a few of the names in Slade's eighteenth-century Battle Harbour ledgers that reappear later among the ranks of Settlers or historical records.

They are joined in the early nineteenth century by Joseph Cribb; Thomas Painter; Moses Brown; Thomas & Stephen Groves; William & Jonathan Coombs; John Deer; John Gillingham; William Holloway; James Goodenough; William Reed; William Snook; James & Thomas Saunders; John Burden; Thomas Pike; Jonathan Cole; John Yeatman; and the legendary James Smoker, among others. In many cases the Christian names differ from those given for family progenitors in oral genealogies and legends, but it would be a strange set of coincidences indeed if there were no relationship between most of these men and the permanent Settlers of Labrador on the basis of those surnames.

Most of the planters in Slade's records were trappers and salmoners who went to remote outposts as agents or subcontractors for the company before striking out for themselves. The list of purchases in the ledgers suggests that although they returned periodically to Battle Harbour for supplies, their main objective there was to obtain liquor and a few other sundries presumably unavailable closer to their homesteads in Hamilton Inlet and Sandwich Bay. The ledgers and diaries also allude to men who shifted among employers, like Tilsed, whose story may be typical of many. Tilsed originally worked for George Cartwright at Ranger Lodge before transferring to Cartwright's friend, Lester, in Trinity, Newfoundland. He returned as boatmaster to Cartwright in 1785 before signing on with Slade's when Cartwright left Labrador the following year.

Mary's Harbour, Fox Harbour, Cape Charles, and Lodge Bay filled with the families of Slade's servants and sharemen, eventually becoming "suburbs" of Battle Harbour. By 1850 the area boasted a population of six hundred and an Anglican church, presided over by Rev. H. P. Disney. When Slade's sold out to Baine Johnston & Company of St. John's in 1871, many residents of the area allegedly departed for western Newfoundland, Canada, and the United States. By then, the center of activity on the Atlantic Shore had shifted to Black Tickle some eighty miles to the north, her economy had become focused on the codfishery, and her tiny population had been engulfed by the summer flood of Newfoundlanders.

While a small population of Settlers continued to winter in the bays, or moved north in order to be near the fur trading companies, year-round communities of fishermen began to develop near the outer coast. Peopled mainly by liveyers and caretakers of the fishing stations, they offered first choice of fishing berths in the spring but little advantage the rest of the year. Winters were brutal, the hunting grounds distant, and the only pelts to be had on the coast were those of the ubiquitous fox. Black Tickle was one of these settlements.

Most other coastal harbours were used only in summer. Venerable fishing and sealing stations such as Spear Point, Francis Harbour, Hawke Harbour, Venison Tickle, and Seal Island were operated through much of the nineteenth century as outposts for West Country firms based in Newfoundland or near the Straits like Birds, Slade's, and

Noble & Pinson. The Cape Charles/Lodge Bay station has been in continuous operation since 1735, when Frenchman Antoine Marsal arrived. Many on the islands had been used sporadically since the 1500s. In time, these too were taken over by Newfoundland companies like Earle's and Rorke's of Carbonear, and new ones opened along the archipelago to accommodate the growing summer fleet. By 1820 there were small fishing establishments at Petty Harbour, Fishing Ships Harbour, Occasional Harbour, Square Island, Cape Bluff Island, Snug Harbour, Double Island, Island of Ponds, Spotted Islands, Partridge Bay, St. Michael's Bay, Black Bear Bay, and Table Bay.[6]

By the end of the century there were nearly five thousand Newfoundland vessels on the coast and over twenty thousand floaters and stationers each summer. Like migrating seabirds the schooners beat to favorite anchorages as soon as leads opened in the frozen ocean, their tawny sails racing north against the dense tide of broken ice. Dormant harbours sprang to life. Forests of spars, their halyards slapping in the wind, swayed and creaked at crowded moorings. Wives, children, even livestock stumbled from fetid holds into the bright cold Labrador air to rejoice in reunion with friends and reclaim the musty one-room huts they had left the previous fall. Merchants unbarred their stores. Heavy boots drummed on boardwalks and over the lattice-breasted stageheads that serve as docks in rocky Labrador. Children called to each other from the hillsides where they had rediscovered last summer's hideaways. Smells of tar and hemp, cutch, sawdust, rum, wood smoke, baking bread, tobacco, canvas and fish offal enriched the clear air, mingling with the sounds of Newfy banter, squealing winches, hammering, and the eager cries of gulls. It must have made a strong impression on the liveyers.

The summer stations of the Atlantic Shore have an especially precarious appearance, for few of the areas fine harbours are surrounded by level ground. Cabins, storehouses and stages cling to steep encircling rocks like barnacles, haphazardly scaffolded against the wind and the pitch of the shore. Weathered to the same silvery sheen as the rocks, they become all but invisible on a gray day. As most needed major repairs or reconstruction after the ravages of a North Atlantic winter, there was little point in building anything of substance.

In spite of salmon's importance to Labrador's early Settlers, fish in that place has always meant cod. A man standing in a dory knee deep in salmon will answer the question, "Got any fish?" with an honest, "No, by, nary a one." If you want salmon, you must ask for it by name. This was always so in the British fishery, for no other marine resource had ever equaled cod in abundance and economic value. For over a century, the Labradorians too were caught up in the excitement of an annual race to harvest a resource from which they themselves would gain little.

The fishery began in late June when the great schools of cod followed the sardine-like capelin toward their spawning beaches. From the time Portuguese first came to Labrador in the fifteenth century until the introduction of the trap net in 1875, cod were taken one by one with double-barbed, fish-shaped lead hooks called jiggers. The huge trap nets—box-shaped corrals anchored across a known fishing ledge or berth—are expensive, arduous to clean and repair, require several men to haul, and are frequently carried away by ice, storms, or whales. This was an investment few Labradorians could afford. But traps gave the larger operators and more prosperous liveyers a significant advantage over their less well-equipped neighbors, and the fishing industry an advantage over the fish, precipitating a search for ever more efficient harvesting methods that would lead ultimately to the demise of the industry.

Needless to say, a man's success at fishing depended also on having a good boat. Here too, the Labradorians were almost always behind the offshore competition. Though most were able boatbuilders, few had schooners or, later, longliners. They fished from shallops and large, open dory-like boats that could be rowed or sailed. After the introduction of motors in 1918, those who could convince the merchants to extend enough credit installed them in their open vessels. The result was the ubiquitous Labrador trapboat whose funky single-cylinder beat characterized summer on the coast until the inshore fishery finally gave out in the 1980s. With the advent of motorboats, Labradorians were able to venture farther from shore and add trawl lines to their fishing arsenal. These were used in the fall to intercept cod on their way back out to deep water.

During the fishing season, days began at three in the morning. By five o'clock boats had left the harbours for the family's traditional trap berths, if they had them, or for their jigging holes. If the catch was good, the day might not end until midnight when the last fish had been gutted, headed, split, salted, and stored in the stage. This operation was done at great speed by the fisherman and members of his crew and family, including women and young children. After three hours sleep the new day began, day after day except Sundays, until the cod headed back out to sea in October.

On days too rough for fishing there were nets to be mended and cleaned, and boats to be repaired. Idleness was unknown. Near the end of the season, the salted cod had to be washed and dried in the sun, spread out on flakes—rocks or raised stick platforms—and packed in quintal (112 lb.) bales or large barrels called "tierces." Fish were graded, priced by merchants at the nearest fishing station, and shipped to Newfoundland ports for transport overseas. The value of each man's catch became the basis for winter rations allocated to his family. In a bad year, there were those who left the store with little more than a jug of molasses and a gallon of kerosene, for the irony of the codfishery was that the price was good only when the fish were scarce because it all went to market at the same time.

By any measure, the Labrador fishery was a grueling, dangerous, and unrewarding occupation, but it was not without its pleasures. Saturday evening the rum kegs were tapped, the fiddles and pipes brought out, and all hands gathered at the largest available house for a good old "time." Then it was the pounding of rolled-down hip boots— 'rubbers'—on a hollow plank floor that echoed across the harbour.[7]

Early British trading vessels ran circuits from home to Newfoundland, then to the West Indies and back. The dried cod they carried to places like Jamaica was exchanged for molasses and rum, much of it for consumption on board and in the northern colonies. During the frontier period, therefore, rum was cheap and people drank it like water. Missionaries and government officials tried to discourage merchants from using it to seduce and enslave the native people, but only missionaries frowned on its use by whites. However, persistent lobbying by the churches and the rising price of rum gradually altered public attitudes. By 1900 liquor consumption and sale was illegal in Labrador. These factors along with the increasing stability and order of family units led to at least partial temperance throughout the Settler population. Most households continued to make berry wines for medicinal and ceremonial purposes, while potent home-brews concocted from yeast, hops, spruce and birch, and fruits replaced rum for those determined to have an occasional bash. Drunkenness at special times such as the end of the fishery seems to have been tacitly condoned by all but the most rigid Wesleyans and Moravians.

On this coast, Sunday was another working day for some of the Newfoundland fishing crews, like it or not, but as elsewhere, the predominantly Protestant Settlers considered the sanctity of the Sabbath inviolable. In 1848 when Bishop Feild of the Church of England surveyed the spiritual condition of the fishing stations he counted twelve hundred nominal Anglicans, most south of Black Tickle. Nominal was the operative word. Few had ever been to a real church; fewer still could read or follow a service, but groups of devout families across Labrador had for some time gathered on Sundays for improvised services of their own invention. By 1860 when Feild had established summer Missions at Battle, Seal, Spear, and Henley Harbours, and at Camp Islands, he found that attendance by all but the local Inuit was poor, the Settlers preferring their homestyle gatherings. Soon after the C of E chapels were constructed, the diocese of Newfoundland followed by opening Catholic Missions for the Irish and Newfoundland-Irish communities at Mary's Harbour and Black Tickle (also Pinware in the Straits), apparently with better results.

The fishery came to define life on the Atlantic Shore, and every fall it packed up and went away—merchants, missionaries, magistrates and all. Flocking ducks left the bays with a sound like sudden bursts of applause to join others already gliding southward over the surface of the water among the shadows of windblown clouds. Discarded feathers and trampled shorelines were all that remained of the growing companies of geese that had been muttering anxiously among themselves for weeks in hidden tundra ponds. Harbours emptied, grew silent, and then froze.

The men who stayed to tend the main fishing establishments through the winter, or simply stayed to try their hand at independence, must have found the abrupt solitude stunning. Little wonder their winter landscape was peopled with phantom dog teams like Old Smoker's. Between Battle Harbour and Black Tickle at the southern and northern extremities of the Atlantic Shore, Settlers wintering in the isolated bays had no access to services and little social contact until the 1930s, but at least they could hunt and get a few furs to supplement their income. The small communities of liveyers near the coast were neither hunters nor trappers by training or inclination, although they took seal and ducks when they could get them and trapped the island foxes. When the fish began their long, halting decline, and the price of salt exceeded the price of cured fish, leaving them destitute at the onset of winter, they had no choice but to join the baymen in pursuit of diminishing populations of game in the interior. Caribou and porcupine had all but disappeared from the area by then, and a long arduous hunt was apt to yield little more than a few ptarmigan and rabbits.

As the twentieth century approached, the center of activity for the Atlantic Shore shifted from the Black Tickle area back to Battle Harbour. This was due in part to the location there of the first Grenfell Mission hospital in 1893, and to the other services it attracted and reinforced—churches, schools, stores, and visiting government representatives. Schooners flocked to the harbour and Settlers again filled the old salmon posts and winter homes around the bay. Although Battle Harbour's prominence declined in tandem with the schooner era and the fire that destroyed its hospital in 1930, it remains a colourful historic site, with its old wooden buildings fitted with original hardware and trim, its pathways and gullies inlaid with antique refuse. The store itself sits atop a prehistoric Dorset midden. Many of the buildings have now been restored, and the site is run as a museum for the benefit of tourists, since most residents of the island moved to Mary's Harbour after the fire.

The twentieth century has been characterized by attempts to develop alternatives to the declining fishery. Newfoundlanders ran a two hundred-man whaling operation at Hawkes Harbour from around 1910 to 1950, employing a few of the liveyers. In 1933, just when the full-force of the Depression hit the Atlantic Shore, the Labrador Development Company under John Hope Simpson opened a logging operation on the Alexis River, establishing the town of Port Hope Simpson for workers and offering cash wages across the board. While once again, most employees were from Newfoundland, some jobs went to Labrador families. They came from as far north as Seal Island and set up their own community across the bay at Blackwater Brook. Bowater Ltd. took over the logging operation and kept it afloat until the 1960s. By then, wage employment was available at Goose Bay and other larger communities.

In the 1950s, two enterprising Newfoundland-born brothers started a sawmill in beautiful St. Michael's Bay. This provided work for fishing families in the vicinity of Square Islands and led to the development of the present-day village of

Charlottetown. The sawmill is still in operation, and by 1980 the new town boasted several churches of diverse denominations, a medical clinic, and two schools. During the resettlement period, both Charlottetown and Port Hope Simpson were designated economically viable communities by the government and therefore received some of the families resettled from nearby outports. In all there are nine year-round communities in this part of Labrador today. In 1980 they ranged in population from fifty to four hundred. All have schools, medical clinics, stores, electricity, telephones, satellite television, churches, and airstrips. Many have recreational centers, running water, and sewers or septic systems. Everyone has enough to eat.

No part of Labrador was a stranger to poverty and hunger, but the Atlantic Shore in its time knew hardship more intimately than most. While the average yearly income of a family in Sandwich Bay around 1930 was $600—$1,000 in western Lake Melville—it was but $160 in this area, and many made far less.[8] When the merchants cheated the fishermen, as was common in the early nineteenth century, or there was a spell of bad years for fishing and trapping, as in the 1860s, or the costs of fishing exceeded the gains, as in the 1920s, people "went down." That means they had neither cash nor credit with which to obtain cod traps, the twine to repair them, or ammunition for hunting. They went hungry and their health declined, they lost the strength needed to struggle with the sea and the wilderness, and they raised undernourished and debilitated children. Some went down about as far as one can go, and for many years there was no one to lend a hand but neighbors as hard up as themselves. Before Confederation with Canada in 1949, the sporadic "poor relief" programs offered by Britain's colonial government were so inadequate they did little more than fuel frustration and anger.

During this period the people of the Atlantic Shore were called "the despised liveyers" of Labrador by at least one outside observer.[9] American Alphonse Packard, who visited the coast in the 1880s, wrote: "Dirty, forlorn tilts, smoked and begrimed with dirt, the occupants in some cases thoroughly harmonize with their surroundings. Their features and hands are smoked dark and their rough life is more or less demoralizing, but certainly law and order are well maintained on the coast, and no cases of immorality came to our ears."[10]

In 1923, John Abbott of Newfoundland, imploring the governor for better attention to the needs of the Atlantic Shore peoples, summed it up this way:

In referring to the temporal affairs of the people I may say that the condition of the greater portion of the permanent Settlers of the coast leave much to be desired. For the most part they are poor with very little chance of improving their condition. Of course, there are exceptions and the coast from Blanc Sablon to Battle Harbour [The Straits] is decidedly ahead of the other portion.

Most of the people in that vicinity live continuously at one place and have good homes and fishing property, but from Battle Harbour north, nearly all people migrate to the bays every fall where they have shacks of a very poor kind in most instances. These shacks are mostly small and they are built of round sticks filled in between with moss and covered with felt. They are usually all one-roomed affairs and the whole family live, eat and sleep in the same compartment.

Their general avocation during winter is trapping furs. I was informed that quite a few years previous to 1922 repeated failure year after year on the hunting ground made the hunters very depressed and disheartened. But there was a fairly good supply of furs, also seals, last year the proceeds of which enabled them to procure the common necessities of every day life, thus lessening poor relief and preventing some poverty.

In some places I found quite a few fishermen, who formerly had good fishing gear, experiencing great difficulty in keeping it in repairs. In fact some have discarded much of their twine [nets] as worthless and have no means of having it replaced. Similar conditions apply to many of the hunters. So these people in both cases have their means of production considerably lessened, and the government must suffer the consequences.[11]

The worst of it, according to George Poole from Fox Harbour, was from 1920 to 1939.

There was nothing for you to get. Nothing at all. If you didn't get a skin of fur there was no more cents, no more dollars, no nothing. I can remember at least fifteen years when I didn't have enough money to post a letter. Take every cent you had to get a bit of food. Your clothes wasn't too stylish at that time either.

I seen some hard times on the Labrador. I seen people starve to death for want of some relief. Taking the bitter with the sweet I always managed to get along. There was times I had a little extra to share with others.

It is characteristic of the "despised liveyers" of eastern Labrador that, given the worst odds in the game, they not only managed, but managed with considerable patience, good humor, dignity, and selflessness, as did most Labradorians. Had Packard and other outside commentators troubled to look beneath the swarthy complexions, they might not have been so quick with supercilious judgments.

I WAS BORN TO WILLIAM'S HARBOUR and raised there, and when I got married I went to George's Cove, which is on the same island as William's Harbour. William's Harbour is twenty miles from Port Hope Simpson, which is where I live now.

My father was John Russell from William's Harbour and my mother was Mary Anna Burden from Carbonear. My mother died when I was four years old, and my father married again when I was six. Then when I was fourteen my step-mother died, so I was left with a family of nine to raise. The youngest two girls—her girls—one was a year old and the other one was goin' in three. I raised 'um 'till I was twenty-six, then I got married.

I can remember when my mother died, and I can remember before she died. I can remember now what she looked like. I can remember how she wore her hair and everything, although I was only four. I wouldn't be five until the next June, and she died in December. I'm eighty-two now.

My father lived alone and looked after us for a little while. There was four of us. My youngest brother was a month old when my mother died, so my aunt took him until my father got married again. I was second oldest. I had one brother older than me and two younger brothers. There's only meself now and one brother leaved. He's eighty. I reared 'en up.

Our tables and all used to be board then. We'd make our own tables and benches; different ones used to make chairs. We used to make our own mats. I had a house when I was in George's Cove—five bedrooms upstairs, three downstairs, and I'd have mats on 'um all, made 'um meself. Hooked the mats meself. Sometimes I'd be a long time before I'd get cloth enough, you know. I'd make the mats out of old clothes. My aunt used to give me some clothes belonging to the boys. I'd take it, wash it and make mats. When they'd get dirty, we'd scrub 'um out wit' soap and bring 'um down to the landwash, put 'um in the salt water, sweep 'um wit' the broom and put 'um on the rocks to dry. We'd put our own designs on the mats. Sometimes we'd see a flower and pick it, seal it on wit' a bit of thread, git a needle and stab it right around and then mark it on.

I made all me brothers' and sisters' clothing. Many times I cut over old articles and made suits for them. I had to learn it all out of me own head. I had no one to show me. I made skin boots and slippers for me brothers and sisters, that's me step-sisters. I had two step-sisters and two step-brothers, see? I thought the world of them.

I got one livin' now, that's the one I reared from a year old. She's sixty-seven now. I thinks the world of her.

I made the skin mitts, too. I've made the suits, the cossacks and the pants, out of sealskin. I did all that wit' me fingers. I made me own patterns for the mitts, boots and suits. I made one sealskin suit fer me husband the second year we was married. You can see me hands is wore out from workin' at the sealskins. I've worked hard in me day.

My husband was Fred Burden. We had six children. I reared five. I lost one when he was three years old. He took a germ and got tuberculosis meningitis. There was no doctors then, no nurses, nothing. He was three years old, that was our youngest. We had our own remedies, and we done all we could fer this little feller, but we didn't know what was wrong. I had a sister-in-law, see, and she died wit' TB. The doctors claims that's what it was when they come.

I had no learnin', never went to school—never inside a school door in me life. I picked up so much with the children learnin' in the house, and I'd go to church a lot and follow along what the minister was sayin', so it give me a chance to read the Bible. I can read the Bible.

The mailman used to come from south. He used to stay at our house—Uncle Billy Murphy. He'd come from Battle Harbour. He had a son used to come wit' 'en—Neddy. They used to come on dogteam. Sometimes 'twould take 'um two days to come from Battle Harbour to William's Harbour. He'd go from that to Norman's Bay, sometimes go to Cartwright. Sometimes he'd come down wit' messages—no sendin' messages like it is now.

Uncle Billy Murphy was a funny, nice old man, you know. He'd always call me Sade, never called me by me own name. "Sade, maid," he'd say, "'twas hard goin' yesterday, but 'twas nice today." Or, "Sade, have you got any herring ready fer me?" He'd eat three herring fer his breakfast. He'd be takin' his stuff out of the house and lashin' it on his komatik and he'd come in and take a piece of herring, go out and come in and do the same thing again. After he got too old, his son Neddy took over, and he used to stay to the house, too. They'd have their komatiks piled right up with bags of mail. They'd have to go through the hard and the soft wit' it.

Uncle Billy Martin used to come from down the shore. He'd stay to the house too. We was the only ones used to stay on the outside, see? We used to take in the fur buyers that used to come. There was Mr. Clarence Birdseye, Uncle Tom Fequet, Uncle Harry Fequet, Steve McDonald and Manuel Pardy. Then, not only the men would come. You'd have to put the boilers on and cook fer the dogs. Lots of times they'd get the tubs and cook outdoors when I'd have too much else to cook. They'd just come and eat, they'd never pay nothing, them days. Uncle Bill Martin was nice; he'd always give me two or three dollars when he'd be goin' through the door. Sometimes they'd have something in their box and they'd get that out in the morning. Uncle Billy

Murphy would have ducks in his box, already cooked. He'd take 'um out and say, "Now, Sade, I'm goin' to take out something fer you to have fer supper."

The doctors would stop by our place, too—there was not many nurses used to come, them times, 'twas all doctors—Dr. Grieves and others.

I was only young when Mr. Birdseye used to come there—fifteen or sixteen. When I'd see 'en comin' I'd flash up, frightened. I used to say, "What's that old thing comin' now fer." I'd be washin'. He'd bring candies and give 'um to the children and the people what was there, pass the bag all around. He'd say, "I got to go and put one in Clary's mouth." Boy, if you was there then you could have lit a match on me face. I would feel some embarrassed when he'd come. He'd always want me to come down to Muddy Bay to work fer 'en. He said he'd pay me big wages. I'd say, "No, Dad. No, Dad, don't say yes."

Lots of old people used to go around them days and after they'd go away I'd have a big lot of work to do. No canvas to wash up then, no carpets to do or anything like that. Lots of parkas there. They'd all have their sleeping bags. You'd come down in the morning and they'd be all stretched out, one here, another one there, and so on all around the house as high as five or six. They'd pick up their bags and get ready fer breakfast. You'd get breakfast be the lamp light, no other kind of light then. They'd be gone by eight o'clock.

The first time I was ever in the hospital was at Battle Harbour. I went there to have some teeth out and I was runned right down. I was nineteen then and I'd been lookin' after a family from fourteen to nineteen without any help. I was there a month and I couldn't stay no longer because I was thinkin' about the crowd at home. Dr. Grieve give me some medicine. They thought I was runnin' TB, but I never got that.

The *Maraval* used to come down here then. They had a big operation one Saturday when I was there. They had six operations one Saturday, the doctor did. Dr. Grenfell was there himself, and there was other doctors there. They took off one little boys legs and turned them around. That was some operation. His two feet was turned right around backwards. All I knows was he was a Caines. I got sick of the hospital that day. Mrs. Butt had to have her finger taken off—well, wasn't I some glad when she had to go in because then I had to take her baby and go outdoors. I was some glad I got out of it. Nice hospital, though. They was nice to me.

After I went home from the hospital the doctors used to came to the house and they'd send me a parcel, clothes for myself and some things for the house, things you had to use like dish cloths and table cloths and sheets and stuff like that. I had a big parcel; I was some tickled wit' it, too.

— Clara Burden
[4.1:52]

I'LL TELL YOU HOW BATTLE Harbour come to get its name. Cabot come out from England and when he come it was all savages. They had to have a battle to get into the harbour. That's how it come to be Battle Harbour. Right down from where the church is now and up along the shore, before it was all built up, that was all graveyard. The holes were dug and the bodies lowered in. They had no coffins or nothing like that then.

Then people began comin' down from Newfoundland in schooners. They'd come to Battle Harbour, put up, fish and go back. More and more schooners began to come and soon some began to build on the land.

My old grandfather, he come from England as a cabin boy on a schooner and went to Twillingate, Newfoundland. Then he come to Labrador and pitched his tent on Big Island. That's how come we was all reared on Big Island. We had a great house built in a cove on the front side of the island. On the back of the island it used to be wonderful rough. There's no one livin' there now because it's a hard place to get off of durin' freeze-up and break-up. You could be there for weeks not able to get off....

I'll tell you now, when I left Big Island and we moved to Battle Harbour, the difference between then and now you wouldn't believe unless you could have seen it yourself. On Jessie's Point there was two coves. There was Manning's Cove and Trap Cove, just a little ways apart. There was stages, flakes, houses, men and youngsters. There's not one of them livin' today. At Battle Harbour you could hardly put your foot on a rock there was so many bridges and things. There was bunk-houses, big houses and stores. There was a big store, under the bank, over forty feet long. You go out on the point and there was a big seiner for hauling seines up in. You go along the eastern side of the island and there was a big stage halfway across the cove. There's hardly a stick there now except for what Baine Johnson got there, and there's a house and a stage that we got. All the rest is all gone. We had a small schooner out in the Tickle and Uncle Ned Ashley had three or four of them moored up in the mouth of the Tickle. Jim Snook had one too. Murphy's was on the western side of the Tickle. It was all built up with houses and stages.

—Levi Joe Spearing
[2.3:23]

FIRST WHEN I WENT FISHIN' I wasn't very hardy. The old man used to put me in the cuddy of the boat. I was ten year old. I was seventy when I give up. I wouldn't have knocked off then but I got too old to manage proper.

Back when I started fishin' we used to have jiggers, dappers and grounders and, for boats, we had dory rats and bullies. Dory rats was smaller boats, and bullies would hold about ten to fifteen quintals of fish.

Schooners used to be swarmin' here for years and years and years. Black Tickle used to be swarmin', Batteau would be full of schooners. Most people lived aboard their schooners.

When I was small we used to come here in the fall. You'd hear an old feller down in the cooper shop makin' casks—hammerin' away night times. I heard that dozens of times. Every night, sir, you'd hear 'en workin' away. I wasn't afraid. You'd hear the old fellers talkin' about it. They never minded. I never seen nothing at all 'cept a scattered light. Lights, you see swarms of 'um over to Spotted Islands. Every night you'd see 'um. That's from where people got drowned—schooner people—and they never found their bodies. I've heard 'um singin'. Have a big storm come on and you'd hear 'um singin'.

There been people lost here, drowned. Years and years we've seen one of the fellers walk across here and go back again. A young feller almost struck 'en one time. He had his oil clothes and all on. The young feller got an awful start, almost touched 'en before he seen 'en. 'Twas the token of a feller that got lost.

There was three more fellers lost out here off some schooner. They're buried down in the bottom of the cove. I don't know the name of the schooner; that was before I was born.

There was a schooner lost down here on the Fox Bawn. Most every fall, if there's a breeze comes on, you'd see it all lighted up; the whole length of her. We went up on the hill one fall and come back and said the steamer was comin' up through the Run. We went back and never seen no sign of her after. 'Twas a schooner that was wrecked.

I never minded anything. I spent my lifetime around here. I'd be out hours before daylight, sometimes, gunnin' in the woods all day long.

—Alex Turnbull
[13.4:23]

THEM TIMES, ON THE LABRADOR, we didn't know what kind of prices we was going to get for our fish until we shipped it in the fall. All you knew was you caught fish. Well, this particular year fish turned out to be a dollar and fifty cents a quintal, and salt was seven dollars a hogshead. It took a hogshead of salt to salt five or six quintals of fish, so the more fish you caught, the further you went in the hole. If a quintal of fish can't pay for a hogshead of salt, you go in the hole.

So we settled up in the fall, me, me father, and me brother, and we didn't have a cent comin' to us. I was seventeen then and me brother was married with some kids. I was just a young feller so the old man took my share and paid off me brother's account. Comin' on spring, after spendin' our bit of money that was left the year before, we was hard up. We didn't have any food and no money to buy any.

Me father was sick in bed most of the winter, something wrong with his kidneys. At home there was me father and mother, meself and me younger brother. Well, we had to eat. We set off for Battle Harbour to look for "relief." When we left home there was no food. I didn't even have any breakfast before I left.

We got to Battle Harbour and went to the Relieving Officer, as they were called at that time. His name was Ned Neil and he belonged to Bay Roberts, Newfoundland.

His office was in the house of a man named Charlie Mangroves. Me brother had no trouble at all. All he had to do was go to the Marconi station to Mr. Stan Brazil, who was the Justice of the Peace as well as the Marconi operator, and swear an oath that he didn't have any food and no money to buy any. Then you'd take the affidavit down to the Relieving Officer.

When me brother was finished talking to Neil, I asked him, "What about me?"

"Are you married?" he asked.

I said, "No sir, I'm not."

"Well, there's nothing I can do for you," he said.

"I didn't come lookin' for help, meself, personally," I said, "although I got to eat. I come lookin' for me father."

"Where's your father to?" he said.

I said, "He's home sick in bed."

"Oh, he's sick in bed," he said.

I said, "I'll tell you what I'll do: the food you're goin' to give me brother Fred, he's able to haul that and you too. He got a good team of dogs. So you go with him and see me father, which is about seventeen or eighteen miles away, and see his condition. Then you'll be able to decide for yourself whether he's able to get in a coach box and come to Battle Harbour just for the sake of swearing an oath."

"Oh no." he said, "I'm not here to do that kind of thing. How much fish did you get last summer?"

"We got between five and six hundred quintals between the three of us." I told him.

He wanted to know why we didn't get more than that.

I told him that was a pretty good voyage for three hands. And it was, considerin' the fact that you had to make all that fish, dried.

"I can't do anything for you," he said again, "I got to see your father."

We talked back and forth a bit then we decided to go to the Marconi station, so me brother could take the oath and go to get his food. When we was there we told Mr. Brazil our story and I asked him what he'd do in my situation.

Mr. Brazil was an awful man to swear. "By Jesus, I don't know what you'd do," he said, "But I knows what I'd do if 'twas me." And that's all he'd say.

So me brother took the Bible, made his oath, and we left. On the way down to the Relieving Officers we had to pass this church, and we stopped there. Fred said to me, "George boy, it's no good for you to go home without food in the middle of April. The time is come to break-up. With the bit of food that I got, it's no good to add on four or five more mouths because we'll never make it. It'll only last about two weeks and then nobody got none. It could break up and we'd starve to death. Other people wouldn't be able to help us because they got none themselves. So you got to get food before you leaves here."

We were down against this church and the wind was blowin' from the narwest with a little old drift blowin'. We went in to the shelter of the church and held a council of war. Like I said, I was a young man and I didn't care much whether I lived or died, but I didn't want to starve to death because that was too slow a way to go. So I said we'd go down to Neil again and if he wouldn't give me food, I'd have to make it rough for him.

We went down and walked into his office. Now, he's office was in a room off from the kitchen and this was where Mrs. Mangroves used to pass his meals through. It was just about dinner time and they had fresh meat for dinner. I could smell it cookin'. It was about one in the afternoon and I never even had breakfast, so I was feelin' pretty hungry. The smell sought me crazy.

Neil said, "I thought I told you not to come back here."

"I'm back," I said, "for you to make me a note for food."

"I told you I wasn't going to," he said.

"Well, I said, "I'm tellin' you to go ahead and do it. Is you married?" Me brother was just standin' there, not saying a word.

"Yes," said Neil.

"You got children?"

"Yes," again.

I said, "Do you want to see them again?"

Now, his family was in Bay Roberts. He said, "Yes, I would very much like to see them. I'd see them today if I could."

"Well, sir," I said, "you'll never see them no more if you don't write that note; now write it damn good and fast or I'll kill you with this." And I took this big white enamel chair and put it over me head and brought it down on the table.

"Now," I said, "that's the first one; the next one is goin' through your brains."

He got kinda scared.

While I was doin' this, the woman of the house went and took off for Mr. Brazil's.

"Yes," I said, "I'll kill you with the chair." And I meant it, too, my son.

"Yes," me brother said, "There's two of us and you can't get away," and he began to haul off his cossack and he put it on the floor and jumped on it. By that time the old feller was shiverin' too much to even talk almost.

"Hold on," he said, "I'll write a note for you. I'll write a note."

I said, "I thought you couldn't write nare note? I thought you couldn't do anything for me? Do it now and do it fast."

Now this feller had been in the Dardanelles in the First World War. I don't think he got such a fright when the British tried to get up through the Dardanelles as he got that day. I had no trouble when he seen I meant business. He told me not to ever come back because he didn't ever want to see me again. And he told me I'd be going to St. John's when navigation opened for makin' a racket. I didn't mind that very much.

I took me note, without lookin' at it, and we left to go to Baine Johnston's store. On the way we met a man comin' down the road.

"My God!" he said, "Mrs. Mangroves is dead. She just got to Mr. Brazil's door and she fell in the snow bank. They got her dragged in the house now."

I said, "Very good, boy. Well have to hold Mr. Neil responsible for that. It wasn't my fault."

We never bothered about the poor old woman, just went off to the store. She used to have fits when she'd get confused or upset, and she'd faint away. She was all right after a bit.

Anyway, we went to Baine Johnston's and Fred got his note took care of first. Then I give my note to Charlie Hoff, the store manager. Now, if I'd got the same rations as Fred, we could've hauled it all on one komatik. Mr. Hoff said, "By God, you'll never haul all that." I made three trips to Battle Harbour to get the food that Neil give me. Three times. Three komatik loads. I landed it here at Fox Harbour and pretty near filled the old man's little wood house that he had there. We never had to get anything charged to our account before the middle of August.

— George Poole
[2.2:44]

THERE USED TO BE HARD times in Black Tickle. Food was scarce lots of times. Well, there was no stores, so we had to walk to Cartwright for every mouthful we'd eat. 'Twas a clever ways to go, sixty miles down, sixty miles back.

When all the dogs perished, that was another thing. We lost all the dogs in Black Tickle, sove two out of eighteen. Everyone lost all their dogs. We had to walk then, just a couple of dogs clippin' along. 'Twas a hard lookin' fit-out, eh? You had to take two or three dogs on a sixty-mile jent. 'Twasn't very nice. Take three or four days, up and down, takin' your time. You had to haul along your bit of food wit' it. 'Twas years before we got the dogs back, years and years and years.

Used to get relief then; that's what we used to get, relief. Two dollars and fifty cents a head, a month. We had to live on that, six and a half cents a day. But a dollar then was as good as ten now, eh? You get a barrel of flour for seven dollars, now you got to pay twenty for a fifty-pound sack. Sugar was seven cents a pound, salt beef was fifteen cents a pound, pork was ten cents a pound. Everything was cheap then.

We been months without food here. We was the whole month of May, one time, without one mouthful of flour in Black Tickle. No molasses, no tea, no nothing. For all of that, now, poor ol' Grandfather Keefe, now that was me poor ol' father's father, it wasn't fer regard of money because he had thousands a money, barrels of it... It just couldn't be got. There was none here, none to Cartwright. Cartwright was gone dry. There was fellers went up as far as Battle Harbour on dogs to try to get some food, but there was none anywhere on the coast.

'Twas terrible. Yes, sir, used to be hard times then, I'll tell ya. Lots of times we used to go to bed wit' a hungry stomach. That's all you could do about it. The children don't know nothing about that now, and I hope they never will. My wife, Maude, here, often seen three or four days wit' not a mouthful to eat. She seen it bad.

The funniest part of it, I couldn't see through, it must have been handed down by the Almighty, surely gracious… You know, you could go and kill ducks when you like and seals, wind up or wind down. You'd have duck fried up fer breakfast, seal p'haps fer supper—still and fer all that, seemed like there was nothing to eat. We had nare bit of strength in the world, in our bodies, eh? Sweat rollin' off ya all day long. If you only moved around you'd be sweatin' all day long. Sure you could hardly lug a bucket of water. We was starved to death.

One of them years, too, the measles was around. That was another thing, another beautiful thing. 'Twas an awful lot of people died here wit' that. I believe there was sixteen or seventeen altogether between Batteau, Spotted Islands and Black Tickle. Uncle John Dyson up to Batteau, his wife and son, all three of 'em died the one time. I wasn't sick at'all. Me father was right blind wit' it, broke right out, pickled all over. 'Twas one of them years—I don't know—I expect near about 1930. We never had no fire ider, the fire was gettin' burned out where everyone was laid up so long. I used to marle off with me bit a rope in me hand and go down to the gulch down there, and I'd tear up some a them big long weeds. I'd boil the kettle then, but sure, there was no tea, no sweetness, nothing.

—Jack Keefe
[3.4:42]

I CAN REMEMBER ONE TIME we had a relievin' officer come there [Battle Harbour] givin' out grub. He's orders was to give out grub. He come and put the grub in the store and never give Charlie Hoff any orders to give it out. Before he left I went and told him I had to have grub. He never give me no answer, just got aboard the steamer and went off and that was the last trip. When I got so hard up that I had to have food or die, they was gone.

Brazil was there keepin' Marconi and he was the Justice of the Peace. He wouldn't send no messages about a man with no grub. He'd say he sent it in but couldn't get no answer, but he was tellin' lies.

One day me and Arch Rumbolt went for grub. First we went up on the hill to Brazil and he told him we had to have food or die. Then we went to Charlie Hoff. Brazil come in and went in with Charlie. Poor old Arch went in first and he come out again and said I had to go in.

"God," says Alf Snook, "He's goin' in. He won't be like you, Arch."

"Ah," I says to Brazil, "You drove Arch out but you won't be able to drive me out."

I caught'n be the throat and hove'n across the floor.

I said, "I wants grub and I'll have grub before I lefs this. I got me hatchet out here and if I don't get grub I'm goin' to chop the store out."

"You is," he said.

"Yes," I said, "There's fellers up in St. John's like you. I knows all about them. Now, I'm goin' to have me grub."

Charlie Hoff stood ag'in the counter. He wouldn't give in. Me and Charlie had a few words and what he said was none of his business because he wasn't there that summer. He said I wouldn't go fishin' because I was lazy. He didn't know what he was talkin' about.

"Look here," I said, "Charlie, you're goin' to catch it for that. You'll pay for that."

He never said another word.

"I catch you before you goes to bed tonight," I promised'n.

Well, I went home and was cuttin' a bit of wood. After a while I asked the old woman what time it was. She said 'twas such and such a time so I knowed Charlie was comin' handy about then. I started to walk up and just as I got to a bank at the back of the church, he come over the rise with an iron poker in his hand. Garge Smith was comin' behind me but I didn't know he was handy 'till after. Anyhow, I grabbed Charlie Hoff and he rose the poker. Well, I tell you, he come down quick enough, he and his iron poker. I knocked'n in the big bank of snow and poor old Garge Smith went down on top of'n. Charlie jumped up and I caught hold of him and took all the buttons off his coat and I up with me foot and give it to him in the ass and put him down over the bank and fired his iron poker after'n.

Poor old mother wanted to go down to the store and put the buttons back on his coat.

Next morning I went back to the store and I had no trouble gettin' me grub.

When we come back to Battle Harbour from Port Hope Simpson we had nothing. What we left there was all destroyed and gone. Anyhow, we fixed up some kind of room with old sticks and stuff, got a bit of grub and went fishin'. Before we started fishin' some fellers come here to build up on White Point and, b'gar, they wanted men. Me boys went off and me and Garge stayed and made the fish we had. We caught a lot of fish and done well. The next year we done well again and ever since we got on.

— Levi Joe Spearing
[2.3:24]

THERE WAS AN OL' FELLER we used to call Joker—a little short, stoggy feller. He was strong as a bear and smart. He used to be always carryin' on wid the maids.

There was a girl on Green Island and she was right mad after the boys. She'd have a new one every night if she could get one. When we'd go over there we'd find out who she wanted that night and he'd go off wid 'er, or pretend he'd go wid 'er or something.

Then all hands would chase 'em and get 'er started. She'd get right mad, fight and everything.

One night, after we was landed there and talking on the bawn, some of the maids found out it was me she wanted that night.

"Come on, Jessie, lets go for a walk." I said.

I didn't know what was goin' to happen. The boys wouldn't touch anyone she was wid, 'twas only she they'd do anything wid.

We dodged on but we didn't get very far when I heard Uncle Joker comin'. He grabbed 'er by the two legs and hove 'er over his back. All she could do was bawl. She couldn't kick because he had 'er hold so fast. She had a pair of white pants on. The boys got all around callin' at 'er and she was bawlin' blue murder. At last he put 'er down. She had a good smack at 'en but she couldn't hit 'en because he was too smart. She scravelled to get some rocks, she was goin' to kill 'en. By the time she got the rocks he was gone out of sight in the dark...You talk about a racket!

That ended the walk that night.

"No good to take a walk wid you, Jessie," I said. "The boys won't leave us alone."

Another night when we went over there—and we only went over once in a while—she went wid Ray Wells. That was the night of the BIG racket, the night she had Ray.

'Twas time for 'er to go in, see, when Ray found out who it was she wanted to be wid that night. He took 'er into this little ol' fish house that Uncle Art Crummy built. The boys got a big rock, oh, about as big as a boiler—took two of 'um to lift it. They got 'en up on the roof thinkin' he'd go down through. Sure if he'd gone down through he'd have killed 'um both stone cold. When the rock went on the roof, Jessie scravelled out through the door. She thought she was goin' to be killed. She scravelled out through the door draggin' Ray.

That was all very well; the boys disappeared.

Ray said to 'er, "Jessie, maid, 'tis no good. If that rock had come down we'd have been killed stone cold. I'm goin' home."

Anyway, they dodged on down the path towards the house. Ray had his boat to the stagehead. When they got to Uncle Art's house they stopped ag'in the house. Now, Uncle Art wasn't gone to bed; he was sat to his table writin'. They could see 'en through the window.

Uncle Art had an ol' big vessel spar lodged between the roof of the house and some rocks. That was a brace to help the house stand ag'in the wind.

Anyway, Jessie and Ray dodged down aginst the side of the house and stood longside the door talkin'. Harvey Richards got a big ol' sod that he tore off a rock, tore off like a sleepin' bag, rolled 'en up and tucked 'en under his arm. Then he started to go up this spar, goin' up to heave this sod down over Jessie and Ray. We was all standin' round watchin' the fun.

I thought to meself, That spar is goin' to break to once. He was there a long time. Sure enough, when Harvey got about half way up here it smashed down in two pieces and come down, Harvey, sod, and all. We all thought he was killed. 'Twas an awful racket.

Uncle Art scravelled out through the door but the only one he caught was Jessie. He made her go in. He come out ag'in after to see who he could find, but all hands was hidin' away among the rocks—clear of Harvey, who was under the spar wid the sod over 'en. He was knocked stunned and couldn't get up for a spell. Anyway, Uncle Art didn't see 'en, all he saw was the broken spar. He went back in the house.

After 'twas all over Harvey got out moanin' and groanin'. He wasn't able to go anywhere else that night. In fact, he done very well to get down to the boat and get home. He thought he was killed and 'tis a wonder he wasn't. He was up about seven or eight feet or more when the spar broke. If it'd come down on 'en he'd have been killed for sure.

That was some of the best sport we ever had.

— James Burdett
[14.4:38]

Now, I GOT A STORY to tell about Battle. True story, as true as the sun shines. Do you believe in ghosts or spirits? Well, after I tells you this story, you're goin' to believe in something.

This dog Battle always obeyed me, clear of a couple of times, and I had 'en thirteen years, so I got to forgive 'en for that.

Now, I lived wit' me foster father. He was me uncle, but you know, he raised me up. Me mother died when I was sixteen and me youngest sister come and lived wit' us. There was three bedrooms upstairs, so me sister slept wit' me. Battle always slept on the couch. He never, as a rule, bothered to go upstairs unless somebody was sick in bed and he missed 'um. He'd usually go up, take a spin around the rooms and come down, and that's all there was to it.

So this night everybody was gone to bed. Uncle George was home and I was home and me sister was home, and there was this man on the stairway. The dog start to bark. Oh, he was barkin' crazy, barkin' crazy, and this was laughable you know, but 'tis true.

The dog started to bark downstairs and Uncle George bawled out to 'en to be quiet. Now when the dog start to bark, I was turned inside and I t'ought I heard someone step on the stairs, so I turned outside, and when I did there was this man standin' by me bed. I could see 'en as plain as I can see you now. Them times they used to wear what we called long-johns, fleece-lined underwear and khaki shirts most of the time…when I turned outside, here he was right by me bed. On account of 'en creepin', I didn't know what to think.

Well, I didn't have much time to think anything, I just sat up in bed and stuck me arm out as far as I could reach but I never touched the man even though he was right close to me bed. Then he disappeared just about long enough for a person to get downstairs.

Well sir, that dog was barkin' and yappin' and Uncle George bawled out to 'en. He went back and jumped up on the day-bed, or couch. The couch was like a leather couch wit' curled legs on it, all done up, you know, and when you touched the back of it 'twould vibrate by the wall. When the dog hit the wall, the couch vibrated, he hit wit' that force. He only jumped on the couch once, then back to the hall and, this time, up over the stairs. Well, he was really mad.

Well, me and Uncle George both bawled at 'en, but he kept on barkin', so I told 'en to come in wit' me. I told me sister to slide out. Now, 'twas in me mind that if there was such a thing as ghosts, Battle seen it. Anyway, me sister slide out and the dog jumped in over the two of us. He was makin' a noise, like a spitey way of breathin'. That dog was scared to pieces.

Me sister said, "What's the matter wit' that old Battle? I won't get no sleep tonight."

I took the top quilt and put it over the dog, like you would to keep the quilt down, and that dog was tremblin' for at least an hour, I'm sure.

I was awake now, but me sister went back to sleep. I just lay there thinkin' about what I had seen and thinkin' about the dog, why he should get such a fright. Then the time came to get up.

Uncle George said, "What in the buggerin' hell (that was a sayin' he had) was wrong wit' that dog?"

I said, "There was a man in my room last night. Did you hear 'en?"

He said, "No."

I said, "I never heard 'en but I seen 'en."

Now, my dear, that's all I can tell you. Just long enough for a person to come in through the house, the dog start to bark, and long enough for a person to go downstairs, and the dog went crazy. Now that's all I knows. That's all I knows about that spirit. I almost forgot about it, but sometimes someone will bring up ghosts and spirits and twill all come to me mind again and keeps me renewed.

— Alex Poole
[6.2:50]

I THINK A GOOD ONE to tell you is the first time I went to North West River and then to Makkovik. I was sixteen years old, now I'm seventy. The first time I went to Cartwright from Indian Tickle I pulled a load of freight to Roaches Brook with a dogteam. When I was there talking to the Anglican minister, Parson Lawton, he wanted a team of dogs to take him from Cartwright to Porcupine Bay. He was talking to me and asked me would I take him. I had a very good team of dogs, so I said yes. So, I took him on with a load of freight and landed at Roaches Brook for the night, then I come on the next morning, and we went to Porcupine Bay.

When we come back to Cartwright the next day, he asked me if I'd go north with 'en as far as Makkovik. He had to have a team to take him to North West River and then along the coast to Makkovik. I said I didn't know the way, I was never down there before. I was only a young feller. He said he knowed the way, he guessed. He could figure out the way, no problem. It was going to take about two months, and he'd pay me. The pay was $1.50 a day, and he'd find the food for the dogs. That was very good, I called it, but I didn't know the way—that was the worst.

So we took on and got ready. We had a bit of food. It was poor times then on the Labrador. We had to carry something to eat 'cause lots of times, when you'd go into a place, a feller wouldn't have anything in the house.

Anyway, away we goes. After we left Cartwright Bight I didn't know where to go, but I had a good leader. You put him on the track, or footin', and he'd go all day. We had eight dogs. We went over to North River, and the minister figured we wanted another dog—eight was hardly enough—so we got the loan of one there. He was a great big old gray dog he was, and strong…and saucy, I thought he was. Every time I'd go alongside him, he'd growl. When he overstepped and came out of his harness and I put him in, he made a big yap and I give him the back of the chain drug in the side of the head. He never bit me, but he'd growl all the time when I'd go alongside him.

So we went to West Bay and then to Back Bay and on to North West River. It was wonderful bad going. The snow was too deep, the dogs couldn't get along. I put my rackets on and got set to walk the ninety miles up the bay to North West River. On the way up, the dogs got right mad 'cause there was seals on the ice. We got one—a jar he was.

After we got to North West River and spent five or six days, we went over to Double Mer and we come to a house with nobody in it. Come to find out, the man was after gettin' astray in his head, and his family took off out of the house. He went silly! He called hisself the King's man. He had a gun and cartridges with 'en. It was a risk to go where he was—he might shoot you. He used to come back to his house and get food at night.

The next day, some people from Rigolet brought him back there. When we got to Rigolet, he talked to the minister. He went to the service and, when we kneeled down in prayer, he went for the door and got out. We had an awful chase. Bill Davis from Cartwright and I caught 'en. He was right savage. We carried him back and got a straightjacket on him and put him in a house with bars on the windows. He was there until the *Kyle* picked him up in June.

So we went on our journey. We went down to what they calls Killer Man's Neck then. There was about a foot of snow again that night. Buddy put me on the path and told me to go that way. When we got down over the hill there was two leads, one going north and one going northeast. The minister didn't know which one to take but he said we'll take the one going this way. We could see Cape Harrison. I said, "Ouk, ouk," to the dogs and they turned off.

When the leader went so far he stopped and looked back. I never said anything, and he went on again a little bit and stopped and looked back again. I said we were going wrong. The minister said, "Oh no, we can't be going wrong," but I said, "Come around," to the dogs. When we got to where we turned off from, the leader put his nose right to the ground and took off. The minister said, "I never seen the like of that before." I said, "He can go on to Nain now, snow or no snow." The next day we got down to Tuchialik and the next day we got down to Makkovik. That was hard driving, down that way.

We was down there about a month, going one place or another. If a place was handy, he'd have a service two or three times a day.

On our way back to Cartwright it turned mild. It was good going, but it was bad for the dog's paws. They cut their paws. We had to get a green sealskin—and it was a job to get one—but we got one to make boots for their paws so we could get home. This old big gray feller that we got in North River, when I went to put the boots on 'en, he grabbed me hand in his mouth. I had a hold to his paw, and he had a hold to me hand. I didn't know if the best thing was to get the minister to shoot 'en...He never bite hard, he wasn't even nippin'. When I'd haul on the boot string, he'd nip; when I'd slack up, he'd slack up. I said there was something queer about that. I'd haul on the string and he'd breathe down hard on his teeth. The harder I'd haul, the harder he'd bite. I thought if he got the taste of my blood, he might get me then. Anyway, I let 'en go and when I did, he let me go. Then he attacked the boot on his foot and started to eat the boot.

Of course, dogs wasn't all that easy all the time. About forty years ago a Newfoundland feller took a man's youngsters and his team of dogs. He wasn't real used to dogs. He took them about five miles up the lake near Port Hope Simpson for a picnic, and when they got there the ice was bad and they fell in. The boy was eight years old and the girl was ten. When they fell in he got the girl up on the ice and the little feller had to hold on to a rock and he told 'en, "Hold on, my son, hold on. I'll get you 't'once."

The dogs turned around, they got on the ice. They went back to where the girl was and attacked her. They eat her on the ice. They tore her up on the ice. And when the little feller seen 'em eating his sister, he was bawling to the dogs, screechin' and bawlin' at 'um. Then he slipped off the rock and went down. The man had to get away from the dogs or they'd have attacked he in the water. So he swum away from 'en after a spell and got on the ice.

And the dogs, some got on the ice, some got in the water and got their traces off and harnesses off and started to go all over the place. Then they eat the poor little girl. The boy drowned. Then the man had to go back to Port Hope Simpson and tell the father and mother. They got a feller to go and shoot the dogs. The youngsters' father and mother were Gilbert and Bella Russell.

— Billy Parr
[7.3:39]

I NEVER SEEN OLD SMOKER but I've heard tell of 'en lots of times.

Poor old Eli Hopkins, one time, told me they seen Smoker and they heard him up in Partridge Bay. He said he had some wood cut up inside the houses. He lived to Apollo's Cove—that was about four miles from Partridge Bay. The people lived to Partridge Bay. Eli said he forgot something. 'Twas a fine night so he said he'd go home and get whatever it was. After supper he harnessed up his dogs and drove along in by the houses in Partridge Bay and come back out on the pat' they used, a pat that went right around. After that the people said they seen Smoker, heard him and everything. Eli never told them the difference; he said he supposed they seen him yet. That's one Smoker.

Mr. Moores told me about another Smoker up there to Riding Pond, comin' across Black Bird Bay, or there somewhere. He said they come down on the pond when 'twas gettin' dark, and the trees on the other side of the pond formed like a man on a komatik with seven or eight dogs in the team. He said they were goin' along and that made this other thing that look like a team seem to be movin' along, too. Well, he said that was Smoker for sure. When he got over to Open Bay he told 'um about this team he seen goin' along by the side of the pond. They all said that was Smoker because they was after seein' or hearin' him a few days before that. He never told 'um the difference. That's another Smoker.

I don't know how many more Smokers there is, but that is some that I heard tell of.

Uncle Jimmy Davis told us a funny story about Smoker. He said that Smoker had a daughter married up to Open Bay. She went outdoors one night and was gone for a long time. They was beginnin' to wonder where she was gone to. After a spell she come back and told them she was off fer a ride with her father. She said he come along and she jumped in the box and went on. He always had a komatik box on with the old woman into 'en most of the time. She jumped in the box with her mother and went off fer a ride. They don't know yet anymore than that. They never seen nothing or heard nothing that time.

— James Burdett
[4.4:5]

IN 1929, ON OR AROUND July 15th, Tom Campbell (fourteen-and-a-half years old) got me (barely fourteen) to go duck hunting. Tom got his father's old twelve gauge, single-barrel, breech-loader, and away we went in along Martle Pond, across a short neck to Sandy Pond and on to Island Harbour. Altogether it was about a mile. There we saw a little clinker-built, two-stemmed boat belonging to Tom's father. The boat, about ten feet long, was hauled up on a rock. I noticed that there were two paddles. Tom put the gun aboard the boat and we launched her out and went up along shore.

As we travelled along by the shore we looked for ducks or anything else that we could get. Near Herring Pond Brook we saw a few ducks, but they were too smart for us. Then we went out on an island, hauled up the boat and walked to the top of the island to have a look around. I noticed that this was just one of the many islands that barred the inner harbour from the outer harbour. Looking towards the nor'west was the whole expanse of the outer harbour and the lower part of St. Michael's Bay, which was dotted with islands and rocks. There wasn't a ripple on the water. All at once I saw Tom drop down and he said to me in a hoarse whisper, "Get down."

I got down in a hurry and looked where he was pointing. I saw ducks coming from behind another island about half a mile away.

Tom said, "Brass-wing divers."

At first there wasn't many, but as they came, the company got bigger. The first company started to thin out and then a second company came and thinned out, and finally a third company swam out. There must have been thousands. By the time the last company thinned out the vanguard was almost to another island about a mile farther out in the harbour.

There was not a word spoken all that time, then Tom said, "When they get on the other side, we'll go down on this side of the island."

As soon as the last ones were out of sight we launched the boat and started off. I was on the fore thwart and Tom was on the aft thwart pulling on the one set of paddles. We tried to be as quiet as we could but even then we must have made a good bit of noise—it was so calm. When we got out we landed on a flat landwash among boulders of all sizes sticking out of the mud. Tom left me to look after the boat. I got out into the mud and tried to haul the boat up by her stem. I got her half out of the water and looked around for something to tie her on. I found a fathom of six-thread rope with one end tied to the risens. I took the other end but couldn't find anything to tie on to, so I put the end of the rope on one rock and placed another rock on it, then I followed Tom.

At the top of the island there was a little low cliff with five or six stunted fir trees, their tops just above the cliff top. I found Tom lying down peeping through the top branches, but I could tell by the way he was stretching his neck that he wasn't seeing too much. Something had gone wrong. When Tom got up higher to have a good look, I got up too. There wasn't a duck in sight. As we were on the lower end of the island, we couldn't see around the upper end, which was where we figured the ducks must be. We went up around and discovered that it wasn't one island but two joined by a low sand bar, forty to fifty feet long by twenty feet wide and about a foot out of water.

We couldn't see anything on the other side of the bar, so we went over to and up on top of the island, which was the higher of the two. There was no sign of the ducks there either. We kept on crawling and peeping until we were right on top of the summit on the upper end. We could see the water about a hundred feet below, and only then did we realize the ducks had flown away, for now we could see right around on both sides of the two islands and all down over the water where we had come out about two hours before.

I looked up to the nor'west and saw something I had never seen before. Tom must have seen it too but he never said a word. It was calm all around and for about a mile out in the bay, then the water was white. It looked like it was smoking in a straight line all across the bay. What looked like smoke seemed to be coming towards us with great speed. It struck us off the summit and onto the land under the top of the hill. The water around the island was calm for a few seconds. This smoke was feather white and passed us almost as fast as our eyes could follow on its way to the bottom of the harbour.

From where we were standing we could see right in over the island on which we had landed. All of a sudden I noticed something: a little boat was blowing along with the wind about two hundred yards from the shore. At first it didn't dawn on me that it was our boat. Tom must have been looking in another direction because when I said, "Tom, look at the boat," he took one look and started down over the hill towards the sand bar. I followed right behind him but when we got there the sand bar was under water. The puff of wind had pushed the water, for even as I watched, I could see the water rising. Tom didn't hesitate. He jumped right in and splashed across. The water was over his knees. I jumped as well, knowing the longer I lingered, the deeper it would get. By the time I got to the little hill, Tom had reached the landwash and was standing to his knees in the water watching the boat drifting away.

The first thing we noticed, after we realized there was nothing we could do, was how cold it had gotten. All morning the temperature must have been around 80 degrees Fahrenheit. Now it was almost freezing. The wind wasn't blowing nearly as hard. In fact, it seemed to be dying down as fast as it had sprung up. Even though the sun was still up quite a bit, we were starting to get cold. I don't remember emptying any water out of my boots, so we couldn't have had much on our feet. Neither of us had a cap. Tom was dressed in a light shirt and pants; I wore the same but also had a light windbreaker.

I thought about putting up a signal, so we went to look for a long stick. In by the cliff we found a stick about three to four feet long and brought it out to the point towards the harbour. We propped it up with some rocks, and now we needed something for a signal. After talking it over for a while, we decided on using my windbreaker. Next we went to look over our domain, and about all that was there was blackberry bushes with rocks sticking up here and there but no berries. I suppose the gulls had eaten them. By this time we were getting very cold so we looked for a place to lie down. The only place we found that would give us any shelter was under the little cliff. We crawled in as far as we could, only to find that there was loose rocks in there. We crawled out again taking what rocks we could and then moved the rest to one side, after which we must have fallen asleep.

The next thing I remember was waking up very cold and finding it was also very dark. I thought about my windbreaker and how nice it would be to have it to cover us. Then I thought, They can't see our signal in the dark. I ran out and got it. We put it over our heads and went back to sleep. I don't know how long we slept for when I woke again it was daylight. I jumped up and ran to put the signal up again, went back and went to sleep again. The next time I woke to the sound of a motor boat.

I rolled out, jumped up and ran towards the signal. As I ran I could see boats coming from all quarters. Nobody was making a sound as I looked around and saw Tom just crawling out. The men in the boats began to cheer. The reason I had been runnin' in and out of the cave all night, and the first one out now, was because Tom was on the inside and I was on the outside.

When two of the boat crews saw we were both all right they turned around and headed for home. The other two came in on shore. One was John Batten and his crew: son Charlie and Bob Boon, now in Harbour Lodge, Saddle Hill, Carbonear. They were from Bareneed, Conception Bay, fishing in Square Islands. The other was George Kippenhuck, Uncle Sam [his father] and his brother Sam, now in a home in Clarks Beach at ninety years of age. George also had part of another crew: Uncle Billy Bourne and his grandson, Cecil Bourne [the Carbonear crew].

Next thing we knew the grub boxes were on shore and someone had a fire going. Someone called "Come and have something to eat."

John Batten asked us if we had our signal up all night. We told him that we did. He said he didn't see it when he looked through his spy glass from Burned Island, but when he got part way out the harbour he looked again and saw it. The others must have seen it when he did for everyone arrived there at the same time.

Uncle Billy Bourne began telling stories. I remember he told us one about when he was a small boy. He told us where the incident happened but I didn't catch the name. Anyway, it was about a cave and a skeleton had been found, standing up by a slanted rocks with all the bones attached. Uncle Sam asked where we had slept. We told him and pointed under the cliff.

Uncle Sam said, "There was a grave on this island. Come and show me where you slept."

I went and showed him. He got down on his hands and knees and dug around the rocks we had moved before we lay down. He found a large rib bone.

He said, "Whoever buried this old fellow must have picked the warmest spot on the island as well."

We left in George Kippenhuck's boat and got home around eight a.m. The little hunting trip that was to be about three hours had taken us twenty-four.

— Roland Powell
[14.4:59]

ME AND ESAU DYSON WAS in the country trappin' one fall. We went in to Black Bear Bay country, that's about twelve or fourteen miles south of Spotted Islands. We was quite a ways in from that, but that's to the mouth of the river. It was in November and it turned mild. The bears, I guess, decided to come out for another root around for a few more berries. I dare say their cave was quite close by, although it don't take them long to go a long ways just the same. Anyway, me and Esau, we seen this bear on the marsh eatin' berries. All we had was .22s.

We crawled across the marsh and got over longside 'en. He'd eat berries and every now and then he'd walk back up over, still eatin' berries. When he'd go down over we'd follow 'en and when he'd come back up we'd stop. Finally we got over close and when he come up we fired at 'en. Only crippled 'en. Struck 'en in the foreshoulder, only for that he would have caught me. He runned for the woods, a narrow strip of woods between the marsh and the brook, and a clear place up above. There was only about a quarter of a mile of woods and the rest was all marsh. I said to Esau, "You run up to the clear place and I'll walk up through the woods and drive 'en out to you, see."

There was some thick alder bushes beside the woods and he was hiding in that. Now, I didn't know that then, and I must have passed by 'en about six or seven feet away from 'en. I was lucky he didn't come after me then because he could have jumped on me. I went on up to where Esau was and the bear didn't go up, so I said, "I'll run down into the skirt of woods and you walk down through and see if you can drive 'en towards me."

All of a sudden I heard some limbs crackin', boughs, and I bawled out and said, "Is that you?"

There was no answer so I knew 'twas the bear. I fired and struck 'en in the foreshoulder and knocked 'en down ag'in. I only had a single shot .22. I ran over too close to 'en when I should have been gettin' my gun loaded. I was there puttin' a cartridge in when the bear jumped towards me. I slewed and lost the cartridge I had in me hand altogether. I had to bawl then for Esau. That bear would have caught me, no trouble at all, because every time he jumped his nose nearly touched me heels. I wasn't losin' any time gettin' away from 'en.

Anyway, Esau heard me bawl and he come. Just before that, I runned towards a little clear place and I turned right quick, and that time the bear passed along by me and struck his foreshoulder ag'inst a stick and turned clear of me, you know, when he was fallin' down. He went on and jumped in the brook, and by that time Esau was there and he fired and struck 'en in the back of the head and killed 'en. That was too close for comfort.

He was a big bear. We skinned 'en out. He was really fat. The fat was about an inch and a quarter thick on his rump, and that was as white as lard. You could fry that out and there was no scruncheon at all, just went almost like oil. I guess he was all ready gone in for the winter, but we had this big mild and all the snow melted and some of the brooks started to come out. The ponds was still frozen over and you could walk on them, but the brooks was cut out.

A bear will never attack you, I don't think, only when they're hurt or something like that. He was in pain and he was goin' to do everything to get me clear of 'en. I'm glad he never caught me. [10.4:26]

I guess Easter was one of the best times of the year, as far as around home was concerned. Everyone up the coast went to Cartwright. That was the place to go for the "time" on Easter. The whole length of the coast would go to Cartwright, right up around St. Michael's Bay and them places. We'd go down for all the things that was goin' on—dogteam races, football, shootin' matches, and all the goin' ons in the Parish Hall: sales, supper and dancin'. 'Twas a lot of fun, a big change for us, because you was doin' something rather than workin' all the time. Everyone went and really enjoyed it. The only ones that were left home were the youngsters, a few women, and the old people, ones that were a little too old to move around.

The distance from Spotted Islands, which was my home, to Cartwright is fifty miles by air, a little further by dogteam, but 'twas only the crooks in the path that would make the difference. 'Twas pretty straight, anyway.

We'd usually wait 'till the Saturday before Easter to go down. There was people already down there then, of course, because all along the coast they was comin' there. You could get there in a day in the spring—be all good goin'. There was people that come from Alexis Bay, that's Port Hope Simpson, eh. They'd be a couple a three days comin' down, so they'd stop to two or three different places along the way. Of course, there was people all along livin' at every little brook or place anyway, them times.

Most times 'twas better if Easter come around the middle of March, because any time after that you was likely to get a mild, so 'twould be water and sloppy. In the middle of March 'twould still be cold enough for good travellin'. Of course, the first part of April even, 'twouldn't be too bad because one thing then, there'd be lots of snow, so it took quite a bit of rain to make it real sloppy. Right now, sure, if you get a shower of rain 'tis right sloppy everywhere because there's no snow for the water to sink into, anyhow.

I came down a couple of times when 'twas real stormy. One time, in April I think it was—because everyone was moved out to Spotted Islands—we left and got into a storm and 'twas bad. Once we got into Bill's Brook it wasn't too bad then. We went in there and boiled up, and by that time it slacked a bit. We went on in to Sandy Hills that night. Bill's Brook is in Rocky Bay, and that's about twelve or fourteen miles from Spotted Islands. The ones that lived there in the winter had moved out to Spotted Islands fer the spring. Yes, 'twas really stormy. You couldn't see nothing ahead. Everybody kept as close together as they could so they wouldn't lose each other, you know. We made good time. There might have been some people out all night if it wouldn't have cleared in the evening, because there was a lot of people on the go then.

'Twas all dogteam then. The usual team was between six and nine dogs. Six and seven was the most I used to have. I often wondered about when we'd get to Cartwright there, look at the hundreds of dogs that there was and no one ever got bite, and they'd be runnin' around loose all over the place. You could hardly step clear of dogs.

Everyone stayed with the families in Cartwright, and there was lots of houses that was filled. I guess every place was filled, and some were overfilled. I usually stayed with Theodore Davis, myself, or to Don Martin's and scattered different places. One Easter I stayed to Petten's, Charlie Petten's. Usually though, when I didn't stay to Theodore's I stayed to Uncle Jim Martin's. I could name several places that were over-filled. There'd be people there from Paradise River, up around the bay, up around our way, and I suppose there'd be people from north, too, no doubt. Cartwright was big then, compared with any other places on the coast.

I went to school in Cartwright, so I went to the Easter Fair a good many times while I was goin' to school at Lockwood. You finished school at twelve or thirteen, so I'd say I was about thirteen or so the first time I came down for Easter.

Something else too—there was no shops up around home, them times, so you had to go to Frenchmen's Islands, which is around sixteen or seventeen miles from Spotted Islands. That was the closest store, and most of the time they didn't have too much, just rough food and that was all. So 'twas good to get to Cartwright to get a chocolate bar or something like that. 'Twas a change from gettin' nothing.

'Twas the one time of the year that everyone got together and seen everyone else. Christmas 'twasn't froze up, most of the time, to go around anywhere, so you was around home just in small places. Easter was one time to get together and have the biggest 'time' of the year, which is what it was, then anyway.

I never went in the dogteam race many times, just a couple. I always took part in the shootin' matches, football, sales and other things. I'd never miss the shootin'.

Most of the things at the sales was homemade, stuff made up, like komatiks, komatik boxes, grub boxes and things like that. There was things made up by the women, too, like parkas and things like that. 'Twas all good. It used to go up to a pretty good price. There wasn't much money on the go then, but I guess everyone just saved a bit for that time. That's the way it seemed to be, quite a bit of money on the go at Easter.

The baskets were something else—Oh, yes! They used to be sold off on bids. The girls would make 'em, and the fellers would buy 'em. Most of the time you didn't know whose basket was whose, but some fellers used to find out so that they could bid on the right one. There'd be a meal in them or, if there wasn't, you'd go somewhere to have a meal with the girl whose name was in the basket you got. They used to be sold fer good prices. A lot used to go very high. Some fellers would drive 'em high just to keep another feller from gettin' a basket that he thought might be the right one. That was the point anyway.

Abe Dyson was good at drivin' the prices up. If he knew who owned the basket, he was bound to drive it up. I never got up very high, I think somewhere around twenty-five dollars was the most I ever paid for a basket. I think that one was Ethel's, but she never told me what her basket looked like, all the same. Most of the time you'd get them fer around twelve and fifteen dollars, something like that.

The next day after the time, a lot of people would start off fer home. Some of us would stay around fer a day or two and do some shoppin' and things like that before we'd go home. There'd be an awful lot of people leave the next morning. Boy! There used to be a lot of people around then.

— Herb Webber
[3.3:50]

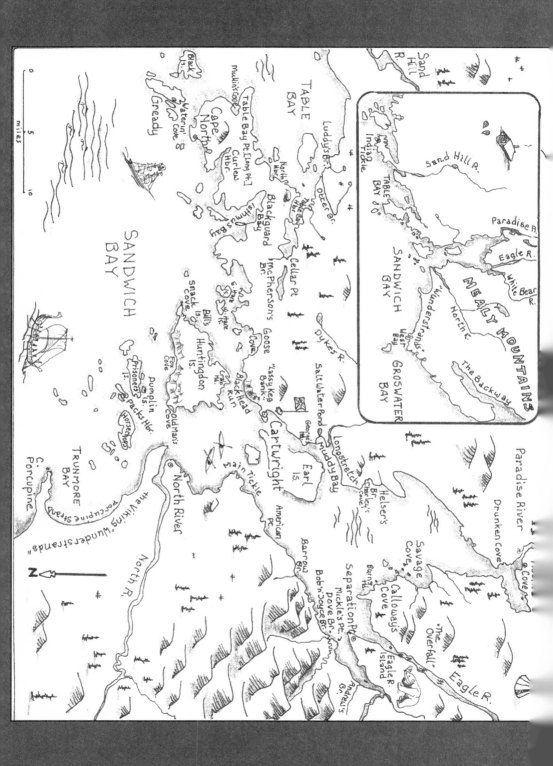

CHAPTER

Four

PARADISE

ABOVE INDIAN TICKLE THE COAST of Labrador begins its long sloping traverse toward the arctic northwest. From here past the Vikings' *Wunderstrands* and on to West Bay is George Cartwright country, with its economic center of Sandwich Bay. The stations he opened there in 1775, believed to have been the first in the vicinity by Europeans, have been used almost continuously thereafter by commercial enterprises holding exclusive charter to the bay and its nearby islands. The site of Cartwright's headquarters and homestead, now one of Labrador's principal village centres, still bears his name.

Approaching Sandwich Bay from Indian Tickle, one first passes Sand Hill Cove, where Jeremiah Coghlan had a "settlement" in Cartwright's day. In the summer of 1777, when his crew was exploring Esquimaux Bay, an associate, John Peyton, allegedly lured Coghlan's salmoners John Wrixson, John Nooks, and William Phippard to Sand Hill from stations in the Alexis and Black Bear rivers and conspired with them to usurp his partner's posts.[1] A century later when the Hudson's Bay Company acquired the Sandwich Bay stations from Hunt & Henley, they purchased Sand Hill and its fine salmon river as well. When the salmon fishery declined it was left to local residents, perhaps descendants of servants from these old companies. Some families still return there for the salmon season.

Across Table Bay and down its long arm to the pretty, round lagoon at its head, an equally rich history lies moldering in the forest floor behind a tight phalanx of spruce. Coghlan's former servant Wrixson drowned there while wintering with a crew of men in 1778, the year William Phippard and John Nooks were abandoned in Esquimaux Bay, probably by Peyton. Some years later, around 1815, an independent Nova Scotian planter named McPherson settled in Table Bay. He built a schooner with his bare hands; it caught fire on the blocks and burned before its christening. He built a house with a cellar hole, perhaps for vegetables from a garden, but the legends say that it was the smell of rum that drew bears to rout in its ruins after he too drowned and the house rotted away. The Davis children remember the bears. Their family lived in Table Bay since 1830, when self-described "renegade" Charles Francis Davis of Plymouth settled there five years after arriving in Labrador at the age of 17. His descendants are scattered all over Labrador now. A few Reeves still live in the area, too, relatives or descendants of the lad old McPherson rescued just before the rising tide swept him away. No one lives in Table Bay now, and the forest is fast consuming the last traces of human occupation.

From Table Bay the coast veers sharply eastward into the Atlantic. This is North Head, the cape that marks the southern approach to Sandwich Bay. Gready Harbour, on an island just off the headland, has been an important codfishing station since the Napoleonic Wars. Cartwright named it for his servant James Gready. Homesick Norwegian whalers operated a rendering factory there during the 1930s. Its crumpled rusting ruins look today like the fragmented skeleton of a monstrous dinosaur too ungainly for the earth to swallow. North Head itself is almost an island. It takes a good half day to circumnavigate by boat but can be crossed on foot in minutes from the head of Table Bay to Goose Cove or Isthmus Bay, where Cartwright hid from pirates. Today, hunters on skidoos use the shallow connecting valleys in winter and spring, and the sons and daughters of fishermen return to cabins in the old harbours of Cape North during their summer holidays, taking a few trout and salmon to smoke for their own use.

Opposite Cape North, the northern approach to Sandwich Bay is defined by the elegant southeastern front of the Mealy Mountains, separated here from the main northern ridge by a stream that spills off its lap into the Atlantic. Inuit families lived at nearby Main Tickle through much of the historic period, perhaps families of the first Settler wives. North River itself was used extensively by aboriginal peoples in prehistoric times, judging from the artifacts collected by summer residents. It was called Cartwright River in the eighteenth century. Phippard and Wrixson are said to have stayed there in 1777. Charles Williams settled on its banks in 1828. Later a branch of the Davis family moved there to trap along its headwaters in the Mealy Mountains. Some of their descendants still have salmon fishing cabins near the mouth. During the resettlement period the tiny community of North River won a reprieve from the government since the resources available at Cartwright were accessible to its residents, except at freeze-up and break-up. The Williams of West Bay relocated there rather than go to the town.

Between Cape North and North River, Huntingdon and Earl islands effectively conceal the entrance to Sandwich Bay from the sea, giving to the outer shoreline an aspect as uninviting as any in Labrador and possibly discouraging further investigation by the French and other Europeans who had sailed the coast before Cartwright. Like the broad-shouldered downs on either side, these islands also shelter the hidden bay from the assaults of the cold Atlantic. Once inside the narrow passage that leads to Cartwright Harbour, the incessant growl of surf subsides, and the climate assumes a more temperate disposition. Ten miles farther down the neck, around Earl Island, the inner bay slowly opens up until its dancing waters extend to the horizon in a picture-postcard vista more like primeval New England than Labrador.

Roughly twenty miles deep, not quite as wide, Sandwich Bay is expansive enough to provide a complete resource base for a relatively large number of families, yet small enough for a person in the middle to feel the sheltering embrace of surrounding land. The blue flanked Mealy Mountains sweep across the northern skyline from the west, a formidable if enchanting barrier between the world of Sandwich Bay and that of Lake Melville. In summer, their luminous crest carries the circling day, holding its fading radiance above the rising tides of night until—not quite extinguished—it is rekindled by the dawn. A dense forest of black spruce, rent by the lighter green of birch, alder, and larch that marks watercourses and old burns, spills down the mountain slopes to the bay and stops at the waters edge behind a lacy collar of alder and willow. The south shore of the bay is far less dramatic. Thinner woods not yet recovered from fires in the early decades of this century are scattered across boggy hills. No streams of any consequence crease the slopes between Muddy Bay and Paradise, and game is scarce.

For most of the historic period, human activity in the region was concentrated at the western end of the bay where three of the best salmon rivers in Labrador tumble from the high plateau in a profusion of noisy cataracts. When George Cartwright arrived in 1774, white bears congregated here by the dozens to gorge themselves on the roiling masses of spawning salmon and trout in the pools. Delighted with his discoveries, he named the rivers Paradise, Eagle, and White Bear. He named Dove Brook, another good salmon stream, for the unexpected little bird that greeted his first visit to its banks.

Grassy aprons of land ideal for homesteads spread out at the mouths of the rivers. Here an abundance of fruits and berries grow wild, and the sandy soil will yield a crop of short-season vegetables if amended with seaweed. Trees near the river mouths once grew tall and straight enough for schooner masts. The Dickie Lumber Company ran a sawmill at Dove Brook in the early years of the twentieth century. Today, driftwood polished smooth as antique silver necklaces the shore.

Such archaeological research as has been done in Sandwich Bay suggests that the Montagnais Innu were visitors rather than residents, at least while Inuit were in the vicinity. The prevalence of Indian Harbours, Tickles, and Islands nearby would suggest the opposite if they had not been named during a time when whites called all Natives 'Indians.' More compelling evidence of pre- (or proto-) Innu occupation is found in the Beothuk-like artifacts turned up in gardens at North River, Dumplin, and other islands at the mouth of the bay. During the historic period, the Eagle River headwaters area was a territorial nucleus for members of the St. Augustine and Lake

Melville Innu bands. Moravians mapping the region in 1872 noted the presence of twenty Innu families at that location.[2] When hunger or better fur prices compelled them to leave their usual routes between the Gulf and the main caribou highways west and north of Lake Melville, they descended the Eagle into Sandwich Bay. Some remained to work as free-lance furriers for the trading companies. Long accustomed to and interbred with Europeans from the Gulf coast, members of this southern Montagnais group were less reclusive than their northern cousins, and a few even married into the Settler population of Sandwich Bay. Family networks between the St. Augustine Band and the Sheshashiu Band in Western Lake Melville remain strong even today.

Inuit groups apparently moved into the area about the same time as European whaling and fishing crews (although their forerunners, the Dorset peoples, had preceded both Inuit and Europeans as far south as the Gulf and Newfoundland). The Netcetumiut, who occupied Sandwich Bay (Netsbucktoke) in the summertime, may have joined the raiding parties that bedeviled Basques in the sixteenth century and French and British during the seventeenth and eighteenth centuries. Their numbers declined sharply after 1750, the result of Innu massacres, European diseases, their predilection for rotten meat, and curiosity about the Moravian stations. Caubvick's smallpox epidemic of 1773 and an outbreak of botulism from an old whale carcass that killed forty Netsbucktoke and Ivuktoke Inuit in 1794 dealt severe blows to the Inuit of Sandwich Bay. But populations recover from illness and wars. It was not these, but rather intermarriage with white Settlers that led to the extinction of the Netcetumiut. By 1872 all the Inuit daughters had married Settlers, and only two Inuit men remained in the area—Peter Shelmuck and a man named Henn—names that have survived only in Slade's records and an old Moravian map.

Cartwright was the first European to establish commercial operations and an extended residency in Sandwich Bay. Landless son of British gentry seeking fortune and freedom in the New World, the man was as complex as the revolutionary times in which he lived. Cartwright relished outdoor life and idolized his naturalist friend Joseph Banks, to whom he sent crates of Labrador flora and fauna. Yet he loved nothing so much as sport hunting and was oblivious to the contradiction implicit in the destruction of beauty so much admired. His own account of the carnage he wrought on the white bears of Eagle River will take your breath away. Cartwright also shared with his friend Captain James Cook a respect for the dignity and rights of indigenous people, yet he did not hesitate to have servants and Inuit neighbors beaten for what he believed were moral infractions. He considered himself a progressive thinker and sought escape from the constraints of British society, but he was dogmatic in his defense of British mores when they were disregarded by others. He was a Tory to the bone.

Cartwright's story is fascinating in itself but relevant here because he document-ed an important and otherwise opaque period in Labrador history and left an indeli-ble impression on Sandwich Bay. The current names of almost every point and stream are those that Cartwright gave them. The places people settled were the sites of his posts and stations. And a few of his servants able to evade the mandatory return to England eventually became part of the Settler population.

George Cartwright personally managed his Sandwich Bay operations from 1775[3] to 1786 employing large groups of artisans, furriers, sealers, and fishermen at stations around the Bay and along the coast as far as Ivuktoke. While it is unlikely he would have permitted his servants to take up residence in Labrador against government pol-icy, he could not have prevented their shifting to other employers and thereafter to independent status when he retired. Financially ruined by American privateers and relentless misfortune, Cartwright returned to England in 1786, but his Labrador oper-ations were sustained under surrogate management until at least 1793. Arch-rival John Noble purchased them at that time and held them with successive partners Pinson and Hunt until 1816.

During the Napoleonic Wars (1803-1815), the stations seem to have been occu-pied only sporadically, if at all. Especially during the period of embargoes leading up to England's "War of 1812" with America, transatlantic shipping virtually ceased. The ensuing decrease of commercial activity in Labrador, both by English and North American companies, probably created the first real possibilities for permanent set-tlement in the region. One can imagine that men willing to remain in Labrador were encouraged to work on shares, rather than wages, and many of the outpost stations were closed. The growing population of independent planters dealing with firms like Slade's and Noble's now had access to prime locations formerly used by company ser-vants. Men capable of surviving on their own in this formidable environment, with-out access to European goods and markets, might have seen this as their first good chance to avoid both impressment and creditors by retreating into the remote bays of central Labrador. It also offered Newfoundland, Nova Scotian, and American fisheries a chance to set up seasonal stations among the coastal islands and coves.

When the circuit court from Newfoundland began making its rounds on the Labrador coast in 1811, one of its seven stops was Huntingdon Island at the mouth of Sandwich Bay, a site undoubtedly selected for its population of summer fishing crews at Indian Harbour and Snack Cove, as well as at nearby Dumplin Island, Pack's Harbour, and Gready. But the court was also instructed to serve "Europeans or Americans who remain the winter."[4] At the end of the wars, when Philip Beard & Company of Dartmouth arrived with the charter to Cartwright's holdings in Sandwich Bay, the seasonal interlopers were obliged to move on, but the planters were allowed to stay. One of the interlopers was a Nova Scotian salmoner named McPherson, whom Beard found ensconced in Table Bay. In response to Beard's suit against him, the Court ruled that McPherson could remain if supplied by a British ship instead of a Nova Scotian. He thus became a planter.

"Eight or nine families" of British Settlers were living in Sandwich Bay in 1818.[5] Some may have been Cartwright's former employees, like the shipwright Learning, said to have been in the area since the 1700s,[6] or James Goodenough, who came to the bay in 1807 after a term of service with Slade's. Laws prohibiting settlement were by then enforced only where they infringed on areas specifically granted to and current- ly used by the merchant adventurers. But as Joseph Bird discovered, it made good business sense to foster a resident population of workers dependent on the company for supplies and access to markets. The merchants of Sandwich Bay certainly seem to have embraced this approach.

Hunt & Henley, or Hunt & Company, first appear in Labrador around 1830 when they bought out Noble & Hine's operations in Temple Bay.[7] By 1836 they had obtained the rights to Cartwright's Sandwich Bay posts from Beard, and within a few years were the most important commercial firm in Labrador. While the Hudson's Bay Company would immediately vie with them for that distinction, the Hunt Company succeeded in dominating the Sandwich Bay area until 1873, and maintained strong northern posts at Snook's Cove near Rigolet, Davis Inlet, and Webbek Harbour on Cape Harrison until the 1860s. Their principal interest at these posts was salmon, which they marketed smoked or salted until canning became feasible around 1850. Thereafter the company operated canneries at both Eagle and Paradise rivers. They also maintained a trading post at Cartwright, and a sealing post at Dumplin Island, as well as sealing and fishing stations at Francis Harbour on the Atlantic Shore. Most of the current residents of Sandwich Bay came as Hunt employees during the half- century after 1830—John Burdett of Derbyshire; George Rendell, Charles Davis, and Charles William's of Plymouth; the tinker John Lethbridge of Exeter; and former planters mentioned in Slade's eighteenth-century ledgers, Moses Brown of Devonshire and ships carpenter William Dicker among them. Lethbridge came to Labrador after a stint in Nova Scotia with Noble & Pinson. He brought his Iroquois- Micmac bride, Mary Ann Louis, with him. They had nineteen children.

Freed artisans either settled in the bay, like Lethbridge and Dicker, selling both skills and produce to the company on a freelance basis, or moved north to do the same for the Hudson's Bay Company. Furriers and traders like Amos Voisey and pos- sibly Samuel James Thomas and John Ford, who had manned Hunt's northern out- posts, established their own small trading posts nearby, arranging independent sup- ply lines and markets with the captains of summer fishing vessels.

In 1873, when the collapse of Jersey banks brought down many of the old British-based Labrador companies whose operations they financed, the Hudson's Bay Company finally succeeded in acquiring the Hunt establishments in Sandwich Bay. By then, HBC was importing few employees other than factors and clerks, who rarely settled and consequently contributed little to the area's population. Preferring the traditional methods of pickling and smoking salmon, they closed down Hunt's canning factories and centered their operations in the town of Cartwright, which became the company's Labrador headquarters. Local men were encouraged to increase their winter trapping activities, so former Hunt employees built homes where the old canneries used to be and began extending their traplines ever farther into the interior. The western bay henceforth belonged to the Settlers.

The intense commercial activity generated by Cartwright, Beard, Hunt & Henley, and finally Hudson's Bay Company in Sandwich Bay helped sustain among the residents a sense of connection, tenuous as it was, with the outside world until regular mail and steamship service came to the coast in the 1870s. The introduction of the steamer service ushered in a new era for Labrador. Steamers now transported Newfoundland fishermen to and from their summer stations. They also brought mail, merchandise, missionaries, doctors, teachers, entrepreneurs, and the first adventure tourists to the coast. For residents, they provided access to competitively priced goods and markets independent of the local merchant. Savvy Labradorians took advantage of these new opportunities to establish commercial relationships with outside vendors as well as contacts with distant relatives. But in order to avail themselves fully of these opportunities, the people had to read and write, skills largely absent from Sandwich Bay until the twentieth century.

Circuit preachers from the Wesleyan mission began making winter visits to the bay in 1861. Notwithstanding that most residents considered themselves Church of England, and C of E services were offered on the islands during summer months, the Wesleyans thereafter claimed Sandwich Bay as Methodist territory. Seminarian Arminius Young, charged with the winter mission to Lake Melville and Sandwich Bay in 1903, spent "fruitful" weeks at Paradise, where he lived with the Meshers. He observed in his published diaries that the people there, notably his host family, were even more devout than their northern counterparts, and also more knowledgeable of the outside world. But Robert Mesher and his wife, Eliza Hamel, had imported their religion and such learning as they possessed from Lake Melville. As for awareness of the world, credit must surely go to the continuous shipping traffic to the bay and the work of the C of E teachers.

We learn from Mr. Young that a Church of England schoolteacher was in residence at Cartwright during the winter, providing instruction for the few families in the village and holding services on Sunday. Travelling teachers also held school sessions for a few weeks each winter at Dove Brook and Separation Point, the community that developed between Eagle and White Bear Rivers after Hunt Company left. People remembered these short sessions as being academically ineffectual, but they did expose the families at the western end of Sandwich Bay to information and concepts from the outside world.

In 1920, a Grenfell-inspired missionary, Rev. Henry Gordon, opened Labrador's first real school in Muddy Brook, five miles west of Cartwright. The history of the Muddy Bay School was short and dramatic, but it had a lasting impact on all of Labrador. Intended as a boarding school for children of coastal communities not served by the Moravians, it had immediately to serve as orphanage for the children of the Spanish Influenza, which devastated the adult population of many coastal communities and claimed sixty-nine of the three hundred souls in Sandwich Bay. During its eight-year existence, the school not only provided the country's children with their first taste of formal education, it exposed them for the first time to their contemporaries from distant settlements and to the ways of the outside world as represented by fresh-faced young teachers from England and America. A little boy who resented some necessary infringement on his liberty burned the school to the ground in 1928, nearly incinerating his classmates in the process. It was not rebuilt, but others soon took its place in Cartwright and Paradise, and it became a prototype for boarding schools at North West River and Makkovik. People had seen the light and wanted it for their children. Thenceforth, all across Labrador schools became magnets for families during the winter months and precipitated the development of villages.

Professional medical service reached Sandwich Bay early in the twentieth century when doctors and nurses from the International Grenfell Association began winter and summer circuits around the Labrador coast. By 1935 the IGA had made Cartwright its regional headquarters and opened a hospital and an industrial shop where women could supplement their husband's meager incomes with piecework. By the time the Depression hit, Grenfell clothing, hooked rugs, baskets, dolls, and carvings from the "industrials" of Labrador and northern Newfoundland were bringing hundreds of thousands of dollars into the regional economy. The rugs were especially popular, and prolific producers became significant breadwinners for the family. Today the hooked rugs made from the used silk stockings of American housewives are prized collectors' items across North America.

Grenfell was committed to liberating the Labradorians from their dependence on the trading companies and took every opportunity to create jobs and local enterprises. Unfortunately, not all of his schemes succeeded. An ambitious reindeer-husbandry venture failed utterly, as did the fur farm he underwrote near Muddy Bay in 1916. Its manager was a young American named Clarence Birdseye. While his foxes all perished from neglect, Birdseye learned about flash-freezing foods from Garland Lethbridge of Paradise River and subsequently became a millionaire back in the States. Mr. Lethbridge received not so much as an acknowledgment, but of course, everyone in Labrador knew that game or fish caught when it would freeze quickly retained its taste and texture. In time, the Hudson's Bay Company adopted the flash-freeze method and began sending frozen salmon to its markets in England and

Canada. For the past three decades, most of the salmon exported from Labrador has been frozen fresh or smoked.

Sandwich Bay and its adjacent coast is considered today to mark the southern limit of "Central Labrador," an area defined as much by its mixed population as by its geographic location. Indeed, by the twentieth century one would be hard-pressed to find a settler family with anything approaching ethnic purity. As in all coastal Labrador at least as far south as Cape Charles, the lifestyle and resource exploitation patterns too were a blend of Innu, Inuit, and European. Trapping/hunting activities were pursued October to March from winter homes in the river mouths. April was the month for ice-fishing, woodcutting, transport of supplies and wood to summer fishing stations, and seal hunting at the ice-edge for dog food, oil, and skins. In May, everyone hunted migrating water birds and set out small potato beds before moving the family to its salmon station. Some also had small gardens at their fishing places. June and July were the salmon months. After Hunt Company left, people sold their catch to HBC on the way out to the codfishing camps, usually around the twentieth of July. There they remained until mid-September—or October if they were taking herring as well. After selling their catch to the fisheries' merchant and "settling up" at the store, they headed back to winter homes, hoping to find a good crop of potatoes where they had planted eyes the previous spring.

The entire circuit from summer to winter cabins took most families a distance of no more than twenty miles, while the Lake Melville families might have to row over 150 miles from a cabin in Grand Lake to a fishing hut near Smokey. But Sandwich Bay men took fewer furs than the trappers of Lake Melville, fewer quintals of cod than the people of the Atlantic Shore, and salmon brought a poor return 'them days.' In spite of the diversity of resources within easy reach of the Settlers, the average annual income here was just 60% of that in North West River during the peak of the trapping era.[8] Still they fared better than some.

By the 1930s, the town of Cartwright was a thriving regional center, attracting people no longer able to survive in isolated coastal areas as well as those eager for access to schools, churches, and a more stimulating social environment. In the 1960s, Premier J. R. Smallwood's relocation program brought a new influx of families from outports on the Atlantic Shore, many unwillingly. But relocation did not immediately solve the problems of the desperate fisher folk resettled from the coast and initially made them worse. Where prosperity depended on a good catch of salmon and fur, and where all the good traplines and salmon berths for miles around were already claimed, newcomers had no way to make a living.

While Cartwright was growing in size and importance, people in the small winter communities of Dove Brook, Separation Point, and Paradise River continued to live much like other isolated Labradorians, relying on survival skills learned generations before from Native companions. These including an arsenal of home medical treatments that ranged from the efficacious to the injurious. The Grenfell hospital at Cartwright was a blessing, but even here, too far away for most illnesses and injuries. When the Spanish Flu struck in November 1918, it hit Sandwich Bay with a voracity equalled only in the Inuit far north. There was time neither for home remedies nor Grenfell doctors.

In this and in other respects, Sandwich Bay is a microcosm of all Labrador, of its peoples and its history. With the exception of the Moravian episode, she has lived it all. In 1941, when word reached the bay that sturdy Labradormen were wanted at the head of Lake Melville to build a great air base in the wilderness, the young men responded. Some would eventually return to Sandwich Bay, preferring the freedom of the trapline to the tyranny of the clock, but it would be by choice, not necessity.

Today there are about seven hundred people in Sandwich Bay, all but forty or so at Cartwright. They are on retirement incomes, or they work at a job in the village—storekeeper, mechanic, crab-plant worker, post office clerk. Although the codfishery ended there in the 1960s, a thriving crab fishery has since taken its place, and the wharves near the old HBC store—boarded up now but nicely maintained—bustle with activity throughout the summer. The Paradise River community is fading away, its population down to a couple dozen from over a hundred in the last decade. Most of the houses strung along the dirt path round the narrow shore are boarded up. The foundations of Cartwright's station and the Hunt Company fish factory can still be seen under the eroding beach sods. At Separation Point most of the houses were abandoned long ago and stand in various stages of decay. A few are kept up as summer homes. Footpaths back in the woods lead past the humped remains of old storage cellars, a feature seemingly unique to this region. At Dove Brook, only the little white church still stands, kept up by former residents for special gatherings and old times' sake.

The bears have returned to the rivers now, black bears. It is their tracks that break the tide-smoothed sand along the beach where children used to run, their shuffling feet that keep the footpaths open—wiry brown fur on a gray gate post. But the white bears have never come back to Eagle River.

1775-
July-

Of all the dreary sights which I have yet beheld, none ever came up to the appearance of this coast, between Alexis River and Cartwright Harbour, on my late voyage to Sandwich Bay. The continent is all of it mountainous, except the peninsula which parts Rocky Bay from Table Bay; the extreme point of which forms one side of Indian Tickle. All the islands, the Isle of Ponds, the Seal Islands and some of the small ones which are within the bays excepted, are high; the faces of all the hills which front the sea, are scarce any thing but bare rocks. The spots where any verdure was likely to appear, were covered with drift banks of snow; the shore was barricaded with ice, seven feet thick; most of the best harbours were then not open, and all the rest had so much loose ice, driving about with every wind as to render it dangerous to anchor therein; the water which we had to sail through had abundance of scattered ice floating upon it, and all towards the sea was one, uniform, compact body of rough ice. How far it reached from the shore must be left to conjecture; but I make no doubt it extended fifty leagues at least; perhaps double that distance. There was however some advantage from it, since it kept the water as smooth, as land would have done at that distance. The badness of the weather also contributed to increase the horror of the scene.

But we no sooner entered Cartwright Harbour, than the face of nature was so greatly and suddenly changed, as if we had shot within the tropics. There we saw neither ice nor snow; the hills were of a moderate height, completely covered with spruces, larches, firs and birch, the different hues of which caused a pleasing variety, and the shore was bordered round with verdant grass. The water too, instead of pans of ice, was mottled over with ducks and drakes, cooing amorously; which brought to my remembrance, the pleasing melody of the stockdove. That nothing might be wanting to complete the contrast, there was not a cloud in the sky: the sun had no sooner attained sufficient height, than he darted his rays upon us most vehemently; which were reflected back, by the glossy surface of the water, with intolerable heat; while zephyrus played upon us with a tropical warmth. The scene was greatly altered on our return, for the jam ice was not to be seen, the barricados were fallen off from the shore, most of the snow melted, all the harbours were open, and we had much pleasanter prospects, since we ran within several of the largest islands, and of course saw their best sides.

— George Cartwright[9]

MY MOTHER WAS AN ANTHONY before she married my father; she was a 'come-by-chance'. One of my grandmothers was a Reeves, but I don't know who the other one was only that she was a Phippard afterwards. She married William Phippard, but I don't know where he came from either.[10] My father was John Davis and my grandfather was Tom Davis. Tom's wife was a Reeves.

There was an ol' feller there in Table Bay; he's name was McPherson. He must have been there a long time. He had a good house in Table Bay, cellar and everything. The place is now called Cellar Point. He had a little boat for gettin' around in, around the bay and one thing and another like that. He had no big boat so he went to work and build a vessel to try to get home in. He had a fortune back home. One time he was out somewhere in his small boat and he had a young feller wit' 'en by the name of Reeves. When they come in the bay they got on a rock, a place now called McPherson's Rock. He couldn't get his boat off, so he swimmed ashore, got the young feller ashore and left 'en there. He swimmed back to his boat to see what he could do about her. I don't know if she was wracked or not but he couldn't get her off the rock. Then the tide come down too strong for 'en to do anything and he got drove away wit' the tide and drowned. That was the end of McPherson.

This young feller, Reeves, he growed up, got married and had a family. I don't know if Grandmother was part of that family or if there was a family ahead of them. Grandmother was one of those families. There was Aunt Betty who married a Morgan and there was Uncle John Reeves and Joe.

When McPherson built his vessel, there to Table Bay, they was what they called 'brimmin' 'er. They'd put a piece of birch rind on the split end of a stick and set that afire and melt tar wit' that. Wit' a stick they'd rub the tar in the seams. That's what they called brimmin' 'er. They was workin' away at that and dinnertime came so they all went to dinner. When they come out the place was all ablaze, schooner burnin' on her blocks. That's how come he was gettin' around in this little boat, tryin' to do something for himself.

I heard Dad say, lots of times, there was seven fortunes in Scotland that nobody owned, all belongin' to McPherson. Nobody ever claimed them. McPherson might have been one of them McPhersons. The other McPhersons might have been scattered around, like he was, and never got back home. Seven fortunes in a bank in Scotland. I don't know what happened to 'um.

McPherson had a cellar on the point and that's where he used to keep his rum and stuff like that. Poor ol' Uncle Mick can remember smellin' the rum. When the barrels rotted I s'pose they fell abroad. The bears used to be diggin' there, but they never got down to the cellar. They smelled the rum, I s'pose, and was diggin' around to see if they could get some.

— Tommy Davis
[10.4:51]

THE FIRST PLACE WE LIVED to in Table Bay, the first house, there was always something queer goin' on there. Different people seen stuff in that house. One time poor old Arthur Hamel was there. Uncle Mick McDonald was livin' in our house that year. Arthur Hamel was tailin' his fox traps in the fall and he come in to Table Bay for the night and stayed 'long with Uncle Mick. After supper they was sot down in front of the stove yarnin' like a couple of old fellers would, you know. They was sot on a chair, each facing one another and all of a sudden the chair Arthur was on just floundered, went clean out from under him. Arthur thought the chair went to pieces, you know. He went down and bumped on the floor. He got up to see what happened to the chair and the chair was all right, only it went out from under 'en that's all. The chair wasn't hurt. It went out just like that and nobody knowed the cause of it.

Another time, poor old Uncle Jim went to Table Bay 'long with poor old Uncle Mick McDonald for a load of wood in the summer. Uncle Mick and they stayed to their own place, and Uncle Jim went up to our place and went in for the night. After he went to bed he heard a crowd of people talkin' downstairs. He thought that was awful strange—there was no one around there in the summer, there never do be anyone there then. He got up and went down to see who it was, and when he got down then they were upstairs where he had just come from. With that he took to his heels and went down and stayed to Uncle Mick's all that night. I heard Uncle Jim talk about that lots of times, poor old chap.

Another time, now this was the years that we'd be spendin' the winters out to Gready, so our house was available for whoever wanted to live there. Anyway, this time poor old Uncle John Pardy and Aunt Violet was livin' there. One night when Aunt Violet went up to bed and after she got into bed she blowed the lamp out and the house lighted right up again. She looked at the light and this was a rabbit runnin' across the floor and it was lightin' up the house. She didn't know the cause of it. 'Twas never a rabbit in the house, but that's what it looked to be like, a rabbit poppin' along across the floor lightin' the house up, and when he got across to the other side the light went out again and there was no more rabbit or no nothing.

Now I'll tell you the story about the teapot. This happened one night when me and poor old Tommy Curl was at the house.

There was a lounge on one side of the door and the staircase was on the other side. The staircase had a rung from each step right to the loft, and those rungs was only so far apart. The Waterloo stove was right again' those rungs. We always keeped the teapot on the oven. He was a big old blue enamel teapot, he was.

Me and Tommy Curl got a cup of tea and he straightened away, covered up for the night, and I started to go upstairs. When I started to go up, here I meets the teapot coming down, bumpity-bump, bumpity-bump on the steps, you know. Now, I was just after puttin' 'en on the oven not five minutes before that and here he was comin' downstairs as I was goin' up. When he got down, he struck the floor and the tea in 'en went up over the room door. That tea left a stain that we could never get out. I thought 'twas awful funny for 'en to go in through the rungs and get upstairs when there was nare place between the rungs that was big enough to get the teapot through, he was too big. But he got up there somehow because he come down. That's something that is unbelievable.

Uncle Mick McDonald figgered the house was build on a crossed road. There was an old vessel build there one time and the people who lived there while they were buildin' had a path goin' in to their schooner and there was a path goin' up around the shore, where people went huntin' and one thing and another. Right where these two paths crossed he figured that's where we had our house build. There was no sign of a path all the same when we build our house, you know, because that was long, long years before the paths was there.

There was always something goin' on there in that house so we went to work and tore 'en down. We took the same house and carried 'en down to Luddy's Brook where we lived for years. We build 'en back the same as he was before but we never heard nothing in 'en down there. So whatever it was must have had something to do with where it was build.

I know if I told most people about what I saw they'd say I was makin' it up.

— John C. Davis
[3.1:42]

IN THE FALL OF 1883, there was a very severe gale of northeast wind. No one knows how many gales there were before that date, but the facts of the 1883 gale were told to me by the older people who could remember what happened.

Right up to the late 1800s there was no employment in Newfoundland except fishing and farming. Several big fishing vessels were lost in the gale of 1883 and many Newfoundland fishermen were lost, also women and children in some cases.[11] We have no record of how many lives were lost in Groswater Bay. We do know that White Bear Islands, on the north side of the big bay not far from Indian Harbour, was the hardest hit. One schooner went ashore and hit the rocks with her deck and masts facing the land. There was a girl on board, eighteen years old. She had the quickness of wit to run ashore on one of those masts, thus saving her life. The ship was swung facing the sea by the next big swell and the rest of the crew drowned.

One schooner left Indian Harbour, near George's Island, which is on the south side of Hamilton Inlet or, as we call it, Groswater Bay, in the morning of the first day of the gale. It was homeward bound. That must have been a large vessel, because when it reached the entrance of Curlew Harbour it was blown ashore on the rocks, and because of the high winds and heavy sea, the ship was wrecked and eighteen members of the crew perished. There must have been several of the crew left and having enough strength and energy they dug one big grave and buried those who did not survive. There may have been a few men here in Sandwich Bay who knows where that grave is at Curlew. Curlew is a small harbour facing north east and about four miles in the bay from Cape North. The grave site is quite well covered over now with small vegetation and blackberry bushes.

The merchant dealing with food and supplies for the fishermen was named Roderick David MacRae. He had a schooner at Black Island, four miles south of Gready, ready to sail for home. On the morning of the third day the storm sprang up again and twenty-two people drowned. They were swinging women and children ashore on a halyard, as the mast of the ship was leaning over the rocks. The captain of the ship was Isaac Mercer. When his wife was swung ashore, she hit the cliff and broke her neck.

There was one schooner anchored at Cartwright Island, a little farther in the bay. In order to save her from being lost the captain ordered the heaviest mast to be cut off and let it fall overboard.

At Snack Cove, where my grandfather lived, their stage and store were blown down on the grass in the bottom of North Cove. There were big puncheons blown across the neck of land between North Cove and South Cove.

At Gready, where R.D. MacRae carried on his business, his wharf was all washed away. Three Learning brothers agreed to take a small schooner in to Sandwich Bay to get repaired the next spring, and to cut firewood to take to Gready for the following summer. They were anchored at Crab Head just outside Black Head Run on Huntingdon Island shore. They went adrift, evidently breaking her moorings, and then they ran ashore on one of the small islets in Goose Cove channel. That small island has been called 'Hit or Miss' after the merchant's vessel which went ashore on the high tide but never beat up. They had a row boat, so after the wind died down, they rowed in to Goose Cove. In Goose Cove they went to a house owned by my grandfather, Thomas Davis. There was a stove in the house but no stove pipes. They sawed a hole in the roof and used an empty barrel for a stove pipe. Bill Brown told of a man, from this crew, who walked up across Goose Cove marshes carrying the one possession, the only thing he saved from the wreck, a new pair of leather deck boots.

— Frank S. Davis
[4.4:54]

THIS HAPPENED WHEN I WAS livin' to Goose Cove, livin' with Andy Toomashie. That was in the thirties, I think. We had our white fox traps out on Hare Islands. This particular morning I told Andy I was goin' to check me traps.

"Yes," he said. "I'm comin' out when I gets ready."

I went on to the upper island and seen me traps, then I went to the house there. That was in March month, but there wasn't a bit of snow hardly. I went in and put in a fire to boil the kettle for when Andy got there. I was boilin' the kettle when three loud knocks come on the house.

I yelled out, "Don't be so foolish, boy. Come on in."

It rapped three times again. I runned out and right around the house, but there wasn't a soul, not a sign of a soul. I didn't know what to make of it. I went in and looked after my kettle and here come these three knocks again.

"Come in, boy, come on in," I sung out again.

That was six raps each time. I went out and struck her right around the house in the other direction. Not a soul, not a soul. I went back in and had me dinner. I was all alone, just meself on the island, Andy never come out all day. It must have been a ghost, eh?

One time I was goin' fer a day's hunt up around Charlie's Cove and one place and another lookin' fer partridges, rabbits or whatever I could find. Uncle Jim Pardy told me there was a brook up there and I shouldn't try to boil up there.

Comin' home in the evening, I come to this brook and decided I'd boil up, so I put the fire in and put on my kettle. All of a sudden my kettle turned over in the fire. I had to scravel and get my kettle and fill 'en up again. There wasn't a thing there that would trip up anything, but just after I put 'en on he tipped over again. I wouldn't give in, I tried to put 'en on again. He tipped again.

I said I better get home, in the name of God, because I'd never get my kettle boiled there.

The name of the brook was Helser's Brook. Uncle Jim tried to boil his kettle there and couldn't. He told me there'd been an old, half-crazy feller died around there and he was the one that wouldn't let nobody have a boil-up there.

I was workin' with Hudson's Bay Company in Cartwright one time, I don't know what year. Aunt Mary Lemare was the cook. In September month she went out to Old Man's Cove to spend her holidays with her son Finley, so I was the only one stayin' in the Kitchen, which was what they called the HBC staff house.

One Saturday Grandma took sick, so I went down and stayed with her until ten o'clock in the night. When I told her I was goin' back to the house, she said, "Yes, my dear, go home and have a rest."

I went home and got ready for bed, just took me bedclothes and hove them back, never covered meself up. While I was layin' there, I heard the door open downstairs and I thought it might be somebody comin' to tell me that Grandma had died. This person come in and walked up the steps. I could hear her as plain as day. She went to the empty room then come to my room. It was a little short woman. I thought it was Grandma. She took the blankets and covered me up and put her hand on my head. I went right to sleep.

In the morning, five o'clock, Fred Groves came and told me that Grandma was dying, so I went down to see her.

'Pon my soul, it was that dear little woman who came to me that night.

— Edward Pardy
[4.4:9]

UNCLE BEN WILLIAMS WALKED UP to Cartwright from Goose Cove one time. They used to come up fer grub, a week's or a couple a' weeks' stock of grub. Before he got home this night, gettin' dark, four or five fairies come to 'en. They all had red caps on and they used to take his cap and put 'en on their heads. Every time he'd stop they'd be tormentin' 'en. By'n'by he sat down on Lassy Keg Bank, that's half way between Cartwright and Goose Cove. He took his bag off his back, an old strap bag that you carried on your back, and put 'en on the ground. The fairies took everything out of his bag and lugged it all around the woods everywhere, and they was only little ol' tiny things, a couple a' foot high. Uncle Ben said they'd take a big ol' parcel and run off with 'en.

Next day somebody went back with 'en and they found his stuff scattered everywhere.

There don't be no fairy stories now like there used to be. I used to be afraid to go outdoors one time, listenin' to people tellin' ol' stories.

— Henry John Williams
[4.4:4]

CHARLES DAVIS ARRIVED IN SANDWICH Bay around 1825 according to his own statement on an 1835 petition signed by Labrador planters. It is thought that his homeland was Wales but he sailed from Plymouth, England, with Charles Williams, who also settled in Sandwich Bay.[12] The reasons Charles left his home are unknown, but oral tradition has it that he may have been a convict or a draft-evader, since his surname was originally Francis. He settled in Labrador as Davis.

Charles married a woman of Labrador, the youngest daughter of a Mr. Pardy of Sandwich Bay. They settled in a beautiful little spot known as Goose Cove, about seven miles from Cartwright. It is thought that he chose this spot because of its ideal living conditions. The cove is situated in such a way that the mid-day sun shines directly in through the glade on to the dwellings. — Joyce Davis

I often heard my father say that old man Davis came from England over a hundred years ago. He was seventeen when he came over. He lived and died in Labrador. Most people in Sandwich Bay came from England, not too many from Scotland in our bay.

Great-grandfather Davis married old man Pardy's youngest daughter. I was told that old feller's name was George Pardy. There was a lot of Pardys.

Two of my grandfather's brothers went back to England and never came back. Old Uncle Bill Davis went over when he was seven and came back here again when he was seventeen. He was well educated.

I heard my father say that Grandfather was a doctor, a midwife and a minister. He used to perform weddings. When I was a boy, Grandfather lived right near us. My father and I would go to see him on Sunday Mornings. He'd be sitting up with his long-stemmed pipe, reading his newspapers. Years after he died my father still got those papers from England.

On my mother's side, her old gentleman was from Wales. His last name was Perry. He married an Indian woman.

— William Davis

Grandfather Davis, the first old Davis, took a fiddle over with him when he came. It was the only fiddle in Sandwich Bay at one time. Whenever there was a wedding she had to go. She'd come home all flagged off with ribbons. I still got the body of that old fiddle....

The Davis' all had fine big families. My grandfather, he had seven sisters and they married every different name around Sandwich Bay almost. You might say that half Labrador begin with the Davis'. Nearly all Sandwich Bay came from the Davis'.

— Tommy Davis
[6.4:4]

OLD GRANDMOTHER SHEPPARD WAS THE nurse in Sandwich Bay years gone by. Her brother, James Davis, was the doctor. They weren't trained but that's not to say they weren't experienced. Grandmother Sheppard delivered well over two hundred babies. People all over the place would head for Fox Cove [about twelve miles from Cartwright] if they had something they couldn't cure themselves.

Years ago hundreds of schooners would come from Newfoundland. One particular summer one of the fishermen got a badly infected hand. They heard about Grandmother Sheppard, of course, so he was brought to her. She operated on him. She made a cotton bag, sort of like a mitt, and told my mother to go and get several maggots to put in it. She put the bag with the maggots in it on his hand and left it on overnight. Next morning the hand was cleaned right out. In the meantime, Grandmother had steeped out some ground juniper bark and prepared a salve out of the pulpy part of the juniper. She mixed a bit of cod oil into her juniper salve. Next morning she bathed the hand in steeped juniper, applied some of the salve and dressed it. It wasn't long before the fisherman could go back to his schooner.

If there was a big job needed doing, Grandmother Sheppard and Uncle Jim would get together and tackle it. Uncle Jim had a doctor's kit that come over from England with the first Davis.

They were brave people. They did a great deal of good for many people.

— Margaret Davis
[2.4:44]

MY MOTHER WAS A BRAVE woman when it come to a showdown. She took my brother Willie from six dogs one time.

Uncle Micky 'Dan'l [McDonald], over on Long Point, had dogs that used to run around. He had one, a black one, [wolf] half-breed or something, and she was vicious. This day they come over to our place at Mullin's Cove. Poor little Willie was playin' on the bawn about a hundred yards from the house, all by he's self. These dogs come and fastened right into 'en. I don't know if Mother was lookin' or if she hear'd something. I was another hundred yards across the cove playin' in the beach. Mother went up on the bawn and started peltin' rocks at the dogs. When she started peltin' rocks at 'um, all the proper dogs went away, all but this old black one. He just stayed there and tore away at Willie.

There was lots of small rocks there. 'Twas on a bawn made with small rocks, so she could pick up a rock anywhere. She pelted that ol' dog 'till he left Willie. She must have hurt 'en, I suppose. She picked up Willie and had to carry 'en under one arm and pick up rocks wit' the other hand to keep that old dog away. Then she seen me over across the cove playin' in the sand. Of course I seen what happened but I was too stupid to know what to do, whether to come over or what. Mother kept bawlin' out to me to come home, go in the house and close the door. After a while that's what I done. All the while I was comin' over, she had to keep peltin' rocks at the dog to keep 'en round her so he wouldn't get me. When I got to the house, she runned for the door and got Willie inside.

Poor little Willie had his head all tore up. You could pull his skin back and see his skull, and he had a big cut under he's eye. There was no doctors around them times, you know. So Mother and Grandmother had to fix 'en up. They put bandages on 'en everywhere there was a bite. They had to do it whether they knowed how or not. He was tattooed all over where the dogs was bitin' 'en under he's clothes. I think all the dogs was bitin' at 'en, but not too hard except for this one that was tearin' at he's head.

Now, Dad and Uncle Bob Pardy, who was wit' us that year, was gone somewhere. 'Twas early in the spring and as soon as the trout'd come out of the brooks in the spring, you could take a net on your back and there's a place over across the point where you could tail a net wit'out a boat. Now, I thinks that was where they must have gone. When they come back and went in the house, that's the first they knowed about what happened. Dad grabbed he's gun and went out and shot every dog.

I'd say Willie was about three years old then. He was able to get about on his own. I don't know how old I was. Let's see, there was me, Frank, Edgar and Willie. That would be about eight years between me and Willie, so I would have been about eleven year old then.

Poor little Willie got drowned after, he and Edgar.

— Tommy Davis
[6.4:24]

IN 1927, A MERCHANT, MR. MacRae, was carrying on considerable business, supplying Newfoundland fishermen and Labrador liveyers at Gready and the surrounding harbours. When he packed up in the fall, each year, and went home to Harbour Grace in Newfoundland, his business premises would be deserted, so he engaged my father to stay in one of his houses throughout the winter, and to take care of his property. It was during one of these summers, when I was seven years old, that a large whale factory ship from Norway came to Gready and proceeded to build a factory on the land at Waterin' Cove, just about a quarter mile from Gready Harbour.

Thus it was that, next fall when our family moved to Gready for the winter, we were the only neighbors to these seamen, and almost their only friends and helpers. I was the only child nearer than Table Bay or Cartwright, twenty miles away. They literally had me for a mascot. We could not converse, of course, but that made no difference. I was with them all the time trying to help, but perhaps being underfoot mostly. This is how I got to know and love the Norwegian people. I would be over there every day, and there was always a place set for me at the staff table. I learned to like the Norwegian way of cooking, all kinds of fruit mixed into every dish.

The Norwegians worked hard around the clock. In those days Norway was no nearer to Labrador than the moon, and these men were cut off from their families with no correspondence whatsoever.

On Christmas Day, they dropped everything, dressed in their Sunday best, and all seven of them came over to our house. I was glad to see all my friends here at the same time. I started to play records on our old square box gramophone. After playing several records, I was halfway through another when I noticed that every one of the seven Norwegians was crying. To me that record was just another nice tune, but to them it was their national anthem.

Once, when I stayed home all day, I went over to the factory in the evening and met the last man, the captain, coming up from it. He invited me to come and see what they had done that day, and he took the trouble to go back to the boiler room, climb up on the boiler and turn on the steam, and then take me out to the guano drying room where he started up the two steam engines that they had installed that day.

In the spring, they had my brother Jack, and Michael Bird from Cartwright as steam-winch operators, and they were good at it, too.

They had a water supply tank on the hill, higher than the buildings. It was supplied by a steam-driven pump in the boiler room. Sometimes they would run out of water and at other times the tank was overflowing. One day the captain said to me, "Can you learn?" Thus it was, I became a steam engineer at the ripe old age of seven. I went home feeling as big as a giant, and they never ran out of water after that.

In the years after, Father would ask them for some whale meat for his dogs in winter. They would give him a backbone to pick, and he would get eight or ten barrels of meat off one bone. Some years they would give him a complete whale to tow away to the back cove of Cape North, and then everybody, north and south, would get into the act, with lots of meat for everybody's dogs. Meantime, I had grown to ten or twelve years of age. One day, my brother Tommy and I were leaving the whale factory with half a load of meat in a small motor boat. Three men were towing a whale ashore with a banker's dory, so we took the line and helped them. When we got close to the shore, we stopped and let the whale go on in, but the whale kept on coming and we couldn't get our engine started! The whale's tail pushed us in over the rocks, completely out of water, and then pushed us off again, so that the boat slid into the water once more, with nothing broken.

In the mid-1930s the price of oil went down, and the factory went out of operation and was deserted. Vandalism wrecked the whole place, with the help of the wind and the weather. Vegetation grew up and covered most of it. All that is left now is some concrete and some steel frames. On Sundays we would often visit the place and wander through the ruins. On such occasions, uppermost in my mind was the thought of the friends who had been there. They are gone, but will never be forgotten. [3.2:13]

How often have I heard Mother say to me, "Waste not, want not," and in them days, when goods were scarce and money even scarcer, this was good advice.

The first I remember, flour was brought in wooden barrels, 180 lbs. The empty barrels were used for many purposes—wash tubs, bakeapple barrels, dogs' food tubs, blubber barrels, for storing salmon nets in to try and protect them from mice (which was almost impossible) and the staves made into skis for kids to slide on. In later years flour companies began packing their product in cotton bags, about seventy-five lbs. These cotton bags were even more useful. There was Ogilvies, Cream of the West and Robin Hood flour. Robin Hood had a statement on the bag "FIT FOR A PRINCE." Most families used the cloth for clothing, pillows, bed sheets, shirts, and even women's underwear. Someone said he saw a woman climbing up over the stage head and he saw written across her rump, "FIT FOR A PRINCE!" [10.2:62]

In them days weddings were fun! How well I remember my oldest brother's wedding. Tommy was getting married to Maggie Williams from West Bay.

Them days people had to wait for the winter or summer visit of the clergy from Cartwright or from other larger centers, depending on which part of the coast one lived. In this case, it was winter at Table Bay. The word got around and people started to arrive from Sand Hill River and Otter Brook and, of course, all the people in Table Bay, young and old.

There was no money around them times but that made no difference. Everyone made a cake or something to bring along. I remember Mrs. Austin Pardy. She claimed she could make the best custard in the bay. She made a sizable pot full and my brother Jack went and picked it up with his dog team. He left it on the komatik in the coach box, temporarily, just as the dog teams started arriving. One team got into the coach box and ate all the best custard to be found in Table Bay!

About then the sky clouded up and by the time all the teams were fed it started to snow. A storm was coming on.

Tommy and Maggie were married in the evening about four o'clock and then the wedding feast. There was plenty for everyone. A little boy like me was bound to get a tummy ache from all that sweet stuff. When the dishes were all cleared away, the furniture was put to one side and the dance started. They danced all night and all the next day while the storm was raging outside. They danced the next night, with just enough break times to get something to eat, and this went on all through the storm, about three days.

When the storm petered out, the teams got ready and took off for the various winter places. It seems there was no end to the energy of these young people. Of course, on arriving home, it was off to the wood path and haul wood. It took all week for the Davis household to return to normal.

— Robert H. Davis
[8.2:24]

JANNY-TIME WAS FROM BOXING Day night, December 26th, to Old Christmas Day, January 6th. Jannying we called it, but I don't know where the name come from. Newfoundland people calls it mummering. 'Twas a lot of fun. 'Twas a tradition.

We'd save up old clothes in the fall, perhaps an old oil jacket, an old pair pants, some odd boots, anything that could be used for janny-time. The idea was to dress up so that people wouldn't be able to recognize you. We'd put on the ugliest old clothes we could find, put it on inside out, backwards and everyhow. There was no masks to get in those days so we'd put soot on our faces, colour them with crayons and lipstick, or make masks out of cloth, perhaps an old piece of sheet. We'd stuff ourselves with pillows and make wigs out of old scraps of wool, anything to make a good costume. The more ragged and stuffed you were, the better. We'd disguise our voices by talking high and squeaky, gruffy, or by talking and inhaling our breaths at the same time, janny-talk.

When we lived at Sand Hill they always knew us because there was only three houses there. There wasn't many adults at Sand Hill so 'twas only the young people out. At Mom's house, she'd get her accordion out and we'd have a good old square dance. They had a great big kitchen. Of course, then you'd start to get warm so there'd be jannies pulling out their pillows and stripping off some of their outer garments. 'Twas an awful lot of fun.

At Table Bay there was seven houses and at Cartwright you could go to a dozen houses, or more. At Cartwright a whole bunch of us would go out together, fellers and girls. Everyone would be expecting you so you'd usually get some cookies or buns. Uncle Sam Fequet always had a big pan of apples and you were sure to get one. You wouldn't get something at every house, you wouldn't expect to. You were out more for the fun. We'd be climbing snowbanks, rolling around, carrying on. There'd be different groups of jannies out and perhaps you'd meet up with another crown and there'd be a little fight, or scrummage, trying to find out who was who. Of course, sometimes you'd want a certain feller to know that it was you. You'd hook up with him and go for a walk and join up with the others later on. Goose Cove path was our choice place. More than once me and George hid behind a snowbank and had a little kiss or two, then, take off to catch the rest again.

From Boxing Day to Old Christmas Day there'd be jannies out every night, not the same ones, but every night you could depend on seeing some jannies. It was great entertainment and great fun.

— Minnie Hefler
[2.2:10]

Cartwright Village
Thursday 27
August 1778
S.S.W

At one o'clock this morning, I was alarmed by a loud rapping at my door, which when I had opened, a body of armed men rushed in; they informed me that they belonged to the Minerva *privateer, of Boston in New England, commanded by John Grimes; mounting twenty moderate nine-pounders, and manned with a hundred and sixty men; and, that I was their prisoner. They then demanded all my keys, took possession of both my vessels, also the* Otter, *then full of goods which she was going to land from the brig, and of all my stores, which were on shore. About nine, the* Minerva *worked into Blackguard Bay, and came to anchor there. I then went on board her, and was received with civility by Captain Grimes, who told me that, some days ago, he had entered Temple Bay and taken three vessels from Noble & Pinson, which he had filled with fish, and stores from the shore and sent off for Boston. He said that many of the fishermen had entered with him; among whom, were two men who had lately lived with me, and who had informed him where I lived. From thence he went to Charles Harbour, where he had taken one vessel from Mr. Slade, another from Mr. Seydes, and had plundered my possessions there at the Ranger Lodge; at the former place another man who lived with me last year, and one of my salmoniers at the latter, had entered with him. I requested the release of Mr. Daubney, who was kept prisoner on board, but he would not grant it. He sent an officer and a party of men in my baitskiff to Caribou Castle, to plunder there also. The skiff was piloted by that villain Dominick Kinnien, who went out baitmaster of her for the first time yesterday; and who, together with his whole crew of six men, had entered with the privateer's people the instant they got on board. In the course of the day, they shipped what was on the* Otter *on board the* Countess of Effingham, *and in the evening sent her off for Boston. In going out of the harbour, they ran her on shore off the low point on the east side, but soon got her off again, and went to sea through the north-east passage. In the night I slipped a skiff out of the harbour with four hands, to inform the boats, and order them to go into North Harbour, in Table Bay.*

A fine, clear day.

Friday 28

The Minerva *came into the harbour this morning, where she moored, and filled her empty water-casks. The* Otter *and* Stag *were sent to Caribou, to bring down what was there; and they shipped off some of my dry fish, and most of the goods which were here. By this time, many of my people had entered on board the privateer, and some of them had informed the captain of the four men going away in the skiff last night; which enraged him and his people so much, that I found it prudent, to send Indian Jack[13] by land with orders for the boats to come in here.*

A cloudy day.

Saturday 29
Wind
little and variable

In the course of this day, the remaining part of the dry fish, and most of the goods which were here, were shipped off on board the Reconciliation. *In the afternoon, the three shallops which were out a fishing, came into the harbour, the people were set on shore, and the sails were unbent: but the Indian boy, was kept on board. In the afternoon, the surgeon of the privateer drove the two Indian women on board, and the child, Phyllis, was soon sent after them. In the night, the* Otter *and the* Stag *returned from Caribou, with all my property from that place. At supper, having heard that they intended to send to Paradise and White-bear River for what was there, I dropped a hint, of expecting a frigate here immediately; and it had the desired effect.*

Sunday 30
S. moderate

Early this morning, I found the enemy in a great bustle. They took on board the privateer, all the goods which had been brought from Caribou, except a chest of baggage, which Grimes returned; but many things were pillaged out of it. He then gave me a small quantity of provisions, returned my boats and most of their sails, and by noon, the ship together with my brig went to sea through Western Tickle, and steered away north-east by east; passing to the westward of the Gannet Islands. May the devil go with them!

The Minerva's *guns formerly belonged to one of his majesty's frigates, which was cast away near Boston; I think the* Syren. *The first lieutenant's name is Carlton; the third, Cushin; the master's, Ogilvie; lieutenant of the marines, Larey; and the surgeon's, Elliot. Carlton and*

Elliot are two of as great villains as any unganged; the other three behaved exceeding well, particularly Mr. Ogilvie, of whose civilities I shall ever retain a most grateful remembrance. I should be particularly happy to have it in my power to reward properly the infamous behavior of Carlton and Elliot; and the villainy of Thomas Adams, lately a mate in the service of Noble & Pinson; also of Michael Bryan, Luke Ryan, Dennis Ryan, and Dominick Kinnien, lately my servants, who were by far the most active in distressing me. They were the persons who gave information where I lived, piloted the ship to this place, and discovered to the enemy the places where great part of my property lay. Grimes is a lying rascal; for, he voluntarily made me many promises, and afterwards broke them all. Many of my people entered, and went away in the privateer; and most of the remainder would have done so likewise, under the apprehension of being left here destitute of the means either of subsisting, or getting off the island: but I thought it my duty to my king and country, even in my then distressed situation, to prevent the desertion. Grimes turned two rascals on shore again, and I immediately gave them a most severe beating with a stout stick.

The rest of this day was spent in landing the provisions which Grimes had returned, and in picking up the few things which were left scattered up and down; and I had the pleasure to find, that they had forgotten a puncheon of oil, and my three live swine. As soon as they were gone, I took my gun, walked out upon the island and shot a curlew.

A very fine day.

— George Cartwright

THERE USED TO BE AN old box up on Flagstaff Hill. 'Twas made of plank, chopped out. I guess every inch of that box was carved with initials; some dates was in the 1700s. The box was eight to ten feet each side and eight to ten feet high with a flag pole on the top. I don't know how long ago it got torn down or who tore it down, but it's gone now. A lot of the old boards were rotten.

Some of the old initials were weathered so bad you couldn't read them, but others must have been carved very deep. I remember several dates 1700 and something. It might have been put there by Captain George Cartwright.[14] Some of those old names, and I don't know if it was the way they were spelled or mis-spelled, or if that was the real names first... Learnings was one, that was spelled L-a-r-n-e-y, and Pardy was P-u-e-r-d-y, almost sounds Spanish. Heards was H-a-r-d-s. And there was names there that weren't here as far back as I can remember, whole families died out I suppose. There was Follett (Follett's Pond), Goodchild (there's a place on Earl Island named that.) The old boards should have been kept. It should have been preserved.

Most of the dates was the late 1800s. I dare say I carved my name in there too.

There was a couple of old cannons up there, one each side of the old box. That was a perfect spot to guard the Run back in George Cartwright's day.

— Leslie Pardy
[12.1:43]

CARTWRIGHT IN SANDWICH BAY, LABRADOR, is my home town. I was born there many years ago and I know every rock, hill and valley there, like many others who were born and raised there. And like everyone, those childhood days were the happiest days of my life—no cares of any kind. I remember Cartwright, at the time, as the prettiest little village you would see anywhere, especially in summertime. There was no other place I'd rather be.

There was only a few families living in Cartwright in them days. They were the Davises, Martins, Pardys, Fequets, Birds, Coombs, Learnings, Lameres, Heards, Painters and MacDonalds. There was one little church where most of our grandparents and parents were married and all of their children were baptized. There was a little road that led from the church to the churchyard. When you stood on the church steps you could look up the road and see the big brick-colour gate of the churchyard at the end of an avenue of trees.

There were little roads and footpaths leading everywhere, little bubbling brooks running from the woods down to the shore, and little wooden bridges joining the roads over those little brooks. The roads were well kept up. A few men were hired each summer by a government official whose name was Martin Murphy from Harbour Grace, Newfoundland. He was known by everyone as Judge Murphy. He would come to Cartwright in June and stay 'till the last boat in late fall. He did this every year for about twenty years. These men that he hired worked with pick, shovel and wheelbarrow to keep our little roads in order. The families would paint their houses and clean up their property. There was always one day in June, known as 'cemetery day,' when people would go and do up the graves of their loved ones and paint the fence. Every spring this was a must in them days.

A lot of families moved out to their fishing homes in early June. There were families who moved to Cartwright for summer jobs with the Hudson's Bay Company or do road work until the fall when they'd move back into the bay again. Everyone looked forward to moving; it was a happy time when everyone was getting out to their fishing places. Our family moved to Pack's Harbour with many more families from Cartwright and from the north and south sides of Sandwich Bay. As soon as our feet touched the rocks us young people were gone all over the hills. We spent summers of fun and frolic, in boats, fishing, and berry-picking with our many friends and relatives. Women and young girls could all handle a boat and row anywhere we wanted to go. I remember so well wherever you looked you'd see boatloads of people off for the day getting their bakeapples for the winter. Then there were the men and boys on the fishing grounds, some jigging and others at their cod traps. It was nothing in them days to see the motor boats coming in from the traps with just the stems and sterns out of water, boatload after boatload of codfish. You could see people working on their stages 'till twelve and later, cleaning their fish by the light of the old oil torch-

Above: Forteau, ca. 1930. [BESSIE FLYNN]

Left: Elsworthys from Wales.
[DORA HUDSON]

(L–R) Mary Ellen O'Dell, Catherine Beals and Gertrude Hawco, Pinware 1910.
[JOSEPHINE O'DELL]

Bessie Flynn, Forteau 1981.
[JUDY McGRATH]

Fishermen boarding the mailboat, Battle Harbour, 1909. [PANL]

Above: *Harmony* at Battle Harbour, 1909.
[PEARY-MACMILLAN ARCTIC MUSEUM, BOWDOIN COLLEGE, BRUNSWICK, MAINE]

Below: Newfoundland "floaters" working at the fish.
[NORTH WEST RIVER UNITED CHURCH COLLECTION]

Attuiock drawn by Nathaniel Dance, ca. 1733.

Caubvick drawn by Nathaniel Dance, ca. 1733.

Cod flakes at Gready. [PANL]

Left: William and Esther (Mesher) Goodenough.
[MARION THARP]

Below: (L–R) Back: Henry Pardy, George Hefler, Edward Pardy, Butler Martin, and Bernard Fequet, Cartwright, ca. 1928.
[MINNIE HEFLER]

(L–R) Bob, Edith, Clarice, Joshua with John, Lizzie and Jim Burdett, Sand Hill.
[REV. LESTER BURRY, NORTH WEST RIVER UNITED CHURCH]

Christmas Eve service at Okak. [MORAVIAN MISSION LABRADOR, THEM DAYS ARCHIVES]

Left: Clara, Ramah, ca. 1930.
[KATE HETTASCH, THEM DAYS ARCHIVES]

Below: Children outside the Moravian Mission fence, Okak; (L–R) Sybilla Boase, Frieda Merkuratsuk, Rosina Nerrokiasiak, Eleanora Millie, Judy Tutu, Agnes Pamack, Andreas Martin, Augusta Merkuratsuk, Tamma Millie and Sophia Harris. [SUSAN MARTIN, THEM DAYS ARCHIVES]

Bottom: Spanish Flu orphans outside sod house, Okak area. [DOROTHY SMITH, THEM DAYS ARCHIVES]

Nathaniel, the school teacher, Nain, ca. 1905. [S.K. HUTTON]

Inuit lady with toddler in seal skin packing parka. [DOROTHY SMITH]

Martin Martin, holding Benigna, and his wife Susan, Nain 1922.
[JERRY & REGINA SILLETT]

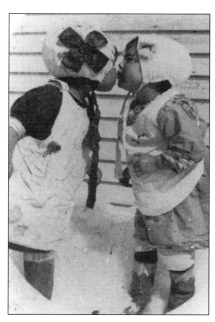

Hulda Hunter and Elizabeth Green, Nain, ca. 1940. [KATE HETTASCH]

es. Rain or shine, the harbour was always alive with activity. Early in the mornings the hills would echo with the sounds of motor boats. Those days are all gone now....

As a young girl from twelve to sixteen, I often went out fishing with my father. I'd help him to row and jig fish. Very often we went out early in the mornings when the beautiful red sun was just rising. It was a wonderful life.

After the fish was shipped off everyone would be happy to move back to the winter homes. For us that was Cartwright. In them days moving was a big job because most people had to take almost all they owned with them. There'd be stoves, beds, pots and pans, dishes, flowers and everything. If anyone had hens, they took them with them, and then there was the husky dogs. It was nothing strange to see the motor boats coming in the harbour with one or two little boats in tow with four or five dogs in them. There were some people who had their families, luggage and dogs all in the big boat. On our way to Cartwright we'd call to some island and pick up our dogs, which had been there all summer. As soon as the boat touched the rocks the dogs would jump aboard. You'd think they were going to eat us, they were so excited to see us after all summer.

Cartwright in my young years had a one-room school and three stores. There was the Hudson's Bay Company, S.B. Fequet and Son, and Porter's Post, an American general store. We had a Parish Hall where many activities were held. There would be children's Christmas and Easter concerts and grown-ups' concerts. There were billiards, table ping-pong and boxing for the men. Everything was booming. People would come from north and south to get to the Easter fair at Cartwright as that was a big 'time.'

A little later on I married Percy Davis, who was a native of Cartwright as well. Together we had a family of ten children, nine of them had lived to be fine men and women. Our second child died at the age of three weeks of whooping cough. There was no prevention for whooping cough in them days and for a baby it was fatal. That was one of the sorrows we have had to face. Nine of our children were born in our own home and the last one was born at the Cartwright hospital. I had one all alone without the aid of a midwife or doctor. A young girl stayed by me until a nurse came fifteen minutes later. Everyone in those days had some kind of experiences but it all came out in the wash.

A lot of women in them times had husbands who were trappers, so they spent a lot of time alone while their men went off to make a living. In the fall Percy would cut up a winter's supply of wood to last until he got back. It was a lonely time when the steamer blew her horn and Percy left with his canoe, guns and gear to go up the coast to his trapline up the Alexis River or one of the many rivers that he has trapped. He's trapped on the Hawkes River, Sand Hill River, Eagle River, Alexis River, North River and the Adlatok River near Hopedale. The fall him and his partner and two brothers went up the Adlatok they left the seventeenth of September and never got back home until March. That was a long trip.

While Percy was off trapping I kept the home fires burning and looked after the family. I fed the Husky dogs that was left home, carried all my water in buckets and made all the fires on in the early morning to warm up the house and cook breakfast for the children. That's how it was then.

After my parents died it was so lonely. My mother died in 1942 and my father died on August 18, 1948. The fall following Dad's death, Percy was going to trap at North River. It was so lonely that I wanted to go with him, so he said if he could get us a house he'd take us with him for the first part of the winter. He managed to get a house from someone and we moved over. North River is about seven miles from Cartwright. After we got straightened away, Percy went up the river to set his traps. He'd be gone from five to seven days. That was nothing compared to his earlier years of trapping.

Living among the woods was strange at first but I soon got used to it. The older boys made themselves useful by taking their .22s and getting partridges from nearby. Before long it was Christmas, and what a wonderful Christmas it was. That was the first Christmas Percy and I spent together since we had been married, and that was five years. Percy's youngest brother had been living at North River for a number of years so with him and his family we had an enjoyable time.

Percy and his brother later built a little schoolhouse between our two houses. We got a teacher and our children went to school. From then everything fell into place. We made our own fun and everyone was happy.

One fall after we moved in from our fishing place the men thought there was a black bear prowling around the schoolhouse. One morning early in November, after a fall of snow, they saw the tracks not far from the house. Percy, his brother, our oldest son and Uncle Charlie Williams each set off in different directions to corner it. By dinnertime they had it shot. They hauled it home. It had a white star on its chest. Uncle Charlie said it was the biggest bear he had ever seen and he saw lots of bears in his time.

In the winter time the men would go to the Mealy Mountains to get their deer. They would come home from most trips loaded down with deer. They could kill as many as they could handle in those days. One time Percy come home with a couple of legs of venison after killing eighteen on that trip. He got his friends to help him haul it out, giving each man a deer for his help. This is how it was them days.

We got lots of smelts in North River. Around the middle of February all we had to do was run down to the river and catch away at the lovely silver smelts. No polluted water then. There was also plenty of partridges and rabbits. There was full and plenty of everything.

Our summers at North River were enjoyable. There was all kinds of wildlife on the go, raccoons, black bears and caribou strolling on the sand bars and swimming the strong tide of the river. We'd often see beaver and otter swimming near the river bank. Late in the evening there'd be the howling of a wolf. We've watched salmon splashing here and there in the calm water and watched trout jumping. We've listened to the call of loon and heard geese calling from the bogs where they were nesting. After we were gone to bed we'd hear the last call of the grass snipe. Our children had a good life all through the summer months. They lived with the wildlife, spent all day long in the water, running from sand bar to sand bar, laughing and shouting. There was always something new, the days weren't long enough. Now they are all grown up and gone away from North River.

Percy and I are now living in Happy Valley but we still get the urge to go back home to Cartwright and over to North River for the first part of each summer. We catch a few salmon and trout. All we have now is our little grandson and at times it's rather lonely. We often sit on the river bank and talk about how it used to be. Before I know it I'm blind with tears so I have to leave and go up to our little house, but there too I can hear the children's voices, I can hear them shouting "Mom." I got to pull myself together and get to work at something. We spends most of our time on the nets, going for walks and showing our little grandson things and telling him stories about our children and about the wildlife. I can still hear it all as I did so many years ago.

— Margaret Davis
[2.4:52]

TRAPPING PLACES WAS HANDED DOWN from your fathers and your grandfathers, places where they trapped all their lives. If the younger ones was interested, well, they would take it over and that's how it went from generation to generation. That's the way they owned trappin' grounds. I mean, each trapper had a certain branch on the waters to branch off to and they didn't bother no one else. That's all different today. You got people now goin' all over and, be God, they'd set a trap on yourself; not a bit of snow or under a tree or anywhere if they thought they'd get a skin of fur. That's the way it's done today. I was talkin' to a feller the other day and, be gar, he said, "I s'pose that's all you can do about it. You set on one side of a tree and buddy comes along and sets on the other side." There's not too much you can do without you got trappers' rights or something.

Be gar, one time, when everyone was livin' out the coast there was thousands of ducks. You'd go and kill a fresh meal of ducks whenever you wanted 'um and that's all you did bother. You didn't kill ducks and let 'um rot, spoil or anything else and throw 'um away. You just killed what you needed. Now today there's hardly anyone at it and you hardly even see one anyway.

I think half that's wrong with everything, the ski-doos we got is frightening everythin' to death, or poisonin' it. You could poison yourself on one of them almost, not to mention birds and animals. We went just as far by foot or with the ol' dogs them days than you'll ever go with ski-doo. The only things is that now they can go faster.

When we lived out on the coast half our livin' was there. As long as you had the hardware stuff you had nothing to worry about. There was fresh fish, fresh birds, fresh seal and so on, the main part of our livin'. And why did we leave Spotted Islands to come to Cartwright? Government promises. 'Twas like poor ol' Joey Smallwood said when they took over, he said they could burn all their boats and everything and every man, woman and child would have a job. That's why people started to resettle. Now we're here in Cartwright from Spotted Islands, Batteau and Seal Islands and, be God, that's where we got to go to if we wants to fish or hunt, and the same with our trapping ground. We never trapped or anything in Sandwich Bay or anywhere like that and we don't want to bother with anyone else. I mean, we was in a place where we was botherin' no one and there was lots of places to set traps and all the rest of it. It's not so around here. And we was forced to move because they wouldn't give us a teacher, they wouldn't give us any medical services, they wouldn't give us any mail service, so what choice did we have? I mean education is supposed to be the main thing. Now, be God, the funniest thing is they're educatin' 'um and they still got no jobs. They're no better off than the ones that never went to school in their lives. Well, most is worse off.

When I come back to Cartwright I usually don't come here 'till October, and I don't want to come then. There's nothing to do only get a bit of firewood and get a drop of water. There's no place to hunt. People is just not comfortable here, not the people that resettled, because they haven't got the freedom they was used to before, freedom to hunt, trap and fish. Cartwright will never be home and that's the way it goes.

— Jack Holwell
[14.3:37]

I CAME TO CARTWRIGHT IN 1930 from Bolster's Rock, which is a place south of Frenchman's Island. Years before I was married to him, my husband Jim used to trap, but after we got married he went to work for the Hudson's Bay Company, for I don't know how many years. We never moved to our fishing place those years but most of the people in Cartwright then moved outside fishing.

When Jim worked for the Hudson's Bay Company, salmon collecting, mending twine and all that, in the fall he'd bring home what we called our winter supplies. There'd be flour, butter, molasses, hard bread, pork, beef, beans, peas, rice, rolled oats. There was no such thing as apples and oranges them times. We had dried apples and dried apricots. There was no such things as canned fruit, meat or soup. There was no tea bags or pound tea, it was all loose tea. Sugar came in butts not bags. Molasses came in great big barrels. Everything was bought by the pound. Later we begin to get tinned meat. In 1938 corned beef was fifteen cents a tin. That's the first time I can remember....

You take mens' wages. First when men began fixing up the roads here at Cartwright they were getting fifteen cents an hour. That was working with pick and shovel. That was the road around the Point since World War II, but before the American Base was put on Black Head. The Grenfell Mission had an old van first when I come here but the rest of the people had dogteams and rowboats.

I used to scrub the S.B. Fequet shop four times a month for a dollar a day, and I scrubbed the Hudson's Bay Company shop for a dollar fifty a day.

We knew what hard work was. I was ten years of age when I left home to go out to work. I went to work to save what I would eat at home for the next one in the family. That's how bad off we was. My father was always sickly. I had a brother older than me and we, being the oldest, did all the hard work. We had a team of dogs each. We got all the water and wood. It was no such thing as go out to earn money; you went out to earn a bit to eat or for a pair of boots. From that day until I was married the highest pay I ever got was $20 a month. That was 1930. People are getting hundreds of dollars a month now for nothing, just press a button and go on. Them days 'twas kerosene lamps and very often we never had that.

One time when we was all home, there was seven of us in family, 'twas a spring that the ice was around very very thick and you couldn't get anywhere. This spring was what we called "a hungry spring" and it was hungry too. If you was a millionaire and there was a shop across the harbour, you couldn't get over. There was too much pack ice. There was an old man and his wife on the other side of the harbour and on our side there was six families. We had nothing to eat so my mother and my aunt picked their way across the pack ice to this old couples' house. The old lady gave them some crusts of bread. Then my mother and aunt went to an old store that was there and come across some molasses kegs that was left by some people who had moved to Hawkes Harbour wintertime. They washed out the kegs and got two bottles of molasses water. They each took a bottle and divided the crusts between them. When they got home this food was divided among the smaller children. There was nothing else to get.

When the ice slacked off a bit, three or four of the men pushed their way across quite a long bay and walked across an island to Hawkes Harbour. The whaling boats used to come down then so they got food from them, molasses, tea, butter and whatever else they could carry in their grub bags. That lasted until the ice cleared off and they could get to Seal Islands. There was people to Seal Islands that always had plenty. There used to be merchants who'd come in the summer and certain men would be caretakers of their places during the winter. They got paid with food and through the means of this they always had plenty, and they'd help us. We never did have full and plenty because, as I said before, my father was always sickly. When he was able he'd get fur.

Old Abe Clark was a caretaker at Comfort's Bight. This was how he got his supplies. When he'd run short he could take from the store. Hopkins looked after Munn's place at Seal Islands. Uncle Chris Green looked after Crocker's place at Seal Islands. Through the means of this they always had plenty and through them having plenty, we had it too. However, we had to go a long ways in boat, rowing or sailing, to get there. No motor boats. Not even the Newfoundlanders had motor boats them days, just the old row boats. It breaks my heart to see such waste today.

People wouldn't stand up to work today like we had to do. I knew a man and a woman who lived up in Porcupine Bay. Uncle Tom and Aunt Eliza Circum. They come to Cartwright one time hauling six long ladders that they'd made for Hudson's Bay. Pulled them down on komatik with the lash lines on their shoulders. From Porcupine Bay to Cartwright must be fifty miles or more. They got the worth of those ladders in food. Can you picture a man and woman doing that today? You wouldn't even see a man doing that now.

First when welfare officers come you'd get dole orders. He'd give a person a slip of paper with so much food a month on it, according to the size of the family. If you got pork this month, you'd have to wait 'till next month to get beef. You couldn't have both the same month. You'd be surprised at the little bit they'd get. That was just rough food. That would've been around the 1940s, I suppose....

First when the Grenfell Mission started here it was a benefit to us in every way. We had doctors, nurses, good aides and even an X-ray machine. The nurses them days had no roads to walk around the harbour on. If they couldn't get over by boat they'd walk around the shore. They'd visit every home, not missing one. They'd make regular rounds with their packs on their backs. We had to pay hospital fees but it was worth it. We paid five dollars a year per family and for that we'd get the best kind of attendance. You didn't have to move out of Cartwright to North West River or Happy Valley to get an X-ray of your finger. The nurses we had here them days was as good as any doctor that comes around today. They could even operate if they had to.

Then Mrs. K.M. Keddie started an Industrial Shop on the Mission side. She learned us a lot. We'd get our material from her, already cut out, and we'd make it up. When we'd bring it back to her we'd go to her clothing store and get our clothing. There was nothing in the other stores in way of clothing to fit a child. Very often you'd have to get something and cut it over. You didn't mind getting a woolen garment to ravel out and knit up something else. I did that more than once. We'd make a pair of mittens, a coat or something and Mrs. Keddie would give us a slip saying the amount we were owed and we'd take it up in clothing or get cash, whatever we wanted. It was really a good help. This was in the '40s. Everything was in full swing them days. We'd walk back and forth across the bight and never mind a bit. Seemed like when Harvey Bird died the Mission side went just like that. The dormitory closed and the school closed. No more hearing the dorm children playing on a calm day....

— Joanne Martin
[2.1:41]

WE WAS LIVIN' TO AMERICAN Point when the flu was on. We skinned clear of the flu, but there was everyone dyin' all around us. There was only Mike, meself and Flo born then. That flu was harder on older people they said, which was the reason Muddy Bay Orphanage was built. There was so many orphans left, almost cleaned out the entire families in some places. Rev. Gordon went from house to house workin' to save people. My sonny boy, he was up early and late and he wasn't that strong either. He was some hand to go. He was a remarkable man.

Pretty well every year, before we was sent to Muddy Bay school, a teacher would be sent to a place for so many weeks, or a month. Go right 'round the bay like that, goin' and teachin'. I can remember three: Blanche Davis, Miss Bright and Nellie McKenny. I wasn't very old then. The only books we had was the *Royal Readers*. I went through the number four *Royal Reader*, I believe 'twas three times. Different teachers eh? I had to repeat, but I wasn't slow, I was quite smart. I could remember it all. When they sent me to Muddy Bay, the teacher was Miss Ashall and the nurse was Amy Astbury.

I called Muddy Bay School a nice school. We had all the freedom we wanted after school. The first year I was there we went to school all summer long, but we didn't mind, I know I didn't. I went to school from about eight years old and I finished up a year or two before it burned down.

— Willis Bird
[5.1:21]

MY HUSBAND ARTHUR'S FAMILY HAD a hard time in the flu. They was all sick—John, Arthur, Lizzie and Bob, the adopted boy.

John seemed to be getting better and, when he was able to get about the house, he got dressed up one evening and went to watch his brother feed the dogs. Later, he told his mother he'd like to have a cup of boiled partridge berries with sugar. Supper time they was all around the table when John stood up and turned to his father.

"I think I'm going now, Dad," he said.

"Going where, my son?"

"I'm going now, Daddy," and with the same he fell dead into his father's arms..

Arthur began to get ready to go to Cartwright.

His father said, "My son, how can you leave us at a time like this?"

"I don't know, Dad. Someone got to go," Arthur said and left.

He walked all in around Salt Water Pond. 'Twas dark, I believe, when he got to Rev. Henry Gordon's to see about John's funeral.

He got back to Muddy Bay about one in the morning. The lamp was still lighted and his mother met him at the door.

"How is Lizzie?" was his first words.

"She said she felt wonderful when I looked in on her half hour ago," his mother said.

He throwed off his clothes and went off upstairs. His sister Lizzie was dead on her bed.

Arthur used to cry and cry about that. Even just before he died so many years after he would still cry about it.

— Miriam Hamel
[1.1:27]

AFTER MY FATHER DIED, I went to live with my mother's people, Grandma and Grandfather Learning, at White Bear River, about twenty miles from Cartwright. When I was eight we shifted down to Separation Point and stayed there one year. Then my mother died. I was ten years old. Then I went 'long with Uncle Charlie Learning from April to August.

I went to school in Muddy Bay, in the Orphanage, in August, 1924 and I left there again in 1927. I stayed there all the time except for perhaps a month in the summer. That wasn't just a school, it was an orphanage.

Henry Gordon adopted me when my mother died and he put me in the Orphanage. 'Twas good there in lots of ways. There used to be as high as seventy children there. Most of the children lost their parents in the 1918 flu. There was children there from north, North West River, Sandy Hills, Spotted Islands, Sandwich Bay, Rigolet and all those places. Clarence Holwell was there.

We used to go to school from nine to twelve in the morning and one to three in the afternoon. We used to have to cut up all the wood. We didn't have to cut it and saw it, but we'd go in the basement and split it up and carry it along to the stoves. There was quite a few stoves there. There was two schoolrooms, a big dining room, a staff kitchen, storerooms and everything. We used to light all the fires except for the kitchen fire. Everybody had his own stove to look after, the biggest boys. There was two boys to get water for the kitchen and two to get water for the laundry. The other little boys, they'd just go and play until they were old enough to work. When you were ten year old, you were old enough to work. There was a lot of little boys. You take sixty or seventy children, that's a lot, three rows of tables in the mess hall, big, long tables about thirty feet long.

They used to have lots of wood, four and five thousand all the time. They had a motor boat and a big old scow. You could tow about six or seven hundred turns of wood in that old scow. One load. The biggest boys would go and load her.

The food used to come in on a big schooner. People used to bring in fresh meat, rabbits and partridges. The last couple of years they had cows and hens.

The staff was three cooks—Clarence Holwell's mother was a cook, and there was two younger girls under her, Jane Williams was one. Charlie Bird was the boss, he runned it. He said how the outside work was done, trips they'd take and all that kind of stuff. He used to make all the things for the school, things built. The first year I was there we had a principal whose name was Miss Hamilton, a Canadian. There was an English teacher, Miss Wasserman. Dr. Grenfell took over in 1924 and then we had American teachers.

I left Muddy Bay in October 1927, and it burned down in February 1928. The feller who burned it down said that he had to go without his supper. He was bein' punished for doin' something wrong. He said he and a couple of more got to work and stuffed the chimney with shavin's, in the basement, and they hove kerosene on it and sot it afire that way. I was a young man and married before I saw the feller who told me about it. He said she went up fast. They was havin' supper when it caught fire. There was a scoutmaster broke his leg jumpin' out the window. They didn't have far to go for shelter because Cartwright was only five miles away. We used to run down there without stoppin'. We used to come out of church and not stop runnin' until we got to Muddy Bay, run every step of the way. There was always a hard path between Muddy Bay and Cartwright.

— John Dicker
[5.1:19]

I RECALL EVENINGS AT HOME when we were little children gathered around the warm stove talking about the great things we would do when we grew up. I was always going to "find babies." Suddenly, Ma would speak up, "First of all, all you children got to go to school and get all the learning you can, eh John?" and Pa would say, "Yes," and that was it for their decisions were final.

I started school in Rigolet where there was a small one-room school and where, each year, some young person came from Newfoundland to teach. In the fall when the rest of my family went to our winter home in Double Mer, I was left behind in care of friends so that I could attend school. Their daughter Eva and I became fast friends and rabid competitors for first place. I loved school from day one.

I was heart-broken the final year at the Rigolet school when I was beaten by my friend, by a few marks. Taking my second prize (a skipping rope) home, I threw it on the floor and burst into tears and would not be comforted even when Ma told me how pleased she was with the good marks I got. During the summer months my wound quickly healed. I was very happy when my parents told me that they had made arrangements for me to attend boarding school at Muddy Bay, a place not far from Cartwright and a school owned and operated by the Grenfell Mission Association.

Ma was busy the last few weeks of the summer getting me ready for school. She made my older sister's clothes over to fit me, made skin boots and duffels for the winter, helped me to knit long woolen stockings, and all the while telling me, "Always be a good girl. Don't forget to say your prayers morning and evening. Be respectful to your elders. Listen to the mistresses, and try to let us know how you are getting along."

The day finally came, early in September, where the *Strathcona* steamed into Rigolet Harbour, and I, dressed in my Sunday best and very proud, was rowed aboard, after saying good-bye to my family. I was the only child on board and was placed in the dispensary of the boat, with a warning not to touch anything. The half-door was barred for safety and I found myself alone.

As the houses of Rigolet faded in the distance, I became very homesick and stood at the door crying and miserable until, finally, Dr. Grenfell came in. He sat me on his knee and started leafing through a magazine, telling me about the things and places pictured there. Finally he came to a picture of a grand lady and he said to me, "If you'll be a good girl and work hard and get all the education you can, you'll be a lady like that someday." I have never forgotten the words he said to me and, like all children who knew him, I loved him dearly.

Finally we arrived at Muddy Bay. The school building looked monstrous to me. As the *Strathcona* drew up to the wharf, the children and staff of the school poured down on the wharf to greet us. I was taken by someone up to the school building and handed over to the head mistress. She just looked at me without smiling or making me welcome by offering me a cup of tea. Calling one of the working girls to her she said, "Take her upstairs and show her where she is going to sleep, check her head, give her a bath and put some decent clothes on her." I was devastated.

This being my first time away from home I suffered severe homesickness for quite some time. Gradually I made friends with the other children, but life at the school was very strange at first. There were so many rules and regulations to get used to. You must "never go into the staff rooms, knock on the door if you want anything, ask permission to go outdoors and to come in, eat everything on your plate, make your bed before leaving your room, button the clothes of the smaller ones, take your cod oil without fussing" and so on.

But the hardest thing to hear was that there was no one to put their arms about you when you were feeling bad and no one to tell you how pleased they were when you did well. No one understood how you could miss your family and home so much, but would tell you how lucky you were that you were in a place where you could get better food and nicer clothes. No one understood that, for children, there is nothing that can compensate for the love and understanding and the feeling of security that you have in a close-knit family.

I soon learned to adjust, as children do, and my happiest hours were spent in the classroom. I could read quite well by then and was hooked on books. There was a small library and often I hid away behind a chair or in a dark corner and would read anything I could lay my hands on. Once I was caught and wasn't allowed to have a book for a week.

Early in the school year, our teacher told us that someone had offered a prize of a five-dollar gold piece each for the girl and boy who got the best marks at the end of the year. I intended to work hard for it.

In that first winter I became a Brownie and then a Guide and at ten years old was considered old enough to be responsible for playing with and minding the little ones. We all had our chores to do. Some peeled and prepared vegetables (when there were any), others scrubbed the wooden bedroom floors, cleaned, filled and trimmed the lamps, and it was considered a privilege to be allowed to tidy and dust the staff rooms or to mend their clothes and darn their socks and perhaps iron some of their clothing. They had such nice things—clothes with lace on them, pretty beads and flowered hand mirrors.

Sunday was a special day. There was no studying and we spent the day reading, playing and having services, each of us saying aloud the Bible text we had been set to learn that week. Then for an extra special treat each Sunday, as we filed out of the dining room after eating our supper, we were given a candy. We all looked forward to Sunday, especially for the candy.

The winter flew by and we had our school examinations. When our grades were handed out, I was very proud to find that I had won the five dollar gold piece for the girls, and John Heard was just as proud to win the boys' prize. Our money was locked in a drawer in the office for next year.

Most of us returned to our homes for the summer holidays. A short trip of the old S.S. *Kyle* brought me to Rigolet and oh, was it good to be home with a loving family.

When I returned to school for the second year a brother and sister accompanied me. They too suffered the pangs of homesickness, but I was now an old hand at the school and, hopefully, made things a little easier for them.

I think it was early in the fall when there was an outbreak of scarlet fever at the school, and those of us who were affected were all isolated in one room. Once the fever stage had passed we had great fun. That year there was a nurse with us and she must have had her hands full. As soon as she left the room we were out of bed, dashing about and throwing things out of the window to the children below, who were always there when they weren't in class. They in turn would try to throw things up to us until we were all caught and were forced back to bed.

Long before Christmas we were all well and back in the classroom in time for all the excitement and talk that precedes the visit of Santa. Although I can recall Christmases earlier at home, even to what was in my stocking, I cannot recall the details of those two Christmases at Muddy Bay. Maybe it was because we had too many items to remember. The thing I remember best was the holiday time when we were free to be out sliding and playing, and best of all, there was time for reading in the library.

One cold Sunday evening in February we were all in the dining room eating our supper and sneaking peeps at the candy we would get when we filed out, when one of the working girls came in and said something to the mistress. She always stood by the food table watching us while we ate, and she said to us, "Children, get up immediately and file quietly out into the hall and go straight out the front door." We did as we were told, though we all felt like grabbing our candy as we passed by the table. As we passed the stairway, there was smoke coming down and we could hear the crackling of the fire. Outside the door someone told us to go out on the harbour and then up to Bird's Eye cottage and wait there. We could see the school burning from the window. I had found my brother and sister and we all tried to help the little ones. It was very cold and the snow was deep and we had to leave without our coats and parkas.

In Cartwright the people saw the glow of fire in the sky and hastily made ready their dog teams. They came for us with komatik boxes and whatever blankets and wraps they could find. Soon we were wrapped in blankets and on our way to Cartwright. It was only a short drive but it was very cold. The manager of the Hudson's Bay store had opened the store, built a warm fire, and had hot cocoa and biscuits ready when we arrived. It was so good to be in a warm place again.

It wasn't long before the kind people of Cartwright came and took us into their homes and fed and comforted us and gave us what clothing they could spare. I wondered where my brother and sister could be, for by now we were separated.

Next morning we learned that our school had burned to the ground and that one little girl, who had been sick in her bed upstairs, had just escaped when one of our teachers had managed to get her out by handing her to people standing below the roof of the porch. Then he was forced to jump himself and broke his ankle or knee, I don't recall which. It is tragic to note that the same little girl lost her life when a new and safer school dormitory, built at Cartwright, was destroyed by fire some time later.

The laundry building near the school was left standing, so it was decided that those of us who were in the sixth grade would finish our school year. The laundry was turned into a classroom and a bunkhouse, formerly used by the Birdseye people, was now our dwelling quarters. The Hudson's Bay gave us ledgers for scribblers and sent us pencils and wooden crates for desks.

As soon as we returned to Muddy Bay, I went poking through the ashes with a stick to see if I could find my five dollar gold piece but I never did.

The people along the coast gradually learned of the fire and came to get their children. When Pa came to get my brother and sister, I didn't mind at all because I loved going to school and wanted to get my grade six. Pa said if I stayed and got my grade six, perhaps I could go on to St. Anthony and get as high as grade eight.

We had a lovely time getting our grade six. There were six of us, five girls and one boy. We all passed our grade six and I got more for my five dollar gold piece than money could ever buy.

— Millicent [Blake] Loder
[5.1.36]

1775.
June
Thursday 29.
Wind variable.
a very hot day.

> *At day-light I sent the people on shore to build the wharf on a point which I named Paradise.*
> *At six o'clock in the evening the wharf being finished, we heaved alongside and began to deliver the goods; but were soon obliged to desist, as the tide was near carrying away our new fabrick We had six slinks in the net.*

August
Wednesday
Wind calm

> *Four hands were at work on the house 'till five in the evening, when they were driven off by rain; they afterwards picked oakum. We caught one hundred and sixty-seven fish, and packed four tierces. At noon I went up the river, landed on the east side, about half a mile above Friend's Point, and walked to the top of a small hill, from whence I had a good view of the surrounding country. I observed a very fine lake, about three miles long, and one broad, lying on the south river, a mile higher up. By the side of the east river, there were some large marshes; and most of the adjacent country is covered with good birch, fit for making hoops and staves: the whole had a beautiful appearance; and particularly so at this time of year, when birches have a richer, and more lively appearance than spruces and firs. Nor are the hills either so high or so steep as in most parts of the country, and they are divided by a variety of little brooks and rills, which adds to the beauty of the prospect.*

Monday 21
Wind calm

> At five in the morning we set off again, and soon came to the mouth of a large river, which I named Eagle River, from seeing several of those birds by the side of it. The mouth being very shallow, I sent the skiff to the point on the north side, and went up in my kyack to the head of the tide; which I found broad, rapid, and discharging a deal of water; the sides were bounded by high, rocky hills, well covered with wood, appearing to be much frequented by salmon and bears, but difficult to fish; nor did I see a proper place for buildings to be erected upon. Returning to the skiff, we rowed round a sharp point, which I named Separation Point, into another large river, to which I gave the name of White-Bear River; the mouth of which is full of sand banks. At four in the afternoon we got to the head of the tide, where a smaller stream falls in; and a little higher, there is a most beautiful cataract, the perpendicular fall of which is about fourteen feet, with a deep pool underneath. It was so full of salmon, that a ball could not have been fired into the water without striking some of them. The shores were strewed with the remains of thousands of salmon which had been killed by the white-bears, many of them quite fresh; and scores of salmon were continually in the air, leaping at the fall; but none of them could rise half the height. The country all around is full of bear-paths, leading to the fall. We watched there 'till dark, but saw no beast of any kind. Returning to the mouth of the small river, we made a fire under a high, sandy hill, and lay there.
>
> The day was fine, but it rained most part of the night.

Tuesday 22.
Wind
W. fresh
strong
moderate

> At day-light the greyhound awoke us by barking; we jumped up and found it was a black-bear, which was at the foot of the bank. He immediately ran off, when one of our people going about fifty yards from the resting place, came close upon a large wolf, and was glad to make a speedy and safe retreat. Captain Dykes and I instantly went after him, and saw the beast not far from the same spot: when I sent a ball at him, and laid it close to his heels. We then walked to the cataract, but saw nothing. Returning to the boat, we put our things in and were just going off, when I perceived a wolf coming up on the other side of the river, and expected he would have to come within shot; but he turned off on winding the smoke. About a mile below, we saw a large stag crossing the river, and I pursued him in my kyack; but he winded me, and galloped off into the woods. At the mouth of the river, we landed and walked round a flat, sandy point; covered with tall bad wood, to the mouth of a small brook, which comes down a valley from the northward, close under the foot of Mealy Mountains and on the west side of them; the bed of this brook is a fine, white quicksand. Near the mouth of the brook we saw a pair of doves[15], and I killed one with my rifle; it was much like a turtle dove and fed on the berries of the Empetrum

Nigrum. I never heard of such a bird in the country before, and I believe they are very scarce...

1778.
July
Wednes.22
calm
N. W. little

At four o'clock this morning, we weighed anchor, towed out of the river, and anchored again a little below the mouth of it, where we moored. Leaving one man on board the shalloway, to take care of her, I got into the yawl with captain Kettle, Jack, and the other two sailors; and rowed up Eagle River to bring some of the salmon-craft from thence. On entering the river, we observed a wolverine going along the south shore of it, which is the first I ever saw alive, unless in a trap. When we got to the first rapid, which is as high as a boat can go, we saw a brace of white-bears in the river above; and a black one, walking along the north shore. I landed on the south side with my double barrel and rifle; ordering captain Kettle to land Jack on the opposite shore; then to follow me with one of his men, and leave the other to take care of the boat and keep her afloat. I had not gone far, before I observed a very large black-bear walking upwards, on the other side of the river; which soon took the water and swam across, but landed at some distance above me, and went into the woods.

About half a mile higher, I came to a very strong shoot of water, occasioned by the river being pent in between two high points; from thence I saw several white-bears fishing in the stream above. I waited for them, and in a short time, a bitch with a small cub swam down close to the other shore, and landed a little below. The bitch immediately went into the woods, but the cub sat down upon a rock, when I sent a ball through it, at a distance of a hundred and twenty yards at the least, and knocked it over; but getting up again it crawled into the woods, where I heard it crying mournfully, and concluded that it could not long survive.

The report of my gun brought some others down, and it was no sooner re-loaded, than another she bear, with a cub of eighteen months old came swimming close under me. I shot the bitch through the head and killed her dead. The cub perceiving this and getting sight of me, as I was standing close to the edge of the bank, which was near eight feet above the level of the water, made at me with great ferocity; but just as the creature was about to revenge the death of its dam, I saluted him with a load of large shot in his right eye, which not only knocked that out, but also made him close the other; during which time, he turned round several times, pawed his face, and roared most hideously. He no sooner was able to keep his left eye open, than he made at me again, quite mad with rage and pain; but when he came to the foot of the bank, I gave him a second salute with the other barrel, and blinded him most completely; his whole head, was then entirely covered with blood. The second shot made him act in the same manner as the first, until he struck the ground with his feet, when he landed a little below me, and blundered into the woods; knocking his head against every rock and tree that he met with.

I now perceived that the two others had just landed about forty yards above me, and were fiercely looking round them. As both my guns were discharged, the ram-rod of my rifle broken by loading in too great haste the last time, and as I had left my shot, and ball-bag belonging to the other in the boat, I freely confess, that I felt myself in a very unpleasant situation. But as no time was to be lost, I darted into the woods and instantly loaded my double-barrel with powder only; that I might singe their whiskers at least, if I were attacked; for the rifle balls were too large. Having loaded my rifle also with as much expedition as a broken rod would permit, I returned to my former post. The bears having advanced a few yards, were at the edge of the woods, and the old one was looking sternly at me. The danger of firing at her I knew was great, as she was seconded by a cub of eighteen months; but I could not resist the temptation. She presenting a fair broadside to me, I fortunately sent my ball through her heart, and dropped her; but getting up again, she ran some yards into the woods; where I soon found her dead, without her cub.

The captain, his man, and Jack coming up, I was informed that Jack could not get a shot at the black-bear; but had shot one of those white ones which first passed me; that the beast had landed on this side of the river, and had gone upon a small barren hill, some little distance within the woods, and there died; that they were going after her, but thought it best to come immediately to my assistance, when they heard me fire so often.

Leaving them to skin this bear, I advanced higher up the river, until I came opposite to a beautiful cataract, and to the end of a small woody island which lies near the south shore. There I sat down upon some bare rocks, to contemplate the scene before me, and to observe the manoeuvres of the bears; numbers of which were then in sight.

The cataract is formed by the river being confined between two elevated points, with a flat rock extending across the bed of it; the perpendicular fall of which is eight feet; from whence there was a gradual descent for about forty yards, with several rude cubical rocks standing upon it. These made a most complete and magnificent cascade; far superior to the best artificial one I ever saw. Immediately beneath was a deep pool; and the river widened in a circular form, into a spacious basin of three hundred yards in diameter, which, taking a short turn below, resembled a circular pond. The water being low, there was a space of some yards between it and the woods: some parts were composed of fragments of rocks; others, of gravel, sand, or flat rocks, with bushes of alder growing in their interstices. The whole was surrounded by small, detached hills, covered with spruces and firs, interspersed with larches, birch, and aspen, forming a most pleasing landscape; a drawing of which I greatly regretted that I was not able to take. In the lower part of the pool were several island-rocks, from one to two yards over; with salmon innumerable, continually leaping into the air, which had attracted a great concourse of bears. Some of them were diving after the fish: and I often observed them to get upon a rock, from whence they would take a high leap, fall head foremost into the water, dive to the bottom, and come up again at seventy or eighty yards distance. Others again were walking along shore; some were going into the woods, and others coming out. I had not sat there long, ere my attention was diverted, from the variety of objects, which at first presented themselves, to an enormous, old, dog bear, which came out of some alder-bushes on my right and was walking slowly towards me, with his eyes fixed on the ground, and his nose not far from it; at the same time he presented a fair forehead to me: I turned myself round to front him, drew up my feet to elevate my knees, on which I rested my elbows, and in that position suffered him to come within five yards of me before I drew the trigger; when I placed my ball in the centre of his skull, and killed him dead: but as the shore was a flat, reclining rock, he rolled round until he fell into the river; from the edge of which, he dropped at least four yards.

On casting my eyes around, I perceived another beast of equal size, raised half out of the water. He no sooner discovered me, than he made towards me as fast as he could swim. As I was not then prepared to receive him, I ran into the woods to make ready my unerring rifle. Whilst I was employed in that operation, he dived and brought up a salmon; which he repeatedly tossed up a yard or two in the air, and, letting it fall into the water, would dive and bring it up again. In this manner he diverted himself for some time, falling slowly down with the stream until he was shut out from my sight, by some bushes, which grew a little lower down. Being now ready, I advanced to the attack, and presently perceived him, standing in the water with his fore paws upon a rock, devouring the salmon. I crept through the bushes until I came opposite to him, and finding myself then within fifty yards, I interrupted his repast, by sending a ball through his head; it entered a little above his left eye, went out at the root of his right ear, and knocked him over; he then appeared to be in the agonies of death for some time; but at last recovered sufficiently to land on my side of the river, and to stagger into the woods; where I found he bled so copious a stream, that it was impossible he could go far. Captain Kettle and his assistants had now finished their work, and joined me a second time; and as I wished them to skin the other bear, I sent them to him for that purpose.

Never in my life did I regret the want of ammunition so much as on this day; as I was by the failure interrupted in the finest sport that man ever had. I usually carried fourteen balls in the box which is in the butt of my rifle, exclusive of the load; besides a couple of bags, tied to my bandoleer, for the use of my double barrel; one containing six balls, and the other shot. But this morning, I had inadvertently neglected to replenish the box, which had only seven balls in it, and had left my bandoleer with the bags in the boat, as I mentioned before; otherwise I am certain, that I could with great ease have killed four or five brace more. They were in such plenty, that I counted thirty-two white-bears, and three black ones: but there were certainly many more, as they generally retire into the woods to sleep after making an hearty meal; and they could not be long in doing that here, for the river was quite full of salmon.

— George Cartwright[16]

WHEN THE FIRST OLD PEOPLE come over from England and them places, I can almost think they got homesick for their homes when they got old. Some of them old people used to lose their minds when they got old, they wouldn't know anything and they'd run away sometimes.

I heard old Grandfather Brown tellin' this story. This is an old story: They was fishin' up to the Overfall where the graves is now, up on Eagle River. I think the old man he was talkin' about was a John Brown.

Now the first time they knowed there was anything wrong, his daughter went up to see 'en. She told them, when she got back, "Daddy is quite a bit different today than every other time I went to see 'en."

Grandfather asked, "What's the trouble?"

"Well," she said, "He told me a lot of things that I never heard about before, things that happened before he left home. But I don't know where 'home' was."

They told her that his home was England.

She said he told her a lot of stories and she found it wonderful strange, 'twas things he had never told her before. But we don't know what the stories were because, like Grandfather said, she never told 'en what was told to her.

— Roland Lethbridge
[15.1:50]

MY FATHER WAS LEVI PARDY and my mother was Sarah. Mother was a Davis. All the first old fellers come from England and those places. I can remember my grandfather Pardy, his name was Jim. He was a proper Englishman who come across and jumped ship to stay in Labrador. That's the way most of the old fellers came...

The women in the earliest days were Eskimo or part Eskimo because the people in Labrador when our first old people come over was Eskimo, them old Englishmen—Martins, Pardys, Learnings and the rest of them....

Tom was the oldest in our family, then there was Bill, Alvina, Manuel, Jim, Harriet, Edward, Eliza and I. 'Twas a wonder we was all so small 'cause father was a big old feller. Mother, of course, was real small.

White Bear River, when I was a young feller, had thirty or so people livin' there. The Learnings lived furtherest up the river, and we lived about a mile down below them, and about half way between the two was where Charlie Learning had a little house of his own. There was just Charlie, his wife and little daughter, Mary Frances. There was two or three families of Learnings. The Davises used to live there too but that was before my time. The old Browns used to live there but they shifted to Separation Point.

My parents weren't very strict but, now, the Learnings were. I can remember when I was just a little boy. There'd be Jim, Harriet, Eliza and I. That was after poor little Edward died. Now, Charlie was a man, almost thirty I s'pose, and he'd ask his father if he could walk down so far with us children. They all did that, asked their father if they could go anywhere. Now, I don't know if they ever asked their mother, but I know they asked their father. Any time I ever heard him he always said they could go ahead if they wanted to. The old man used to read. I been there and spend the night there and the old man would get up and read the Bible in the morning, have family prayers.

My brother Edward got shot through his leg with a breech loader, accidentally. He was fourteen when he died and he used a gun about two years before that. He was crazy about goin' around with the gun and huntin'. That spring we got the loaned of a boat from Old Paradise Bill Martin to shift out the bay. We'd take everything the one time that way. There was some ballast rocks in this boat that Old Bill had put in her.

We started that morning from White Bear River to come to Black Head, but the wind come in so we turned back ag'in. There was no engines in them days. We went back to the house and had our dinner.

Edward left his gun in the boat and, of course, he had to go back and get her to go huntin'. Jim went down 'long with him. Edward leaned down and was haulin' his gun, barrel first, right towards his knee. The hammer hooked into one of those ballast rocks and bang she goes.

There was no need of him dyin' because of that. If only we'd tied something around his leg, but we were so frightened we just didn't know what to do, see. That was four o'clock in the evening and twelve that night he died. The only time he spoke he said, "I wonder will I die? I wonder will it kill me?"

Jim was on the deck of the boat when it happened and he hauled him out of the hole and back on the deck. That was a hard old time, a hard old time for us all.

I was sixteen years old the first time I came to Cartwright. I went with my brother Jim. That was the first time I saw a drunk man and I thought he was out of his mind. I thought he was crazy. Yes, that was the first man I ever saw drunk. He was a real nice, sensible man but he came here to Cartwright and somebody gave him some rum.

There was an awful lot of people drunk that night. I said to Jim, "By Gar, if that's the way that stuff makes people, well, I'm certainly not goin' to drink."

Jim used to fish, go shareman with people, with the Birds, Bob Bird at Gready, Sam Learning to Cape North and with Bill Martin out to Fox Cove. He didn't knock around the world, or Newfoundland or Canada, but he had a lot to talk about, things he'd seen and done.

You know he was able to stand on his head on the stem head of a motor boat while she was goin'. He'd take hold of the gunnels and stand on his head and the boat goin' through the water. I've seen him do it. And I saw him one time, comin' down across from Pack's Harbour to Fox Cove, sit on a thole pin, a thole pin stickin' up through a rowlock. Balanced hisself and sat on that right good. Sat up on one thole pin.

He was always doin' comical things like that just to make someone laugh. He could sure stand on his head but I never saw him walk on his hands the way our brother Manuel could. Manuel could walk the length of this room on his hands.

Jim was like me, he never had no learnin' poor old chap, but you talk about a country man. I'll guarantee you he was some country man. From the time I was seventeen 'till I was past forty I went in the country with him. He'd always go ahead no matter how bad the goin' was and if I'd go ahead, well, he wouldn't like that very good. I never ever seen him tormented or out of sorts. I used to get three times the fur he got but he didn't mind that one bit. If he got two or three minks, or something like that, he called that all right.

Jim was my favourite brother. We hung around most of the time together. We used to have some good old times trappin'. There was four of us used to trap together, in souther'd. There was Tom and Bill Coombs—two brothers—and Jim and I. We went that way for years. We'd go 'way in across there to Hawkes River, generally, but we've gone in past that to Alexis River. We had traps all around, set out as we went along the river

One evening, just before we got to where we was goin' to set camp, we saw three deer. There was a big lot of crust on the snow and the deer couldn't run. Tom and Jim saw the deer comin' up through and they off with their rifles. There was a little, small island about the size of this house, with several trees on it. They ran down on this island with their rifles ready. They fired and fired but they never struck one.

The deer couldn't go in the woods because there was more shell on the snow in there than there was in the open, so they turned back on their tracks ag'in. Tom and Jim had rifles but me and Bill only had .22s. We wouldn't go after them with .22s, foolish like. We might have killed them. I thinks if I'd have fired I would have struck them. Tom chased them for a while.

While Tom was gone we set up camp. Bill, he was up on a high bank cuttin' a great big dry stick—oh, a lot bigger than a six-inch stovepipe, and he was long. Tom come back and was walkin' up the bank. When he got in breast of this old stick that Bill was cuttin', he stood there talkin' to Bill. The stick begin to fall.

I was lookin' at the tree and saw exactly what was happenin' and all I could say was "Tommy! Tommy!" There was Tom lookin' about and bang goes the stick right across his head. It hit his head so fair that the stick broke in half, one piece goin' one side of him and the other piece on the other side. Well, that's what looked comical. But it knocked him out. Yes, he went right down across the snow. Bill thought he killed him. What a laugh we had after it was all over.

Yes, Jim and I had some wonderful times together, travelled the country a lot. One day after I come back to Cartwright, after livin' in Happy Valley for so many years, I went in to where we used to go and I come to one of our trappin' places. Jim used to make the stove legs, you know, and drive them in the ground or the snow to put the stove on. Well, here was one of the stove legs still there. I cried a little. [10.2:33]

My brother Jim was the first one from our family to go to Mountaineer Cove after our oldest brother and his wife died in the 1918 flu. Jim told me all about it when he came home but there's lots of things I don't remember now.

We were living to White Bear River then. We were hearing tell of everybody dying and we didn't know what it was, eh. We didn't even know the name of it. It was wonderful frightening because we all expected to die, you know. We were all sick but we wasn't too bad. We broke out with…there was an old 'breaking-out' with it that they called 'Herpes.' We was all laid up with that, couldn't get around. Poor old Mother, she was the worst. She got up one morning while she was sick and she said, "Whoever else is not dead, Tom is because he spoke to me last night. He said, 'Come on, come ooonnnnn'." She told us the way she heard it. 'Twas a while after, of course, before we heard they was dead. No one died in White Bear River but everybody was sick and got over it.

As soon as we was all well enough to go down to Separation Point, Jim and I went down in boat; wasn't froze up then. There wasn't a sign of anybody walking around in the snow, no tracks of anything. We went up to the first house, that was real old Uncle Fred Brown's, and his wife come to the door and told us not to come in. She told us how many people were dead. Oh, there was a lot dead. 'Twas proper ridiculous. All my good old friends that I liked so well was dead, the Brown boys.

One day, when it was all froze up, Dad was going down the run a little piece, catching rock-cods. There was a man come up from Separation Point. We could see them from where we lived up in White Bear River. The man come to poor Dad and was there talking to him quite a long time, and then the man turned and went away again and Dad started to come home. When Dad got home he had the news that Tom and his wife were dead and a lot of others. Oh, 'twas an awful thing, 'twas a very sad business.

We had heard from the Cartwright people and all around the bay everywhere; Paradise was the last ones that we knew that were dead.

'Twas early in December that we heard about the death of Tom and his wife. They got sick in their own home and they died and their five little children were left all alone. Louie, the oldest child, was away to school somewhere. The little children were there with their parents dead in the bed together for a week or more. There was only little Jim to look after them and he was only eleven years old.

After Jim, my brother, went up, the children were taken to different places. I can't remember where the baby went. Some of them went to Steve Brown's at Separation Point, and we took the rest of them with us until further arrangements could be made. Somehow they all survived it, poor little things.

— John Pardy
[3.1:16]

I WAS BORN TO PARADISE River, in Mountaineer Cove, on October 23, 1907. I'm the third oldest in the family. Louisa was the oldest and then Jim, and there was Henry, Alvina and Harriet after me. ...There were four families lived to Mountaineer Cove. There was my mother's brothers, William and John Winters, my father's brother, Bill Pardy, and us.

My dear old father was Thomas Pardy and my mother was Elizabeth Winters. I'll never forget my darling mother. The only learning she had was what she got from the dear old Bible, which was the only books they had at that time. ...Mother's mother was Maria Smoker, whose father was from England and whose mother was part Indian. Mother's father was Silas Winters. My grandfather Winters shot himself before Uncle Si was born....

Father wasn't home much, always away working to try and keep us from starving. The year of the Spanish Flu I used to go round with my father. I was ten years old that fall, turned eleven in October. I remember the first place I went with my father was down to Drunken Cove to tail some fox traps, and we went up on Drunken Cove Hill to tail some mountain cat traps. My brother Jim used to get around with Uncle John Winters.

In November 1918 my parents died with the Spanish Flu. Mother died Sunday night at twelve o'clock and Father died the next morning at six o'clock. Not long before Mother died Uncle Bob Mesher came for her to born his wife's baby. This was Uncle Bob's first wife, Mary Ann [Snook]. Mother borned the baby but the mother died. The baby was named Mary Ann; she grew up and married Sid Pardy, Judson Pardy's brother, and when Sid died she married John Davis, and his son Manuel married my daughter Cynthia.

Anyhow, Mother was sick when Uncle Bob came after her. After the baby was born Uncle Bob was trying to get Mother back home. It was very cold and it took them a long time to get across the river. That was the Sunday night that Mother died. I'll never forget seeing her on the floor. She was old-fashioned but she was good and she loved her God.

Father died in the morning with baby Harriet in his arms. Uncle John Winters, his wife and daughter died. Uncle Bill's wife lived but she wouldn't stay with us after Uncle Bill and her son died. She went across the river. So there was only we Pardys left by ourselves for about two weeks. Uncle Bill Mesher and a couple of men came and buried the dead. No coffins.... [12.1:40]

...We must have been there by ourselves a week or more after Father and Mother died. The poor little baby was in a bad state when they took her away from us. She was almost dead. Aunt Alice Heard took her across the river after help came to us. Poor little dear, her napkin was matted on her. She lived through it somehow but she's never been able to stand a lot of cold or heat and she was left deaf... [3.1:16]

After Christmas, Father's brothers John and Jim came and took us to White Bear River with them. Later that winter Uncle John Learning took little Harriet, and I went with him in May. I liked Uncle John Learning. I stayed with Uncle John and Aunt Eliza until I was fourteen years old and then I went for myself.

I worked to the Hudson's Bay Company for eight year for fifty cents a day, which was big money them days. We worked from six in the morning 'till six in the evenings, with time off for meals and two fifteen minute lunch breaks a day. In the winter we'd get a half day off on Saturdays.

Dr. Grenfell took Jim and Henry to St. Anthony to go to school until the school was built at Muddy Bay. Henry lived with Uncle Si Winters for a little while and he also lived with Uncle Ned Lethbridge for one winter. Alvina stayed at the school one winter and then she went with Grandmother again. When Henry married, he took Alvina and Jim to live with him. I was a bird alone....

— Edward Pardy
[12.1:40]

WHEN OUR BABIES WERE RIGHT tiny, just born, we used burnt flour to keep diaper sores away. Goodness, we never saw babies with sore bottoms in our day. When they got a bit bigger, we'd put black bear oil on them. I got that from Mother. You'd render out the fat, boil it out, and drain off the oil and make a real salve.

We used bear oil on our hair, too, to keep our hair from drying out. Rub it right into the scalp, leave it for a while and then wash your hair. Mother scented that with Florida water to make it smell good. 'Twould be right nice, good as anything you can buy.

We used juniper [tamarack, larch] poultice for risin's, such as boils and carbuncles, and any other type of getherin'. We'd get the juniper rind and scrape off the inside. You'd take that pulpy mess and beat it into a salve. When my daughter Linda was small, she had an abcess on her leg. When the doctor came from north he give me a jar of salve and I used the whole thing. Sure, for goodness sake, it never done a bit of good. I fixed up some juniper poultice and cleaned it up in no time, took everything out, core and all, and that was that!

To keep our blood clean we'd drink spruce and juniper steeped out. We also used ground juniper root. It was a long, yellow, thread-like root that ran along under the ground. Every fall we'd dig up a whole lot of it. Us youngsters had great fun at that. We'd chew bits of it while we was collectin' it. Mom used to steep it out and bottle it up.

Turpentine from the fir trees, now that was just wonderful. That was good for several things. You'd eat it for a sore throat. You would also use it on cuts. Nothing else was ever used on cuts as I know. We'd collect bottles and bottles of turpentine bladders off the trees, just cut the bladders and let it run in the bottles.... [7.4:53]

Years ago, we had berries to last us all winter long. We'd put away berries as they ripened and had them right up 'till the following spring. Nobody, them times, picked berries before they got ripe. They were bottled, boxed, barreled or whatever and put in a ground cellar, or root cellar as some calls it. Just about everyone had a cellar or shared one with someone else. Dad had one little cellar underneath the schoolroom[17]. When 'twould come mild enough to open the big cellar, which was away clear of the house, Dad would take out enough stuff to last a while and put it in the house cellar. Things kept right nicely in that little cellar. In winter time, the cellar kept things from freezing and in the summer it kept things cold. Each cellar had its porch, and that was the coldest place around September.

Our cellar was about five feet underground and high enough to stand up in. I don't remember the measurements, but I do know 'twas a nice size. It was made of logs. On the top was a layer of logs, then a layer of ground, then logs again and then ground piled high on the top of it all. I suppose a person made his cellar according to how many people would be using it.

We had a portable kerosene stove for going into the cellar during the winter. You'd put that stove in the cellar porch for a while. You had to warm the air, you see, before you'd open up the main part of the cellar.

Anything you wanted to keep for the winter, well, you just put it in the cellar. Berries, now, was one thing we always had. Labrador got all kinds of berries so I'll try and go right down through them all.

Raspberries grows up in the bays. In August they begin to get ripe and we'd pick them as 'cording as they ripen. The riper a raspberry, the better they are to keep. Some we'd make into jam and bottle, others we'd put in bottles and add sugar to them. After the sugar dissolved and it got syrupy, we'd run hot wax over the top of it. We'd save bottles of all kinds for our berries. We'd melt down candles to pour on the top of the berries.

Squashberries [*Viburnum edulum*] would grow up in the rivers and bays too. We'd boil them until they got right tender. They were very sour so we'd add lots of sugar. Once they were tender we'd drain off the juice, some of which you'd bottle off as drink and the rest you'd add a gelatin to and make squashberry jelly. We also poured hot wax over the top of the jelly.

Redberries, or partridge berries [*Vaccinium vitis-idaea*, mountain cranberry], ripens about September. The best place to find them is where there been a fire. Mickles Point was a wonderful spot and so was Pond Hills. You'd pick barrels and barrels of them. We'd sell some, of course. Twenty-nine gallons in a barrel for nine dollars. According to prices now, my, we'd clean her. We'd always put a couple of barrels in the cellar for our own use if we could at all. I'd say redberries was the main berry.

Magna berries [*Gaultheria hispidula*, creeping snowberry] is a white berry that you find under some little green leaves in among tall trees. We'd eat them without cooking. We'd put sugar on them and let it dissolve then eat them. That was good for cleaning up the blood.

There's three types of blueberries. There's sugar herts [*Vaccinium augustifolium*], a small, very sweet berry that grows on bushes off the ground. I've seen them so plentiful on Newfoundland Island I could pick a gallon a day. Ground herts [whortleberry or bilberry] grow on bushes right on the ground. They're not sweet like sugar hurts, but they're delicious. Tobacco herts grow up off the ground. We never bothered much with them, just pick and eat. The three types are good for jam and wonderful for pies.

Bakeapples [*Rubus chamaemorus*, cloudberry] grows on marshy land, mostly. They were numerous home this year, so I heard. A good summer you could go in a marsh and as far as your eye could see 'twould be red with bakeapples. My, what a beautiful sight.

One time my brother Bill went bakeapple picking, he said he knew as soon as he got home someone would ask him how many berries he got. He counted up to a hundred. Sure enough, soon as he got home someone asked him how many berries did he get. He said, "Well, I don't rightly know, but I do know I got over a hundred." I thought that was right good.

I never set out to spend a whole day picking, but by darting in when I felt like it I got about five gallons a day at the most, I suppose. We put our bakeapples in tight kegs and put them in the cellar. Dad used to put his in a little small keg and bury them in a puncheon of coarse salt. That would keep them cold. After I was married we just used to bottle them and wax them over on the top to keep the air out. Them old gallon jars we used to have was wonderful for keeping bakeapples in.

Dogberries [*Pyrus decora*, northern mountain ash], now, we never picked until they were frozen on the trees. You'd put them in a tight container too. Where our dogwood trees were at home was right close to the house. We'd leave the berries on them and pick them as 'cording as we felt like it. We didn't cook them. I just loves dogberries.

Blackberries [*Empetrum nigrum*, crowberry], like redberries, could be kept in almost anything in a cold place. We'd try to put away a barrel or two of them for each winter too, if we could at all. Blackberries grows by the salt water best. They are black and round with a little white spot where they're attached to the branch.

We used to get wild pears [*Amelanchier*, service-berry, June-berry, shad-bush, sugar pear, Indian pear], too. They were right plentiful by the side of the big marsh at Separation Point. They were a real treat. We'd pick them and eat them right there....

I always says things kept better in a cellar than in a refrigerator. Once you freeze something it's not as good after....

Talking about berries and home reminds me of bangbelly. That's a cake-like thing. You save up your bread scraps. When you get what you think is enough, you soak them just enough so you can crush it up. To this you add molasses, pork scrunchions, baking powder and enough flour to stick it all together. Stir it up with a spoon, and throw in some raisins or berries—we use to find blackberries wonderful good in bangbelly. You'd put it in a pan and bake it. We never used measurements at all, just banged it all in, one ingredient after another. I dare say that's where it got its name.

— Jemima Learning
[1.2:20]

WILLIAM FRANCIS LEARNING, BORN AT Paradise River, Labrador on April 24th, 1847, married Dianne Pardy of Paradise River. Their children were Belinda, Emma, Selina, Eliza, Harriet, Arthur, Mary-Jane, Maria, Levina, Samson and Frances Albert. The second son and second last child grew to be a very large man, standing eight feet and three inches, and was known to all Labradorians and Newfoundlanders as The Giant.

William Learning, with his family, left Paradise River during the summer months to fish at Cape North. Mr. MacRae had a big fishing station there where salt cod could be sold when cured and ready for shipping back to Newfoundland. Mr. MacRae, who owned the station, built bunkhouses and living quarters to house his hired men. A spot was chosen to put the building. All was fine except for one large size rock which was sort of in the way for the entrance to the house. Different big men or strong-looking men were asked to try and remove the rock. It seemed lots tried but all failed.

One day a schooner came with more fishermen who also had homes at Cape North, and as soon as word got around that there were two big men over six foot among the newcomers, so the builders of MacRae's station decided to go after them to see if they could move the rock. One man proudly boasted there wouldn't be any need for both, and he volunteered to take on the job alone. The other six-foot man decided he would go along to watch. Both went.

The first man stood over the rock for a second then bent over putting both hands around the rock where it had been dug around to provide a better hold. He moved it slightly but couldn't rise it. He gave up, telling the second man it wouldn't be any use for him to try. The second big man who wanted to bet he wouldn't lift it. Bets were made. The man placed both hands around the rock and got it up a small bit higher but couldn't bring it out of its resting place. So the game was over. It was decided to go [put the entrance] to one side of the rock.

A few days passed and another schooner came into Cape North with four men from Sandwich Bay bringing wood and household goods before bringing the families. Word soon got around that there was a very big man who looked like a giant. One Sunday afternoon, two young lads from MacRae's station decided to go over the hill, thinking this man would be a bit over six foot. They found instead an eight foot man, a real giant. This was Samson Learning. Also in the house at that time was Samson's father William, his oldest brother Arthur, and his father's brother, Edward Learning. When asked by William Learning what brought the lads there, he was told about this rock that nobody could move and that it was a bit in the way. Samson asked about the size of it and he was told about the two six-foot men who couldn't rise it. Samson said he didn't think he could do any better.

William asked the young lads who they were. "Fishermen, sir, and Catholics. We live with MacRae. We been fishin' all marnin' before we got the chance to come 'ere."

William gave them a hard look and then said, "We, me sons, are Anglicans belongin' to the Church of England and we don't work on Sundays. You will have to look elsewhere for someone to move your rock."

The next day or so William and Edward sailed off for Sandwich Bay leaving William's two sons to tidy up the premises. That night Samson and Arthur decided, for the fun of it, to go over the hill to MacRae's to have a look at the rock. A crowd gathered around and jeered and shouted when Samson said he didn't think he could lift it. Arthur came alongside and told Samson to give her a lift. Samson stood with his legs apart and asked where they wanted the rock put. Everyone was shouting that he couldn't do it. Samson bent over, placed his hands around the rock and lifted it over his head, then he placed it down well out of the way for the door. As the story goes, the rock could have been well over three hundred pounds.

Samson died during the flu of 1918-19.

There have been some quite large men in the Learning family since that time. Arthur and Frank were a bit over six foot, Arthur's youngest son, Frank, stands six and a half foot and Frank's oldest son stands at seven foot three inches the last time he measured. There is a good chance that Duane could reach eight foot [he was nineteen then]. Duane, too, looks like a giant. Arthur's oldest son, Arthur Forward, has two sons six foot and over, and his oldest son is five foot eleven.

The date of the Learnings at Cape North was around 1913, 1914. Samson was then around twenty-one or twenty-two years old.

— Gladys Mesher
[12.3:46]

JUST ABOUT EVERYONE AROUND THE Paradise River, Cartwright area who have ever been up around Savage Cove have heard the Savage Cove Devil. It's been heard for years and years. The sounds are still the same. There been people who even went as far as to search for whatever was making the noises but they couldn't get close to the noises even. You can't get close because the sounds are always the same distance away.

I was out on the rocks in front of the house at Calloway's Cove when I heard it. 'Twas a real pretty evening, right calm. You could hear for miles. 'Twas so hot that evening that there wasn't even any flies. Most evenings when there's no wind the flies are thick enough to carry you away.

The sounds I heard was like someone callin' out for help. 'Twas so human sounding that my step-mother told Bob to go up around the shore and see if there was someone drove ashore with engine trouble. Bob told her that was only the Savage Cove Devil.

The sounds started like someone callin' for help, then it changed. Sometimes it was like people fightin', then people cryin' and babies cryin'. 'Tis all kinds of sounds, people sounds. 'Twould be a bad thing to have to listen to if you was up there alone in the night. Awful scary. After we heard it I couldn't get to sleep all night. I kept my brother Bob awake for company, I was so nervous…

Daddy been there lots of times, years ago, cuttin' wood for the Hudson's Bay Company. He said it used to be so bad it would keep the dogs howlin' all night. He'd have to get out of it.

Some people believes 'tis something in the rocks. P'raps the way the wind blows among the trees and the rocks. It can't be that though because we heard it on a flat calm day. Others believes that years and years ago there was white people there and the Natives killed them all. Where the bodies fell was where they rotted and their souls haunt the place now.

When someone tells you a story like that, you don't pay much attention to it. You thinks they're puttin' you on. You got to experience it yourself before you believe it. All the years I was growing up I heard about the Savage Cove Devil and I just took it to be another ghost story. Not anymore. I heard it and it's real. Whatever it is, it is real.

— Ellen Learning
[2.2:28]

THERE'S ALWAYS BEEN A SAVAGE Cove Devil ever since I can remember. Don Martin and Roll McDonald and, I think, Butler Martin was camped in there one summer, or spring, or something, and they heard this noise. Don feared nothing on earth, eh. He went on in lookin' for it, by the side of the hill somewhere. It must have been late spring, I s'pose 'cause they had dogs. Anyway, he was goin' about the woods lookin' for this 'thing' and all of a sudden he heard it comin'. It ripped—whipped right between his legs. You know most men would have fainted with the fright. Don never batted an eye. He never feared nothing, that man. 'Twas one of the dogs got clear and chased him.

One dark night in the fall, early fall, September, I think it was, me and Burton was up to Savage Cove. We had a house-cabin boat. I woke up in the night, thirsty, and we had no water. Burton was still asleep. I got up, got the boat and went ashore to Eagle River Harbour. Samse Learning got a little cabin there now, I think. Dark as the devil. I rowed ashore. Not a breath of wind, just flat calm. I was just takin' my paddles in when I heard this god-awful noise. I don't mind admittin' to anyone…that I could feel the hairs movin' on my head.

I was nervous and I nearly went back, but there was no water and I said, 'If I do go back, Burton will laugh at me.' So I went ashore. I had no flashlight or anything. I did have matches. So I was lightin' matches and goin' to find this little small stream that was there; this little spot of water, you know, you could hear trickle. Just before I got to get the water, those noises came ag'in. You'd get this creepy old feeling, you know. I can't explain it. Sometimes it's like an infant cryin', or wolves howlin' in the distance, you know, mournful, and then those bitter screeches.

I nearly went back to the boat without my water but I felt sure Burton would laugh at me. 'Twas only nonsense, only a bird or an animal. Got to be, eh?

Lots of people, people my age, have heard the Savage Cove Devil, you know, like Max Pardy and Horace and George. Max was Jud Pardy's brother, Uncle Arch Pardy's son. They was camped on Saddle Island down there, right in the mouth of Savage Cove one time, gettin' a load of wood. They had it cut there for Pack's Harbour or something. They was lyin' in camp when they heard this noise. The younger guys wouldn't go and get water. Max went and got the water and when he left, they left camp with him. They wouldn't stay in camp alone. That was the kind of noise it was, 'twould nearly scare you. I don't know; no one knows, what the hell it is for sure. Must be a bird or animals or something, maybe water pressure, air pinned up. 'Tis hard to know what it is, but it's been heard now for many, many years.

— Neil Lethbridge
[10.1:48]

THE SAVAGE COVE DEVIL WAS a very interesting thing. You wouldn't notice this in the middle of the summer, you had to be there in the fall of the year when 'twas icy. Sounds funny but, I mean, that's the way it was, eh.

Me and Forward was camped out on Saddle Island, a little island there in Savage Cove not far from the brook. We had a flashlight each, of course, and like I say, I was a devil myself, not afraid of anything and game for anything. So we took our flashlights and followed the little brook up through the hill, zig-zagged through willows and grass. We could hear this noise up there.

There was a wee bit of snow on the ground and 'twas icy. There was water streamin' down and, of course there was the tide from the current comin' down. There was a big tree with bare roots out on to the rocks and the sod was liftin' where the root was growed on. When the tree would rock, 'twould choke the water, see, and 'twould bubble and then when the tree would lift, 'twould squeak and grind, make a very mournful sound. Me and Uncle Far shined our lights in and this was what it was, just the tree, water, turf and woods that was makin' all this fuss. We went back in the morning and cut down the tree so there's be no more noises to bother the hunter in the fall.

— Samson Learning
[10.1:50]

MY FATHER WAS NORMAN LETHBRIDGE and my mother was Gertrude. My grandfather Lethbridge was Garland, and the first Lethbridge was an old John Lethbridge. Old John Lethbridge came here to work on Eagle River Island. He was a tinsmith, that was his job. He married a Lizzie Michelin. I believe she was Old Joe Michelin's sister, from up in Lake Melville somewhere. They had seven boys and one girl, which was Elizabeth. I don't know the names of all the boys, but there was Phillip, Garland, Tom and John. The rest I don't know. In Grandfather Gar's family there was seven boys and one girl, Mary Ann. The boys were John, Joe, Chris, Norman, Mick, Tom and Frank. Frank and Tom are buried over in Eagle River, at Tinker Point.

I heard Dad tell a story about when Tom was real sick one fall. One day Dad said he went out and killed a tomtit, a little bird. He thought it would make Tom feel better. Tom was only a little feller, about seven or eight. Dad said when he went in and showed Tom the little tomtit, Tom said, "You shouldn't have done that. You shouldn't have killed the tomtit."

Dad said that ever since that day he remembered Tom and the tomtit. It was only a day or two after that, he said, that Tom died.

Dad and Uncle Joe died with cancer in the stomach and Uncle Micky died with some other complaint. He swelled up right tight. That's how Uncle Micky died.

Aunt Mary Ann married Jonathan Pardy.

I got four sisters and two brothers. Gar is the oldest in the family, then it's me, then Ella, Liz, Kate, Myra, John, and Irene. I think that's how it goes. They all married except me and I don't expect I'll make it now, but it's all right, I guess. I'm doing very good yet. I can still get around.

I was born at Separation Point on May 2, 1923. I got the same birthday as the Hudson's Bay Company....

— Roland Lethbridge
[15.1:50]

My mother was a Lethbridge first, Mary Ann Lethbridge, and she married Jonathan Pardy. I can't remember my father at all. He was brother to Uncle Austin and Uncle John Pardy. I was born March 25th, 1917, down to Burns Harbour, but I growed up in Separation Point. There was two older than me but they both died. One died the fall of the flu. We had a school in Separation Point and teachers would come there from Newfoundland, Charlie Petten and they. Charlie Petten was to Dove Brook and he used to come over to the Point for a while. I got as far as grade three in school, but I learned a lot from books since then, and from kids that goes to school. I been lookin' at their books and I learns quite a bit from that....

When we was livin' to Separation Point the Indians used to come there, Shimoon and them. Shimoon was the oldest feller and I think his wife's name was Pename. They came out in March one year, when we was livin' there, and they stayed until open water and then they went away somewhere. I suppose they went to North West River. They'd stay up the river from us in tents and we'd go up there for a cruise after supper. After we got to know them they would come down to see us. Of course we couldn't talk much to them because we couldn't understand them, but we liked going up there just the same. They were real friendly. Shimoon could talk English very good. They used to full [lace] rackets for people and make moccasins.

We moved to Paradise River twenty-six years ago, the fall Mother borned Rod Mesher. There used to be a lot of people, them times, to Separation Point, Dove Brook, Bob 'n Joyce, but they all moved. We felt bad about movin' but we had to because there was no school then on that side of the bay. We had gardens over to the Point. We used to have wonderful greens and lettuce and stuff like that. There was good ground over there.

We liked livin' to Separation Point. It seemed strange when we come to Paradise at first but now I wouldn't want to leave it, except to go to Cartwright for the summer months. I likes Cartwright in the summer 'cause it's so warm and flysy here.

— Polly Lethbridge
[11.2:38]

I often think back on the days when I was a child at White Bear River. I loves that place. There were so many things you could get to eat there—fresh meats and all kinds of fish. All we had to do to get smelts was to run down over the bank by our house and catch them through the ice. In the fall and winter we would set out our rabbit snares and then when the nights would come with the big moon and stars shining, we would go and get rabbits and bring them home. Then in the morning we would get some more. In the summer there would be lots of berries growing—raspberries, strawberries, squashberries and currants. In the fall we would go up in the bottom of White Bear River and pick our redberries for the winter. There was also plenty of good drinking water from the big running brooks.

White Bear River had sand bars and banks sliding into the river like the Hamilton River, only it isn't as big as the Hamilton River. We used to go up to Andrew's Brook and play on the sand. It was nothing to see a deer swimming across the river. In the spring we often saw deer walking across the sand bars on the ice. It was so pretty to look at.

White Bear River was surrounded by forest, and when the Grenfell Mission used wood for fuel, they would come and load up their boats with thousands of turns of wood.

My sister Florence used to set out traps and get foxes on the bank not far from our house. Sometimes she would catch minks by the little brooks. She always caught some fur.

We lived five miles from Dove Brook and Separation Point. There was only three families there. We didn't move to Separation Point until after my father got sick. One night, when there was only Mom, Dad, Lewis and me at home, we were playing a game. That was how we enjoyed ourselves in them days. Dad fell down. When they picked him up he wasn't able to talk so that we could understand him. I was four years old. People would come up from the Point to stay up with him all night. They said it would be better if we moved to the Point, so that's what we did. Dad died on November 29, 1937, less than a week after we moved to Separation Point.

Lots of trappers used to come by our place on their way to their trapping grounds hundreds of miles inland. Uncle Donald Martin was one of them and he was like a father to us. When it was time for him to come out of the country we would run out on the river to see if we could see him coming. A while before he would arrive Mother would bake redberry pies and cook up a big feed of deermeat, turnips and greens. We grew our own vegetables them times. When Uncle Don came he would take us in his arms and kiss us. Sometimes he'd stay with us for as long as a week and while he was there Mother would wash his dirty clothes before he'd head for Cartwright. That's how it was in them days; you'd help people who were kind to you.

We made our own fun in them days, playing games and things. We had lots of fun even though there was only three families living there at White Bear River. We had no fancy sleighs, but we made our own. We'd take a piece of birch, cut it, plane it and put it over a boiler of steaming water to put the turn at the head. That was our sleighs. We also made sleighs out of barrel staves. They went fast too.

— Greta Davis
[9.2:40]

ONE TIME WHEN ME AND Henry Mesher and Reg Pardy was up the river there, someone made a noise. I don't know what it was. Me and Reg was gone to bed. I put in the fire and I heard a ski-doo come down over the bank. I heard that ski-doo as plain as anything. I bawled out and told Reg he'd have to get up because someone was come and we'd have to boil the kettle for 'en. That ski-doo come and stopped to the tent same as they always do ….not a darn sound after. There was nothing come. I called poor old Reg for nothing.

The next weekend I was expectin' Eldred to come up. I was layin' down readin' a book and all of a sudden I heard someone call out my name. I put down the book and called out, "Hey," as loud as ever I could. There was nobody there and nobody ever was there, but I heard that as plain as ever could be.

The next weekend Lewis came. I heard his ski-doo and I heard 'en call my name. I never answered, just stayed there and read my book. I never spoke to 'en until he poked his head in through the tent door. He said he thought I was asleep or dead. I told 'en I thought he was a ghost, so 'twas no good to answer because he wouldn't come in anyway.

Old Grandfather Lethbridge told me he'd be back to see me after he was dead. He asked if I would be afraid. I told 'en I wasn't afraid. He said if he wasn't back in three years that he wouldn't come back. He's been dead about fifty years and he hasn't come back yet. I guess he couldn't get back, poor old feller.

There was three of us shook hands one time—me, Edward Pardy and Fred Pardy. We said whoever died first would come back and tell the others what it was like wherever we was to. I think 'twas Edward Pardy. Fred been dead now for a long time and he haven't showed up yet, so I'm beginnin' to think they can't get back once they dies.

If there is such a thing as a ghost, why don't everybody see them once in a while? Why should some people see them and others never see them? That's what I can't understand. And if there is such a thing, why should people be afraid of them? I don't think I ever did anyone enough harm on earth that they'd come back and do me harm.

There's some old people I'd like to see again if I could.

— Harold Brown
[9.2:41]

HUDSON STRAIT

Button
Islands

Port
Burwell

Killinek

UNGAVA
BAY

C. Chidley

N. Aulatsivik
Is.

Seven Islands
Bay

Nachvak
Fiord
Sealupiat
Ramah

Korok R.

Saglek
Fiord

Hebron

Inglisuatutuak
[George
River
Post]

Ford R.

Napartok

KAUMAJET MTS.

Ittiplersoak

George R.

Olik.
Divak

Okak
Nutak

Sillutalik
[cutthroat]

Tessialuk

Falcoz R.

KIGLAPAIT MTS.

Nosingukuluk

Kingurutik L.

Whale R.

Fraser R. Tasisuak L.

Indian
House
Lake

Anaktalik Br.

Kangittdok

Nain

Ikkilitsimavik [Rhoades b
Aupalutuk
Atanqiak
Nukasusatuk
[nakasetjatuk?]

Kogaluk R. [Frank's Br.]

Mistinibi

50 mi.

Five

TORNGAT

BY THE TIME THE NARRATORS of "Paradise" were born, the mixed-race culture that developed in isolated bays between Cape Charles and Kaipokok during first half of the nineteenth century had become the dominant culture of Labrador. Its father was European, usually British; its mother was Aboriginal, almost invariably Inuit.

To understand the Inuit component of the Labrador equation, we must skip over Ivuktoke and Kaipokok for the moment and visit the far north, land of the *torngat*,[1] where old legends of 'The People' have survived, frayed and faded with time, and the drama of their entry into the civilized world has been meticulously recorded, albeit through the heavily filtered lens of Moravian missionaries. This was, by English charter and Inuit consent, Moravian territory after 1771. Within the protective enclaves of the Mission stations, other whites were unwelcome, and the missionaries provided a level of social stewardship and order for their converts that the rest of Labrador would not know for more than a century and a half.

There is no clear boundary, social or geographic, between the Northern Inuit and those of Ivuktoke. In 1763 the Ivuktoke band, by then accustomed to coexistence with Fornel's men in Hamilton Inlet, called their northern cousins "*karalit*" and warned the English that they were a bad lot. However, the two groups reconverged at the start of the Moravian period to diverge again gradually in the nineteenth century. By 1850 the Inuit north of Hopedale were quite different from those in the secular 'Southlands.'

The coastline from Hopedale to Nain resembles that of southern Labrador, barren and severe in aspect but on closer inspection graced with pleasant wooded vales and tundra meadows. Inland, however, the forest has retreated from the plain and now huddles in steep-walled river valleys and elongated bays, leaving a high barren ground that gradually gathers into the bony spine of northern Labrador. North of Nain the country changes once again. Except for a few of the more sheltered bays and river valleys, northernmost Labrador is almost completely barren. Her mountain ranges—Kigliapait,

Kaumajet, and Torngat—are bereft of plant life, terrible dead heaps of ancient rock sloughing rotten crusts into the sea from headlands towering thousands of feet above the tide. Only among the low islands in protected bays, or deep in the heads of fjords, or on the narrow aprons of glacial till and leveled scree behind the capes is there any place for turf and shrubs to grow, kayaks to be pulled above the tide, legs stretched, and tents pitched.

For some five hundred years—until the evacuation of Hebron in 1959—this austere coastline was the heartland of the Labrador Inuit and their Thule forebears. Before that, it was where the leading edges of Dorset and Pre-Dorset migrations reached the Atlantic and turned southward, one after the other, only to vanish from the continent like wavelets on the sand. In a much earlier, warmer time, it was the northern outpost of the wide-ranging Maritime Archaic Indians and destination of their expeditions in search of Ramah chert, the translucent stone with which they made their ceremonial blades and finest tools.

Each of northern Labrador's early tenants left its own unique cultural footprints on the islands and landing places—stone tent rings and house pits, cairns, duck blinds, tools and tool-making debris, caribou fences, deadfalls, hearths, *inuksuit* on the hills, hopping stones on the beach, soapstone figurines and net plummets. In a land that consumes organic material,[2] and where pottery was not used, most of what we can learn about the people who lived here before the coming of Europeans must be read from stone and soil. It is a text that leaves much to the imagination.

Labrador Inuit were the last to trickle down the coast from arctic barrens, replacing the people they called "Tunit," those gentle giants and boulder-movers of legend. They recycled the sturdy foundations of Tunit houses, cleaning out their neatly leveled stone floors and walls, adding new superstructures of wood and sod. Now the ruins of these Inuit renovations, along with those of their own more typical sod huts, dimple sheltered coves with lush, grassy pits visible even from the air; and bold stone rings that once anchored hems of summer tents themselves lie pinned beneath crusts of heath and lichen on the shore.

These long-abandoned dwellings housed families who saw the ships of Frobisher, Hudson, and Franklin nose into the fierce currents of Hudson's Strait in their search for a passage to Cathay. Their sons joined flotillas of kayaks bound for the European fishing stations in the south, confident in the self-deprecating way of the Inuit, fearless, and eager for iron implements and wooden boats. They were the homes of families who greeted the first Moravian missionaries, and of shamans who competed with the Christians for the souls of their people. The detritus of their daily lives chronicles the changes brought about by European economic interests and a growing dependence on European goods and services. Nearby, mossy skulls in hastily assembled burial cairns bear mute testimony to the ravages of European disease.

Fortunately, rocks and bones are not the only record of Inuit life before and during contact with Europeans. The people of the *torngat* also passed on legends bearing traces, however fragmentary and distorted, of pre-historic memories and states of mind. We seek in these cryptic accounts clues to the character of "the most treacherous, cruel and barbarous of all Savages ever known,"[3] a people soon to become the mothers of modern Labrador.

The 'civilizing' of the Inuit—those who survived initial contact—took three different pathways: spontaneous assimilation of white genes and values in central Labrador; deliberate and persistent indoctrination in the Moravian mission stations; and a combination of economic necessity and osmosis in the far north, where a number of Inuit families firmly rejected Christianity and had almost no contact with whites. While there are no longer any 'savage' Inuit, it would be an oversimplification to say all pathways have as yet brought them to the same place. By the time TV and compulsory state schooling flooded all of Labrador with the ubiquitous culture of the modern world, they had in fact become quite different. One cannot help but wonder which, if any, was the better way. The answer is by no means clear.

In northern Labrador, pacification of the Inuit was from the very beginning the exclusive province of Moravian missionaries dedicated to creating true 'children of God,' innocent of European secular vices, liberated from heathen superstition and vice by the love of Jesus, preserved indefinitely in their natural state, forever dependent on the missionaries for spiritual nourishment and secular protection. Whatever the merits of this undertaking, it was one that required enormous dedication and sacrifice from missionary families and, to the extent that it was successful, represents a remarkable feat of social engineering. Its story, documented in the annual diaries and Periodical Accounts from the mission stations, is one of the far north's most extraordinary sagas. In this, too, one finds clues to the Inuit character as it responds to an alien culture single-mindedly dedicated to its modification.

Having witnessed the effect of rum-toting European traders and settlers on the Greenland Natives, the Brethren who founded the Labrador Mission were determined to establish an enclave in which they alone would have temporal and spiritual access to their would-be converts. In 1769 the British government reluctantly accepted these terms as a means of keeping the troublesome Inuit away from the nascent enterprises on the south coast. Two years later the Moravians opened a station at Nain. This was closely followed by Okak in 1775-76 and Hopedale in 1781. By 1904 there were eight stations extending from Makkovik in the south to Killinek at the northern tip of Labrador.

Some five hundred Inuit are said to have welcomed the Moravians to Nain, compelled perhaps by curiosity and opportunism as much as by the exhortations of Mikak, who had met Brother Jens Haven on her trip to England with Lieutenant Lucas and Governor Palliser four years earlier. In the exchanges that followed, the Inuit seemed enthralled by Bible stories and open to aspects of doctrine which corresponded with their own values and experience. But they found the notion of sin and guilt perplexing and the idea that they were morally inferiority to Europeans absurd. 'The People,' were not only secure in their sense of ethnic superiority, they had acquired a particular disdain for Europeans during two centuries of contact.[4] The Moravians saw that bringing this proud and strong-minded race to the point of conversion would take time and a great deal of patience.

While the missionaries initially wanted the Inuit to live permanently at the stations in order to complete their conversions, they were neither capable nor in favour of sustaining them with goods and food. The Moravians' refusal to provide trade goods was disappointing for the Inuit; their reluctance to share food was immoral. When in the 1780s new traders appeared in Kaipokok and Hamilton Inlet promising guns, liquor, food, and relief from the relentless moral observations of the missionaries, the Inuit (among them those who had earlier flocked to Nain from the south) left the stations en masse. It was the Mission's first major crisis, precipitating its decision to enter into trade with the Inuit. In time, this would prove profitable, then addictive, and ultimately, compromising.

Groups of Inuit began returning to the stations in 1792 sick, famished, and shaken by their exposure to the first allegedly rough bunch of Settler-traders on the southern coasts—just as the missionaries had predicted. To the Inuit, such foreknowledge of events, and the ability it implied of being able to control outcomes, was the province of great shamans. The Moravians seized every opportunity to reinforce the impression that the power of Jesus was greater than that of the *torngat* by challenging the *angakkut* in contests the missionaries were bound to win by virtue of their superior understanding of natural phenomena. One after another, the leading *angakkut* were humiliated in this way, and the Inuit, feeling both chastened and impressed, began to take the words of the missionaries to heart. It was the inauspicious start of a striking transformation.

From 1800 to 1805 a tidal wave of religious enthusiasm swept through the Inuit communities. Mission schools were crowded with eager children and adults, many of whom by then could read and discuss Inuktitut translations of scripture. Everywhere the people could be found praying and weeping, confessing sins, and witnessing to one another. At last, the Brethren were convinced that some of these conversions were genuine and began to accept the eager Inuit into the Church. By the end of the "Great Awakening," most of the population in the vicinity of the three stations had been baptized.

For the Brethren, the Awakening was God's magnificent validation of their purpose and labours, surpassing all their expectations for the success of the Mission. Some social psychologists today explain the phenomenon more in terms of ethnic capitulation and cultural collapse. Confused and depressed by the relentless denigration of their way of life, demoralized by the loss of their cultural supremacy, unsuccessful in their attempt at rebellion, the only remaining escape from collective despair was the protective embrace of Jesus. This white *torngak* promised a reintegration of the Inuit soul and a place, however small, in the inevitable new world order. If nothing else, conversion offered some relief from incessant social pressure.[5]

The stations enjoyed thirty relatively prosperous years in terms of harvesting souls. Mission Inuit seemed devout and happy. Many had learned to catch seals with nets, to net and cure winter supplies of codfish, and to trap foxes for the station. They looked forward to the numerous Moravian festival days and proved able and enthusiastic musicians. Every village had its brass band and string orchestra, organist and choir—choirs that performed what are thought to have been North American premieres of Haydn and Handel and which must, in any case, have been the only Inuktitut performances of these works in the New World.

The missionaries established schools soon after each station opened and encouraged the Inuit to send their children at an early age. Until a complete Inuktitut translation of the New Testament became available in the 1820s, students inscribed their own copies from texts learned in recitation. They also copied hymns and instrumental music. Later, the missionaries were able to provide translations of *The Pilgrim's Progress*, *Christy's Old Organ*, *Jessica's First Prayer*, hymnbooks, and a book of short readings in natural history and general knowledge. The speech and writing of elder narrators in this chapter reflects the sentiment and Biblical elegance of these texts.

By 1810, Mission Inuit were almost completely literate, a fact that astonished European visitors at a time when literacy was extremely rare among whites. Children and adults alike attended schools while at the stations. They studied some geography and math, but almost no other secular topics. Instruction was in Inuktitut, the Mission Inuit being forbidden to speak English until 1950, when the provincial government mandated English instruction in all Labrador schools.

By the end of the Great Awakening it seemed even the wild 'heathen' north of the stations, whom the Moravians called "Northlanders," were on the verge of conversion, but soon after Hebron station was established in 1830 the tide turned. The Hudson's Bay Company's new trading posts on Ungava Bay would seduce the Northlanders across the peninsula with liquor and European foods the Moravians refused to sell. When these tenuous posts closed in 1842, and the Northlanders returned to trade at the mission stations, their minds were set against conversion, preferring their own uncritical *torngat* to Jesus, independence and pride to the self-abasement of the Mission Inuit, and their male-oriented moral values to the gentle ways of the Christians.[6] Rebuffed missionaries had to admit that, rough looking as they were, some of the so-called heathen in fact behaved better than members of their own flock, among whom criminal and moral lapses were not uncommon.

South of the stations, the 1830s brought other changes that would threaten the Labrador Mission's monopoly over the produce and allegiance of the Inuit. Trader-Settlers were filling bays and island harbours around the stations with relatively comfortable wooden houses. Many of the newcomers were offspring of mixed-race families in Ivuktoke—now called Hamilton Inlet—and Sandwich Bay. Southlander Inuit working for or with them, like their white counterparts, had adopted the Anglo-Inuit-Innu lifestyle that would prevail in settled Labrador. Some seemed to enjoy equal status and a similar standard of living to the newcomers, and unlike the Mission Inuit, all were free to make the most of such opportunities for advancement as existed in the area, limited though they were.

The mission stations greeted these new arrivals with ill-concealed hostility, and the planters responded in kind, launching a campaign of disinformation that succeeded for a short period in seriously discrediting the Brethren in the eyes of their flock. Many Mission Inuit again moved away from the stations, joining the newcomers and, in the process, injecting Moravian religious values and literacy into the Southlander and Settler population. After some unsuccessful early attempts at direct confrontation with the planters, the Brethren bowed to the inevitable and extended a reluctant welcome. The psychological warfare ended, but so did the Mission's original dream of an exclusive society of Christian Inuit.

By mid-century, the Inuit of Hopedale and Nain had switched to European-style frame houses and begun wearing European clothing, and Settlers were attending services at the stations. In 1853, John Reed and his Inuit wife were not only accepted for baptism in Hopedale but also allowed to build a home in the village. By 1907 a quarter of the thirteen hundred Moravian congregants would be Settlers.

During the 1850s and '60s, a relentless streak of famine and gruesome epidemics precipitated a new period of disillusionment and unrest among the Mission Inuit. Taught that God would reward those who worked hard and followed his teachings, the zealous redoubled their efforts to meet His standards so that their families would be spared these plagues. When year after year the truly virtuous and industrious members of the community suffered along with the slackers, even the strongest faith was sorely tested.

It was also becoming apparent that crises like this were exacerbated as much by the Mission's social policies and trading practices as by those of the non-Moravian Europeans against which they were trying to shield their people. Area resources could not be depended upon to sustain centralized communities, and the growing emphasis on trapping and codfishing during traditional hunting seasons deprived Inuit of gamefoods required for good health. Even the Moravians began for the first time to admit a connection between the annual onset of infectious diseases and the arrival of the Mission ship from Europe, a relationship long obvious to everyone else.

Adding insult to injury, it became known that Mission Inuit received less than the going rate for furs. The Mission's explanation that it accepted all pelts at this price, including those of inferior quality rejected by other traders, did little to assuage the father of a starving family who knew he could sell his better pelts elsewhere for a higher price. He could also obtain foodstuffs like flour and biscuits that, however detrimental to his long-term health, would put something in the mouths of his children today. And as a last resort, he could count on at least some of the traders, including the Hudson's Bay Company by then dominant in the area,[7] to advance enough credit or, in some cases, charity to see him through the worst. The Mission's charitable allocations were made with great reluctance, on moral as well as practical grounds, and were barely adequate to sustain life, let alone the productivity of the family provider.

Discontent with the Mission grew so great that normally diffident village elders and chapel servants openly confronted the missionaries. It was clear even to the Mission in Europe that its Labrador operations were in trouble. In 1861, Bro. Leo Reichel conducted a thorough investigation of the Labrador Mission on behalf of the governing board, which unanimously approved his astute recommendations. In sum, these would have amounted to a complete overhaul of trade practices and social relations with the Inuit. He advocated adoption of fair market prices; more generous charitable allocations; more comprehensive education including trades, secular topics, and English; opportunities for Inuit to join the Brotherhood and serve as teachers; more social interaction between missionary wives and Inuit women; and so forth. The Mission's objective, the report said, was to prepare the Inuit for participation in the modern world, not for eternal childhood in the care of reclusive and paternalistic overseers. The report went so far as to suggest that the best indication of the missionaries' success in achieving this objective would, in effect, be their own obsolescence.[8] Needless to say, the Brethren in Labrador were unable to compass a view so antithetical to everything for which they had laboured over the past century. The report was voluntarily implemented only to the most superficial degree, but time and circumstances would eventually take care of the rest.

It was the Spanish Influenza of 1918-19 which, more than anything else, loosened the Mission's grip on the Inuit. Although no blame was cast, no renunciation made, a trust had been irreparably broken. Perhaps it was the ultimate revenge of *Tuurngaatsuk*, giver of seals, fish, game, and laws — Moon Man to some — perhaps greatest of all the *torngat* deposed so long ago by the clever missionaries. "*Torngak*," says Tanner in 1947, "through his unreflective Christian optic was no less than the spirit of the dead. He would worry and trouble people so that they should tire of their existence on earth and their spirits desire to move over to *Torngak* and live with him. For this reason he attacked people of all ages; hunger, disease, and death he sent out to catch the desired spirits of mankind and bring them to him."[9] Indeed, suicide has become one of the most virulent plagues presently afflicting native peoples all across the Arctic.

In 1926 the nearly bankrupt Mission was obliged to abandon its trading operations to the Hudson's Bay Company, arch-rival for nearly a century. In 1949, when the Canadian and provincial government assumed control of social institutions, what remained of the Mission's prominence in the temporal life of the community began to evaporate. The Moravian Church is now one of several denominations in Labrador, its lovely mission buildings little more than cultural relics in the largely secular Inuit and mixed communities of Makkovik, Hopedale, and Nain.

Nain is the end of the line today, the northernmost settlement on the Labrador, its population of twelve hundred swollen in recent years with outsiders poised to begin mining the nickel deposits discovered in 1994 at nearby Voisey's Bay. On the distant horizon rises the serene frosted peak of Mt. Thorsby, broad white shoulders spread protectively across the skyline as though to keep her wayward children from venturing farther north. Beyond this gentle guardian, the old mission stations of Okak, Ramah, Saglek, Nachvak, Killinek, and Hebron have been reclaimed by the polar bear, the deer, and the spirits. Here is now another set of cultural footprints— ceramic stove tiles under hummocks of snow-bent grass and a rhubarb patch struggling through a fallen picket fence near the hollow-eyed ruin of a magnificent Teutonic building large enough, it would seem, to shelter all God's children from the demons of this land and the advancing forces of the modern world.

Ramah station was dismantled and removed in 1907, Okak torched in 1920 after the Spanish Influenza. Only Hebron and Killinek—closed in 1959 and 1979 because they were too remote from government social services—still stand, silent and deserted amid the fireweed and nodding cotton grass. Hebron's historic buildings are under nominal protection of the park service, but each year this astonishing specter in the wilderness diminishes, gone to bones like the hills around it.

Far northern Labrador is not uninhabited. A few Inuit families and young men quietly return each year to the hunting and fishing places of their forefathers rather than succumb to the torpor and dependency of village life. It is an option, as is college, entrepreneurialism, temporary jobs, and community leadership—or alcoholism, early motherhood, and suicide. Inuit have dwelt with their *torngat* for a long time. They have learned to outwit them; they can laugh in their face. They will find their own way to prevail even, perhaps, against the one they are facing for the first time—the possibility of economic prosperity.

The narrators in this chapter tell of Inuit life in the northern stations from various perspectives—Inuit, Settler, missionary, and trader—and lead inevitably toward an episode that has dominated the collective memory of this region above all others. While the Spanish Influenza of 1918 cut a deadly swath around the world, its impact on native peoples, who lack natural resistance to foreign infections, was especially devastating. In Okak, a healthy village of over 350 souls, it was genocidal: only a handful survived, most of them children. Of all the northern communities, Ramah alone escaped because the Moravian mission supply ship *Harmony* which carried the infection to Labrador was unable to stop there.

Accounts of "the sickness" enable us to see key players in the Labrador epic at their most focused and transparent—missionaries struggling with the realization that they have inadvertently brought about the destruction of the people they came to save; traders and Settlers on the sidelines, horrified, helping, but seeming to understand that they are witnessing the culmination of a drama in which they have been but bystanders. Mainly, the accounts provide some rare glimpses into the subtle dimensions of the Inuit psyche, as a group and individually.

The trials inflicted by this event would not be unlike those experienced in times of famine, warfare, or sickness throughout the history and prehistory of the Inuit, and it is not difficult to detect their collective response strategies. The ingrained stoicism and irrepressible determination to take pleasure in life are as useful in this environment as a warm coat. But the multiplicity of accounts—more than are warranted on literary and historical grounds—should also dispel any notion that aboriginal people respond to events with less individuality than others.

Anthropologists tend to seek cultural generalities and common denominators that distinguish one group from another. First-hand accounts such as these support that as well, but they also allow us to appreciate the variations of personality that transcend culture. Ultimately, the epic of the *torngat* coast—which continues to play out in its MTV-computer-Reebok generation—may be about the ephemeral nature of cultural overlays and the triumph of human personality. But with first-hand accounts, you can draw your own conclusions.

TAIKKOA MAGGOSIMAJUK KAMMASUIT kangiane unnuasiuviuligamik.... There were ghosts up by Kamarsuk, south of Nain. Even they used to frighten the people so bad that the people used to weaken from the fright, mostly at night. I knew the people in Kamarsuk so well. That place was no good for travelling during the night. I really knew that place, now it's not like that anymore, not the way it was that time. In that place the people used to go walking on shish ice to go seal hunting around Kamarsuk. Even if the people were just walking along the beach, along the shore, they'd get a good fright from them ghosts. That's how powerful it was when it tried to frighten the people away while they were hunting and going home in the night. It used to do that, not only to one person, but to a lot. Even when was no one living there only the leftovers from the old stone house foundations. It used to be really bad them days but it's not like that there anymore. [4:4:13]

I will tell you a short story, only as I have heard it from my father and mother and other older people.

A long time ago Nain was not yet a settlement, only down there just across from Nain, an island called IkKilitsimavik. Like around here, we all know that there are old places where the stone houses were once built, and there are left-overs there from the old sites. That's how they lived there in IkKilitsimavik before Nain was a settlement. The people there in IkKilitsimavik got killed in the war. There are ghosts now. They got killed in the war. The ghost's head moves. Want to go and see 'em? I can take you there.

When the people were living there in IkKilitsimavik, the women used to go fishing there to the Annainak River, just across from Nain. They used to block the river with rocks and wait for the low tide so that the fish wouldn't go no further than those rocks that they had put in the mouth of the river. They used to put the rocks just where the char would have to come to the water. The women and children used to fish that way in the old times. I never heard tell if they used to fish that way in the fall too, only in the spring and summer seasons. I never really heard if they were all women, but I heard that the men used to go hunting the caribou down to Kangitldok, and when they didn't go caribou hunting they went to Kitak. The Annainak River used to be called the fishing place.

While the women were fishing, they used to make all kinds of noises and do all sorts of things, and while they were doing that the white bear came. The bear was the kind that would kill anything on sight, so it was a fearful creature. As he was nearing the fisher-women and their children and walking slowly towards them, it turned into a rock. It is there ever since. A long time ago some outsiders used to try and say it was just painted. It is not just painted. If it were, the paint would have worn off long ago.

That's the story I used to hear from my parents and older people.   [4:3:60]

Down there at Atangiak, close to Paul's Island, on a little island, there was a woman who turned into stone a long time ago. You could even see it but it is almost gone now. What happened to that woman was that she wasn't married. She had a child, and the people used to treat her really badly. They didn't want anything to do with her. When the ice broke up and it was time to leave the winter camp, the leader went and told the woman that she would not be coming along in the boat. She would have to live there by herself all her life. No one would come to pick her up from the island, and she would be left there by herself. When the people were leaving she couldn't do anything but watch them leave on their boats so she went to the top of the hill to watch them as they were crossing to the other side. She watched them, standing with her baby in the hood, then she turned into stone.

A long time ago the features of the woman used to look real even though it was a stone. Even the baby in the hood looked real. That was a long time ago. It wasn't chipped or anything then. Now the features aren't very good anymore; now it's falling apart. [8:1:55]

I will tell another story that I have heard. This happened when the missionaries had already arrived in Labrador and settled and had houses. This guy who lived in Aupaluttuk had a brother who lived in Nakasetjutuk. The leader at Nakasetjutuk died, the brother of the leader in Aupaluttuk, while the people were watching. When he died he had wanted to have his mitts on and his sealskin pants on and wanted all of his belongings to be put on top of his grave, his sword too. He also wanted to be buried on the top of the hill overlooking Aupaluttuk, where his brother lived—right on top of the hill. So he got buried there. In the night he started making noises like he was using his sword...a dead person! He started to make the snow slide down the hill to the people in Aupaluttuk. That's how he killed off the people in Aupaluttuk. There were two people left out of the whole community and that's the two who went and told the minister that the dead leader of Nakasetjutuk had killed all the people in Aupaluttuk and they were the only ones left. The brothers used to have matches all the time before one of them died, like who is the stronger, who is the smarter and things like that. That's why the dead brother killed the people in Aupaluttuk.

There is an old saying from long ago that they should leave two people out so they can tell the other tribes that there had been a killing. I forgot how that is. A long time ago there used to be wars like that.

— Manase Fox
[4.4:14]

SIKULIAK SIUYUTUK WAS AN *inupanavualak* [giant] who was too heavy to go hunting on thin ice. He had to wait until the time that the ice became very thick and cracked by frost. During this time the other people were out hunting.

In the summer Sikuliak used to hunt alone in his kayak. Sometimes he killed whales. If a storm arose and the other Eskimos couldn't stem the wind they would tie on to his kayak. He would tow them right into the wind regardless of how many there were.

One winter a man was out hunting seals on the thin ice and killed a seal. When he was hauling the seal home Sikuliak took the seal away from him and frightened him. This same thing happened on other occasions and the Eskimos wanted to kill Sikuliak.

One day Sikuliak went out to the *sina* [ice edge] with the Eskimos to hunt for walrus and seals. This happened before the Eskimos had dogs so they travelled on foot. They went to a place called Qingaluk and made a snow-house. Then the Eskimos started plotting to kill Sikuliak.

This was the first time that Sikuliak had ever been to the *sina*. He asked an Eskimo the proper way to sleep in a snow-house. The Eskimos told him that his feet had to be bound together and his hands tied behind his back. Then they tied him well.

When Sikuliak fell asleep the Eskimos started to stab him with their lances. He started rolling and thrashing and was able to kill two men with his weight alone. The lines started to break but Sikuliak was getting too weak to free himself completely and he died.

The Eskimos started homeward in a line. They filed past Sikuliak's mother who was standing in the doorway of her house. She knew that her son had been killed because she was an *angakkuk*.

She asked each of the Eskimos whether he had killed her son. Most of the men didn't answer her. However, the last man in the line replied, "No, the others did it."

She said to the man who answered, "When the crow caws don't look around."

Later the first of the men who had refused to answer had to leave his house to urinate. While outside he heard a crow but when he looked up he saw nothing. The man died.

The other men also went outdoors and heard the crow and the same thing happened to them. Only the man who had been last in line remained alive because he had been warned not to look up.

Sikuliak's mother wanted to have another son so she started having relations with some of the men. She gave birth to two sons and said that those two would get revenge on the people that had killed her son. One of the sons had arms like a polar bear because the mother wanted it that way.

When the brothers grew up they started to kill Eskimos. They stuck lances into every kayak they saw. The Eskimos fled from the place.

The two brothers had a married sister. Their brother-in-law helped them kill the Eskimos that came to their place, which was called Silupait. When they got an Eskimo in their house the brother-in-law kept watch while the two brothers drilled a hole in his forehead and killed him.

When they saw a kayak they pursued it in the *umiavik*. When they got up to it the brother-in-law, who was steering, recognized the Eskimo as a man he had grown up with. He shoved the tiller back and forth and broke the rudder because he didn't want to kill this man.

One of the brothers said, "You broke the rudder again."

The brother-in-law replied, "Because you never made it strong enough."

The Eskimos escaped and people didn't come to Silupait any more.

The three men at Silupait used to kill seals and walrus and store them in a cave for the winter. One day two *angakkut* came to the men's house. The three men started to kill the *angakkut*, and while they were doing this their mother blocked the doorway. One of the *angakkut* jumped out through the window, which was made of *udjok* [square flipper] gut. He became a crow. The men drilled a hole in the other *angakkuk*'s forehead and his eyes popped out.

When the Eskimos heard about this they wanted to kill these three men. For an excuse to visit the three men they said that they had no meat. The three men offered them meat from their storage place and helped them get it out. The meat was frozen and difficult to remove.

The crowd of Eskimos had a strong man with them who was a Tunit. This Tunit had a knife tied to his wrist. When the brother with the polar bear arms jumped down in the place where the meat was, the Tunit jumped down and drove the knife in his back. Because the knife was tied to the Tunit's wrist the brother was unable to get away from him and he died.

When the other brother saw this he started running away to a wooden scaffold [used for meat storage] to get his bows and arrows. Just as he was almost up on the scaffold another man grabbed him and hauled him down. Because there was a large crowd of Eskimos they killed him without difficulty.

Then the Eskimos were going to kill the brother-in-law, who was also there. The brother-in-law told them that he had not wanted to do the things that he had done, and that he had only done them because he was afraid of the two brothers. He reminded them of how he had broken the rudder and so the Eskimo spared his life.

When the Eskimos went away they took the woman and her daughter's husband to their place. They forced her to cook for them. When she was cooking seal meat they had her remove it from a boiling pot with her bare hands. They made her do this because she had seen her sons kill people, and had once blocked the door while they killed people instead of trying to stop them. By removing meat in this manner the woman's finger bones became exposed.

One day the woman ran away and lived by herself. A man came and stayed with her for a while but then went away again. She wanted to have another son to help her get revenge.

The woman hunted caribou for herself. When she cooked the caribou meat, people came to her and she fed them. She saved the grease, melted it and gave it to her visitors. The grease hardened in their stomachs and they died. She did this for revenge because they made her remove meat from scalding grease.

She became pregnant and went to Saglekh, where she gave birth to a son. She placed the son in a *matsavik* [large wooden tub] full of water so that he would learn how to swim. She still wanted revenge.

When the son grew up he got a kayak and started hunting different kinds of animals to feed his mother. Several Eskimos were out in kayaks one day and saw him. They started after him and when they got close they recognized him.

The mother saw this while she was eating caribou sinew to make her son strong. She cried out for wind and the wind came. When the men got close to the boy he turned his kayak over and slipped out of it. Then he swam under all the other kayaks and split them open with his knife. He sank every one of them and swam ashore to his mother. [10.1:16]

The Tunit were very strong men. They lived formerly at Naghvakh, Saglekh, and Nosingnukuluk. They put up big rocks which can still be seen. They made caves to put their winter food in. They didn't take the fat off of harp seals and ringed seals to make their clothes. Instead they just cut off the seals' heads and flippers. They did the same for their sleeping bags. They did not want their flesh to dry up. They used caribou skin when they didn't have any seals.

The Tunits used to kill Eskimos in the night. They bored the Eskimo's foreheads until their eyes popped out. Naghvakh was formerly known as Udliujak. Two brothers ran away from the Tunits at the latter place. They wanted to return to their camp but first they wanted to find out if the Tunits were still killing people. The Tunits told them that there were no more animals at Udliujak. They kept the two brothers. The two brothers always held knives under their foreheads so that they wouldn't drowse off to sleep. They thought that if they slept they would lose their strength. *[Told to J.O. by Qingalinuk of Saglekh.]*

— Joshua Obed
[11.2:24]

NASAKULUK WAS AN *ANGAKKUK*. HE lost his father, as a boy, and had to teach himself how to hunt. His father had been shot in the head while he slept. When Nasakuluk's sister heard the shot she tried to rouse her father but, when she went to shake his head, her hand went right through the bullet hole.

When Nasakuluk was strong he went to see the man that had murdered his father. When he was ready to leave he told his cousin to get things ready because he was going away. Nasakuluk said that he wanted a drink of water. Somebody gave him a drink of water inside a person's skull. Since Nasakuluk didn't want to drink the water from the skull, he told the person to drink it himself.

A man was waiting outside of the house, with his knife, ready to kill Nasakuluk. However, Nasakuluk sensed danger and got his own knife ready. He ran out of the house and ran his dogs so fast that the man didn't have a chance to kill him. The man got on his komatik and started to pursue Nasakuluk but his dogs were not fast enough so he got off and chased him on foot. When he found that he couldn't catch Nasakuluk he gave up and returned home. He told Nasakuluk that he could not beat [him], so he [Nasakuluk] could stay in the village. [Told to N.K. by Hulda Saurak of Ramah, who heard it from Nasakuluk of Killinek. 11.4:32]

There was once an Indian woman named Iavaganak who had an Eskimo husband. She told lies that caused the Indians to come to the Eskimo camp when the men were away and kill all the people. All the people in the Eskimo camp were killed except for two women who hid away. When the men returned they looked for the Indian woman. Her husband found her and brought her out of the tent. Four Eskimo men were waiting outside and they tore her apart. This happened near Okak.

— Natan Kaujasiak
[11.4:34]

WHEN I WAS A CHILD there used to be plenty of seals anytime in the spring, in the fall. We would have plenty of dried seal meat. We lived in a tent, with a place for a bed and lots of food, seal meat, blubber and all kinds of meat right there in the tent. I did not grow up with my parents. The people I lived with had plenty seals to eat all the time. When we finished hunting seals in the spring we would go to Paul's Island where we would fish. There was lots of codfish and we had plenty of *pitsik* [dried codfish].

When I became bigger I did not go fishing with the others because I was a pet of the people who took care of me. I couldn't even cook, only Harriet, who would also fish, would cook when she got home. She would cook in big metal pots. I was given the job of fetching water. When I woke up in the morning, while everyone had gone fishing, I would find some candies by my pillow. These are things I remember when I was a child.

There would be lots of fishermen and many schooners. They had no motors or engines. Those days they rowed the big schooners. If it was a calm day you would see some of them being towed into Paul's Island. The fishermen from the schooners would come ashore and we, not knowing how to understand or speak English, would make each other understand by motions and hand talking.

The fishermen would come in their schooners and anchor out in the harbour at Paul's Island on Sundays. The grown-ups would go aboard while the children stayed at home in the tent. Sometimes when we stayed at home like that we would pretend that we were white people. We used long clothes that weren't anything like the real white man's clothes. We would think that we were so pretty once we were dressed as *kablunaks* [white people]. The other children who were staying home with me, when they saw the boats coming ashore, would hurry and take their make-believe clothes off...not me though. I would be wearing Harriet's long skirt and her blouse and I thought I was so pretty and elegant. When they got ashore they would have a big laugh at me, who was the only one dressed up and being so proud.

Long ago and many years back, when there was no white people, the Eskimos would make things out of flint. They would use diamond to sharpen tools. That is why we would be looking for flints all the time when we were children. That was the only thing that would be able to break the rocks or stones, the diamonds. I don't know much about the real early days. They did all kinds of bad things, even had wars among themselves, and fighting. And the Indians had been around at different times. They said the Indians could not be seen, they even said the Indians turned into rocks or stones. The Indians and Eskimos feared each other. The Indians were called Naskaupis. These are stories that have been passed down to me.

In earlier days all the men used kayaks, only, to hunt seals in the spring. They would bring back lots of seals. They would dry sealskins by stretching them and pegging them to the ground by wooden pegs. They would take the fat off by rubbing them on rocks or land. The skins would turn out so clean without even washing them. The women would make plenty of skinboots. These days nobody knows how to clean skins, make skinboots, or make kayaks. I don't remember too much now. When I was a young girl I was able to clean skins and make skinboots. I learned by watching. These days we are all wearing old store-bought shoes, all of us.

I don't want to tell a story anymore.

— Susan Martin
[2.1:32]

WE, THE INUIT HERE IN Labrador, right to this day still have the traditional ways of our forefathers. Right to this day we eat what our forefathers used to eat, food with no price tags on it, food created for us ever since the earth was created. People have different foods according to their land. This I was not aware of in the past. Some eat only what is grown in gardens, others eat whatever food they can get their hands on and we, the Inuit people, have a different diet because we are people of a cold land. Because we are people of a cold land, wildlife is our main diet. Our forefathers were strong because nothing was scarce, everything was plentiful in those past years. We, the younger generation, think we are hungry but we are not because there is plenty of the white man's foods available for us to obtain at any time. We are only hungry for wildlife meat because some years are plentiful and some years there is none at all. This I have found.

Our forefather's ancestors, which we have just heard of but not seen, taught our fathers how to share any kill made amongst their people. So my father taught me to share my kill as it was the traditional way. When I was a young man every time I went hunting and came back successful I invited the poor, the less fortunate and the old Inuit to share my kill. After they had eaten they would joke around and tell stories of the past. When I heard these happy people I was aware that this was a blessing. I had made my fellow people happy through sharing. Our Creator had blessed me and I had carried on this blessing by sharing because this was meant to be. It is sad how this tradition is being forgotten. Young people now keep their kill to themselves. Some will give a little to those they wish to share with. I have said what I have seen and experienced and I am aware that this tradition is no longer practiced. I hope this will be written down so that our children can be made aware of what used to take place in past years.

We have not lost all our traditions and culture yet. We have not lost our ability to hunt wildlife game. We know how to locate and hunt the game. Our young men still try to hunt in the traditional ways but they have difficulties because there is less game now. But our young Inuit have not given up trying their best to hunt for wildlife food. This will never be lost as long as there are Inuit in Labrador.

I am one hundred percent pure Eskimo. I was never educated in the white society way because when I was a child this was not practiced. Our school term lasted only six months and our main subject was studying the word of God. We had to memorize Bible verses and speak them out from memory while our teachers listened. The only time we were given a new verse was when we mastered the one before. Because of this teaching we, the elderly Inuit, can still speak out by heart many verses of the Bible, at least I always could. I don't know of my fellow elders but I'm sure they too can speak out what they memorized as children. In this generation our children have almost a whole year to learn and study but they are learning only the white society way. No wonder they have a better knowledge than we, the elderly. I am not happy that they are only being taught the white society system. I would be happy if they were taught first the word of God, then how to deal with life....

In such a short time we, the Inuit of Labrador, have changed in many ways. We do not carry on many of our traditions. We are forced into many new ways which we do not even understand. Also in these days we have seen the Inuit from other regions, those we had only heard about but we did not know if they had traditions and cultures which were similar to ours. Now, we see them in the flesh and see that our fellow Inuit share our traditions and culture....

I wish you peace on earth. We may never see each other on earth but through God's will we will see each other in Heaven when we are removed from the earth. So, let us look forward to meeting each other where there will be no pain or sorrow but happiness and eternal life. I am an old man now. My name is Martin Martin. I wish all a happy and successful life.

— Martin Martin
[2.2:56]

GOGUSIUTILLUTA HEBRONEME NALUJUALUIT tikitldaKattalauutut Nalujune Januar 6-ime Nalujulluasiagaluit...In Hebron, when I was small, the *nalujuks* used to come on Nalujuk's Night, January 6th. Real jannies, they were, wearing seal skin and caribou skin clothing and face masks. Some had swords, some had sticks and they had real guns, too. They used to even come inside the church, and me sitting in the front with the rest of the kids. They used to have a lot of goodies, candies, clothing and much more. You were told to sing a song or a hymn before you got your present from them. They used to have real big bags in front and on their backs. I think the *nalujuks* used to get the things to give away from the local store.

Some of the *nalujuks* wore *amautiks*, and they'd tell the children that if any of them were bad in the past year, they'd carry them in their hood and take them away, faraway somewhere. One time old Abel Atsatata was staying with Markus Lidd and two *nalujuks* came in and told him to sing, and he started to sing. He was only trembling, and he was making too many mistakes. One of the *nalujuks* had a real gun, a .44. He cocked the trigger, ready to go off. Abel went into hiding under the table, and the *nalujuk* really made it look like he was really going to shoot him, even though he didn't have real bullets. Abel went hiding under the table and I was sitting on top of the table. Abel was some scared!

Our parents used to let the *nalujuks* in the house and tell them that we never listened to them, and our parents would tell the *nalujuks* to take us away.

When my wife was a child, some *nalujuks* came to her house by breaking the door in half with a sword. And one time when my wife was small and the other kids' parents told them to go out and light candles outside, so they went and lit up the candles. All of a sudden, they saw two *nalujuks* and they started running to the house. They used to fall down, and when they got to the porch, they were so many of them that they couldn't get the door opened. The *nalujuks* couldn't get in the house either. The kids were all crying too. One *nalujuk* had a real scary face and the other one was limping, had one of his legs all bandaged up in canvas. They were some scared that time.

When I was small we used to find things in our stockings on Nalujuk Day [Old Christmas Day, January 6], anything from candies to homemade toys. But when I became a teenager I used to smoke on the sly. Then one Nalujuk Day, I found old pipe tobacco ashes, not new either, old ashes I found. I didn't like what I found one bit, even though I found some toys and candies along with the ashes. We were very happy though that time. Later on we never found anything more, maybe because I peeked at the *nalujuks* when they were filling our stockings during the night, because after that I never found anything anymore. Some bad, nothing in your stocking on Nalujuk morning.

— Boas Obed
[6.2:14]

THE EARLY ESKIMO HAD no music [instruments] except for the drum, and the drum dance was not so much music as a feat of strength. If you have seen pictures of the drum dances, you will realize that the people who performed these dances were athletes in their way. But the Moravians, of course, I'm afraid, drove the old drum dances underground. I don't know why. Because they were connected with heathenism, I suppose, the people became ashamed of them in the course of time and didn't use them any longer. I have never seen the drum dances, except on films. They beat the drum and wave it around. It needs a strong man to keep the drum going, I can assure you. He doesn't just sit down with the drum in front of him, but he moves around with it.

I remember my chagrin and disgust, on going through the diary for the Mission station at Nain in the year 1771, to get to a point where the missionary said that tomorrow the Eskimos were holding their Festival of the Sun. This was the heathen Eskimo of course. And then the writer went on, later in the diary, to say that the heathen ceremonies were too disgusting and tedious to mention. I thought that I had really come across something about the old dances and the old customs, and here I was disappointed in this.

The Moravians brought church music, many of the Bach chorales and the music of the church, to Labrador when they came in 1771. The scripts of the music along the coast is mostly hand-written, being copied from books which the Moravians brought over.

The real name of the Moravian Church is the Church of the *Unitas Fratrum*, or United Brethren. The Moravian Church began in Czechoslovakia, and it was the first church to give the people of the congregation a hymn book in their own language. This was early in the sixteenth century. The Moravian Church was driven underground and was renewed in Hernhut, in Saxony, in 1722, and they came to be known as 'God's singing people.' There are all sorts of services in which there is just singing. For instance, in the Saturday evening singing meeting on the continent of Europe, the minister sits down in the church and starts the hymns himself, and there are probably ten or fifteen hymns with a reading of the text. Most of the ministers were good singers. In 1824, the Mission introduced stringed instruments to the Eskimos.

Incidentally, just last year the Nain choir went to St. John's, Newfoundland and gave a performance in the cathedral there. There were fourteen members in the Nain Choir under the choir director, Jeremias Sillitt of Nain. There were ten singers and four instrumentalists. There was a television broadcast and performance in the cathedral and a special performance for the Premier [Joey Smallwood] at his ranch. I just can't remember all the names of the choir members but most of them are children of the people who sang in the choir when I first came to Labrador. It's surprising how the musical ability seems to be handed down from generation to generation. It's a tradition for certain families to support the choir...

If you went into the church in Nain, you would notice that there are letters on the [organ] keyboard, the notes of the scale. They go up to the eighth, and all the octaves are marked on the keyboard. A boy would go up there and he would sit down and start fingering them out, then someone would come along and show him a little bit. The boy will persist and, in the course of time, he will learn to play the organ. He is allowed to play the Voluntary when people go into the church and then, later on, he'll be playing hymns. Then he is really self-taught. He has had some help from the organist, or some other interested person, but he has done most of the work himself. It's the same way with the violins and cello. David Harris, who is the organist at Nain, gave quite an amazing performance for a man who had never seen a church organ before. He was a pupil of my wife for three months, and that's all the training he had. David is quite an accomplished organist.

It is common for the choir members to have their music hand-written. There is printed music, of course, which had been copied by the Eskimos, and then the old books got destroyed, gradually, and people copied them out. There is a supply of note paper, music paper, on the Mission station for the Eskimos to copy out their music, and they are always copying out some music. It's usually the work of one person, and in Nain it's David Harris, and I think that his manuscripts are really amazing.

The church choirs have certain numbers that they perform every year, for example, the Hosanna Anthem, which was written in the sixteenth century and is traditional in the Moravian Church, and is sung at Advent and on Palm Sunday.

The Eskimos also had brass bands. I don't say that they are the best brass bands in the world, but they play with plenty of enthusiasm. On Christmas morning they are out, about six o'clock, going around from house to house giving the call to 'awake,' I suppose to those who are not already awake. Then on Easter morning they start out about an hour before sunrise, or before the sunrise service, which starts half an hour before sunrise, and they go from house to house. Sometimes they get out at three and half-past three in the morning and play. In the early mornings it is rather difficult conditions to play brass instruments, out in the cold and snow. They take spare players with them, and each instrument is covered with a duffel bag and they play underneath the bag, as it were. It doesn't muffle the sound very much, as I can attest to since I've been awakened on many occasion by the brass band. However conditions are difficult and sometimes, as I said, the instruments freeze up.

The brass bands also play at other festival days, such as the Single Brethren's Festival [young men's day], and the Single Sister's Festival [young women's day], Children's, Married People's, and Widow's Festivals. Also before a celebration of Holy Communion the brass band stands outside the church and plays as the worshippers are going in to Holy Communion. When everyone is inside, the band members then come in and take their places in the congregation. This is traditional and I think it comes from the continent of Europe.

The Eskimos love music, there is no doubt about that and, while in the churches they love the old Bach chorales and old German hymns which have been translated into Eskimo, they also love the western music. When I had my own radio station in Nain, I used to have a group called The Nain Singers and they sang cowboy and western type music. Their leader was Sidney Dicker. Sidney doesn't sing in the church choir, but his wife does. Sidney is the nephew of old Jim Dicker who used to be the old cooper for the Hudson's Bay Company at Rigolet...

— Rev. F.W. Peacock, *Unitas Fratrem*
[12.2:26]

KESEK KAYAK ELLONE SENEVEUGAME tusanedlamat sogosaudlonga... When I was a little girl, I was eight years old, my dad used to take me in his kayak. When I got very sleepy, he used to put me inside his kayak, up front. I used to hear him ask to sing him a song about the waves lapping against the side of the boat.

Little Maria, sleeping on the tiny waves,
When she's inside the kayak.

Takseakujauvogalo emak
Mariagolak
persekapuk
malleagolait
kangetegut
sajokaumejarlone.

— Judith Solomon
[3.2:20]

THERE WAS A LITTLE MAN, Albert Jararuse. He was almost too old to hunt but he was always on the go. He gave up keeping a dog team and everywhere he went in winter he walked. He was a widower and, because he was so happy, he was welcome anywhere. So I'd see him with a bundle on his back leaving to go visiting. He usually came to say good-bye. He'd say it was probably the last time because he was getting so old, maybe he'd die this time. He'd go off laughing…be gone perhaps a couple of months, and every so often someone would bring in a pelt or two or a roll of new sealskin line or something to trade for him. Then one day I'd hear him chuckling in the porch and he'd come in, all smiles, and shake hands. He'd be around for a while and then he'd be gone again. In the summer he'd come and go by kayak. During the trout and cod seasons, he'd fish with someone or other. I don't think he'd get much more than his food, but that's all he wanted.

Albert came up to my shoulder and was half again as wide. He was enormously strong. He could go day and night and never tire. His teeth were worn level with his gums from being used as a third hand, and most of his fingers were damaged from harpoon lines and the like. I would go a long way off my track just to see Albert. Anyway, when he'd run in from his camp and had told me how old and tired he was, I'd give him a mug of black tea and all the hard biscuits he wanted. Then he'd put his packsack on, sing me a little song about himself, something foolish to make me laugh. Then he'd be away. He had a brother, Conrad, about the same size and about the same age. They might even have been twins, but I don't think so—someone would have told me.

Well, once Willie Mille walked up in Hebron fjord to pick up a small boat that he had left. He said he'd go hunting while he was up there and if I'd give him a few days he'd probably have meat for the whole camp. He suggested that I come up in the motor boat and pick him and the meat up. He also said that Albert and Conrad would be glad to go along and help bring the meat to the boat, in case he made a kill far from the water.

So a few days later, the happy brothers and I left and spent all day going up in the head of the bay. There is a lovely little harbour there and some willows big enough to make a fire. So we camped there. Willie's boat was there but there was no sign of Willie.

It was early fall, gorgeous weather, no flies. I had a tent which we put up and we had a meal. It was still light so Albert and Conrad went down to a gorge in the rocks that must have been there for many years to wait for a possible seal. I went down to take a look. They had it very comfortable. There was a big flat rock to sit on and enough shelter that a seal could only see two round heads together. He might even mistake them for a couple of ducks on the rocks. Conrad had a monstrous old Martini-Henry rifle, a relic of the Boer War, and Albert had a Winchester 44/40, I'm sure one of the first ever made. Looking at them and their equipment I figured no seal would have a chance, or perhaps all the chances he needed, so I went back to the tent and lay on my sleeping robe, very content indeed. It is one of the prettiest places I've ever seen, and the valley runs straight west so I had a magnificent sunset to admire.

I guess I was half asleep when Conrad's old Martini-Henry went off and shook the tent and sent every gull and duck for miles squawking and flying around. I looked out and there were the two chuckling hunters launching Willie's boat to retrieve a small seal. A few moments later they came up the hill with the choice parts of a young ranger. They had already collected a huge bundle of dry willows and in a short time had a fire going and a pail of meat cooking.

Those two old men, who had never been very far apart, seemed to have an enormous lot to talk about, and when they talked they laughed. I sat with them and listened. They were in their element, lots of tea and tobacco and a big pot of meat on the fire.

When the meat was cooked I ate a few choice bits they picked out for me and went to my bed. They sat there in front of the fire, their sleeping bags rolled up to lean against, and they went to work on the pot of meat. I woke once or twice and they were still eating and talking. Then I woke, it was dark but there was some light from the fire. My two heroes were sound asleep just sitting there with the empty pot between them. They had sealskin clothing so they would be warm. I went back to sleep.

I was awakened an hour later by a hail from across the valley. It was Willie announcing that he was on his way up. I took the boat to go across the river to pick him up, and my two jolly boys got going on the fire again, in the full hope and expectation that Willie would have some nice pieces of meat for the pot.

Willie had a heavy load and, as soon as he dropped it by the fire, Albert gave him some hot tea and a bit of seal to keep him happy while the deer meat cooked.

You wouldn't believe what those two little gourmets ate, you'd think they'd been starving for weeks. While he ate, Willie told us where he'd got the deer, quite a long way, and he said there were lots of wolves so we'd have to get the meat soon as a pack of hungry wolves can foul and spoil much more meat than they will eat.

So, wouldn't you know, the two little old men said they'd leave right away, in the pitch dark. I wondered how they'd ever find the meat in that darkness, but Willie only grinned. He said they knew where to go and when they got close enough, about a mile or so, they'd smell it. So, instead of waiting for Willie to have a sleep and go with him, I decided to go with Conrad and Albert. I figured they were pretty old, they'd eaten two huge meals, I'd have no bother keeping up.

They must have been able to see in the dark like cats. We went across the level valley to the foot of the steep hills at a pretty good clip. When we started to climb they went along like it was day. I kept putting my feet where I thought there was rock only to find there wasn't and nearly falling on my face. Then I'd put my foot where I was sure it was level and I'd end up with it on a high rock. In a short time I realized that the Natives were slowing down, not because they were old and getting tired but because of me. All I could see in the dark was a faint white shadow, a flour sack that Conrad had on his back to bring home the deer sinew in. So I followed the sack. I'd never been over on that part of the valley and I was willing to swear that the hill was twice as high as Everest and many times steeper. Those two little men with their short bow legs were completely tireless. We climbed and climbed. You know how long a road is when you don't know it, I began to wonder if we'd ever get to the top, much less ever find the meat.

Albert was behind me, Conrad was leading. Suddenly I felt Albert's hand on my arm, he whispered to be quiet. I just stood there and in a short time I was aware of the smell of wolves, very close. At the time I didn't know we were travelling on a narrow ledge and that the wolves would have to be directly ahead or behind. I knew there was no danger but it was an eerie feeling, just standing there, knowing that there were wolves also just standing and listening to us. In a little while we could hear the whisper of their feet as they went away from us. They were ahead and I guess they had waited for us to catch up to find out what kind of creatures we were. At this point the lads decided to stop for a smoke. I got up just to move around a little and Conrad quietly told me to be careful. I asked why and he picked up a rock and threw it out in front of us. My heart nearly stopped when, after a long time, it crashed far down the side of the hill. I knew then that we were on a ledge for sure. Conrad lit his pipe and in the light of the match I could see his eyes looking at me with a world of mischief in them. His chuckle and Albert's answering gurgle were enough.

We went on and believe me I stuck very close to my guides. They were like goats, never a misstep, never a stumble. I, in all my life, never wished more for a flashlight or any source of light.

By the time I realized that we had reached the top of the hill and were walking more or less on the level, the moon, which had been hidden by the hill on the far side, became visible. It shone right into the valley. The river, now far below, looked like a strip of molten silver. The side of the mountain where we were was bathed in its radiance and the far side was darkly forbidding, but what a scene! I suppose we may have been two thousand feet up, and we had a clear view of all around. To the east we could see all Hebron Bay like a great looking glass. To the west, a wild jumble of mountains that looked impossible to reach but which I knew had many passes all familiar to the two little men who stood beside me. They too were moved by the great panorama under the great silver orb. Miles and miles of unimaginable beauty, lovely and silent. I thought, 'how many moons had lit this fantastic scene, over how many centuries?' And all that beauty had been seen by only a minute number of people. The land may have looked empty but we had reason to know that a great life pulsed under the myriads of stars that seemed to come down to the very hills around us. The air was completely still. Albert lit a match and held it over his head and pointed across the valley. There was an answering twinkle, so small as to be almost invisible. Willie had seen and had answered.

I could hardly tear myself away but the small men were moving restlessly and we moved on. I could see much better. The climb was behind us and we would move faster. In about an hour more of steady trotting, with me making all the noise and my two little men stepping almost noiselessly along, we stopped again. They stood, with mouths wide open, inhaling the fresh cool air. One of them gave a grunt of satisfaction and we turned at right angles to the left and started down a steep incline into another valley. But it wasn't far. In about half an hour we had found the deer, all neatly butchered and laid out on the rocks to cool. They had smelled the meat.

Conrad and Albert had two large sealskin sacks each, which they filled with meat. I hefted one and found that it was considerably heavier than I would have wanted to carry across that mountain and down into the valley. These fellows contemplated carrying two. I had a regular packsack. In the division of meat, they gave me solid joints with little bone protruding to hurt my unaccustomed back. There were strips of back fat which we ate raw, and we had a drink from a little clear lake. Then we started back. It was somewhere near midnight by the clock. There were many hours of darkness ahead. Conrad and Albert had enormous loads. They had put their sacks, securely roped together, on their backs, with a thin strip of seal skin across the front of their shoulders and chests. A most uncomfortable way, as far as I was concerned, but that's how they all carried in that country.

Then they rolled up the deer skins and, with many chuckles, loaded them on one another's backs 'till all that could be seen in the moonlight was two very large bundles with an exceedingly short pair of legs under each and a bright spot of fire from the two pipes, which lit up two good humored faces as they alternately glowed and darkened as their owners drew the smoke into their mouths.

I slung my packsack on my back, with some misgivings that I had bitten off more than I could chew, and they loaded a couple of deer hides on me. There was no weight but the size of the bundle made me feel top heavy.

Most of the way back was downhill and only now did I realize that it's not all fun going down a steep slope in darkness, because the moon had now moved across the valley. The site of our camp was now lit but we were in total darkness as soon as we started down. That was a long night. I knew now that we had passed across some dangerous spots on the way up. Those places were all that much more dangerous now that we were heavily loaded. Conrad and Albert never faltered, their feet seemed to have sight. Now and then one or the other would put a hand on my arm and direct me across places that I couldn't see.

You can believe that I was more than a little weary. I had been born in the country and I'd had my share of walking and carrying, but never under those conditions. We stopped now and then for the quiet little men to light their pipes, and once while a dozen or so deer slipped past almost without a sound. I could smell them and had no difficulty understanding how Conrad and Albert could smell the meat so far away.

When we reached the boat I was glad to dump my packsack and take the oars to row us across the swift river. Conrad and Albert kept their loads on and sat chuckling while I rowed. On the far side they slipped out of the boat like men who had not gone farther perhaps than the river's edge.

Willie had tea ready. I drank a cup and headed for my bed. My companions sat near the fire drinking tea and telling Willie their story. Some time later, Willie came in and lay down. I could see the old men still muttering together, sitting as they do with their legs stretched out in front. The tea pail was sitting near them.

Dimly I remember Willie getting up some time later and preparing to leave to get the last meat and skins. I looked out and could see my heroes sound asleep sitting just where I had seen them last.

The sun was high and the air was cool and fresh as only a Labrador morning can be, when a gentle hand patted my arm. I looked up into a wrinkled brown face, a most friendly, smiling face, and smelled the freshly cooked meat that Albert had brought to me. The partners had decided to show me some of the country in the daylight while we were waiting for Willie to return.

We climbed the steep hill behind the tent, a long climb and, as the sun was up now and the air was warm, we took it easy with frequent rests to look at the scenery. Far away to the southwest I could see the road we had taken the previous night, and with a telescope I could make out the narrow ledge across the face of a steep cliff that we had climbed. I didn't even try to estimate how far a man would have fallen had he tripped.

The view from the top of the hill was also impressive. One could look down a long valley out on Hebron Bay and an extensive scope of calm water. To the northeast one could see into another valley which I could see must come to the coast somewhere north of Hebron. The valley on which we were camped went straight as an arrow to the foot of a range of high mountains. The river, making many twists and turns, followed the valley. At our feet was the little harbour with the motor boat looking like a toy on its placid surface.

Where we were standing there was a large *inukshuk*. It had been built many, many years ago. All the surfaces were covered with a deep mass of lichen, which takes hundreds of years to develop. The only sign that modern man had ever been there were two ancient 450 Express shells, carefully filled with sand and stood in a recess of the stones. They too had a growth of lichen. Seeing that the 450 Express was an elephant gun in the days of the British conquest of India, one could surmise that the shells had been put there by someone so long ago that he wasn't likely to be above ground now, unless in a cozy pile of rocks some place. I was right. Neither Conrad nor Albert could tell me anything about the shells. They had been there as long as they could remember.

Albert was serious for once and he held my arm in his strong fingers as he pointed out the various valleys and told me where they led and what could be found in them. In the valley where we were camped we saw several small herds of caribou. The brothers hooted with laughter to see them as we had gone to so much trouble and effort to bring meat down from the mountain while it was in the valley all the time. It was no accident that Willie had gone to the hills for his deer. He wanted sleeping skins, and that was where he could find them. Most of the animals in the valley were does and fawns, neither the meat nor the skins had time to mature.

Away up the valley we could see the remains of a large snow slide. Albert said that it was a dangerous place to be as snow collected on the side of the hill and could fall at any time. He told me of two young men who had been caught there many years before. They had escaped by running up hill, but had lost their team and equipment.

The valley was the bed of a great river at one time. It rose in half a dozen terraces, ancient beaches. On these terraces the caribou grazed and from our hill they could be easily seen. A man on a hill therefore had visual command of miles and miles of country. Several men placed in strategic places would be able to wait in comfort for game, never having to make long, perhaps unproductive hunts.

Albert pointed down to where our solitary tent stood and indicated a collection of tent [rings] and turf igloos. "Very fine place to live in old days." And I could see that it had been, the river teeming with char—I had seen them there in their millions in spring and fall—seals to be had on the ice and in the sea in Hebron Bay and the northeast fjord; caribou in the valleys and on the hillsides. It was also easy to see how a whale might follow a capelin run into the narrows and might be prevented from going out by a group of kayaks and umiaks. And Albert pointed out that if they could herd the huge animal into the bay and keep it there, the falling tide would expose the rocks at the entrance and the whale would conceivably ground. If not it could be harpooned and lanced. The Tunits were reputed to be big people. They had huge harpoons. They could easily kill the whale. How much of that last was imagination, how much true, I don't guess, but the country as he pointed out was ideal in all respects.

It was a lovely day and we sat there a long time scanning every possible area with our telescopes. Conrad had one and I had another, but Albert looked so left out that I gave him mine. They would lie behind a rock and hardly move for minutes before they went on to the next spot. When they were finished there wasn't a thing of interest, from the top of that hill, that they hadn't seen.

At one point they laughed heartily, almost rolling on the ground. Albert gave me my telescope and pointed to the area in front of the tent, far below. Directly in front of the gorge, where the two rifles still stood, was a huge square flipper, lying flat in the water, just enjoying the sun. The most valuable seal there is to the Natives, and there they were on top of a hill while it floated only yards from their guns. The greatest of all possible jokes.

Finally, far across the valley, on top of the mountain, Conrad spotted Willie returning and we watched his tiny figure cross the top and start down towards the valley. When he was directly opposite and about at the same level as we were, Conrad gave his strange melodic call, and after a while we heard a faint reply. The irrepressible Albert immediately sent a chorus of goose honks and raven belling across the valley, so true to life that if I hadn't seen him I'd have been looking for the birds. All he got in reply was one derisive honk from Willie.

We got down to the tent and had everything collected and loaded into the motor boat when Willie got there. The first thing he did, after putting down a load of heavy meat, was to chase Albert all over the camp site, honking like a goose while Albert, bursting with laughter, jumped around and over rocks to evade capture by his much younger attacker.

We finally got away just as the tide started to fall and thus had a fair current with us on the way home. Then, with Willie at the tiller and I comfortably lying in the bow, Conrad and Albert had their first real sleep since we had left Hebron. Side by side, half sitting up, with their heads against the side of the boat, they slept like babes. They were old men, more than that, they were tough old men. They carried more than their own weight for hours on end. Short and stocky, faces wrinkled and marked by storms of half a century and more, their powerful hands bearing the scars of all sorts of accidents, they were indestructible men. They were two, perhaps, as far as I was concerned, a special two, in a camp where they were by no means exceptional. Gotran de Poncius defines Inuk as "a man pre-eminently." Conrad and Albert would be convulsed with laughter, but de Poncius wasn't in any way in error. They were exceptional men and you can understand how much I respected and admired them. I saw a lot of those cheerful little men; never once did I hear a word of complaint, not one remark that wasn't happy.

— Leonard Budgell
HBC Factor, Hebron
[13.1:53]

AN ESKIMO NAMED PAUNGALUK [JOSHUA'S first wife's father, later known as Jako Jararuse] once saw an *ingaraulik* [dwarf]. It had a kayak just as big as any Eskimo's and it had two polar bear skins inside of its kayak. The dwarf was skinning an *udjok* [seal] beside its kayak and started to eat some of the meat in spite of the fact that Paungaluk was watching. When it was putting the meat in its kayak, it saw Paungaluk and gave him a share. Paungaluk said "Thank you!" Then the dwarf started paddling out to sea. When he started the wind came.

— Joshua Obed
[10.3:40]

IT WAS THE YEAR 1918. The month, October. The place Okak, my home and birthplace. The Moravian Mission freight boat, *Harmony*, just arrived after a long journey across the Atlantic and up the coast to deliver food and supplies to small Eskimo communities for the winter. There was great joy at the sight of the small freight boat. Hundreds of people were on the shore shouting, singing, and even shooting to salute the arriving of the boat. I have never heard so many voices as that day in my life.

After all the unloading has finished, when everything is done, we would then leave for our hunting grounds for the fall. We would remain there until the ice is strong enough for us to travel on dogteam. Then we would return to Okak. That fall the *Harmony* would take more families to their hunting grounds, for each family would have a house of their own. The last family to be brought was Jerry Sillitt.

The doctor there in Okak warn people and predicted there was going to be a flu. The sign was the Northern Lights were bright red. Even the snow was pink from the reflection. Then we know there was going to be something happening which we never thought would be anything as bad as epidemic flu.

Jerry Sillitt, father of Gustav Sillitt, was the first person to die. He was already not too well when they arrived on the *Harmony*. Not long after his death we found that everyone was sick with flu. Hardly any person was able to stand up. Finally, my husband and two children died and few more members of the house. There was only myself and another woman left. We moved to my house and left the other house for there were bodies lying on the floor and on the beds. There was fewer bodies in my house which we share night and day. During towards night after we go to bed we would look at the unusually large star moving westward. We would wonder what it is.[10]

The other family living pretty close to us came over when they finally gain more strength from their sickness. There was only two women and two young men left from their family. All the rest died from the flu. One of the young men was Gustav Sillitt. One woman was Maria, Gustav's sister. Her child died soon after they moved to us. Gustav sang a hymn and placed the child next to the other bodies.

Nobody was strong enough to do anything, even to chop wood for firewood. There was plenty enough food, for those people saved enough fish, meat, and berries from the fall. We would not have any light in the house even when it was dark.

Those people who got sick did not suffer any pain, except they would have a very bad cold in their chest and they'll be very sleepy. Some don't even wake up and die sleeping.

There were many dogs. None of the dogs got sick and were roaming all over.

As the Flu went on, we did not even know what day it was or even what date. Then we realize through the full moon that it must be near Christmas. By that time, everyone who was left was well enough. We started out for Okak. When we got there, only a few people were left. There was not one grown up man left, only young men. There were few women and children. The only men left was the minister, doctor, and store manager. The manager's wife died in the flu. Those men dig a huge hole in the ground and placed in it three or four hundred bodies altogether.

When the houses were cleared up, there were many belongings and clothes lying around outdoors. Even now I don't like to see clothing lying around outdoors. Also I don't like to see people sleeping on the floor. These things are reminders of the horrible sickness that once happened when I was still in my young life. I still don't know how much courage we had to face all that terrible sickness. I still often look for this unusual star we used to watch and never seen again.

A person will never die unless the day has come for his end. My name is Emelia Merkuratsuk. I am now seventy-nine years old.

— Emelia Merkuratsuk
[1.2:54]

IN THE LATE SUMMER AND autumn of 1918 we in Hopedale were visited by an epidemic of what is undoubtedly a modified form of small-pox, which swept through the whole village, only one member of the Mission staff, one Eskimo woman, and a few children escaping. It carried off six adults. Br. Bohlman, who attends to the medical work, was kept busy for some weeks attending to the sick, but, with the sufferings of the afflicted the sisters were likewise called on to do their share by making large pots of soup daily for those who had no appetite for native or home-prepared foods. We did not get clear of this epidemic 'till well on in January, when boils, sore eyes, showed themselves very numerously, and caused quite a large amount of inconvenience and pain. After communication with our scattered members opened, and intercourse became more frequent, the disease gradually spread to the isolated homes in the bays, and some of these are even now (end of March) not free from the sickness. Among the Settlers and half-breeds the attacks were much milder than among the pure-blooded Eskimos, giving clear proof that the native is not able to withstand the white man's diseases as well as the white man himself is, even though conditions of life are exactly similar in both cases.

When the *Harmony* arrived from Nain in November 1918, we received news that the Nain congregation had likewise been passing through an epidemic of small-pox. It had been brought to Hopedale and Nain by patients who had visited the Indian Harbour Hospital. But Nain had an epidemic of measles at the same time. They escaped in 1916, when the other stations passed through the measles epidemic, but now had to fight the two complaints at the same time. The ravages wrought by the two epidemics raging simultaneously were severe, and the result at Nain shows a considerable reduction in membership for the year 1918.

These visitations we thought very heavy, and all our people felt that the hand of God had been laid heavily upon them. Little did we dream of what was happening at Hebron and Okak and that our experiences were not a patch on what the missionaries and their flocks there were passing through in their terrible isolation. Immediately after the departure of the *Harmony* from Hebron—even, in fact, before the *Harmony* left—the natives showed signs of having contracted the Spanish Influenza from a sick sailor. Captain Jackson had forbidden the natives to visit the crew's quarters, warning them of the infectious nature of the sickness, but they paid no heed to him. The result was that in the course of about nine days nearly two-thirds of the Hebron congregation were corpses. Indeed, if one reckons the people who were in Hebron itself, the percentage is nearly nine-tenths, for out of 100 people at the station, only 14 survived. That so many names are still on the Hebron books is only attributable to the fact that the Ramah and Napartok people had no connection with the ship or with their afflicted fellow-countrymen.

One cannot describe what the Hebron brethren and Sisters must have passed through during those dreadful days. More or less sick themselves, they did what they possibly could for the stricken natives; but in reality they could do nothing to stop the fearful epidemic. Bishop Martin fetched water and wood for houses where all the inmates were sick, and with what help was available removed the corpses as one after another died; but at last there was no one to help, and Sr. Martin went with her husband to perform the gruesome task. They could not carry the dead bodies, so they had to haul them by a rope; but at length even that became impossible—the number was too great. They had perforce to desist from the work—it was more than they could manage—and the few living had to leave the houses where the dead were and congregate in a couple of houses that had been cleared of dead bodies. Then the true nature of the Eskimo dogs showed itself. Probably excited by the smell of the dead bodies, they just went wild, dashed through the windows of the houses, and pulled down the doors and fell to eating human flesh. In some cases they seem even to have attacked the living who were not strong enough to beat them off, and tore them to pieces before life had really left their bodies. Providentially, the weather was cold and the bodies froze. If this had not been the case, who can imagine what would have happened.

Of the disposal of about 80 bodies, by burying them in the sea, the Brethren's letters will tell. It was the only way they could think of, as it seemed an impossible task to undertake to dig a grave large enough to hold all. Many of the native huts were then set fire to—the quickest and safest way of disposing of mangled human remains and nests of filth and indescribable horrors. Br. Merklin (the store-keeper) and an Eskimo started shooting the dogs, as soon as they were strong enough to handle a rifle, and probably some 80 to 100 of these are lying in the village buried in the snow and will have to be disposed of as they thaw out in the spring. Much work of a most disagreeable nature still lies before the Brethren as they will need stout hearts and strong arms to accomplish the task.

But meanwhile the *Harmony* had gone to Okak and there the Eskimos immediately opened intercourse with the sailors with results as at Hebron. When the *Harmony* left Okak the people were beginning to fall sick, and the sickness spread like wildfire. Crews went off to their sealing places only to fall sick and die. Some tried to get back to Okak and failed, portions of the boats crews dying on the way. In some settlements a small remnant survived to tell the story, but at some places all died. I will not attempt to repeat what I heard from the Brethren; their letters will tell of the tragedies. The Brethren Waldmann, Asboe, and Ward have done an immense amount of work in disposing of the dead and caring for the living.

In Okak and at several of the sealing places the dogs played havoc with the corpses. At Sillutalik 36 persons died, but only 18 remained to be buried. The only visible remains of the others were a few bare skulls and a few shank-bones lying around in the houses. Possibly other remains will appear when the snow melts. Most touching was the case of a little girl of eight years of age. The Brethren received the news that the family at Olearsuk was sick and dying, and Br. Waldmann made an attempt to visit them by boat, but had to give up owing to very heavy weather and high seas. They could only conclude that during the interval of freezing up all had died, as no one came from there. Before Christmas two lads went to the place from Okak to fetch a barrel of berries and, looking through the window of the house, saw someone moving about, but concluding it was a ghost they beat a hasty retreat. About three weeks later the Brethren went to bury what remained of the corpses and to shoot the dogs. Br. Ward entered the house and was about to shoot a dog when he heard a voice, and looking around was surprised to find a little girl alive. She had had sense enough to thaw snow by the heat of a candle, and thus obtained a little water to drink, and had made use of a tin of milk and some berries to keep body and soul together, but was living there with the dead which were being eaten by the dogs. When the lads visited the place her little brother was still alive and might undoubtedly have been saved had the lads been more sensible, but before the Brethren came to the place the little fellow had also succumbed. They immediately packed the little girl on the sledge and conveyed her to Okak, where she soon regained strength.

These are the facts as nearly as I can remember them but doubtless the Okak letters will tell the story more fully.

We received the first letters from Hebron and Okak on February 20th. Till then I had not been anxious about the two stations, as I knew certain alterations had been made in the running of the winter mail, and thought that if anything very serious had happened the Brethren would have sent a special messenger at Mission expense. But the first Okak letter I opened revealed the tragic state of things. They had sent no sledge for the simple reason that there was not a man left to send. Two men still survived in Okak, but both were sick. One, a Settler, has recovered; the other, an Eskimo, had by this time probably joined the great majority. The Brethren requested me to go to Okak as soon as possible to see what could be done; so, after making hasty arrangements for church services, etc. while I was absent, I started on February 22, but owing to my being held up at Nain by bad weather I did not reach Okak until March 4th. It was clear that the only thing possible was to decide to abandon Okak and divide the 59 surviving souls between Nain and Hopedale. No one wished to remain at Okak; the majority were eager to get away as quickly as homes could be found for them and arrangements made for their transport to the South.

— Br. W.W. Perrett
Report of the Superintendent to the S.F.G., July 1919
[11.3:38]

WHEN THE *HARMONY* WAS LEAVING Hebron that time it did a really unusual thing. It blew its horn three times and even fired its cannon. It had never done that before, not even when it came or left Hebron. The captain told our minister he blew his horn and fired his cannon because he thought it would be the last time he would ever see Inuit people. When our minister was telling the Inuit people this, I even heard him.

It was late in the fall, in November, when the *Harmony* left. My parents left Hebron to go netting seals, but as soon as they started putting out the nets they began to get sick. Since some of them were still able to work a little, they started to go back to Hebron. There was a sea on and they had to go sideways to the wind. They didn't have a motor boat, the *Harmony* pulled them when they left, so they had to row back to Hebron. When they got to Hebron they were too weak to unload the boat, so Willihatus, the brother of Harriet Nochasak, had to unload the boat himself and right after he finished the unloading, he too got sick.

As soon as the *Harmony* left Hebron, Abraham Kura and his wife, who had come for supplies, left to go back to their home in Napartok Bay. They only got as far as Manetuasuk and Abraham's wife got so sick she was nearly dying, so they started to go back to Hebron. They had a little pup with them and they put him in the cuddy. When they got to Hebron, Abraham went to anchor the boat and while he was at the anchor, his wife died. Mrs. Kura was the first person to die of the Spanish Flu in

Hebron. I think it was about a week or two after Mrs. Kura died that everyone seemed to start taking turns dying....

Later on, when most of the people were sick, a man named David went and told the minister that his wife, Helena, was dead. Not long after David left the minister's, Helena walked in to tell the minister that David was dead. The minister was shocked when Helena walked in, because David had said she was dead. When Helena found out that David said she was dead, she didn't want to go home, so the minister let her stay in the school, which was attached to the church. She stayed there a long time, even 'till the middle of December, after Advent. The minister gave her bedding, clothing, food, and kept her woodstove burning. When she wanted to come with us, we went to the minister's house to get her. Carolina, my aunt Paulina, Piasta, Ernestina and myself went to get her on a komatik. At that time Helena had long hair and it was sticking right up with lice, so the minister got someone to cut it and put it outside. As soon as they put her hair outside, Helena couldn't talk anymore. She really tried to whisper in people's ears but they couldn't make sense out of it. She even tried to write with a pencil, but no one could make sense out of that. She was trying to tell us about the bad things that used to happen to her, like she was confessing. Finally her writing started to make sense and she was understood. When she finally could talk, there was a knock on the door, but we were the only people left, all the others were dead. Aunt Paulina, Piasta and Carolina were staying close to Helena by the stove where it was warm.

When Helena could talk she started to confess. She said her relatives told her if she ever told on them that they would kill her. Her family used to steal from the store. They even made their own key so they were able to get in the store. They used to get whatever they wanted. They used to steal when the people were asleep at night. They also stole wood from the woodhouse where the wood was kept for the missionaries. There used to be a lot of wood already cut in the shed, so they used to go and load up sacks in the night. When the people were asleep, they would go along the beach and behind the hill and steal whatever they wanted. Helena said they really had it made, they were rich and didn't need much 'cause they were living off stolen things. She used to tell her family not to do all these things but they wouldn't listen to her, instead they would threaten to kill her if she told. Helena used to pray out loud after she confessed. She died a good woman.

Before Helena died, when she was trying to confess, we had two little boys who were sick but getting better. They were little Benny and his brother, my little namesake. They were in a bed close to the stove almost by Helena. Those two little boys both had crew cuts too. They made fun of poor Helena who was so helpless and trying so hard to talk. When Carolina told us about how Helena's husband used to baby her because he loved her so much—he used to say to her, "*Asuilla, ausilla*," meaning "See, it happened"—those two little boys, eight-year-old Benny and his nine-year-old brother, started saying, *"Asuilla, ausilla"* and making fun of Helena. We couldn't help but laugh at them, even though little Helena was really sick. We all laughed at the two little boys who had their hair cut short like Helena's and they were pretending like they were Helena.

After Helena died, we wrapped her body in a caribou skin which was used for bedding. Carolina, Aunt Paulina and myself took her to the house where we kept dead bodies. We were pulling her along in the caribou skin and since she was so light we started to run. All of a sudden we bumped her head on a little rock that was sticking up. Poor Helena, we bumped her on the rock but not on purpose. We took her to my grandmother's house where the dead bodies were kept, but it was so full of bodies, even the floor was full, we put her on the porch. She was so light we put her on the porch with no difficulty. We just made sure the wind wouldn't blow her off.

After Helena died, me and Aunt Paulina used to go to the storehouse to get dried meat, caribou and sealmeat and also rancid seal fat from the containers. We had dried meat 'cause my uncle and them made a lot of *nikkok* [jerky].

One day when we were going for dried meat, we saw my mother's old dog that we had been after for a long time. Aunt Paulina told me to see if I could shoot him. I hit him but only wounded him. 'Twas the dog me and Mark Lyall had been after for a long time, since we began killing the dogs when they began eating dead bodies. We had a lot of dogs to kill. I used a lot of bullets which Mark gave me. Mark used to even shoot from his window. My mother's dog was one we couldn't get. That old dog used to come by our house when I was chopping firewood and I used to pretend I was going to shoot him with a little stick, but he wouldn't go away. Whenever I went to the house for my gun, he used to go. He went towards the house where the dead bodies were and I never seen him after, not even when we were putting the old dead dogs away. At the time I shot the dog I wasn't sick yet, only later I got sick. Them old dogs, when they were eating dead bodies, there were many of them. They used to come up from down the beach just like a herd of caribou. There was some lot, that's why me and Mark Lyall was killing them off.

The same time we were killing off the dogs, there was a lot of ravens, I think about a thousand. They were eating all the dogs we had killed. Some of the ravens were eating seaweed along the beach. Some were eating cod fish that was left in the boats anchored in the ice. Sometimes those ravens would be flying before daylight even. Them old ravens were as many as the snowbirds in the spring, when they're flying south. Those ravens were a different colour from the ones we see today, they were almost gray, not black like now. Sometimes as soon as daylight they'd be flying like crazy. Sometimes they would be flying all night. I never seen so many ravens before. I think they were death itself.

When we were sick with the Spanish Flu, we were really thirsty. Some people died with thirst. Samuel Angottak came to our house to see if he could get a drink of water.

When his nephew said, "Sorry, we don't have any water," he just went out again without saying another word. How I pitied him, that poor old Samuel. I still see him today as though it had just happened. I really felt love for him when he had to leave without even a drink because we didn't have any water at all. I still think of old Angottak, his hair sticking right up with lice, poor old man.

That time when we were all sick there was a man next to me in the bed. All of a sudden he started to lean up against the wall and then he fell dead on the pillow. My brother, even though he was sick, dragged that man to the door.

Before my brother died everyone was sick and we were all so thirsty and there was no water. Later on I told my sister-in-law, "Jesus can make water come through the wall, hey?" When I said that she only looked at me lovingly. On that same night, just before daylight, I started to feel better. As soon as I felt strong enough, I put on my brother's sealskin pants and his skin boots and went to get some water from the brook.

When my brother died, my sister-in-law tried to wake him up, but he was dead. She told me my brother just died, and since there was nothing I could do, I just said, "Yes." Then she said to me, "I don't want to die during the night 'cause you might be left alone."

There was a young girl named Naeme—I called her Naemiatsuk (little Naeme)—and her baby brother who was only about a year old, he was almost walking. They were the only ones left in one of the houses. Their mother was dead and the little baby still needed his mother's milk, so Naemiatsuk used to make the baby drink the dead mother's milk. I think the baby died, I can't remember. Naemiatsuk was one of the people who didn't die in the sickness.

The dogs that were left over from the ones we killed were Timothy's dogs. There was five, six or seven of them. We kept them from going outside, so they wouldn't eat the dead bodies. One morning I thought they were gone so I went to look for them. I went near the house with the dead bodies in it and as soon as I got there and started calling I heard a person crying in the house. I got kind of scared 'cause I was all alone and there with all those dead people. I started running home really fast. As soon as I got home I told everyone that I just heard somebody crying in the house full of dead people. That was early in the morning, just before sunup, and it was still dark outside. Aunt Paulina, Carolina and Akko started to shout at the dead people saying, "Why do you want to cry when you are dead?" Afterwards we never heard anything else.

At the time of the Spanish Flu I was thirteen years old, old enough to have my 'Day,' Single Men's Day [January 25], held for boys thirteen and up, and unmarried men. I never had my Day 'cause the sickness came. Besides that, I was the only single man left in Hebron. That was before the people came over from Saglek Bay. The minister came to bless me on my Day anyway.

After a while no one else died, and we were the only ones left in the whole community. There was not more than twenty of us. That was a really bad sickness. Before they died, the people had dark spots on the insides of their hands and lips. My brother had those dark spots before he died.

As soon as the ice formed, Danny Kura came on dogteam to see if his brother Abraham and his wife were all right in Hebron, 'cause they never went back to Napartok. As I mentioned before, they were the first people in Hebron to die with the Spanish flu. Danny only came as far as the point, never even came to the village, 'cause he thought maybe everyone was dead. When we were told to go and greet the dogteam, me, Piasta and Aunt Paulina went. We were told not to run, but I did because I didn't know what to think. When we told Danny his brother was dead, he just started to cry right away. We all started to cry and hold each other, all of us. Danny didn't even stay, just took off again for Napartok.

When the people came from Saglek Bay, the ones left, we started to work on the dead bodies. We had to smoke out the house where the bodies were kept 'cause it was such a bad smell and the bodies were half eaten by the dogs. There was one body that didn't even get dark. We smoked them out with tar and all of them came out full of soot and ashes except one, the body of Timothy's wife. She was wrapped in a red blanket and there was not even one little spot on her, she was really clean. We could not believe our eyes, but that's the way it was.

We had to bury the dead in the water 'cause that's how Bishop Martin wanted it done, so we went along 'cause there was nothing we could do but listen to him. After each body was put in the water the minister would say a prayer for it. We had to tie heavy rocks on them so they would sink. There was one body that wouldn't sink no matter how many rocks we put on it. We even put two brand new anchors on the end of the rope, but it still wouldn't sink. His name was Nathaniel and before he died he said he didn't want to be buried in the water. I think that's why he never sunk for so long, not until we put real heavy rocks on him. The rocks and anchors would sink but not him.

And that little dog Abraham Kura and his wife had in the cuddy of the boat, well, when Danny Kura came back from Napartok in the spring to work on Abraham's boat, he found that little dog still alive in the boat. The little dog had been there since November and it was May when Danny came back to Hebron. When Danny put him on the ice, he fell down 'cause he was starved. I think he lived that long 'cause he licked the snow in the boat during the winter. When Danny put him on the ice he tried to walk up to the village towards the houses. Danny shot him afterwards. That dog lived a long time without food. He was a brave dog having lived that long without food.

When the *Harmony* used to come to Labrador, when we were children, it used to be a lot of fun. We kids used to have fun playing "Going Across." It was a game that we played. What we used to do was put a little piece of wood, or anything, inside the *Harmony*, maybe push it into a crack or something and then it would leave on the *Harmony*. The next season when she returned the little things would still be there. I never knew where they went, but wherever they went they came back. They never used to be taken off, went overseas somewhere.

Old Tobias Kura, the father of Abraham and Danny Kura, used to tell me about the time when he was a child how they used to play that same game, sending something off on the *Harmony*. One time he put a small piece of shit on the *Harmony*, just for fun 'cause he was a child. When the *Harmony* came back the next year, sure enough, there it was, Tobias's little shit, still stuck on. That was what old Tobias told me himself one time.

I have told only what I can remember, that is all.

— Joshua Obed
[6.1:13]

I WAS KITORA PAMACK FROM Okak. My father was Gustav Pamack and my mother was Rosina.

Let me talk about my childhood. When I was a child we used to play and play, undeterred by the cold of winter. Our mittens would freeze and we would arrive home with icy mittens, even duffel ones. As we threw them down on the floor, my younger sister and I, they would make the sound as a rock hitting the floor. But we weren't cold. Maybe the reason we weren't cold was because we wore sensible clothing, duffel *atigiks*, or Eskimo designed parkas and mitten and boots which were all designed to keep out the cold. I will tell you about what I remember. A whole bunch of us kids would go sliding together, as Okak was usually deep with snow. We would slide down on small sleds and those who had no sleds would make do with their bottoms. The teenage boys usually had skis. Even us teenage girls used skis, even myself when I was turning into a teenager. My legs were fine then; maybe I was strong....

When we were children, all of us teenage girls would slide all the way from the top of the hill to the ice below. Later in April, the time for real sliding, a whole fleet of komatiks would slide down all the way from up there to the ice below. What fun in those days! One time, when we were sliding, two long komatiks filled with teenage girls spilled over. The second komatik, which was tied to the first, came crashing into the front one causing it to lose its *napoks* [komatik bars] and fall apart from our weight as we crashed. The next day everyone who had been on the komatik that broke were searched out and we all had to pay for it, since we had to pay for the cost of the *napok* rope. After that we tried not to bump into each other, as there were always so many of us sliding together. The next morning, after we each paid and saw each other again, we couldn't help giggling at each other. Lawrence, the little old man whose komatik we broke, was said to be really angry. That day, as soon as we broke it, we had all immediately abandoned the broken sled. When he found out we had broken it, he asked that we pay for it.

Now I will talk about a few other things that I remember. It seems to get harder and harder to talk about things as there are so many memories to choose from.

There were so many of us teenage girls on Young Women's Day, which was held on March 6, we had to be split into two groups and hold the celebration in two houses instead of one. As was the usual custom on Young Women's Day we were treated to tea at church at 3 p.m. and then went visiting the white missionaries afterwards. That was what was expected of us on that day. The porches of the mission house were huge. It was the custom that when we visited them after service and all the girls were assembled on the porch, the minister, as was usual on that day, would throw out treats, candies and nuts, and there would be a terrific scramble for them, each of the girls squealing and some getting a little hurt in the effort to grab what we could. It was fun in those days with no worries or cares, unsuspecting that soon there would be many lives lost through death from the Flu, lives of people with whom we led happy lives. Maybe it was meant to be that way because people here became too numerous. That is the reason why we just act happy.... [10:3:31]

In the winter all the people would stay at Okak. We went to school when we were there, which was in the church. There were three different groups of us. The minister would teach the oldest group, the middle group was taught by Benjamin, an Inuk, and the youngest ones were taught by the women. There were no *kablunak* teachers then, only the minister. We were taught in German then, not English. We heard German all the time, German and Inuktitut. We were taught to count in German, not one-two-three like today.

When school was over we would go to our hunting camp by dog-team where my father would hunt for seals. My sister and I would be in the komatik box all covered up in blankets and my mother would be sitting at the front of the box, keeping an eye on us. We would try to get as close as possible to the edge of the ice where there is open water. We set up our tent on an island close to the *sinak* [open water]. The tent was big enough for all of us and all our food. This would be from early May until the end of June. My father would get a lot of seals too. We used to have a lot of fun at that place.

When it was June, when it was almost open water, my father used to go to his own camp. We used to kill white whales there and all kinds of seals; jars and all kinds. There was never any shortage of food.

I am sure you have seen those thick layers of ice that form along the shore in winter or along the edge of islands when the sea ice gets broken up by heavy seas. When we travelled to our spring camps we often had to travel through that kind of ice. It was really frightening sometimes because if our komatik slipped we would fall right down into the sea. That would be June month. When my father started fishing we would move to still another place—to Sillutalik—by boat. The first part of July and August were fishing seasons. I can remember those things though I was just a child. In those days they used to jig for codfish. Even the women worked at the fish. When August came they would dry the fish so that it would be ready when the *Harmony* arrived.

I can remember the times we used to put the fish out to dry and then go out in the boat to get bakeapples and blackberries. We'd come home late and gather up the fish for the night only to spread them again the next day.

After the fishing season the men would start trapping foxes, hunting for partridges, rabbits and anything else. Starting in October and November they would hunt seals again, storing up food for the winter, and storing dog food for the winter. When Christmas season came we would all go back to Okak by dogteam. [11:3:45]

I can remember when my father died because I was twelve years old at the time… When I was fourteen I started taking care of the minister's children, a family of German missionaries. They used to give me a lot of clothing, dresses, hats, jackets and everything else that you could wear. I used to wear them too. I used to wear the hats and jackets. The clothing had real small waists. I think the things we had in them days were a lot better than the things we have nowadays. They were valuable, I guess, because they were made in Germany.

We use to be real happy and have a lot of fun, because we were all well. And then the sickness came. I was twenty years old at the time. That was in the fall, November, just after the *Harmony* left Okak.

People used to look forward to the *Harmony* coming. There was always excitement in the village. Three or four men would be sent up the hill to keep watch and as soon as they saw the ship they would fire their rifles into the air. The people used to be very happy then. There were two small cannons in the village and they would be made ready and fired as soon as the *Harmony* came into sight. Everyone would gather down to the wharf. As soon as the ship anchored, the Okak choir would sing and then the brass band would play. Everyone would be so excited.

It was like that too in 1918. There was no thought to the catastrophe that was to occur.

When the *Harmony* arrived there was no sickness in Okak. All the people helped with the unloading of the cargo and then all the fish caught in Okak that summer had to be loaded on board. After the *Harmony* departed there was a church service. There was a lot of us at that service. The very next day, though, there was a Communion service and there were very few of us because people were already ill. It was so sudden. People said that the sickness came from the cargo.

People said that one of the crew of the *Harmony* was sick and that the captain told the people not to go aboard. People always used to go on board for a visit so some people did not pay attention to the captain and went on board anyway. In this way the flu spread among us. In just a short time a lot of people were sick.

My mother, my younger sister and one of my older sisters were living in the house with me. They all died. I was the only one of our family left in our house. Later, my other sister came to live at our house because she was the only one left of her family, all the others being killed by the sickness. My sister and I took care of a lot of the children of others who died. There were many of us together in my father's house.

The dead people, young and old, men and women, were all taken to the big house next to the hospital. All the dead people were gathered together there—men, women, children and babies. Babies couldn't survive that sickness. It came so fast. By December it was over.

All the people who died were well looked after by the minister and the storekeeper. The women were given the task of sewing together tent material to cover each of the dead. Even the babies were covered in this way. The dead were buried at a place called Kakkolak. It was the only place they could dig because the ground was frozen, the men had to pour oil onto the ground and light it. This would make it easier to dig the hole. From afar the smoke looked like a ship's smoke. They dug a big ditch and the dead weren't just put away, they were buried proper by the minister. They put all the bodies onto komatiks and took them to the grave. It was done well. They were treated with respect.

I was working for the minister when the flu started and every time at 3:30 p.m. I would bring them tea and buns when they were preparing for the funeral. That was how I helped them. My sister was taking care of some of the children. They were children who had lost their parents. Most of the children did not have any parents, aunts, or uncles left at all.

Later, in February, people started to come to Okak from the fall hunting places. They were just women and children. Some by dog-team, some walking. No men amongst them! It wasn't good. That's the reason the people of Okak consisted mostly of women and children that year. All of the men died of the sickness.

We were sad over it and yet we were not. There was nothing that we could do about it. We just had to go on and be as happy as we could. I think we were thankful that we were still alive.

For a long time after there was this sense of decline as far as yearly activities were concerned among the Inuit and all the northern Labrador communities. A sense of let down was in the air for a long time. Whenever November comes I think back about it; my friends and all my own family and how they were killed. I try not to dwell much on the losses but try to be happy and think of the good times we had. Although Okak was my home as a child, I feel that Hopedale, where I am now, is my home.

My sister Eleanora and I didn't leave to go to Hopedale until October. We had to go there because Markus Pijogge and his family had sent for us. We went to live with them, but we had to move to Michael Friday's soon after. Michael Friday and his family were nice.

I was in Hopedale for a whole year that time. I was single then. As soon as spring came, William Barbour came for me from Nain. He married a girl we knew from Okak. I had to leave my sister behind in Hopedale and go back to Nain. I liked it in Nain and was happy there because I could see some people I knew from Okak. Noah and his sister Ruth were staying with William while I was there. I knew them both. They were the type of people who always joked around and were really nice to be with, so we had a lot of fun and were happy.

We used to go to Nain for Easter. One time when we went there were all kinds of people that come from other places and one of the men who come from Hopedale asked me to marry him. His name was Boase Boas. I said "Yes," so we got married there in Nain. Then we went back to Hopedale after that. We had four children altogether, all girls. One of them died but the rest are all right.

Boase and I were both church elders and we were married for a long long time, altogether for over fifty years. Right now I am alone, because my husband died last year on the eleventh of October, 1978. I am now eighty years old and I am really thankful for being blessed and living that long. I hope my grand-children, my great-grandchildren, relatives and all my friends will be blessed the same way each and every day of their lives.

— Kitora Boas
[4.4:28]

I CALLED OUT TO MY mother and there was no answer, so I went over to her bed and put my hands on her, tryin' to wake her up. My hand popped back, just like it was something I wasn't expectin', see—hard body. I went to my step-father and told him my mother died and he didn't take a bit of notice. He just went off to sleep like, you know. They had no pain or nothing. I can remember they had a job gettin' their breaths—bad colds. Choked right up it seemed like. It came on all at once. My mother was sick only a couple of days and she died, and my father.

I didn't notice my brother until after my mother died. I had to look after him then. I used to give him the bottle of molasses after we got out of milk. When I got sick it was worse then. I got right sick and my two aunts were too sick to look after him. I just had to try to look after him. I'd be in bed and couldn't breath hardly.

The old dogs were the worst. They were so hungry they used to try to break in the houses, see. Eat the bodies. One feller told me he was tryin' to haul out a dog, he thought, from under the bed to drive it out of the house. He hooked at it with a stick or something. All that time this was his sister's head—he thought it was a dog. No wonder he cried—couldn't stand it hardly, when he was tellin' us, you know.

When Uncle Tom and Aunt Bella [Gear] took my sister and brother, I cried. Broke my heart! It was nothing at all for my mother and grandmother and them to die but to separate from my brother and sister, that was awfully hard.

Captain Jackson, he was captain on the *Harmony* then. I seen him quite a few years after. He said he could never forgive himself for that—bringin' the sickness to Okak, killin' all the people out. He blamed himself, you know. It's cruel 'cause that sickness was all over the world, they said, not only in Okak and Labrador and Newfoundland. There was a big war on, you know, First World War. People died all over the world and Okak was the worst, the hardest place hit with the sickness.

—Rosie [Pamack] Ford
[11.3:56]

I WAS BORN IN OKAK. I remember a li'l bit, just like I was dreamin', you know. I remember a big hospital, a big meeting house and a church. There was stores and lots of houses.

I was seven years old when the ol' Flu came to Okak. My grandmother, my mother and aunt, they was all sick and they died.

In August we went to Nain with my Aunt Eleanora. Aunt Kito was gone already while I was in school. She had people or something in Nain, and if they wants we then we got to go with them. We went to William Barbour's. He was married in Okak and his woman was our second, third cousin, or something, you know. I don't want to leave from the minister's. I was only cryin'. I remember I was goin' on the li'l ol' mail boat, smaller than boats now. They was all in the window, wavin'. She [the minister's wife] was like my mother. I was right used to her. She wants to take me away but my aunt said no because my mother told her she got to mind me. That time we went to Nain and then to September Harbour.

We stayed down in September Harbour all the time. We'd never go to Nain, only sometimes in Easter, and Christmas if there's good ice. At September Harbour they was fishin', sealin' and gettin' foxes. Lots of seals them times and lots of fish. We got to help dry the fish. All the rocks are right fulled up with ol' fish. All the children got to work all the time. There was four or five other families, I s'pose. I remember David Barbour, that's William Barbour's son, and William Barbour, that's his namesake. Tom Barbour's father and them was there and Isaak Rich and his wife, and somebody else. There used to be lots of people all around you know, on the islands. They used to come and visit us sometimes. A lot of people used to live to Evilik, too, one time.

Old William Barbour was workin' for himself. He used to be makin' lots of boots and send them away to St. John's, I s'pose. They sent fish to St. John's too, I think. I can't tell proper, but I think it was like that. He used to have food come from somewhere and that was St. John's, I think.

William Barbour got his seals with net. In the fall he got to go in motor boat around the island. When they'd can't go in the boat, they used to walk around the other side of the island. Leave early in the morning before daylight and not come back 'till dark in the evening. Sealin' and sealin'. Lots of seals them times, 600, 700 sometimes. All up around here and around Evilik, too, they used to get lots. We wasn't hungry at all them times.

The women used to be makin' boots and other things, cleanin' the floors. They'd be makin' vamps, mitts, washin' clothes, makin' bread and everything. They used to have one, two, three, four, I s'pose, fixed up in the house, Late in the nights, sometimes, the women would be makin' skin boots by the lamplight, li'l ol' oil lamps. They was makin' boots all the time, ol' boots for the Newfoundlanders. They'd never stop workin'. Sometimes when the men was finished workin' they'd play cards and li'l ol' checkers. Sometimes, just like, it sounded like they was goin' to get cross. The women would play cards sometimes. They used to have li'l ol' tobacco or something and matches. Some of them got lots sometimes. I used to see them, not mind them too much, just see them. I wasn't thinkin' to play. I was too young at that time to think to play.

Lots of Newfoundland schooners used to come down around September Harbour. They'd come in small boats first and put out lines where they was goin' to have their cod traps and a week or so after the schooners would come. There used to be lots of schooners, right full sometimes. Everywhere Newfoundlanders fishin'.

The young girls used to have to work, cook seal meat all the time, you know. In the morning sometimes, they had to cook seal meat for breakfast, have a big ol' pot right full with seal meat, before they wake up the older people. Have to get up five, six o'clock. When the men is gone we got to cut up some wood, too, sometimes. We got to have a fire. We bring in wood and get some water and everything before dark, you know. We got to work hard all the time them times, but it was fun, too. We likes it....

When I was about 14 or 15, William Barbour was gettin' old and kind of sick, so we left September Harbour and went back to Okak. We all left—his wife, his son David and Ruthie Ikkiatsuk and Noah Ikkiatsuk. We was all 'long with that old man to Okak. When we got there we went up to Tessialuk to stay in the fall. We don't know at all why we went there. We was there in a li'l ol' house, not much good, not very big. We was all there and two more families besides we. David Barbour had an *iglosoak* [sod house] they made for themselves in the hill. About November that old man, William Barbour, died. No minister. No nothing. Right up there inside Okak at Tessialuk he died that same year we moved up there. In the spring my Aunt Eleanora came there from Nain, she and two men on komatik and dogs. She got us then and took us to Nain. Aunt Eleanora was married to Lucas Tuglavina then.

David Barbour and his wife moved to Nain, but William Barbour's wife never. She went to Hebron or Nutak. I don't know yet, I can't understand why William Barbour moved to Okak. He had everything in September Harbour, a nice house. I didn't mind at all at that time but when I think about it now, just like William Barbour was a rich man. That old man had everything. He had a big house in Nain, nice, everything in the house and lots of stuff in September Harbour. He had big houses and warm. I remember we used to get mail, maybe twice a winter on komatik. He used to get newspapers come, from St. John's I s'pose. He told us that when some more years come we was goin' to be able to hear people talkin' from all the world. He was tryin' to tell us about radios. He read that in the newspapers, I s'pose. He was a boss, too, in Nain, like Martin Martin, an elder.

— Sybilla Nitsman
[11.1:31]

WE HAD GONE TO OKAK wooding when we started getting sick. In four days we were all sick and could not carry wood. We wanted to return to Sillutalik so the *Harmony* towed us from Okak to Sillatulik. There were some people sick in Okak then but not too many. When we arrived I found that my father had already been dead for three days. My brother-in-law died when we arrived at Sillutalik and the other people kept on getting sick. I fell asleep on the floor and when I woke up there was only a few alive. I had to take care of the ones that were left. My mother died while winding up the big clock that my father had bought. She was talking as she was winding the clock and all of a sudden she fell. I went to look at her and found that she was already dead. I had not seen my father die because he was gone with the other men.

I was taking care of Jerry Sillitt, Maria, my sister, and a baby girl whom I did not know. I thought we were the only ones alive at Sillutalik. I fixed the door with seal nets then so the dogs couldn't get in, and climbed out the window. We went to the first house but most of the people in there were dead. I was frightened then. When we went to another house we found some girls who had all gathered in that house: Amelia Merkeratsuk and Tabea Boas. Before Tabea was married she was Tabea Kakkak. We were all living in the same house by that time. There was also Simeon Henock, I think, and Martin Millik from an island outside Sillutalik.

Simeon went to see how his parents were and when he came back he was crying. He told me that all his relatives were dead and eaten by the dogs. I told him when my feet didn't hurt I would go with him and we would see them together. When I was able to go we went. There was nothing left except bones and skulls. The skulls on the floor looked like they were looking at us through the window. There was no flesh on them, they had been eaten to the bone. I had to get away from that house. I told Simeon, "It can't be helped." Then I wanted to leave for Okak. That was around the beginning of December.

When we arrived at Okak, there were no lights in the houses except for a few. The lights at Okak could be seen from afar. The few houses that were lit were the *kablunaks'* houses and a few of the Inuit houses.

When we arrived the *kablunaks*—the storekeeper, doctor, and minister—were making a big ditch. We helped them with the ditch and to get things ready. There were people who had died sitting up. We went around to the houses getting bedclothes to wrap the dead, and for some that we couldn't find bedclothes for we wrapped that in tablecloths and Grenfell cloth. We would take two komatik loads and bury them. In Okak alone there were about a hundred dead. When we finished at Okak we went to Sillutalik and buried them under the rocks, because the rocks weren't frozen to the ground. Outside of Okak there were more people who had died. In Uivak there were more dead people, most of Martin Millik's people. Some that arrived from Uivak told us that there was no one alive there.

When we heard the people of Uivak were all dead, we went to see for ourselves. There were skulls lying outside of houses and also some bodies. When the dogs saw us they began to chase after us. The person with me had a whip and I picked up a piece of wood and we drove them away. The dogs were really wild and were coming out of the houses. Benigna was the one who told us that there were no people at Uivak. She was from Olik.

There was a young girl who had arrived in Uivak. With her there was a widow by the name of Ada. The widow Ada was fine when they put the punt to shore and they went towards a house. When they went to the door, Ada died right across the doorway. The young girl was Justine Martin. I really liked her. There was a child with them and Justine thought she might die on the way to Okak so she left the child, Amelia [Merkeratsuk's] son, behind. Before she died, Justine told us that she left Martha there too. Our minister tried to get to her twice but fog and storms made him turn back.

After we had beaten the dogs away, we were able to get to the houses. When we went to one house we heard someone say, "*ittialiut*," which means 'damn old shit.' It wasn't too loud. It was said that there were no people so I thought I heard a ghost. I wanted to go in but the person with me wanted to leave, so I just followed him. Later, from outside the house, I called in and said, "If you are alive, come out." But no one came out or spoke. This is why I was sure the person in the house was a ghost. I didn't really mean to leave Martha there.

…After Old Christmas, January 6, we were going to bury people at Uivak, at Martin's land first. It was then that we found Martha. We had rifles with us to shoot the dogs. The store-keeper and I went to the house where we had heard the voice. We went in and saw that she had a dog that was taking care of her. When the dog showed at the door, I shot him. It was only later that I found that it was not wild. I heard crying and I thought it was the dog, but it was Martha who was crying.

After we took Martha out, we burned the house down. Martha was fed and taken care of by the minister. We found a barrel and made a bed for her on the komatik and took her to Okak. She had been in Olik since fall until Old Christmas Day—all that time. The door of the house had been open, but she was well. There were small candles that she had kept lit in the night and her food had been a few biscuits. She hardly had any water.

In 1919 I went to Nain. All of us from Okak left to go to other places—some went to Hebron, Hopedale, Nain, and Makkovik. I was adopted by Martin Martin.

— Gustav Sillitt
[14.2:5]

WE LIVED IN OKAK WHEN I was a child. I stayed with my grandparents, my father's father. His name was Samuel Menzel. We had gone away for the summer to a place not far from Okak. The name of the place was Okliasuk [Olik].

That fall—I was seven years old—we were still at Okliasuk. My grandfather was out chopping wood and as soon as he walked in he died. It seemed like he wasn't sick at all. After I had gone to bed my grandmother came to lie down beside me and she died. There was also an old woman with us and a child. There were only three of us then in Okliasuk. We lived in a sod house with windows made of seal gut and two beds made of dirt.

I was alone for three months before I was found. I kind of lost my mind. I didn't have any clothes so I put on my grandfather's shirt. The dogs used to come in through the window and the door. I couldn't shut the door because there was a dead woman in the way.

The dogs came into the house and ate the bodies while I watched. They were eaten and dragged outside, too. I just stayed on the bed, hardly ever moving from the bed. I stayed inside the bedclothes. I never even thought where my clothes were. All I know is that I put on a shirt, my grandfather's shirt. I also had on a pair of old pants.

The little boy who was with me lived for quite a while. I may have starved him to death because I didn't know how to feed him. He wanted tea. I remember him getting out of breath. I had him on my lap for a while, then I put him down beside me when it was getting dark. As soon as I put him down he was taken by a dog and torn to pieces. He was still alive, I think. This is something that haunts me even to this day. I didn't know how to feed him because I was just a child myself.

I remember I was always crying. The door was always full of snow because I couldn't shut it, but I was able to go out. I used to go out without any socks on because

I didn't know I was without socks. I used snow for water and I ate hardbread. I ate very little. People used to never come to the place where I was at. I had long hair and my head was covered with lice but it never used to itch. I cut my foot really deep one night when I was going to look for some live people and to get some snow. I cut my foot on broken glass and wrapped it with rags. It healed by itself but I don't know how.

I wasn't bothered by dogs too much. There was one dog that looked after me. I think he was my grandfather's lead dog. The people who came for me thought he was wild. The minister, store-keeper, Gustav Sillitt and a Martin from Okak came and found me.

All the dogs were shot when the *kablunaks* came, even our lead dog. Even though they were shot right next to me, I was never hit. They only saw me when I started shouting. Maybe they thought I was one of the dogs because my hair was so messed up, so tangled up.

I couldn't eat or drink on the way to Okak, but after a long time I could eat and drink again. I wasn't able to sleep lying down, only sitting up with my head on my knees, because I was used to sleeping that way.

My father's sister, Amelia Merkeratsuk, took care of me after I was taken to Okak. When I was yet a child I was taken from Okak to Nain, to my father's uncle, with Amelia. We went to Nain by dog team.

I can only remember what I am telling you now.

— Martha Joshua
[14.2:8]

Presumably, this will be the last report from Okak, it is the saddest ever written.

The station has existed for 143 years. During that time 1,607 children have been baptized, 793 persons have been confirmed, 450 couples have been married, and 1,740 people have died. The 60 members who are left, adults and children, have been removed to Nain and Hopedale, and some have been transferred to Hebron by marriage.

During the 143 years, 155 missionaries have been called to Okak to work among the Eskimos there. Seventy-seven children of European parents have been born here; and in all, 11 missionaries and 20 children have departed this life.

Unfortunately, the spirit of the times has filled the hearts of the Eskimos also, and has drawn them away from the one thing needful. This was especially observable on Sundays during the last few years. Owing to the motor-boats there was no quiet on Sundays. Backwards and forwards they went all through the day....

It was about December 8th, when we began to dig a large grave in which to bury all the people who had died during the epidemic. This was no easy matter, as the ground had already frozen to a great depth. When we got down to about three feet we came to the old frost and we were obliged to make large fires and we used up a considerable quantity of petroleum, otherwise we should not have been able to get down far enough. In this way we dug down seven or eight feet and the length of the grave was 32 feet.

On January 4th, 6th, and 7th, we conveyed the corpses to the burial ground and laid them to rest in their common grave. Those that were not already clothed we wrapped in calico, of which we used about 100 yards. On January 8th the dead bodies were brought from Simmikutak and we buried them with the rest—101 in all, adults and children.

On March 30th there was a double wedding here, the last one to take place at Okak—one couple for Nain and one for Hebron.

Then came Passion week; but, alas so very different from former years! On Maundy Thursday we celebrated the Lord's Supper in the church with five communicants! The rest of Passion week meetings were conducted in the house of a sick man, Moses Torarak by name. He had been brought here on January 4th from Ittiplersoak along with one boy, as being the only survivors out of the whole company that had been at that place. Eight Okak people died there. On April 29th this man died too— the last of the Okak men. I made his coffin and dug his grave, and on April 30th, we buried him. He died in the faith. We could only wish for him to die, for he had suffered a great deal—but he was also quite resigned and calm.

Now that the snow has melted, what was once the village looks more desolate and dirty than ever. We have broken up most of the houses, making great heaps of household furniture and rubbish, and burning the lot. Other houses which stood by themselves, we saturated with petroleum and burnt them to the ground. The whole place ought to be thoroughly cleaned and disinfected, but we missionaries can not do it alone. What native people there is required by the store-keeper for the purpose of drying codfish that was purchased last autumn in a wet state, in order to help the natives.

We cannot yet get accustomed to the thought, when looking at the ruined village, that everything has gone so completely; that practically the whole congregation has been buried, and that we shall have to forsake everything and go too!

— Annual Station Reports to the S.F.G.,
June 1919, Okak
[11.3:44]

There is but little desire [among the people] for spiritual things. After the terrible experiences of the preceding year one would have thought that the soil of their hearts would have been loosened and the desire of something higher and better than what the world can offer would have been aroused. But I regret to say there is but little of this to be seen. Since the time of the epidemic it has scarcely ever happened that an adult of his or her own accord, has come to the missionary in matters of the heart and if I try, in one way or another, to reach the heart of the individual, I often have the impression that I am knocking at a door that is closed.

— Annual Station Reports to the S.F.G.,
December 1920, Hebron
[11.3:46]

NO ONE REALLY KNOWS HOW MANY of the old stone and sod houses in the Hebron area have never been discovered. It would seem that an area so rich in sea and animal life must have had a relatively large population in the days before the white man came. There are great cairns on the tops of almost inaccessible mountains, so high that they cannot easily be seen from a boat close inshore. I asked a wise old man why Eskimos would build such cairns that would be much more useful for craft approaching from offshore, and he said, "Not made by us, before us."

I suggested Tunit who had been on the land before and he said, "Maybe before that."

I am convinced that there is a story to be found on these mountains and islands, a story that may never be told.

But the stone and sod houses that in some cases were originally Tunit houses do exist, and in my time several were occupied at one time or another. To my eye they were much alike, but people would say this was once Tunit, this was Inuit. Of course any artifacts around the occupied houses had long since disappeared. The nearest to the old settlement are within walking distance.

The construction of the houses, especially those that had not been recently occupied, was very similar to the houses at Nuvuk near Repulse Bay, North West Territories many miles to the northwest and across Hudson's Bay. Almost surely built by the same people.

The lower walls, which could be as much as four feet into the ground—actually less ground than loose gravel and small boulders—were of stone, as were the sleeping platforms. The stones were quite large and heavy and showed evidence of having been split along natural crack lines. In general, the work was well done, especially the inside walls, and the sleeping platforms were quite level and smooth.

The stone walls in the houses that had not been occupied were usually in good shape, but the whale bone rafters had fallen and the sod roofs with them, so very little of the interior was visible. The still-occupied houses obviously had been cleaned out and new roofs had been put on. There was no whale bone to be had but there are small trees about forty miles south and a few poles and sods made acceptable shelters out of the ancient houses.

The late Bill Metcalfe and I were walking back to Hebron, one dark night, from a place further up the fjord, when we came upon one of the occupied underground houses. It was surprisingly dry and comfortable, possible because the ground had been frozen for some time and all run-off had ceased. The walls had apparently not been touched; all the debris had been carefully shoveled out and a new roof put on. There was a seal gut window in the roof which must have given a good deal of light during the day. The floor was clean dry sand, partly covered with deer skins and a square of heavy canvas that looked like it might have been part of a vessel's sail at one time.

There were two apartments. One entered the main room down a sloping sort of tunnel from outside. It contained a large sleeping bench, and here the elderly wife of the present occupant tended her seal oil lamp and watched her two grandchildren playing on the floor and on the sleeping bench. A smaller apartment had been excavated at the side of the main house. The sand and gravel were held back by a neatly built wall of stones and pieces of driftwood and plank. The roof was the same as the roof of the main house. This room had been added comparatively recently. The end result was a very warm and cozy place looking into the main chamber. Here the young son and his wife had their sleeping bench and *kudlik*. Here also was collected much of their hunting and fishing gear. There was no door on this room, but the only entrance to the house from outside boasted a wooden door where the original inhabitants would have used animal skins.

Seals had been plentiful and two *kudlo's* were burning, the place was warm and well lit. The older hunter sat smoking his pipe, his wife was softening a small seal skin, the son was repairing a *kakivak* [three-pronged fishing spear] while his wife tended a pot of caribou or seal hung over the kudlik. It was a picture of domestic contentment. There was meat in the caches outside. There was dried cod and char in apparent abundance. The dogs were clean and well fed. We stayed a while to rest, to take tea and dry fish with the family then left on our way home.

I passed that little dwelling several times in the next couple of years. The older man living there told me where to find several other houses that had been occupied in comparatively recent times. He pointed out that these houses bore no relation to the sod houses that were in Hebron years before. These he said were only sod houses with no stone and most were miserably wet and cold. They had been gone long before I came to Hebron but I had seen pictures of the Mission which showed sod houses where the Mission gardens were in my time....

Sometimes [the stone house] was occupied, sometimes not, as the family moved to other areas to fish for char and cod and to trap white fox, but they were usually there in the late fall as the fjord started to freeze over. The harp seals on their southern migration in the fall trim the shore and go into every bay and cove. They would go up the fjord in herds consisting of a dozen or hundred seals and come back the same way. The house was in a good sealing spot. However, all year there was some sign of occupancy—a pole framework for drying fish and meat, perhaps a kayak high on piles of stones to preserve it from dogs and wild creatures.

The location was grand; the fjord is wide there. Behind the house the mountains went steeply up and their remarkably smooth sides swept away north and south in a great semi-circle. The people living there had a good view of anything that might pass either by water or land. Just above the house a low wall of stones had been built behind which a man might lie at his ease and with his telescope see anything of interest for miles.

Then one spring I passed away out on the ice of the fjord on my way inland hunting caribou. There had been much snow that winter and a huge cornice hung menacingly several hundred feet above the little house. There was no one there. They had seen the signs and had moved to safer quarters.

Some time, no one knows when, that huge mass of snow, sodden with the heat of the spring sun and with the melt water that had accumulated behind, suddenly burst free and hurtled down the steep slope. Wet compressed snow, hundreds of tons of it, dug a path through the sand and when the pile melted the house was gone as if it had never been. Every vestige had been swept out on the ice of the fjord and had disappeared at break-up. We landed there once to see the extent of the damage. There was only a jumbled mass of broken stone that had come down with the snow, or had fallen later as the scanty soil melted and allowed minor landslides to flow from the damaged area far up in the mountain. Several large landslides were to follow over the next two or three years as the disturbed area stabilized.

We found a piece of evidence to show that people had lived there. Among some rocks near the water's edge Bill [Metcalfe] picked up a tiny toy kayak, cunningly made, exactly as the hunter's own kayak is built. It was covered with membrane from a seal's stomach. Miraculously undamaged it lay there cut off from the sea. I expected that Bill would take it home to his young son, but without a word he placed a small stone in the hunter's seat to give it balance and carefully put it in the water. We watched it 'till we lost sight of it in the blaze of the sun on the fjord. The very last kayak had gone out from the old dwelling under the ancient mountain.

Time heals; the signs of the landslide are probably invisible now, the stones of the house lie mingled with those that fell. Nature has restored the balance and erased the damage.

War came [World War II] and the people were taken away. Lamps no longer shine through seal gut windows, their light and warmth is gone, the walls are no longer there to give shelter. The tiny kayak's voyage is long over, and in the years much snow has blown across the silent land. Winter gives way to spring and new life, and in their time summer and autumn have completed the cycle.

The birds arrive in the spring and leave in the fall. The harp seal migration follows its ancient route and the caribou come and go after the manner of their kind. The *sik-sik* [ground squirrel] whistles from the hill and the eagle swoops for its prey. The land is there waiting.

But the people are gone. Slowly the moss and lichen accumulates and soon the signs that the Inuit left will be as faint as the traces of the Tunit in my day.

I think often of that ancient house and of the people who lived there. They had food, warmth and light in the shelter of a primitive hut. They also had content and the knowledge that much of what they had came by their own skill, for they were Inuit.

— Leonard Budgell
[16.3:59]

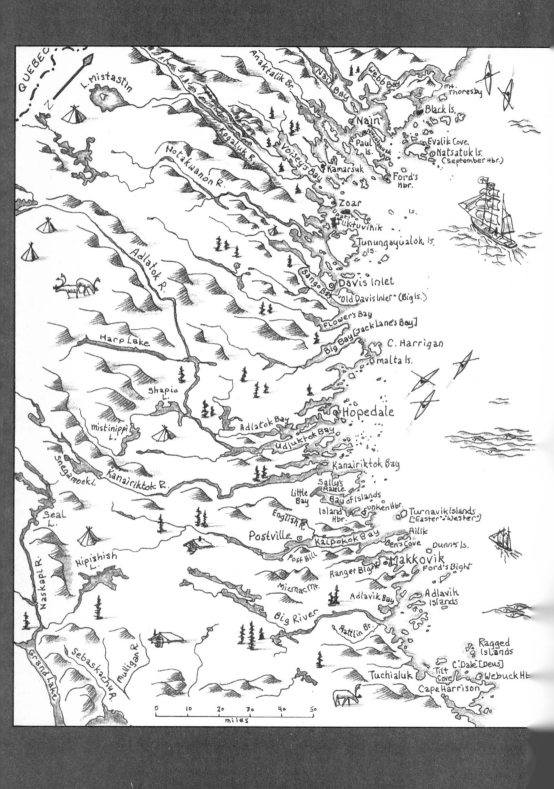

THE MORAVIAN COAST

BY 1782 THE PATCHWORK OF territories ceded to the Moravian Mission extended south as far as Hopedale, but the Mission's influence resonated nearly to Cape Harrison on the brink of secular Ivuktoke. Mission stations at Nain and Hopedale took the place of seasonal villages like Arvertok as social nuclei for most of the region's Inuit. Even members of resolutely independent families from the Cape Harrison-Kaipokok area availed themselves of some educational and economic offerings at Hopedale, and later Makkovik. Basic and austere as they were, the Moravian stations provided the most comprehensive examples of European social organization in the country for 150 years, but for more than eighty, they were open only to the Inuit. Newfoundland fishermen, Innu,[1] and a growing population of northern Settlers were denied access. The history of the Moravian Coast is in many respects a study in the micro-dynamics of segregation and integration, of cultural overlays and infiltrations. It is curious that peoples who shared the coast—Inuit and Settler—merged rather easily in spite of Moravian suasions and sanctions, while the Innu never sought and in fact passively resisted integration.

From earliest times, Labrador's northern-most Innu procured marine resources and wood from the bays of the Moravian Coast. Later they also came to trade their furs for ammunition and tobacco, and to seek help in times of need. These were the Mushuau Innu, the 'Naskapi,' hunters of the barren highlands west of Kaipokok Bay, brothers to the Waske neken Innu of Ungava Bay, cousins to the Montagnais of Laurentian and central Labrador, and perhaps (like the Montagnais) distant relatives of the Beothuk of Newfoundland and the Cree. Although the Moravians quickly lost interest in this race when they learned of their Catholicism, they promoted reconciliation between the Inuit and Innu for the sake of Inuit souls and access to hunting and trapping grounds in the interior. With further encouragement from priests and traders, the two Native groups in time learned to co-exist, and several cases of intermarriage are known to have occurred. But the Innu as a whole remained aloof, spending as little time as possible on the coast and then avoiding the Moravian stations in preference to the secular outposts at Kaipokok, Voisey's, and Sango Bays.

During the first half of the nineteenth century, the bays once frequented by precursors of the Innu and Inuit, more recently by the Inuit themselves, gradually filled with trappers and petty traders then or previously employed by the merchant adventurers in southern Labrador and Esquimaux Bay. A few were already second or third-generation Labradorians with Inuit blood in their veins, but most were relative newcomers from Europe. By mid-century, many of the latter had married local women or Newfoundlanders and adopted the prevailing trade-oriented hunter-gatherer lifestyle of Settlers. Together, the old and new families created a coastal community distinguished by its multi-national origins and relative success at achieving economic independence from the country's mercantile overlords.

During the period of exclusion from Moravian lands and society, the Settlers established family enclaves deep in the unchartered bays peripheral to the stations. They called themselves "baymen." Like everyone else in Labrador, they moved to the outer islands to fish for cod during the summer. There they mingled with Newfoundlanders, who became their bridge to the outside world, and with Inuit, who ultimately became their bridge to the Mission.

The Mission's resistance to Settlers broke down first at Hopedale. By 1850 there were over a dozen Settler families within a fifty-mile radius of the station, many of them married to communicants and eager to join the Church community. As most had given up their small trading operations and no longer posed a threat to the Mission's monopoly over Inuit goods, it became increasingly difficult to justify denying them access to God's Word. At Easter 1853, Settler John Reed and his Inuit wife Jane were admitted to the Hopedale congregation and, after considerable soul-searching by the missionaries, allowed to build a house within the village.[2] Settlers John Lane and John Ford officially witnessed the agreement. By contrast, Ford was allowed to attend services at the station but not to live within Mission territory or join the congregation because he remained an active competitor in trade.

Reed's baptism in the Moravian Church of Labrador launched a new era in which the Mission and Settler communities began slowly to converge. As early as 1860 missionaries began to sanction intermarriage on the grounds that European blood, with its resistance to Western diseases, might protect the Inuit from extinction. As the number of Settlers and Newfoundland fishermen desiring religious instruction increased, the brethren were obliged to offer an English-language service in addition to those in Inuktitut, but only Inuktitut was spoken in the schools at Nain and Hopedale until 1949. As a result of this and the increased co-mingling of social and commercial activity, the stations and eventually the coastal population became bi-lingual.

Economic collaborations developed between the Mission and Settlers where previously there had been fierce rivalry. In one case, a Settler who produced sealskin boots for an English trading company in Newfoundland persuaded the Mission to act as middleman in procuring additional boots from its congregants.[3] At Nain, where missionaries had once cautioned each other not to let John Ford assume too great familiarity with the station, his son William was hired to run the productive Black Island sealing station, which he later purchased.[4] By 1896, when the Mission opened a new station at Makkovik predominantly to serve Settler families of the Kaipokok-Cape Harrison region, the resident population of Hopedale and Nain was becoming almost as mixed as the Settler families of the adjacent bays and island harbours, and the job of brethren on the Moravian Coast evolved from one of conversion and paternalistic stewardship into one of ministry.

Due partially to the bi-racial population's enhanced resistance to infection, the 1918 Influenza gave the Moravian Coast only a glancing blow. In its aftermath, however, pure-Inuit survivors from Okak, most of them children, were placed with relatives at Hopedale and Nain, where they adapted quickly to the Europeanized culture while providing a fresh infusion of Native blood. A larger wave of Inuit followed in 1959 when the Newfoundland government resettled hundreds of Hebron residents at the southern stations, including Makkovik. These Northlanders had few relatives on the Moravian Coast and, arriving as they did in family units, assimilated with difficulty if at all. However, their grandchildren are now joining the mainstream, genetically as well as culturally, and the number of pureblooded Inuit is again on the decline. In fact, it would be very difficult to find in the population today a Labrador Inuk under the age of fifty with no white genes.

This chapter is primarily about the Settlers of the Moravian Coast, a group of families whose origins are as diverse as any in Labrador—French-Canadian, Norwegian, Scots, Irish, Welsh, English, Newfoundlander, Inuit, and Cree. While they have had a foot in each of the country's Western systems, that of the exploitative mercantile companies and that of the Moravian Mission, they maintained an uncommon degree of independence from both. Some also achieved, by Labrador standards, a measure of prosperity and mobility. Read the history of this coast through the lens of the Moravian Periodical Accounts and you will barely see them, yet these Settlers have become pillars not only of the Moravian Church but of the socio-political organization representing Labrador's Inuit population today, the Labrador Inuit Association (LIA). By virtue of LIA's geographically-based membership, the Settlers of northern Labrador are today called "Inuit." Their personal stories provide a counterpoint to the meticulously documented history of the Mission stations and a slightly different perspective on the dynamics of survival in this precarious wilderness.

Below Mt. Thorsby the towering coastline gradually gentles and subsides, the bays become longer and narrower. Inland, the northern limit of the treeline runs just about level with Makkovik and Hopedale, but the bays and river valleys are well wooded throughout the region. In fact, just inside the dense island passages is a captivating stretch of country where the forests are relatively loose and open, the tundra carpet is thick and lush underfoot, and the firm, bounding rock of bald hilltops is quickly gained. From this vantage, chains of open ridgeline roll invitingly from one to another as far as the eye can see, spanned by the wistful laments of white-crowned sparrows—slender filaments of sound so clear that they compress the intervening distances, like Sirens, luring the visitor on and adding to an illusion of infinite possibility. These are vistas that lighten the soul of superfluous ballast and give it wings.

The coast attracted traders very early in the frontier period, but this was undoubtedly for its proximity to the remote hunting and trapping grounds of the Naskapi rather than its natural beauty. French Canadians established posts in Kaipokok Bay, possibly as early as Fornel's tenure in Hamilton Inlet. Inuit hostility to whites was at a peak just then, and the villages of the Canybucktoke band at Aillik and the Ogbucktoke near Hopedale guarded the approaches to the bay. Brother Christian Erhardt's small party of Moravians seeking its first contact with Inuit near Aillik in 1752 is assumed to have been murdered nearby.

In 1782, thirty years after Erhardt's death, the Moravians finally opened a station near Arvertok, calling it "Hopedale" in reference to the martyr Erhardt. However, its function by then was less to commemorate the legendary expedition than to staunch the exodus of Inuit to southern trading posts. Br. Crantz wrote in his account for the year:

> The spirit of traffic had become extremely prevalent amongst the southern Esquimaux; the hope of exaggerated advantages which they might derive from a voyage to the European factories, wholly abstracted their thoughts from religious inquiries; and one boat-load followed another throughout the summer. A Frenchman from Canada, named Makko who had newly settled in the south [then at Chateau], and who sustained the double character of trader and Catholic priest, was particularly successful in enticing the Esquimaux by the most tempting offers. Besides the evil consequences resulting from these expeditions in a spiritual point of view, so large a proportion of their wares was thus conveyed to the south that the annual vessel which brought out provisions and other necessaries for the brethren, and articles of barter for the natives could make up but a small cargo in return, though the brethren, unwilling as they were to supply this ferocious race with instruments which might facilitate the execution of their revengeful

projects, furnished them with the firearms they could otherwise, and on any terms, have procured from the south.[5]

The traders responded to the southward expansion of the Mission territories by moving north to meet them, eager to take advantage of the Inuit's new congeniality and appetite for trade, and determined to arrest further expansion of Mission holdings. Around 1784 Pierre Marcoux and Louis Marchand reopened the old French posts at North West River and Kaipokok, where Marcoux "established an apparently friendly connection with the members at Hopedale, and succeeded in enticing half the congregation away with promises both of trading and religious advantages without such irksome restraints as were imposed within the pale of the Brethren's Church."[6]

In 1795 the Moravians at Hopedale recorded their observation that Marcoux and George Cartwright's former associate Collingham were the first whites to "settle" in Kaipokok Bay. They were accompanied then by "an Englishman, and two other Europeans,"[7] the first of several small groups of whites to come and go from the coast during the ensuing decade. By 1797 two of these men had taken Inuit wives.[8] According to the Periodical Accounts, all had vanished from the Moravian Coast by 1806.

One can only speculate as to the fate of these first nameless families. Some may simply have retreated to the relative security of Quebec, Newfoundland, or the southern stations until the European wars ended and supply lines re-opened. But if the would-be colonists left progeny, they seemingly had little impact on their acculturation, for only one origin story survives from this period—that of Ambrose Brooks in Ivuktoke.

It seems plausible that some mixed children from early unions were abandoned or orphaned by their fathers and raised in Native households. The Inuit Lucy,[9] Brown, Cole, and Mucko families in the Kaipokok-Ivuktoke area could well have acquired their names in this way.[10] In 1857 when Brother Elsner travelled the coast he noted an Inuit family called "Markuse" near Pottle's Bay and another called "Makoo" near Rigolet where the Muckos now live—names of Inuit men that traded at Slade's in the summer of 1798. You will recall that the Inuit called Marcoux "Makko." They may even have named Makkovik after the place of his residence—although there are alternative theories regarding the origin of the village name. Peter and Tobias Lucy were also designated by Elsner as Inuit, although Peter's homestead deep in Kanairiktok Bay south of Hopedale—an uncharacteristic location for an Inuk—suggests a Settler upbringing. But one must remember that throughout the nineteenth century Inuit were as likely to have appropriated a familiar white surname as to have inherited it. By the 1850s Lucys, Tooktoshinas, and Serkoaks (later "Shiwak") had adopted Christian names as well. Manak, Markuse, and the rest of the Ivuktoke Inuit families would do so within the next fifteen years.[11]

Permanent settlement of the Moravian Coast began after the Napoleonic Wars ended in 1815. When British adventurers and merchant fisheries returned with charters to Southern Labrador stations, some of the displaced freemen and petty entrepreneurs who had taken over in their absence came north to start over in Ivuktoke or the virgin bays of the Moravian Coast. Others came to trap furs and open outposts for companies like Slade's and Hunt & Henley, but it would be another fifteen years before a sufficient infrastructure was in place to support anything but the most tenuous Settler existence. As elsewhere, those who came before the 1830s are the men whose early family history remains most obscure—Thomas,[12] Broomfield, Reed[13]— lost, perhaps, in a generation raised by mothers who spoke only Inuktitut.

The opening of trading posts on the Moravian Coast in the 1830s increased the viability of settlement and brought a wave of immigrants to the area from Europe and Canada. Thomas Bird re-opened the Kaipokok post in 1830; A. B. Hunt Company established the first post at Davis Inlet in 1831. In 1834 ownership of Kaipokok passed briefly from Bird to Quebec-based Bostonian David Ramsey Stewart, reestablishing its original position as part of the main Esquimaux Bay concession. Stewart sold out to the Hudson's Bay Company three years later after a tenure in which his Kaipokok agent, a Mr. Brown, committed suicide. Might he have left offspring? A family of Browns lived in Bay of Islands at mid-century, and local people have not forgotten the story of old Tom Brown, described as Inuit, who was widely thought to have murdered a succession of wives, children, and neighbors in Kaipokok Bay during the 1890s.

Although the earliest Moravian Coast Settler to pass on his history was John Ford of Kingston, there are reasons to believe that the first permanent Settler in the region may have been a Broomfield. Family members generally attribute their origin to a Joseph Broomfield of Dartmouth who married a Coveyduc from Newfoundland with whom he fathered Samuel James, Abram, Eliza, and Charles in the Rigolet area during the 1850s. Samuel James, born in 1852, is thought by one narrator to have been raised by old Charles McNeill in Bay of Islands. He himself claims to have been born near Rigolet and moved to the Moravian Coast in 1875. Once settled in Big Bay, he produced a large family and became widely known for his white whiskers, English pride, fiddle and accordion playing, and his diligence as game warden for the north coast.[14]

Other accounts, however, tell of a family of mixed-race Broomfields (sometimes spelled Bromfield or Brumfield) which preceded Samuel James and his siblings by sixty years or more. Its progenitor was William Broomfield, "servant" on Slade Company's books as early as 1791. Or possibly even John Broomfield, "planter," who traded with Slade's at Battle Harbour from 1783 to 1792, when he "retired to England." By 1794 William had a family, and by 1810 he was in business with partner George Dempster, working the salmon posts in Hawkes Bay. The gravestone William erected there for his friend Dempster, "a patron of England," is reported to say he died in 1802 at age 65, but George Dempster & Company did engage in trade with Slade's in 1811. (John Thomas had some of his earnings credited to the Dempster/Broomfield account that year.) Labrador gravestones are rife with errors, and this one should probably read 1812, but it is also possible that the company (or partnership) name outlasted the man. As for William, he was obviously successful. By 1806 he had earned an expenses-paid trip home, which it seemed he planned to take. If he did, he was back in Labrador within two years, apparently to stay.

One of William's mixed-race children was indeed named Joseph, but the similarities with the story of his namesake end there. This Joseph was born in the second decade of the nineteenth century and orphaned young. Old Mark Ansty raised him at Collingham's Tickle in Ivuktoke.[15] Joseph and Tom Broomfield signed an 1835 petition as "planters and merchants of Esquimaux Bay" objecting to a Bill then before the colonial government of Newfoundland which would have extinguished all existing title to salmon rivers on the Island "and its dependencies," principally Labrador. Their signatures suggest they were both of legal age by then. Joseph fathered several children (among them a daughter named Mary who married George Pottle in 1860) and lived to be an old man on the south Moravian Coast near Tom and William Broomfield. All three names appear on Brother Elsner's mid-century maps.

Cobbling together the scraps of information from the narratives of descendants, we can imagine that Slade's William Broomfield, planter, drowned sometime around 1820, leaving half-grown, half-breed children. Eliza would have been among the oldest, Joseph among the youngest, William, Tom, and Mary in between. As his Inuit wife was unable to care for the family, his young children were raised in other households. Eliza married French Canadian Peter Hamel around 1830 and took her teenaged sister Mary in for a year or two before arranging her marriage to Englishman Samuel James Thomas, also from Dartmouth. The grizzly story of Eliza's murder is told by Lydia Campbell's family in the narratives from Esquimaux Bay. Mary's story is told in this chapter by Caroline Jacques. Her daughter, also named Mary, became the wife of Norwegian immigrant Torsten Andersen later in the century.

It is possible that Slade's John or William Broomfield had an English son or grandson named Joseph who came to Labrador after the war years to start the branch of this family tree described by descendants of Samuel James Broomfield of Big Bay. Perhaps it is just a coincidence that so many offspring from both branches bore the same Christian names. But it is also possible, because the children were so young when their father died, that selective family memory has reinvented its origins, compressed the first two generations, or that the mixed-race second generation of Settlers still considered themselves Englishmen and their place of origin that of their father's family. This would be fairly typical of the Settlers of that era who viewed their stay in the New World as temporary, an opportunity to advance themselves before returning to homes many of them would never see again. Today most of the Broomfields live in Happy-Valley Goose Bay, but many of the old families from Cape Charles to Nain are laced with their bloodlines.

Ford family lore claims as its progenitor John Ford of Kingston, who came to Labrador in 1815 with four grown sons, at least one of whom, William, remained in the country. John or his namesake son later served as factor at Hunt Company posts on the Moravian Coast, settling at the Paul's Island location. It could be coincidental, but the Fords employed by Slade & Company in the 1780s and '90s also bore the Christian names John, William, Thomas, and Joseph. It is possible that they left Labrador to fight in the wars with France, returning immediately thereafter to settle. In Labrador, the family as a whole was successful in trade and had stores on several of their premises. Prolific and peripatetic, they had homesteads in Big Bay, Voisey's Bay, Paul's Island, and Black Island, north of Nain, and possibly at Ford's Bight near Kaipokok. Many travelled to Newfoundland and beyond, or to outposts in the North West Territories. John Ford, Sr. remarried, this time to a Newfoundland woman with whom he raised children of roughly the same ages—and with many of the same names—as his grandchildren, to the consternation of future genealogists.

John Lane, another name in Slade's ledgers for the years 1786-88, had settled permanently in Labrador by 1830 and was allegedly the first to build a homestead in what is now called Big Bay, between Davis Inlet and Hopedale. For many decades it was known as Jack Lane's Bay. Descendants lived there and in adjacent Jim Lane's Bay (also called Flower's Bay) until the 1950s, when most moved to Postville, North West River, or Happy Valley.

Amos Voisey (1817-1887) came from Plymouth to Cartwright as a cabinboy around 1835. He signed on as furrier for Hunt & Henley, eventually working for their agent John Ford at Paul's Island. In 1844 Amos married Clare, an Inuk from the Nain congregation, and settled at Kangeklualuk Bay. When Clare died in 1855, he married Rachel, a communicant from Hopedale. In 1864 the couple moved to Kamarsuk and, four years later, established the family homestead in Voisey's Bay. From 1871 until his death in 1887, Amos ran the Mission's store at Kamarsuk, serving both the small community of Inuit and Settlers around the Zoar Mission (1866-94) and the Mushuau Innu who came down from the barrens via the Kogaluk River. After Zoar Mission closed, his son George moved the store to his own homestead at the head of the bay by then known as "Voisey's," but which the Innu always called 'Emish,' their rendition of Amos.

Canadian Antoni Perrault and his Indian wife came to the Moravian Coast in 1843 following a six-year stint with HBC in Rigolet. It would be interesting to know if he was related to the Perrault, "sealer" on the Lower North Shore who, in 1770, petitioned the Crown to return Canadian and southern Labrador as far as Esquimaux Bay to Quebec.[16] Antoni and his wife settled at the head of Kaipokok Bay and established an independent trading post for the Innu in direct competition with their former employer, whose main Kaipokok post was barely ten miles away. Perrault's operation, supplied by the illustrious Captain William Bartlett, was so successful that he became the only independent trader on the coast to prevail in a contest with HBC. The Great Company packed up and left the bay to Perrault in 1879. Both Perrault and Jean-Baptiste Jacques,[17] who also came to Kaipokok in the 1840s, had large families whose descendants now live in Makkovik and Postville. Thorwald Perrault led part of the exodus from the coast in 1941 and helped found the village of Happy Valley, now home to his descendants.

Charles McNeill, youngest son of Scottish crofters, sailed to Newfoundland with his father in 1820 and joined a fishing crew operating around Cape Harrison and Ivuktoke. Ten years later, having accumulated enough capital to outfit his own schooner, he married Wealthiness Metcalfe of Clark's Beach and brought her to Labrador to seek an isolated spot in which to create the ideal homestead he envisioned. It was not until 1849, however, that they selected the site for a permanent home and settled down at Island Harbour with their growing family. The McNeills of Island Harbour are unique in having sustained over several generations the semi-agrarian lifestyle of the Scottish isles, with its orderly crofting routines and traditions. The old buildings are nearly all gone now, along with the gardens, livestock, and all but a few of the McNeills, who until recently have returned when they could on holidays. However the homestead remains one of coastal Labrador's hidden Shangri Las, a cluster of weathered buildings tucked in a wooded cove just round the point and out of earshot from the Atlantic's noisy shore. Here it is the murmur of wind in the tall spruce and the jazzy riff of a fox sparrow that one hears, mingled with the splatter of a waterfall that tumbles off a mossy cliff into the lagoon. Against its backdrop of darkly steepled spruce, the silvery gable of Rupert and Peace McNeill's house sails on a billowing tide of window-high delphiniums that now run wild in the tall grass of the surrounding meadow. Since Rupert's passing, I am told, she too is beginning to sink beneath these cheerful waves.

George Lyall (1818-1884) of Grenoch came to HBC's Kaipokok post as a cooper around 1855.[18] On completing his service to the company, he married Charles McNeill's daughter Margaret and settled in Kanairiktok Bay just north of Island Harbour.[19] Most of the Lyalls, like the Voiseys, later gravitated toward Nain and the northern Moravian stations. But branches of the Lyall and Ford families took root at Island Harbour through marriage to McNeill women. Like the Fords, the Lyalls and McNeills often married Newfoundlanders, conducted business directly with Newfoundland merchants, and sometimes sent children to St. John's for schooling or apprenticeships. A few made their way to the outside world and never returned to Labrador.

Torsten Andersen of Norway, *né* Torstein Kverna, first came to Kaipokok Bay with the HBC after a short period at its Rigolet post. He left the company in 1854 and set up as petty trader at "Maggovik" or Makkovik Bight, just south of the entrance to Kaipokok Bay. With its mountainous backdrop, it would have reminded him of home. Torsten married Mary Thomas, daughter of his neighbor Samuel James Thomas and Mary Broomfield, his half-Inuit wife.[20] Thomas was a prosperous fur trader, and Torsten's future bride grew up in a comfortable home with a garden deep in Thomas's Bay, now called Makkovik Bay. Torsten and Mary Andersen raised a large family remembered for its extraordinary pioneer women and Torsten's insistence that the children marry only whites to preserve the purity of their Nordic blood—a pretense most of his offspring considered impractical if not absurd. Torsten did not attempt to replicate the farming life he had grown up in but did pass on to his children the Protestant values and work ethic of his homeland. It was probably Mary who made them strong Labradorians. The family today is proud of its Native blood; in fact, the first president of the Labrador Inuit Association in the 1970s was an Andersen, and descendants are still active in civic affairs.

Edward Mitchell (who married a daughter of John Ford), William Metcalfe, and William Flowers also had homesteads on the Moravian Coast by 1857. No history has come to light for Metcalfe, who is probably a relative of Wealthiness McNeil from Clark's Beach in Newfoundland. We can surmise from Elsner's helpful Moravian maps that the first Flowers was a Charles and that he arrived in Labrador relatively early (possibly from Newfoundland, where there is a Flowers' Cove near the Strait of Belle Isle, or the Channel Islands), because at mid-century there were apparently already three adult generations. They seem to have lived first in the Rigolet area, as some still do, and are presumed to have come with HBC. The Moravian Coast branch—William's family perhaps—gravitated toward Hopedale, where they have since played a powerful role in local business and politics.

By the end of the nineteenth century, most of the new arrivals to the north coast were second or third generation Labradorians from Sandwich Bay and Ivuktoke, like William Dickers, Harry Webb, George Sheppard, Irishman Richard Gear, Nathan White, and later, Freeman Saunders. Webb's story exists in fragments, some of them contradictory. The progenitor arrived around 1826, possibly working for Hunt at Cartwright and later John Ford at Paul's Island. He married one of Ford's daughters but died shortly afterwards on a return voyage from England. His widow then married George Sheppard, who raised Webb's young son near Rigolet. The son, apparently also named Harry, went to Davis Inlet as cook for the Hudson's Bay Company when he was twenty-one. Since HBC did not take over the Davis Inlet post from Hunt Company until 1869, Webb would have been born after 1848. In any case, he settled in Webb Bay with Sarah Jane, his Inuit bride, when he was thirty-seven.

Thomas Evans of Liverpool "ran away" to Canada around 1865, eventually finding his way to the Makkovik area, where he married Harriet Broomfield and settled in Ben's Cove, named for Ben Monamie. Monamies are more often associated with Sandwich Bay and the Atlantic Shore. The origins of the Monamie and Edmunds families have so far eluded this researcher, but Edmunds lived in Kamarsuk, at the mouth of Voisey's Bay, and later at Sango Bay/Davis Inlet, during the last years of the nineteenth century.

When HBC left Kaipokok Bay in 1879, the focus of the local economy shifted from fur, salt trout, and salmon to codfish, and the population spent more time among the Newfoundland fishermen and traders like Dunn's and William Bartlett who operated fishing stations on the islands. Expansion of the Newfoundland fishery into northern Labrador began after 1850 but did not peak until the end of the century. The Turnavik Islands outside Kaipokok Bay and Queen's Lakes outside Nain were their principal stations, but floaters gradually filled the good fishing harbours as far as the codfish ran, even to the north of Okak. Settlers welcomed the fishermen, with whom they initially shared exclusion from the society of the Moravian stations. Like Perrault, they found them convenient channels to Newfoundland markets, merchandise, and sometimes wives. At least one of the fishermen, Abe Morgan of Clark's Beach, became enamored of a Labrador woman and joined the Settler community on the Moravian Coast.

As the century progressed, the Settlers became increasingly involved in Mission life. Families like the Andersens who brought a strong Protestant orientation with them from abroad embraced the Moravian Church and became influential in its local leadership. It was for these families, especially the Andersens, that the Moravians agreed finally to establish a Mission (1896) and school (1897) near the original Andersen homestead. The school in turn provided an incentive for families like the Evans, who lived nearby, and the McNeills, who valued education and family togetherness, to establish temporary lodgings in the village during winter months when the men were off trapping. In 1919 the Mission followed the example of the Grenfell Association and opened a boarding school for children from the southern Moravian Coast. However, as was true across Labrador, the Settlers did not abandon wilderness homesteads for permanent homes in the village until the 1950s and '60s. Makkovik remained Labrador's only non-Inuit Mission village until 1956, when the government moved a group of families from Nutak into the community. By 1961, following resettlement of Hebron families, the town's population had doubled and its ethnic composition become at least as mixed, though not yet as integrated, as other settlements in northern Labrador.

When I last saw it in 1989, Makkovik was a pretty village spread across a crescent beach against a backdrop of purple-faceted mountain peaks. Fishing vessels from Portugal and other distant ports still visited the little harbour looking for fuel and girls and, as of old, conducting a clandestine trade in illicit substances. Old frame houses with scalloped Norwegian eaves and decorative trim relieved the terraced rows of tract housing in the village center. Komatiks leaned against the houses next to turquoise planters made of inverted inner tubes with sawtooth rims. Gargantuan geraniums pressed against the panes of lace-curtained windows, gaily watching the sea from assorted coffee cans and pickle jars on the sill. Elderly matrons whose grandchildren had gone to Goose Bay and a more promising future groomed them absent-mindedly as they, too, watched the sea and waited. In the woods behind the Moravian church, twice rebuilt since fire destroyed the village in 1948, a hand-lettered sign almost hidden within the branches of a spruce tree overlooking the graveyard read:

> The tired winds are hushed
> to rest
> The shadows deeper grow,
> The evening star shines dimly
> Like a taper burning low,
> The flames of evenings alter fires
> Light all the western sky
> And God's sweet peace
> [Bodes] over all
> As sunset hour draws nigh.

The village of Postville was founded in 1949 when a Pentecostal missionary built a church and lumberyard on the site of the old HBC Kaipokok Bay post. Lanes and Jacques, Sheppards and other families desperate for work followed. Lumberyards, boat yards, and uranium mines have since come and gone, and with them the promise of a viable livelihood within this deep bay. The latest plan, proposed by the current Pentecostal minister, grandson to the founder, is to reopen the lumber yard and provide building materials for the Voisey's Bay mine site when development proceeds. Meanwhile, the community remains idle and isolated. Well, not quite idle. I imagine its rickety smoke-houses still turn out some of the best smoked trout in Labrador, the church bell still calls people to worship at intervals throughout the day, and kids, I hope, still play a wicked game of stick hockey.

The historic village of Hopedale is a good day's boat trip north of Postville. When On my last visit, a huge fuel depot at the head of the cove, featureless as a shoebox, dominated the approach to the harbour. A cluster of government-issue houses had sprouted around it, and clouds of dust rose from the wake of vehicles traversing the half-mile roadway between the new and old town. But the old village at the mouth of the bay had changed little in twenty years. Its imposing Moravian buildings, one of them said to be the oldest frame structure in Canada, still commanded awe and admiration. Today much of the space in the long Mission house serves as museum for the relics of a time when hope for a heavenly community on earth was still vivid. A ghastly collection of eighteenth-century surgical instruments stands out from the rest, jarring symbols not only of the enormous corporal obstacles to be overcome by the missionaries, but of their extraordinary hubris. Not until Dr. Grenfell put them to shame in the 1890s were any of them prepared with more than a rudimentary training in medicine. Now its entrepreneurial Settlers, not the church, rule the town. As a result of their schemes (which included opening the coast's only beer store in the 1970s), it has waged and to some degree won an especially hard battle with alcoholism. It has, however, been unable to solve the problem of its unaccommodating location. The puddled bedrock on which it sits prohibits introduction of modern water supply and sewage systems; pro-growth local businessmen have resisted relocation; and the political heat generated by this issue has left the community divided and embittered.

Leaving the village by sea, the red roofs and green cupolas of the Moravian Mission's venerable buildings drop out of sight below a rise in the rock. The last glimpse of Hopedale is of the ancient sod house foundations of Arvertok crumbling from beneath the roadway.

Davis Inlet is the only Innu village on the coast of Labrador. The Naskapi called it Utshimassit, "place of the boss." Its location had no traditional importance to the Innu, who rarely ventured so far out in the bays, but it was convenient for the trading companies needing a deep-water anchorage, and so the Innu annually sent delegations out to the station for the ammunition, tea, and flour on which they had come to rely. When the Hudson's Bay Company acquired the post from Hunt & Company in 1869, it actively courted the Naskapi for their furs by encouraging the visits of Catholic priests, providing inoculations against smallpox, and importing birch bark for canoes. Settlers were welcome to trade there, and did, but the assumption that Inuit would not do so was reassuring both to the Innu and the Moravians.

Until the 1960s, Innu visits to Utshimassit/Davis Inlet were brief and unpredictable. In most cases they found Settler-run posts like George Voisey's more convenient and hospitable. When a shift in deer migration routes caused wholesale starvation in 1916, it was to Voisey's place that they went for help. When they did visit Utshimassit, they usually stayed at their camp in Sango Bay until 1927, when Father O'Brien began his annual summer ministry. Then they began to prolong their visits to the post, using the time on the coast to repair canoes and tents. HBC built a church for them in 1945, but it was not until 1952 that a missionary was assigned to the community year-round, and part of the encampment shifted to Utshimassit, bringing with it the alcohol-related problems that had already developed at the Sango camp. The last Innu shaman died five years later.

In the early 1960s, the priest and government encouraged the Innu to take up codfishing, providing those selected by the priest with boats and equipment, sometimes to good effect. "Through the missionary, the Naskapi also expressed a desire to live in houses. The government was in favour of this and in the period between 1966 and 1969, a new community was built on the nearby island of Iluikoyak, to which the Naskapi began moving in the fall of 1967."[21] The traders and Settlers called it "New Davis Inlet." To the Innu, it remained Utshimassit. By 1969 most had moved from tents into houses for the first time ever and given up the winter migrations to the interior. They went on welfare, exchanging deer meat and fish for Coca-Cola and stale potato chips. Optimism soon gave way to disappointment. Water and sewer systems were never installed in the houses. The island may have been good hunting and fishing country for Inuit, but not for the Innu, who found themselves trapped there for weeks on end by forming or breaking-up ice.

Efforts by the priest and store manager to prepare the Innu for participation in the mainstream economy of the coast created a schism in the community. The drinking families shunned by the priest segregated themselves from the non-drinking families who were rewarded with job opportunities, fishing boats, and other favours. The village soon turned into a breeding ground for dissipation, rancor, and despair. Come autumn, when the men returned to hunt in the interior, these social problems quickly gave way to traditional patterns of leadership and cooperation. The families left in the settlement began to long for the freedom of their old nomadic lives. They felt trapped, disempowered, dispossessed. A quarter century later, they still do. Alcoholism, gas sniffing, drugs, and suicide reached such epidemic proportions in the 1980s that the plight of this tiny community made news around the world.

Through social and political activism, some of the Naskapi are finding ways to revive the spirit that once sustained their people only in the wild. But so far they have won no battles—not the fight to stop the damming of Churchill Falls which flooded much of their hunting grounds, nor the low-level NATO flight training and aerial bombing from Goose Bay that daily destroys the exquisite peace of Nitassinan. Even their success in obtaining government approval and funding for a new community at the old campsite in Sango Bay has a hollow ring as they realize another move, even to a more traditionally favourable location, will not eradicate their social problems. They themselves will have to find a way to leave them behind.

On a larger scale, the Innu of Utshimassit/Davis Inlet, in concert with the northern Inuit and some of the Settlers, are today waging what may be the most important battle of their lives—the right to a voice and a stake in development of Labrador's resources. Because they have never signed a treaty, never extinguished their rights in exchange for the trinkets and tokens offered by colonial regimes, never abdicated their stewardship of the land, only the Innu and Inuit can legally challenge the government over "ownership" of Labrador. It is therefore they who must hold the line of defense against the formidable forces of greed that are driving the mining, logging, and hydroelectric interests and the financially desperate government of Newfoundland in a barrage of planned mega-developments across Labrador. The future not just of the Aboriginal people, but of all Labrador, is in their hands. To the surprise of many observers, they are turning out to be extremely capable hands at that.

When the HBC moved its Davis Inlet post to Iluikoyak in 1968, Freeman Saunders, the retired store manager, took up residence on the original site. Saunders came from Cartwright to work at the Davis Inlet post in 1917. His son Jim, who was eight years old then, grew up among the Naskapi and learned their language. Jim and his wife, Maggie Gear Saunders, a survivor of the Spanish Influenza in Okak, raised their family at this 'Old Davis Inlet' homestead. Saunders and Edmunds were the only Settler families in that area during the twentieth century.

Settlers began moving into the Nain station after 1926 when HBC took over the Mission store and opened a nursing station, and Captain Donald Macmillan of the US contributed a new school in the tradition of Wilfred Grenfell. With the introduction of government stores (1947), Canadian schooling (1950), and an IGA hospital (1957), more Settler families moved into town—Lyalls, Voiseys, Fords, and Webbs among them—taking jobs in the stores, fish plants, and service industries that grew with the town. Accustomed to a peripheral status at the station, most originally congregated on the opposite side of the Mission buildings from the enclave of Nain Inuit and its "suburb" of identical box houses the government built for the displaced Hebronemiut. When Hebron station closed in 1959, Nain effectively became the northernmost village on the coast of Labrador, as the Killinek station was too small, too remote, and too oriented toward Quebec and Baffin Island to count.[22] Growth of the town and continued intermarriage in recent decades has all but effaced the economic and ethnic distribution of the population.

In contrast to modern Hopedale, Nain enjoys a setting that is both accommodating and dramatic. The Moravians early on declared the vigorous spruce forest that covered the sandy terrace on which they erected their station as a "Park," to be preserved and protected for all time. Its remnant trees still tower behind the Mission buildings like an honor guard, erect and inscrutable at the foot of the hill that rises behind the village. Across the bay, the silvery dome of Sophia, named for the maiden said to have thrown herself from its brow into the sea, lends majesty and pathos to the scene. In summer, when the sun rides behind the shoulders of the town, it is Sophia who catches and magnifies the first glow of dawn, the blaze of watery sunlight after storms, and the sheen of moonlit nights.

In recent decades Nain has become an important center for northern Labrador affairs, attracting a large community of outsiders as entrepreneurs, social service providers, and government representatives. Since 1994 its population has undergone another surge as preparations began for the mining operation at nearby Voisey's Bay. The town has spread around the harbour almost to the feet of Sophia and back into the land, but the old white frame Moravian compound still presides at the head of the wharf, gracious as a welcoming committee. A succession of fires destroyed the original buildings, but those standing today are distinguished enough to impress tourists. Yellow, white, and orange poppies planted by the early missionaries nod gaily in the unmown grass at their feet, surviving somehow the haphazard traffic of children, dogs, ATVs and trucks that tumbles around the Mission House like water around rocks in a brook, filling the air with the pineapple scent of crushed chamomile.

For most of Nain's residents, the land of the *torngat* no longer exists but in their veins and souls. They look now to the sea, where only the larger vessels can venture far enough to harvest resources as yet spared from extinction—shrimp, scallops, and deep water fish disdained when cod and salmon schooled near shore. They look with a mixture of hope and apprehension to Voisey's Bay, wherein lies their future, for better or worse. And they look to the south, to St. John's and Goose Bay, gateways to a world more accessible to them now than it has ever been, but so very far from the scent of chamomile raised by the feet of ancestors, generation after generation, under the shining face of Sophia.

Nain, 1900.

The weather, upon which so much depends in the case of a people like the Eskimos who live by hunting and fishing, was, unfortunately, very unsettled in the autumn of the year 1898, extreme cold interchanging at short intervals with great warmth. True, the sea froze over at the usual time, but so quickly did the cold give over to milder weather that no one dared venture on to the thin ice, with the result that the seals that were there in large numbers escaped to the open sea before they could be captured. Foxes and reindeer were fewer than for some years past; ptarmigans and hares likewise. The prospects for the winter were, accordingly, poor.

Christmas and New Year were furthermore saddened by discouraging experiences with the people at the station, many of whom had to be placed under Church discipline for frivolity and sin. On the other hand the missionaries were also permitted to see fruits of the work of the Spirit of God in the hearts and lives of others at the station. At Easter two youths belonging to settler families were confirmed, and at their own special request a goodly number of such [Natives] as were under exclusion or suspension were re-admitted to full Church fellowship, before starting, as they were about to do, for their hunting and fishing grounds. Sad to tell! ever so many of these fell into sin again during their absence from the station....

Reference has repeatedly been made to agents of the Hudson's Bay Company in the reports published of our Labrador Mission, and with pleasure we read in the diary of the Nain congregation of a friendly visit paid to the station by Mr. and Mrs. Swaffield, the Company's agents at Davis Inlet, the HBC post situated between Hopedale and Zoar on the coast. Mr. Swaffield and his good lady take a great interest in the spiritual as well as the temporal welfare of the settlers who trade with them, and have again encouraged our missionaries to visit these people, who belong to the poorest on the coast, as frequently as possible.

— Moravian Periodical Accounts
[13.3:41]

1921 IS A DATE NOT to be forgotten for it was in that year that Nain caught fire. All the mission buildings were destroyed by fire, in that year, 1921.

At that time I was cod-trapping at Natsatuuk with William Barbour's crew.

The *Harmony* had arrived in Nain and all the able-bodied men were told to go to Nain to unload the freight and the winter's supply of food. Consequently, a lot of people came in to work. When the *Harmony* was unloaded, it left in the morning travelling north towards Hebron. It was a beautiful morning. It was warm, a little hazy, and the sun was shining brightly.

Before we had to go back to our fishing place, we tried to get to the store, before dinner, to buy our provisions. There were so many people also buying their supplies that we were not able to leave before dinner. We just left without going to the store because we were in a rush. We were fishing at Natsatuuk and our work there came first.

When we got to the western end of Uigumigali, by that island, someone saw smoke. We stopped to watch where it was coming from because it was just getting bigger and bigger. When we realized that it was coming from the direction of Nain, we started heading back to Nain.

All the Inuit who were able to work were away at their summer places. They were all spread out around Nain; some were at close places, others further away.

When we came in sight of Nain, we saw that Nain was burning. When we saw that, we unloaded all that we were carrying in the boat on a rocky bank on the landward side of Nuvutannak, on the island facing Nain Harbour. With great speed we proceeded to Nain.

As it happened, the store was on fire. Because there was such a wind from the west, the flames from the fire were shooting up and were being blown to the missionary houses. The roofs of the mission houses were caught afire. Before we reached Nain the roof of the church was in flames. When we reached the wharf we all started running to our houses. I just kicked the door open to our house and began taking all the things which were most important to us down to the beach. My wife and I carried everything to the water-line of the shore. When all the possessions which we valued most were out of the house, we went to see the fire. The heat was too great to go near the church. The fire was still raging and as I wanted to see the store, I went over there. The day before the store had been full of everything, but we saw nothing as everything had been burnt.

Also burning were big puncheons, huge barrels of seal oil, rendered from seal blubber, readied to be transported by the *Harmony* on its way south. There were also many, many barrels of trout ready to be shipped out on the *Harmony*. Right there from by the store there was a river of flames right down to the water's edge from the seal oil that was burning.

There was no food left.

All the *Quallunaak's* [whites'] possessions were swallowed by the fire.

Not one Inuk house caught on fire that time that there was a fire in Nain.

These things can be replaced, that we understand.

All these things I saw with my own eyes and perceived with my own credibility. This is not just a story.

— Martin Martin
[3.4:52]

Affidavit of George Voisey
In the Matter of the Enquiry into Newfoundland
Territorial Rights on the Labrador

District of Labrador, Voisey's Bay, to wit:

I, GEORGE VOISEY, of Voisey's Bay, Kekitonjak Island, make oath and say as follows:

1. I reside in Voisey's Bay, a settlement about thirty-one miles from Nain and about sixty miles from the waters of the coast.

2. My father [Amos Voisey] was born in Plymouth, England. He came here about sixty-five years ago [1844], and lived up here to the time of his death about twenty-two years ago. I am fifty-seven years of age. I have resided here all my life. My father was a trouter, salmon catcher and furrier, and used to go into the interior on hunting trips for fourteen and fifteen days at a time, going in as far as one-hundred miles. He exercised the rights of citizenship here during his lifetime and was subject to the laws of the Government of Newfoundland, the same as we are now. I have been subject to the Governor and the Government of Newfoundland all my life, paying duties to the Collector of Customs since he has been coming on the Coast. I have fished, trapped and hunted, and have been in the interior a hundred miles on hunting trips. I never had any intimation from the Canadian Government that I was on their territory, or anything of that sort. I have been all my life under the Moravian Mission, obeying the laws of Newfoundland.

(Sgd.) GEORGE VOISEY
Sworn before me at Voisey's Bay aforesaid,
this 19th day of August, 1909.

(Sgd.) F.J. Morris
Judge of the Court of Labrador

— Privy Council Records, vol. VIII,
Section D, No. 464 , p. 1353
[18.3:3]

MY GREAT-GRANDFATHER, AMOS VOISEY, he runned away from England for some reason, nobody knowed why. He worked his way over on one of the boats that used to come across to Cartwright. He didn't land in Newfoundland first, he landed on the Labrador coast at Cartwright. He worked his way over as a cabin-boy, whatever that is, a steward or a cook's helper or something like that. When he got to Cartwright he got a job with the Hudson's Bay Company, I s'pose, or some other trading post [probably Hunt & Henley]. In them days the company would outfit fellers to go trappin' fur for them, then in the spring they'd turn in their fur and they'd get so much for what they caught. That's what he was doin' first when he came to Labrador.

He left Cartwright and the next place he showed up was Paul's Island at Ford's Harbour, with John Ford, another Englishman, the first Ford. He spent a couple of years trappin'. John Ford would fit him out with traps and grub. I don't think it was his own store; I think he might have been tradin' for the Hudson's Bay Company [Hunt & Co.]. One time when the Moravian supply ship *Harmony* didn't make it to Nain, and they were runnin' low on grub and supplies, he [John Ford] helped them out a little bit with what he could spare.

After my great-grandfather got married he settled in Kamarsuk—that's where the Winters lives now. He didn't do any tradin' there, he trapped marten. Them days there was marten around to be trapped. What they was after then was marten and seals, seals mostly for dogs feed, skin boots and stuff like that. When he was dying he told my grandfather, George Voisey, to leave Kamarsuk and move up in the bay closer to the martens. Now, Edmund Winters was livin' with my grandfather—he adopted him like—so when Grandfather left Kamarsuk he left the place to Edmund Winters....

I don't know how many years it was after Grandfather moved up Voisey's Bay that the Moravian Mission set up a store there. Anyway my grandfather took charge of it for a year or two. He didn't like the job so he quit on them and then my father, Amos Voisey, took it over. When the Hudson's Bay Company took over all the Mission stores, my father stayed with them until he got pissed off, wasn't makin' a salary, just gettin' a commission, as they called it. That was along around the wrong time, too, 1934-35-36, the hard years....

My father would come to Nain for supplies in time to get it up in the bay before the fifteenth of October. That would be the time for settin' traps and he wouldn't want to waste no time. He get up and have everybody outfitted before the fifteenth of October if he could.

He'd trade with the Winters, the Edmunds, Voiseys and the Indians, but he got most fur from the Indians. He'd buy foxes, otter, not many mink, no marten then because they had been caught up long years before I could remember. He'd take the coloured foxes, not many white. The Indians used to bring out white fox skins from inland some years, and otter, bear skins and a wolf skin now and again....

In them days the Indians did nothing only trap and hunt. What they used to do, in the wintertime, January when 'twas cold and rough, they'd be all out in the bay instead of goin' back inland deer huntin'. There's a brook up there in the bay where they used to live off trout and hunt partridges. When the days got longer, around the middle of March, they'd leave their families at the brook while the men would go up on the barren land deer huntin' and trappin', then a little bit later, if they happened to have deer killed, they'd move the families up and they'd stay there until around the end of April or early part of May and bring out their furs. They'd be in and out all winter tradin', sellin' fur. Some would come to Voisey's Bay and others would go to Davis Inlet. The 'Bay Indians' we called them, they'd stay around the bay until the end of June or early July and then they'd go to Davis Inlet to see the priest, old Father O'Brien. Then in August they'd go in and you wouldn't see them no more until October when they'd come to get a fitout for the winter trappin'. They'd go in as far as they could and as it got colder they'd move out to the shorter brooks, and by January they'd be out to the bay for two or three weeks and then move up to the brook....

— Jim Voisey
[18.3:6]

I WAS BORN [IN 1898] to Chesley and Mary Ford at Nain in a little log cabin belonging to Uncle George Voisey. My mother was a Ford married to a Ford. Dad was adopted by old William Ford, my grandfather's father, down at Black Island. That's how come he was a Ford. Mom was a Ford before she married Dad, so I'm a natural Ford....

The first Ford, John Ford, came out from Kingston, England in 1815, I think it was. His first wife died and he come out to Labrador with his four sons. Later he married Mary Ann Summers and they started another family. The four sons that came over with him were John, Tom, William, and I can't remember the fourth one. The second lot of children were Jim, my grandfather, Aunt Mary Ann Mitchell.... I can't remember the rest, but Henry was the youngest.

The first Fords came to Nain and then they moved to different places. They came out as joiners and carpenters and that. I think Uncle John Ford went to Ungava Bay and one of the brothers went to the States or Canada or went back to England, no one ever found out where he went. They came over to work with the Moravian Mission, some of them worked with the Moravian Mission. They are all Moravian now in their religion.

Uncle William Ford went out to Black Island—he got married and went out there. My grandfather, Jim Ford, he was out to Paul's Island. Uncle Bob was over to Upatik. Uncle Henry, my husband's father, was out to Paul's Island. Uncle George Voisey went up around Ungava Bay somewhere.

Uncle George Voisey's first wife was Aunt Harriet. She's buried up in Davis Inlet. They had three children, Lizzie, Henry and Solomon. Afterwards he married a woman from Newfoundland and they had two more girls and a boy. Cardelia is nursing somewhere in the States. Selma used to live in Catalina, but I don't know if she's still living or not. And I think the boy died.

Aunt Mary Ann married old Uncle Edward Mitchell from Hopedale. Probably he was the first Mitchell come over from England. Old Uncle Harry Webb married two sisters. He married Sarah Jane first and when she died he married her sister, Susan. They had Sarah, Jim, Chesley, Clara, Louisa and Mary Ann, and there was a little one named Henry. He died when he was just an infant. Uncle Bob Ford married a Susan. I don't know what her last name was, but they lived at Upatik. They had no children but they raised one of his brother's children. So that's the old generation.

One time when we was small we had some young puppies, just big enough to break in to harness. We were always at Dad to let us go across Nain harbour to cut a few sticks of wood. We thought it was great to get across. 'Twas juniper over there and not much limbin' on them. We had an axe each, Jim and I, and we had Alf on the komatik. He was about three or four. Dad said we had to take him with us so we took him. We went and cut about five or six sticks of wood, and we thought we had a fine load. It was a job to get the pups to go. You had to lead 'um. Comin' home Alf got cold so Jim and I pulled our parkas off and we put one over his own and the other over his legs. Now we were doin' fine because we had lashed Alf on the sticks. We were gettin' well along when the pups must have smelled the village, and didn't they take off! My goodness, didn't they go! And we couldn't catch them. And there was Alf lashed on to the komatik! Dad happened to see and he had the dogs stopped before they got to the ballicaters. If they would have got to the ballicaters, Alf would have been killed. Dad told us not to ever do that again. We were frightened to death so we never done it again....

I went to school at Nain under the Moravian Mission. In the summer they used to have a teacher come out on the first *Harmony*, and she'd go back on the last one. Through the winter we'd go to school with Mrs. Smith. It was her husband christened me. They were Charlie Smith's parents.

Charlie Smith used to be a real imp when he was small. One time Mother was doin' something in the kitchen and Charlie come in and said to her, "Aunt Mare, guess what I got in me pocket?" She told him she'd never guess what he had. Anyhow, he pulled his little sister's finger out of his pocket. Mother asked him, "Where did you get that?" He said, "That's Trixie's finger. I told her to put it on the block and I chopped it off." He chopped her finger off! She was only about five years old. Another time he hung his sister Mona. He tied a string around her waist and he put her over the head of the wharf, and the tide was comin' in and the dogs were howlin'. Mother sent me down to see what was goin' on and here was Mona over the side of the wharf where Charlie had lowered her in the water. He done it for devilment. He was about nine years old, I s'pose. He was up to all sorts of mischief. Of course, we was all mischiefs anyway. I used to climb trees, get in the boats, fall in the water, and do everything a boy does.

When I went to school, you didn't have a regular classroom. You went to some-one's living room and sat around a table. I went to grade five. My first teacher was Mrs. Smith, then it was Mrs. Perrett. She taught us when Rev. Perrett was away. Then we had Miss Francis for some time, and we had Miss Dickson from New-Castle-on-Tyne. I didn't know the two oldest Perrett girls but I knew Mabel, Gladys and Edna. My two best friends were Leah Stone and Matilda Lidd. We stuck together.

Leah was married three times. She married my uncle first. He married her so she wouldn't be harassed by the others. We were always friends, and after I went away she was kind of lost like and she was being harassed, so Will Ford, my uncle, married her, but they never lived together. When Uncle Will died, Leah married Elias, some-one, and when he died she married again. The last time I saw Leah was in 1927 up in Burwell. She had a baby born on board the *Ungava*, her and her husband were on their way to Baker Lake. Mother had to go on board to born this baby and when she got there she discovered it was Leah. I didn't get to see her 'till three days or so later. They brought her ashore for a short time and then she went off again.

Mother should have wrote a book. She was a wonderful woman—what she went through, you know? She had her leg amputated when I was nine years old. She sprained her ankle a few years before that and 'twas gettin' to be worse all the time. For a year she couldn't bear anything on her leg, couldn't walk, and then it turned to gangrene. In 1907, Dr. Wakefield or Dr. Armstrong, some doctor from North West River or St. Anthony took Mother right to the hospital in Okak and took her leg off 'cause she was really gone. He said she wouldn't have lived another week like that. They cut off her leg to save her.

Mother sent for me to be with her, to get her drinks and do little errands for her. So Uncle Harry Webb said he'd take me down. Now, that was in January or February. We got caught in a snowstorm and we was stuck there off Kiglapait for three days. The first night Uncle Harry just dug a hole in the snow and put the canvas right over and I crawled in the sleeping bag and that's where I stayed. Next morning Uncle Harry went out and he was gone all morning. I thought he was lost and I was there all alone, so I started to cry. I dug a hole to see if I could see him and the snow drifted in. It was driftin' to beat the band. Anyhow, there he was buildin' a snow house. He built a lovely big snow house, the first one I was ever in. On one end he had like a chimney built. He took the two ends out of my komatik box and one of the boards off the side, and that was the fire wood. The snow melted where the fire was but it made it real hard.

So there we were. We had nothing to boil the kettle 'cause we was only gone for a day and a half, so he melted snow in an old white mug he had and he held the mug over the candle to melt the snow. He gave me a drink of the tea but I didn't like it 'cause the tea was all floatin' on it so I spit it out. He drank it then he melted more snow and made some more tea. We had no milk, just a little sugar, and he made the tea too strong. He liked it. I drank a few mouthfuls and I thought it was poison. We had only enough buns to last a couple of meals, so the last day we had nothing to eat. I was hungry and cold. Uncle Harry'd say, "Cheer up, now, girl. We'll be there soon." When we finally got on the go, I was glad when we seen Okak.

When I saw Mom, she was paralyzed on one side. She couldn't shut her hand or anything like that. She'd lift her hand but she couldn't get it to her mouth. I was frightened.

There was a little kitchen opposite Mom's ward. She'd tell me what to do. Dad sent down some grub and I'd try to cook it. Imagine, I was nine years old! I did very well though 'cause Mom taught me home. I used to make her a cup of tea. The bread wasn't very good, 'twas heavy. One of the girls used to make it. There was a big jar of redberry jam there and I tasted it and there wasn't a bit of sugar in it, the berries was just boiled to keep them. I put sugar in them and put it on Mother's bread for her.

There was an Eskimo woman, Sepora (her husband's name was Juiley), she used to bring Mother and I soup made from partridge and raisins dumplings in it. Another woman, Juliana, used to do our laundry and mending. Her husband was Abia. They were very kind people, as were Lukas and Maria, who would bring us good things to eat, as there was no cook at the hospital.

I stayed there at Okak a long time. Dr. Nixon was the doctor there. There was a girl from the village, she had something wrong with her chest. She couldn't breathe and Dr. Nixon put a tube in through her chest. He said to me, "Now, you help me." He put a white apron around me and tied a white thing on me head and I stood on a chair. He named all the things for me and he said, "Now when I asks for them you give them to me." He was operatin' on this girl, see. I was doin' fine and I passed him the things as he asked for them until the blood came and that was all I knew about it. I flopped. Whoever was there put me somewhere. Dr. Nixon was always tormentin' me after that. He used to say, "You're a nurse now, you konked out." The girl lived for two weeks after that, then she died. That was my first experience as a nurse.

They amputated Mother's leg to the ankle first, and it was always weeping. They didn't cut the bone short enough to lap the flesh over, you know, and 'twas always weeping. So she had two more operations after that, the last one was in 1922. They cut the bone shorter and cleaned it, and she never had no more trouble with it after. She wore out three artificial limbs, but you'd never know she was lame. No one would ever know she had an artificial leg, unless they happened to be to the house and she took it off or something. But she was some cute, she had a bag and she'd put that on the leg and take the whole leg off and shove it under the bed. Mrs. Peacock didn't know she had an artificial limb. Mom stayed with the Peacocks [Rev. Peacock, Nain Mission], see, after Dad died. She was in the kitchen one day and she felt something down around her leg. The Peacocks had a rabbit and it had nibbled the boot off around her leg. This was when Mrs. Peacock found out about Mother's artificial limb. She never limped. She lived to be eighty-four years of age.

I wasn't in Nain when the church burned down. That was about two or three years after I left. Well, I cried to break my heart when I heard Nain was burnt. There was some really nice old buildings. I can just picture it now. Every family had a garden, and there was a big kitchen garden right up from where the bridge is right down to the Mission houses. They grew everything there, grew all their own vegetables. 'Twas really nice! There's not a garden there now. It's all built up or all tore up in them places.

Bishop Martin had a park, come down from his garden. He had rustic seats and tables all built and the trees all trimmed underneath. He had a fence around it, painted red. I can always see it, you know. That's where I shot my first partridge, up in that park. Dad crippled it for me so it wouldn't get away, then he come and told me there was a spruce partridge in the tree and to go shoot it. I used a twenty-two. That's the first partridge I ever shot....

We stayed in Nain summer and winter. When I was ten years old, we went to Okak and stayed for two years. There was mostly Inuit at Okak then, except for the missionaries and ourselves and Johnny Gear. Johnny Gear married Beatrice Watts' grandmother, Tabea. Tabea used to always have her daughter Rosie dressed different from the other girls. She used to have her dresses kind of short and she wore black stockings. Rosie was always on the run, always runnin' like them little birds. They used to call her *Kanaiqik*, which means nansary, a long-legged little bird we see on the beach.

When we were at Okak, I remember this missionary, Mr. Baldwin. He come down one evening and 'twas startin' to freeze. He started flappin' his arms around and he was sayin', "Chesley, when the wind blows now and it freezes, the komatik will fly." They used to have a sail on the komatiks up there at one time, you know, and it used to help the dogs when the wind was fair. Anyhow, Mr. Baldwin was right excited. I'll never forget that. He had a whisker, and Mrs. Baldwin, she was very tall and very sedate, always wore the high-neck collar and long dress. She was right slim. She was a nice person, always nice to me. Now some of the missionaries were kind of surly like, you know, with children, but Mrs. Baldwin was always nice.

Kate Hettasch and them lived at Okak. When the two of us got together there was nothing we wouldn't do. She had an older sister, Ermela, then there was Katie, Elsie and Greta. Greta was the youngest. I remember when Seigfried was born. It was a real snowy day in February, snowin' to beat the band. The oldest one was a boy. Kate is two years younger than me.

When I was twelve, my parents and brothers went to Burwell, and I had to go to Hopedale because there was no room for me. It was only two bedrooms and we were too big to sleep in one room, boys and girls. So I went to Hopedale with the Hettasches. But I got lonesome for me brothers, you know, and Mom and Dad. When my grandmother came south for Easter, I wanted to go home with her. She wouldn't take me so I made all kinds of fusses until finally they let me go. I stayed with Grandmother then at Paul's Island until Mother and them came back from Burwell.

I enjoyed living in Nain when I was a child. Whatever was there I enjoyed it until I got to seventeen and I wanted to get out and see the world, so when I was eighteen I went to St. John's to work at Maunders [tailor]. I went up too soon. It was hot and I wasn't used to the dust and the dirt and the town. Like when you're used to fresh air, eh...? By the time Maunders opened I was too sick to go to work. My brothers had come the year before and through they being there we got in touch with the minister and he got me a boarding place. That's how I came there, and I stayed until October. Maunders opened in September and I was down to work three days but I was too sick to hold the iron even. The last trip of the old *Harmony*, Captain Jackson came to see me and he asked what happened to me and I told him. He told Mrs. Reid, the woman I was stayin' with, to get a doctor right away. Dr. Roberts, old Will Roberts, came up and sounded me. He said, "Where does she come from? Where's her home?" Captain Jackson told him. Dr. Roberts said, "Take her back. If you wants to get her back alive you better take her now."

[In 1930] I married Abe Ford, Christiana's son.... Abe Ford worked with Dr. Grenfell with the reindeer, down in St. Anthony years ago. That's before I knew him. He was with the Hudson's Bay Company after, and he was to the First World War, him and his brother Jim. Jim got the measles and died in Scotland. They had another brother, Henry, who died when he was about eight or nine. Christiana and Henry Ford was their parents. When Henry Ford died, Christiana married Johnny Lyall. They had a number of children by the two marriages. Christiana lived to be eighty-four or eighty-five. We always called her Aunt Stana.

My father died in 1945 at the age of sixty-seven. He is buried at Boat Harbour near Zoar. My mother lived to be eighty-three. Her and my husband, Abe Ford, are buried at Thorold, Ontario.

Our family is scattered everywhere like weeds in the wind. I am now eighty-one [1979] and living with my daughter in St. John's, Newfoundland.

— Clara Ford
[5.3:4]

I WAS BORN IN CHIMO on June 18, 1928 [to Clara's brother Jim and his wife]. I was there until I was two years old, when we moved to Killinek-Burwell. When I was three I went with my grandparents to Newfoundland and I was there until I was five years old, when I went back to Labrador with my grandparents [to live at Zoar, the abandoned Moravian station]. I learned to trap and fish and a lot of other things....

...I was sixteen years old when I saw my parents again; that was when they came out from Chimo. I think I saw Dad when I was seven. He was out to Newfoundland to see a doctor and on his way back he spent a week or so with us. He couldn't get out very much because he was so busy up there, and it was hard to get out in those days. When Dad decided to come out with all the family—Mom, Lavinia, Billy and Norman—I was sixteen. I think that's the year they went to Newfoundland, 1944....

I had three brothers, George, Tommy and Johnny. George was in Goose Bay, Tommy was up in Voisey's Bay, and Johnny was living with us [at Zoar]...that was in 1945, I think. I was about seventeen....

Grandfather was sick for a while and he knew he was going to die, so he told me what to do, where to get my brother. That was in September and the weather gets very rough up there that time of the year. He told us to keep him in the house for three days after he died and maybe by that time the weather would be calmed down for us. So we went to Tommy's place, about ten miles from Voisey's Bay. Tommy said he would go up Voisey's Bay and tell Uncle Amos and them, and we could go back to Zoar. On the way back another storm came up so we went right up to Antoine's place and stayed there for the night, anchored out. There was another boat came over from Nain and stayed close by.

In the morning we saw Tommy and them passing. 'Twas quite windy but they went up, so I thought if they could go so could we. I hauled up the anchor to chase them. We were doing all right, going along pretty good and then it got real rough. The water got in the motor and it stopped. There was just Grandmother, my twelve year old brother and me. All we could see was the Atlantic and old Tuktuvinik.

Grandmother said, "We're finished now."

"Like heck we are, " I said, "I'm going to put the sail up." So we put up the jib and sailed her right past Tuktuvinik Point and got in real close and anchored. We were going up and down on the waves like a mussel shell. I wasn't scared. To me it was just a challenge. We stayed there tossing around, up and down on the waves.

Tommy and them got home and when they got there he went up on the hill to see if he could see us. When he couldn't see us he thought we were lost for sure. The people that were there from Nain were up on the shore because their boat was high and dry...you know how the water rises and falls? They couldn't come and help us but they could see us. They were watching us.

We left in the morning around ten o'clock and it was in the afternoon that we broke down. In the evening we got in to the shore. I pulled up two of the three anchors. I left the anchor with the chain on it out because I thought the chain would hold, but it snapped off and it's still there. Grandmother thought we would be wrecked for sure but I managed to steer the boat right in between the two big rocks that were there, went right up on the sand. We got ashore and Johnny and I got Nanny out of the boat and made a fire. I said the people would see the fire and know we were all right. Then I went up on the hill to pick some berries because we didn't have much grub with us. We figured we would be going right back so we didn't bring much with us, so we lived on berries for a while. It was too rough to fish.

In the evening a boat came to get us and, in the meantime, Tommy got Grandfather ready for burial. It was at night when the Nain boat got to us. I went out with a lamp to show them where to come in to the shore. They came in and asked how we were. We were okay. Then we got Nanny in the boat, left our boat where it was because it was anchored so it would be okay to leave it. It was three o'clock in the morning when we got to Zoar. . . .

The next morning we got ready and went down to what we calls the Neck, where Grandfather said he wanted to be buried. We couldn't get right up on the hill so we dug the grave on the side of the hill. There was Uncle Amos Voisey, Bobby Voisey, Rosie and me dug the grave and we put him in it.

Then we went to Voisey's Bay and then to Nain for a while. After a week we came back and got ready for the winter. We had everything in and I knew how to handle everything—the dogs and the boat. . . . George was in Goose Bay and Tommy was up in Uncle Solomon Edmunds' place, but he would come down when he could. The Voisey's used to come and check to see if we needed anything.

October was berry picking time and we got a lot of berries for the winter. We had fish and trout and we made sure we had enough dogs' feed. Tommy and Rosie came down and stayed with us and Tommy and I went out and got seals and that, got partridges. . . .

After Grandfather died, in September, my brother Johnny was perished in January the following year. He went to Nain with Allan Saunders to get dogs' feed. He was supposed to go to Kamarsuk and stay there, but he never gave the message to the Winters that he was supposed to stay with them. About ten days later Johnny and Allan were found six miles from Nain. Johnny was just thirteen.

Johnny was next to Lavinia and then came Billy. In 1947 Billy was accidentally shot up in Frobisher Bay. So we had our sad times too.

The year after Grandfather died the dogs got the rabies. I lost my dogs. When my brother George got back from Goose Bay he got me a dog, and I got another one from Voisey's Bay. That was fine, I could start another team. . . .

The last spring I was up there we had dogs. Tommy went to Nain and Rosie, Nanny and I were home with Margaret Ann, who was about six or seven months old. We had four little puppies about four weeks old. A team came from Nain and he left his female dog with us because she was going to have pups and he didn't want to take her any further. She was a nice dog. The time was when she had her puppies, five real nice puppies. That day she kept eating a lot of snow. I wondered what was wrong with her. The next morning I got up real early for some reason and I looked through the window, and the dog was looking at us with froth at her mouth. I heard puppies bawling, Tommy's pups, so I grabbed Margaret Ann and put her upstairs in a bed. I went outside and the dog had the jaws and everything tore off the puppies. Just as I went out around she started after me. I ran back and got in the porch.

I yelled, "Rosie, get the gun and shoot."

Rosie got the .44 and shot but it didn't seem like she hit the dog. She shot quite a few times but the dog kept running so she couldn't hit it. We used to have German windows that opened like doors. The puppies were right in front of the back porch window.

Nanny said, "Open the window a bit and when she comes to get at the puppies, shoot her.

Rosie waited and when she come she shot her behind the ear. She just keeled right over.

Nanny said, "Thank goodness, you got her."

Not five minutes passed and she was up again. That kept up from six in the morning until twelve o'clock noon. She'd come out of the woods with one eye hanging out. She come out and walked along the edge of the bank on the side of the hill. Nanny said to make sure to get her in the heart, which Rosie did. But there was no way we were going to go up and get her.

That dog killed all the puppies, Tommy's and her own. When Tommy got home I told him we had nothing left—and we'd had nine puppies and a dog.

...We used to go to Nain for Easter. Easter was a lot of fun. I would meet all the girls. They had a day they called 'Udlishuking Day,' Girl's Day. It was a day for the girls. We all dressed up and put on more ribbons than you can think of to put on. I went along with them and had lots of fun. Nanny used to say I didn't have to dress up like that, but I enjoyed it.

When it was Boy's Day they would borrow all the jewelry they could from the girls. I believe they would try and see who could get the most jewelry on their hats.

On your 'Day' you wore your Sunday best—best boots, best dress, parka and so on. You'd have ribbons! It was quite a day. You'd have a special little bonnet.

We'd get up in the morning, get ready, get your ribbons and white bottom boots on and go to church. Then you'd come home and visit the different houses in the village. It was at Martin Martin's house we had a big dinner. There was everything on the table, different kinds of food. Martin would say Grace. After dinner we would go around visiting again and then back to the church for another service. It was a special day for visiting and it was really nice....

I was nineteen when I went to Newfoundland and worked as a domestic for five years. I didn't really like that so I went to work in the hospital as an aide and ended up as a nursing assistant. I was twenty-five or twenty-six when I met Karl. Then when we got married we went to Ontario to live and we've been there ever since. But I will never forget my life in the north. Where you grow up, that's always your home.

They say you can take people out of Labrador but you can't take Labrador out of the people.

— Betty Ford Koch
[8.4:52]

THE SAUNDERS REALLY COME FROM Cartwright....I was eight years old when Dad went to work for the Hudson's Bay Company. He went from Cartwright to Davis Inlet to take over the store there for five years. When his term was up, he liked it up there so much he wouldn't go back to Cartwright. He quit HBC and went on his own. That's how come the Saunders settled in Davis Inlet.

I went to St. Anthony to school one year. There was no school in Davis Inlet when I was a boy. Reg went to school in St. John's. He was in the orphanage out there. When Gil got married he took Reg and looked out to him until he got to the age where he could look after himself. People kept the family together in them days. That's how Reg Saunders come to be in Davis Inlet....

The first Saunders came to Labrador from some part of Newfoundland. I don't know what part. I think the Perrys [her mother's family] come from Newfoundland too, but I'm not rightly sure about that. [4.3:51]

...When I was a real young man, about eighteen, and my cousin Reg Saunders was about a year older, we built a house over on Big Island for Reg to go trappin.' There was me, Reg, and his mother, Aunt Bella. Down below where we build Reg's house we found an old sand pit. There was an awful lot of old spear heads and arrow heads and stuff like that, you know, where the Indians used to make them. We picked up about ten or twelve of 'um. I went back a few years ago to see if I could find some more but all I found was pieces. I made an awful mistake; I gave them all away....

In my young days the Indians used to make spear heads for spearin' deer in the water. They made them out of deers' horns. They'd take the spear head and put it on a long stick for stabbin' the deer that was in the water, caught in the lakes and stuff like that. The ones me and Reg found must have been a long way back 'cause you could see where they used to have a fireplace. You could see the fireplace with the old coals.

The Indians used to have dances when I was young. They had their drums. Ol' Sam Rich, he was the one that used to make those old drums. There was scattered others, but Sam always carried his drum, a great big drum. Every once in a while they'd have a *mukashan*, like a big 'time,' and they'd beat the drum and sing. I used to get in on this.

Ol' Sam really gloried in the old ways. He had his wife make him a deerskin coat, almost like the cowboys' coats, sleeves with frills on, and he'd have them painted, you know. They'd get dye from Richard White's tradin' place. He used to have different dyes for paintin' snowshoes, and Sam would have his coat painted too, and a deerskin hat. Then he'd get playin' his drums. He was always a real good hand, we'll say, like that. Same way with his family, all dressed in deerskin clothes when they'd come out from the country. Little caribou dickies on the children with the head and ears on. That was summer skins, see. But they're all got away from that now....

I wouldn't have come to Happy Valley then, but in 1947 the Indians was havin' a hard time. The caribou was away back in the country so they was goin' to move the Indians to Nutak—better place for huntin', more deer. So they moved the Indians and closed down Davis Inlet. Oh, they gave me the opportunity to go to Nutak with them. I wouldn't go. I was born in Cartwright and I moved to Davis Inlet and that was home. I wasn't goin' to go no further north. I had me own boat—that's the motor from her out there stuck up in the grass. Before that there was dog sickness and I lost all me dogs except for two and two little puppies. Now, to go to Hopedale, forty miles, to try to haul home grub, I couldn't do it. So I said we'd move to Goose Bay. We got ready and we left the 27th of September, 1947....

I moved to Davis Inlet when I was eight year old. I grew up with the Indians, we'll say. I travelled the country with them, trapped with them, hunted with them and everything. I got to be part of them. This is why I goes back year after year. People used to ask me why I always went to Davis Inlet on my holidays when my relations was all here in Cartwright. I couldn't explain it, only that I felt that was my place to go. Just because I moved away and got a job didn't mean I had to forget them. The way I look at it, I'm part of them. The Indians always treated me good, took care of me and helped me in any way they could. They took me as part of the tribe and they always treated me with respect.

— Jim Saunders
[13.2:20]

...some members of the Davis Inlet band owe their inception to the mating four generations ago of a Scotsman (or Scots-Cree half-breed) with an Ungava Eskimo woman. This family, called Rich, is completely Indianized....

[Tanner, p. 594]

...The Rev. Paul Hettasch, the Moravian missionary, which lived in the country for forty years told me that he knew of only one mixed marriage, namely the parents of Edward Rich, whose father was a Naskaupee Indian and his mother an Eskimo; the Riches now form a kind of clan which usually lives apart from the others....

[ibid, p. 444]

THE FIRST GEAR IN LABRADOR was Richard Gear—they said he was a runaway. He was one of them that had to like get away from Ireland because they was havin' a hard time there. He got a job with the Hudson's Bay Company in Rigolet and married a girl, Margaret White, from—I don't know if she was from Rigolet or North West River. Anyway, she was Hiram White's father's sister. Her brother's name was Ted White. They lived at Burnt Wood Cove near Rigolet and had a big family. I used to hear my uncle Tom Gear talk about them. Why he used to talk about it so much, he was from around Rigolet and after he moved up around Davis Inlet the Goudies moved up there too. They used to talk about the people at Rigolet and North West River.

When Grandfather Richard Gear died he left a bunch of healthy young men. There was nothing much to do around Rigolet in them days so Dr. Grenfell took them, girls as well, and their mother, and put them to different places, like where there was sealing places or some work for them to do. Uncle Jim, the oldest, went to North West River, Uncle Nath went to work for Dr. Grenfell in St. Anthony, Uncle Tom went to Big Bay, Uncle Sandy went to Sango with the Edmunds, my father, John Gear, went right to Okak to work with the Moravian Mission in the store, and Uncle Edward joined the service and was killed in France in the First World War....

Uncle Tom married Bella Lane and they never had any children. Aunt Bella was the one that reared me. Oh she was wicked, but that was the style in them days. She'd send me fishin' in the cold, me freezin' and cryin' with the cold, and if I didn't catch any fish I'd have to go to bed without any supper. That's how it used to be in them days. She used to treat Alec and me terrible bad. They said my little brother Alec died from TB in the bowels. He was only young. After Aunt Bella died Uncle Tom married Maria Dickers. Her father was Herbert Dickers. Uncle Tom and Aunt Maria had two children, Ted and Selma.

My daddy, John, married a partly Inuit woman, Tabea Pamack. Her mother had her for a German storekeeper or something before she married old Mr. Pamack, but she went by the name Pamack. My mother had my sister Rosie before she married my father and then they had me and Alec. After our parents died in Okak in 1918, Uncle Tom Gear took me and Alec because we were his brother's children. William Ford took Rosie and Dick Pamack to work for his parents because they were old. Rosie said she knowed for a long time that she had a sister but she didn't know where I was. She was married before she found me. I was in Davis Inlet, see....

—Maggie Gear Saunders
[18.1:34]

I HAD A REAL BAD miscarriage one time. The Indians were travelling out of the country at that time and I was callin' for a midwife. There was an old woman called Aunt Lizzie Adams and she was livin' up to Adlatok with Uncle Bill Abel. That's the only lady we could think about callin' and we wrote a letter up. The Indians came with a letter sayin' that Uncle Bill Abel was comin' first open water with a midwife. We was some overjoyed. At the same time I was workin' around the house doin' heavy things and I been kind of hurt myself, and it happened that I lost the baby. The Indians was the ones that helped me. They come up from their tents and they done everything to bring me around and get me well.

The Indians had young girls out diggin' holes in the ground then puttin' rocks in a pan of hot water, makin' them steam. They was steamin' me out inside because I never lost the afterbirth and 'twas all inside me and they couldn't get it. The only thing they could think to do was to melt it away. I didn't have no pain 'cause I was gone, like not dead, but past frightened, I suppose. One Indian took off with a canoe. I looked through the window and he was takin' off with the canoe on his head, runnin' from icepan to icepan and put the canoe in the water and paddled off, tryin' to get to where there was white people. They was afraid if I'd die the white people would think that they killed me, see. I told them not to think that.

There was a Newfoundland woman there, Jim Lane's wife, Olive. My uncle come up from down the bay and he said that the Indians was doin' wrong. Olive said to me, "You better let the Indians do what they can. They're only doin' the same as the doctor would do but instead of usin' hot water bottles they're usin' hot rocks."

There was an old woman there and one other one, they was doin' all the work. And there was Joe Rich, he was interpreter for the woman that was doin' the work for me.

Joe Rich said, "My woman says that if they can work at you again they might be able to do something about it. If my woman could only do again what she was doin', they might do something for you."

My uncle still thought that they were doin' wrong, so Olive brought him up to her house to talk to him, and the Indians went to work again.

After they got the afterbirth they was goin' to put me in an Indian tent to sweat me out, to get my insides clean, but they got it all out. I went through it and I lived but I was thin all summer. The Indians used to come and see if I was working too hard. Oh, they was good to me, really good to me.

I remember I had a great big old long worsted coat, nice warm one, from my aunt [Lylie Saunders] who was livin' in Goose Bay. These two old midwives what tended to me, they wanted that coat. I told Andrew, my first husband, that whatever I got I'd give to them. But there was only one coat and there was two of them. I couldn't give it to only one.

I said to Joe Rich, "What's they goin' to do with that coat?"

He said, "They're goin' to cut it up and make stockings for themselves for travellin' in the country."

So I give them the coat and they halved 'en, old Joe's woman and the other one, halved the coat. They wanted scissors and they wanted worsted, and they wanted needles. They sat down and chippered and 'twasn't long before they had two pairs of stockings for themselves so their legs wouldn't be cold. The small woman had the arms and the big old fat woman had the body part. That was good, I told Andrew, I was some glad. Joe said they was goin' to be warm now. Another thing, I used to save all Andrew's boots and tap them up and save them for the men. I had no money to pay them for what they done for me so I had to do things like that to show that I had regards for them, was thankful for what they done for me. They were the only ones that helped me, the only ones that were able to do it. I always says I likes the Indians because they done all their best for me.

— Mabel Manak
[2.4:40]

MY OLD GRANDFATHER, BILL DICKERS, came out from England with the Hudson's Bay Company as a ship's carpenter. That was on the first old *Pelican*. I think the first place he went was to Cartwright and he got married. They spelled the name D-i-c-k-e-r-s back then. Now they tries to spell it with a D-e-. I won't let them do that but they leaves off the 's' most times. Grandfather had a big family. There was John (my father), Bill, James, Harry and Tom and some girls in between somewhere. I know one girl was named Rachel. My father and Uncle Jim was born to Cartwright and p'r'haps some of the others were too, I don't know.

My father married Lavinia Broomfield, Samuel James Broomfield's daughter. My grandfather on mother's side came from England, too. He was Joseph Broomfield. I was born in Old Davis Inlet.

Old Grandfather Dickers put Father and his brothers to school in England. Father learned his trade, boat buildin', in Liverpool. Grandfather worked for the Hudson's Bay so 'twas no expense to 'en and he had people over there like his father and mother and uncles and so on. They all came back educated. I often heard my father talkin' about civilization and stuff like that. I thinks meself that the old Labrador was more civilized....

— Walter Dickers
[11.4:36]

In the Matter of the Enquiry into Newfoundland Territorial Rights on the Labrador.
Labrador, Jack Lane's Bay, to wit:

I, Samuel James Broomfield, of Jack Lane's Bay aforesaid, make oath and say as follows:—

I was born in Grois Water Bay in 1852. My father was an Englishman from Dartmouth, England. I came to Jack Lane's Bay 34 years ago [1875]. I have been fishing and trapping ever since. I have gone into the interior trapping every winter, a distance of about 50 miles. I have paid revenue to the Government of Newfoundland ever since revenue was collected on the Labrador, and have been obeying its laws and recognized myself as a citizen of Newfoundland and under jurisdiction of its Government. I have never had anything to do with any Canadian officers and have traded with Newfoundland traders and the Mission traders and no one else, and nobody ever interfered with me in my rights as a resident of Labrador. I have never heard that Canada had any claim or made any claim to the interior of Labrador.

(Sgd.) SAMUEL JAMES BROOMFIELD
Sworn before me at Jack Lane's Bay aforesaid
this 25th day of August A.D. 1909.
(Sgd.) F.J. Morris Judge of the Court of Labrador

— Privy Council Records
Vol.III, No. 609, p. 1557
[3.3:37]

Tucked away somewhere between Hopedale and Davis Inlet lies Jack Lane's Bay—the home of the late Samuel Broomfield. Uncle Sam, as he was known from one end of the Labrador coast to the other, died last year at the good old age of eighty-eight years, and with his passing went a gallant gentleman, a true friend and a most hospitable host. There remains, however, a memory as long lasting as the rocky coast on which he lived.

Short of stature, and rather thick-set, his piercing blue eyes peeping out from beneath heavy white brows, and with long, flowing white whiskers, he presented a most picturesque and somewhat patriarchal appearance.

Uncle Sam hailed from Groswater Bay originally, but lived most of his life much farther north in the vicinity of Hopedale, where he made his living at trapping and fishing. He was also Game Warden for the Newfoundland government, which position he held until the day of his death.

In latter years, after he retired from active work, he was to be seen in a long-tailed black coat and stove-pipe hat. One thing he always wore, day in and day out (and there are some who say he also wore it at night), and that was the Gold Medal commemorating the 250th anniversary of the Hudson's Bay Company, which was presented to a few of the oldest and most loyal of their customers. This medal was presented to Uncle Sam by Mr. Ralph Parsons, Fur Trade Commissioner, on behalf of the Hudson's Bay Company.

He was a musician of no mean talent, and played the violin exceptionally well, providing entertainment to the many wayfarers who habitually frequented his house. He was the first Labrador man to ever speak over the radio, which he did on one occasion from the good ship Bowdoin, *owned by Commander Donald Macmillan, famous explorer and close friend of Uncle Sam's. At one time Uncle Sam made and sent to His Majesty, King George V, a fine sealskin pouch and a letter expressing his loyalty to his sovereign. In return he received a letter of thanks from the King. Needless to say, this letter was kept among his prized possessions....*

— Newton Morgan from *The Cartwriter*
December 9, 1939
[16.3:46]

OLD SAMUEL JAMES BROOMFIELD WAS my grandfather. He was a game warden. I remember he used to have a great big bag with S.J.B. marked on it, that it was to keep all his papers and stuff in. He'd carry that bag when he went around seein' people....

I hardly know the way he come to be in Big Bay. I think he used to live at Island Harbour Bay with old Grandfather McNeill and them when he was a little boy. He used to tell me the story about how he went to look for his woman, my grandmother Eliza [Learning], up around Rigolet, or Cartwright. He had to travel away up there to look for a wife. He used to laugh about how he had just a small komatik, just long enough for his komatik box and this young man he had in company with him, Uncle George Lane....

I used to hear Grandfather talk about Hunt & Henley days, that was before I can remember. I think that was the place Grandfather built up his place from—the houses that was there and what he built up on his own. He had a good lot of houses, like for puttin' stuff in, and he had stages and all that. He had young boys makin' paths between the houses and the stages. He had a lot of little stores for puttin' his nets in and things in and net racks for hanging the nets on.

Grandfather was only a short kind of man with a long whisker. He'd always have the radio on and when he'd hear a good tune he'd grab his fiddle and play along wit' the radio tune. He was a man that used to ke'p services, like when he was home there wouldn't a Sunday pass but he'd ke'p service. He could preach as good as a minister yet he liked his dances between that.

— Mabel Manak
[20.2:45]

...I CAN MIND A TIME when we was caught out in the rough.... We was coming from Big Bay to Hopedale by dogteam. Johnny Broomfield was only a boy then. Uncle Sam Broomfield was living then. He was game warden.

I had me mother, brother and sister in the riding box. I had five dogs and an old Eskimo feller with us. Uncle Sam and his son Abraham was on their komatik.

When we left in the morning 'twas getting a bit rough. By and by there was times when we could hardly see Uncle Sam just ahead of us. Before long we had to put a line fast to the side of my leader and on the back of Uncle Sam's komatik.

We crossed the land and was going on. By and by this old Eskimo feller begin to get restless. He told me Uncle Sam was going the wrong way. If we follied him we'd be lost for sure. I didn't know if he was right or not 'cause I was only a boy. We went on again for a bit longer, then the old feller jumped off and went over to Uncle Sam. He told him he was going the wrong way. Well, Uncle Sam said he figured he was going all right, but the old feller said that he wasn't. He told Uncle Sam he could go on his way but we would go our own way. They argued a bit. The old feller was going by the wind. He was noticing the snow banks on the ice, the way they was going and how the wind was cutting them. That's what he was going by. He said if we went he's way we'd find the right path. Uncle Sam finally agreed and said he would go with us. Sure enough, the old feller took us right to the proper path.

Now, we still had a pretty good distance to go before we'd get to Hopedale. And right in the height of it they stopped the dogs again. I didn't know what was happening. This was Nath Gear coming out the bay and heading straight out to the ocean. He was lucky he runned into us. After a bit then we got to Hopedale.

When Nath Gear left the bay, that was a different one from ours, he had old John Lane in company with he. Mr. Lane had his own team, and he had his wife and young feller with him. Somewhere along in the storm the two teams got separated from one another. Poor old Jack Lane and his family got perished.

— William Edmunds
[1.2:43]

Hopedale, 1900.

The year under review has been a sad one in more ways than one for this station. Sickness and death have been frequent visitors among the missionaries and people alike. On June 6th the young wife of Br. Nestle was called home to her eternal rest, and was buried shortly after alongside of her still-born infant—a terrible blow for the poor husband and the mission-band in general. Great sympathy was also shown by the Eskimoes at the station. About six weeks afterwards a little daughter of Br. and Sr. Lundberg was also laid to rest in the burial-ground. Several of the Eskimo families were likewise called upon to surrender one or another of their children; indeed, so great has been the mortality among the children of the genuine Eskimoes of late years that, if this congregation depended, numerically, on them alone for the future, it would in a comparatively short time become extinct. Fortunately, the settler families and those in which one of the parents only belongs to the Eskimo race, are on the increase, and the missionaries do all they can to encourage marriages of this latter description. Hopedale, we are told, is feeling more than any other station on the coast the weakening influences of civilization and all therewith connected....

The Hopedale people have again been brought a great deal in touch with the Newfoundland fisherfolk, but, sad to say, not to their advantage. In the first place, the Newfoundlanders have again robbed them of their best fishing-places, and, then, they have exercised the worst possible influence over them morally. In order, however, to counteract these baneful influences as much as possible, our missionarues have, as in former years, last year again done all they could to benefit the troublesome visitors spiritually. Prayer-meetings with addresses have been held whenever there seemed to be any desire for them, and on Sunday afternoon a regular service was held in English for all who cared to attend it. Tracts were also frequently distributed, and a good many schooner people were also treated medicinally and otherwise by Br. [Paul] Hettasch, who, as our readers will remember, underwent a one year's course of training at Livingston College, London, in the elements of medicine and surgery before he sailed for Labrador.

Br. Hettasch was away from home several times during the year, visiting both in the north and in the south, and combining with these visits medical and surgical work wherever called for.

— Moravian Periodical Accounts
[13.3:32]

HOPEDALE WAS CALLED, WHALE BAY before it was called Hopedale. There was a shoulder blade bone down at the back where they got the houses now and that's what it used to be called 'Whale-shoulder-blade-place.' So there must have been whales there one time.

The best thing I remember about Hopedale, in my young days, was Festival Days, Christmas and days like that. We used to always live away from Hopedale when I was growing up. My Dad was a hunter in winter, catching foxes, so we had to move away from Hopedale to get a better place for catching foxes. We had a winter place at Little Bay, we called it, five miles froπm Big Bay, south. We had a summer place for fishing. Our summer place was at an island called Malta, just outside Little Bay. We'd go from place to place by boat or komatik and dogs. I enjoyed shifting from one place to another. It was fun because that was all the excitement we had.

I was a Mitsuk before I got married. My father was Solomon Mitsuk. My mother was Emily Edmunds. She was an Edmunds from Sango, which is further up in the country from Davis Inlet. My mother couldn't talk Eskimo, not 'till she was nurse-maid for the missionaries. She used to speak English and Indian before that. When she was a little girl she used to play with the Indian children. Her father was William

Edmunds and he had a brother called David. The first Edmunds were pioneers. They come to Labrador in the 1800s. My mother was born in 1890.

We had wood houses from the time I can remember. It was cabins and they were very warm. Frost wouldn't come in them like it will around the walls of these kind of houses we got today. I remember one time before Dad made a house for us, we was living in a hut [sod] house and the only window we had was up on the top of the hut. That hut was made of logs and sods, the sods was put around to keep the wind and the rain out. We didn't have a glass window-pane, we had seal's gut, cleaned and stretched. What I remember about that seal gut window is that two times the dogs fell into the house through it and frightened us. You had to try and keep the dogs away from the house so they wouldn't fall in. The roof was only about five or six feet high. The house was dug down a little but not so we had to step down into it. We was only using it for a little while 'till our other house was fixed up....

— Susannah Igloliorte
[3.1:48]

OLD CHARLIE MCNEILL BROUGHT THE first livestock to Island Harbour: sheep, goats, pigs and hens. I don't know how this livestock was brought up from Newfoundland, but it seems that he always had this little schooner, and I'm pretty certain this is how he got the animals up. He got more later when his son [Samuel James McNeill] went out and started comin' up on this trader.

The reason they had sheep was because they could get their own wool. They had a spinning wheel. They used to knit their own stockings, socks, cuffs, and underwear, everything, all for their own use. I don't know how many sheep they had but it must have been sufficient to take care of their needs.

The also had pigs for pork, and hens. They only kept four dogs and they had a big log house built, what they called the dog house. The dogs were kept there to give the animals freedom. That little hill where the house was is still called Dog House Hill.

They had goats for milk and butter. They didn't give much milk in the winter, but in the spring, summer and fall they'd get a lot of milk. They also made butter from the milk. They say the very best milk is goat's milk. My father told me that in the winter the milk used to taste funny because they used to give them these little green trees, little fir trees, when they were short of hay, and after a while you could taste it on the milk. Grandfather told me they used to cut the hay with these big old long scythes. He said the hay would fall in tiers, just haul the scythe right through it and then tie it in bundles and store it. They got enough grass in that area. That grass grows right to the height of your head. You can go right out of sight there in the summer, just see the grass movin'.

I can remember yet when the old goat house was there. There was two parts to it, one part was the goat house and the other end was the cook-house. They used to cook in there over an open fireplace in the spring when it was too hot to have a big fire on in the house. Island Harbour is a hot place because it's landlocked. We used to cook in this place even after I can remember. The end was all built up with rock, stowed up just like brick, the whole end. The rocks went up and joined the wooden chimney on top. Half that house had a rock floor, these flat rocks. There was old bellows there for pumping wind to get the fire going, and they used to have those old hooks hanging from the beams for putting the pots on for if the fire was goin' too high, you'd rise up the pot. We used to cook trout and stuff in a big iron pot, and we'd have a big iron kettle too. I can remember that.

In later years, after old Charlie McNeill died [1855], my grandfather and them started movin' out to Turnavik Islands[23] to cod-fish and go back to Island Harbour in the fall. They had two goats left, and I heard them say they had one real mischievous one, liked to steal things. They had a box of hard bread left down on the stage, the kind of stuff you use for makin' brewis. This goat went down and eat whatever she could, then she started drinkin' water. She swelled up and died, killed herself. They had one goat left, but they weren't fussy about them because they were buyin' milk now, things were startin' to change. So they used to put that goat on an island, and she'd live there by herself all summer until they'd pick her up in the fall. When I was a boy, I can remember seein' the old beds she used to have under big trees with the branches growin' out over, a hollow where she used to sleep. That's Goat Island now.

One night they heared the dogs makin' an awful work, snarlin' and everything, so they looked out.... Here was this old white bear with his head in a barrel after some [dogs'] food, so they got their guns and fired at it through the window. They had one of these old Schneider guns with a great big ball in the bullet. This old feller was in the Boer War over in Africa and this was what they used to use when they were on horseback. It's only a short gun, Schneider they calls it. I got the bayonet that come off her. Anyhow, they said they never killed the bear dead, just put this big ball into 'en. They heared 'en when he growled and went over the fence. He broke down the fence when he went over it. There was a little bit of snow on the ground, in the fall it was. 'Twas a black dark night; they couldn't see a thing. Next morning, when it got daylight, they followed his track 'till they come to 'en. I don't know if he was right dead, but he was doomed anyway.

There used to be old documents around, right from early days, because I can remember lookin' at it, seein' where they got so many seals in Drunken Harbour. There's a harbour six miles from Island Harbour where, when he was lookin' for a place to settle, Charlie McNeill anchored one night. His men got into the rum he had on board and got so drunk that he couldn't sail all the next day. He named it Drunken Harbour and that's what it's called to this day. The documents were more or less like diaries. It stated what they killed, when they started diggin' potatoes and how many barrels they got, how much turnips they got, and I seen where they said they killed a pig a certain date and what they did with the meat. Says like, they went to Drunken Harbour and how many bedlamers, young harps. It recorded things like that.

Turnaviks was a big fishin' place. My grandfather and my father used to fish there. They would get supplies from William Bartlett, father of Bob Bartlett who became the world famous explorer. Old William Bartlett used to supply about forty crews besides what he kept on his premises. He had people on wages; they fished but he owned the fish. The rest of the people sold their fish to 'en but they weren't on wages. He had two crews on wages, that's eighteen or twenty men.

Bartlett had a coopershop and a blacksmith shop on his premises. I can remember the big old bellows and the forge. They could do any kind of iron work, fix rudders for boats. The blacksmith was on wages all the time....

My father had a schooner and I can remember when she was lost. I was three years old then. I can remember well about the men cleanin' away the fish on the deck of the schooner. He used to have six men. The schooner got lost up in Island Harbour in a hurricane. They said the water was driftin' like snow, right white. One of her anchors dragged and she went in over the bar rocks. Every two weeks or so in the fall you get these real high tides. She went ashore during one of these very high tides and washed in on the rocks and by the next high tide 'twas froze up. She got hung up high on these big boulders and the weight of her strained her. My father got her off in the spring, but he couldn't keep her out of water and she sunk.

— Rupert McNeill
[5.2:27]

CHRISTMAS WAS SUCH A WONDERFUL time home. There are so many things I remember. Half the fun of Christmas was getting ready for it. We always had a tree in its permanent place, between the end of our old chesterfield and Mother's bedroom door. We had no store-bought decorations for our tree. We made it all. Mother would save pretty bits of paper through the year. I remember half pound cocoa came wrapped in bright red paper with shiny silver on the inside, and that was so pretty when cut in little shapes and tied on the tree. We used to paper our rooms and the left over pieces we'd cut and fasten to make chains to go on the tree. Of course, our gifts were homemade and as Christmas approached Mother would be up late sewing and dear old Dad would be working in his shed.

Christmas Eve had its customs. Dad always ate a baked salt fish for his supper. The house would be all straightened away and after dinner, Mother would put on a clean white apron to get ready to make the pies for Christmas dinner. Us children would help or watch, depending on how big we were, and when the afternoon grew darker we'd all be looking out the kitchen window to see if we could see Santa coming over the hill. We never did, of course.

After supper we would hang our stockings up. There was a metal rod in the kitchen that went across two, p'haps three beams that Mother used to hang the mens' wet clothes on when they came in for the evening. That was where we'd hang the stockings. The Christmas brother Will was six (I was only three) he climbed up on the table and in trying to hang my stocking for me, fell off and broke his collarbone. I always found that bad, being Christmas Eve and all. Later Christmas Eve, Dad would always read the Christmas story to us from our big old Bible.

Christmas morning, Mother was always the first one up. She would have the dinner on by the time we'd wake so she could enjoy the fun with us children. We used our black knitted stockings and we'd often have to hang two of them since whatever gifts we got were in the stockings. Usually we'd get a new pinafore, sometimes a pretty new dress made over by Mother from clothes relatives in St. John's had sent in the fall. Always we'd have an apple or orange that had been kept from the early fall, out of our sight. And down in the toe, the last to come out would be our Christmas candy. Those candies were so good! We never did find out where Mother's hiding place was. One Christmas Dad made us all little komatiks and had something lashed on the back of it. When we opened it up, it was slices of Christmas cake for our 'grub.' Christmas dinner was always a real feast, a big goose killed in the fall and lots of vegetables and pies.

There wasn't much visiting at Christmas, only between us and the Lyalls—Uncle Ernie's and Uncle John's families. Later, when our boys were older, the Jacques boys would come down to spend Christmas with them. We found that good. When the Lyalls came over to our place, we'd be singing and eating and, of course, the older ones having a drop of mother's spruce beer. She'd have it made in a wooden keg. We liked it best when she used molasses sugar because it would be so clear and a good sting on it, too.

Besides singing carols, we had one song we made up about "Happy Christmas is here again." I heard from Goldie Lyall only a few years ago and she said she'll never forget going over to Aunt Susan's at Christmas and singing that.

In the afternoon Christmas Day the men would go shooting. They would set up bull's eyes on the trees and have contests. These days the women shoot too, but then the women and children watched. Each man would put up a prize, p'haps a cup of raisins saved or some Christmas candy. When the day was over, we went to bed feeling tired and happy and wishing it could always be Christmas. It was so good.

— May McNeill Pardy
[5.2:30]

WE GREW UP IN FATHER'S old house at Island Harbour. When I worked for the Air Force at Goose, we started going back to Island Harbour in my boat, the *Mystic*. We would go when I had annual leave in the summer....

One spring I went to Island Harbour to have my first trial at salmon fishing there. Our ancestor away back had salmon fished there before they ever started fishing at Turnaviks. I couldn't get anyone to go with me so I was there alone except for my little dog, Flossie.

One morning, a beautiful morning, I woke up with the sound, "Leonard, it's time to get up."

I stopped a bit and the voice came again. I thought I was dreaming. There was nobody there only myself. There was nobody to speak but it sounded like my mother's voice.

I had the alarm set for five o'clock. I looked at the clock and it was quarter to five. I was wide awake by this time. I got up and started dressing.

While I was wide awake the voice spoke again, the third time. "Leonard, it's time to get up."

I really recognized the voice. Many a time my mother called me when I slept in my room in the old house when I was growing up. She would call me and tell me it was time to get up.

I thought about it several times during the day and I went on my nets. I wasn't nervous. I had never harmed my mother in any way and she had never hurt me. She was a good woman, a good mother. As far as people gone before us is concerned, they're not going to hurt us. I sort of forgot about it after a while.

That spring I had cleared the underbrush from around the trees and had piled it by the edge of the water. It got too dry to burn it, so I waited for a rainy time to do it.

One evening there was a real high tide and it started to rain a bit. After supper I said to myself, "Now is my time to burn that old pile of brush." I got some old diesel fuel, lube and stuff I had around there, and threw it over the brush and set fire to it. Flossie was there with me. She always had to chase me wherever I went. I begin to hear noises up in a cove on the other side, I thought. Sounded like gulls when they're after bait, when there's capelin around.

I said, "The bait must be in the cove on the other side again now." Even thinking perhaps if I had some nets on that side it might be better than where I was to. There was quite a few salmon down there.

All of a sudden a voice seemed to say, "Leonard got a fire in over back."

I thought it was somebody come, perhaps Rupert or some of the boys. I thought they came and I didn't hear them and now this was them talkin.' I was certain.

The fire was about burned out so I started to walk over. It got quiet. I went on and brought the place in sight. No sign of a boat. No sign of a person. I came back and never heard it after. But that voice was as plain as could be. It reminded me of when people were living there and they would be talking back and forth from one house to the other.

The last I heard in Island Harbour was the same year my first wife died. There was only a nephew, one of my sons and myself there. The two boys was sound asleep and this rap came on the wall. A voice came right behind it saying, "Hark, there's somebody knocking."

I thought for certain that somebody had come and was wanting to get in. I jumped out of bed and looked but there was nobody there. I asked the boys if they spoke. They both said they never. I thought about my boat that I had left, not hauled up. I thought this knock must be a reminder. If my boat was left where she was she could have a hole beat in her from the rocks. I pulled on my clothes, took the flashlight, and went down and hauled her up.

Shortly after, my wife died. I thought that could have been a sign, you know, that something was going to happen.

— Leonard McNeill
[15.2:48]

ONE YEAR SEVEN INDIANS WALKED out to Makkovik. They had their main camp about forty to fifty miles further to the sou'west. They came out to do some tradin.'

They brought lots of furs out to the Hudson's Bay Company, so they bought a lot of stuff. They hired myself, Alfred Winters, Uncle Albert Mitchell, Bob, his son, Bob Wolfrey, Toby Perrault, and Uncle Sam Broomfield. I think 'twas four teams went in all, all full loads of provisions. They had all kinds of stuff. They had all kinds of fur.

They hired us, so the next day we started. We got to Adlavik the first day and the next day 'twas quite bad. It was blowin' and windy like you see it in January. We wanted to start. The Indians was talkin' among themselves. Charlie, I don't know his last name, was the interpreter. He could speak good English.

He said, "Too cold. Indian no good, too cold."

After a while we started anyway and got in to Rattlin' Brook and camped. The Indians never had any tents. On the way out they spent a night out. So we camped and they was watchin' us, so we, Alfred and I, told them to take our tent, because there was three or four tents among us. So there was seven of 'um in this little small tent, but they made out all right.

Next day we started again. We went up through Rattlin' Brook and got on the barrens. The old chief, Penashue, he stayed back with us, and the other fellows went on haulin' their sleighs, just light sleighs. They was walkin' ahead and after a while they disappeared. We just followed their tracks. I guess 'twas about fifteen miles we never seen the other fellers, just their tracks. Talk about walkin'! I never seen nothing like it. But they had no loads, just light sleighs. We figured they left this old man with us in case we lost their track, you know, he was a pilot. He knowed where their camp was.

We reached the camp about three o'clock in the afternoon. There was, I believe, five tents, five families there. When we got there the fellers that walked on ahead come out of the tents like they hadn't been anywhere.

The next day was a poor day so we stayed there all day. They had lots of grub, lots of fur. They was truckyin' all day, tryin' to buy our stuff. They wanted to buy our boots, wanted to buy our dickies, and socks. We could have sold it all if we'd wanted to.

When we was stickin' up our tents, the night we got there, we asked Charlie if they could cook us a pot of deer meat for supper.

Charlie said, "Yes, Gimme your pot."

He come back about an hour later with the pot of stew. That's the best deer meat I ever tasted in my life. It was the way they had it cooked, lots of grease.

Me and Albert got a little Indian cracky. We had 'en in a dogs' [feed] tub, with a little piece of line around his neck, tied on to the lash line. By and by we got off for something or other, come to see the little puppy was draggin', hung up by the neck. He was almost choked, not makin' a sound.

We got to Adlavik that night but we had a poor time, bad goin'. The next day we got back home to Makkovik. [16.3:40]

I think it was 1947 or 1948 when there was dog sickness and dogs died out all along the coast.

Me and David Mitchell used to go in the country trappin', you know. That year, the first part of April, we took off in to strike up our traps. We had eleven dogs. We were goin' about fifty miles towards Double Mer from Makkovik, on that length of land. There was dog sickness around when we left but our dogs was perfect, good healthy dogs—and we came back with three. Boy, what a time we had with our dogs dyin' all along the way.

I remember the last night we were camped, we had five dogs left. One was a big ol' woolly one I called Slim. We were in camp, had our wood in and the camp door shut. We had our tent pitched by a big tree. We heard something so David looked out and he said, "Slim is gettin' mad." Sure enough, he was tryin' to climb the tree. Didn't look very good and he with the froth comin' out of 'en. He come right around to the tent door, tryin' to come in like. I had my 30/30 and I shot 'en. We couldn't take no chances, you know.

The first day they started to get sick, then we lost one or two as we went along. Some would go blind. I remember the leader we had went right blind. We had to shoot her. Her eyes glazed right out and she was no good at all. Shoot them was the only thing we could do, because we couldn't handle them, you know. If you get bite, well, you'd be gone too. I don't know what it was, but they died all along the coast that year.

We had three dogs left and we had to haul ourselves, like on banks and that. We didn't have too much of a load, like on the level, because our dogs' feed was all consumed. We got back by helping our three dogs. And they died after we got back. We never got fur to pay for the trouble we had.

Alfred Winters had one old dog left, ol' Lukey he was called, a big ol' husky dog, and he was all right except there was something wrong with his back. He seemed to be weak in his rump like, so he was goin' to destroy 'en. Lavinia asked if she could have 'en.

Lavinia said p'r'haps he'd get better. So she took 'en over against our house, right 'longside Alfred's. I don't know what she give 'en, some medicine or something, and he begin to get better. He got right perfectly well. He was a big old dog, too, he was. I got another one from Uncle Sam Broomfield, a big ol' woolly one.... That was two good dogs, very good.

The ice was still all right for seal huntin' outside. One day I took the two dogs and went out, ridin' along like everything. The first seal I got after, I stopped my dogs, took my *taluk* [screen] and left the dogs lied down. I was gettin' up pretty handy to the seal when it seemed startled, seemed to be alarmed. I knowed it wasn't me. I looked back and there was my two ol' dogs fighting. They were from different places and not used to each other so they were havin' the biggest kind of fight. They'd stand up, you know, like two men. I just stayed there watchin' them. They fought until they got tired and then they lay down. My seal didn't go down and after a while I got 'en. I got six seals that day. Came back with two dogs, riding along with six seals on the komatik—perfect.

It took a couple of years, two or three years, then to get up a team anything worthwhile like.

I think that year, the year the dogs was dyin' out, there was a boat up north collectin' dogs for the South Pole. He was up as far as Hebron. 'Twas a big schooner, you know. They came to Makkovik that fall and two people came ashore, Mr. Rockwood and another man. They said they were buyin' dogs for the South Pole, all they could get. They was payin' seven dollars a dog. I think I sold them two. 'Tis likely they lost their dogs too, but they might have been taken far enough away to escape it, unless it was in the animals. I don't know what they wanted them for, just that they were goin' to the South Pole.

— Edward Anderson
[11.2:50]

THERE WAS AN OLD FELLER one time lived over in Ben's Cove, near Makkovik. He was supposed to have poisoned his wife and daughter. Old Dr. Grenfell had to go and find out what happened to these people because they died from unnatural causes, died sudden. What happened was they couldn't get any tea so they steeped this Indian tea that grows around everywhere. Well, this old feller [Tom Brown][24] steeped his tea and put some hemlock in with it and his wife and daughter died.

This same man was supposed to have killed another woman one time. Nobody knows what happened to her, just disappeared up in Island Harbour Bay. He sent her down to Island Harbour to get some tobacco for him. No one smoked in Island Harbour (I was probably the first one to smoke there) but they had tobacco there— Lyalls used to have it on hand for when they wanted someone to work for them. But I don't think they had any at that time, so she left to go back on her dogteam.

Some time later this old feller come lookin' for her, askin' if anyone had seen any sign of her. He said the dogs came home but Sally didn't. Some of the Lyalls went back with him. When they got to his place they stopped their dogs against the end of his house. He ran right to the edge of the water and looked down. They asked him what did he see, and he told them he sunk a seal there last fall and he thought he seen 'en floatin' down through, now, in the tide. When they went in the house his young daughter told them that the girl came back and her father killed her and hove her in the rattle. That rattle is known as Sally's Rattle to this day.

Everyone was scared of that old feller; he used to get queer spurts.

I heard Uncle Will Jacques telling a story about once when he was a boy. He said he and his brother, both in their teens, was comin' out from trappin.' They came to this old feller's place and he was sick, walkin' about the house groanin' and makin' an awful ugly noise. They was kind of scared because this was the noise he used to make before he'd get into these tempers, get funny like. Probably he wasn't all there. He told them they would be stayin' there that night..., so they told him they was goin' to secure their boat for the night. He said he was goin' to see they didn't go any further that night. When they went in the porch they saw his old muzzle-loader gun and he had the cap and all on 'er. They went out, give their boat a shove, jumped aboard, took the oars and rowed as hard as they could down the bay. That was right late in the fall.

After it froze up Uncle Will said they saw a dogteam goin' down along the other side of Postville, haulin' the old feller down to bury him. He died not long after they left him. Uncle Will said after that they used to say there was nothing then to be afraid of in Kaipokok Bay because that old feller was dead.

— Rupert McNeill
[19.2:48]

I WAS BORN TO BEN'S Cove not far from Makkovik, just across the portage. When we were growin' up there was eight of us children. We never found it lonely. There used to be an old woman live with us. She was Annie Brown from Kaipokok Bay. She come to live with Tom and Harriet Evans, an old couple, and after she lived with us. She used to go fishin' and salmon catchin' in the summer, just herself, to Ben's Cove when we'd go to the island. Sometimes Daddy would go and see how she was gettin' on.

She'd salt her salmon and trout. She used to do very good. Of course, there wasn't a very good price then.

Ben's Cove was a good place for berries—red, black, blue, marsh and bakeapples. I fancy I can see it all now just in over the barrens. Plenty trout and salmon in the summer. We'd go to Turnavik, which is not too far from Ben's Cove. My daddy had a crew of one or two men. He used to trap codfish. When my brother Tommy got bigger, he helped Daddy. When he was about ten years old he'd be prongin' fish in the box. I used to work in the stage, headin' fish. Sometimes we'd work 'till midnight. Not every night but a few nights a week. We'd be up again early the next morning and work all day again. Later 'twould be wash the fish and dry them. Whoever was big enough to work would be up early to spread the fish on the bawn as soon as the rocks was dry.

That was September month. Myself and Annie Brown used to go troutin' on fine days. We'd get little trout through the ice. Later years we found a bigger pond so my daddy said we'd try up there. We got bigger trout in there. Later on 'twould freeze top to bottom and we'd have to give up fishin' there.

Mr. Chard used to have a store at Aillik, not far from West Turnavik. Daddy got his supplies from them. We used to charge stuff, then when we'd get our fish we'd settle up. We used to make out very good. We'd get enough food for the winter. Later on Daddy would get fur and he'd go to Aillik for more grub....

I was seven when I started school first, that was to Makkovik boarding school. We'd come over in January month and in May I'd have to go home and mind the smaller ones. I don't know at all how many years I went to school. It must have been a couple I think. After I left school I helped look after the other children 'cause I was the oldest. When I was eighteen I got married. My mother said she didn't know what she'd do without me. That was 1937 I got married [to Alder Ford].

Last fall we went to Island Harbour for a visit. Willie come 'long with us to drive the boat. Ernie Lyall from Goose Bay was with us; it was his home too one time. We went to Turnavik first and me and Alder picked some redberries. Ernie and Willie went for a hunt in speed boat and tried for fish. All they got was rock cods. We cleaned and cooked them for supper then went on to Island Harbour. Oh, we had a nice time. We stayed in Leonard McNeill's father's house. Our old house is there but he's nearly fallin' down. I felt sad when I saw it, but Alder is thinkin' about fixin' it up to stay in when we goes over.....

It's a lot better over to Island Harbour than it is here. I didn't want to come back. I been livin' in Makkovik for twenty-four years but I don't call it home, not altogether. I sooner be over to Island Harbour.

— Margaret Ford
[2.1:39]

THERE WAS A LOT OF hardships for the hunters and fishermen of Labrador when I was a young boy and up until Confederation, which as we all know, brought better living conditions, better wages, more benefits for large families as well as small.... Looking back on the days when I was old enough to get out and help earn for the family (I was thirteen years old) in them days, you were supposed to be a man even though not in strength, you had to get to work, the work being fishing, hunting, trapping and bringing home firewood and so on.

The whole year was filled with self-employment, no unemployment insurance then. The winter months from January to the end of March was the trapping season [in Kaipokok Bay], travelling inland for mink, otter and other short-haired animals and hunting caribou. Then back to the coast to the coloured fox trap lines, then off to the outside islands to the white fox lines. It was a continuous battle to earn enough money to survive on. Late March and early April would be the time to gather in firewood for the summer and the next fall and part of the winter, and some to sell to the Moravian Mission or Hudson's Bay Company. All wood was burned for heating during them times.

May month was the month to hunt the jar seal on the ice. The meat and fat was for dog food, none wasted. If more was taken than could be used at the time, the balance was preserved in oil or salted away for the following winter's dog food. When the weather was bad, the men would be found in their twine sheds mending seal nets, salmon nets, trout nets and the big thing, the cod traps.

In June we all went in the Bay with our seal nets to capture some of the migrating harp seals. This gave the women folk an extra busy two weeks or so, cleaning the skins with the ulu and spreading them in frames to dry, ready to be made up into seal skin boots. This took up the evening from suppertime until midnight. These women could be found, at that time, sitting by a kerosene lamp with the square top needle and the caribou sinew making boots.

The codfish came in July and I tell you they used to come in abundance, but for our part of the coast it was a short period with the trap, averaging about two and a half weeks. The old timers knew they had a short season of plenty and often referred to it as make the hay while the sun shines. We would be out hauling that cod trap when the sun broke over the horizon. In July that would be around quarter to five, then we would work constantly. The meals were bolted down. We kept at the fish 'till about eleven-thirty at night, and sometimes after twelve. When it got too dark, a cod oil lamp was lit. You had just a glimmer of light, enough to manage to clean the fish. Four o'clock in the morning you were out again. This went on from Monday until Saturday. After the codfish slacked with the trap, the old trap had to be taken up, hauling eighty pound grapnels out of twenty-five fathoms of water. This gear had to be dried and stored away for next year. Then 'twas take the jigger for another three weeks. I can tell you when you were young it was no trouble to see bladders on your hands. When you got out in the morning you could hardly move your fingers until you got them soaked with salt water again. You'd jig again and burst some of the bladders and cut a few more places. Tough going for a while.

After the middle of August, 'twas start handling the same old fish again. You had to wash the salt off it and spread it out on the bawns, the smooth rocks, or built up flakes [wooden drying racks] to dry it. It had to be spread in the morning and stacked back in piles in the evening. This had to be done for three days, sometimes four, depending on how good the drying was. After all the catch was dried, which could be five to six hundred quintals. This was between three men and a boy, or four men. Around the first week of October a vessel would come to pick up the fish. After all that handling you got paid for your labour at a rate of $1.50 to $2.50 a quintal. Out of that would come your salt, gas, food, maybe an engine and all your rope (one could not use old rope on cod traps because they hold too much tide). All this stuff had to be deducted from your catch before you had any take home pay.

Then 'twas hurry back to the winter home to get a couple of boat loads of firewood from the Bay to put on your winter pile for insurance in case of accident or sickness. Then out with the fox traps again. A few would take off inland for the country furs but most stayed back on the coast and trapped foxes. In December the seal nets had to go out again to capture some of the harp seals migrating south.

So our years were spent continuously on the go, but we had our fun, not that often, but there were the special celebrations and gatherings when people would come in from the bays to celebrate together. One special day was New Years. The last Monday in January was a special day for single men and women from thirteen years up. That would be a big "do" with plenty of dancing, my father's home being the dance place as there was no hall here then. In February there was a special day when the married couples, widows and widowers would gather for their celebrations. I often wonders now how these people could have so much fun and be as lively with not a stain of liquor involved. Easter was a time when almost every family from around the Bay would gather in to Makkovik for church services and sports day on Easter Monday. This is still celebrated in a big way here. Christmas, of course, is celebrated and always has been in a big way, but it's a time for families more than big gatherings until after Christmas Day.

— William Anderson, Sr.
[1.3:48]

Makkovik
October 3, 1901

My dear brothers and friends,

    It is now a long time since I heard from you in our old Norway. I thank God that all of us are still alive and healthy, but I begin to feel my age. However, it is no wonder as I was born in the year 1834.
    We receive letters each year from our relatives who live in the United States, and find there that they are all in good circumstances. I will now send you a photograph of me and my wife. She was born in the year 1837 of English parents,²⁵ who lived here on the coast for many years. We were married in 1859, so that we naturally both seem old, but the time speaks to us all in Labrador as well as in Norway. We have had ten children, who are all still alive to this day, but there are only three of them who are not married. One, a girl named Bertha Andrea, plays the organ in our church, and the piano and the harmonica which we have in our house. My two unmarried sons are known as good hunters in the winter and fishermen in the summer. However, there has never been such bad fishing on this coast as there was this summer, although the fishing was good about 200 miles south of us. The point from Davis Inlet was taken out of the coast, so that the fish could not come to land. As a consequence, I am afraid that there will be poor living for many people around here in the coming winter.
    When I think of the days of my youth, I still think I can see the old places where I used to go, when I was a shepherd on the "Saeter" [summer farm], and many places where I and Anders used our fishing rod in the Buvas River, and other places in Begne Valley. Yes, it is now about fifty years since I left my place of birth.
    I'm still a merchant in this place, but it is not easy to make money with trade as there are so many poor people among us and I find it hard to see families with small children who have not much to eat. I cannot hold back, but must give them something and thus goes many, many dollars from me, one year after another. But I do not think about it as long as we have enough for each day.
    Be so kind as to write to me when you receive these lines, and let me hear about all the old places in Begna Valley. Who is now owner at Haugsrud? Is there much timber on Huget? Have you many new boats on Begna River? Is there a railway now through the Begna Valley? Is Oslo now a big city, and how many inhabitants does it have?

All right dear brothers and friends...
My address:
Mr. T. Andersen
Mission Station Makkovik
Labrador

TORSTEN ANDERSEN'S REAL NAME WAS Torstein Kverna. Torstein is an old Norwegian spelling and pronunciation of Torsten. He changed his surname to Andersen in Labrador because Kverna was too hard to pronounce, and because his father's name was Anders....

Torsten grew up working in a sawmill in winter and taking sheep or goats up to the mountain pastures in the summer. He had no formal schooling. When he was in his teens, he left the valley and went down to Christiania, now Oslo, the capital of Norway, and became a cooper, or barrel maker. After about three years he got an offer from an English company, probably HBC, to go out to Canada, which he did.... He married a woman of Welsh descent in Labrador [Mary Thomas]. My grandfather, Ted McNeill, sang Welsh hymns and the National Anthem of Wales, which he learned from her family when he was a child growing up in northern Labrador.

One of Torsten Andersen's daughters married a McNeill, and they are my grandparents. My grandfather, Edgar (Ted) McNeill, who was with the Grenfell Mission in St. Anthony, spoke of Torsten Andersen sometimes. He said that he was a Norwegian, a God-fearing man who had painted on a rock on the coast, "Prepare to meet thy Maker." He used to be layreader in the church in Makkovik. His sermons were a bit tedious, I gather, because he spoke in heavily accented English. I didn't get too much else out of my grandfather about Torsten, because, at that time, I was not too interested in these matters.

— Curtis McNeill
[3.3:17]

OLD GRANDMA THOMAS [MARY BROOMFIELD] was seventeen years old when she got married to Samuel James Thomas, but she didn't want to marry him you know. She was gettin' around wit' this Scots feller, a Hudson's Bay Company manager or something, and he went out for his holidays, like they do now. They wasn't engaged but she'd promised to marry him when he came back. So she didn't want to marry James Thomas at all. She said afterwards that she didn't want to marry "this old big-headed Englishman" but they forced her to.

What happened was that her father drowned when she was quite young and her poor old Eskimo widowed mother, she couldn't keep them very good. It seems like Mary was one of the older [probably younger] girls. She had a step-sister who had married a Frenchman, and they had to keep her. This step sister tried to get Mary married off, I suppose, so she wouldn't have to keep her. It was hard times, them days, and p'r'haps they was poor off, I don't know. Anyway, she told Mary she had to get married. On the back of the house there was a big marsh with a big rock. She runned out as far as the rock but she couldn't get across the marsh so she stopped on this rock. The next thing she knowed they were there. They told her she had to come back and get married, the minister was there, so that's how poor Mary got married.

I think James Thomas must have had some money gathered up, because after he got married he bought a boat, what they called 'bully-boats' long ago. It had two masts in it, and he fitted her out, bought a whole lot of grub, and they come on down looking for a place to settle down. He must have heard talk about there was good places down this way for huntin'. He wasn't much of a hunter or trapper, I don't think, but his wife was. Mary trapped like a man. They come and went up in a bay, but I don't know if they knew where they was to. I don't know if it had a name...might have had an Eskimo name, I never heard. So they went up in this bay to a place, like in a brook, but they thought it was a river. They runned in when 'twas high water and when the water falled they was in shoal water. They got out of there and went down a little farther and built a house at the head of Makkovik Bay.

They had three girls, Eliza and Susan and Mary, and two sons, Samuel and James. Samuel and Eliza died, Samuel when he was about twelve years old. Mary married Torsten Andersen. He was from Norway. And Susan married a man named Johnny Walker from Cape Cod, and they went outside and lived. James married Susan Broomfield, a cousin, and they lived to Adlavik just south of Makkovik. They had one son, Sampson, then Susan died. Next James married Sarah Edmunds from down around Big Bay and had a daughter, Ellen. Sampson married Eliza Broomfield and after her he married an Eskimo woman from down around Hopedale. I don't think they wanted him to marry her because the Andersens, them days, although they was mixed with Eskimos themselves, they was particular, eh, the old man especially. He wanted his children to marry their own kind, white. I heard Antoine say that Grandfather wanted to marry an Eskimo girl but his father said that he couldn't.

— Caroline Jacques
[8.2:9]

MY AUNT ELLEN [ANDERSEN] MARRIED a man when she was eighteen. He was Solomon Broomfield; I don't think he was any relation to John Broomfield what was here. He was a man from south somewhere. Aunt Ellen told me that when she first met Solomon, he had killed some deer and brought them to the Mission where she worked at the time. She said his face was all frozen badly, and she thought he was the ugliest young man she ever saw in her life. Later on she married him.

She had a very hard time because he developed TB and she couldn't get to Island Harbour, which was seventeen miles from where they lived. It was neither ice nor water. She stayed there with her dying husband and as soon as the ice became strong enough she put him on the komatik and she drove to Island Harbour where her sister Susan was living. I suppose what she had gone through all that fall was too much for her; just as she reached the place, she dropped on the snow by the komatik. She was beat out.

Abram Morgan came from Clark's Beach. He came out fishing with a man by the name of Rose. Morgan and my aunt meet—she was still no more than twenty-two or twenty-three, having been widowed very young. They must have fell in love that summer. Abe Morgan went home, and when he came out the following summer, he told me, he packed his trunk. After the fishing was over, and Rose was going back to Newfoundland, he took his trunk and went ashore to my grandfather's home. He married Aunt Ellen shortly after and never went back to Newfoundland again.

Aunt Ellen never had any children, but they adopted Aunt Mary Jacques when she was a little girl. She was a Pardy. Her father, Jim Pardy, had accidentally shot his arm off.

Aunt Ellen was a good old soul. She wasn't too old when I remember her first, probably in her forties. She could be awful rough sometimes, too. She was a hunter, she hunted rabbits, partridges. She was a good shot. She had one of these old muzzle-loading guns called a musket.

One day Uncle Abe was off hunting and he never came home that night. There was a lot of wolves around because the deer was out close to the salt water. She was very uneasy about her husband because the wolves was plenty. She couldn't do anything about it, just stay home alone and wait and hope that he was all right. Sometime that night she heard a fight and she thought it must have been her brother's dogs. Her brother lived not too far away, and sometimes his dogteams would run down to their place. When she opened the door she saw it was wolves. A wolf's eyes in the dark is very fiery and bright looking. She shut the door, took her old gun off the rack, opened the door again and had a shot. They already had two of her dogs killed. She knew she had killed one wolf. She loaded her gun again; it took some time with those old guns. She had another shot and that was two wolves dead. She fired at another wolf as they were running off and she saw one fall down. She finished off the crippled dogs and shut the door.

She told me this story herself. She said she told herself that no old wolf was going to keep her from sleeping that night.

Next morning she went out and there was a wolf tumbling about on the bank. She said she told the wolf, "You're not worth wasting a load on," so she finished him off with the axe. She looked over the bank on the ice and saw another wolf getting up and falling down, and taking the axe she went on and finished that one off. She counted sixteen tracks, so there must have been twenty wolves, and some of those were bleeding.

The next day Uncle Abe got back home. What had delayed him was that he had crippled a silver fox, chased him but never got him, so he decided to stay out all night and wait until daylight. He got his fox the next day and went home.

Years later, after they shifted to Kaipokok Bay, where Postville is situated, her husband and a young Eskimo man who lived with them decided to go to Micmac Mountain. I been on that mountain many times. I would say you could walk to it from Postville in a day with good snowshoe walking, but from where Aunt Ellen lived, farther in the Bay, it wouldn't be quite so far.

Aunt Ellen didn't take her gun, instead she took some sewing. She told me they had eleven dogs, big husky dogs. They always had big black dogs, and they were always a little vicious, a little. I don't know what it was, but they were always a little vicious. However, she was in the tent sewing and the men were on the mountain hunting, when she heard her dogs making a fuss. She looked out and saw a deer standing at bay, tired out. He'd been chased by wolves, four wolves. He could not go any farther. One of the wolves was cutting the tendon on the back of the deer's leg. That's what wolves do when the deer is tired out, they cut the tendons so they can't walk. Another wolf nearest Aunt Ellen was tearing the deer's ear down. The other two was on the other side. Aunt Ellen grabbed the axe and went to the wolf that was tearing at the deer's ear, and instead of chopping him on the neck or head to kill him, she chopped him in the middle of the back. Then she ran to the one at the deer's leg and got him in the same place. She ran around to the third one, she had the axe in that one when she heard Uncle Abe say, "Helen!"—He used to use the "H"—"Helen, get the 'ell out of that!" A rifle shot was fired and the fourth wolf fell down.

Then he asked her, "Why did you chop the wolves in the back? Why didn't you chop them in the neck or head and kill them out dead?"

She said she didn't care what she done as long as she put them out of commission.

— Thorwald Perrault
[3.4:60]

IN THE YEAR 1910 MY father, the late Joseph Chard, moved from Bay Roberts, Newfoundland, to a place called Aillik. In the winter, our nearest neighbors was the Andersen family at Makkovik, and Thomas Evans at Ben's Cove to the west.

The Andersen family was a very fine family indeed. I knew them all personally—John, James, Wilson, Sam, William, Aunt Ellen Morgan, Aunt Christina Perrault, Aunt Susan McNeill, and last but not least, Aunt Bertha. She was known as Aunt Bertha by everyone from Nain to Rigolet.

What can one say about that marvelous woman? I would have to call her the patron saint of that part of the coast. She devoted her life and energy to others less fortunate that herself, and they were many. She had an unshakable faith in God and an undying love for her fellow man and woman.

...Aunt Bertha Andersen was the local midwife on that part of the coast. She would travel to Nain by dogteam to deliver a baby for one of the missionaries; also she would travel to Rigolet to the Hudson Bay Post to answer the call of mercy. She would travel by boat in the summer no matter how great the storm. Storms wouldn't stop Aunt Bertha when the call came in if she could get the men with enough nerve and courage to take her. The last two times she was out of Makkovik on a delivery case was at Aillik to deliver our two kids. She was in her seventy-sixth year then and our child was her eightieth delivery. She never lost one case in childbirth and she had no medical training. I would say this was a marvelous achievement. To offer Aunt Bertha money for her services was an insult to God and herself.

How did Aunt Bertha Andersen make a good standard of living for herself? First she was a good trapper, and a good hunter as well. She could use a gun with any man and give lots of fellows tips on how to take good aim with a gun. She had her own seal nets, salmon nets, and trout nets. She could look after herself, that is to say, haul nets, clean and split salmon and trout and salt them. The men from the community would look after her seal nets, but many a cold day she'd be over at Ranger Bight helping the men clean and mend the nets for resetting. The seals that Aunt Bertha would get from her nets she would skin, clean, and make them into skin boots and mitts. She would sell these articles for top price. When a pair of skin boots or mitts left Aunt Bertha's hands they were perfect in every way.

Aunt Bertha as a trapper: She would have out fox, mink and weasel traps around Makkovik. It would take her a day's travel to see each trapline. One day would take her up around Ranger Bight, another day around Aillik Neck, and another day around Ford's Bight. Looking at her traps and hunting partridges she would have at least ten or fifteen miles a day on snowshoes, no ski-doo for Aunt Bertha. Then, too, she would always have a few traps on hand to give to someone that was going into the country for a month or so. They would take along a few mink traps and anything they caught in those traps would be Aunt Bertha's. In March when the white foxes was coming south, Aunt Bertha would have a few traps to give the boys to take out on the island to set for her. She always come up with a few white foxes. Any buyers buying Aunt Bertha's furs had to give her top price or no deal.

Aunt Bertha was the local counselor for the area. Anyone with any kind of trouble would always call on Aunt Bertha for advice and she was always ready and willing to pour oil on the troubled waters. One could always depend on Aunt Bertha for sound, solid, and dependable advice. One always left her feeling much happier.

All the time I knew Aunt Bertha, she lived with her brother Uncle Wilson, as we called him. He and Aunt Bertha always had a team of black husky dogs. Auntie was a wonderful lover of dogs. She would look after them like they were part of the family. In those days they were the only means of transportation in winter. I've often heard it said, when Aunt Bertha used her own team to go out on a mercy call, her dogs knew they were on a special mission. They would go all out. They needed no coaxing, no driving. Aunt Bertha would just say the word "go" and they were gone. I can back this statement up because I've seen it happen.

— Samuel Chard
[4.1:56]

I WORKED TWO YEARS FOR the Moravian Mission at Makkovik. In the summer time the minister used to go out to the summer places and hold services. We'd leave Makkovik on Saturday. First stop would be Aillik where the Chards, the Edmunds and all the Jacques from Kaipokok Bay lived. The minister would hold a service there then we'd go on to Wester Island. Evans, Lyalls and a lot of Newfoundlanders from Brigus lived on Wester Island. William Bartlett was living there too. He had a big place there from his father's time. When the salt vessel would come they'd come right to the wharf. Awful deep water there in that harbour. Next was Easter Island where the McNeills and more people from Brigus was. They used to sell their fish to Bartlett too. After that was Dunn's Island where the Andersens, Mitchells and a lot of Eskimos stayed. Tom Dunn had a big place there. The island must have been named after his father. They come from Harbour Grace. There was a lot of people from Harbour Grace on Dunn's Island. Then we'd go to Upper Island Cove and Lower Island Cove and on to Ragged Islands. Monday now we was going in to Tilt Cove. There was only one family there, Broomfields. Johnny Broomfield. Not Big Bay John, but another John Broomfield. 'Twas blowin kind of hard right from the southwest.

John Thomas Lucy told me, "Alfred," he said, "when you get to Cape Dale that's where you're going to hit the wind."

Sure enough. When he was getting handy the lops begin to come more and bigger. By and by they got real big. Big ugly. I was to the engine. Uncle Sam Jacques was steering and the minister, Mr. Sach, was behind. We had a hard time. By and by the fly wheel began to take the water. I was bailing with a big bucket but I couldn't keep her free. Couldn't keep her free at all. Blowing a gale of wind. She used to come right over. She was a thirty-five foot boat, deck boat, with a house on her, you know. Max Jacques was only a boy. He was in the cabin and the water was almost to his knees. That's how much water was in the boat. Our grub box was floating from side to side. I bawled out and told Uncle Sam I'd have to stop and try to bail the water out. The motor was white with pickle. I tried but couldn't keep her free so I said I'd have to start her again. She started, white with pickle like that. It was a long time before we could get her turned up to the wind. We made a big circle. We went on and on and I was bailing all the time. Mr. Sach was seasick.

By and by we got to the lun of the land. 'Twas better then and we runned in to Tilt Cove. The tide was out. Two fellers went ashore and two stayed aboard bailing. High water we took her to the wharf and tied up. Low water we went and looked at he with the lantern. 'Twas dark now, see. The water was running out of her. There was a piece of plank, about six inches long and four inches wide, gone right to the ceiling. You could put your hand right in and touch the ceiling. In a boat, see, there's the bottom of the floor of the boat, well, that's the ceiling. 'Twas a solid plank. We must have hit a stick in the water, I suppose, a piece of drift wood. I don't know. Anyway, low water we got a piece of board from Uncle John and we fixed her up. High water we left as good as ever and went back home.

— Alfred Winters, Sr.
[1.1:51]

ONE OF MY GRANDMOTHERS WAS Julia Lucy. She married John Broomfield. She had my father before she married John Broomfield, and his Aunt Charlotte took him and reared him up, she and her husband. They had no children of their own.

Before Aunt Charlotte got married, some people came and took all grandmother's family, Aunt Charlotte too, and took them to the World's Fair in Chicago, USA. When they come back my grandmother married John Broomfield.

My other grandmother married Tom Edmunds first, that was my mom's father. She was Sarah Winters and her mother was Elizabeth Williams. She was married to a Pardy first and then she married John Winters. There was Jim Pardy, Bill Pardy and John Pardy and Mary Pardy. Mary Pardy was my husband Kenneth's mother. And there was Aunt Rachel Pardy, she was Uncle John Lethbridge's and their mother. There was Susan Winters, she married a Sheppard, and there was Edmund and Tom Winters. They lived to Hopedale.

I heard mother say that Grandfather Winters was still living when she was growed up. He come from England and he was a runaway from a ship. They used to treat them bad on ships in them days.

Up here in Back Bay there's a Peter Lucy's Brook. Well, Grandmother said that's where the Lucy's come from. Great-grandfather Lucy, that's where he come from. Grandmother's parents both died there around Cape Harrison. I think her mother was related to the Pallisers, because when they went to the World's Fair she said they took Pallisers and one was her uncle and another was her cousin. I think her mother was a Palliser.

Dad's people, I don't know them. I s'pose they're in the States somewhere. Grandmother says the captain of a ship was his father.

We got an Uncle Charlie married in the States. He went out to be in the World's Fair in Chicago and wouldn't come back. He was the youngest one.[26] There was

Grandmother Julia Lucy, Aunt Hilda Oliver's father, Abe Lucy, and Simon Lucy, Nancy Monamie's father.

Grandmother didn't tell me too much about the World's Fair but Uncle Simon used to tell stories about it. Grandmother told me one story. She told me when the ship was going to come take them there was people picked them to go. She said they wanted them to take something along with them so they picked some blackberry bushes and some crackerberry leaves and took some seal skins. When they got out to the Fair, people used to pay a lot of money just to come and see them and see what they had with them from Labrador.

Uncle Simon told me that he used to go to shows and one thing and another. He and his brother and some more, he said they took them into a big building and sat them around a big table. He said the one that took them in told them they would see something to once, right in the center of the table. Uncle Simon said they all begin to look around to see where something would come from the table, but they couldn't see anything. They couldn't even see a seam. By'n'by he said they could hear like a little noise and up popped a woman's head, right in the middle of the table. She talked to them he said, a real pretty girl. Then she went away and they looked under the table but they couldn't see anything. Then he said the noise came again she come up that time with two heads. She done that three times and the last time she had three heads. He said they looked everywhere on the table to try and find a seam or something but they couldn't find a thing. He said he don't know what they done, he couldn't figure it out.

Uncle Simon used to be tellin' me about the bananas. Apples and oranges was all we ever got. He'd say to me, "Apples and oranges is no good, Susie. Get pinanas." That's what he called bananas, pinanas.

Uncle Simon got killed with a stick of wood. He was livin' with a family in Makkovik. He went to cut up some dry wood and they had their good pile on a flat rock. There was a big stick of wood in the pile and in trying to get a dry stick out, this big stick fell down and knocked him down. It come down across his head and he hit his head on the rock and it killed him. He only lived a few hours, I think. He couldn't speak or anything after, he just died.

— Susie Pottle
[8.3:35]

I WAS REARED UP WID' old Simon Lucy, when I was only a little kid, 'cause he was always around home and I always seen 'en around. That was around Tuchialik and in the summer time around Ragged Islands, our fishing' place. This old feller told me he could *angakkuk*.

"Well," he said, "I could but not in a bad way."

I thought this was funny he couldn't *angakkuk* in a bad way. I thought it would have to be in a bad way.

He'd always say that he could only *angakkuk* in a good way, but he'd have to fight seven devils to do it, seven devils! I thought that was funny, but he said it was right.

One time he took a silver fox that he got in the winter time and the next spring, when the boat was runnin' down the coast, he took it aboard the *Harmony*. I think a silver fox ran upwards to $500. So he took it aboard and gave it to the captain or mate, who promised to bring or send back the money when they could. I suppose there'd only about three trips for a summer. Anyway, he didn't get his money that year. The next spring she come down again but she didn't stop in at Aillik, where he was that summer. He wanted the money from his fox but he couldn't get aboard the boat because she was passing down outside Aillik, so he said he'd stop her in the run.

"Yes," he said, "I'll stop her flat."

He went up on the hill and by'n'by the boat stopped out in the run, stopped right still. He walked down off the hill and got aboard his flat and rowed out to the boat. He was there quite a little while and by'n'by we seen 'en start to row back, and later the boat went on. He really done it! He come back with his money.

The captain said after that the boat was steamin' along and all of a sudden she was just a tremble. The motors was goin' but she wasn't makin' a bit of headway. She stayed that way 'till the old feller got aboard, done his business and left.

— John Edmunds
[4.4:8]

DOGS WERE DEPENDABLE THINGS TO HAVE. I had one lead dog that was really good. He could take me home anytime it was rough. Just let him alone and let him go on. Sometimes you couldn't even see the nose of the komatik. Once I know I come out of the country and it come right rough. I was down around Ticoraluk Hills, and that's high hills. From the knobs of them hills 'twas rough enough to blow you away. I just let me dog alone and he took me right home. I didn't know where I was myself. 'Twas the dog I was trusting to. That was a good leader....

I often come from across the Big Neck, down from Ticoraluk to Fox Cove and Tom Luscombes [Brook]. When we couldn't get north for supplies we'd go to Rigolet. Uncle Austin [Flowers] used to keep a bit of trade at Ticoraluk and we'd go to he. When he never had it we go to Rigolet. Course we used to trap to Tom Luscombes too. The first time we went across we didn't know a thing about it. We sort of thought we'd get across out on the bay. We went over the barrens and found a marked tree there. From that we follied right out to Tom Luscombes. Uncle Austin and Jerry used to always trap in there I been told....

Talking about old times, well, 'twas harder again in me father's time. Hunting and carrying on in them times, you never got much. 'Twas just trade and that's all.

You gave so much furs for a gun, so much for something else and so on. Things was cheap, real cheap, but you hardly got anything for your fur. 'Twould end up you'd only get enough to cover your food and gear. If you didn't have the fur, well, you had to get the old pit saw and saw a bit of lumber to get something to eat. I can mind about that.

I was fourteen years of age when me father died. I was on me own from then on. I had a mother a brother and a sister to look out for. I'm still looking out for meself…just a bit slower now. I'm more than thankful we're getting our pensions now. That's a wonderful thing. The memories of the past is wonderful too. It helps to be able to look back on it all.

— William Edmunds
[1.2:43]

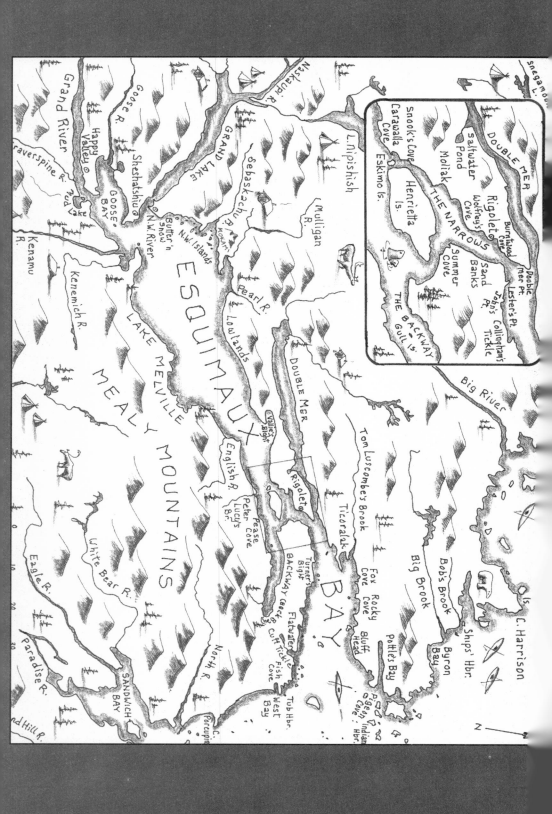

CHAPTER

Seven

GRANDE BAIE
DES ESQUIMAUX

RISING A THOUSAND FEET FROM the sea like some monstrous Jabba the Hutt, Cape Harrison presides over a devilish brew of opposing currents, fickle winds, and rebounding ocean swells intimidating to the ablest mariners. Small, shore-hugging boats risk it only for errands of some importance and under favourable weather conditions and tides. Perhaps for this reason it has always served, at least in the summer months, as a boundary between the Moravian Coast and the heart of the Hudson's Bay Company's territory in Labrador—Esquimaux Bay, now called Hamilton Inlet. No other region in the world produced furs as thick and lustrous as those from Esquimaux Bay District.

Over one hundred-fifty miles long in all and up to twenty-five wide, Hamilton Inlet encompasses both the inland sea of Lake Melville and the broad estuary of Groswater Bay. The Inuit called it Ivuktoke. On seventeenth-century maps it was named the Grande Baie des Esquimaux, and so it was known by most Europeans for over three centuries. The very name evoked such apprehension among sailors that until the nineteenth century few even ventured into the Narrows, which consequently were often mistaken for its headwaters. Winter villages of the Aivitumiut, the reputedly barbarous Inuit of Ivuktoke, clustered on the shores of its guardian islands. Mariners who dared to slip past them, bucking the currents, rips, and whirlpools of the channel, found themselves on the threshold of a tidal lake some hundred miles in length. Sailing into the wind along the thickly forested hem of the Mealy Mountains, the northern shore soon falls away, lost in a haze of spindrift. On clear, still days it recedes in the distance to an irregular line of blue between the other blues of water and sky, between seeing and imagination.

Through the glacial trench of Lake Melville flow all the rivers draining the flanks of the snow-capped Mealy Mountains to the south, the Moravian Coast highlands to the north, and the central Labrador plateau extending over two hundred miles westward to the borders of Quebec where lay the Innu's watery Nitassinan, the trappers' "Height-of-Land." Its thickly wooded shores and river systems provided ideal habitats for fur-bearing mammals, or rather, their pelts, for while the creatures themselves were probably never numerous, the quality of their fur is without equal. Seals congregated at the river mouths to intercept the passage of salmon and trout in their annual pilgrimage to spawning grounds.

Chief among the western rivers is the mighty Grand. Renamed Hamilton and, again later, Churchill by map-makers; to the people of Labrador it will always be the Grand River—Kessessasskiou to the Innu, which means the same thing. The Innu who lived near western Lake Melville and its tributaries took its name. Transformed by time it has become the name of their community, Sheshatshiu.[1] The Grand is joined by the Traverspine, Kenamu, and Kenamish in feeding the sandy southwest corner of Lake Melville. These waterways cascade from the hunting grounds of the Montagnais and headwaters of rivers running south to the Gulf of St. Lawrence and west to Hudson's Bay. Thirty or so miles north, the Naskapi and Red Wine rivers flow through Grand Lake, then Little Lake before decanting into Lake Melville through the short, swift channel sometimes called North West River today. Originally, North West River referred to the whole Naskapi River system draining Lake Michikamau. This system led to the hunting grounds of the tundra, or Mushuau Innu, whom others called "Naskapi," and to the headwaters of rivers flowing north to Ungava Bay and east to the Moravian Coast.

The north shore of Lake Melville is favoured by more than its southern exposure. Salmon and trout once swarmed at the mouths of rivers that crease its thickly wooded slopes. The Sebaskachu, Pearl, and Mulligan—old Naskapi highways—abounded in marten and provided Settlers with overland winter routes between game on the barrens and the families and traders in Double Mer and the bays of the north coast. Clusters of wooded islets protect the shoreline from Lake Melville's fickle winds while furnishing a pretty foreground to the panorama of snow-capped mountains looming across the inland sea. These islands and the rivermouths between the Sebaskachu and North West Point were the principal fishing grounds of the Naskapi, whose modern-day campsites are still to be found behind the screen of alders framing the shoreline. Not surprisingly, this became a choice location for Settlers.

English River and Peter Lucy's Brook, which fall to the colder southeast shores of Lake Melville from the highlands of the Mealy Mountains, were frequented by some of the area's first English trader-trappers, possibly due to their proximity to winter trails between the Lake and English stations near West Bay and Sandwich Bay. They must ultimately have proved unsatisfactory or unnecessary, for they never became important outposts and were again in the hands of Inuit families when the Hudson's Bay Company arrived in the area six decades later. Some historians believe English

River is the site of Thorvald Eriksson's death at the hands of *skraelings*, described in Norse Sagas, but his burial cairn has never been located.

Together the rivers of Lake Melville wash over its ponderous salty depths, spilling into Groswater Bay through the Narrows, a sixteen-mile-long bottleneck choked by Henrietta and Eskimo islands. In this tight passage, the turbulent contest between fresh-water and salt, current and tide, creates an exceptionally rich marine environment and year-round ice-free water. Teeming with migrating salmon and trout, a playground for whales, porpoise, and seals, the Narrows of Ivuktoke was the heartland of a prosperous community of Inuit, now considered the southernmost Eskimo band in the world.[2]

On early eighteenth-century French maps, the Grande Baie des Esquimaux meant, or included, Lake Melville, suggesting that Inuit dominated even the inland sea soon after their arrival in the sixteenth century. Archaeological evidence, however, indicates that they were concentrated in the eastern half of the Lake, while its western shores have long been Innu territory. The people of the Kessessasskiou congregated at the mouth of the Kenamu, Naskapi, and Grand rivers, and at Mud Lake since prehistoric times. North West River has been inhabited sporadically for some six thousand years by both proto-Innu and proto-Inuit groups, and the village of Sheshatshiu has been used by Innu for well over a hundred years. In the eighteenth century, the Innu of Lake Melville had the advantage not only of firearms but of a privileged relationship with the French traders in North West River and its western outposts. Fornel employed Montagnais from the Gulf stations as guides and servants. While discouraged from aggressive behavior toward the Inuit, these Native companions probably assumed a defensive role, in keeping with the other measures Fornel took in anticipation of Inuit raids. The Inuit, for their part, appear to have kept mainly to the islands of the Narrows, where they were courted by traders at the posts in Rigolet and Groswater Bay. They rarely ventured farther west than Mulligan, about half-way down the Lake.

Because Inuit first reached Ivuktoke from the north about the time Europeans began arriving from the east, their earliest living sites in this region contain remnants of traditional tools fashioned from iron nails and fittings. By the time French traders appeared on the coast, china, glass, pewter, mirrors, and beads had became part of the southern Inuit household. Within a hundred years the Aivitumiut had also begun to use firearms, alcoholic beverages, sugar, flour, and tobacco.[3] Their population had experienced a steep decline in number (due in part to the lure of the Moravian stations), and the future of those who survived the massacres and epidemics was beginning to merge with that of European Settlers.

In 1824 Methodist minister Thomas Hickson estimated that there were a hundred full-blood adult and sixty juvenile Inuit in Ivuktoke, plus nineteen European and sixteen Canadian Settlers with sixty half-breed children.[4] This would suggest that not even the Canadian men brought families with them to the area, and up to half the available Inuit women had already married whites, initiating the core family lines of the Labradorian. Among these progenitors were the Englishman Ambrose Brooks and his Inuit wife Susan whose story is told in this chapter by their descendants. By 1850 the Ivuktoke Inuit headcount had reportedly dropped to fifty,[5] though even then the distinctions between pure and partial Inuit were apt to be more cultural than genetic. European blood ran in many of the families, for the earliest liaisons were often informal, and mixed children whose father's perished or abandoned them were likely to have been raised as Natives.

Once European commerce and settlement began to take hold in the bay, the adaptable Inuit began speaking English and acquiring European ways. In the 1840s the Moravians observed (in a comparison that could as easily have been inverted) that these Southlanders already differed little from their Settler neighbors. However, to Charles Hallock, visiting the coast in 1860, families like the Pallisers and Ikeys were still discernibly Inuit. As late as 1893 when Labradorians were selected to represent Eskimos at the Chicago Exposition, members of the Palliser and Lucy families agreed to go, clearly satisfying that designation both to the recruiters and to themselves.[6] Tanner counted eleven Ivuktoke Inuit families in 1937—six of them Pallisers[7], two Shiwaks,[8] two Ikeys,[9] one Adams,[10] and one Mucko.[11] He missed the Shuglos.[12] Like the Adams family, the Lucys[13] and Tooktoshinas[14] of the south Moravian Coast also had ties to Ivuktoke Inuit families, as did most of the Settlers on both sides of Cape Harrison.

By the end of the nineteenth century, the distinction between Settler and Southlander was based largely on custom, self-perception, and often enough, on self-deception, for as the Settler population struggled to emerge from the primitive conditions of the frontier period, some of its number began to deny or forget their Native roots. Embarrassment would change to pride when affirmative action and land claims legislation was initiated in the 1970s, along with publication of *Them Days* magazine and other accounts of Labrador life.

European settlement of Esquimaux Bay began in 1778 when Jeremiah Coghlan's man William Phippard and his partner John Nooks [var. Newhook and Knox] are alleged to have been abandoned in Esquimaux Bay. They were said to have been there three years, suffering terrible privation from which they barely survived. Lydia Campbell recounts stories her mother told her of their marriages to Inuit women, settlement at English River, Nooks' murder at the hands of his wife's half-brothers, and the subsequent death of his son. As a child, Lydia herself lived in a house with Nooks' blind old widow, then wife of John Whittle. Nothing more is known of William Phippard's story, but he appears on Slade's records in 1782 owing the company for passage on *The Sisters*, presumably to England.

The charismatic rum-dealer, trader, and self-styled Jesuit preacher Pierre Marcoux and his partners arrived next, possibly as agents for the Gulf firm of Lymburner & Grant. They seem to have been the first to reopen the old Fornel posts at North West River and Rigolet after a vacancy of some thirty years (although Jacob Pozer held title), and also established a staging ground for these operations in Tub Harbour at the southern entrance to Groswater Bay. Marcoux and Marchand were at North West River in 1784 and Rigolet in '85, when rivals and eventually associates Dumontier, Dorval, Beliveau, and Plante took over at the former. Marcoux himself is said to have settled near Makkovik by 1795, but at least one genealogist has proposed that the Inuit Muckos of Ivuktoke are his descendants.[15] In any case, he remained in Rigolet through 1788, when Nicholas Gabourite of the Quebec Fur Trading Company assumed management of the post. By then Slade & Company had opened an outpost in Snooks Cove just above Rigolet in the Narrows. In the 1790s, Joseph Bird & Son established themselves at the Tub Harbour post, extending their activities to the Kenemich River in 1810.

Dumontier, Beliveau, and two new partners managed North West River through 1799, when their permits were denied, possibly on account of England's war with France. In 1815 when the wars ended the widow Dumontier sold her late husband's share back to Jacob Pozer. During the next twenty years, ownership of North West River post would turn over more than a half-dozen times, gradually reverting from Quebec-based merchants to those from New England with a Canadian affiliation.

These, then, were the principal conduits and support system for the pioneer Settlers in Hamilton Inlet: the Canadian firms at Rigolet and North West River, and the Slade and Bird outfits at Tub Harbour and Snooks Cove, all of them undoubtedly cut off to some extent from the slender lines of communication with the outside world that had begun to develop before the wars. It was during this period that the Ivuktoke Inuit experienced the dramatic events recounted in the *Diary of Lydia Campbell* and the Moravian and Cartwright journals. The last three decades of the eighteenth century was the era of Caubvick, Mikak, Tuglavina, Paulo, and "Susan"; of the Inuit's struggle to cope with, adjust to, and, if possible, profit from the enormous changes happening in their land.

Oddly enough, it was the English companies who seeded Esquimaux Bay with its first Settlers, perhaps because it was easier for the Canadians to return home without getting caught up in the war. William Blake, William Broomfield, Moses Brown, and William Reed came to Esquimaux Bay with their Inuit wives in the late eighteenth century as agents for Slade's, although they also seem to have done work for Bird's. Robert Best and James Mesher [Mercier] of Jersey apparently found their way up from the Straits at that time. The origins for Ambrose Brooks and John Whittle remain elusive (unless their first names were really Benjamin and Joseph, in which case they were Slade's men seeking anonymity during the wars), but will probably be found in ships' manifests for Bird & Company or Slade's in the 1790s. All remained in Hamilton Inlet when, in 1820, Hunt & Company took over Slade's post in Snook's Cove and opened another at Webbek Harbour on Cape Harrison.

During the first three decades of the nineteenth century the pioneer Settlers were joined by Thomas Groves, John Mudge of Devonshire and John Williams of London, who traded or settled near West Bay (Groves had a trading post at Tub Harbour). Mudge started out in Sandwich Bay around 1806 and moved to West Bay in 1834. Williams came to Sandwich Bay in 1818 at the age of nineteen and had a place at North River before settling down at Flatwater and West Bay.[16] Peter Hamel, another early arrival, may have come from Quebec, a descendant perhaps of Pierre Hamel, Constantin's attorney and son-in-law, who ran his concessions in the Straits durings the 1730s. Peter married Eliza Broomfield in the 1820s or '30s. Mersai [Marcel] Michelin, a *coureur du bois* of French Canadian and possibly Montagnais Innu extraction from Trois Rivieres, arrived in 1834 and settled at Kenemich, trapping the Innu country west and south of the Mealy Mountains. Mersai married the widow Hannah Brooks and fathered three sons and several daughters whose bloodlines, like Hamel's, run through most of the old families of Esquimaux and Sandwich Bay.

On the north shore of Groswater Bay, Newfoundland fishing companies opened summer stations at Indian Tickle and Smokey Harbour—notably William Langley & Co., Angus Brownson, and John Leaman (or Lemmon), whose Brigus-based company was operated by Captain Nathan Norman. Steve Newell came to the coast as a servant for Norman; George Pottle operated some of Norman's stations and ultimately vied with him for ownership rights. Mark Ansty (originally 'Anstey') settled in that area as well after completing his service with Slade's. They were all there by 1835.

As on the Moravian Coast, names of many early planters disappeared through emigration, want of progeny or, like Ambrose Brooks in the first generation and John Mudge in later ones, failure to raise male offspring. Some, like Bird, Phippard, Broomfield, Brown, and Reed would later settle permanently in other parts of Labrador. Blake, Best, Mesher, Pottle, and Groves are among those whose names survived in the early twentieth-century population of Hamilton Inlet.

These men were probably among the planters encountered in the 1820s by Wesleyans attempting to initiate a ministry in the Narrows. Within four years the missionaries left in disgust due to "the opposition of the traders, and the excessive indulgence in spirits on the part of those who were the object of their labour."[17] The fact that most of their subjects were staunchly, if nominally, Church of England[18] and as such considered themselves superior to the puritanical Methodists was undoubtedly a factor, but this is not the only reference to alcohol abuse in the region before the arrival of the Hudson's Bay Company.

HBC came to Esquimaux Bay in 1836. Within two years it had bought out all competitors and established a monopoly over the fur and salmon trade in the district.

D. R. Stewart (who then held the North West River post), Hunt Company at Snooks Cove, and independent traders like Thomas Bird, Thomas Groves, and William McKenzie were among those compelled to sell. Groves remained to settle in the area, Bird evidently settled in Sandwich Bay, and McKenzie and his sons (probably members of the prominent métis family from the Gulf) signed on with HBC in North West River.

During the early decades of its tenure in Labrador, HBC was still obtaining a majority of its employees from Scotland and the Orkney Islands, as it had done in northern Canada during the eighteenth century. Preferring to have honest, hardworking, God-fearing men as personnel and neighbors in an otherwise lawless wilderness, the Company was selective in recruiting servants for duty in Labrador. But its meager compensation was insufficient inducement for them to remain in service for more than the requisite five-year term, especially since most recruits were motivated by the prospect of passage to the New World and a chance to forge an independent life for themselves. Those who elected to strike out on their own in Esquimaux Bay contributed many fine qualities to the Settler population. They include Scotsmen Daniel Campbell, Thomas Baikie, John Montague, Malcolm McLean, the Finn called 'Fred Hope' because it was easier to pronounce than his real name, Englishman George Flowers, Irishman Richard Gear, possibly Eamon Chaulk, and Norwegian Torsten Andersen. Gear and Andersen ultimately settled on the Moravian Coast with HBC's northern recruits, George Lyall and Antoni Perrault.

The first Goudie in Labrador, John, was the Quebec-born son of an Orkeyman at HBC's Moose River post on Hudson's Bay. He, his Cree wife and three children were transferred to the Ungava posts in 1835 and, the following year, to the new HBC post in North West River. He ran their trapline at Traverspine, buying it from them when his term ended in 1844 and passing it on to his son Joseph when he moved to Double Mer. The Rich family of Rigolet and North West River, said to have had a Scots progenitor, also spells its name Riche and Ritch, variants that even occur among siblings. The Inuit Isaac Rich of Nain is not considered a relative. Nor are the Innu Rich/Riche families of Davis Inlet and Sheshashiu, whose ancestors are said to have included old Ned Richards, another métis patriarch from the Gulf Posts, and an Inuit woman from Ungava. Isaac (Ike) Rich of the Rigolet-North West River group, a founder of *Them Days*, presents himself in his narratives as the quintessential Settler. It is recklessly tempting to speculate that his facial structure, knowledge of Innu customs and language, and his apparent empathy for the Naskapi reveal a relationship he was reluctant to admit. One can even imagine a marvelously peripatetic and prolific HBC Scotsman on the Labrador Peninsula in the early days of settlement, a man who by baptism or charm, assured that his progeny by women at each of his assigned posts would bear his name regardless of who raised them.

From the very start, HBC considered the choice river mouths of Lake Melville prime real estate, subject to official rules of ownership, which they dictated. Early occupants unable to successfully exploit their resources sold out to the Company, which made sure that only the most capable trappers and salmoners used or purchased them thereafter. It was a kind of un-natural selection that favoured the population of Lake Melville, especially former Company employees. Until the trapping boom began, these families lived like everyone else, alone from September to June in isolated coves, women tending the family while men walked the traplines. For four or five month a year ice on the lake was hard enough for travel, and people were able to visit neighbors and the posts at North West River and Rigolet. In June they would pack the household, bedding, dogs and all, into an open boat and row or sail sixty, a hundred, hundred-thirty miles down the Lake, through the Narrows, and out to the fishing grounds in Groswater Bay. There they obtained a winter's supply of codfish, wild eggs, and berries and a haul of salmon and herring to trade at Rigolet before rowing home.

Unlike the fishery, in which large families and a few neighbors were an asset, trapping was a solitary occupation requiring men to work and live at considerable distances from one another. Older sons had to find new territory far from that of their father when they married, while the youngest son stayed with his aging parents and inherited the father's traplines. When both the Settler population and the fur business began to boom in the twentieth century, the exploding younger generation of Lake Melville trappers had to move into the long rivers feeding the head of the Lake where men could find unclaimed trapping grounds deep in the interior. Most were alone on the traplines for six or seven months, but the good ones, the lucky ones, could obtain enough top quality furs in a season to provide for their families throughout the year. The exhausting trip to the coast was no longer obligatory, though some went anyway simply for a change of scene and some relief from the insects that plague the interior in summer.

While European immigrants took over the prime coves in western and northern Lake Melville, the Narrows and Backway (or Back Bay) of eastern Lake Melville reverted to the descendants of the Aivitumiut who had previously lived together on the islands but now needed to disperse more widely for trapping, woodcutting, and salmon fishing. A few participated in the cod fishery, but their annual circuits were short, and they lived relatively well on an abundant supply of marine mammals and trout. The occasional fox pelt and odd jobs for HBC-Rigolet provided them with the equipment and supplemental provender needed to sustain the Settler lifestyle they now preferred.

With the ascendancy of the Hudson's Bay Company and establishment of Newfoundland fisheries at Indian Harbour and Smokey, commercial activity shifted to the north shore of Groswater Bay. Most of the West Bay Settlers drifted back south toward North River and Cartwright, or north to mingle with the Inuit and mixed families of the Rigolet-Cape Harrison area. A few individuals remained into the twentieth century, and great grandchildren who are themselves great grandparents still return in July to net a few trout and salmon for themselves.

Groswater Bay was a cold, hardscrabble places to make a living in the winter. Even the best of the trapping grounds at West Bay and Tom Luscombe's Brook (named for an eighteenth-century Slade Company employee) were exhausted within a couple of generations, and once-stable families fell on hard times. Some left to begin anew elsewhere. The north shore of the bay near Rigolet was settled by year-round employees of HBC, like members of the Flowers family. The northeast coast was settled by caretakers of Newfoundland fishing stations like Steve Newell, by diehard fishermen whose main objective was first chance at choice berths in the spring, or by runaways, castaways, and stowaways with no sponsors in Labrador and nowhere else to go. As a rule they married Inuit women from Ivuktoke and Cape Harrison families, or second-generation Labradorians as destitute as themselves. In spite of these unpromising beginnings, some managed to survive, to rise above abject poverty, and even to join in the relative prosperity of the Lake Melville trapping community. They include Broomfields, Olivers, Allens, Newells, Chaulks, and Pottles, descendants of Thomas's presumed brother George.

George Pottle, whose signature is on the 1835 petition, had a winter home in the Backway during the 1850s and fished near Pottle's Bay on the northeast coast of Groswater. In 1860 he married Joseph Broomfield's daughter Mary with the understanding that she had inherited old Mark Ansty's fishing properties at Collingham's Tickle. His fruitless struggles with Captain Norman over ownership are documented in the narratives. Thomas Pottle "of Dover," perhaps a son or brother, came to West Bay in 1840 and married Mudge's daughter. Tom Oliver was 'cast away' on an island near Indian Harbour and rescued by Inuit sometime between 1820 and 1850.[19] He survived to found a large family that has lived along the north shore of the bay and Narrows ever since. Like most Groswater families, his became part of a community that extended across Cape Harrison to the southern Moravian Coast. Eamon Chaulk of Scotland is said by descendants to have been a "runaway," though he may have come with HBC or even Slade's, which listed Chalks on its early ledgers. He appears to have settled first on the northeast coast of Groswater Bay before his family made its way into the trapping communities in western Lake Melville. Charles Allen came to Groswater from England in the last quarter of the nineteenth century and settled at Bluff Head. William Mugford arrived in the 1860s from Cupids, Newfoundland. He came, wrote Methodist missionary Arminius Young, "to make an easier living."

When the Hudson's Bay Company consolidated commercial activity in Hamilton Inlet, it became the center of a web connecting the lives of all the area's residents. It was loose-knit by design, as people were encouraged to continue living far enough apart to maximize the harvest of furs and salmon. Though the Company's basis was exclusively commercial, it unwittingly provided the rudimentary infrastructure for evolution of an orderly, coherent society.

In time HBC developed local if not international markets for almost anything the planters could produce—pickled herring, handicrafts, komatiks, sealskin boots, snowshoes, boats, preserved berries, seal oil, net whips, ladders, planked logs, whatever. The one product it did not deal in until very late, and then only marginally at Rigolet, was fish. The codfishery and outer islands of Groswater Bay were the province of established firms, most based in Newfoundland. From 1832 or earlier until the end of the nineteenth century the main dealer in this region was Captain Nathan Norman at Indian Harbour. Norman gained possession of several prime shore stations in the northeast sector and collected fish from planters up and down the coast.

HBC-Rigolet, for many decades the larger of the two Hamilton Inlet stations, was mainly a salmon post, shipping its product dry-salted in barrels to England. It also became the destination for official and unofficial visitors to the bay—magistrates,[20] missionaries, doctors, tourists—and the staging ground for major social gatherings such as the short-rubber dances at end of the codfishery and week-long celebrations of the New Year. Leonard Budgell, son of HBC factor George Budgell, grew up at the Rigolet post during the early years of the twentieth century. His evocative descriptions of the old station could apply in many respects to all its forerunners in Labrador—Hunt & Henley at Paradise River, Slade & Company in Battle Harbour, Noble & Pinson at Charles River, and George Cartwright's headquarters in Sandwich Bay. Budgell was at Rigolet during its peak, and he reflects the romantic idealism of his father and the sense of company pride and loyalty common in the upper levels of HBC management but seldom expressed by the rank and file, even those in skilled positions like James Dickers. Accounts by other HBC employees and neighbors spin a sometimes dissonant counterpoint to Budgell's glowing tributes, and a Labradorian perspective on the "Great Company's" impact on their lives.

Until the twentieth century, outside visitors wishing to go into Lake Melville disembarked at Rigolet to hire a smaller boat for the voyage to North West River.[21] North West River was mainly a fur trading post, although in the early years it supervised crews of salmoners as well as furriers at Kenemich, Traverspine, and other river mouths in western Lake Melville. The only residents at the post were the families of servants and factors. Donald Smith, chief factor for Esquimaux Bay District from 1848 to 1868, transformed North West River post into an experimental farm inspired, perhaps, by the success of the Mission gardens on the Moravian Coast and his desire to show Labradorians that with industry it was possible to live well in their country. Visitors marveled and Settlers made plots in their little coves for the potato sets he gave them, leaving mother nature to tend them during their summer's absence on the

Hopedale. [SYDNEY W. WOODWARD]

Voisey family, Nain 1910-11; (L–R) Back: Jim, Emma (nee Dicker), Lily and Amos, Middle: Susan, George, Alice (nee Ford) and Emily. Front: Selma, George, Henry and Alice. [JIM VOISEY, THEM DAYS ARCHIVES]

Matthew Pualo, Hopedale 1928.
[ALICE PERRAULT]

Thomas and Mary (Mudge) Pottle.
[VIOLA BIRD]

Log Cabin built by Horace Goudie at Voisey's Bay 1978.   [JUDY McGRATH]

Naskaupi boy with bow and arrow.
[PERRY-MACMILLAN ARCTIC MUSEUM]

Lillian Broomfield, Big Bay.
[JIM GEAR]

Falls at Frank's Brook, Voisey's Bay. [PERRY-MACMILLAN ARCTIC MUSEUM]

Left: John and Mary Jane Pasteen, Davis Inlet, ca. 1930.
[MON. EDWARD O'BRIEN]

Bottom: Joe Rich, Davis Inlet.
[PEARY-MACMILLAN ARCTIC MUSEUM]

Lydia and Dan Campbell, Cul de Sac, ca. 1880. [FLORA BAIKIE COLLECTION]

Hudson's Bay Company store, Cartwright, ca. 1901. [PEARL PYE]

Perry Chaulk's house, Mulligan. [ESTHER CHAULK COLLECTION]

Joseph Michelin (1845–1940), ca. 1900. [PAPERS OF W.T. GRENFELL, YALE]

Muskrat Falls, 1980. [D.J. SAUNDERS]

Montagnais Innu Camp. [NORTH WEST RIVER UNITED CHURCH]

Above, left: Montagnais Innu girl.
[NORTH WEST RIVER UNITED CHURCH]

Above: Austin Montague, North West River.
[NIGEL MARKHAM]

Middle, left: John Michelin, North West River
1976. [NIGEL MARKHAM]

Below: Montagnais Innu.
[NORTH WEST RIVER UNITED CHURCH]

Left: John A. Broomfield, Happy Valley 1975.
[D.J. SAUNDERS]

Below: Surveying for Goose Bay Air Base, 1941.
[NORTH WEST RIVER UNITED CHURCH]

Bottom: Happy Valley 1943-44.
[RALPH MURRAT]

fishing grounds. The small harvest of potatoes, greens, radishes, and rhubarb with which some were occasionally rewarded provided but token supplements to the high protein and carbohydrate diets of the Labradorians but undoubtedly contributed to a healthier start for many of the children. In a country where nutritional deficiencies were rife, this was not a trivial advantage.

Smith was the first trader to take a personal interest—if a relatively passive and pragmatic one—in the well-being of the planters. It became customary during his tenure for post managers to assist in performing weddings, funerals, hearings, and church services, and for the Company to extend credit when the families fell on hard times. Smith and his wife provided some rudimentary medical assistance, helped families to obtain books, and actively recruited Moravian and other missionaries for work among the residents of the bay. HBC also provided under-compensated but often lifesaving jobs, apprenticeships, and seasonal work for the local people.

While northern and southern-most Labrador each enjoyed the advantages of organized community life and rudimentary social institutions early in the nineteenth century, the residents of central Labrador, Hamilton Inlet in particular, had no stationary institutions or permanent services other than those provided by HBC. But what these people were denied from outside, many were able to achieve for themselves. Industrious, more or less devout, and sometimes literate HBC men married Inuit or half-breed girls who, unlike the earlier generation of Settler wives, spoke English and were familiar with European customs. Many had a Moravian education, which for a century was superior to that found in any other group in the country. The combination of Inuit skills, resourcefulness, humour, stoicism, and generosity with the Protestant work ethic of the Settlers helped elevate their families above the almost bestial conditions in which they lived. Some taught themselves to read and write, generation after generation, observing religious practices handed down by parents and grandparents who had themselves never entered a church. Like all Labradorians they were also their own doctors, pharmacologists, and midwives, and they were their own keepers of law and order.

No other documents provide better insights into the history, heart, and soul of the Labradorians than the recollections of Lydia Campbell and her daughter, Margaret Baikie. Like old window glass, the semi-literate view they offer of the first years of settlement is as tantalizing in its suggestiveness as it is frustrating in its lack of clarity. But these glimpses of the Labrador character as it was being forged of European and Inuit components is invaluable, particularly in tandem with the slowly emerging historical record of this "dark" period.

The bloodlines of Lydia's parents, Ambrose Brooks and his Inuit wife Susan, are woven deeply into the fabric of Labrador's population. Most of Hamilton Inlet's leading families are descendants, but the connections range across the entire coast. Although Ambrose Brooks offspring were exceptional in some respects, their lives exemplified the experience of most early Labrador families whose histories have been lost. In a very real sense, the epic of the Brooks clan is also a history of Lake Melville, which would in time become the center of modern Labrador. It begins when whites made their first tentative forays into the land of Innu and Inuit and leads to the establishment of large and relatively prosperous trapping settlements in Mud Lake and North West River in the early twentieth century.

"Susan" was born on Eskimo Island around 1788 and orphaned in her early teens. We have no idea what her Inuit name was, or what family she came from. Tormented by superstitious relatives, she escaped to seek shelter with Europeans seen in the bay. After a sixty-mile hike along the shores of Lake Melville, she was rescued by two French Canadians working at Mulligan. By then there were several English and Canadian crews in the bay. The following year Susan's band reclaimed her and later gave her in marriage to the young Englishman, Ambrose Brooks. Brooks had come to Esquimaux Bay in the 1790s "as an apprentice" in one version. In another version he is said to have jumped ship to escape the press gangs then recruiting for England's interminable wars against French and American colonists. Both may have been true.

Ambrose named his wife Susan after his mother, and the couple settled down at Mulligan River. Their summer place was at Mulliauk, near Rigolet. Together Susan and Ambrose raised three daughters, Elizabeth (b. ca.1808), Hannah (b. ca.1813), and Lydia (b. ca.1818). Ambrose taught the girls to read the Bible and follow its precepts. Susan taught Ambrose and her daughters to trap and live on the land. She also told them harrowing stories of her escape and of the first Englishmen to settle in the bay, William Phippard and John Nooks.

Lydia married twice, the first time to William Blake, Jr. who had come to Labrador with his father in the early 1780s to work for Slade's Company. After Blake's death, Lydia married HBC cooper Daniel Campbell, who came to Rigolet from Orkney in 1845. Her sister Elizabeth had married William Reed, a "young half-breed," probably brother of John Reed, who was in Esquimaux Bay in 1835 before moving north to become the first white to settle in Hopedale. Newlyweds Elizabeth and William reportedly drowned in a boating accident around 1824, leaving no children. His father was said to have perished with them. Hannah first married William Mesher and, when he died, Mersai Michelin. She had children by both. The third generation—Lydia's and Hannah's numerous children—married Baikies, Goudies, and virtually every other family name in the Lake Melville area in the first half of the nineteenth century.

Near the end of her life, Lydia was encouraged by Methodist missionary Rev. Arthur C. Waghorne to write down her memories and the stories she heard from her mother. This retrospective diary was published in installments of the St. John's *Evening Herald* in 1894 and 1895. Selections have been transcribed here with most of the original punctuation and spelling errors. While Lydia could read, she did not learn to write until she was an adult.

Margaret Baikie, Lydia's daughter, also transcribed her recollections when in her mid-seventies, inspired undoubtedly by her mother. Her eye for detail and remarkably keen memory bring nineteenth-century Lake Melville to life more vividly than any other existing document from the period. Two generations later, this family tradition would be continued by Elizabeth Blake Goudie, whose autobiographical book *Woman of Labrador*—also written when she was in her seventies—would be celebrated across all of Canada, receiving the Canadian Book Award in 1976.

After an epoch in which life changed little if at all in Esquimaux Bay, the twentieth century swept in like a spring flood carrying several unrelated groups of outsiders who would each leave an indelible mark on the country. In 1883 the Wesleyans returned to Groswater Bay and built a church at Lester's Point across the Narrows from Rigolet. It had a small, lukewarm following but gave them a foothold at last in Esquimaux Bay. From there they preached to the fishermen in the summer and send itinerant teachers to homes around Esquimaux and Sandwich bays in the winter. In 1905 a minister of this denomination (renamed the "United Church of Canada,") tried to established a "headquarters" in western Lake Melville at Mud Lake. The Dickie Lumber Company of Halifax had begun lumbering operations there several years earlier, attracting newcomers to the small community of Settlers. Dickie paid cash wages to the local people in its employ—another important first. They also paid for home-cooked meals, laundry services, and home-brew. On Saturday nights there was music and dancing for all, to the horror of the starchy Wesleyan, who wasted no time consigning them all to hellfire. Needless to say, this made him rather unpopular and, unable to find lodgings the following year, he packed up and went to North West River where the Grenfell and HBC employees gave him a more cordial reception. So it was that the United Church headquarters finally took root on C of E and Catholic soil.

Among the most important newcomers at the turn of the century was the French fur company Revillon Freres, which opened a trading post at North West River in 1901, forcing HBC to match the fair prices it offered local trappers. This helped initiate a trapping boom in western Lake Melville that gave many Settlers the boost they needed to begin the long climb out of poverty. Its location on the southwest side of the river with the Catholic church, along with its care for the Innu, contributed to the development of a permanent Innu community on the riverbank opposite HBC which would in time become the autonomous village of Sheshashiu.

Another important newcomer was Dr. Wilfred Grenfell. Grenfell's hospital at Indian Harbour opened in 1894, and while it primarily served the Newfoundland fishing fleets, it also treated nearby Labradorians. In 1912 Dr. Harry Paddon opened a small hospital for Grenfell at Mud Lake. This was moved to North West River four years later, and Paddon began making regular trips to Settler homesteads around the bay during the winter months. For a period, North West River became the epicenter for the International Grenfell Association in Labrador, and the trading post began to evolve into a settlement, attracting families whose men worked the rivers feeding Grand Lake and northern Lake Melville. In 1926 when the IGA boarding school opened there, more families moved to the village for jobs with the Grenfell Mission and to be near children enrolled in the school.[22]

The trapping boom that peaked in the 1920s crashed in the 1930s with the onset of the Depression, and hard times returned to the people of Esquimaux Bay. In 1941 a small party of surveyors arrived in an airplane, quietly hiring local men to guide them to a broad sandy escarpment overlooking Blake's and Groves's trapping grounds in Goose Bay. Measurements, elevations, and soil samples were taken, maps were made, and nearby anchorages sounded. The rest is history, and the subject of another chapter.

THIS IS A STORY THAT I heard many times.

It was said that one time, a long time ago, there was a big ship come to Eskimo Island near Rigolet. The Eskimos thought it was a big bird, so they took out after it in their kayaks. When they got almost to the ship a cannon was fired out over them, not to shoot them, just to give them a fright. The Eskimos all went for the shore again. When all the others got ashore there was still one kayak left and the people from the ship got in their boats and they went and got the kayak and there was a woman in it. When they got her on the ship they discovered that there was a baby in the hood. They were so excited because they had two of them and not just one as they had thought at first.

They took this Eskimo woman and her baby to teach her right from wrong. They wanted to see if the Eskimos could be civilized. They took them away somewhere, I don't remember now where it was they took them. They had to give them a name so they called them "Palliser," which was the last name of the ship's captain. This is the story that I heard of how the Pallisers got their name.

This Eskimo woman and her baby stayed away a long time. I heard that before they took them back home that the Queen give the baby some gold buttons to put on his coat when he got big. She also gave him a crown and many other things before he come home. It wasn't so very long ago that Joe Palliser had that same stuff, 'till once his house burned down and it got burned except for the crown, so I heard, oh, not so very many years ago, no more than twenty years ago.

This story is one I heard. Now, I don't know if it's true or not but I was told that a real lot. It must have been a long time ago, so whether it's true or not I don't know, but I believes that it's true.

— Edna Campbell
[3.1:56]

Captain came to Rigolet on a schooner. Queen Victoria [Charlotte] had wished to see Eskimos from Labrador. So he made the old man drunk and got two women and a little boy on board and carried them to England, where they stayed all winter. They did not like living in England. They found it all too sweet when they had been used to seals and fish. One of the women died but the little boy and his mother came back all right. I remember seeing a very pretty dickie, a present from the Queen to the woman. It was made of white cloth all trimmed with little gold hangings all around the lower edge. I remember seeing them, the shape about this size. They found it too pretty to wear. She never took it with her. I don't know what became of it. My mother had two of the little gold drops someone gave her. There are some of the Pallisers still living yet.

— Margaret Campbell Baikie
Memories p. 51.

My mommy died when I was only nine years old. I've been working ever since. I've worked in the house and out doors. It was a hard life. I used to go hunting with the men to try and help out. We used to row all the way from English Harbour to Rigolet. We'd go way down there fishing. Sometimes in the fall we'd go for weeks and weeks. We'd row all the way.

My father died before I was born. He drowned over to Summer Cove Point. They found a piece of board on a rock where my father wrote "My days is ended. I hope God will help somebody to go and see my family." Tom Palliser and them found it. He took my poor mother and sister to his place. A week before my father died, my sister froze her legs and he had to chop them off to save her. After my father died Dr. Grenfell came and took sister away. She stayed away until after mommy died. We hardly knowed each other when she came back because I was only small when she left.

I am half Eskimo, half Newfoundlander. My mommy was from Newfoundland and my father was a northern Eskimo. Mommy married twice. Her last husband was George Palliser. I had one brother and one sister. My brother was Tom Palliser. He went to Cartwright for three years then went North as an interpreter. He died in the North.

— Alice Palliser
[1.1:34]

OF ALL THE TIMES OF the year I think fall had to be the best when I was a kid. Labrador falls seem to stretch out longer, maybe because things weren't so hectic then. I remember the mornings when it was flat calm, when all the birches had changed colours. The water was so cold that a trip to the trout net was a test of endurance, but the fish were worthwhile, as with colder weather they were firmer and fatter. I'd get to the house, my hands numb, and my mother would pick out what she wanted for the day and I'd split any left over, salt them lightly and put them out in the sun 'till the salt melted, then into the smoke house. Put them close to the fire in a puncheon we had rigged for that purpose, and by evening they'd be smoked and cooked, just take them from the smoke house to the table....

After a heavy frost every tree, every building, even the boardwalks were snowy white and there would be a light fog over the water that vanished with the first ray of the sun. And quiet, incredibly quiet. There was no one there, of course, except for the Hudson's Bay Company people. Every boat in the harbour had a reflection of itself under it and their moorings would go straight down, if you loosened them they'd sit there, not a motion of wind to move them.

The first real sound you'd hear outside was James Dickers closing the office door on his way up to the 'men's kitchen' for breakfast. Well, that wasn't really the first sound. Mrs. Flowers would have already rung the quarter-to-seven bell and the seven o'clock bell. But if you were outside you could hear James' footsteps as the boards in the walk creaked with the frost. James had a slow deliberate walk, and you could hear the 'crack-crack' as he made his way along. Once, I remember, I was across the cove looking at some rabbit snares along the side of the hill and I just happened to be sitting where I could see the Post, enjoying the absolute stillness and the beauty of the morning, when James came out. I watched and listened as the boards sounded under his feet and it was an extra bonus as he went inside the door and, due to the stillness of the air, I could hear his last footsteps and the bang of the door seconds after he was invisible inside.

...Sometimes I could see Freeman and George Pottle away over by Sand Banks hauling seal nets. Every sound would eventually reach me, but seconds later than my eyes told me I should be hearing them. They used to land first, make a fire, leave a pail on to boil and go look at the first net. I'd see them chopping wood but the motion of the axe and the sound wouldn't have much relation....

I could see all the houses from the Point and each seemed to have a straight finger of smoke pointing at the sky. The big old Company house was up on a hill above the others. It would have two columns of white smoke pouring out, the rest usually had one. Now and then a little pattern of air would cause some to sway a bit, but soon it would be perfectly perpendicular again.

The water in the harbour and the cove were dimpled with breaching smelts and little tom cod. The old saddleback gulls that nested, year after year, on top of the hill opposite the Post would cruise back and forth and, when they saw a good opportunity, would do a remarkable wing over, just dip a bill and get their fish, while their lazy young sat on the rocks along the shore screaming to be fed. They had good living all summer as their parents hauled all manner of fish up to the top of the hill for them. Once their wings could support them well enough to manage the long glide down to the water, the free meals were cut down. The young would paddle around at low tide snapping at anything that may have been left by the falling water, and they created all kinds of ruckus about who got what.

The man who said 'little birds in the nest agree' never saw a gang of saddleback kids fighting over a dead starfish. The old birds are so dignified, especially when compared to herring gulls, but their young are dumb as clowns....

Now the big graceful fish hawks are another matter. They don't need anyone's help. There were several nests within sight of the Post, and my dad kept a close eye on them. No one dared ever point a gun in their direction. I'll never forget how mad he got when one of the Grenfell WOPs ("workers-without-pay") stood on the Company's wharf and took a pot shot at one as it flew by with a fish. If that WOP is still alive I'd be glad to bet he doesn't forget either. My dad just happened to be walking out on the wharf and he saw the whole thing. Luckily the fellow missed or he would have been over the deep end, but he did get an earful. The Old Man wasn't one to whisper when he was mad. He took the gun, a brand new repeating shot gun, right out of the fellow's hands and for a second two I thought it was going over the side, but he unloaded it, threw the cartridges in the water and handed the gun to Jack Watts who had just come on deck. He told Jack to keep that young so-and-so aboard from then on. Jack had no idea that the WOPs, who were waiting for the *Kyle* on their way back to the States, were carrying guns. He made a search and rounded up several more. There was another lecture and some pretty quiet WOPs hardly dared put a foot on the wharf afterwards.

That was before DDT and the fish hawks were plentiful and, because they were protected, we saw them all the time at Rigolet.... My dad's desk was by a window and the office was only twenty feet from the water. He'd sit there for the longest time just enjoying those birds. They would hover over the harbour sometimes for a few minutes before they saw the right fish then they'd drop like a stone and seldom would they miss. We always had a trout or a salmon net out, and I remember Austin Flowers once telling my dad that having those birds so close would scare the fish away. The Old Man said that when the fish got so scarce there weren't enough for him and the osprey he'd go for salt beef and the birds could have the fish. He meant it too. [15.1:59]

I grew up on a Hudson's Bay Company Fur Trade Post. I was privileged in that it was Rigolet, Labrador. It was a small place, which from its relatively isolated situation had retained more of the old HBC atmosphere and traditions than had some of its more 'favoured' neighbors. Its main attraction was the old buildings, their contents and the work that still went on in very much the same manner as it had been done when they were new, back in the 1800s.

They were constructed of local timber, hand squared and pit-sawn, with huge knees supporting the rafters, thick floors, heavy ceilings, and massive doors with handmade iron work. They had been well-maintained by a succession of careful managers including my father, George Budgell. In repairs, squared logs was replaced by squared log and pit-sawn plank by pit-sawn plank. [14.4:3]

Rigolet, at that time, was a 'Fur and Fish' post. Probably the returns from the salmon and cod fisheries represented the greater part of the local peoples' yearly income, however, fur revenue was not inconsiderable and, in common with other Labrador posts, the fur was of high quality. The fur mark 'E. B.' was known through-out the Fur Trade as being the finest. E. B. represented Eskimo Bay. At the fur auctions in Montreal and New York there was always special interest when E. B. collections were shown.

World War I had caused a brief interruption in the normally placid life of the trappers and fishermen and the Great Company, but in most essentials life differed lit-tle from that in the last quarter of the 1800s. Several of the permanent Post employ-ees, who were proud to call themselves Company Servants, had been hired around the turn of the century. James Dickers, cooper, John Blake, schooner master, and William Shiwak, foreman/carpenter/talented master of almost any trade, were the three stal-warts who carried out their respective duties with a degree of competency and loyal-ty that was remarkable, even in 'them days,' of honest service to the Company they chose to serve.

In light of today's trade stores the plant at Rigolet was impressive. The buildings were strung along the rim of the little harbour in a straight line terminating at the salt store and cooper shop, then turning to the right to include the last few structures. A wide boardwalk connected all the buildings, most of which dated from the mid-1800s....

As I remember, Number One was the office, a two-storey building that incorpo-rated a private office, a large general office and two bedrooms on the main floor. The bedrooms were occupied by James Dickers and his apprentice Walter, who was also his nephew. The upper floor was a long loft where salmon nets were repaired during the winter and where general carpentry, such as komatik-making, was carried out as the main carpenter shop was unheated.

Number Two was the trade store, a large two-level place. The sales shop occupied half the lower area; it had shelves all around three of the walls and a continuous counter separating the customer from the merchandise. Almost nothing was self-serve. All goods were displayed on the shelves and were handed down by the clerks for purchase or inspection. The variety of goods was extensive. Food stuffs, generally in bulk. Sugar in 300 lb. barrels swung on a pivot under the counter. Rolled oats, peas, beans, hard biscuit, tea, confectionery and other goods were in bins or barrels. Tobacco, raisins, currants and other dry fruits came in boxes and were retailed out of the same containers. Margarine, lard, and shortenings were in 10 or 20 lb. pails and tubs. Salt beef, pork and spare ribs were in 200 lb. barrels and also retailed from the containers. Fishery and trapping supplies included steel traps, rifles and shotguns. At that time the old-time muzzle loader was holding its own with the new breech loaders. There were jiggers, cod lines, bank lines, rope, tar, pitch, red, white, black and green leads and oxides for making paint, wire and galvanized boat nails, ammunition, powder, shot, empty shotgun shells, primers, lanterns, babiche, oils, greases, pocket knives and a host of general hardware.

The dry goods shelves carried yellow oilskins and sou'westers, tweed caps, leather and rubber sea boots, shirts, trousers and heavy wool socks and mitts and Native-made sealskins and moccasins. There were yard goods, blankets, duffel, stroud and knitting wool, or worsted as it was called locally. There were plain and glovers' needles and denim, khaki, cotton duck and, every year, a few bales of 'pound goods.' These were known by the trade as Fents and Limbrics. The bales, large and tightly packed, were mill ends of cotton, velvet, silk and other materials. When a bale was opened and the released contents spilled out on the counter it was a veritable sunburst of colour. The material was bought and sold by the pound. I remember in my first year of apprenticeship that Limbrics, which were solid colours, and Fents, which were patterned fabrics, sold for a dollar a pound. A pound averaged six yards and could be almost any material. In the days of low prices, in the pre-Depression years, these bright colours helped brighten many a small child's life, I am sure. We carried the usual ginghams, poplins, shirtings and prints, but the pound goods were the real sellers because of their incredible variety.

The second half of the ground floor of Number Two was given over to the storage of barrels of flour, biscuits, oats, dried peas and beans all in neat piles. Molasses, which was used by many in preference to sugar, came in ninety gallon puncheons and was sold by the gallon in the summer and by the pound in the winter. Some customers would require ten gallons or more, and it was never an easy task to handle molasses. There were also barrels of redberries and bakeapples that were purchased in the summer and sold again in the winter to those who had been unable to collect for their own use.

Number Three was thought to be the oldest building on the Post. It was a single-storey structure of big squared logs faced on the outside with pit-sawn clapboard and it was limed white in common with the other buildings. It comprised two long narrow areas: a blacksmith shop and a cooper shop. The smithy was not in regular use but William Shiwak would sometimes fire up the ancient forge and make various ironware for use around the Post or on the vessels. James Dickers operated the cooper shop alone at first but later his nephew was hired as an apprentice. He worked for a number of years at Rigolet before being transferred to Frenchman's Island to follow his trade there. When I was about six years old, to the great regret of my father, who was conscious of the historical value of the old buildings, the cooperage was torn down and a new building was constructed.

Numbers Four, Five and Six were all under one roof, in an archway building. Number Four was the net loft and it ran the full length of the structure on the second floor. It held all the fishing gear; the nets, floats, leads, rope, twine, grapnels, bales of cork and all the necessary equipment for the salmon fishery. The nets were stored in separate bunks on each side of the loft and each bunk had the name of the fishing station in elegant script carved and painted on a board over the door. I never knew who was responsible for the calligraphy, but whoever it was took a lot of time and pains. I only hope the boards, if not the building, have been preserved. It gave one a pleasantly eerie feeling to go into the net loft in winter and see the long row of bunks, silent in the half darkness, and to remember the busy days of summer when the loft was full of fishermen coming and going. Now the nets were idle, waiting for the next season when the Atlantic salmon, surely the most beautiful of fishes, would again start its great migration into the rivers of its birth after an absence of four or more years.

The attic of Number Four was a repository for ancient fire-arms, old whaling guns, ship's blocks and fittings, lamps and all the memorabilia of an age just passing, stored there by my father and his predecessors because of their historical potential. There was an arms chest marked H.M.S. *Perlican*. I have often wondered what became of it. There were kegs of flint for old rifles, ammunition, similar to those used in the Indian Mutiny, and Boer War bayonets—long, sharp, rust-stained things that had gruesome implications for us youngsters. They had probably never been used, however, youthful imagination is hard to suppress.

The lower part of the net loft comprised the carpenter shop and the barrel storage, Numbers Five and Six. They were separated by a passage through the archway with a large double door at each end, and here visiting people stored all manner of travelling and hunting gear. It was possible to see modern rifles, muzzle loaders, old Schneider rifles and Native-made harpoons, as well as dog harnesses, molasses kegs and oil cans. The passage, as it was known, was never locked; it was open to all.

Number Seven was the oil store and seal fat rendering shed. Seal oil had never been exported to any great degree at Rigolet but there was a hand-operated grinder and several large vats. Seal fat was purchased but most of it was sold again to people living away from the open water to be used as dog feed. In late spring a couple of not-too-interested men would grind whatever fat happened to be on hand and barrel the resulting oil for shipment.

Number Eight was the salt storage. In those days all fish was shipped salted: salmon in tierces in brine and cod, dried, in casks or, more frequently, in bulk. Number Eight could hold a huge quantity of salt and it was a considerable chore, when a shipment arrived, to move it ashore from the ship and trundle it by wheelbarrows along the boardwalk to the shed. Obviously every grain had to be returned to the wharf by the same method as it was purchased by the fishermen.

Number Nine was the powder house and ammunition storage. It stood some distance away from the other buildings.

Number Ten was originally for feather storage. At one time feathers were an important item of trade. They were accumulated in bags over the year and before shipment were packed in barrels. It was surprising how much could be packed into a barrel by using a long wooden rod with a wedge-shaped tip. As one man fed the feathers into the barrel, another thrust the rod repeatedly into the loose mass compressing it into an almost solid form that weighed many pounds. Sugar and flour barrels were carefully saved all year for packing feathers. As the feather business declined, Number Ten became a storage for products such as coal tar, pitch and cutch (used for barking nets) and a variety of wooden boxes and cartons for use around the Post.

Number Eleven became the new cooperage, which was built by James Dickers and his apprentice Walter, and was operated by them. It was the only building on the Post which did not have a key hanging on the big circular board in the office; James, and James only, opened and closed that door.

Number Twelve was the wharf freight shed. It was used to hold the cargo as it came ashore from the ships. After the ships left the cargo was moved to permanent storage.

Big iron keys, for the massive locks on all the doors, hung on a board in the general office. They were taken as required and left in the doors until just before closing, when it was the responsibility of one of the clerks to collect all the keys and return them to the board.

In addition to the various stores and warehouses, there was the Manager's dwelling, a handsome, bell-roofed building which housed my father and his large family, plus one-to-three clerks or apprentices.

There was a second dwelling, said to have been Lord Strathcona's house. It was torn down when I was quite young. It had been repaired at some time in the past and when the newer lumber came down there was a compass rose painted on the floor of the living room and an identical one on the ceiling. They had been hidden for many years as none of the local staff had any idea that they were there. In 'them days' there were no heritage associations and many irreplaceable things were lost forever.

The Men's Kitchen, or 'Comers and Goers' house stood near the water across the boardwalk from Strathcona's house. It was a busy place, in the evening and especially in the fall. There would be as many small boats as could crowd into the little beach.

It was close and convenient for people to bring their luggage ashore and much easier to watch the boats if the wind got up at night. It was a large, two-storey building with a number of small rooms upstairs. The labourers who were hired from time to time lived and ate there, and travellers put up for the night. There was usually a family there to look after the place. Tom Pottle and his wife, known to everyone as Aunt Meg, were there for a number of years. They were succeeded by Jesse Flowers and his family, who were still at Rigolet when I left many years later, but they were then in the new 'Kitchen' as the old one had been torn down.

There was a bell in a little steeple on the roof of the Kitchen and one of the Keeper's duties was to ring the bell every day. The first bell sounded at a quarter to six in the morning, the second at six was a signal to start work, the third at seven signalled breakfast, the fourth at seven-thirty meant 'back to work', the fifth at noon was the lunch break, the sixth at one meant 'back to work again' and the seventh at six, the final for the day, called the men to supper. On Sunday only the meal bells were rung and in winter the two early bells were omitted.

William Shiwak had a house at the south end of the boardwalk and John Blake had one on the side of the little hill behind the office. There were two dwellings that did not belong to the Company. They were the Customs House and the school, which stood a little apart from the rest of the buildings.

Each of the Company buildings were painted or limed white with black roofs. In the late twenties the colour of the roofs was altered to red and this came about almost by accident. When my father was at Davis Inlet he found that the man he had relieved had forgotten to order any material, usually tar, for the post roofs. It was unthinkable that they should not be coated so he and Gilbert Saunders mixed up a concoction of red ochre and seal oil and coated the roofs. It so happened that Mr. Ralph Parsons, District Manager at that time, when he arrived at Davis Inlet in the spring, was so taken with the white buildings with bright red roofs against the tall green spruces on the hill that he had all the roofs in the district painted red thereafter. The stores and the warehouses had red trim and the doors were also red. The dwellings and the office had green doors and trim. Rigolet, situated as it was in the little bay, with its white buildings and the intense green of the trees was a pretty place when you came to it by water.

One of the things that marked the Hudson's Bay Company Posts, aside from the Old English lettering on a big sign, was the flag pole. At Rigolet it stood on a little rise in the centre of the complex. The first one I remember had been erected by H.M.S. *Cotter* early in this century. It was a top mast affair with crosstrees and a short boom. When it rotted at the ground beyond a safe limit it was replaced by a single pole which stood sixty feet above the ground. It was a beautiful spar, as straight as a gun barrel. It was carefully trimmed by William [Shiwak] and his brother Wilfred. It had been cut and delivered by Big Joe Palliser who always referred to it as "my tree." It was securely mounted in the ground with a small crib around the butt. It had no stays or shears to support it and when it was new it bent with the wind to a degree that could be seen, but later as it dried and stiffened the movement was not so obvious. We used to lie on the crib on really windy days and watch the tip, far above our heads, move in a little circle with each gust of wind. It was inevitable that many attempts were made to climb that pole and Walter Dickers probably got up as far as anyone, but I remember that even he only made it half way up. One day the halyard seized up in the pulley and broke. It looked like the pole would have to come down, no mean job with a stick that size. However Big Joe brought his younger brother Hugh along and, for the price of a pound of black pipe tobacco, Hugh climbed the pole, freed the broken halyard and reeved a new one. How did he do it? Simple. He turned his sealskin boots inside out, wet them slightly so they stuck to the wood like glue and went up like a squirrel.

This was Rigolet sixty years ago [1926], a comfortable place situated on the north side of Hamilton Inlet, or Groswater Bay as it was then more commonly known, and at an earlier time had been known as Esquimaux Bay. The hills around are not too high but are relatively steep and at that time were well wooded with spruce and balsam fir with enough birch, alder and juniper thrown in for contrast, especially in the fall when the colours were brilliantly spectacular....

I never tired of watching the action at the wharf. The boats would come alongside and carefully pass up the huge fish, which had been split down the back and laid out flat for the preliminary salting which took place at the salmon stations. They were washed in a large trough, where John Blake was in charge with several young fellows to do the washing. They washed off each fish and piled them by the scale where William Shiwak culled them for size and quality. Then they were packed into tierces which had been made by James Dickers, the cooper.

There was an art to packing salt salmon. The packer picked them up one by one and twisted the tails slightly to conform to the shape of the tierce, laid the fish flat and salted them again. John Blake and James Dickers watched the salting carefully. When the full 300 lb. net weight had been packed, the tierce was cut across the wharf to James or Walter and quickly headed. It was then turned on its side and rolled away into a big storage area on the boardwalk to be filled with brine, which we called pickle, and bunged for shipment in the fall. The head was stenciled: *Hudson's Bay Company, U 1, Rigolet, #1 Large*, or whatever it might have been. Most of our salt salmon eventually went to Holland, and by the time it got there the word Rigolet had been accepted as a brand name. It was a source of pride to all concerned that Rigolet Brand was considered to be the finest available and always found ready for sale.

In contrast with North West River, which being a 'Fur Post' was usually quiet in the summer, Rigolet was always busy. Fishing operations consumed a great deal of the time and in between there was firewood to be hauled in by scow and mail and freight to be taken to North West River, as the coastal steamer, the *Sagona*, did not go beyond Rigolet. The Company operated a small schooner, the *Thistle*, built by my mother's father [Silas Painter, from an old Sandwich Bay family]. She hauled the mail and freight and picked up salmon from the only salmon station at the head of the bay. This was operated by Mr. [Malcolm] McLean and was situated at Kenemich. The *Thistle* was strictly a sailing vessel when I knew her, but later she was fitted with a primitive three-cylinder Acadia engine. John Blake was the skipper of the *Thistle* and after the engine was installed William Shiwak or his brother Wilfred would go along as engineer.

By September the last of the dry cod had been brought in and people were beginning to move from their fishing places to their winter homes, further back from the coast. Usually two or three families would have snug winter homes close together for mutual support and assistance, especially those who owned larger boats, as several men and their families were needed to haul them out for the winter. Once everyone had shipped his fish and received his 'Start' for the trapping, Rigolet became a quieter place with only a few of the nearby customers coming in now and then. This did not mean that it was less busy. On the contrary, the rush was on to get the fall work done....

For a short time at freeze-up, Rigolet became totally isolated; no one came or went. The staff took up their winter work and inventory was taken of the trade goods, with so many items and so many warehouses, this could be a cold process and everyone was glad when it was over. William and at least one helper started on the long monotonous task of repairing the salmon nets. Each net was checked for damage and for signs of rot. Old nets were replaced with the work being done locally. People would take several large bundles of hemp twine away to their winter places and during the quiet nights would knit it into new mesh using home-made needles and cards. The netting would come back in during the winter and William would 'bring them to' with new head and foot ropes and corks and leads. A net improperly 'brought to' will not fish properly and is a waste of time and material.

James and Walter would have been hard at work making new tierces as soon as the last of the fish was shipped. They worked at this all winter and by spring the barrel storage in Number Five would be filled with beautifully finished new tierces. They also made hogsheads, barrels, kegs, [puncheons] and a host of other containers but their main work was with the big salmon tierces.

Jesse Flowers and Bill Wolfrey cut all the wood used on the Post. They started early in the fall. The wood was cut in pole lengths and calculated by the turn. One turn is what a man can carry on his shoulder. Once sufficient had been cut, they would haul it by dog team to a convenient spot on the shore where it would be picked up by the scow next summer.

We knew that the bays were frozen over when the teams started to arrive. They came in from Double Mer, Backway, Ticoraluk, Vallies Bight, English River, Pease Cove, John's Point, Flat Water and Turner's Bight. The bright fox pelts, mink, otter and lynx would start to accumulate in the fur room. It was an experience for a small boy to go there, though I can remember having some doubts about the huge silvery lynx with their tufted ears and large feet hanging there so motionless and silent.

As the teams arrived, the stone hearth in the dogs' feed house would be strung with rows of pails and iron kettles as drivers cooked for their dogs. The Company's dogs were usually fed on seal meat and cullage salmon, but the kitchen boy would find time to be there to cook for the younger dogs and small pups and enjoy the gossip. The Post kept at least two big teams for fur buying trips and the like, probably thirty or more dogs. The tired dogs lay outside quietly waiting for their one meal of the day. Favoured dogs and small pups were sometimes allowed inside. The dogs, conscious of their special position, usually lay quietly and the pups tumbled all over the place, occasionally getting stepped on as the atmosphere was none too clear what with the fire and fumes of the black pipe tobacco. For light there was one old lantern hung from a beam but it was never properly trimmed and the glass was usually black with soot. Now and then someone would take it down and shove a handful of grass through it and that distributed the smut a little more evenly and improved the light not at all. It was a noisy, friendly place. We would slide on the hill behind the office until dark, then run to the dogs' feed house to get warm and see who was there.

The old custom of Christmas keeping was very much in effect. A few days before Christmas the teams started coming in again; this time the women and children came too and soon every bit of available space was taken up. There were hundreds of dogs and komatiks everywhere. The first event was the grading and pricing of fur. One could see the trappers standing in a group near the office door, each man with a white cotton sack or two stuffed with his catch. No one ever said what he had and no one ever asked. It was only now and then that some said, "How'd you do, b'y?" The answer was invariably "Not so bad."

Only a single man or possibly two relatives entered the office at a time to have fur priced. Many guesses and estimates were made by those outside, but only the trapper's family and the office staff ever knew what he had sold. This secrecy applied only to fur catches; cod, salmon and seal catches were openly discussed.

The fur being sold and necessary purchases made, Christmas Keeping became a fact and people got down to visiting. Perhaps some had not seen one another since last Christmas. Square dances were held every night in the Mens' Kitchen and, since everyone wanted to get out on the floor, there would be a second dance going on at another of the houses and people circulated from one to the other. The rugged construction of the buildings was put to the test when dozens of active feet started stomping out the old dances.

On Christmas Day my father would make a point of greeting each and every visitor, and there was a flurry of gift-giving between the women—the men seemed to be exempt. Some of the teams would leave shortly after Christmas Day, but a greater number stayed for the New Year. On New Years Eve at midnight everyone who had brought a gun, and everyone did, lined up on the boardwalk and saluted the New Year with a volley. There were always a few misfires and what was called hangfires so that the volley had a notably ragged echo, but no one minded and a dance started immediately and carried on until broad daylight the next morning.

A couple of days after New Year there would be no evidence that there had been a gathering, except for the hard packed snow in every direction around the Post. The next gathering would be at Easter, but this was always more restrained and on a smaller scale.

In January my father left on his first fur buying trip. He'd be away for more than a month at a time, using a Post team. He might have William along as teamster, or perhaps some other trapper, who was having poor luck, might come in off his trapline to take on the job.

The mailman came three times each winter from Cartwright. The mail had been relayed up from Battle Harbour, as ships could reach that point much later in the fall and early winter. At Rigolet it was split. George Pottle took the North West River packet and Old Steve Newell took the bags for north to Makkovik. Freeman Saunders then delivered to Hopedale, Davis Inlet and Nain, and Amma Pannigoniak made two trips from Nain to Nutak and Hebron. The mail was by no means new when it got to us, but the arrival of the Mailman was an important event. He brought the local news from other centres and that probably meant more than the letters and papers that came in the mail.

The only other winter events were the Doctor's visit from North West River and the Church of England minister from Cartwright. It was many years before a United Church minister or a policeman made the rounds.

By the middle of March the 'coloured fur' was becoming faded and rubbed and the season ended. Mink, otter and lynx were 'springy' and almost valueless; the beaver season was closed and would be that way for a long while. White foxes were still good and the men who trapped on the 'outside' would move their traps to the islands to trap the white foxes that, every year, came down from the north on the floating ice. The Inuit people, who lived near the open water in The Narrows, spent this time hunting the beautiful silver jar seals on the ice of Hamilton Inlet or Lake Melville.

April was another rather quiet month; travelling was usually getting bad and most people stayed close to their winter houses. This was when logs were cut and pit-sawn into lumber for new boats and flats, built during the warm spring days and shown off with a great deal of pardonable pride when they visited the Post to 'fit out' for the salmon fishery.

In May people started moving back to their fishing stations again. The people from North West River would come down, and once again Rigolet became busy. The *Thistle* and all the other boats were painted and launched. The buildings were freshly limed and the nets were brought out for barking. This was done under John Blake's supervision. A mixture of water and cutch was used to give them some protection against rot and to render them harder for the fish to see. Cutch was the sap of a mahogany-type tree growing in South America, and there it was boiled and poured into paper-lined wooden boxes where it solidified. We received it in 200 lb. cases. John used 22 lbs. to a hundred gallons of water, boiled in a large iron pot and poured hot over the nets, which had been carefully coiled down in puncheons. It had a strange, exotic smell especially when combined with new hemp twine. After two days and nights of soaking in 'bark,' as it was called, the nets were taken out, drained and hung on poles to dry. They were then taken back to the net loft and put in the bunks to await the arrival of the fishermen.

Fitting out was quite a process as everyone seemed to arrive together, probably by design so that some visiting could be done. Some of the fishermen operated quite close together but salmon fishing leaves little time to visit.

Bill Wolfrey spent his spring around the Post helping John at the barking, raking and cleaning up and liming the buildings. He was usually the first man with a net into the water. He prided himself on being 'first fish' each season and there were not very many when he wasn't, as I remember. He must have longed to eat that first fish, but he never did. It always came to the Post. He was a shy, gentle man and I remember seeing him sidle into my mother's kitchen with a large silver fish, neatly cleaned, on his finger. He always said the same thing. "'Spect I got the first ag'in, Missus."

And the spring would again merge into summer. If there was a good salmon season, the boats would come day and night for salt and supplies. The fishermen spent their days in the boats, hauling and cleaning nets and processing the catch. Always there was the net cleaning. The Inlet is tidal and a mass of seaweed and kelp is flushed backward and forward with the tides; the nets were always full of it. A man could spend hours cleaning a fleet of nets only to find them as cluttered as before on the next turn of the tide. Salmon fishing for a living bears little resemblance to the sports version.

Soon salmon fishing was over and it was time to ship the catch and prepare for cod fishing, and when that was over it was time to get ready for the fall again. The time went by so pleasantly and so fast. I can't think of no better place for a boy to grow up.

I have been asked what we did for entertainment in such a small and isolated community with no radio, T.V. or movies. It never seemed to be a problem. During the winters, which are comparatively mild so near the open ocean, we made our fun in the snow as kids do everywhere, and in the summer there was all the activity around the boats and warehouses. We may have sometimes been in the way but the staff was unfailingly kind and if we were a nuisance we never felt it. If there was no danger involved we could usually do pretty well as we wished. There was quite a gang of youngsters of various ages and one could be pretty sure of having another to aide and abet.

As we grew older we learned to hunt and fish. There was no refrigeration other than natural, so that all fresh meat came from the bush and the sea. We went with the wood scows and hung around the schooner and the boats. Our days were full. Perhaps the older girls had a thinner time of it, helping out at home occupied a lot of their time. My father, William and John had large families. Jesse had two at home when he came to Rigolet at first, and one of the events that affected us all was the accidental drowning of his daughter. It is impossible to describe what such an event can do to a small group of people who know one another intimately.

For the adults, there were the Christmas and New Year dances and get-togethers; there were the constant card games. Auction, a simplified form of Bridge, occupied many hours and created tournaments that actually went on for years between groups. There were checkers and various board games. There was yarn spinning and ballad singing; nearly everyone had a tale to tell about 'them days.' On the Post Jesse Flowers was the principal yarn spinner. He had a phenomenal memory and once he heard a yarn or a song he could recall it at will. He had a pleasing tenor voice and could sing old hymns by the hour. Recently I saw a collection of ancient songs and ballads and was surprised at how many of them I had heard Jesse sing.

There was also work to be done during the long winter nights. There was dogs' harnesses and snowshoes to be repaired, guns to clean and, for the lucky, furs to skin and dry. William Shiwak was hardly ever without a sharp tool in his hand. He made komatiks for those who needed them and oars and paddles. If it could be made out of wood, William could make it. He was a pleasant, kindly man who received little for the work he did in his spare time. I would guess that no one was refused.

John Blake was away all winter so we saw little of him then. He was a good trapper. This was a hard way for a man with one hand to earn a living but it did not seem to bother John. As skipper of the *Thistle* he was active and never seemed to mind his disability. Around the Post he did practically whatever the other men did. It was not unusual to see him high on a ladder with a paint pot or repairing a broken plank on the boardwalk. He was a little shy and was not much of a talker. He and James Dickers had known one another and worked together many years. Now and then one would see them during 'smoking time' yarning together, and he used to enjoy sitting in the forecastle of the *Thistle* with his crew. Sometimes he'd take a hand at cards. He had been an employee at Rigolet when Mr. R. Parsons, the last Fur Trade Commissioner of the Company, had served his apprenticeship at Rigolet, and they were good friends. R.P. never went past Rigolet in his inspection boat unless John was along. He always said that John was one of the best men the Company ever hired—no small praise from a man whose favorite expression was "The best is none too good for the HBC."

Walter Dickers was a good cooper and always full of fun and jokes. He was a born mimic and could reproduce any voice perfectly—it was a game and no one was offended. I remember William's grandmother, an ancient lady with a high pitched voice. She'd go over to the cooperage now and then for an apronful of chips for a quick fire. Walter would have the wood ready and he'd load it into her apron, all the while talking to her in her own voice, and she'd totter off laughing. I suspect she came as much for the laugh as the chips.

James Dickers was a master cooper, tall and straight as an arrow. He never married. He lived in his room in the office and ate his meals in the Mens' Kitchen. He was quiet and had a severe manner which said he had little time for fun and games. However, one Christmas he surprised us by getting up and dancing a very active Sailor's Hornpipe. He was absolutely loyal to his employer and a strong Royalist; these were two subjects that might cause James to take fire. He would listen to no criticism about either and had a remarkably effective way to deal with anyone who affronted him.

James started to work for the Hudson's Bay Company in 1878 and served as cooper for sixty-seven years, surely a record. As his trade became more or less obsolete with the introduction of new methods of handling salmon, he became the last of the Great Company's coopers. Fortunately there was enough to keep him occupied 'till his death, as he refused to quit work because someone in Winnipeg Head Office thought it was time he retired. He had the first contract that he signed as an apprentice of twelve and all the succeeding ones, the clause that he was to defend the Company's property with his life if necessary I am sure he took seriously. [11.4:5]

Now most of the buildings are gone—the dog feed house of many happy memories for me, where the big kettles hung and steamed while forty or fifty hungry and tired dogs lay relaxed in the snow and waited, the Trade Store where I served part of my apprenticeship and where the Fur Trade Commissioner served his, Strathcona's house and the big old Manager's dwelling with its sturdy lines and its view of the harbour and Inlet. And now what I thought of as the new cooperage has gone.... It is progress, it is inevitable and, in some ways, essential. The things that cannot perish are the memories of the old buildings and the exceptional men who worked and lived in them.

No one is exempted. We serve our time and retreat into the obscurity of retirement. I think of the craftsmen who have laid down their tools: the Painters, who were my own folk, the Blakes and Flowers, the Birds and Groves, the Shiwaks, the Voiseys,

Fords and Lyalls, the Swaffields and many others, the Fur Trade Commissioner, George Budgell, my father, and James Edward Dickers.

Could any Company have a greater tribute than the loyalty of these men? It could not have survived without them and their like. Men like James Dickers have ceased to exist, and we are the poorer.

On the wall in James' room, in Strathcona's office, hung the motto of the British Overseas Club, of which he was a member. It read:

We sailed wherever ship could sail
we founded many a mighty state.
Pray God our greatness may not fail
through craven fears of being great.

— Leonard Budgell
[14.4:16]

MY FATHER WAS MALCOLM MCLEAN. He come from Stornaway, Scotland. That's up in the north of Scotland, I believe.... He was seventeen or eighteen when he come over from Scotland. He come over for the Hudson's Bay Company. There was two or three of them. They come over on an old wooden ship he said. She sprung a leak and they had to come in to Rigolet. The first place he ever put his foot in Labrador was at Snook's Cove. In the fall they come up to North West River.

They had about thirteen men in HBC then. They was kind of slaves, I suppose you'd call them. They worked for what they eat and for clothes to wear. My father used to tell us that the first winter he was here they sent him across the bay with an old feller and his wife. They belonged to the country. They was sawing with the pit saw.

This old woman was the cook. She'd cook porridge for breakfast in an old iron pot. What was left in the pot was cooked with rabbit for dinner. What was left over then was cooked with salt codfish for supper. The leftovers was all cooked like this for all winter long, just went round and round in a circle. Father was only young then, 'bout eighteen....

There was some of these men trapping. Some were up Grand Lake, some were up to Gull Island. Some men were cutting spars for schooners. There was a big demand then for spars. All sailing then. No telephone poles them days. There's a bunch of spars in Kenamu yet. If I could get in there I could take someone in to it to get pictures. That was my father and old John Blake (he's dead too) cut them trees. Great big brutes. My father told me where they was and the last time I was in they was still there and they'll always be there. They'd fell them and cut the limbs off the top side and cut the tops off. Now, to get them out of the woods was something else. I asked old Uncle Johnny Blake how they rolled them over to get the limbs off the bottom side. They did it with block and tackle. They hauled them out the same way. There is a bunch there that they never did get out.

Hudson's Bay had men hunting, men fishing and men around the Post. Saturday evening each man would go to the store and get a handful of loose raisins. Now, you could throw them in a pan or you could eat them. You could please yourself. The ones in the pan was put in a raisin pudding for Sunday dinner. If you eat yours, well, you never got no raisin pudding.

There was no such thing as money. They was getting everything free, so called. You was never out of debt. You'd get something and 'twas marked against you. When your month was up you was a dollar or fifty cents still owing. Away years ago, when Aunt Lizzie Goudie's father was young, he told me about when he was working for HBC and he had to take up his wages. No such thing as cash. Well, he said that he took up the things he wanted and there was fifty cents coming to him. There was nothing else he wanted. The manager told him that if he wouldn't tell anyone he'd give him fifty cents cash. He couldn't tell anyone because everyone would want cash and that wasn't allowed. Old Uncle Joe told me he had that in his pocket for years. He said he'd like to have showed it to someone but he promised he wouldn't so he just couldn't. That was the first fifty cents he ever saw and the first he ever owned. People was gypped and double gypped because they had no way of knowin' what their work was worth. In my father's time there was no knowin' if you was in debt or out. You was just held there.

— Wallace McLean
[1.4:5]

THE WINTER GRANDMA FLOWERS DIED, that's poor Jesse's mother, Mr. Budgell sent for Jesse to come to Rigolet and cut wood. They used to cut five thousand [sticks] a winter, you know. Jesse got paid for that, and Mr. Budgell wanted me to take the Kitchen. That was the first year I took over the Kitchen. I don't know what year it was, but Rene was quite a big girl then. The next year she drowned.

We was salmon catchin' then, in the summer. Poor George [Flowers], Jesse's brother, was sick. He had a paralyze stroke and couldn't row, and poor Jesse had to tend the nets. There was an old Mr. Sheppard come down here from Vallies Bight and fished to Old House Point and he was goin' to get some salt. Poor Jesse said to write a note to Mr. Budgell to get a bag of salt and send it by Rene because she was goin' along with Mr. Sheppard. There was Mr. Sheppard, a girl they had with them named Minnie Hope, Sam Hope's sister. And Rene was with them. On the way back the wind come on to blow and they had a puncheon of salt in the boat. The boat capsized and they all drowned. That ended our salmon fishery after that. We come up to Rigolet then and poor Jesse used to cut wood every winter for the Hudson's Bay Company.

I can't remember what year it was that Rene drowned. She was a young woman, fifteen goin' sixteen. She used to work and that. She was older than Gus. I almost went out of my mind when I heard she was drowned.

Peter Sheppard, old man Sheppard's son, come in their boat with a flag half-mast. I spied at them and told them all that there was some bad news for us. I never got over that for a long time. Poor Jesse couldn't get over it either. She went so sudden. I was wishin' we didn't send her at all but poor Jesse wanted to tend his nets because the salmon would be soft and spoiled and poor George couldn't work at all.

The people in Turner's Bight, Peter Sheppard and his wife Louisa [Flowers] and they, they seen the boat capsize. Louisa said it looked like somebody was in the boat. She wasn't sure but it looked like somebody in the boat. It was blowin' so hard the boat blowed out the bay. It blowed so hard.

When I went to work in the Kitchen, they [HBC] used to take me down to Burnt Wood Cove in the summer to cook for the men down there. I used to go down there and poor Jesse used to be down salmon fishin' to Tom Luscombe. That's the way we lived. A queer way to live, eh, and we had to work for it, hard. I don't know how many men was there, and there'd be men comin' down with boats of salmon. They'd always eat their dinner, sometimes get there dinner time and sometimes after, and I'd have to give them dinner.

They used to collect salmon at Burnt Wood Cove. The collector used to come there, see, and take the salmon from there. They worked down to Burnt Wood Cove because 'twas a better place to work than at Rigolet or something. They had ice there. Afterwards they moved up to Rigolet but I don't know what happened, I'm sure, but they come up here and got an ice house and everything.

Uncle Jim Dickers used to be around in them days. He used to always have a big crock of jam out to the end of the table. He'd never share it with anybody. Ike Rich took it one morning and passed it around and took some himself. Uncle Jim didn't like that at all.

— Mary Flowers
[11.4:39]

THIS IS A STORY MY father told me.

The old trappers wouldn't speak about their fur, they'd keep it quiet. My father told me about when he was livin' up here to Double Brook. Uncle Albert Flowers, I believe, was livin' up to Fox Cove, not too far apart. Uncle Jerry Flowers, down to Ticoraluk, about seven miles from where Dad and Uncle Albert lived, used to have trade there. Then soon as the brooks would get fast [frozen], they'd go to Uncle Jerry's and get some groceries. My father had a silver fox but he didn't want to let Uncle Albert know about it. He was up to Uncle Albert's the evening before and Uncle Albert said he was goin' to Jerry's tomorrow and he asked my father if he was goin'. Dad told him it wasn't much use for he to go because he never had any fur so he didn't s'pose Uncle Jerry would let him have any credit if he had no fur. Uncle Albert said he never had any fur either but they couldn't starve, so he'd go up and try to get something. Dad told 'en p'rhaps he'd go too. Now, all this time the old man had a silver fox.

They used to get molasses then, drawed out of molasses kegs, so the way the old man got his fox up to Uncle Jerry's without Uncle Albert knowin' about it, he washed out the molasses keg and put the fox skin in the keg. They went up to Ticoraluk the next day. After supper Uncle Jerry asked Uncle Albert if he wanted to go out in the store. Uncle told 'en he did but he didn't have no fur. They went out anyway and was gone a long time.

When they came back Uncle Jerry said, "John, I suppose you got no fur either?"

Dad said, "No."

Uncle Jerry said, "That's pretty tough, boy. I can't see you go home without nothing so you come out and I'll see what I can do for you."

The old man said, "I'd like to have a bit of tea, molasses and butter if you'll let me have it."

They went out and the old man said he'd like to have a couple of gallons of molasses, so Uncle Jerry took the keg and was goin' to run the molasses in it.

The old man said, "God, no, not yet. I got to take the head out!"

Uncle Jerry said, "There's no need to take the head out, the molasses is not froze that hard."

Dad took off the head and pulled out the silver fox.

Uncle Jerry said, "John, I thought I was cute, but you're a damn sight cuter. I'd never think about doin' that. I just bought a fox like that from Albert."

And neither of them had any fur! Oh yes, them old people was very keen over their fur.

Another time my father was goin' out through the Portage Path, goin' out to Ticoraluk one evening gettin' late and Uncle Jerry was goin' out ahead of 'en with a cross fox on his back. When he heard the old man's dogs, Uncle Jerry took the fox off his back and hove 'en out in the woods. The old man come along, stopped his dogs, went out in the woods, got the fox and shoved 'en in his box.

That evening after it got dark, I s'pose Uncle Jerry got kind of uneasy about his fox, thought the dogs might get 'en and eat 'en. He went out and was gone a long time and when he come back he never had nothing. I s'pose he seen the old man's footin', 'cause he come and said, "John, you got my fox."

The old man said, "Got your fox? You told me a few minutes ago that you never got nothing today only a toe or something."

Uncle Jerry said again, "You got my fox."

The old man went to his box and took out the cross fox and give it to 'en. And Uncle Jerry just told 'en he never got nothing, only a toe or something. That's what 'twas like a long time ago.

Some people would roll their fur skins around the inside of their boots, a fox skin, and you'd never know they had a fox. When I'd get a fox I'd always be so glad I got 'en that I'd tell everyone.

There used to be fur buyers goin' around and they'd try to keep the amount of fur they had on the quiet, because the Hudson's Bay manager would try and get all their furs because they might owe a debt, so the Hudson's Bay Company figured they shouldn't sell to anybody else even if they could get a better price.

— George Rich
[8.3:58]

MY HUSBAND WAS A TRAPPER. He used to travel a long piece in the country. Some years he got lots of foxes. There was lots of meat in them days. Good fresh meat. Lots of berries too. We lived at Rocky Harbour, just outside Rigolet. I can't remember how many years. We had hard times and some good old times too. There wasn't much in them days.

We had a winter place and a summer place. We liked shifting from one to the other. We found that real good. It was always good to get back to the summer place in June.

We didn't live too good them times but everyone was happy. We had plenty meat and berries. There was always something to do, trapping and fishing. We used to get about in the old bully. That was a big kind of sailing boat. All hands would get aboard with our stuff. There was no motor, just sail. She had a deck and a cabin. If there was no wind we'd just anchor, or if 'twas blowing real hard, we'd find a harbour to anchor. It was hard work but good fun. We didn't mind it. 'Twas what we had to do and we did it.

My parents [Taylors] come from Newfoundland but I lived in Labrador all my life. I never been to Newfoundland.

We got more now than the old days but we didn't mind then. It was a different kind of life. The government is doing more for us now.

I reared my family up and some of my grandchildren. I reared up May, Curtis, Benny and Sarah. Mike, Sarah and Benny were only babies when their mother died. I think I've done a good job with my life.

— Ann Oliver
[1.1:35]

I WAS BORN AT PIGEON Cove, which is somewhere between Rigolet and Indian Harbour in Groswater Bay. My parents were Thomas and Ann Oliver. We were quite a big family, nine girls and three boys. There was Jimmy, Stanley, and Lawrence, and Ethel, Mary, Jemima, Maude, Tabitha, Victoria, Elizabeth (me), Elsie and Jane. The three oldest ones, Jimmy, Ethel and Mary, died with the whooping cough. Stanley died when I was working up to Muddy Bay; he had pneumonia, I think. There's only Elsie, Jane, Lawrence and me left now.

When we were growing up, we spent our winters at Double Mer and our summers at Bluff Head. We had good times and hard times. We used to have hungry times some springs comin' down to Rigolet from Double Mer, which was about fifty miles. Me and my sisters rowed that distance one spring with only a few raisins to eat. We had what they called a 'trap boat' that you rowed with big oars and a scullin' oar. I can't remember how old I was but I was big enough to hold an oar. We didn't seem to mind being hungry ourselves but we felt for Mom. Lawrence was the baby then and it was hard for Mom. One year, on our way down, we saw a boat in to Ships Harbour after wood, so Dad went in to see if they could give us something to eat. They gave us salt meat, pork, butter, hard bread, sugar, and milk. We put on a big fire and all hands kept runnin' around to keep warm. Dad cooked up a real feed. Then we were afraid to eat, scared we'd all get sick, not havin' anything for so long. We'd wear old brin [burlap] aprons to keep us from gettin' too wet when we was rowin'. People wouldn't be caught in a flour bag apron now. We used to make clothes out of flour bags once. I still got some sheets that I made years ago. Flour bags wears everlasting....

— Elizabeth (Oliver) Coombs
[2.2:40]

I CAN REMEMBER CLEARLY BACK TO 1921, and Christmas from 1921 to 1941 were very similar to the Christmas times that went on a hundred years before that. In 1921 I was around nine years old and I lived in a settlement or community that was very rural, an out-of-the-way place in the Rigolet area. Christmas was a thing that was brought over by the old Europeans, our old forefathers. They remembered and celebrated Christmas. In order to have a company together there had to be a certain place to gather in to. They always knew they were going to gather in to the Richs' or Flowers' place or something for Christmas time. Usually in our area, the people came from as far away as Bob's Brook, that's about half way to Makkovik. They gathered in to my grandfather's place in Rocky Cove. That's a little settlement of our families, Grandfather and his two sons. Other people, maybe about ten families, would gather in there to celebrate their Christmas. Like here in Labrador everything was isolated and you couldn't go and buy all those things in the stores. There was no Christmas toys. If we were able to get to Rigolet, which was thirty miles away, we would have all gathered there, I imagine. Due to Double Mer, which is a big inlet of water and it was just bad ice, between ice and water, you couldn't get there by dogteam. So Christmas time the people in our area gathered to Rocky Cove....

The older people, well, their main thing was the dance. My grandfather was about seventy-five years old at that time. When it would come Christmas Eve night and it would be come time to start the celebrations, just after supper, Grandfather and one of the women, my mother or some other woman, would start the dance by having this cutting out bit as they called it. It was kind of a promenade about the place. This would start the dance. Then other people would get out and call for other couples to start the ball. Usually in those crowds there was always someone who could play the fiddle or the accordion. My uncle could play the fiddle and I had an aunt who could play the accordion, so they usually took turns. They had those old dances and enjoyed themselves. They had the Cotillion, the Quadrille and Newfoundland sets, all these kinds of old time dances that come out from Europe. They had someone to call them off and they really kept it going. They didn't have the real dance slippers, you know. You usually had your deerskin slippers or sealskin ones. They were very light so you didn't exert yourself too much, but everyone really did enjoy themselves. They kept that up for three nights.

Being old Europeans and being the white men, they still had this idea in their heads that they should have their beverage, so there was a lot of spruce beer made for Christmas. It was really a light drink which was usually made in kegs, about five gallon kegs. These people who would come to our place like from Bob's Brook, Wolfrey's Cove, Bluff Head, Pottle's Bay and those places would all take along a little keg of spruce beer. This wasn't very intoxicating at all, but you did want something more like a little boost to your spirit, so you had another keg of hops beer, you see. This really could make like a little cloud come over you once in a while, and you'd wake up, then you really could dance. So you had your beverages and this was the way it was and everybody enjoyed theirselves.

That's the way it was then and I remember it clearly. These families would gather in to our place and celebrate all Christmas week. By that time you were able to get across Double Mer ice and get to Rigolet. Everyone was on their way to the Hudson's Bay post for New Years. That was really another time.

— Ike Rich
[1.2:39]

ONE FALL, BEFORE I WAS born, Irene Pardy's grandfather was livin' to Tom Luscombes, down the bay. In those days there was big boats called whaleboats, big two stemmer boats. The people to Tom Luscombes furred and caught salmon.

Late that fall Irene's grandfather, Jesse Flowers, looked out and seen a whaleboat comin' in the river. The man in it was a stranger. He asked them if he could stay there for the winter, himself, his wife and a small child. The Flowers told him he could stay, so he told them he'd go on the lower side of the river. He went over there and camped, and he had all kinds of supplies. He was a dark man and his wife was right fair and she could speak the best kind of English. The Flowerses all joined together and helped him build a log house. Oh they got along real good. He didn't want to tail any traps. He told them he just wanted to get enough meat to eat.

Nobody knowed where he came from. There was no radios in them days. Nobody never seen him pass north. Nobody never seen him pass south. He lived there all winter and Christmas time come.

In those days all the people living to Tom Luscombes and Fox Cove would go to Ticoraluk and spend Christmas. There was two more Flowers' families there and a family of Broomfields.

Anyway, Christmas time came and the Flowers came up from Fox Cove and wanted this man to go over and spend Christmas with them. He wouldn't go but his wife said that she'd like to go and see some fun at Christmas. He told her she could go but she must be sure and come back the day after Christmas. She got ready and some of the young fellers took her and her baby in the riding box. She went and never went back until two days after New Years. The same two fellers carried her back and they stopped out on the river to tie on their dogs. They thought they heard a gunshot. One feller said he thought it was the ice cracked. They was goin' up over the bank with her and when they pulled back the bedclothes they found she'd been shot in the head. So those young fellers, both unmarried, decided they better rush into the house. When they burst in, this man had a big ladle full of lead and he was runnin' it in his gun.

"I'm not goin' to hurt youse," he said, "My wife disobeyed my orders. This is two days past New Years."

He took the little child and he stayed there the rest of the winter. In the spring he got in his boat and left.

In some ways there was no law in them days, but in other ways there was more law than there is now.

— Arthur Rich
[9.2:33]

Mulligan River, May 24, 1894

They [the Inuit] had it to say once upon a time the world was drowned and that all the Eskimos were drowned but one family and he took his family, and dogs and chattels and his sealskin boat and kayak and komatik and went to the highest hill that they could see. They stayed there 'till the rain was over and when the water was dried up they descended down the river and got down to the plains. When they could not see any more people they took off the bottoms of their boats and took some little white pups and sent the poor little things off to sea and they drifted to some islands far away and became white people. Then they did the same as the others did and the people spread all over the world. Such was my poor father's thought, "Poor people they can read it for themselves in the Bible, what few there are in this bay."

— Lydia Campbell from *Sketches of Labrador Life*
[2.4:47]

I MUST TELL YOU OF my grandmother. She was an Eskimo in the long ago days when they were not civilized. She was an orphan with one brother. They were talking about killing her for they said it was her who was giving them bad luck. They had cut her finger thinking it would give them better luck. There was one man and his wife who were better to her than the rest. When the men went hunting he put her across the bay. They were living on Big Island as we call it now. They put her across on the north side of the bay where we live now in summer at Snook's Cove. She was going to run away. They gave her a small piece of meat and she had her Eskimo knife called a ulu. They used it for all purposes. She heard of some white men who were going up the bay to live, some going one place and some another. They were Englishmen, the first white men to our country.

My grandmother was dressed in sealskin. She wore sealskin boots tied up to her knees. She wore a cossack made of sealskin. She had a very long way to travel. She had a very large bight to go around, many miles. It is called Vallies Bight. Many who have passed up and down the bay in steamers and schooners have seen it. Sometimes she would have to cross rivers, some were quite wide. She would dig up roots of trees to tie her raft with and gather driftwood to make her raft to cross the rivers on. Sometimes she would have to climb cliffs and more times go through the woods. One day she saw a large bear coming along the shore, right for her. She took her ulu in her hand, the only weapon she had to face anything with and she went behind a large rock and the bear passed on. She went on again. She saw a spruce partridge and she killed it with a stick. When night came she would be under a big tree and she would start off again when it got light enough for her to see. How lonely she must have felt! All alone and so many wild animals going about.

Then after a good many days of travelling, she came to Mulligan River. There was an island in the middle of it. She had begun to make a raft when she saw two men in a boat, crossing a way on the other side of the river. It was two Englishmen going to set traps. One of them was going to be my grandfather. She ran out on a sand bank waving and calling to them. When they saw her they were scared, they knew no one was living near. They took her in the boat and tried to talk to her, but she could not understand. They were living at Mulligan Point. So they took her home to stay with them for the winter. They said she was handy to make their sealskin boots and skin mitts. She was willing to do anything for them what she could do, and after a while my grandfather got married to her. She learned to talk a little English, but she was ashamed. She thought she could not talk it right. There were no ministers near them so the best learned Englishmen were the ones to marry them. Nearly all the Eskimo girls were marrying the Englishmen. My grandmother bought her a cotton dress but she was ashamed to put it on. She wore a white cloth dickie and white and black pants and sealskin boots. She never wore a dress.

They had three daughters—Elizabeth, Hannah and Lydia, who was my mother. Elizabeth married William Reid [Reed], Hannah married William Mesher and my mother married William Blake. My Aunt Elizabeth and her husband were drowned together. My Aunt Hannah married a second time to a Frenchman from Canada [Mersai Michelin] and my mother married a second time, Daniel Campbell from Orkney. Mother wore a cotton gown and a white lace cap when she got married. When I was married I wore a silk dress and white collar and white cuffs. So you will see the difference in our dresses.

— Margaret Baikie
[8.2:4]

You must please excuse my writing and spelling for I have never been to school, neither had I a spelling book in my young days—me, a native of this country, Labrador. Our dear father had no school book to teach us in, nothing but a family Bible and a Book of Common Prayer. We learned a little in that way.

If you wish to know who I am, I am old Lydia Campbell, formerly Lydia Brooks, then Blake, after Blake now Campbell.. So you see ups and downs has been my life all through and now I am what I am, Praise the Lord. [December 25, 1893. 2.3:51]

...When I was a little girl my mother used to tell me and my sister how when she and her little sisters and brothers was left alone, orphans, that the older Esquimaux took them and used them very hard, and while any of them—the master or mistress—got sick, that they would take hold of their hands and cut a place in it, to draw blood to cure the sick. They thought that was a cure for them, as the orphans was witches. If that was not enough of superstition, I don't know what to say—to see poor little ones bleeding in that way—the friendless was used pretty hardly. I suppose it is the case in many a country besides this. Poor mother, when she grew up to be a woman she ran away from them before there was any ice to keep her, on October some time, and she went along shore, crossing rivers on drift sticks and wading in shalow water, crossing points, throu woods, meeting bears, no gun, no axe, no fire works, but lye down under juniper tree and spruce tree. Who does this represent in the Bible. She had to travel all the way—70 miles—on foot. All she had to eat was 2 dry fish and berries, and the only wepen she had was a mooloo [ulu], a woman's knife. She went until she came to a large river called Muligan in French language. There she got stock, (as people call it about hear); but while she was standing and wondering what to do and gathering some sticks to make a raft, she saw a French boat with 2 people in it—Frenchmen—and she took off her outer garment and waved to them, and they thought it was a deer, and they rowed towards it and saw it was a person, and, what a strange sight, miles and miles away from any habitation, and the mountaineers [Innu] went into the country. When they came they could not understand each other, but they took her in their boat and went back to their trading post, and she stayed the winter with them, and was loved as a sister to one and a daughter to the other. How she did their things, and how did she pick and gather berries in the fall, for the winter; how she drest and rellen and tap their boots.

In the spring they [her Inuit tribesmen] came up the bay sealing and took her away again. She was sorry to go. That was the custom of the Esquimaux, to go up the big bay to kill and hunt seals and pitch their tents on the ice near the seals with their dogs, komatiks, tents, men, women, and children. What a time they would have when it would come bad weather. The women firing to let the sealers know whereabouts they were, the women going ashore for wood to cook their meat, and the seals was inumerable at that time. The reason they pitched their tents on the ice, was that they were afraid of the mountens [Montagnais Innu] might come out of the woods and kill them. So we was told when we was young, and in that way they [Inuit] would go to a French post called Muligan, at the point of Muligan. There was things for their seal, and going ashore they found my dear, good mother and carried her off, and as there was no other kind of woman to marrie hear, the few Englishmen [in the area] each took a wife of the sort, and they [were] never sorry that they took them for they was great workers, and so it came to pass that I was one of the youngsters of them. [January 22, 1894. 14.3:56]

This country has been my home ever since I was born. When I remember first to see things and to understand, I thought this was the only place in the world and that my parents and my sisters were the best in the world. Then our good father [Ambrose Brooks] used to take me on his knee and tell me that his was a better country only it was hard to live there after his good old father died. His mother could not keep him so he stayed with a good old minister until he, too, died. Wars were raging then, between England and France and other parts of the world and press gangs were forcing young men into service. My father and many other Englishmen came out to this shore. Woodcutting, seal fishing and cod fishing was plentiful in those days.

There were very few white men, much less women, so the men had to take Native wives. Those men would have been happy together with their wives if it had not been for the cursed drink that the agents and the few merchants had here.

We lived up in the river at the head of a long bay, no one nearer us than seventy miles. We lived happy together until our dear sister, Elizabeth, got married to a young half-breed, as we were. That was my first grief, to leave her behind. She got married down to Cuffingham, near our summer houses at Cul de Sac. Well, this is about 68 years ago, that break-up in our family circle. [January 1894. 2.3:52]

Now I will go back about 90 years ago, when our poor father was what we call an English youngster, when he was going about his work with another young Englishman, the Esquimaux was so plentiful and they was so fond of the few white people. He and the other young man was rowing down Dubble Mare [Double Mer] bay, they saw an Esquimaux rowing around the point and paddling so nice in that pretty skin boat called a kaiak, paddling along the shore, and they saw another man come across the point through the woods with a gun in his hands and sat down behind a rock and as the other got opposite to him he aimed at his head and the old flint-lock missed fire, and

Father and the other [English] man was leaning on their oars to see the result. The Indian [?] took aim again and missed fire again, and he would not hold on to the gun any longer, when he [the Esquimaux] paddled past the other [his assailant] and got out of sight. Father and the other man went on shore where the man with the gun was. He trembled and would hardly get into the boat, as they took him aboard the boat, and landed him to their tent, and as his wife was holding with him, they waited for him, the man in the little boat, and rare enough, when he came back, he [Esquimaux] was up to some of the tents and took his meat as usual before crossing the big river (for his wife and children were on the other side). While in the tent, this wife of the other man took an noole [ulu], a woman's knife, and went down to the kaiak and cut long strips in it to sink him as he was crossing, but even in that they failed, but as he was nearing the other side his little boat was nearly full of water and he began to call for help, but no one heard him at that side, so he got safe to land after all amidst the strong tide and wind and people trying to take his life away. He died a few years after. He was a step-son to the first English settler to this country; his name was William Phepherd [Phippard] and he took another English[man and his] wife with him by the name of Knocks [Nooks], as the elder [Phippard] took a widow woman and her 3 children, Esquimaux people, Knocks took her daughter; the mother and daughter was married to two Englishmen—the first settlers of white people is to this bay. [May 8, 1894. 14.3:61]

After my poor mother died (I was about seven then) [1825] my father took me to live with an old Englishman, John Whittle and his wife. The little woman was blind and lame. I used to listen to the poor little woman talking about her young days. She was a native of this country and before John Whittle took her she had been married to one of the first Englishmen that come to this country [John Nooks] One day her husband was going to find two large keels to build a boat. Him and his wife's half-brothers was going to a place about ninety miles from Double Mer and when they were about half way across her half-brothers killed her husband. Then John Whittle took her and her little half-breed boy. One day the little boy died while he was outdoors playing in the snow.

Well, that was a long time ago. I was not thought about then and I am now seventy-five and my sister Hannah is older than me and our oldest sister, Elizabeth, was five years older than Hannah.

I remember the time so well when father met us at the door, as we came home from our snares, with a book in his hand and told us Mother was dying. We all went and kneeled down near our good mother as she was breathing her last. By the time father had done reading and praying she was gone. Oh, what to do? Where to go? only five of us and so far away from any other habitation but the Lord was with us.

My mother died saying the Lord's Prayer and my dear old father died singing a hymn with "Oh, Lord remember me" at the end of every verse. So died my poor parents. I hope to meet them in a better world. My good mother has been dead and buried so long ago that the people who lives near her grave says that the juniper and white spruce is growing large on her grave.

After I went to live with John Whittle's poor blind and lame woman, John Whittle and my father Ambrose Brooks decided to get a woman to help me because I was too young to make all the clothes needed for the winter. I was glad to think that I was going to have a chum. Off they went and returned, a day or so later, with a paralytic woman. When this poor thing tried to show me how to cut out the things I had to make, she was worst than me for she jumped and trembled, so did poor native Betsy. She would give up and poor blind Sarah would slide along the bench, for she could not walk, and put her fingers on the work and tell me what to do. I was then about eleven, no wonder I found it rather hard at times.

I would laugh at those two women when they had rum. They'd have a 'booze' as they called it. They were jealous of each other, the blind woman and the paralytic, while the liquor lasted, one speaking Eskimo and the other, broken English. Sometimes they would laugh and old John Whittle would call at them so roughly that they had to be quiet. That was strange to me.

The time came when Betsy had to go home and I missed that poor Eskimo woman.

That winter the weather was such at one spell that John Whittle and Father did not get home for about a week. I was so afraid I would be stifled in the drifting snow while getting water from a drifting brook. Behold me, about eleven, dressed in my little dickie made of jersey with my serge frock underneath.

"Are you afraid to go?" the little woman asked me.

"A little," I said.

"Well, then," she said, "I will sit here and sing as loud as I can and that will keep you a little company."

But when I got as far as the porch, I lost the sound of her voice. Poor little woman with her native dress, a dickie, breeches and a pair of little sealskin boots on her feet. She sat on a little stool plaiting deer sinew to be used for sewing on boot taps.

The morning after the storm Sarah woke me saying, "Alaka louksvah," a pet name she called me. I told her it was dark yet, very dark. She told me the sun must be shining. To please her I got up but told her I could not see without a lamp.

"Ah," she said, "We are snowed up. The house is buried child."

She told me it was nothing strange after a storm. She told me to go in the porch and look up and I should see some green light. I saw it. When I opened the outside door there was nothing but a hard wall of snow. I did not sit and cry but took a wooden shovel and made a hole big enough to crawl through, then I took an axe and chopped an opening big enough to walk through. The two men came home and found us alive. Ever after that I was sorry to see Father going away.

Times have changed now from the times I have been writing about. When my dear old father first came from England there was not so many white people here. It was lonely, no one to see for miles but Esquimaux and Mountaineers [Innu] and they was plentiful. Father said that the dozens of canoes of Mountaineers would come out of the Big Bay, as it was called then and what is now called Hamilton Inlet or Large

Lake. They used to come skimming along like a flock of ducks, going outside egg hunting on the Islands. Well I know it is a pretty sight to see a lot of birch canoes shining red in the sunshine, I have seen them. I have seen men steering the canoes, women paddling and children singing or chatting. Where are they now? We hardly ever see a family of them now except in winter when we get a visit or two. Oh, our Indians have been killed with liquor, strong tea and dirty tobacco. How few they are now.

Hannah and me would slide on the Mountaineer sleds father would buy for us. We were thought a great deal of by the Mountaineers and they would bring us pretty snowshoes and deer skin shoes for wearing indoors or out, all painted so pretty. [August 1, 1894. 2.3:54]

It was thought that if anyone had deer's meat cooked and seal's meat cooked at the same time and someone eat it at the same time, they had to eat a little white moss between the two to keep them from quarrelling inside the person. So we heard in my young days. And the children were kept from eating different kinds of berries according to their names. Those laws and customs are all done away with now, and there are so very few left. In that time the Eskimos was very plentiful all along the shore and on the islands but now there is only about six or seven families. Where are they gone now, the poor souls had no religion whatever, besides the rum bottle, more shame to the white people that sold them the rum and tobacco—that wretched weed.

How pretty and tall the first race of Eskimo was, so lively when I first remember seeing them but they have dwindled down so small with the cursed drink and tobacco smoking and kept pressed down under debts to the Agents. Now they are few and small, half-starved and possibly naked. One blessing is done them—that the Agents or Hudson's Bay Company does not bring rum or spirits for sale, but such as they bring is for the higher sorts, I suppose no fear for them to be found fault with.

About forty years ago there was a gathering at our house on a Sunday. We saw two smart young men rowing or paddling along by the shore, going home. They had been to the Post and bought a gallon or two of rum. Two nice little boats, kyacks, skimming along so pretty in the sunshine. We looked at them for the last time, poor boys. As the evening was drawing near we heard them call out to each other, they was on the opposite side of the river from us, the river was about a mile across from where we were. While we were kneeling down to prayer we heard them fire two or three gun and then we heard them call out. We thought after it was done that one must have upsot and the other was going to his aid but both found a watery grave. That bad rum sunk both body and soul into where.... How many lost their lives in the same manner?

I knew one large family, a nice lot, they was thought a good deal of. They seemed happy together, the old lady was proud of her big grown up sons, four in number, her daughter and her husband. Ill luck befell them. The youngest, a young man, fell through the ice and got drowned, one shot himself, so I heard, accidently, another brought some rum and started to go outside with his wife, both got drunk, the wife lay down in the boat and the husband got knocked overboard while steering with an oar.

He was never found. When the other boats came up to them no one was in the boat but the wife, asleep. She was friendless. At the end of the summer there was an English half-breed who wanted a wife. He bethought himself, 'Why not go and try to get that young widow.' So he and his brother took a boat and went off to the island where the Eskimo tents was. He went into one tent with his brother, found the widow and got down by her side. No sooner then when he asked her to be his wife, they heard someone walking very heavy, so they lookt to the door and sure enough in came her husband in size and shape with a dickie on his body, hood up over his head. He came up to where they were sitting and put his hand on her. She leaned back with fear and trembling. When she lookt up he was gone. The people in the tent saw him go out and vanish out of sight. Strange to say, about a month later this man went and married her but after a few years they parted.

When this poor old woman heard what happened to her third son she nearly went out of her mind. When her last child died she did not live long to the sorrow of the white people, for she was the mid-wife for them. One day when the men and women and children were all out of the tent, she hung herself up to one of the poles of the tent. We the Blake's went down that way fishing. She was buried by Captain Norman and his planters the day we got there. What lamentation there was that day. It seems a long time ago but it's not a second in our Maker's eye.

I was about twenty then, I think. I never keept an account of time or how it went. I was teaching the children of the large family that I married into. I could not write then but I could read and teach them to read, sing hymns and to pray oft', as my dear old father teacht me. There was no ministers nor school teachers, them times, here in this country.   [December 10, 1894. 2.4:46]

We hear that there is conjering going on among the Mountaineers yet—so I am told by the men that come down from up the Bay among them. I remember of having the pleasure of seeing the oldest Mountaineer. He seemed to be a nice old man; he had two wives, two sister—well, he had a large family, by the name of Ascenle, meaning neck in their language. As his boys grew up they went into his tent and learned it [conjuring], but one boy was getting up to be a young man, when he got to his father's tent and heard the sounds that the evil one was making, he took great fright and got out, and when his mother and the others saw the condition he was in, they would not suffer him to go in again.

I remember one spring that the Hudson's Bay Company was running short of provisions, no one could get anything from them, until the vessel would come in the spring. So some said that the conjerer would find out where the vessel was, so the master asked him if he would try and find out. So he went on with his work in the tent and told them that he can see a vessel some way below Snook Island, and they looked at each other, and Mr. McKenzie asked some one to go up the hill and see whether they could see any vessel. He went with his glass, and he said there was in the distance a vessel looming up. It seem strange, but Old Neck has many contrivences to get hold of his people; they say that some of the ignorantest can conjer yet.

I remember when I was about 8 years old, that I saw some of the natives trying to lift a woman's head, but when it would mean yes, it would get light; no was heavy, and the person asking would know yes or no. I found it rather hard to see it but if a dog would bark, it would heave up in an instant. It is all gone now, they can't do it, not the Esquimaux can't do it now since Christianity have been preached to them and they can read their Bible. Oh, the heathen lands, poor people, no wonder that they always thought that they saw ghosts going about without any heads, before now. Here at the present time there is a few down at the north that believes in ghosts yet. There is a little rock below this that the Esquimaux used to see a little woman, coming out of the rock, but we passes the rock and can't see any yet: we have not even seen the ghost of that woman that hung herself to one of those trees that grows around this house, long ago. [May 17, 1895. 14.3:62]

There is a large hill above us that is called in the Indian language Mookomee, in the English language it means Drummer's Hill, for before now the Moravians could not put their tents near that hill, for they always heard the drum a-beating....

Well, as we was coming back the other day we past outside on the ice, passing outside Mookomee, the Drummer's Hill, about 4 or 5 miles distance. Still I had to look at the nice looking white spring with snow. I thought about the time me and my poor John went up for a cruise to my sister Hannah's house, about [40] years ago. That a family of Mountaineers had killed a lot of deer on Drummer's Hill. He [Tomas] told Hannah and me that if we would go into his tent mitchwam he would get us a load of deer meat. So we went off to his house. Mr. Meshler [Michelin] and my sister and me and John Meshler—and stays in the house all night. Ah, how sore and tired I was next morning when I got up off the hard bed, for it was sliding down towards the fireplace, and I had a job to keep up from the fire near my feet, and the branches of the fir was so hard under me. I found my loins aching, but my sister Hannah seemed to enjoy her trip. She and her husband was lying on the same kind of bed, but they was more used to the tents more than me.

Their tent was made of deerskin and birch bark and about as large as a good size bed room, about 7 feet long and about the same width; a ridge of snow covered with fur [fir] branches for their pillows around the tent: all looked so happy with the deers meat stuck up on sciverw made of wood.—good looking meat dreping with grece. They evokt a nice piece for us though, to let us see how kind they was to us white peopel as they called us. This was about 4 miles in beyond Drummer's Hill, what they call Mookomee....

Poor old Tomas is gone, he died last year, his wife this year, 1894, and while we was on our cruise up to Nile River [?] the other day we went in to the tent of their son. All the other Mountaineers got frozen some and some stunned, so they told us the other day when Daniel and me went up to North West River—the company's post. There was only one man left and three or four women and five or six children, [I] found it pittyful to see them speaking about their starved ones. One widow was looking very sad. Sam Nixew's wife—a nice looking woman. They was holding my hand and telling me that I must be his mother now as his own mother is dead and she was a great friend of mine, although we could not understand each other's language sometimes; still we could make it out with sins [signs] and wonders. This was a son of that people that sister Hannah and son and husband went in past Mookomee, after deers meat about 40 years ago. No wonder they are all dead. We had a slead and komatik load to take out, so little John Campbell my son and me took the slead load for us to home to Muligan, while Mr. Meshlin [Michelin] and wife and child took their's home to Sahacatho [Sebaskachu] to their home about 10 miles distant apart. I had a lot of little children then and Mr. Campbell and children were glad when we got home with our deers meat, but how tired we was, my son and me; now he has a wife and 8 children grown up, 3 young women, they are about 1 miles from us, 2 old people. [December 12, 1894. 14.3:58]

Well, I have been writing about Mountaineers, and the Drummer's Hill, sure enough we got a visit yesterday, at last, 2 men and 4 boys brought 3 deer skins dress so soft and white, and 4 deer sinews for making boots or shoes, and to-day 2 women and 2 girls and 2 large boys came hear on a visit and brought a pretty drest deer skin for our boy Huey to pay him for a jacket they had from him 3 years ago. How kind of them. They are now got to be more Christian like, some of them, than they was long ago since I remember, still they would not give us a large piece of deer's meat if they had any, in case we would give the dogs a bone, for they say that would give them bad luck. I knew a man that killed a deer, and a dog eat some of the deer's bones, and all in the night, and he got sore legs ever after, and when I saw him about half a year before he died, and the poor man said that was the reason he had sore legs. I tried to tell him different, but to no purpose. [May 8, 1894. 14.3:60]

Please excuse me when I tell you about my days journey to-day. Well, Esther my young girl and me have had a day in the woods. We got up just dawning, and got breakfast and roust up Mr. Donald C. and Huey, our boy, and my son Thomas Blake and his son Donald out of the other house. All gathered as usel to read a chapter in the Bible and sung a hymn and had a prayer. Then we had breakfast and washt up the dishes and got ready for to go off berry picking far in under some big hills about 4 miles in to the country, a fine frosty morning. We had it nice to go in to the hills, gathered 2 galons of cranberries, now it was time to return but, only if I was not used to put up with all manner of hardships when I was young and all my life, we would be in there yet. The snow got soft, about three feet deep in places, and the bared places bare to the ground, and the little rivers and willows and a heavy kettle and a gun and some provisions and snow shoes on and then I don't know how many pound weight, when got wet is more than a caution, as the men says. Esther had her bundle to carry in to the woods yet. Just now fancy an old woman 75 years old, and a young girl 13 years old, about 4 miles in the country—in past a lot of green woods with a gun, snow shoes, a gallon kettle, a wooden bucket, 2 biscuits, powder and shot, rabbit snares, and knife and thimble and needle, in case of old clothes being tore in the bushes, and a large game bag and a axe, and the sun shining so hot, making the snow cling to our snow shoes. You would laugh as well as me when I fell and loose a lot of my hard earnings, berries. Well, such is life, and where there is a will there is a way, under God's providence.

My son Thomas and his son Donald, and our Huey, started off for 40 miles with 2 dogs and a komatik for a log to build a hut with, and hunt for seals on their way over the bay—the great Esquimaux Bay formily—now called Hamilton Inlet. When Father came hear from England, about a hundred years ago, I suppose, there was hundreds of Esquimaux in this bay, now they have dwindled down to 20 or 30 people, most all dead, but a good many carried up to the World's Fair, as you all know. Well, this day is coming to a close, my husband shot 3 partridges to-day while I was off in the woods, so I must bid you all a good evening for this time. [May 1, 1894. 14.3:60]

— Lydia Campbell (1818-1907)
from *Sketches of Labrador Life*

To the credit of the Hudson's Bay Company be it said that it was always a law with them that their agents on all the posts should conduct services on the Sabbath, for the benefit of the natives as well as their own clerks. This the agents did for many years before any missionary was stationed on that part of the coast and for a long time supplied the only public means of grace among these unfortunate people. These agents not only conducted religious services on the Lord's Day but baptized, buried, and married the people. This work, doubtless, was inadequately done, but it was the best that could be accomplished under the circumstances, and it was certainly a step in advance of the conditions which existed prior to the establishment of the Hudson's Bay Company in Labrador.

A few years ago Mrs. Daniel Campbell, who has recently been called to her heavenly home, gave me the history of her first marriage. This marriage gives a good insight into social conditions existing in Labrador at that time. She was then only sixteen years of age and living at home with her father. Bill Blake, a wild, rough young man, had set his heart upon Lydia, as her name was, but she did not want Bill for she loved another. However he was determined to have her and as she would not consent he planned to force her to marry him. He arranged for a komatik party to Rigolet, a Hudson's Bay Company post, fifty miles from Double Mer, where he and Lydia were then living. An invitation was given to all the people in that place including, of course, Lydia and her father; her mother had died some years previously. The day appointed for the trip was looked forward to with delight by all. No one was more jubilant over the affair than the girl herself. This was her first trip to Rigolet and it was to her what London would be to an English country girl. The day dawned fine and clear, cold and crisp, an ideal Labrador winter's day. All the dogs in the place were harnassed, and soon four komatiks were on their way to Rigolet, Lydia riding on her father's komatik. How glad she was!

Arriving at their destination the usual dog fight began. The large force of dogs at Rigolet rushed upon the strange dogs with vicious onslaught. The men interfered and the savage fight soon ended, after which Lydia was taken to the 'big house' and made welcome. Everyone seemed kind and nice to her, especially Blake's friends. Bill succeeded in making Lydia's father drunk; for by doing so he could more easily carry out his plan. So far his plot had worked well and without the least suspicion on Lydia's part. Presently an old lady carrying a new dress in her hand came to the room where she was and said:

"Lydia, you must take off that old dress and put on this new one, for you have to get married this evening."

"Married," she said, "I never thought of getting married. Who to?"

"You have to marry Bill Blake."

"I will not; I don't love him."

"But you must, your father has told him he can have you and welcome."

Lydia insisted she would not have Bill. Her feelings were not regarded, and two cruel women began at once to remove her old dress. The girl resisted but it was all of no avail; she was powerless in their hands and was forced to submit to the inevitable. Blake came in and she was compelled to stand beside him, while some servant at the station read the marriage ceremony.

It is unnecessary for our present purpose to follow this marriage further, sufficient to say that her life with Blake was very unhappy. He did not live long, however, and some years later Mrs. Blake married Daniel Campbell, a young Scotsman, with whom she lived happily for the long period of fifty-four years.

— Arminius Young
from *A Methodist Missionary in Labrador, 1916.*
[8.2:6]

...ON SEPTEMBER 19, 1848, CHIEF Trader Richard Hardisty wrote from Rigolet to Sir George Simpson, Governor-in-Chief of Rupert's Land:

...Daniel Campbell came to this Country in 1844 in the capacity of Cooper and Fisherman on a five years Contract at 25 [pounds] Stg. per annum. He is a very good man, and very efficient both as Cooper and Fisherman. His Contract expires on the 1st of June next. He is willing to enter into a Two Years agreement from that time at 30 [pounds] Stg. pr. annum but no longer. It was proposed to him to enter into a three years Contract, but this

he declines unless he is allowed 30 [pounds] Stg. pr. annum for the last two
years of his first agreement, being the same terms on which the other Cooper
[George Lyall] came to the Country....

Simpson replied from Lachine on March 27, 1849, that Campbell could be re-engaged for two years at £30 per annum. Campbell entered into a new agreement but he did not renew this second contract when it expired in 1851. He stayed "free in the Country" instead of returning to Scotland.

...When Daniel Campbell had completed his contract with the Hudson's Bay Company, he married Lydia Brooks Blake, a young widow with several children, and settled in Labrador. Daniel and Lydia had eight children. Their descendants are now scattered throughout the world. In Labrador they are concentrated mainly in the Lake Melville and Charlottetown areas.

— Roland E. Powell
[11.4:41]

I first remember when I was two years old of sending [a] mitt to Mr. Smith, who years after was Lord Strathcona, to get candies as my father was going up to [North West River] hauling a sled, for we had no dogs and the snow [was hard]. Perhaps he would be away for a week. [We] lived a long way from anyone. I don't remember when he came home, a while after dark. I was very tired and was asleep when he came. Mother woke me and said Daddy was come. I jumped up; I thought of my mitt. My father took me on his knee and gave me the mitt full of candies. It was sewn up with twine. Mr. Smith had sewn it up. I gave some all around, for I thought I had so much candies.

I found my father real pretty, for he had red whiskers and a red vestcoat. He said that my grandfather [Ambrose Brooks] was very sick and he would like to see my mother for she was his youngest daughter. So a while after Father took us all up to stay a while, for they thought he wasn't long in this world.

I can just remember seeing an old man sitting up in bed with a long white night cap on his head. Mother took my hand but I was afraid to go near him.

I don't remember anymore until the next fall.

My father did not know much about trapping. My mother used to go with him to set the traps. My father had come from the Orkney Isles as a cooper for Mr. Smith, the Hudson's Bay Company. Mr. Smith was in charge then and it was him who married my parents. The next fall we left Lowlands to look for a better place, for we did not get anything there.

My father had given me a little tin cup. As we were sailing along my little brother, John, threw it over and it sank. I cried. I suppose I went to sleep, then I heard them speaking [about smoke they saw] rising under a big tree on a point. I had heard of old Ameal [Hamel] who had shot his wife not long before. It was the same old man, sure enough. So they went ashore to him. He came down to the boat and asked us to come up to the fireplace and get warm. Mother went [but I was afraid] so I stayed in the bottom of the boat. [I was] all in a shiver. I was wishing [we would leave]. His small boat was hauled up on the [shore and] near it was a seal. [He had no flour], so he gave father some traps for flour. It was only when the moon was full he would get silly. He was on his way down the bay looking for a new place to live for the winter.

So that day we came twenty-four miles in our small boat to Mulligan River where I lived until I was nineteen. We stayed in a little log house on an island. The river ran on both sides. Soon after we got there my father started a new house across the river, in where the tall spruce grew so thick. I remember my mother taking me across the river in a small boat to look at the new place. It was getting late in the fall; the ice was making along the rivers.

Jack Hamel and his father had lived, two or three years before in the same log house we were living in. A few years before when he had shot his wife, Jack's mother, she was carrying her little girl on her back in a big hood the same as the Eskimos. He told her to go ahead in the path and then he shot her in the head. He went home and gave the baby to a woman to look after. Jack stayed with his father.

Jack and his father lived nine miles from anyone. One day the old man felt himself getting silly again. He told Jack to hide the axes and knives in the snow and he ran and hid the gun. I suppose he was afraid of killing Jack. Just think how the poor boy must have felt, nine miles from anyone. His father told him to go to North West River after some castor oil. He thought that would make him well. So Jack started on his journey up the river [bay?]. Then he had to go eight miles across a point of land. That evening he stayed at my Aunt Hannah's. He had an axe and snowshoes and matches with him. The snow was quite deep. There were a good many wolves going about in them times but he had not see any. The next day he went to North West River. His father told him not to stop no longer than he could. So he went home thinking to find his father dead or hurt. As he was going down the river, he saw smoke rising. He went in and his father was better....

The first time I remember seeing Jack was at a wedding. Isaac Oliver was going to be married and Jack was best man. His girl was there, poor Nancie Broomfield. She wore a white muslin dress and on her head was a white lace [cap with] roses on it, broad white ribbon strings tied [under her chin]. She looked very pale. She sat back in a chair and cried with a [handkerchief] to her eyes. That spring she ran away. She had a long ways to go to her aunt's place. She had got her feet wet and had taken a chill. Jack's girl had a younger sister who had married a few years later. She had three small girls and was expecting another. It was Christmas Eve. She was wishing for a gull so her husband went out on a point and shot one. It fell a little way out in the water. She went out in the boat to get it but the tide turned and the ice and slob was driving down on her. And before she could get ashore, she was carried away with the ice out to sea. They had no other boat but they wouldn't have got her if they had one. The last time they saw poor Lizzie it was getting dark, she was standing up with an oar in her hand trying to break the ice. That was the last of poor Lizzie. She was a second cousin of mine....

Mr. Smith had sent a family of Eskimos up to Mulligan to try to get salmon. He thought it was a good place for salmon. He gave them nets and a small bag of flour. Not long after they had been there, they picked up a seal ashore on the rocks. They had put it in their tent. Then Fanny, their oldest daughter, began to get sick, getting poisoned, for they had eaten a piece of the seal. The two smaller children did not eat any. The ones that had eaten it were the father and mother and the oldest daughter. When Fanny died the father dug a hole in the sand and buried her just as she was. Then the old people were getting sick. They went across the river as quick as they could with the children and went to our house but the house was locked. They were putting the children there so they wouldn't go astray. Someone may find them, for they knew they were going to die. They hauled up their boat, they knew the children wouldn't be able to launch it. The old people were getting very bad. They went under a big tree and lit a fire to warm water in a can so as to make them vomit. Not long after they died. The poor little children were left with very little to eat. The youngest, Jenny, was three years old and Hughy, nine or eight. He covered their parents with pieces of board, that Father had from building his boat, to keep the dogs from eating them. The blue flies were all over them. Little Jenny used to cry to go to her mother but Hughy would keep her back. I remember seeing a little path trod deep in the [ground] where they would go to eat green berries and leaves that they lived on for two days. Hugh killed a partridge with a stick. They lived [in an old store] house and in one corner was a lot of nets to lie on. The mosquitoes were so plentiful that they could not get any rest. Their father had set out nets before he got sick. Some Indians had come down the river in a canoe and saw some old rotten salmon in the net. They thought the people had been too lazy to haul their net so they passed on.

Mr. Smith was sending two men, in a small craft to go down the bay. When they were about nine miles on their way, the wind came ahead and blew very hard so they had to turn back and run in the river and anchor. They had no small boat with them. My cousin Robert swam ashore to have a look at the place. He saw someone peeping out of the old store. They were children, the little girl was crying and holding on to her brother. She had one bare foot and on her other foot her boot was dried on so hard that Robert had to cut it off with his knife. Robert launched their boat and took them aboard and gave them something to eat. They took them to North West River. Mr. Smith took the boy and sent Jenny down the bay to her aunt. Three years later we heard that Jenny was very sick, so Mother and I went to see her. She was lying in a corner, behind the stove, covered with an old brin bag. Her aunt wasn't good to her. Mother went and put her hand on her forehead and talked to her, for she could talk in her language. Then we went home....

It was sometime in December, Father went to his path to his traps. He had a long way to go in over the hills. He said he would be gone for three days. The weather was very mild and there was snow falling. John and I went down and lay on the ice. John was a seal and I was throwing snowballs at him. Our clothes got so wet we had to go home. Mother scolded us for getting wet. We took off our clothes and went to bed. A quarter of an hour later Tom came in and said a white bear had passed right along where we had been playing. We felt afraid. Mother said it was a good thing we got wet, perhaps the bear would have eaten us. When we put on our dry clothes, we went with Mother to look at the large tracks. That evening my cousin, Ambrose, came. Tom told him about the bear. He said it was the same bear he had been chasing all day with dogs and komatik. He let his dogs run after it and they would bark at it. It would turn around and show its teeth at them. He sank very deep in the snow. He fired two or three shots at him and wounded him. Then he broke his gun rod and had to turn back. He was sorry to lose the bear.

Ambrose was a cripple, from his knee. He had to use a crutch, which he tied his snowshoes to when he walked through the snow.

I remember Mother telling us about when she was a girl, long ago. They always built their store house down by the landwash and their dwelling house a piece in the woods to have plenty of wood to burn. One morning she went down to the store and she saw the door was open, then she saw a large track. So she ran back to the house and told them. Two men loaded their guns and went in the store and waited for the bear. It was a large polar bear, his nose was all covered with flour, for he had eaten a lot of flour out of a bag in the store. They shot him. They went back to the house and told them they had shot the bear and they all went down to see him skinned. He was a very large bear....

The next year Father and Tom went deer hunting. They were going for three days. Mother went down the path to see if she could see them coming. She saw two specks down on the ice. She came in and got the glass. It was two deer coming right for the house. She got in a hurry and loaded her gun with buckshot. Her gun was an old flintlock. Then she peeped through the trees and saw them coming for the river. She told us not to make any noise and when she fired, if she got one, she would call the dogs. She ran down the other path to the river and waited. She rested her gun on a barrel and fired. One fell. Susan ran down the path and I was coming behind with the children. When I came in sight Mother was loading her gun again. The deer would get up and then fall again. The dogs were all around biting him. Mother went in close to him and fired again and he fell. Susan went and got a komatik. It took us a while to get him on the komatik, for he was so heavy. It was a young stag. We hauled him up and got him skinned.

Father and Tom came home the next day. They had killed two deer. They put their deers' hearts in a pan and when they weren't looking Mother put the heart from her deer in. When they saw the other heart they asked who killed the other deer. Mother said, "What do you think?" Then Father had a look at it. He said it was the size of the one Tom got. Then they all had a talk about the deer they had killed. Next day Father and Tom went after their deer with the dogs and komatik. So we had plenty of deer meat for a while....

[Later] Father was away to North West River. When he came home he said there was going to be a wedding at North West River. It was my cousin, Robert Mesher, and Eliza Hamel, Jack's sister. She was staying with my aunt. Robert was a servant for Mr. Smith. Eliza sent for my sister Susan to be her bridesmaid. So Susan got ready for the wedding. My aunt had taken Eliza to look after her children when she would go hunting or trouting. Aunt Hannah would take her sled and her gun and snowshoes to go see her traps and snares. It was she who got most of the fresh meat.

I am passing over two or three years.

I wasn't very well all the fall. Father said he would take me up to see Mr. Smith at New Years for he and Tom were going up for New Years keeping. I found it a long time to wait, three days. Before New Years day we started and went as far as my aunt's that day. The next day we started again with Uncle and Aunt and Peter, their son. I got cold so Father wrapped me up in a buffalo skin and lashed me on the komatik. It was blowing very hard and the snow was blowing all around. The men were going ahead, beating a path for the dogs.

Mr. Smith had twelve working at the Post, some were Scotch, some English and one from Finland. The one from Finland had a very hard name to speak so they called him Fred Hope. He hoped he would do well. I was only twelve years old then and one of the Scotchmen, years after, was going to be my husband. I found it strange to hear them talking to one another.

Mrs. Smith sent for [us to go to] their kitchen where her girl was cooking. So [we went] through with our tea. She sent for us for we were the first womenkind that she had seen that winter. [Father] went out in the men's kitchen. Nearly all the men were out in the shop buying new caps and white shirts with pretty patterns, some with little small stripes with little flowers running up it and others were getting black silk handkerchiefs to wear under their shirt collars. That night every one stayed up until twelve o'clock, waiting for the New Year. Just as the clock was striking the hour of twelve, all the men went out with their guns. And then there was a great firing, bell ringing and dogs howling. Mr. Smith was standing at his door with a bottle of rum in one hand and shaking hands with the other. When he had given them all a glass they came in and went to bed. We went out in the other kitchen to bed.

The next morning, when we were ready, we went out in the kitchen to have our breakfast. We had chocolate, fresh milk, plum cake, potatoes and salmon. At eleven o'clock Mr. Smith sent for all hands. The men had been cleaning up, washing and dressing. Captain Irvin went first, then T. Baikie, then William Spence, then all the rest and then all of us. Old Mr. Goudie and his sons were also there. There were chairs all around the house. Mr. Smith was standing at the table, and on the table were two decanters, one of wine and the other of rum and all around were wine glasses. There were three different kinds of cake, one sort was all shining with white icing and candies. There was a dish of raisins and one of candies. Mr. Smith handed a glass of rum or wine to each man and as the last man took his, they all wished him a very happy New Year. Then they all sat back in their chairs. Mrs. Smith went around with the cakes, James with the raisins, and little Maggie with the candies. Thomas Baikie asked

Maggie to come to him. She went across but she couldn't look up, her face was red. She sat on his knee. She thought so much of him. When the weather was fine she would sit on his shoulder with her arm around his neck. He used to carry her down the bank and back again. She called him her horse. A while after Thomas and the other men were away chopping logs and he cut his foot. They had to haul him home and Mrs. Smith sewed it up. Then Thomas had to stop in bed for a while. Maggie and her brother, James, would carry him in a little kettle of chocolate, milk, and cakes. Sometimes Maggie would give him candies, always asking if his foot was getting well....

The next year we had to kill our dogs, all except one, and our little house dog. Every dog in the place was getting mad. We were afraid to go anywhere for they were running wild. They shot three and got two in traps. Our little dog was Tom's dog, Vanace. Tom would be away for a while and would leave his dog home. She would drag his clothes, or anything of his, to her corner. She would drag it everywhere she would lie, keeping it for him. When he was going to his traps she would bring him his game bag. She would follow him. She was a good dog for finding partridges for him, and in the spring she would always go hunting with him. She would bring the ducks and geese ashore when he shot them.

    One day our dog was howling down the path. Mother said, "Go and see what is making the dog howl." I ran down and listened. I heard a wolf howling down on the point. Tom loaded his gun and put a bullet in, then he put the gun caps in his pocket and started. We were all down the path looking at him. When he had gone quite a distance he lay down and rolled about squeaking like a mouse. The wolf came at a gallop, right for him. We felt afraid. I said, "Perhaps the gun won't go off." Then the wolf would have him. We were finding fault with him, letting the wolf come so near. At last we saw him kneel, take aim and fire. The wolf fell back over, he had a bullet through his sides, right through. John sang out, "He's dead." The wolf jumped up and stood looking at Tom. He had to load his gun, then take his cap box out of his pocket. The cover was hard to open. Then he fired but the wolf was going at a gallop, a string of blood was all along the ice. So next morning Tom went to look for the wolf. He chased him across a point. He saw where four wolves had come on his track so Tom turned back.

    Sometime in April Mother came in. She said she saw something away on the ice. She took the glass and went down the path and spied. She saw two people walking, and when they came near we saw it was a woman and a man. It was nearly dark. It was the same little Jenny, but tall and fat, with her intended husband, going to North West River to get Mr. Smith. They had come a long way across the bay. They said they left that morning. I went down to the river to get water. I remembered the time when she and her brother had been here. She didn't remember....

Mother told us of a young man and his girl who had run away in the night. They had taken a boat when the mother and step-father were sleeping, and they went on an island [Gull Island, Back Bay], the same island. Their boat was driven away and they starved. They had been gathering driftwood to make a shelter. A long time after someone found them lying in each others arms.

An old woman had gone along the shore berry-picking and she thought she heard a sound. It seemed as if someone was waving away across on the island. She went home and told her husband. He said it was crows flying up and down. She felt very uneasy and wanted him to go but he said he wasn't going. She thought it might be someone stranded on the island.

Mother told us she once lived with an old woman [Whittle, previously Mrs. Nooks]. Her husband wanted a girl to stay with his wife when he went to his traps, for she was both blind and lame. Her husband used to beat her with whatever he could get hold of. She told Mother that one day he got a bag of shot and there was a small hole in it, every time he would hit her the shot would fly all over the house. Sometimes he would go away for a week and leave them all alone. One day Mother had to go down to the store to get fish, it was quite a distance. The old woman thought she would be afraid so she said she would go with her if she hauled her on a little komatik. So Mother got her ready and when they were going down the path the little woman rolled off the komatik and down a hole under a tree. Mother was afraid she was hurt. After a long time Mother got her up on the komatik again and hauled her home. Mother was afraid she was going to die but the next day she was better. When she felt better she would sing and talk all day to keep Mother company. It was that little woman's son, Henry, and his Kittie who starved on Gull Island.

— Margaret Baikie (1844-1940)
from *Labrador Memories: Reflections at Mulligan*

I WAS BORN IN MULLIGAN. That's where we always lived. That's about twenty or twenty-five miles below North West River. My father, Thomas Blake was married four times. His first wife was Hester Ann Sheppard. My mother was his second wife, Sarah Jane Blake. I was only two-and-a-half years old when she died. I lived with my grandmother, Lydia Campbell, until Pa married Mary Goudie. She was the one I always called Ma. Pa's last wife was Caroline Osmond.

Gran Campbell's father was Ambrose Brooks. He married an Eskimo girl. He had her christianed Susan after his mother. Gran used to tell us that before her father would go off anywhere he'd tell them not to let their mother eat any raw meat. One time they killed a caribou and Grandfather Brooks went off somewhere. Gran said she and her mother skinned the deer and cut it up. Every now and again, she said, her mother would eat a piece of the fat. Gran said when her father come home she told him. He took a piece of rope and give his wife a hammering. He hurt her, Gran said, 'cause she cried. I says it wouldn't be only me that got the cracks if 'twas me he hammered. Raw caribou fat is real good.

I was married at Mulliauk on August 4, 1910. My husband was Freeman Baikie. I can remember my wedding. It was just like any other day. We had to row down in a little boat to Mulliauk 'cause that's as far as the minister was going to come up. I wore a light dress that I bought or that someone give to me. We all gathered in to Aunt Beck's house where we got married. We got a picture of the people at our wedding. Aunt Beck is there, Aunt Maggie is there and sister Jane. Tom was Aunt Beck's baby. Jane's baby was Pearl, I think. They all had their little ones there. After we was married and went out through the door, some men shot off their guns. Them days when anyone got married that's what they'd do.

People come from all around to our wedding because there was going to be a dance. They all come in little boats with a flag up. The dance was at Cul de Sac, which is just up above Mulliauk and just below Snook's Cove. Cul de Sac was where Grandfather Campbell and his family always lived. He built there after he come from Scotland and was done working for the Hudson's Bay Company. He built houses there and had nets. It was to one of those houses that we went to for our dance. Grandfather Campbell was dead then; Gran was dead and all the old people was dead when I was married. We had the fiddle and accordion at our dance. Everybody had that kind of music long ago. We rowed to Cul de Sac from Mulliauk after the wedding service. That's about three miles or a little more. Sometimes, down the bay, you can get a real fair tide and you can go fast. Nobody had engines them days, never heard tell of them even. I suppose there was steamers somewhere.

We got our groceries from the HBC stores in North West River or Rigolet, that far apart. We was right close to Rigolet. Anybody could go down with the fair tide and come back.

Grandfather Campbell told us once when salmon come right plenty he had to go to Rigolet and get some salt. When he was passing Wolfrey's Point an old man come out and asked him to come ashore on his way back because he wanted to get married. Grandfather Campbell had a license to marry people. This old man told Grandfather that he wanted to marry a little girl but he wouldn't sleep with her until she was twelve years old. He wanted to marry her then because he was afraid someone else would have her if he waited. There was no white girls around hardly and he wanted a white girl for his wife. Grandfather said he went ashore and this old man got his frying pan and smoked salmon and put it on the stove. All the time he was getting married he had his fork in his hand behind his back and every so often he would go and turn over his salmon. I don't believe many men married girls that young but that particular old man was afraid he'd lose her if he waited. Them days a lot of people wasn't too sensible. Of course, there's people like that these days, too.

We always kept Christmas up. More than now I think. Grandfather Campbell and Gran was all for Christmas, Good Friday, Easter and all them days. Whatever days was kept in England or Scotland or wherever they come from. We always had what we don't have now and that's the Bible read before bedtime, and in the morning we'd have a prayer again. That's gone out of style now, I think.

We was never hungry, no time, not even when it was just my father and us children. We always had partridges and rabbits. We always had bread. We used to always get fish. There was an awful lot of trout to Mulligan them days. There was tomcods if you'd go out on the bight. I believe even trout is getting scarce now.

I never went to school. Gran learned us our letters. She give us one of her letters she had from someone and we learned to write a little going by that. We all went through *Tom's Dog*. Gran learned us that. We could learn on our own then. *Tom's Dog* was a spelling book. 'Twas only easy. I suppose people got easy books now for their little children. I haven't got no school learning but I can read a story when I got good light. None of our ones went to school until after we had our children. Then we used to get a teacher a couple of weeks a winter. A Newfoundlander come up to Grand Lake one time for two weeks. Sometimes they might come for a month. The children learned enough to read and do figuring. That was the hardest, I found, trying to figure out things when you was buying up things in the stores....

Grandfather Campbell's place was Cul de Sac, Grandfather Baikie's place was at Snook's Cove, the Blake's place was Mulliauk and the Shiwak's lived to the green place close to Cul de Sac. They lived there summer and winter and they always had good fresh water from a spring close to their house.

Grandfather Campbell had a fine house at Cul de Sac. After all his sons grew up and went for theirselves, he and Gran adopted a little boy, Hughie, and he lived with them until they both died. Cul de Sac was a fine place to live in summertime, but, they say there is no house there at all now.

The Blakes lived at Mulliauk for more than a hundred years for they were old white-haired people when I was a small girl and our old house was there also. People had salmon nets there and got lots of salmon. We always come back to Mulligan when fishing was over. We rowed or sailed up, sometimes our hands were blistered from rowing, but it was good times. We'd put up a tent in the night, cook a duck, a trout or berry cake. My, I wish I could do that again, but them times is over for me.

— Flora Baikie
[3.2:29]

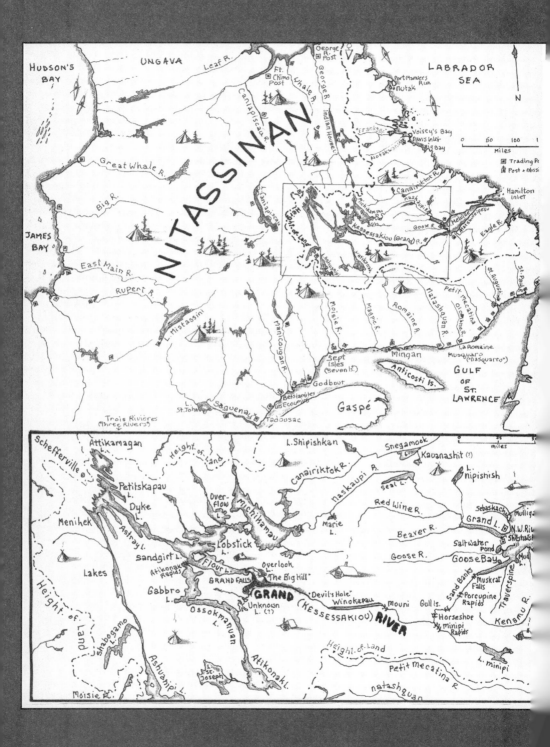

CHAPTER

Eight

NITASSINAN

BOUNDARIES ARE EPHEMERAL THINGS AT BEST, and for the Innu of eastern Canada, none could have less meaning than that separating Quebec from Labrador. Their territory, Nitassinan, encompasses over 250,000 square miles of the Labrador/Ungava Peninsula north and east of the Saguenay watershed. Their migrations, trade routes, and kinship networks have covered the entire area for as long as they can remember, and while they are no longer a nomadic people, they continue to travel extensively and maintain their widespread marriage and kinship systems.[1] The entire upland plateau is etched with the ancient braided trails of caribou and the invisible footprints of their Naskapi pursuers, for of all the Innu, these were most dependent on the deer for their livelihood.

From October to July a mantle of wind-hardened snow impounds the frozen inland plain and all but the hardiest of its tenants in an iron grip. In summer its vast reaches are dappled with lakes, ponds, and bogs set in a filigree of interconnecting waterways, the whole of it humming like high-voltage wires with biting insects. Flying over interior Labrador, as many trans-Atlantic tourists do, is like traversing a shattered mirror. Hour after hour, as far as the eye can see, reflections of sky and glinting sun skip from shard to shard across chartreuse skeins of string bog and broad avenues of pale caribou moss dotted with families of black spruce standing smartly at attention. To the south and in the deeper valleys the spruce consolidate into forests gutted here and there by burns and rockfalls. Outcrops of scoured Canadian bedrock erupt through the vegetation, and eskers up to fifty miles long snake across the land like gigantic mole runs. For all its immensity, it is still a virgin country. Signs of man are almost non-existent except in the iron-mining areas of Schefferville and Labrador City-Wabush on the Quebec border. There the fragile high tundra has been gouged with pits and scarred in every direction by off-road tire tracks, and the watercourses draining the highlands are rusty as blood.

Water from Nitassinan spills down to the surrounding coasts in steep river channels formed by the melt of North America's last ice cap. The largest and longest of these is Kessessasskiou—the Grand River. From headwaters eight hundred miles west in Ashwanipi Lake, its waters once moved slowly north and then east, spreading out through most of the major lake systems of the plateau before gathering again to plunge three hundred feet over its lip through a luminous plume of mist that lifted rainbows above the surrounding forests. The demonic pummeling Grand Falls gave the gorge below shook the ground for miles around like the skin of a monstrous kettle drum. From the feet of the falls the Grand River drops a thousand feet in its first twenty miles, fifteen hundred by the time it reaches Lake Melville 180 miles to the east.

That is how it was before people who had never felt its grandeur began to take it away, first by changing the name to Hamilton, then Churchill River in offhand reference to men whose indifference to Labrador exceeded even their own. In 1967 Newfoundland's first and most controversial premier, J. R. Smallwood, dammed the falls for hydroelectric power, drowning much of the Innu's traditional hunting grounds under a reservoir roughly the size of Lake Ontario and emasculating one of the world's most magnificent natural wonders. The Innu were never consulted and never compensated. Nor, for that matter, was anyone else in Labrador. Construction jobs from the Churchill Falls Hydroelectric Project went mainly to Newfoundlanders, power to the United States, and revenues to Quebec (the result of a business arrangement so desperately shortsighted it boggles the mind). Newfoundland has never recovered from the embarrassment; Labrador, as usual, was left empty-handed and diminished. Today the estuary of the Grand River, as many Labradorians still prefer to call it, is choked with sand flats, and so little water runs down the Red Wine and Naskapi as a result of diversion that local residents say salmon can no longer swim upstream to spawn. The government of Newfoundland, frustrated in its attempts to reclaim rights to the power from Churchill Falls, is now focused on damming the Lower Grand River at Gull Island Rapids and Muskrat Falls. One of the dams is to be 150 feet high, the other 350 feet, and transmission lines will bisect hundreds of miles of wild, roadless country both north and south. Outside Newfoundland, only China still permits hydroelectric projects on this scale.

Other wild rivers that drop from the high plains of Nitassinan have become famous as proving grounds for experienced whitewater canoeists. The Moisie, East Main, Korak, and Kaniapiskaw are but a few that attract the purveyors and seekers of the ultimate wilderness adventure. They too are gradually being harnessed for hydroelectric power. These watercourses have always served as byways for Innu travelling between inland hunting grounds and coastal estuaries in pursuit of seasonal resources, marriage partners, and adventure. For the past two centuries they also provided access to trading posts, priests, and social services on the coast. The *coureurs du bois* of Nouvelle France, men originally imported to hew farming lands out of the Gulf Coast forests, learned to follow the Montagnais back up the Gulf rivers in their capacity as self-appointed middlemen for the trading companies. Many preferred life in the bush to farming and "went Native," introducing French genes into the bloodlines of the southern bands. Eighteenth-and nineteenth-century unions with Hudson's Bay Company employees injected an equally vigorous strain of Scots blood into the mix. The prolific Rich (originally Richards) and McKenzie clans are notable examples represented in Labrador. The Innu's widespread nomadism, small population, and exogamous marriage customs have resulted in the fact that they are in a very real sense one big extended family. Its well-mixed genetic components include Inuit, Cree, Micmac, Abenaki, and possibly Iroquois as well as European, Canadian, and American. What defines them as a people today has less to do with blood than with the intangible attributes of their culture. Innu have traditionally shared a common set of values, a colourful pantheon of spiritual entities, an elaborate system of beliefs, ritual observances and myths (even now interwoven with, rather than supplanted by, those of the Catholic Church) and a philosophy of their relationship to the land which is antithetical to that of its white colonists.[2] Most still share a native language and way of life.

Within the extended Innu family, the bands have for some time been viewed as pertaining to two main groups, the "Montagnais" of the forested mountains between the Gulf of St. Lawrence and the Grand River watershed, and the "Naskapi" (Mushuau Innu) of the tundra barrens and highlands to its north. Each environment required a somewhat different cultural adaptation. Add to this the vast disparity in exposure to new technologies and concepts between the southern and northern extremities of Nitassinan, and you have the ingredients for cultural segmentation. Due to the peripatetic habits of the people, this rift was less dramatic than it might have been, but the two groups did have distinct histories, material cultures, and even physical characteristics by the eighteenth century.

In 1861, Henry Youle Hind observed that the Naskapi were of purer stock, shorter, lighter, more delicately featured and handsome than the Montagnais,[3] whose genes by then were laced with Scots and French. But the tiny Davis Inlet band that he encountered may already have reflected European genes from HBC's Ungava and Hudson's Bay posts. Unlike the Montagnais, the Naskapi at mid-nineteenth-century still used bone, stone, and metal-tipped tools rather than firearms and wore traditional tattoos and decorated skin garments. The Rich family used them until the 1950s. These soft, whitened deerskins, with their exquisite designs so rich in symbolism and aesthetic sensibility, bear testimony to the refinement achieved by this culture at its height. They took similar pains with their persons, ornamenting themselves with tattoos and paint, men plaiting their hair with colored string and feathers, women coiling theirs neatly on either side of their head. Boats and tools were often ornamented, and every household had its carved dolls, toys, stuffed skin balls, and games.

The northern waterways of the Mushuau Innu were rarely ice-free, and their barren lands lacked the trees needed for bark canoes and lodges. Consequently, these bands lived all year in skin tents and, except for the few summer months, travelled the high plains on foot in dogged pursuit of the deer. Trapping interfered with hunting, and having little opportunity to develop a taste for European foods, religion, or alcoholic beverages, they rarely felt compelled to visit the trading posts, though they went as far as Hudson's Bay when the spirit moved them. More often they delegated an elderly tribesman or Montagnais middleman to exchange their few pelts for the little tobacco and ammunition they required. As a result, the majority of Naskapi had almost no contact with Europeans until the second half of the nineteenth century and retained much of their aboriginal culture well into the twentieth. They have often been called the last "wild Indians" of North America.

The name Naskapi originated with the Montagnais of Saguenay, who told French missionaries in the early seventeenth century that their relatives in distant Labrador were called Ounachkapiouek, or "those who live beyond the horizon," of which the name Naskapi is derivative.[4] Those Hind interviewed called themselves Tshe-tsi-uetin-euerno, the "people of the north-north-east," and claim they were once a numerous and warlike nation which inhabited all the land from Lake Mistassini to the Atlantic, a distance of nearly seven hundred miles. They also called themselves the Ne-e-no-il-no, or "the perfect people."[5]

As increasing disparities between Innu bands near the French colonies on the Gulf and those in the remote fastness of Labrador fueled the development of a subtle social hierarchy, the name Naskapi assumed a derogatory connotation and was used by each group in reference to any other they considered more remote and consequently less civilized.[6] Only the barren-ground bands now living in Davis Inlet, Labrador West, and Ft. Chimo were unable to pass the term on to a more distant neighbor. They were the end of the line. During the political awakening in the 1980s, all such distinctions were purged from Innu terminology and replaced by the overall name 'Innu.'

The Canadian government has used the term Naskapi to distinguish the Innu of Labrador from the "Status Indians" of the rest of Canada, who became legal wards of the state in 1867. When the British colony of Newfoundland and Labrador joined Canada in 1949, Labrador's Innu were granted full Canadian citizenship instead of protected status. They had voting rights and paid taxes. But their relationship to the provincial and federal governments remained ambiguous. The Newfoundland government denied them aboriginal privileges with regard to hunting and fined them for infractions of game laws from which, as Canadian native peoples, they were entitled to exemption.[7]

The Montagnais were so named by Jacques Cartier in 1536 when he encountered them on the mountainous north shore of the Gulf of St. Lawrence. They seem to have lacked a collective term for themselves but used an assortment of band names indicating the primary hunting grounds of each family group, as did the Naskapi. In central Labrador, where the Innu of the eastern Gulf of St. Lawrence hunted, the English-speaking Settlers called them "Mountaineers," and found them amiable and capable neighbors on the winter highlands.

The Montagnais of the Tadousac area, where the French initiated their fur trade in the sixteenth century, enjoyed a brief florescence by monopolizing commercial channels between the French and all Montagnais, Cree, and Huron tribes in the region. For nearly a century they had control over the terms of trade and even the price of fur. By 1630, however, the French had rearranged their alliances, the monopoly broke down, and fortune turned irrevocably against the Montagnais and, by extension, the Naskapi. Within a decade the Innu's long slide into poverty and debasement began. Tobacco undermined their health, and, during periods when it was available, liquor subverted the judgment and productivity of those nearest the posts. They toppled like dominoes under the onslaught of European diseases.

Chief Dominique told Hind in 1861 that, once, the deer had been plentiful on the plain, and the Innu had lived well and been numerous. Abundant populations of beaver and porcupine could be counted upon to supplement the caribou during off-seasons. It was when the white men gave them guns and told them to kill deer for hides and trap beavers for the tophats demanded by an aspiring European middle class that the Innu began starving. Within a century the beaver had been driven to the brink of extinction across all of inhabited Canada, and the deer could no longer be counted on to appear in their customary places. To compound the Innu's predicament, a series of immense forest fires swept across Nitassinan in the eighteenth and nineteenth centuries, denuding much of the plateau and destroying the habitat of many important game species. When game was plentiful, Dominique claimed, the tribes all lived together; once it became scarce, they split up and went to remote corners of the Labrador Peninsula, thereafter to reunite only in passing and for seasonal gatherings.[8]

The Montagnais of Quebec were first to feel the encroachment of European colonization. It began around 1620 with a handful of Settlers. By the eighteenth century, white farmsteads were filling the estuaries of Gulf coast rivers and spreading up the river valleys. With encouragement from the French government, colonists cleared the forests for land and timber and probed the hills for minerals. Fish and game populations began to decline under pressure from over-harvesting. When Canadian interests conflicted with those of the Innu, the government placed restrictions on Innu access to fish in their own rivers and on the beaver they depended upon for food. By the middle of the nineteenth century the Innu of Quebec were so hard-pressed that they petitioned the government for reserves of land and protections that would allow them to regain a degree of self-sufficiency.[9]

The Victoria Act of 1851 legislated the first Montagnais reservations on the Gulf. All the Innu were encouraged to settle and take up farming, and although few did, the reserves became their sanctuaries and centers of trade when the original King's Posts evolved into Settler villages. Meanwhile, Oblate missionaries then representing the Catholic Church at the Gulf stations sent Montagnais emissaries to lure the Naskapi from the isolation of their northern barrens. By 1860 increasing numbers were finding their way down the steep rivers from the plateau, arriving at the missions exhausted and emaciated from the six-hundred-mile journey. Most succumbed to epidemic diseases within the year. While the missionaries regretted this inevitability, they are reported to have believed that "it was better to die as a Christian than to live as a heathen."[10]

Relentless waves of epidemic illness from 1863 to 1911 coincided with an unparalleled drop in game populations on the plateau, causing hardship even more severe than that experienced by the Moravian Inuit during this same period. In 1868 when the HBC rationed the Innu's winter ammunition in an effort to compel them to trap instead of hunt, there was wholesale starvation in the interior and a general exodus toward the coasts, where the most virulent smallpox epidemic yet experienced in North America was raging. If this were not punishment enough, the growing population of Euro-Inuit Settlers was beginning to move up Labrador's river valleys into the heart of Nitassinan.

As long as Labrador's Settler population remained small enough to stay near the coasts, harvesting the river valleys in the vicinity of their winter homesteads, they were not in competition with the local Innu, who fished near the river mouths in the summer but spent most of the year on the highlands. The two groups co-existed amicably, engaging in small trade and extending assistance to one another when needed. It was only when the Settler-trapper population expanded to the point where its sons were obliged to find unclaimed "paths" ever farther up the watersheds that conflicts arose. By the 1920s what was destined to become the last generation of "real trappers" reached the 'Height of Land,' the Naskapis' final refuge.

As the twentieth century dawned on Eastern Canada, the few small Innu bands remaining in Labrador were barely subsisting on the plateau west of Nain, Kaipokok, Lake Melville, and Sandwich Bay. Nearly every year more died of starvation. The absence of game had by then forced them to rely for their survival on European foods obtainable only in exchange for furs, and trapping had become an economic necessity.

A century earlier the Innu had readily shared the productive coastal river valleys with the Europeans they considered merely visitors—having no concept of permanent colonization. As the Settlers began moving into the heart of Nitassinan, ignorant of the protocols expected of guests on Innu territory, confrontation began to seem inevitable. Labradorians now, these Settlers were invigorated by their mastery of a hard way of life, confident after more than four generations of their own inalienable rights to the land, and driven by the certain knowledge that their families' survival, too, depended on the winter's catch of furs. In 1901, when the giant Paris-based fur company of Revillon Freres established a trading post for the Innu on the opposite bank of North West River from the Hudson's Bay Company, competition drove the price of furs up to a level more in keeping with their fair market value. For the next thirty-five years many of the Lake Melville trappers, including Innu, were able to inch their way out of the abject material poverty that had so long characterized their lives. But world affairs would overtake Innu and Settler alike, bringing the fur business to a halt before confrontation escalated beyond passive resistance. Although the Innu began complaining to the traders in the first decade of the century about incursions on their hunting grounds, Settlers did not reach the Height of Land in any numbers until the 1920s, just a few years before the Depression sent the fur business into a nose-dive.

The 1930s brought all of Labrador to its knees again, and Settlers were forced to supplement their poor returns from fur and fish with meager allotments of relief from the Newfoundland government. The Innu were suddenly viewed as the responsibility of the Catholic missions, active in Labrador since HBC built the chapel of Notre Dame des Nieges at North West River in 1867. An Oblate priest rendered services there until 1895. The ministry of Monseigneur Edward O'Brien, whose correspondence affords us some relatively intimate glimpses into the Innu character, began in 1921 at North West River and extended to Davis Inlet during the summer season six years later. His dedication to the welfare of the Innu earned for him their trust and lasting devotion, for it was his charitable solicitations on their behalf that saw them through the Depression. Father O'Brien's ministry was abruptly and cruelly terminated in 1945 when care for the Innu of Labrador was transferred to the Diocese of Newfoundland.

True "relief" from the hardship of the Depression did not come to Labrador until 1941, and it came in the form of paying jobs, not welfare. The selection of Goose Bay for a major Allied air base at a time when most of the skilled American and Canadian workforce was already abroad, created an immediate need for as many strong Labrador workers as were willing to leave their impoverished fishing stations and traplines. Hundreds answered the call. Few of the Innu were interested yet in wage labour, but the exodus of Settlers from the trapping grounds gave them back their wild Nitassinan. So many Settlers abandoned their fur paths to work on the Base that all who wished to continue trapping were able to find unused paths nearer home.

Soon after Newfoundland and Labrador joined in confederation with Canada in 1949, pressure was applied on the Innu to settle down in villages. At first it took the form of compulsory schooling. But this resulted in the separation of hunters from their families and strenuous journeys back from the country with game that formerly would have been butchered and dried on the hunting grounds by the women. It turned out to be completely impractical, and in 1956 the agency responsible for Indian affairs began providing round-trip air transport for the men between the villages and hunting camps.

By 1961 Premier Smallwood's province-wide resettlement program reached the Innu. Government-issue housing began to replace tents on the south bank of North West River and on the shores of Utshimassit/Davis Inlet. In 1965 the government gave the community at North West River a small sawmill, which allowed a few men to learn employable skills and operate a business. In 1979 the North West River community became the autonomous, self-governing Innu village of Sheshatshiu. The Mushuau Innu began moving to houses in New Davis Inlet around 1967.

The incurably nomadic Innu did not thrive in the villages. Loss of independence and self-determination and a growing awareness of the fact that the ancient culture which gave meaning and worth to their lives had no value in a white environment inevitably led to a massive collapse of social cohesion and self-esteem. Alcoholism, drugs, suicide, family abuse, and any other form of self-destructive behavior the imagination could invent quickly reached epidemic proportions.[11]

In the 1970s the Innu themselves became politically active, organizing a government funded "outpost program" to transport whole families into the hunting grounds for several months a year. These self-regulated camps are said to be drug and alcohol free, and people seem happy and reinvigorated when they are once again out on the land. But the effect does not survive the inevitable return to the village, where alcohol continues to hold much of the population in thrall. It is the children, of course, who suffer most. In 1988, twenty-one youngsters at Sheshashiu attempted suicide, while the tiny community of Utshimassit/Davis Inlet made international headlines for the extent of self-annihilating behavior among its youth.

Of all the instances of "culture collapse" experienced by native people sidelined and marginalized in lands where once they reigned supreme, that of Labrador's 'perfect people' seems particularly sad because it is happening now, and none of Canada's well-intended social interventions seem capable of arresting it. If there is hope, it is in the political and social activism which has emerged within the Innu community itself, reawakening in segments of the population a sense of power, pride, and purpose which has eluded their people for so long. The Mushuau Innu band has successfully appealed for a new village site closer to its hunting grounds, in fact, at the old Sango Bay camp. Both bands have been campaigning vigorously to halt the NATO bombardments and low-level flight training that regularly shatters the tranquillity of Nitassinan. Now they and the international network of supporters they have inspired find themselves pitted against a host of new intruders, including some of the world's most powerful mining companies hungry for access to the recently discovered wealth of nickel and copper at Voisey's Bay. In opposing development prior to resolution of their land-claims suit, the Innu leadership again perceives itself to be in apposition to the Settlers, whom they characterize as pro-development and whose right to a voice in the assignation of Labrador's resources they do not recognize. Actually, both Innu and Settler populations are divided about development *per se,* and the only Labradorians with even a token voice in resource use are the two official aboriginal associations whose native land-claims suits are pending.

The strongest card in the hand of Labrador's Innu is the fact that, like the Inuit, they are among the few Canadian tribes that have never signed a treaty, never become wards of the state, never accepted less than full citizenship, never given up their lands.[12] It remains to be seen whether justice will prevail in the courts when the land-claims suits of Labrador's native peoples are at long-last settled. What is clear is that in defending Labrador's great wilderness environment and the option to chose non-industrial economic activities that can only be pursued in a wilderness environment, like eco-tourism, the Innu are providing a vital counter-balance to powerful outside forces who see Labrador merely as an unpeopled wasteland to be plundered at will. While some are increasingly willing to reach a compromise with the Settlers and Inuit who espouse modest, controlled levels of development, they are earning through their courage and political stamina a role in the stewardship of Nitassinan which is theirs by birthright.

We have dwelt at length on the Innu because, unlike the Settlers, they have only begun to tell their own stories to the outside world. Few of the Innu narratives collected by *Them Days* divulge much of their character and soul. I have therefore taken the liberty of using excerpts from narratives and published statements about the Innu where first-hand accounts would have been preferred.

For their part, the Labrador trappers have told their story well. Little need be added by way of introduction. Those who participated in the climax of the Labrador fur trade in western Lake Melville recall a life of unbridled freedom, fraternity, and glory burnished, in hindsight, by the very real hardships they endured. The "Height-of-Landers," as the young men who opened new territory on the inland plateau were called, were on the trapping grounds six to nine blisteringly cold months a year, usually alone, sleeping in tiny log "tilts" or in the snow, eating bannock, tea, and whatever game they could get. Most were strict in their observation of the Sabbath, a carry-over from beliefs passed down from family progenitors such as Ambrose Brooks and Daniel Campbell. Some travelled over three hundred miles inland to reach their paths, lining canoes up steep rapids before the rivers froze, hauling gear behind them on sleds after snowfall, and trudging on snowshoes through deeply drifted paths in temperatures that rarely rose above -20° F. By the end of the trapping era, the men from Sandwich Bay were meeting men from St. Augustine and Lake Melville on the high Montagnais country between the Lake and the Gulf. Melville men also met the northern Naskapi as far inland as Michikamau and Lobstick Lakes.

For every heroic trapper there was an equally heroic wife in an isolated cabin near the shore, keeping her family fed, warm, and well as best she could. She hunted rabbits and partridges, fished for trout through holes in the ice, often tended traplines of her own, fended off bears and wolves, bore and buried children, melted snow for water, chopped wood, weathered illness, suppressed loneliness and fear, made handicrafts to sell and clothing for the family, repaired nets for her husband's summer fishing and sealing, and travelled miles to deliver babies and tend neighbors in need. Fortunately, Labrador women have not been reticent about their lives, and they have left us some excellent accounts of trapping life from their perspective, like Elizabeth Goudie's award-winning *Woman of Labrador*.[13]

Yet another chapter in the history of Nitassinan is that of early "adventure tourists" from American cities, men and women lured to the wilds of Labrador in search of a chance to experience the continent's fast disappearing wilderness. As this is a book by and about the Labradorians, the reader will find only passing references to such visitors in these accounts. However, most of the tourists made certain their adventures would be immortalized in print, with the result that there is an extensive literature available for those interested in this genre. Two of these episodes have attained a place in the oral history of Labrador: the tragic 1903 Wallace-Hubbard trip most recently retold in the novel *Great Heart* by James West Davidson and John Rugge,[14] and the equally ill-fated Koehler expeditions, known only from the first-hand accounts of Labradorians who encountered this awesome, driven man and his unfortunate son. Johnny Michelin guided Koehler's 1928 trip, Innu met Koehler's last party just before all perished, and Jim Saunders retrieved one of the bodies. The book Koehler was writing about his trips seems never to have been published.

It is fashionable today to judge the past in terms of the present, the "other" in terms of ourselves. But the reader who approaches these narratives with an animal-rights, feminist, or Innu vs. Settler bias will miss the point and deprive himself of an opportunity to observe the real dynamics of history in action. Settler accounts of trapping life allow us to begin to imagine what life in the interior was like for the taciturn Innu, who lived there permanently, travelled many hundreds of miles each year, were even more severely debilitated by ill health and hunger than the Settlers, and who were obliged to use more primitive trapping and hunting methods for lack of effective hardware. Both groups deserve enormous respect. That they had to confront each other over rights to a land each had "earned" was, as both acknowledged in actions if not in words, regrettable, but no ones "fault."

The future of Nitassinan is another matter, subject to our present concepts of justice for indigenous people. It is devoutly to be wished that through the exercise of law or public indignation the courts return to the Innu, Inuit, and Settlers of Labrador the right to determine how their land is used, and how it may be developed so that it can sustain both the economic well-being and the wildness of this unique and wonderful country.

According to Joe Rich the deer have decreased greatly in the last ten to fifteen years. Joe thinks it's due to Indian killings. He speaks of ten years ago on George River when over a thousand caribou were killed with spears alone....

Now, Joe says, deer come to an area near Indian House Lake, smell Indians and turn back to Deer House. Only a few wander along river or out to the coast where Indians hunt them now. It is this decrease of deer that led Edward Rich's band and the Naskapi to stop wintering in the interior. Few living men have seen Deer House Mountain, and those only with a spyglass. Maybe, Joe says, the mountain can be seen from the ocean for it is very high.

Many years ago a *météo* [conjurer] went to the mountain. He found two doors in the rock, very large, going down. He went down and there were many people, like Indians, there. Finally he was taken to a lower room and saw an assistant chief and, at last, still lower where he saw the Deer god.

He did not say what the Deer god looked like. No one knows save, possibly, some *météos*.

In this house were foxes as big as wolves, deer with human heads, spotted and all kinds of deer. There were big wolves there, too.

[The *météo*] became unconscious and when he came to was on top of a mountain east of Indian House Lake, from which Deer House can just be seen with a spy glass. He returned and after him came many deer to the Indians but very soon after he died. All men who go to Deer House die, hence now no one goes there. But to see this House with a spy glass brings good luck, but the man [spying] may die.

This Deer House Mountain is said to be close to the coast and in the Barren Grounds. All sand and grotesquely worn boulders [like men]. No trees there or large rocks. It is in this house that the 'man who married a deer' lives.

The Deer god has five names:
1. *Te pe nam we su* (Chief Indian god)
2. *Kama pene gas tci uhi* (archaic, meaning lost)
3. *ut nim at tci zu* (Giver of food)
4. *Puk we cem ni magin* (Giver of food to hunters)
5. *Tcam i cum inu* (Grandfather of all)

This seems to be the main deity of these people. He is superior to *Nitan*, the chief of the deer, and lives in a lodge, perhaps the Deer House. He appears in dreams and gives songs to men, which are sung individually accompanied by drum, as prayers for good hunting. The deity sees all that a man does and knows what he thinks. Consequently, if a man does wrong, especially violates caribou taboos, he will have bad luck and probably die soon.

The design [inverted triangle with neck line and head sphere] symbolizes the Deer god and is worn by a *météo* on the back vent of his painted coat. Such a picture is called a *mistapiu, mistapiuits* [plural], or guardian spirits of conjurers.

When Naskapi—North West River [Sheshashiu] people—kill a fox or a deer in pairs, game belongs to the person who did not kill it.

When a boy kills his first deer, his father takes it and gives it to [his own father]. The deer is dried in the house and the guts are burned, then all people [the boy included] come and eat it. The skin is taken outdoors and is kept by the grandfather. After eating, drum is played [with singing and dancing].

A corral was made in the winter time and men, behind, drove the deer into the V made by the women and children. One man runs behind the deer when they are in the corral, with a *babiche* [untanned deerhide] line to keep them in. Men shoot with guns and bows and arrows. Sometimes as many as five hundred are caught. Joe Rich saw this once when he was a little boy. *Akat* [Rich] helped at such drives. Sometimes there were so many deer they could not all get in the corral. Old corrals are still to be seen this side of George River but well in the country.

Edward Rich killed his first deer with bow and arrow. The arrow had a bone dart point. Old times stone heads were used. Arrows had loose stone/bone points. Sticks were scarce and this way they could be used over again and again. Bone points were plenty. Deer arrows were three feet long and feathered.

When hunters sighted deer, one man, said to be lucky, fired first. He shoots deer on the outer edge of the herd, away from the hunters. Then whichever way the deer ran the leaders were shot, then they went wild and all were shot.

When a man wants deer he puts this [vertebrae] outside on a stick at night. In the morning he looks at it. If there is blood or deer hair on the bottom edge means he will kill deer. They say it looks like a deer's face.

The deer spear is light and short, four feet long with a knob at the end. The old type had a bone point, new ones have knife-sharp iron points. The spear is held in the teeth of the bow paddler when approaching swimming deer. When close enough, the paddler takes the spear in his right hand and stabs the deer through the back, under the ribs, with a downward thrust followed by an upward probe for the heart. If the heart is hit the deer dies and floats, if not the deer swims to the bank and dies on shore. One man may kill a hundred or more in a day.

Occasionally an albino deer is seen. If it is killed, good luck results and many deer will be killed. But if it is seen and not killed, then the luck is bad.

Dwarf deer are also seen and killed occasionally. Tracks are seen between those of large deer. These are exactly like caribou and go with them. They are called ma tak wa ti hus. They are said to be borne by male deer, carried in a sack in their skin in various places for six years and dropped full-grown but small. These dwarf deer never have bott fly holes in the skin.

If three men kill game the one who shoots stands still while the other two race for it. The first to reach it gets the game. This applied to everything even silver foxes. If a man is alone he keeps the fox, but deer was usually given away to others.

Joe Rich told about when he, Tuma, and Shinabest saw a silver fox. Joe and Tuma argued about shooting as each wanted the fox. Finally Joe shot, taking a puff of fur out. The fox chased the fur thinking it was a mouse. Then Tuma shot and did the same thing. Finally Tuma killed the fox and Shinabest, who came up then, ran and got it.

When a hunter returns from hunting he doesn't say what he killed, just says he killed some partridges if it was a deer, porcupine if it was a bear, *carcajou* [wolverine] if it was a big bear. If he sees bear or deer footing he says he saw some signs of partridge.

When a lot of deer are killed the horns are put up on posts or trees, never the whole skull. Head bones are crushed and eaten. The hair is put where the wind will blow it away. Dogs are given the guts and meat, if necessary, but never head bones or long bones.

Long bones are ground up and eaten. Gut are sometimes cleaned, smoked, boiled, or fried. It is very bad luck if dogs gnaw on the heads or the horns. Big bones are cracked, the marrow is eaten and the bones are pounded and boiled in a kettle to make grease. This must not be dropped on the floor in the tent—it will cause bad luck in the hunt. A table-cloth is always spread.

Joe says eight bones must not be sold: humorous and femurs. The meat, if sold, must have those bones cut out or all luck ceases. These are marrow bones.

— William Duncan Strong,
Rawson-Macmillan Expedition
1927-28 Field Notes
[16.3:3]

I WAS BORN SOMEWHERE IN the country near Fort Chimo, Atikumek Nipi. My mother was Mary Jeanne Rich (daughter of Joe) and my father was John Pasteen. Charles James was my baptized name, but a long time ago people started calling me Tsinish. It means 'old man.'

We spent our lives then travelling back and forth from Fort Chimo to Davis Inlet. Sometimes I used canoe, sometimes I walked. It would take about four days and four nights from Davis Inlet to Fort Chimo. Sometimes we travelled many days without food. A lot of people were hungry. When a person had no food for his family he would dig holes in the ice and put a net in, shoving a line from one hole to another until it went the length of the net, and then tied the net to the line. They would catch *stikumek* and *mikuasheu* [suckers]. We would use the suckers for bait. There were a lot of them.

The people mostly ate fish in the country. The caribou would be hanging around near the camps. That's why the people got caribou so easy. Sometimes the caribou would swim in the river and the people would chase them using canoes, and then stab them with a long piece of sharp metal or a rock tied to the end. I never used a bow and arrows but I heard some people talking about it, those who used it before. I was about twenty when I first shot a caribou. We used everything from the caribou except for the stuff in the stomachs. Sometimes it was really hard to find food in the winter.

Today I miss it a lot, the places where I used to go hunting and fishing. I knew all the places when I could still walk in the country.

The white men [Herman Koehler, Cornell, and Jim Martin] who died in the country were going to travel from Fort Chimo. They were going to travel down the George River and follow the river out to Upatik then go to Davis Inlet. My *nukumish* [father-in-law] saw them many times. The last time he saw them was when they started to travel down the George River. A lot of people saw them and the Innu people gave them some caribou meat. My grandfather told them which way to go, but he thought the white people travelled very slow. Another Innu told them which way to go but the leader said, "No."

I was still young, not yet married, the year those men died. We were coming from Fort Chimo. It was summer when I saw them. They were looking for George River, so I showed them the mountains and told them George River was over there. I told them to follow the river. My uncle seen them when they were almost reaching the George River. The leader, the big man, told the Innu people they were going towards Notakuan River, then cut in through to Davis Inlet. They were only about fifteen miles from George River. We communicated by using signs. The Innu told them to go to Nain, that was a short cut. Notakuan River is a long way in. It was starting to snow and they would not make it. Their leader didn't want anyone to show him where to go.

The last time they were seen they were in good health but their food was almost gone and they were not wearing heavy clothing. There is a river with a lot of rapids where I last saw them. The river has no name.

The next spring my mother found the fat man's body near the path. He must have gotten sick and died, but he didn't starve because he was still fat. The Innu left him where my mother found him and went out to tell everybody at Davis Inlet what they found. Later my father went in to help get the body. A plane went to pick up the body, which was wrapped in canoe canvas. The body was very heavy. That body was found by the side of the trail where the Innu people used to portage their canoes.

About five years later the little man was found inside the tent where he died. The only thing left was his bones. My brother Katshinak found him. They should have found him a long time before but they didn't know where to look for him. Then a few years later they [the Rangers] wanted to find him, only then was he found. The Ranger, Jim Saunders, Gilbert Saunders, and Katshinak were the ones who went to look for the other two bodies. They used dogteams.

The man with the gold tooth was not found, so maybe it was Jim Martin who starved to death. Maybe the other man drowned. The Innu heard shooting in the fall, after they had seen the three white men. Maybe it was a signal. The Innu thought it was other Innu people shooting.

I saw the place where the white men tore up a canoe and made a sled. They must have been starving when it started to get cold. They had a net and some hooks with them. Maybe they put a net out where they camped. When it got frosty they may have headed to the woods. [16.3:16]

It was very hard a long time ago when everybody was starving. Once I was one of those people that were starving.

When there was lots of caribou tracks everybody would start to look for the caribou. Sometimes they would get caribou and then give it to the other people who didn't have any. Sometimes they got over a hundred caribou. There used to be old-time guns. It was hard to find bullets for those old guns in the country. Once when I was using one of those old guns I froze my hands. Today the guns are very good and with them you can get lots of caribou.

The Innu from North West River and Schefferville would go up to George River and get food from the people up there. Those people from George River sold caribou skins and mittens and bought tea, matches, tobacco and bullets. They didn't get any flour. The Innu didn't eat flour in the country, they just ate caribou and other meat.

The old people were good at hunting. When there were lots of partridges they used to shoot them with bows and arrows. I'm not very good with bow and arrows. When we were starving I wasn't very strong.

One time a lady, her husband and her son left the tribe because everybody was starving. After a while the lady's husband couldn't walk anymore so the lady and her son made a fire for him and left him. They went to George River to get help. After they got to George River they saw some caribou and the son got six of them. The old lady told the people at George River about her husband and the people who were starving to death. That was in the springtime. They had a tent made of caribou skin and a bit of canvas. They didn't bother going to look for the other people—she knew they were dead. The place was far away from George River. That old lady was very old when she died.

The Innu used to chase the caribou when they were swimming across the lakes. Caribou usually swim cross the rivers and the lakes. Some ladies were very good at stabbing the caribou with knives. My mother was very good at it and my father was good at it too.

My mother said one time, when everybody was following a river, they found a deer which had died. The deer didn't smell bad so they skinned it. While they were going to the lake, following the river, they saw lots of dead caribou. The place is called 'Tsinuat Tivis' (Big Brain). The river had big falls on it and the caribou were trying to cross, couldn't do it and fell down over the falls until a lot of deer were dead. They were forced off the falls because the water was too swift. After the caribou fell off the falls and there were a lot of caribou at the bottom, the place was called 'Tsinuativis.' Another place was called 'Katsnatnest' (death for the caribou). The people were not starving then, they had lots of food. Lots of people were skinning the caribou and they saved some meat for the wintertime.

The Innu had lots of *mukushans* [feasts] when there was lots of caribou.

A long time ago when everybody was starving they would go to George River. Everybody knew there was lots of food at George River. Every time there's caribou up in George River. Everybody used to spend time there. Where the dead caribou were found was where they made snowshoes and they got caribou skin for the tents. One time the Innu never used canvas.

— Tshinish Pasteen
[16.3:44]

IN THE OLD DAYS, WHEN I was about twelve years old, I had been hunting for quite a while then. My father had already taught me how to kill small game, like partridges, snare rabbits and recognize animal tracks, some that I still haven't seen, but which I was told by my father that I would be trying to catch in make-shift traps some day. I came to trap by myself in later years but not so much with the old style of trapping as with the modern steel trap.

Anyway, when I was still twelve years old, I made my first caribou kill with a friend of mine. It's a place called Kauanashit in Indian. This friend of mine was Matthew. That day we set off by ourselves. Usually Dad came along because he was teaching us the ways of hunting.

That day was very cold. We could hardly pull the trigger with our bare fingers when we saw the caribou. Finally after much fumbling with the trigger, I squeezed off a shot. That first shot hit the caribou in the leg. The next shot killed the second caribou. The wounded animal got away from us but we didn't let that worry us. We knew somebody would be able to track it down later.

We didn't attempt to skin the caribou after the kill. We hadn't been taught that yet. It was so cold we went home. Next day Dad accompanied us to where the caribou was. He showed us how to skin it. He let us do it because he was the teacher. It took us a long time to finish the job. We did the skinning bare-handed and that day was just as cold as the day before. We had a hard time to keep from crying from the cold. We finally finished the job. It seemed like that job took forever to finish.

Afterwards we were congratulated by everybody at camp. It was a good feeling to have contributed something to our families. Right there and then we became hunters as the men were. I am over seventy years old now and I still hunt. When I think of them days, that first caribou kill was the one I remember most.

— Michel Pasteen
[1.4:4]

I WAS BORN AT SEVEN Islands on June 2, 1902. I was ten years old when my father arrived at North West River, Labrador. I have spent most of my life here at North West River. When I was fifteen years old I killed my first caribou with bow and arrow. There was no guns to kill animals with, we used bow and arrow. There was no traps either so we used devices we made ourselves to trap the animals. It would be set up in a tree. The tree would be bent back and when the animal stepped into the snare the tree would spring up and the animal would be caught.

My father used to trap around Fort Chimo. They would haul sleds from Fort Chimo to Seven Islands.

When we went to the woods, trapping, from Seven Islands, we went a long ways. When we wanted to sell our furs we wanted to go the shortest route. We were closer to North West River so we came here. When we first came, Hudson's Bay Company had a trading post on the north side. We traded our furs to them. There was nothing much in the store and not many people. There was a bit of flour in the store but we couldn't buy very much. Maybe we could have enough to mix a bread once a week. That was all we could get. We used to trade with Hudson's Bay Company until another store was built on the south side, but I don't remember the name [Revillon Freres].

In the fall we would leave Seven Islands to come to North West River in canoes. When the lakes froze up we'd make sleds and haul our stuff over the snow. This wasn't a straight trip; we'd trap along the way. We camp maybe a week here, a week there. Sometimes they used to kill caribou when they were coming out through the mountains. This was the only way they could get food. Now you can get everything you want in the store.

—Joseph Nuna
[2.1:6]

Sept. 6, 1922

During the years that no priest visited Hamilton Inlet, they [Innu] kept alive the faith by occasional visits to the Gulf Posts. Nearly every year some few of the men would get in touch with the Canadian priests in the Gulf, and bring back to the others such objects of piety as beads, medals and crucifixes. But during these years by far the larger number had no opportunity of receiving the Sacraments. The Gulf Posts, some hundreds of miles away, were altogether too far from their hunting grounds to be visited annually. But every year they came to North West [River], came filled with the expectancy of meeting the Priest and receiving the Sacraments, but were doomed to disappointment and forced to return again to their hunting grounds, deprived of the spiritual comforts they valued more highly than all their material returns. They witnessed the taking down of their little church; they saw their bell being shipped back to Canada; they saw themselves utterly abandoned as far as the church was concerned, but still they clung to their Old Faith. Nothing could persuade them or entice them to have any intercourse with the religious sects.... Finally they decided that they would no longer come to North West Post and it was then that the companies [HBC and Revillon Freres] made their appeal on behalf of the Indians. They say that three messages were sent: one to Your Lordship, one to the Archbishop of St. John's and one to Hon. Tasker Cook. It was then that Father Dinn was sent in the year 1920. We followed last year and this.

— Frs. S. Whalen & E.J. O'Brien
from a letter to John March,
Bishop of Harbour Grace, Nfld.
[10.3:8]

Hudson's Bay Company
Labrador District Office
St. John's, Nfld.

20th February, 1933

Rev. Father O'Brien,
Northern Bay,
Bay de Verde, Nfld.

Dear Father O'Brien:

Knowing that you take a deep and active interest in the material as well as the spiritual welfare of the Labrador people, I feel that you will be grieved to learn that the fur hunt of the present season has been almost a complete failure, and in consequence the natives, who depend largely upon each industry as the seasons roll around to supply their needs, and who, as a result of the low price of codfish last summer found themselves more heavily in debt than ever, are now faced with even worst conditions than exist here in Newfoundland, where even the able-bodied may receive support in the form of dole, and help from other charitable institutions.

Unfortunately there are those who write articles which to say the least of them are very misleading, particularly when coming from those supposed to be conversant with living conditions of the Labrador Natives, who brand them as a lazy and irresponsible lot. Naturally such writings from influential sources have their due effect upon authorities, whom we fear may, as a result, consider that their efforts to render assistance have been misdirected....

Recently we received a telegram from Mr. Budgell, whom I think you know is not an alarmist, advising us that destitution was rife in the Rigolet district, which information we passed along to the Secretary of State, (whom I might say right here we have found to be very broadminded and ready to consider any reasonable proposition submitted to him) receiving reply which leaves us to think that he has an exaggerated conception of our responsibilities and may have been influenced by someone unfriendly disposed towards the Company, to believe that we are deriving large profits from our Labrador business, and that possibly might even think we encourage the issue of relief with a view to profit, regardless of the financial position of the country or its taxpayers, who after all have to foot the bills.

If such an opinion of our operations and our methods of doing business is entertained by the authorities, I imagine our shareholders would be glad not only to enlighten them, but be pleased to transfer the heavy losses which they have consistently met with during the past ten years. As a matter of fact, anyone who is intimately acquainted with the Company's methods as you are, and know what native debts we have to write off year after year, wonder why we carry on, and really I cannot answer without feeling that it is part of the game of the fur trade, and like the old prospector who always expects the next find to be a good one, we have like hopes for the next fur season....

Yesterday we received a telegram from Mr. Peters, who is our manager there [Davis Inlet], reading as follows:-

"Furs exceptionally scarce natives have no means of support am unable to get through on relief authorized."

Upon receipt of this telegram we intended to refer it to the Secretary of State for action in the matter, but in view of his previous attitude we decided to advise you and will be governed by any suggestion you care to make which will have for its object the desired result.

We almost dread to hear from our Northern Eskimo Posts, namely, Makkovik, Hopedale, Nain, Okak and Hebron, which as you are aware, we are responsible for in the matter of relief in return for a duty concession presently existing applicable to these posts. Although we have not shirked this responsibility nor do we complain now, it has been a costly bargain to us but of immense benefit to the natives attached to these posts.

Before closing I might add that due to your good offices the Indians at North West River were provided with necessary food supplies last summer to enable them to go inland and engage in the usual hunt. We do not know how they have fared since, but it is just as well to be prepared for the worst, as if the hunt elsewhere can be taken as a criterion in that part of the country 'in which they move and have their being,' in all probability the government authorization of $125 will be but a drop in the bucket towards paying their urgent needs.

Doubtless I have painted a most unpleasant picture dear sir of conditions in Labrador as I see them, but I am not without hope that if we all co-operate and continue to play the game, and above all remove distrust where it is unjustified, we shall win through.

With kind regards and best wishes,
I remain,
Yours very sincerely,
Hayward Parsons

[10.3:13]

Northern Bay
23rd November, 1938

Hon. J.C. Puddester
Commissioner, Dept. Public Health & Welfare
St. John's

Dear Sir,

Acting on information received from Davis Inlet, Labrador, that due to abnormal conditions of travelling, and an unusual scarcity of Deer and fur, a number of Indians were at the point of starvation, I interviewed you in January last about the situation. You were good enough to instruct by wireless Ranger Guzzwell of Hopedale to investigate the matter and relieve if necessary the Indians.

A reply was received that Ranger Guzzwell had handed over the matter to [another] Ranger who had found work for the Indians at Voisey's Bay.

If I was not thoroughly familiar with Indian life, this reply would have given me an easy mind.... Subsequent events justified my doubts, and my personal investigation during the past summer warrant this report to you of the Ranger's inhuman treatment of approximately forty starving Indians....

Here are the facts as gathered from the Indians themselves and from reliable native sources.

In late December 1937, some Indian men came out to Davis Inlet reporting no deer but plenty wolves. That meant no food.

In early January the Hudson's Bay Manager enabled these Indians to return to their families with some supplies.

Late in the month Chief Susapish and more men arrived to report their families starving. The men returned with food in the teeth of a raging blizzard. More and more men kept returning, and about the beginning of the last week in January, the Ranger took over the situation, contending that he would give no relief to the Indians unless they went to Voisey's Bay where deer was falsely reported plentiful and where work would be provided for them. That was an intolerable condition to impose on a number of families whose hunting territory was in a different locality altogether. It involved little hungry children in a journey of approximately fifty miles. One hunter elected to remain with his wife and children and according to the dictum of the Ranger to starve for he would give him no relief. Those who took [the Ranger] at his word were given twenty-five pounds of flour and one quarter pound of tea for a large family and for a small family, the flour was reduced to fifteen pounds. With those meager supplies the journey was undertaken under the most frightful conditions of weather. After a week of extreme hardship Voisey's Bay was reached only to find no relief measures and no work....

In the month of March, the Indians in desperation, decided to return to Davis Inlet and but that Providence had provided one hunting chief with some deer meat, they must all have perished....

When Davis Inlet was finally reached, it was an emaciated band of Indians who staggered in to the Hudson's Bay Company Post.

There is plenty of comment I may make on the Ranger's interpretation of his authority, but the above facts are such to give meaning to what I stated in an interview to the Daily News after my arrival home in August, 'that I am heartily sick of Nit Wits clothed in the symbolic dress of Authority.'

Yours faithfully,
E.J. O'Brien

[10.3:13]

Nutak
Aug. 31st, 1948

Dear Father O'Brien,

We have left Davis Inlet and are going to live in Nutak.

We don't know yet whether it will be better or not but we are going to try it and hope to get more deer that there are in Davis Inlet. We are sorry to leave the Church and we are sorry because we haven't seen the priest. Last year we had a hard winter, three children starved because we were too far in the country and bad weather stopped us before we coud go to Davis Inlet. We ask for your blessing. We don't forget you and we ask you to pray for all of us. Everyone very well now. We ask you to try, if you can't come yourself, to send a priest to see us. Some of our babies are not baptized and some of our young people want to be married. I buried the children who starved, we

*had to leave them in the country. We have no books now, prayer books, and wish you
would send some.*

Good-bye Eamea Appessech,
Joe Rich
[Written for Joe Rich by Max Budgell]

[10.3.26]

I THINK THE FIRST SAUNDERS and the first Perrys (my mother's people) came from Newfoundland, but I always called meself part Innu. I'm not but I grew up with them, know the language, so I feel that I'm part Indian. They were my playmates from the time I was eight years old. Mom and Dad took a little Indian boy and reared him from ten years old 'till he was old enough to be married. He was never adopted but he was just the same as one of our own. His Indian name was Nowishamanku but we called him Sol. All his people died off with the Flu and he was left with an aunt. They had a big family and times were hard. I was in St. Anthony goin' to school so Mom and Dad took him. The rest of the Indians looked to 'en like one of our family. He died in 1947 and is buried over here at Traverspine. I always called him my Indian brother. That's what we were like, brothers. [16.3:16]

Gilbert Saunders was my cousin, eleven years older than me. I learned a good lot from 'en, good and bad as well. When he was teachin' me how to handle the dogs, steer them through the woods, he'd be sittin' up on the box, drivin' 'um through the woods, crooked path, and I'd be jumpin' from one side to the other, 'fraid of me life I was goin' to hit a tree. If I hit a tree he'd hammer me with the whip end. Sometimes I'd be on the komatik cryin' and steerin'. I was so scared of 'en, you know. But 'twas all for me own good. I could steer a komatik, I guarantee you, when I was sixteen or seventeen. I could jump from one side to the other fast. I learned young. Everything I learned about trappin', huntin', and travellin', Gil was the man that taught me. He's the man that made me the man I is today. He was a hard boss and a good boss.

You'd never be lonely with Gil around. One time we was in the country and I had four muskrats killed. Gil skinned 'um out and had them in the tent. I was an awful hand to sleep, when I'd get to sleep I could sleep. Anyway, in the morning Pop—that's what we called Gil later—he woke me just before daylight.

"Go down to the well, boy, and get some water. We got to boil the kettle, soon be gettin' daylight."

I hauled on me boots and went down over the bank to the well in the brook. There was something on the ice right 'longside the water hole—muskrat skins, two of 'um. Now where in the world did that come from? How did me muskrat skins get there? I never thought about Gil. I got me water and went on back. Gil was sittin' up.

"Cripes," I said, "Look what I found, boy, two of me muskrat skins down by the well. How the dickens did they get down there?"

He start' to laugh. "I went down for water," he said, "and I wore them for mitts."

Two muskrat skins turned inside out for mitts, hair inwards. He wanted a cup of tea. He left the skins down there so when I went to get water I'd find them.

Gil was a big, heavy man. I was only skinny and I'm not very fat yet, but when I was that age I was right thin and always cold. Soon as we'd get in the tent I'd have a cup of tea, Gil would lie down and go to sleep and I'd get to sleep about ten. When I went to sleep I'd sleep solid. Four o'clock Gil would be up, finished his sleep. He'd be sittin' up alone and then he's start pickin' at me. He'd gather up the candle wax and make two plugs and shove 'um up me nose, cut off me air. I'd be right up then, just about smothered, candle wax shoved up me nostrils. He used to do some awful stuff to me but for all that he didn't mean no harm, it was just his way. Everywhere he went, if he had to take a trip or anything, 'twas, "Jim, come along boy."

I went with Gil when he was out lookin' for Gillingham.

I think 'twas Bill Coish asked me one time if I knew the "White Eskimo."

I said, "Yes, boy, I knowed 'en well."

He asked me what I thought of the book, *The White Eskimo*.[15] I told 'en "I never read the book but I heard about it. As far as I'm concerned 'tis a bunch of damn lies about what he done." I said, "I knowed Gillingham. It don't say in the book where he was took prisoner and kept in Nain in the old hospital for four or five months, waitin' for his trial. They took old Mark's body right from Okak Bay and hauled 'en to Cartwright for an autopsy." I knowed it, see, I knowed the story. I was one of the ones that was lookin' for Gillingham.

"He was poisonin' the foxes in the country and the Newfoundland Ranger heard about it and he went up, Gil and I went with 'en. We never found anything. They claimed he was goin' along pickin' up foxes that wasn't even in trap and wasn't even shot. This was Gillingham. And this Indian girl he was supposed to have picked up, I knows who she was, too.

Old Bill Carson was standin' 'longside us, "By Christ, Jim, you knows the score on it don't you."

I said, "You better believe I do."

Gillingham wasn't a tall man but he was blocky. He used to wear a black bearskin coat and a black bearskin cap. I don't know if that's what they were goin' by in the book about all his hair. I read parts of the book afterwards but I couldn't read it, I'd get too cross. My brother-in-law, Joe Ford, he got the book up there in Nain. Joe said he tried to read the book but he'd get so cross, to see the stuff that was put in there, he'd heave it down.

Ranger Mercer should be able to contradict the book 'cause he was the one who went up there and took Gillingham prisoner. He and David Barbour, an Eskimo feller, went up. David was the driver, and he stayed outside the ballicaters, wouldn't go inside the house with Mercer. Like Mercer said, he didn't know what he was up against and he knew if he went there after dark he'd catch 'en in the house. Gillingham never put up no fight. He could have broke Mercer off like a match, I mean, the size of him. Gillingham was a cop one time. He was a powerful man there was no doubt about that. He respected the uniform and he went with Mercer, no trouble at all.

That was quite a trip. We had to go over the Kiglapait. You leave Nain and to go to Port Manvers you got to go another fifty or sixty miles to a point, then 'tis something like going to North West River, you go away off and then you got to come back almost where you started from, but at Port Manvers you can cross the hills, the portage. It's high, one of the highest mountains in Labrador. You have to go over with your dogs. There's a brook you got to go through and sometimes that's fulled up with snow, but you can go down with a couple of drugs on, but sometimes its quarred ice and then you got to lower the komatik down because you can't ride it down. I'd say it's about twenty-five miles across on the top and 'tis real barren. A storm could catch you anywhere so you got to know how to make a snowhouse. Of course you generally always wait for good weather to go across....

There was an American up there, Captain Macmillan. He built a house up in Anaktalik. He had a party of men with 'en, stayed there all winter. Now there was a scientist, Dr. [Duncan] Strong, and he was there to find out all about the Indian people, where they lived, where they travelled and all this. So, anyway, they came to Davis Inlet and I could speak the Indian language and knew the Indian country quite a bit. He said the Indians were gone to Big Bay and he'd like for me to go over with 'en, so we took a canoe and went over. But the Indians went over around the end of August and we didn't go until around the end of September so they were gone on.

We thought we might catch them. Now you go up the river for about twenty-five miles and then you come to a big lake, then another brook and another big lake. I thought we might catch them there 'cause that was a very good place for caribou, but when we got there the Indians was gone and I didn't know which way they was gone. From that we couldn't go in canoe, we had to walk over the hill, overland, you know.

We never found them, found some of their campin' place and we picked up a few sticks what they roasted their meat and fish on. Anyway, I had those arrow and spear heads and I was tellin' Dr. Strong about them. I told him where I found them and that. He told me to let him have them and he would take them back to the States and sell them and send me back the money. So I give 'en everything I had. That's the last I seen of my arrow and spear heads, everything and he too. The money must be hold up in the mail somewhere 'cause I never did see it....

The Indians was up in Nutak for one year. They didn't like it there. There was no woods only close to the salt water. It's not the same as Davis Inlet where the woods goes back a hundred or hundred-fifty miles. Up in Nutak they could only go twenty or twenty-five miles and they were out of woods. Where the caribou was it was barren land. Indians don't go on barren land because they got to have their tents and they got to be able to cook their food, they don't eat anything that isn't cooked. They got to have their meat roasted or cooked in a boiler. They couldn't make a go of it at Nutak so they travelled back to Davis Inlet. Then the store was opened up for them again and started to build up for them....

— Jim Saunders
[13.2:17]

1773, Jan. 6

To the Right Honorable Earl of Dartmouth, His Majesty's Secretary of State for the American Department, First Lord of Trade and Plantations, &c, &c, &c.

...The Furring Business requires a thorough knowledge of the interior part of the country which, on account of the deep snows and the rigour of the furring season, is only to be acquired by slow degrees. The country furnishes no other subsistence to the furrier than what his traps provide him, and these require a wide extent of ground to have any tolerable success. In order to penetrate to any distance, each furrier (for they all separate and hunt singly) must, at short distances one from another, build himself huts to live in, proof against bad weather, so that he shall never be too far from shelter in case of storms. Hence it is easy to conceive that, to fur that country properly, each adventurer should have an exclusive right; and otherwise that it never will be practised, except in a very insignificant manner just around the Sealing Posts, by way of something to do at idle times....

All which is most humbly submitted by

Your Lordship's most respectful and most obliged Servant
Geo. Cartwright

[9.3:26]

The territory at and around North West River as far as Hopedale toward the coast [about 100 miles to the north] had been the best of the Indian hunting ground for generations past, but these last few years the [Settlers]...and Newfoundlanders have been making a regular business of trapping, some of them having as many as three to six hundred traps set during the hunting season. In doing this they have overrun the Indian hunting grounds. The Indians are continually complaining to me about the matter, for, as hunting is their only means of living, they are getting poorer every year. Indeed but for the relief which has been given them at the expense of the Government of Canada some of them would surely have starved. They are becoming very bitter against the white trappers and any year trouble may break out.

— Raoul Thevenet
Revillon Freres Trading Company, 1909
Armitage, *The Innu*, p. 47

MYSELF, WILLIAM MONTAGUE, HENRY GROVES, Charlie Goudie and Arch Goudie were the first white men that went in there to trap among the Indians....They didn't like it. They tried to drive us out every way....We were young men then and we didn't care how much, we stuck it out all winter....Arch Goudie had just struck up his [trap] lines when six Indians came out one evening in the afternoon. They were so cross about us stealing their trapping. They had gone to Seven Islands and come back again after the winter. There were six men and they were so cross that one man took his gun and held it to Arch's head while the others robbed away all his grub and burned down his tilt. I came there a little while after, and I didn't know this happened so there we were left without any food, only a little bit I had.

— Bert Blake, ca. 1900
ibid

The greatest industry in Labrador, after the fisheries, is the fur industry. It is safe to say that the whole of Labrador is at times covered by our trappers.
The men from Forteau, West St. Modeste and Red Bay in the Straits of Belle Isle meet not only the men from Lewis Bay, but even men from Sandwich Bay. I have known the furriers from Paradise, in Sandwich Bay, meet the men from St. Augustine and the men from North West River of Hamilton Inlet have covered the country to a hundred miles inside the Grand Falls—that is, 350 miles from the mouth of the rivers.

Wilfred T. Grenfell
Augt. 15, 1924

[9.3:27]

MY FATHER WAS MARK BLAKE and my mother was Ellen Michelin from Mud Lake. My father's parents were William Blake and Jane Williams. Mother's father was Joseph Michelin. Peter, John and Joseph Michelin were sons of Hannah Brooks and Mersai Michelin. Mersai was Hannah's second husband, her first one was William Mesher. Mersai's children were all born down to Sebaskachu....

People lived about in different places in them days. We lived in Traverspine for quite a long time, in the winter time. Father used to have trade there for the HBC for when the Indians used to come out from the Gulf of St. Lawrence. He'd have lots of food there for them so they wouldn't have to haul it in the winter.

The men would come out first and get a load of food then go back to the families and then they'd all come out. They come from St. Augustine, Nasquarro and everywhere. Father could talk some Indian. He'd get so much fur from the Indians and give them food. Father would price the fur so much and they had their bill. Father knew lots of Indians.

You know they used to do a lot for the Indians in those days. Revillon Freres and the HBC had two big teams of dogs and they'd haul all the food to the Indians. The Indians would get down from Grand Lake and both posts would haul food for them to Grand Lake. Father's team was fourteen, and I believe Uncle Joe Broomfield's was the same, fourteen. They always had a few extra dogs because some would get crippled you see. And what big komatiks they used to have—Oh, you talk about big. I'll always remember to see them.

Father was a pretty good hand, made awful good komatiks. He used to make them, big long ones, for takin' big loads up to Grand Lake. That's when you'd see the faces froze. I'll tell you, goin' up Grand Lake in the winter with them big heavy loads and that blowin' and cold, you'd get froze pretty bad sometimes. My, we used to get froze in the old days, travellin', trappin' and that. Face froze. Ears froze. Go on like that, you had to tough it. That was sore. I been had my feet galled so bad my socks was stuck on my shoes with blood. But you had to go on again the next day, try to get it fixed up and go on. After two or three days 'twas all right, hardened to it....

— Alvin Blake
[13.2:55]

TRAPPIN' GROUNDS WAS ALWAYS HANDED down from father to son. A trapper would go to a place where nobody else used and build a cabin, set his traps, and that became his land. Nobody else ever touched that land then. The next feller to come up, he'd go in past the last feller in and set up his ground. After the ground was made, it was handed down.

The first trapper I can tell you about, I guess, would be Uncle Joe Michelin. He was about the oldest man around. I guess he was the first feller to make his ground at Sand Banks. That was handed down to Stewart, his son, who handed it down to his son, Brian, and as far as I know Brian still got it.

Uncle Charlie Groves was to Porcupine Rapid, Judson Blake was to Gull Island Lake, Montagues was to Horseshoe, Joe Blake, my father, was to Slack Waters. Joe Michelin had another place to Mouni's, Henry Blake was to Mouni's, too. Then there was the Goudies, old Willie Goudie was to Winokapau, on the lower end. Walter Mesher had a place up on Rabbit's Head on Winokapau. Henry Blake had another place, then beyond him John Groves had a lot of ground up to Fox Island. Wilfred Baikie had that on the last of it. Edward Michelin was to the Big Hill, Upper Churchill they calls it now. That's the places on the Grand River.

After you got in over the Big Hill, Fred Goudie took a place, Lobstick Lake. Harvey Goudie took Flour Lake, and from that I couldn't tell you, because I don't know. My brother Walter had a place in there, and Jim Goudie had a place to Lobstick Lake. Henry Baikie had a place away up there somewhere. I believe Uncle Bob Michelin had a place up there, too. That's the "Height-of-Landers."

After you turns over the Big Hill you're up on what we calls the Height of Land. When you gets up there, there's water runnin' out north, out to the Gulf towards Seven Islands. 'Tis runnin' out through Churchill River. 'Tis runnin' all kinds of ways, so that's why we calls it the Height of Land. People went there to trap because all the places below the river was took up by other people, so they had to go in there.

Height-of-Landers had to leave much earlier than the Grand River trappers because they had to go so far. They had to leave early in September and 'twould take them about a month to get up there. They wouldn't come back 'till they were absolutely finished. They'd leave their canoes in there, strike up their traps and come out, all finished fer the winter. The Grand River trappers would come out fer Christmas and go back in again.

We used to make our own canoes. We'd make them heavier fer the lower part of the river so you could use them year after year. The Height-of-Landers always made them light, good enough to last fer one year. 'Twas too far to haul a canoe all the way from the Height of Land back to Mud Lake or North West River. They'd scaffold them and leave them up there, then if they got the chance the next year they'd take them out, well, they would, but pretty often they'd be left in there. They might cut the canvas off to cover a tilt. There's an island up there just below the Big Hill, Three Square Island I believe it is. They used to scaffold a lot of canoes on that island. They was out in the centre of the river, clear of the bears....

Trappers made all their own dryin' boards, axe handles, canoe paddles, almost everything. Well, a trapper had to do it all even if he wasn't good at it, as long as he could do it good enough to serve the purpose. You got to make your own toboggans to haul your stuff out in the winter.

To make a toboggan you got to cut a good juniper, cut it out, square 'en down, turn 'en up and lash the bars on. 'Tis a lot of work to a sled when you got to do it all with your axe and sew your bars on with babiche [sinew]. You'd bore the holes with a little awl. You make your holes so the babiche is sunk in and it wouldn't wear off so quick. You'd bore your hole on a slant one way and then on a slant, from the same hole, the other way. You do that on each side of your bar, six places on each side, use good babiche and that never comes off. Babiche will wear better than twine, I knows that.

Trappers got to do all their own cookin' and make all their own bread. You're a jack-of-all-trades when you're a trapper.

— John Blake
[4.3:15]

...THE WAY THAT TRAPPERS WOULD take their canoes through these rough rapids on the Churchill River, always known as the Grand River to us, it was something worth looking at. It was a technique that was handed down from father to son, or from older trapper to younger trapper. I could never compete with some of the older trappers in the skill they had in getting their canoes through the rapids.

I was always with an experienced man when I went through the rapids, although I did take part in some of the tricky things, like steering a canoe through rough rapids when it took three strong men on a long line to drag that canoe through the white water. You'd be there in this 18-foot canoe, loaded with three months supplies for two men, and there was only two inches of that canoe that was above water. You'd look back and you'd see this swell of water that looked a lot higher than the canoe. And if you made the least little mistake, your canoe was gone out into this swirling, boiling rapids, and she was tipped over like a mussel shell, and you lost the whole thing.

So there really was a technique to getting your canoe through. You used this tracking line. Usually there was just one man dragging the thing along, using a thirty or forty fathom line. The canoe was right out into the rough water and he was just barely able to drag the thing along very slow. There was just one man in the canoe, steering it, which was very dangerous.

Now another way, which was very interesting to watch, was where you had these two good old trappers standing in the canoe moving the thing along using what they called the pole. Poling the rapids. These two men were out there in this really rough white water, handling this canoe, putting her through these hundreds, thousands of rocks, and they pushed her through with their own force, standing in the canoe, a man in the bow and a man behind. You'd watch them there with the pole, just hammering on the canoe until they got her through the strongest rise, they called it, to get her over the rise of the swift water of the current.

And so you made that trip and it took you a month. There was a week and a half that you were in rapids so rough and noisy that when you were camped on the shore you had to call aloud to one another to make yourself heard over the sound of the rushing water. Almost similar to when the airplanes first used to start up here on the base. The current was so very loud in places like the Horseshoe, the Minipi, and the Gull Island rapids.

I thought it was a wonderful thing, you know, to be a partaker in that.

— Isaac (Ike) Rich
[1.1:3]

...I CAN MIND WHEN THE old Indians used to go off in August and come back sometime in June, and they used to take mostly only ammunition, you know. They used to make their own canoes...a month buildin' canoes and then take off. I seen them paddlin' down the lake lots of times, gone 'till June, and whole families too. Soon as ever they could paddle down Grand Lake you'd see 'um comin' out. Not even Indians do that anymore.

I was trappin' right in to Marie Lake. I trapped in there one winter, just inside Michikamau. We left here the twelfth of August and never got in to our trappin' place 'till the 22nd of November. We got froze up on the way in, see. It's sixteen miles from the mouth of the Red Wine River to Seal Lake across the land. Uncle Bert Blake told me that was measured. From Seal Lake it's in, there's more portagin' than ever, but I don't know how far it is, perhaps twice as long.

We was seventeen days comin' back. We come back straight and we had a good time. We come out with the Indians. The Indians come out straight, see. If we'd have come out the way we went in we'd have probably been another seventeen days.

That was old Simeon Pone and Peter Jack. They never had no food at all, just dried fish and dried deer meat. We had a little flour and we shared with each other. We had a good time. Simeon Pone went ahead all the ways out and never hauled a sled or nothing. He just walked ahead with his stick and made a track. That's the way Indians travels. We had to camp early on account of the children. We'd camp early and this old feller, what was walkin', he'd go off and hunt porcupines. They'd share with us too. It was all like one. They didn't travel and do theirselves right out. They took their time day by day. We'd leave early and camp early, and they took everything as they went. If there was children that couldn't walk, they'd haul 'um.

When we went in, we went in on the route that Mrs. Hubbard[16] went in on. 'Twas a hard route for a woman.

We mostly had bread and lard in the country and trusted to what we could kill—meat, fish and that, and sometimes that was scarce. I mind one year I left here the first part of October and come back Christmas. I loaded my gun when I left here and them cartridges was still in my gun when I got back. I never got one partridge or one rabbit. I had three or four beaver and I lived on fish. Sometimes we'd get a fox and cook 'en. That wasn't much good, not like other meat.

You can most always trust to fish in the country. There's all kinds of fish. The Indians used to catch fish, dry it and pound it into a powder. They used to do the same with deer meat. They called it '*newagin*' in their language, but we calls it pemmican. That was good, too. They used to make awful good soup. Pemmican was light, good to carry, and didn't spoil. [9.2:52]

I been had a few hard times when I was trappin'. In a year you'd probably get two or three pretty bad nights when you had to barricade out.

We'd travel down around Grand Lake around Christmas, when it wasn't proper froze up. That's about forty-five miles long. That was a hell of a route, comin' down along the shore. You'd be about five days among the ballicaters. Them ballicaters around the shore, they was an awful racket to get around. I came down in 1921, right home in a boat, rowed all the way down. That was a late fall.

I don't know how we ever got as much fur as we did. The old-fashioned traps we had was awful big. We could only have five or six and that was a load to carry. The spring was about two feet long, the jaws was about six inches, old sawed jaws and all iron. The chain on them could almost hold the Queen Mary. 'Twas an awful long chain. The old fellers was awful strong though. They had to carry them old traps.

A tilt was better to stay in than a tent. You made your tilt of logs and chinked it with moss. They was covered with birch bark; they'd never rot. If the tilt was covered with birch bark, the bears won't touch it. Now, if you puts tar paper on your tilt, the bears will tear it off. Porcupines will too. Nothing will bother birch bark because it smells like the rest of the woods. Birch bark was better than anything else for making anything tight. People have tried other kinds of bark, but nothing ever lasts like birch bark.

Uncle Stewart Michelin was Uncle Joe Michelin's son. Uncle Stewart, today, is over eighty. He built a tilt in 1905 and when I saw that old tilt last year, it was still standing....

— John Montague
[4.3:30]

THERE WAS ELEVEN OF US children in our family, and the Old Man and Old Woman. My father was Joseph Michelin and he's father was a Canadian from Three Rivers, Quebec.... He had three sons, Joseph [Traverspine], John [Mud Lake], and Peter [Sebaskachu]. It's spreading out pretty good. I got over fifty grandchildren and damn nigh that many great-grandchildren. Oh, a hell of a lot of great-grandchildren.

I never went to school in my life. Nah! My father used to teach me and I think I was one of the hardest little cusses he ever had to l'arn. The Old Man didn't bother too much with me because the others was a lot easier to l'arn and I'd rather be out. I got along all right without it. Most about readin' and that I l'arned from my Bible.

My father used to trap at a place almost to Winokapau. That place was good for marten, foxes, and all kinds of fur. From Traverspine he had six or seven tilts going south. When he'd go up to the other place, he'd always have a man tend these other places. He bought Sand Banks from an Indian feller who owned it, and he'd always have someone on that. That's where I furred first, before I was married.

I trapped up Naskaupi River once, and I'd go north on Nipishish. That's not very far by plane, but it's a good place where you got to carry your stuff. Oh, I used to get the cramps. That was some sore. Some days I could only get along walkin' on my toes, hardly gettin' along a'tall, and that's on showshoes. Them darn cramps was something. Your feet would get damp so you'd get cramps. I'd try to walk and the next day I could walk but my flesh would be almost too sore to touch then. I was only young then. Afterwards I got clear of it.

I been almost up to Winokapau Lake and go in on the south side of Hamilton River, or Grand River as we called it. I'd go in to the little rivers to the Quebec side, huntin', see. Two or three years I went in there. I was five years just outside of Michikamau Lake. All my traps are still in there, too.

I was about eighteen the first time I went by myself. That was up to Sand Banks up the Grand River. I furred there for years. I l'arned from my brothers and I wasn't long t' l'arn. I loved it....

Many and many a night I slept with a chunk of wood under my head with a bit of brush on it. I'd take my shawl to soften it up a bit. When you're travellin' and carryin' you're not goin' to take anymore than you got to, I tell you. You'd make sure you got plenty dry wood. When one fire'd burn out you'd stick him full of wood again, those little tin stoves. You'd go off to sleep then 'till you start feelin' cold, then you'd wake up and fill her up again.

One-third of my furs I'd give to my father 'till he died, because he wasn't gettin' a pension or nothing. Never heard tell of a damn pension then. 'Twas he's place, and I got it and fixed it up. Before that they wasn't gettin' nothing. I fixed the paths and the tilts I fixed or built new ones. I trapped with the Old Man he's last spring. If I made $900, I'd give he $300.

When you was trappin' as long as you kept goin' you never got lonesome, but if the weather got bad and you couldn't get around, time seemed long. I spent almost all my life alone, only when I'd walk on the long trip in the winter there'd be someone else too. All the best time of my life I was gone from the girls, that's true, but I loved furrin'.

One of my boys was down with a feller from Goose Bay the other day and he said, "You'd never believe what my father walked. It's thousands and thousands of miles." And I know 'tis. I been walkin' all my life trappin' and that all over the place. The Indians found it strange that I went right up ag'in Michikamau huntin' after New Years.

After we was done trappin', in along April, we'd come home and cut our wood for next year. By then the ice is givin' out in places and the ducks and geese is comin'. Then we'd be after them. We'd all have white canoes, white flies [spray covers], and we knowed how to paddle and keep down. We'd have all the ducks and geese we wanted. When that was gettin' over, the seals would come in from the ocean—harps, bed-lamers, jars and all kinds. We'd get all the seals we'd want. No skidoos then, 'twas all dogs. We'd get all the feed we'd want fer our dogs. You could salt the fat and it would render out. When tha' was over, the salmon would strike in and then you'd live on salmon. You'd salt them and if you had a place to sell them you would. Time you had a little blow and get your wood for the fall, you'd be ready for trappin' ag'in. You'd have to cut up and split just about a winter's wood for your family before you'd go back in the country.

Now, the government cut off all that from us. We got no pleasure at all to get out huntin'. You can't kill a bird, they'd take your gun, your canoe and p'rhaps kick you in the backside as well. That's how it's come around. When we was to Traverspine, in the fall, when I was a young feller, we'd catch enough trout to last us all winter. We'd fill up three or four barrels. All that's cut out. They took that from us.

When a man gets seventy they'll give you a pension so's you won't be workin' and takin' a job from a young man. Well, all that was very good on the first of it. I went to work, when they put me on a pension, and I give my trappin' ground to a young man. I give my salmon fishin' place to a young man, and then I s'pose they found me livin' too long so they cut my pension in half on top of it all....

I was married and had three or four children before we moved to North West River. We moved because there was no school to Traverspine.

— Stewart Michelin
[2.1:7]

IN THE OLD DAYS, YOU couldn't sew a button on Sunday. I remember when I was growin' up, you buy a gun and some young fellers might come to have a look at her. They could look at her but they couldn't touch her, not on Sunday. If you wanted to look at her, open her up and aim her around, well, you come back tomorrow. You could hard-ly look at her, even, on Sunday....You wouldn't set a trap or even cut wood.

When I first started trapping, I'd be up Saturday night 'till I had enough wood to last me all day Sunday, regardless of how long it took. You boiled your kettle and cooked your meals and that's all. I knowed some fellers, some years ago, they'd trap Sunday same as any other day, but I couldn't do it. You don't gain anything by work-ing on Sunday.

Me and my half-brother was going up trapping when I was eighteen and we got windbound at Traverspine for two or three days. Sunday morning come fine and pret-ty so we figured we'd move on because Monday might be bad again. If we didn't go that day, we might be laid up another week. I'll never forget that morning. We was getting our stuff ready to move on. Uncle Joe Michelin was the boss in Traverspine and that's for sure.

He said, "What's you fellers going to do?"

"We're goin' to leave," we said.

"There's nobody leavin' here on Sunday," Uncle Joe said.

Well, we told him, if we didn't leave then we might be storm-bound again tomorrow. He said we had to take our stuff back to the house because nobody ever left Traverspine on a Sunday as long as he was there. That was law. You didn't want no judge to back that up. Then he started to tell us how he was young, too, when he started out. He said he started out working on Sundays too and his wife died. He said he kept on working on Sunday and his three children (one was my mother, one was Austin Montague's mother, and a little boy) fell in the ice one Sunday and the boy drowned. So he told us about he and another feller who was in the country with him. They baked all day Sunday so they wouldn't have to bake in the week. There was no baking powder, them days, 'twas old yellow baking soda, and you'd get these old, yellow cakes. Anyway, they made a lot of these, and when they got up the next morning they was all gone. Well, who took them? The devil took them in the night as far as they figured. There was no one else to take them, no one else wanted them.

So that's what he got out of Sunday work that time. Another time he said they built a tilt each, he and his buddy. One Sunday this other feller decided to caulk his tilt from the inside. Sure enough, he spent all day at it. Next time he went back there wasn't a bit of moss to be seen anywhere. 'Twas all stogged on the inside, so you should have been able to see moss all over the floor. Well, that was Sunday's work again.

There was nothing done on Sunday, them days, not like now. And what's the generation coming up going to be like. What the heck is they going to be? 'Tis getting so bad, all you can hear on the radio all day long is murderin', kidnappin', suicidin', bank-robbin' and goodness knows what. If something no good happens you'll hear it on the radio. Well, the world is getting so bad, I figures, one of these days 'tis going to come to a head and, bang, she'll go.

— Wallace McLean
[1.2:36]

THERE USED TO BE FIFTEEN or twenty trappers in beyond the Churchill Falls in the last of it—Lobstick Lake, Unknown Lake, Sandgirt and all those places. There'd be fellers scattered about all over the place. What we used to call Unknown Lake is now called Ossokmanuan Lake. We used to go right around and to Atikonak Rapids to what they calls Gabbro Lake. We used to go up Sandgirt Lake and take in to Seven Islands River, they used to call it, then we'd go down to Ossokmanuan Lake. He's long: 'twould take us about two days' paddlin' down. It could get rough there in the winter.

It must have been over two hundred miles we went in, and we'd walk out all the way. We had to go through rough ice in the rapids where it chokes up. There's danger there; you got to watch it all. You can see this river risin', comin' up, and in about a minute it can be choked. You got to watch this. That ice might break and swing off. You got to be ready to run to the shore.

It would take us right around three weeks to come down, travellin' early in the morning and late at night, haulin' an old, big sled that we made ourselves.

In on the trapline I run a lot of rapids, especially in the spring. I was in there two springs. We runned just about everything clear of Gull Island Rapid. I never runned that one. I don't think anybody ever did. It's awful rocky. Minipi, when he gets high, he's all right because the rocks is gone under. The other ones you can run easy enough. Of course, the Devil's Hole is pretty loppy, but there's no rocks. The Devil's Hole is awful for whirlpools. You got to be right careful and keep right over on the north side. On the right is only a narrow strip, very narrow, and you got to keep right on that. [4.3:28]

...The hardest time I had was when I was only seventeen. We was up there for the spring hunt and just a few days before we left (there was three of us went up) I had a few traps to strike up. Uncle Bob Michelin and Juddy had to go and strike up some more traps up above. The three of us went up on the river and we got up so far...of course, we was young and in canoes quite a bit...we should have gone ashore. We was just thinkin' about goin' ashore. Right there was a big eddy and whirlpool. We never knowed a thing 'till our canoe was tipped over.

I was gone down this whirlpool for quite a while. I forgot all about swimmin' but I come up anyhow after a while. I happened to see Ralph swimmin' and it come to me then to swim. The other boy was on the bottom of the canoe goin' down the river. Ralph and I swimmed to a big rock. We stopped and watched this other boy and he got knocked off the canoe just before he got to a point. He passed this point almost close enough to touch but he was on the wrong side of the canoe. He would have been able to jump right on the rocks. He went right on down, holdin' the canoe.

We watched and thought he was in a channel but he wasn't, 'twas a cove he was in and if he'd stayed on, stayed hold to the canoe, he'd have went right ashore. I s'pose he thought 'twas his last chance and he tried to swim ashore. We watched 'en and he only made it about three strokes and then he went down. He come up once more and we never seen 'en after.

He was young, only fourteen. That was the 11th of June.

We was on the wrong side of the river. We was there just about three days. Our canoe was gone. We could hear dogs howlin' in the evening over to Louie's Rapid. There was nine canoes there and not a soul around. The third evening Bob and Tillie come. That was one of the hardest times I had back in the country.

Bob and them was plannin' to be gone six days, and I don't know what would have happened to us if they'd been gone that long, I'm sure. We'd have been hungry. Our matches got wet but we got 'um dried, dry enough to get the fire goin' and that helped us. 'Twas cold, nights up there, you know. We'd swimmed across two or three coves, quite wide, rather than walk in around them. The water was high then, so we swimmed across them and that wasn't too pleasant either. Water is cold in the spring like that. But the hardest part was yet to come, breakin' the news. That was all part of being a trapper.

Another thing I found so strange was my uncle Fred Goudie. He had some kind of warning before he went up that river, the Minipi. Uncle Fred was in the country for thirty years, p'r'haps more—up and down the river all his life.

I had an old man in the woods with me, Uncle John. Uncle Fred told Uncle John that he planned to go up the river but he didn't know what about it because he was uneasy about this rapid. It was some kind of warning, I don't know what I'm sure.

We boiled up about three miles below the rapid and that was the last thing he talked about—if he could get through this rapid he wouldn't mind. That was Minipi Rapid. The feller we had, Francis Thevenet, told him that if he got through before, he would get through ag'in. Then Uncle Fred's dogs runned across and that put 'en behind us. We should have stayed back and waited for him I guess.

Ernest told us later that Uncle Fred wasn't even thinkin' about his canoe. Ernest was his son. Bob told 'en he couldn't track 'en any farther but he said he'd go on just a little further. Now there was no place to go ashore until he got to a shoal and that was a long ways, you know. He wasn't even watchin' his canoe, Uncle Fred wasn't, 'cause I s'pose he was thinkin' hard about this rapid. Ernest called and told 'en his canoe was comin' ashore and Uncle Fred hove down his line just like a child, among the rocks. You always coiled your line, but he just hove his down and shoved his canoe out, not lookin' at his canoe even, and picked up his line. Ernest called and told 'en his canoe was takin' the tide. Uncle Fred looked up and gave a hard pull on the line and the canoe went down by the head and sunk.

As far as Ernest could see, the line caught around the top of Uncle Fred's foot and dragged 'en out in the river. He passed by just out so far from Ernest, not very far. I asked Ernest after if he thought about his pole. He said it never come in his mind. I asked 'en what about his canoe, why didn't he shove her out? That didn't come in his mind either. He had his trackin' line in his hand. Ernest forgot about his canoe, just let her go, so she was gone too.

Uncle Fred went a long ways before he sunk. I don't think he could swim.

We was gone up to the head of the rapids and we boiled the kettle there and waited for Uncle Fred and them. We waited until half an hour after we was done boilin', then we said we'd have to go back 'cause they must have boiled up back there. We had to go back on account we had two loads. You'd always unload two loads to the foot of the rapids and carry it up. Just after we started back, come 'round a turn, we saw Ernest walkin' up. As soon as he seen us he sot down. We knowed there was something wrong.

What I found so strange was that Uncle Fred had a warning about the rapid, that he was goin' to be…well, I guess we wouldn't have saved 'en anyhow, he had to go. When your time is up you're goin' to go.

He was one of the best in canoe, one of the best on the pole and good at trackin'. He was an expert.

— Harvey Goudie
[9.1:58]

USUALLY IF YOU WERE TRAPPING, we'll say, into the north west of the Churchill River, up in Lobstick Lake somewhere, you got in touch with three or four of the handier trappers by visiting them on Sundays. You got together and you said, "Well now, what time are we leaving to go home?" So they said, "Guess we'll make it around the twentieth of December, we'll leave to go home. It's gonna take us twelve or fourteen days to walk home, anyway." So you start off with three or four men from this area, and there's three or four men in another area, and they're all together the way you are, and you heard from them maybe earlier in the fall, so you might know they're starting back handy to the same time you are. So when you get to the main route of the Hamilton River to come home, by the time you were arriving at North West River, the women looking and expecting the men to come home, they would look out and see maybe ten or fifteen men all hauling their toboggans, walking towards the village.

Now, on the return trip home the dangers were altogether different. I spoke about these rapids, going up in the fall. Now when you were coming out handling your toboggan, you still travelled through these rapids. You had to walk through them, because you didn't want to climb these mountains that are in the Hamilton River area. So you followed the river all the way.

When you got to these rapids, and it's freezing-up-time, it keeps ice makin', more ice, more slob ice makin', and it finally accumulates in these rapids and chokes them. In other words, the water gets pent up, stopped. And to stop the flow of the Hamilton River water is a big accomplishment for anybody. So Nature would try it by slobbin' it with ice, and it would build up 'till it reached the bottom, then it would stop. But it didn't stop for long. So when the water was stopped, and you were coming out up along this dam, it would start to back up. And instead of walking on good hard ice, you began to get into rising water. And it would rise up more and more, until finally you had to start to get into these unwanted mountains, that you wanted to avoid.

So, where you'd be trying to make a cabin that you would have made if you'd had good walking on the ice and no rising water, you maybe had to spend a night before an open campfire in twenty-below zero because you didn't make it to that cabin. And maybe you didn't have a tent because you were trusting to that cabin. And even if you had a tent, you might still have been out in water and you were wet, and it was late, and you were working hard all day walking through the woods, climbing, and clearing your path through the thick woods.

And then, there was the danger involved too if you didn't understand from the older trappers that there was the possibility of the ice that you were on just bustin' up and disappearing on account of the pressure of pent up water at these ice dams. When it got so much pressure up and the ice couldn't stand it anymore, it would just go.

I remember one time when the river did bust up on us. Break up, if you call it; we used to call it bustin' up. I was told about it before by older trappers, but I didn't believe it, to tell you the truth. I didn't think it could happen. And—there was four of us travelling down through the Horseshoe Rapids one time—and there was good ice where we were travelling there. There had been ice there for a long time which was good. There was snow on it and it was good travelling. But suddenly there start to be a rumbling noise of ice cracking and banging, and I, being more or less the greenhorn, started to wonder what's happening here to the older trapper that I was with. And he didn't give me any definite answer, just a command to jump ashore. Get ashore off the ice.

We were no more than twenty-five feet from the side ground; we were out about that distance. And when he told me to get ashore, well we just went for the shore, and the other two trappers that were just about a hundred yards behind, they did the same thing. Well, we just had time to get ashore and get our toboggans ashore, which wasn't very long, within twenty-five feet range, and the river was just clear water from one beach to the other.

That was something unbelievable, and it's something that happened while I was there. It was due to the rapids down below being blocked up with ice, and when the pressure got on it, the water that was swelled up, up here, had this ice rose up that we were walking on. Well, then, when she all went, it took the whole thing, you see.

— Isaac (Ike) Rich
[1.1:8]

I WAS DEAD ONCE. Do you believe that?

My Aunt Ruth, Uncle Job and I was fishin' up to Traverspine River. It was real mild that day and the ice wasn't very thick. There was snow on the ice when we went up, and it was rainin' and mild all day so the snow came off and 'twas black ice.

We caught about five barrels of trout between us. We was takin' two down on the komatik. Me and Ruth was sleepin' on the komatik and Job was skatin' along when we all went through the ice a mile above the house. They heard us bawlin' and come up, Millie, Emily, and the Old Man.

Ruth had her hand out, so they pulled her out. Job got out on the ice, and I was gone...no sign of me! So they hunted and hunted but there was no sign so they give up and went home.

When they got about a quarter of a mile down, Emily saw something shine up through the black ice, in the moonlight. It looked like a grub bag, she thought, floatin' along. She cut a hole with her skate and waited there. When it come by she put her hand in and pulled it up and 'twas me. I had a little white duffel cap tied on me head...I was dead. I had one boot on and one off when Emily got me.

They took us home and worked on us. Ruth started to come around, but I didn't, so the Old Man put me out on the porch, said 'twas no good to work on me anymore 'cause I was dead.

When Ruth came to her senses, Grandmother put me across a chair with me feet on the floor on one side and me head down the other side. She took the board they used for barrin' the door, said she was goin' to hit me across the backside. She said if I was dead, 'twasn't goin' to hurt me anyway, 'twas worth a try.

When she hit as hard as she could, she said I give the bitterly kick and the water started to run out. They worked on me 'till I come around.

And the Old Man had give me up for dead! Dr. Paddon said what kept me alive was that I kept my mouth up to the ice and there's a space of air there. I was nine years old then.

— John Michelin
[7.3:60]

WHEN WE WAS LIVIN' UP the Naskapi River, the men used to go up the river in the morning and stay a night and, almost always, come home the next day. They'd get a few bears.

One spring 'twas real high water and ice, all drivin' and everything. The men never come home when they should've. I wasn't uneasy much because I thought they just stayed a little longer, you know. I looked out and there was a slack in the ice for a little while, just water, and there was these two people comin', sittin' on what looked like a wood komatik with horns stuck up. This was the two men sittin' on two logs that was lashed together, and they had a stick on each side and they was lashed on. They had one axe, one gun, and a little grub bag. They had on their old white huntin' coats. They was comin' down the river, paddlin', sittin' right flat on the water—at least, that's what it looked like.

I watched and watched and they began to paddle in towards the house. They come in as close as they could and they got ashore. They all wore seal skin boots, them days. The side of the Old Man's leg that the sun was shinin' on was all dried up so that he could hardly get his boot off. That was the Old Man and my brother Murdock. They had had to keep as still as they could so's not to fall off.

The men wasn't in the house ten minutes, I don't think, and the whole big river come out. That's what they was workin' for, tryin' to keep ahead of it, paddlin' on those logs. If they'd have lost their paddles they'd have been done for. They were trustin' to ever reachin' home or never reachin' home.

They had to get home that way because they was drove from their tent the night before with the water rushin' in. They managed to grab one gun and one axe. They had to travel I don't know how far to get to the high ground.

It was Saturday evenin' they got home. Sunday morning the ice was cleared out further down, so they went to look for their canoe. They was afraid that the canoe was goin' to come down river ahead of them, floatin' bottom up. She been drove out, sure enough, but we never seen her. They found her drove in amongst the ice, broke up some.

Them old logs was still up there when I last left Naskapi River. [6.3:55]

In our days women and young girls shouldn't wear pants. Nobody was seen with a pair of pants on, not even to fish. 'Twas all dresses for womenkind. 'Twas almost a law.

My father was quite a strict old man in some ways. One day he and the Old Woman went away to the bear traps or somewhere. I was always the rowdy, wild one. When they was gone we used to get right foolish almost. We used to be so glad to get the place to ourselves. We'd be playin' rough and wild. Here I put a pair of pants on and started runnin' after the other ones, playin' and keepin' up an awful fuss. Some of them said to me, "I bet you anything you wouldn't go down on the wharf when our father comes back."

"I bet I would," I said. I'd risk anything almost.

When they was comin' close, down I goes, took a chance on it. Well, he seen me at a distance but he never said nothing first. He was workin' around in the boat and the Old Woman was laughin', she had to.

At last he said, "Annie, you go up to the house and take that off."

Well, I tell you I runned back and I was afraid ever to show in sight all the evening. I very nigh got a hammerin' 'cause I done something that was awful wrong, something that was against all laws. 'Twas counted as kind of a sin for a girl or a woman to wear a pair of pants.

I got a pair of pants now in a suitcase that the girls got for me last winter when we thought I had to go to St. Anthony to the hospital. The girls used to laugh at me about it, but I never had to put them on in the end. [3.1:13]

I used silver pine for poultices. I've made a lot of poultices like that. You bring in an armful of brush, just as well to say. You pick off the little sprigs, backwards like, until you get a little pile, enough to make a poultice for wherever your pain is. If 'tis on your knee, or your leg, so perhaps you might want two, accordin' to. You'd pick all that off and of course your fingers will get all black and sticky, like gummy. Then you got to put it in an old tough bag or a piece of canvas or a piece of thick cotton. You can put it on a big chunk of wood or the anvil and beat it until you can see the green just coming through in places, make it all moist, something like in a partridge crop only it's pounded up more. It got to be hammered up; 'tis no good if it's not. That's the kind I've used.

When you get it all hammered up, you make little poultice bags out of a piece of old sheet or anything. You warm it up in anything. I always used an enamel plate if I could get one. I wouldn't use tin in case 'twould turn black, but enamel or aluminum would be all right. Just put it in with enough water to make it moist but not leak through.

You can keep it hot as you can if your patient is in bed. Put it on the sore spot. Then you can put a towel over it and you can put a hot water bottle on it if you wants to keep it warm a long time. You can use the same poultice twice, that's what an old Indian woman told me. After that the strength is gone.

People seemed to think it done a lot of good for pain. If you had a lot of pain and couldn't sleep for the time being, people have got a lot of comfort and rest out of it. I don't know how long 'twould cure you for.

When I had a bad leg up Grand Lake, there was an old Indian woman brought it upstairs to me. I couldn't walk, not one bit. That year was the year of the Flu when so many people died. My leg turned black. They called it scurvy or beriberi. We was short of the right kinds of food and one thing and another. I got crippled upstairs and couldn't get down, then up comes this old Chief's wife, laughin' away. She hauled down the blankets and I showed her my knee and she put the warm poultice on it. Well, you'd never believe what a comfort. I fell to sleep, and I sleeped and sleeped. Oh, my, that done a lot of good. She warmed it up again that night and put it on again. Next day she said she had to make a new one. Her name was Mrs. Sinish. Her husband was the chief. She was a fine old lady.

— Annie Blake
[3.2:46]

BACK IN THE EARLY THIRTIES, that was when we was still trappers, that was when the Depression was on, wasn't it?

We were trappers livin' apart from all cities. We knew nothing about the Depression, or very little, because there was no radios then, no television, no anything. Now, we as trappers were only managin' from hand to mouth. There was no extra money, none in the bank, none even in your money box. We'd always have to depend on the Hudson's Bay Company to supply us with a fit-out, a supply of food, for three months....

The way the HBC runned it was that you got a supply of food and you had to try and pay that off when you come back from trappin', and if you wasn't able to pay it off completely, it was added on to the bill next year, and then you wouldn't get as much supplies as you did the year before. We would only get butter, sugar, flour, pork, beef, dried beans and dried peas and rolled oats, tea, and a couple of pounds of coffee and some molasses. We had lard for fryin' our fish and pork for stewin' it. My children didn't know what it was to have an apple or an orange. There was no fresh fruit of any kind....

We all had wood stoves and common oil lamps, and our husbands, before they went in the country, would have to cut a thousand sticks of wood and bring it home, saw it up and put it in the shed. Now, the first year we came back [from a failed attempt to make a living in the North] we had to live with my father because we didn't have any money at all. When my husband come back with his catch of fur, he had made a thousand dollars, so we were extra well off. Now we had to go and look for a house.

There was one house standin' from the Dickie Lumber Company, on the sawdust pile we used to call it. It was a tenement house for people movin' in from the coast and places. We got that for a hundred dollars. It was insulated inside with sawdust like you get when you saw a stick of wood. My husband said we couldn't knock the house apart to shift it; we'd lose all the insulation. So we sawed it into sections and moved it to where we wanted to build. The tenth of September Jim had to leave me to go trappin'.

He said to me, "I'll get your windows and doors in but I won't get your bedsteads made and I won't get your dish cupboard or porch built."

I had to undertake that job myself. I built my bedsteads, porch, and cupboard. Now, Horace was seven and Marie was five, and they worked at pilin' the thousand turns of wood in the woodshed. The way they done it, they'd pile it as far as they could reach, then in the evening between daylight and dark, I'd go and finish the pile. We got all the piles done before the snow came....

We never had a pile of anything, no extra dishes, clothes or anything. You had to mend every week, do your laundry by hand, scrub your floors. They'd rip lumber on the saw pit and that was put on your roof and floor. The girls that was big enough would get down and scrub that over with sand and cork. Cork is what you use for floats on your nets. You'd use a piece of linnet, piece of net, and you'd scrub your floors all over for a month, every now and then, until you got all the splinters worn off. Always a wooden floor and log walls.

It was kind of hard all through. Now, I don't know what you call hard times, but when it come to managin' food and clothing, well, before the children got big enough to help me, I had hard times. It was hard gettin' the things made, gettin' the seal skins cleaned, gettin' boots made for my husband, cuttin' over old clothes from the Grenfell Mission. My work started at six o'clock in the morning, when the first fire was lighted, and I'd never lie down 'till twelve in the night. I'd work straight time. A man asked me once when I had my leisure hour. I told 'en I never had a leisure hour, it was work, work, work. He said it must have been a tough life. I told him we didn't look at it as a tough life because we was so busy bringin' up our children and keepin' them healthy and clothed and fed.

We never had any extra money. We were just ready when my husband was workin' for the Americans…he come home one day in October and he said, "Mum, I'm ready now. Our house is paid for and now I'm ready to put some money in the bank for when we get older." I was awful happy. In December they laid him off because of a heart condition, and he never worked after. After everything was straightened out he was gettin' seventy-five dollars a month from the government. We had very little saved up. Chris, who was sixteen or seventeen, quit school. He said he couldn't stay in school and see his parents needin' money. Bill and Joe went on and got their grade eleven, Chris got grade ten and Jimmy got his grade eleven.

The Depression as far as people knew in Labrador was depression all the way. We didn't have any extra money in the bank that we could drop in on when we needed it. I can remember my father comin' home one time after he sold his fur with twenty dollars. He told my mother to put it in the money box and when the minister made his rounds on the coast, he said, they would give him some for the mission work. The rest would be kept for anything extra that might be needed.…

I worked all my life for two dollars a month. Every fall my father would see to it that I got two pairs of winter stockings to help me out. If you got two dollars cash, you could buy some yard goods to make a slip, a nightgown, or a dress, that would be about what you'd get. Everybody was pretty much the same. There was one or two men who made good on trappin' and got businesses for themselves, but the majority of Labrador people were hard workin' people livin' from hand to mouth. [5.1:54]

When I was a young girl I used to dream about carrying water. A lot of times in my dreams I'd go out to a river bank and, this will sound funny—when I'd get to the edge of the bank I would sail down to the sand on the bottom and dip my water up. I'd suddenly be back to the top of the bank, but I'd never know how I got there.

One time I dreamed I was walking around a big hill with a little girl. She was about four years old. We were holding hands and walking around the hill on this shelf. Oh, 'twas good walking there. By and by we come to the end.

She said, "Now, what's we going to do?"

"Well, " I said, "I guess we'll just jump off." And we did. We jumped off and just sailed to the bottom.

I could never figure out why I dreamed that dream.

— Elizabeth Goudie
[3.2:51]

JOSEPH MICHELIN WAS MY GRANDFATHER. He was born in Three Rivers, Quebec, in 1845. There was four brothers of them that left Quebec and come out here to Labrador.[17] Grandfather was married twice. His first wife was Caroline. What her last name was, I don't know. They had three daughters, Hannah, Esther, and Ellen.

Mary Snow was Grandpa's second wife. She came from Bay Roberts, Newfoundland. She was on a fishing boat and before the boat left in the fall, they got married. The captain married them right there on the boat just outside Rigolet. They had eleven children: Jim, Dan, Stewart, Bob, Susie, Emily, Charlotte, Ruth, Mary (my mother), and two adopted ones, John and Ewart.

Grandpa never put any of his kids in school, but they all got high grades when they did go out to school. They knew more than everybody else almost. Grandpa taught every one of his kids. He used to have school in the night, everybody around the table and not a squeak out of them. He had a cane and everything; he was a real teacher. Everyone dreaded the nights when school-time came. I know John was telling us that one thing he didn't like about Grandpa was that he was awful strict. You had to do what you were told and nothing else, no peeping at anyone else's book, that was that. He didn't have school every night, but every other night almost. He used to teach me, too. We used to have to sing hymns and read the Bible every Sunday night. I got right used to it. It just come to me to do that because I was with them a long time and I fitted right in.

Grandpa Michelin and them always lived to Traverspine, but they moved down to Salt Water Pond, just on the other side of Sebaskachu, when they got older. They moved down there just to be quiet, but I know it wasn't much quieter there than Traverspine, but they still moved anyway. Somebody had to stay with them because they was pretty old, so a couple of my sisters went down, but they wouldn't stay no more than a month or so. They'd get lonesome and want to come home. But brave me, of course, I went down when I was twelve and stayed 'till I was nineteen.

Grandpa Michelin was a wonderful person. Everybody loved him, and everybody called him Uncle Joe. He used to always tell stories and jokes, and they'd all be back for more. Walter Blake and others even used to take trips right down from Mud Lake and that, come down purpose to hear Grandpa tell his stories. I'd be sitting down, ears open, listening in to see what I could hear. It was good fun listening to the old stories.

We had a lovely house down to Salt Water Pond, all brand new. Grandpa and them sawed the boards themselves, or they got it from the Grenfell Mission. The house was right up to style, new paint every year, inside and outside. There was two wood stoves in it, one in the kitchen with a square oven and one in the inside part with a round oven. I can't remember the names on them. I should, I've looked at them and cleaned them often enough. On the left side of the kitchen, walking in, there was a cupboard full of dishes. That was beautiful. In the inside part we had another cupboard for our special dishes. The special dishes were only used when people would be visiting us, but the kitchen dishes was just as good.

In the kitchen there was a long wooden lounge with a feather pillow and a black bear skin on it. That was Grandpa's chair for having his meals, and when he'd be sitting on that lounge and talking, he'd be pickin' at the bear skin, and that poor old skin was almost picked bare.

There was another wooden lounge in the study, and the bear skin on that one was right good, because in there he'd usually sit in the rocking chair or on a regular chair. The study was just like going in the library here, all kinds of books. I think Grandpa been having books all his life. After, we left Salt Water Pond, and the next time I went down there, the house was partly torn down, the books was all lying around on the ground, and I had to walk over them. My heart nearly sank. I loved them books.

We had a wooden walk from the wharf up to a little store-house and right up to the house, all wood. You didn't have to walk on the ground at all. We had a real good little outhouse, and that was right stylish too. It was a two-seater. It wasn't like these days, I'm telling you. If you wanted to go out before you went to bed, you'd light the lantern and go to the outhouse—snowing, drifting or whatever.

When they lived to Traverspine, Grandpa had a little store, general store, trading post, or whatever you mind to call it. They used to sell things anyway. When they moved to Salt Water Pond they never had anything like that. I didn't know what it was to pick up groceries 'till after I was married. My Grandma was from Bay Roberts and Grandpa was known from here to Newfoundland to Quebec, so they used to order their groceries and things in the fall. We never used to pick up anything from North West River, only apples and little things like that. We even had boxes of sweet biscuits, all kinds of fancy biscuits. We'd have barrels of flour, boxes and boxes of butter, you name it. We had it good.

We had an awful lot of gardens down there, long ones, like potato gardens, cabbage and turnips…. Dr. Paddon used to come down and look at Grandpa's gardens. Well, the Grenfell Mission was supposed to have the best gardens around, them days, but I don't know, I think our turnips, cabbages and potatoes used to put up a darn good show against the Mission. Grandpa had the big turnips, and turnip tops—wouldn't see my head over them. And give—'twas nothing at all for Grandpa and Grandma to give anybody anything. If you come in they'd give you an armful, and if anybody'd say they wanted something, it was nothing at all for Grandpa to give it to them, never sell anything in them days….

Grandpa was born in 1845 and he was ninety-three when I went to live with them. He used to work like a young feller, cut wood and haul it, run it down over the hill. He had his own little garden in front of the house and the spring he was ninety-five he was out shovelling the snow off his garden and, sure, he fell down in the hole and he never got better after that.

Grandma and I were left by ourselves most of the time after Grandpa died, but Ewart used to come home once in a while. That was all was there except for three or four miles away on each side of us. When I was nineteen Ewart got drowned. About a week after he was drowned, Rev. Burry came over to let us know. They waited that long because they wanted to find his body. That was on December the fourth. 'Twas the time of the year when the ice was just frozen over with no snow on it, and there used to be always a hole. That's what he done, skated right into the hole, like it was between daylight and dark and he couldn't see the hole. 'Twas bad.

I didn't want to leave home, but we didn't have much choice. Uncle Stewart and Uncle Dan come down and shot all of her dogs and locked up the house. Grandma lived with Uncle Stewart then until she went to the hospital. She died with cancer in 1947, so she was born in 1862 and died in 1947 at the age of eighty-five.

Everyone used to wonder how I could stay down there with Grandpa and Grandma Michelin, down there where there was no action, no nothing, not even young people to go skating with, but I loved it there with my grandparents. I found it more like home there than in Mud Lake, because I used to get all my own way.

— Mary Saunders
[4.2:18]

I BEEN A TRAPPER AND a guide all my life. I been guiding since I was fifteen years old. I knows all the water ways, all around the country, right across to Fort Chimo. In 1928 I went across with Koehler and his son, across to Indian House Lake, almost out to Fort Chimo and back again.

Koehler was a feller from New Jersey. He come across from Germany after the First World War. He had a factory where he made engines and different stuff.

He made different trips across the country here. He died over here. He and two more fellers. The guide was from Labrador [Jim Martin] and the other feller was from New Jersey too.

Koehler was a hard man different times, during the full moon and the new moon. Apart from that you couldn't find a better man. He didn't know the country, he had no maps. He was making maps and writing a book while he was going. His last trip in he was going to finish the book and the maps, but he died just before he got to Indian House Lake.

When I went with him, we went in from Voisey's Bay to Frank's Brook and went in across and portaged across to Indian House Lake. From that we went across to where the old Naskapis used to live long ago, when Mrs. Hubbard went across. We had a look at all the old camp places. 'Twas all rotten. We went back up through George's River.

He had a map done by Mrs. Hubbard showing from George's River to Indian House Lake, but he would not go on the river 'cause he said a woman never done nothing right in her life. "If we follow that map," he said, "we might get lost." I told him the map was right, the islands, the rivers and everything. Besides, I told him they couldn't trick me. He took the river up the other end of the lake, and we went sixteen days the wrong route, going due North. I told him we was goin' wrong. He said we'd go that way 'till he wanted to turn back. We come back and took George's River right where we camped first. It never took us sixteen days coming back because we had fair current then.

We never had much grub, but that was my fault mostly. When we was going trapping, a bag of flour was 50 lbs. When I asked Koehler how much flour he had, he said four bags. Well, four bags was plenty. We'd be gone up to perhaps three-and-a-half months. After we was in the bush a couple of days I went to get some flour. I asked him where it was and he said 'twas in a duffel bag. I told him that wasn't all the flour. He said what was in the bag was it. Well, 'twas only 10 lb. bags, so we only had 40 lbs.

We was gone from the middle of June to the middle of October. There was Koehler, his son and me. So we lived on fish for three weeks and a half before we got out. There was lots of fish. All the lakes had fish. They almost smelled like fish, the lakes. In the day, in shoal water, you'd never see a fish, but when you set your net in the evening, you'd have to take it up before you go to bed or he'd be sunk with fish. Trout, whitefish, jack fish and all kinds. Koehler would just take them out of the net and chop them up with the axe and heave it in the pot.

We never clean a fish because Koehler said the fins and the guts and that was the best part of the fish. He said that was where the strength of the fish went. He said that's where the good was to. It certainly was good too 'cause I never used to get hungry. When he'd have it cooked you couldn't find a bone anywhere, not as much as a gill or a head even. 'Twould be all cooked up. He had lots of pork or salt in it. He cooked it good too. I remember the first time I cooked fish, when he got up and found the guts and head, he hove it all in. He took off the cover and I said, "Good God, look at all the insides." I told him I thought that was poison. He said that anything a fish eats that don't poison him wouldn't poison me. He was right.

He was a strong man. In New Jersey he was a boxer and played football too. He was about six foot six in his stockings. His son was a good man, too. But I and his son couldn't talk when the moon was full or new. He told us, before he'd get bad that he didn't want to see us talking to one another. Sometimes he'd get cross and a couple of times he tried to kill his son. One time he grabbed his son and was going to cut his throat. I heard his son making a noise. I runned down and kicked the knife out of his hand and throwed it out in the lake. We was out of grub then a week and a half.

The lake we come to was Michikamau. It was twenty-five miles long and quite wide. I said to him, "When we comes to this lake what's we gonna do? Camp there or go to the other end?" He said if 'twas calm when we got to the lake we'd go on. When we got to the lake he wouldn't go on. There was a big long pole there that the Indians had for putting fish on. He made a smack at it and broke it off. It must have been a full moon then because he was beginning to get bad. His son told me he was getting worst every year. He wanted me to go with him the next year but I wouldn't.

We went from Michikamau, down that lake, took in and come to Overflow Lake, from that to Lobstick, then to Sandgirt and my tilt. That was my old trapping ground. The Indians made me a map at Davis Inlet. That's what I went by. Michikamau is about 140 miles long, bight and all.

Between Overflow and Lobstick we found a silver mine. Some fellers from Quebec had it all fenced off, Quebec mark on everything. Koehler found the big silver mine somewhere in the west. He said what he saw in Labrador was just like what he found out west. It was all running across like silver nails. He wrote it in his book.

Coming across from Voisey's Bay we saw a big red bear about sixteen feet long. I and his son saw the bear. He took our track and went to our canoe. He was standing up to the foot of our canoe and smelling in under the nose of her. The canoe was sixteen feet. We never moved 'till he was out of sight. He was red but his neck and his mane was coal black. Koehler told us a feller got one once and got $1,000 for it. He wanted us to get that one. I said, "The Dickens with that," seeing we wanted to get on in.

We met Juddy and Reggie and Fred Goudie to Lookout Lake. We was there three days waiting to go to Grand Falls. I got a picture taken of us where we went out to where the bottle was. That's the bottle where all the trappers had their names. We put ours in. Mr. Koehler put something in too, I think, but I couldn't say for certain because I and his son went out to look at the falls.

By that time his son was barefooted, everything wore out. I found some old boots and shoes in my camp at Sandgirt, my upper tilt. That's what he wore coming out.

Koehler wanted to go across to Seven Islands. I told him we'd meet Indians down below. He wanted me to go up to Sandgirt Lake to see if there was any there. I told him we'd be sure to meet them below. Next day we left and went down to Bobby Goudie's. There we stopped for the night. Next morning we saw three or four Indians coming in a canoe. 'Twas that blind feller what's here now, Peon Selma, and some more fellers. Koehler wanted them to go to Seven Islands with him. They wouldn't go because they said he took grub from them the year before and they got hungry. They wouldn't have nothing to go with them.

The next day we went down and went to Big Lake and from that went on down and got flour from some trappers. We had a good time from Grand Falls down. We was meeting trappers every day. Juddy and Fred Goudie and them give us some flour.

That was a good trip. Koehler was a hard-headed man but I was as hard-headed as he was. I told him if he'd get flour and snowshoes from the Indians, I'd go across to Seven Islands with him. I told him if he didn't, I was coming on down supposing I left him on the island.

'Twas the middle of June, or just after, we went to Voisey's Bay. We made all that trip across country, and 'twas October we met the trapper's going in. When we got home, I got ready and went in trapping myself, but I didn't go above Grand Falls. I went to the Michelin's place 'till it froze up, then I come back and went in the Longpath and trapped there.

— John Michelin
[1.3:34]

I TRAPPED OVER THIRTY YEARS. That's what I raised my family on.

I was thirteen when I went in with Mr. Goudie and seventeen when I was on my own. The first year I went up the Naskapi River with Grandfather Michelin, my mother's father. That was his place. I trapped three seasons with he....

There was always a few Indians coming or going. They were great old people to have around. They always wanted some stemmo [tobacco] and tea. They were very honest. If they found something in your trap, they'd hang it where you could find it. But they'd never reset a trap. If they come to your tilt while you were gone, they would help themselves to a bit of grub. They would never take it all. [1.1:10]

After trappin' twenty years I moved further up in the country. Before that I never had to portage at all hardly. After the move it took about twelve days to reach my grounds. That was hard work, carryin' a canoe through willows and over banks. The first portage was about three miles long. Gettin' home in December then would take about eight days...

My grandfather and father trapped in around Gull Island Rapid and also the lower part of Grand Lake. I've been told that ol' Grandfather come from Scotland, come out as a clerk wit' the Hudson's Bay Company. Then he took off on he's own trappin'. He drowned at Gull Island Rapid. I often heard Father talk about it. They had big ol' river boats. The trackin' line broke and Grandfather was swept over the rapid with the boat. Fred Goudie and a couple of trappers from Cartwright drowned at Minipi Rapid. But, you know, there was very few accidents for the number of trappers that went up in the country....

There'll never be no more right trappers, not like we was. Boys these days hardly knows how to walk in rackets [snowshoes]. I don't know if they can tail a rabbit snare. The Indians is as bad as our boys.

We'll never get them old days back, not the good ol' days. We didn't have money but we had freedom. The government knows it all now and we knows nothin'. They tells us what to do and how to live—fellers from Ottawa tells us how to trap. Let's go and tell them fellers in Ottawa how to run their lives.

But, of course, when we speaks they don't listen.

— Austin Montague
[9.1:55]

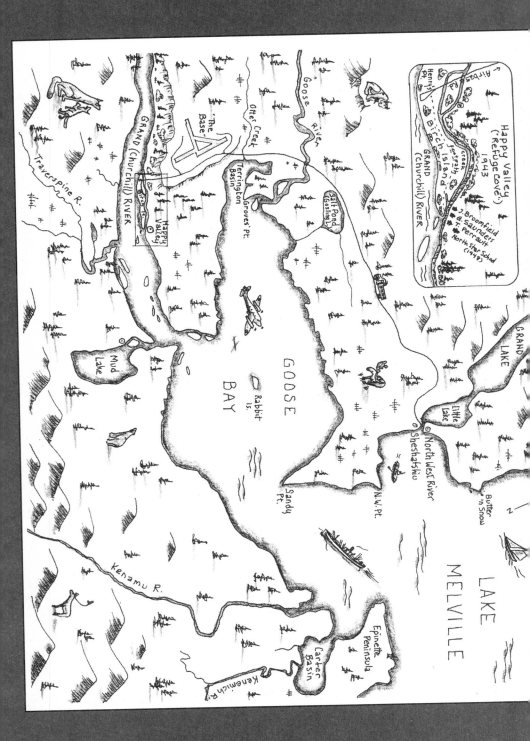

CHAPTER

THE JOURNEY TO GOOSE

IN THE FALL OF THE YEAR that Goose Air Base was started, I had a strange dream. I dreamt there was an angel hoverin' over the treetops at Rabbit Island, and when I got closer to it, it seemed to be Aunt Annie Groves. Her head was turnin' from north to south and out to the east. She seemed very uneasy. That fall Goose Bay was started. I often figured it was that she knew the base was startin' and that everything was goin' to change.

After the base was here two years, I had another dream. This time I dreamt I saw one of the prophets in the sky over Goose Bay. He looked like the pictures I have seen of Moses. He was lookin' down on Goose Bay with a very sorrowful look on his face. I been thought about that dream a lot.

These two dreams disturbed me, kind of. After Goose Bay started our lives did change so much. It changed so completely from what we was used to. I thought that those dreams was a warning of things to come.

—Elizabeth Goudie
[7.1:34]

BEFORE RADIO 'TWAS JUST OUR little world. You went from place to place visiting in the fall of the year and in the night. Of course, you were trapping, hunting, cutting wood and all other things in the day but in the night if you wasn't too tired, you just went off to see someone. From place to place you knew each other so you was always glad to see anyone.

There was no problem like crime back then. We were just livin' in a little world of our own and never thought about the outside at all. The only way you heard any news was if you'd go to Cartwright to the Marconi station, unless someone told you what they heard from the station. I think everyone was happy with it. Well, you had to be because if you wasn't you'd never stand it, eh!

— Herb Webber
[*Goose*, 12.4:24]

THEM TIMES, IF I WANTED a shirt, Mother had to make 'en out of flour bags maybe, pants the same way, and she'd make all our underwear, but that was made out of flannelette. The old man would buy so many yards and she'd make 'um. And a pair of pants, you couldn't get a pair of pants. My pants, them days, was nothin' but patches from head to foot. There were pants there in the store but you couldn't afford 'um; there was no money to buy it. It was like that until I come to Goose Bay in 1941.

— Lawrence Saunders
[10.2:62]

THE PORT OF GOOSE BAY actually came into being in World War Two when a refueling base was urgently required for servicing the new war planes being flown to the war zones overseas. As the United States and Canadian governments were both involved, each sent a survey party in to Labrador to find a suitable site.

The Canadian party under Mr. Eric Fry, a noted surveyor, commenced their search from North West River, a small township of trappers and their families 130 miles in from the Atlantic through Hamilton Inlet and a series of inland lakes. On his arrival, Mr. Fry was delighted to be informed that there was a fog-free plateau on Terrington Basin...a three-by-one-mile inland lake with access to the sea, fourteen miles to the southwest. On visiting the plateau, he found its sixteen-square-mile area an ideal site with practically a ready-made airstrip. He advised Ottawa accordingly and stressed it was FOG FREE the year 'round. His advice was accepted by both governments, and a contract was let through the Canadian government to the McNamara Construction Company on a cost-plus basis with orders to lose no time in getting started. The lease for the area on the American side being included in the 'swap' for fifty over-age destroyers from the U.S. Navy, so vitally needed by Britain at the time.

In September 1941 the Canadian icebreaker *N.B. MacLean* arrived at North West River towing a floating crane. There they hired Russel H. Chaulk, who was familiar with the area, to pilot her into Terrington Basin. Sounding ahead of the ice-breaker from his canoe, Russell found a channel through the shallow waters at the outer end of Goose Bay (nothing to do with the name of the port) fifteen miles from Terrington Basin with a depth of nineteen feet six inches at the inner and shal-lower end. After a boat's crew of nineteen feet six inches at the inner and shallow-er end. After a boat's crew from the icebreaker had buoyed the channel with empty oil drums, she passed safely through...then through the deeper water of Goose Bay to Grove's Point Channel, the narrow entrance to the Basin, where they found a least depth of thirty-five feet. After this was buoyed the *N.B. MacLean* was the first ship to enter the Basin. A few days later the cargo vessel *Erika* arrived in the Basin with a full cargo of equipment and supplies for the contractors. After anchoring close in to the low-lying land on the south shore, her cargo was rafted in and a camp was set up.

Work was then commenced on driving a road the half-mile through the bush to the foot of the sixty-feet high plateau...then up on to the plateau itself, with men specially flown in to do the work. There the shallow-rooted black spruce which covered the plateau in profusion were felled. After several inches of moss and lichen were cleared away, a firm base of sand was bared. Some years later a sounding was taken of the sand which showed that the plateau was the top of a huge sand hill dating back to the ice age, with a least depth of 700 feet. A temporary runway was laid, and during the following winter planes were being serviced and sent on their way overseas. Fuels were brought in by small Canadian coastal tankers.

By the summer of 1942, with several thousand men working on the project, a large base was built on the south side of the runways for the United States Air Force (USAF) and a smaller one on the north side for the Royal Canadian Air Force (RCAF) Transport Command. The control tower being on the Canadian side and operated by the RCAF. For the defense of the area, roads were built radiating out from the bases to a ring of anti-aircraft guns mounted on fifty-feet high wooden platforms.

— Capt. Francis Poole
[8.4:5]

US MORE COMMON PEOPLE DIDN'T know too much about Goose Bay or why it was being built up, no more than we knew that the war was on. We had a general idea that they wanted to get their airplanes over here as fast as they could. They wanted to make a chain around their bases in the north. We heard they had bases in Greenland and Newfoundland, so we figured that putting one here was just to link them all closer together. It was all due to the war and we picked up what information we could, us local people. I know I was talkin' to one authority from D.O.T. [Dept. of Transport], that came in to look things over, and I was just bold enough to walk up to him and said, "Well sir, you know, what's goin' on? Can you tell us something about it?"

"Well," he said, "we're all here together, shoulder to shoulder on account of this war, and if we don't stick together we won't win. So we're buildin' these bases for protection."

They had this man come here to Goose Bay and it was a good location, good harbour and sandy soil. 'Twas nothing for a bulldozer just to run over a strip of trees and take everything with it. They started clearin' around September and they were landin' airplanes by Christmas, the same year they started. It was a good location in every way.

Up until 1945, I believe, you could say the people just thought of the Base as a place to go and earn some money to buy a gun, a canoe or something and to go back trappin' ag'in. You had a chance to make a little bit of money, and you had the chance to go in the country and get a few skins of fur. But after 1945 and on people began to realize that the Base was goin' to stay here for a long time, so instead of just makin' enough money to get a canoe or whatever, well, we thought we might get enough to get a better home out of it, a better future, and maybe even change our way of life so that we didn't have to go back to the hardships of trappin' and livin' off the country. It was beginnin' to look brighter.

We always had the idea that we had to work for a livin', and this workin' for wage employment was only another way to earn a livin'. It was like that until they started to take income tax out of our salaries. There was a period of time here when we didn't have income tax taken from us, we were workin' for ourselves, definitely. But when the taxes began to get involved, the government was takin' so much out of our earnin's. We began to realize what the government was doin' for us. They had nothing for us to walk on, only a footpath that we made for ourselves, so why wouldn't they make a road from the Base to the village that we were livin' in? We began to torment the authorities about arrangin' a way of gettin' a road for us.

When the Base started, that was a big jump from dog team to modern machinery, airplane, bulldozer and so on. The ditch-digger gave me some fright one night. I thought it was a horse. It was night time and I was walkin' and there was this thing that had the head of a horse, the neck of a horse, and as far as I could see, it didn't have four legs, but it was movin' its head and feedin', movin' its head and lookin' up. It was dippin' down in the ditch and lookin' up. It was dippin' down in the ditch and movin' out, the same as a horse.

And they had those gravel trucks. One of our guys asked me what they was supposed to be.

"Well," I said, "Boy, those red things down there, that's trucks and they're very dangerous. They're goin' to do a lot of good, but they're goin' to do some harm, too. I dare say, before fall, I guess someone'll be killed on account of those things."

One of our neighbors was killed by a truck that fall. We were unloadin' lumber one night. Around twelve o'clock we were waitin' to go to work and they told us there was no work that night. We were just out of hearin', almost, when the foreman called out to us to go back, and the four of us went to work. One of us was killed that night. He went to take the sling off a load of lumber and the truck backed in and broke his neck, ya' know, between the lumber and the truck.

There were three killed durin' the construction of the Base, three natives.

I think the majority of the people around here were glad to have all those people move here, as long as they didn't move too far away from the Base and interfere with our trappin' grounds, which we figured we were goin' back to some day.

— Isaac (Ike) Rich
[7.1:34]

BACK IN 1941 THE GOOSE Bay airport was getting ready to be built, and contractors were calling for men to work on the job. A few of us decided to take a crack at it. As the saying goes, we were heading for the gold-rush to get rich. Sad to say it didn't work out that way.

On September 24th, 1941, we left Cartwright on board the *Fort Cartwright*, which was owned by the Hudson's Bay Company. A decked boat, about thirty-five or forty feet long. There was Clarence Brown from Eagle River, Charlie Lethbridge, Eugene Martin and Howard Lethbridge from Paradise River, Butler Martin and Tom Elson from Cartwright, Selby Smith from Batteau and me, William Elson, from Bob 'n Joyce Brook. The day was fine but blowing a good stiff breeze from the west-southwest. We called in to Pack's Harbour, a little fishing village nine miles northeast of Cartwright. We spent a little while out there and then Skipper Joe Reeves decided we would try to get on down the shore—maybe up around Fish Cove—for the night, so we started on our way. The wind still kept blowing and most of the boys were seasick. It was a bit cramped up in the boat, so many of us stowed away in the mid-ship (the main carrying space). We pushed on until it was time to pull in for the night. We spent that night in Cuff Tickle, some of us went ashore and spent most of the night just wandering around the beach. I think we all managed to get a few winks of sleep that night.

The next morning it was still nice weather so we started on again, expecting to make Rigolet that night. About noon we ran into engine trouble and had to go into Tinker Harbour to fix it. John Heard, the man looking after the motor, wasn't long getting things fixed and we moved on again. We put into Rigolet late that afternoon thinking we were going to stay there all night and get some badly needed sleep. We never got that chance because the *Fort Rigolet*, another HBC boat, was waiting there to take us on to North West River. Mr. Budgell was the HBC manager at Rigolet.

We shifted all our things from the *Fort Cartwright* to the *Fort Rigolet* and were soon on our way again, this time heading for St. John's Island at the entrance to Lake Melville. We were about half ways through Rigolet Run when Mr. Bill Shiwak, the engineer, got gassed. Skipper John Blake said we'd have to go back to Rigolet, so he turned around. In the meantime, we were all gathered around Mr. Shiwak. Then Skipper John asked if anybody could operate the motor, and Butler said he could. Can you imagine the look some of us gave him? Our night in Rigolet was out again. Skipper John turned her back and headed for St. John's Island again, and we spent the night there, and what a night it was, September 25th!

They were taking some gas to North West River in forty-five gallon drums, so we couldn't sleep on board. There was also a man and his family aboard from Rigolet and they had the only room that was available, nothing left for us poor souls only to go on shore and bunk 'er down under the stars. We had an old camp but no stove. Four of us tried to sleep but we couldn't, it was too cold, so we had to get around a big fire and that's how we spent the night. We got a nod when we could.

The next day, September 26th, we pulled out of St. John's Harbour and headed up the big bay. It looked big to most of us who had never seen it before. You could see land on either side but you couldn't see land ahead. Late that afternoon we pulled into North West River and just in time, too, because the wind struck from the northwest and it was taking the water up in sheets. If we had been out in that wind we would have had to run for it. It was a real gale.

Anyway, we made it and went ashore to size up the village and look for a place to spend the night. It so happened that Mr. Samuel Fequet owned a store and a house there at that time, so most of us stayed there. Ern Learning, Charlie Bird Jr. and Frank Bird, all of Sandwich Bay, were also staying to the Fequet place on their way up the Grand River. There was a dance there that night and when it was over we lay down to get some sleep, but it was very little that we did get.

The next morning we headed for the end of the rainbow, Goose Bay. We hooked a passage whichever way we could. I got a passage with Henry Blake of North West River.

When we arrived at the site—and a sight it was too—they were plowing up the land with tractors and steam shovels. There was no dock or roads, things were just starting to get going. The first thing we had to do was set our tent, which could room about twelve or fourteen people, using double camp beds. We figured we'd get a darned good night's rest that night…but no rest for us again.

A couple of men came over and said, "Boys, the cook-tent is over there. Supper is at six and after youse have eaten report back here to your tent and be ready to go to work on the midnight shift."

Well, some of us just about gave up right there, but sleepy and tired as we were, we said, "Okay, we're ready to go to work." After supper along came a man that was to be our foreman, Mr. Stan Barney, a good foreman, one of the best. He took us down to where they were driving piles for the dock. He told us our job was to pull the boats as close to shore as we could and off-load them. The boats was called 'Pointers,' something like the Newfoundland dory only much bigger. This was it—we were in business. We pulled on our long rubbers, dashed off, grabbed the boats and pulled them in and unloaded them.

I don't think anybody can imagine how we felt when the time came around for us to go off work at six o'clock. We made off for the cook-tent for breakfast and then off to bed for some very badly needed rest. I guess we got about two hours' sleep and we were awakened by all kinds of noises, motors running, people roaring, and the ring of axes. Some of us got up and went to see what was going on. No more sleep for us that day! And back to work at six o'clock.

That went on for three or four weeks, until they got the dock ready for the ships to come in alongside. Then they used trolleys, a flat-bed with iron wheels on it that ran on an iron track (something like a railway track). We used to push those trolleys to the side of the ship, pick up a load of freight and push it back to the shed. Many's the time I'd doze off to sleep pushing the trolley along.

Nevertheless, we thought we were doing all right. At that times wages were the great sum of thirty-five cents an hour. We worked from seven in the night 'till six in the morning…no overtime.

We worked at off-loading the ships until ice started making and then we had to give up that for the season. Then we all scattered about on different jobs. Some went to work burning brush on what is now the runway. And that was when eight of us decided we were quitting and going home to Sandwich Bay.

The only way to get home was by dog team, or walk. We couldn't afford to hire a team so we had to walk. We left Goose Bay the first of December and walked to North West River, where we fitted out with grub, two tents and sheet-iron stoves. We had to make komatiks to haul our belongings on. We didn't have any snowshoes but that didn't trouble us. If it snowed too much we could make something to walk with. It was still good for walking because it hadn't been froze over for too long.

We left North West River on December 4th and some of us had dinner at Mulligan with Mrs. Stella Baikie and moved on again. That night we spent at Byron Chaulk's tilt. The next morning we travelled on down the shore, which is known as Lowlands, and spent the night at Lowlands tilt. Now, from there we had to cross from the north side of the bay to the south side, which was about eighteen or twenty miles across new frozen ice. New frozen ice is hard to pull a load over, and with that it was only a day or two before that ice-breaker came out of the bay. But who cared about all that as long as there was ice enough to bear us up. In the morning we took off for Frenchman's Point on the south side, and at noon we were about halfway over. We had lunch sitting up on some of the ice the ship broke up when she came out through and after lunch we pushed on again. We camped somewhere between Frenchman's Point and English River that evening. About a month before I had hurt my leg and it was beginning to make me feel lame, but I didn't say anything about it to the other boys. We'd pass the night singing songs and telling stories.

About three o'clock the next day my leg was getting so bad that I couldn't hide it any longer. I was limping quite bad. Butler said that they could haul our cuff and I could hobble along behind. That night we pitched our tent at Pease Cove, about halfway down Back Bay. Now Back Bay is a hard place to travel if you don't know where you are going…and we didn't. There is bad ice there to deal with.

In the morning we hauled out of Pease Cove and headed down the bay again. We did a fair stretch that day and camped well down the bay from South Long Point. That night we talked about crossing from there to the north side and finding the route across to Flatwaters where Uncle Jobie Williams lived. None of us had been over this route before so we wasn't sure if we could find the right place to cross, but by having talked to different people we figured we could make it all right.

Bright and early the next morning we set out for North Long Point. We knew we had to take away right inside of a little island that was standing offshore, so some of the boys walked along the ridge and came to a marked path. We were all set now for Flatwaters, and sure enough, late that evening we camped at Flatwater Pond.

Next morning we got Frank Williams, who now lives in Cartwright, to take me, as I had a game leg, and one of the boys as far as Rabbit Brook. We all got a lift along— some went as far as Cartwright and some of us had to travel on up Sandwich Bay. At that time Wilson Williams was living to Main Tickle, so he took myself, Eugene Martin and Charlie Lethbridge as far as American Point on the north side of Sandwich Bay, where Willis Bird lived. We got Willis to take us from there as far as he could get. The bay wasn't froze up so we had to trim the shore. When Willis dropped us off, we walked the other three or four miles to my house at Bob 'n Joyce Brook, where the trip was over for me. Charlie and Eugene spent the night at my place and the next morning they moved on for Paradise River and home.

— William Elson
[7.1:36]

IT WAS OCTOBER IN THE fall of 1941. Mom took her spy-glass off the cupboard and went to the porch door to spy at a ship that was coming in. It was the *Fort Ross*, the Hudson's Bay Company supply boat which was replacing their previous supply boat *Fort Garry*. This was the first trip to Makkovik for the *Fort Ross*, although her crew, including her Captain, Jim Dawe, were all well known in these northern communities.

When the ship anchored, I rowed aboard and one of the first to meet me was Wilson Cave, a Hudson's Bay Company manager who had been on holidays and was returning to Hopedale to resume his work for the winter. As a matter of interest I started asking him what the news was. His first question was, "Are you fellows going up to North West River to work on the airport?" I was so surprised. I couldn't imagine the facts of what this was all about. I asked him if anybody from southern Labrador was getting a job out of it. He said that was all the talk all along the coast as they came down, people planning on going to North West River for work.

I said, "But they won't carry on working after winter sets in?"

He said, "Oh, my son, the winter won't stop them. They are going to build a big airport only a few miles from North West River."

Well, that was the latest news!

The *Kyle*, which was the coastal boat serving Labrador at that time, made her last trip to Hopedale after that, but we didn't get too much information, only rumors that there would be lots of work going on that winter.... As the fall advanced and winter came on, in January...the time came when we were to make our departure, a time I shall never forget in my life. There was deep snow everywhere. It was a dull, heavy, overcast morning, looking like more snow was coming. We got up early, an hour or so before daylight. Mom cooked breakfast, but the feeling of departure was pressing heavy. The atmosphere was much quieter than usual. We lashed up our travelling gear on the komatik, and as we went to get out of the house, Dad broke down.

He said, "My poor boys, they have never left home to go away like this before."

There was nine of us left Makkovik, and three more joined us when we got up to Tessialuk, making a total of twelve in our group. From Tessialuk we travelled to Tilt Cove where Uncle John Broomfield senior, an independent trapper, lived. Then on to Wolfrey's Cove and Uncle Peter and Aunt Anne Pottle's, and then to Big Brook (now called Michael's River) where Bill Tooktoshina and his wife Lucy gave us a warm welcome. We stayed there overnight and had a good pot of partridge soup for supper— really hit the spot. Next stop was Pottle's Bay to Arthur Newell's, who was the dog team mail courier from Rigolet to Makkovik at the time. Then to Rocky Cove where several families were located—Uncle Ned and Aunt Ann Oliver, Uncle Arthur and Aunt Phoebe Rich. Uncle Arthur had a good bundle of foxes and lots of stories about his trapping. As we travelled south we were very eager to hear any bits of news about the airbase from anyone who had been working there. Then we came to Ticoraluk where Austin Flowers gave us an entertaining night of stories on hunting and general living that went back at least some fifty-six years. The following day we arrived at Rigolet and although it was winter, the big bay was open from one side to the other, one of the most unusual sights we could ever imagine. There was a Hudson's Bay Company store there, a trading centre for the area, with George Budgell as manager and Jack Simpson as store-clerk.

It was Sunday afternoon when we got to Rigolet, and after five days travelling [we were tired], so we stayed there the next day. Mr. Budgell allowed us ten dollars trade each to buy food for the rest of the trip to North West River. While at Rigolet, Uncle Bill Shiwak, Sr. made a chart for us to follow into Lake Melville, as we were all strangers to that area, and it could be some bad around Vallies Bight.

It was a cold trip travelling up the big bay against northwest winds with low snow drifts. Eventually we arrived at Mulligan where there were approximately twenty families. They had a school and, interestingly enough, some of those very students are equal to any of this day when it comes to working and making a living and surviving in their own country. This was an interesting place to spend a night, talking with some of the top trapline people. We were now only a day's travel from North West River, and there was more news about what was going on with the big construction in Goose Bay.

We left Mulligan and later stopped for a nice cup of tea at North West Islands, then on again with one more stop at Butter 'n Snow. When we got to Butter 'n Snow, Uncle Fred Ritch was away so there was only Mrs. Ritch and her daughter. We all bundled in for a cup of coffee. We left there around five-thirty and arrived at North West River long after dark.

Because there were so many people coming from the coast and staying overnight before going on to Goose Bay, at first we just could not get a place to stay for the night. However, with the help of some schoolboys, who naturally were following us around, they very helpfully showed us people's houses where they thought there might be a chance to be taken in for the night. We got in three or four, here and there.

I vividly remember several times that night we got up, like school children, and looked through the windows at the two big steam shovels and a line-up of gravel trucks under the strong floodlights that was erected on towers which kept the gravel pit lighted up. Trucks hauled gravel day and night for the runway that was gradually extending.

The following day we stayed at North West River, and Ed, my brother, and I were invited to Mr. J. Watts for dinner. He was a great friend of Dad's when he was a wireless operator on Dunn's Island off Makkovik Bay, where we fished. After dinner, Mr. Watts took us down and showed us around the hospital, where everything was spic and span and well-organized. He introduced us to the late Mrs. Paddon senior. One of the first comments she made was, "I hear you had a job to get in last night. If I had known I could have put you up for the night." Her husband greatly appreciated the help people gave him when he travelled on his medical trips up north in the winter.

That night a mixed lively crowd arrived from Goose Bay after supper, which was a routine thing for workers coming out to town after the day's work was done. They'd have a break. Up to the community hall a swinging dance got on the way. The fiddler was a construction foreman from Amherst, Nova Scotia, with a couple of his friends with their guitars.

Next morning, around eight o'clock, we crossed the river to where the big trucks were lined up waiting to be loaded. Each driver took two or three men, and we were on our way. It was something we had never experienced in our lives! We were riding over a wide, hard, level road where two vehicles had no trouble passing.

We arrived on the Base around eleven in the morning. The driver stopped and pointed at a row of big bunk houses and told us to see the bull-cook around and he'd see to it where we'd stay. He also told us that the big building on the opposite side was the Administrative Office, and if we preferred, we could go there. We went there and got signed in with the McNamara Construction Company and all ended up with a Company badge with a registration number on it. From there we went over to the bunk house and got settled in, and by that time it was dinner time.

There was two big cook houses that could seat four hundred people or more, each! This was a sight we shall never forget. Waiting there for the doors to be unlocked, there was the Royal Canadian Air Force with uniforms and dress shoes and the small caps. There were office workers, mechanics, carpenters and all kinds of people. Inside it was warm and comfortable, and the food was absolutely delicious. The cook-house staff was around thirty, including cooks, waiters and dish washers.

This for sure was where I wanted to work—nice and warm and plenty to eat and drink. But I was told at the office that I would go with the regulars as a labourer, loading and unloading on a truck, as there were hundreds of tons of materials. There was cement, lumber, steel-work and so on, all piled on the beach where the dock is now located.

Breakfast was at seven o'clock sharp. A couple of days went by. The third morning I was just dressing when Sam Dickers came in the bunk house and he said, "Jim, if you wants a job over in the cook house, come on now. The old man is sick this morning and they need a replacement right away." I got dressed in a hurry and went over. The below-zero temperature was stinging outdoors, and as we opened the back door of the kitchen, the smell of bacon, toast and boiling coffee was overwhelming. Everyone was about their specific jobs. The waiters (or cookees) all wore white pants and jackets. The Austrian cooks looked very capable for their jobs. Sam, who had been there a couple of months, was well used to the crowd.

Sam said to the cook, "This is Jim Andersen to go on with the job."

I had never seen orange juice before, and there was lots of it there to be opened for breakfast.

One of the cooks said, "Okay, before you begin have a drink of juice, make you feel horny." I didn't know what he meant, so I refused. I refused to take anything that I didn't know what the results might be.

Our wages was thirty-five cents an hour.

April came and we headed back home before the ice got bad in Lake Melville. It was late when we got home. As we walked in, Dad was sitting down having a tune on the harmonium.

Mom said, "I just had a good look up towards Trap Point and I was thinking how good it would be to see the boys coming."

It was quite an experience.

— James R. Anderson
[8.4:24]

I WAS BORN IN JACK Lane's Bay, not right here in this house but about three quarters of a mile up the shore from here is where the old house used to be. I was born here in 1909. I lived here all my life until the year I went to Goose Bay and I been there ever since except for summertime when I comes back here. This house is part of the old house I was born in. I tore it down and used what was good of it. I got a lot of fond memories of this place. Even though I don't do any huntin' up there in Happy Valley I still got the hunter's blood in me and I like to be back here at the fishin'. It's not the huntin' season now, I know, but still I'm at the fish and that makes me think I'm back huntin' as well. If I could stay here for a little while longer I would be able to hunt because the season opens the first of September, but I have to go back because I got work to do in Happy Valley; I got to work for a livin'. I comes down here and spends all the money I made through the winter and goes back broke and then I got to make more to come back here the next year, I hope, God willing.

Sheet metal work is my trade that I picked up since I went up to Goose Bay. When I lived here it was huntin', trappin', fishin'; fishermen's life, hunter's life, trapper's life. But in the years before World War II was a time of Depression. It hit some countries a lot harder than it hit this place here in Labrador. It hit us with regard to our gear, and by that I mean our salmon nets, cod nets, seal nets, fox traps and so on, the things that we used to make a livin'. Our gear was goin' down with the use year after year, and there was no price for fish and very little for fur, and the sealskin boots was goin' down in price. Everything was goin' off the market, so the Depression was givin' us a hard time with our gear—although we had plenty to eat and to wear and so on like that. But then you got to have the gear to get the stuff.

I heard tell of them buildin' an airport at Goose Bay, so I decided to go up there. I had no idea what an airport was like, but I'd go there and look for work anyway if the fur turned out poor—and it did. It turned out to be a poor winter.

Myself along with more that lived here from Big Bay, as we calls it, some from Davis Inlet, Hopedale, and one man from Makkovik—fifteen altogether—travelled to Goose Bay. We went up there by dog team. We left here in April but I don't know what time it was in April. We were eight days travellin' to Otter Creek. Otter Creek was where they had a few shacks where people from Rigolet and North West River was livin', people that they wanted to do the work. There was no such thing as Happy Valley then....

Otter Creek was a gravel pit and there was gravel trucks goin' back and forth on the old muddy, bumpy road that was first put through. They had only started in September—that fall—in 1941, and this was April 1942. We were wonderin' how we were goin' to get to the airport. While we were there a couple of pick-ups came, the first trucks I had ever seen except for in motion pictures. There must have been some 'wheels' of McNamara Construction there because there were people taking our pictures, you know, where we were changin' from *mukluks* into rubber boots or something like that. We daren't go up to the airport with our *mukluks* on.

They asked us where we were goin' and what we intended to do. We told them we come lookin' for work. They asked how long we were goin' to stay and we told them we didn't know. They said they hoped we wouldn't go back like some people that came earlier that winter and only stayed about a month then decided they'd go back.

We said, "We can't go back because we sold our dogs and besides that the ice is gone so we'll have to stay whether we likes it or not."

They were pretty pleased about that. One man said he'd go to the nearest phone and call up on the Base. They had these field phones. He went to one and called up, and they sent down a gravel truck to pick us up—my first truck ride. I suppose he was doin' about ten and I thought he was goin' awfully fast. That's the way we got started off in Goose Bay.

When we got up to Goose Bay they gave us a place to stay in the bunk house, showed us around and so on. We went over to the Superintendent, Mr. Durrell, and told him we was there to work. He asked how long we were goin' to stay, and we told him we had no idea but we wouldn't be goin' home until sometime in June, July or August. He said we could take the afternoon off to look around and he'd meet us Monday morning. They worked Sundays and all there you know.

That year I worked with McNamara Construction Company. I came back home in August just to see the folks and help them out with a bit of food and so on because, like I said earlier, the Depression ran down our gear and the ones that were left home were just strugglin' along the best way they could. I had about three weeks home and then I went back up to Goose Bay again and worked with McNamara through the next winter.

Durin' the winter my uncle had some sort of an attack. I lived with my aunt and uncle. He was in the woods and fell down. That was in the spring sometime. I didn't know. Communication was very bad along the Labrador coast in those times. There was a wireless station in Hopedale and, finally, later in the spring I got a wireless message sayin' that Uncle Walter was very sick. I said I'd go back, so I quit my job. My foreman was very good to me, I must say, and he was a very helpful and generous man. He did everything he could. Those times there weren't any bush planes flyin'. The Air Force did have some. My foreman thought he might be able to get a plane to fly up. There was no chance. There was a feller up from Rigolet and he said he'd take me to Rigolet by dog team and from there I would work my way along. That was all right. I went to the office and got paid and that evening I brought my tool box back to the bunk house. When I got to the bunk house this feller from Rigolet was waitin' to tell me he couldn't take me now because he had to take a load for the Hudson's Bay Company from North West River to Rigolet. There was disappointment right there.

Next morning there was nothing else for me to do just go back to work. When I got down to where we were buildin' the dock the foreman was surprised to see me. He asked me what was wrong, and I told him.

"This isn't good enough," he said, "I'm goin' to try again."

So he tried different things, D.O.T. and so on, but there was no chance whatsoever. He took the whole day just goin' around with me in the jeep, goin' to different places. There was no go, so I had to stay until open water.

Uncle Gil Saunders came back in March by dog team, so he left his boat for us to take back when we came down. We quit the first of June to fix the boat—we had to put a new stern post in her. The seventeenth of June we left for back here. We dropped off men as we went along—some to Cape Harrison, some to Makkovik, some to Hopedale, and the rest were from Davis Inlet. There was Tom Ford, Bill Flowers,

Gears, Saunderses, Edmundses and myself. When we got to Hopedale there was no news from home; Uncle Walter was better and everybody was well. At Davis Inlet it was still the same news.

The next day, after we got to Davis Inlet, Jim Saunders decided to take me over here to Jack Lane's Bay. We got here late in the evening. When we got here Uncle Walter and his little family of three girls (the oldest) and two boys (the youngest) were down on the rocks to meet us. Uncle Walter was very glad I come back, but it seemed as though there was something wrong. When I asked where Aunt Carrie was, he just stopped.

"Aunt Carrie left us. She's gone home. She died the 11th of June."

That's how I got the news, just like that. I nearly flopped on the beach. Uncle Walter wasn't well himself. I decided to go back to Goose Bay and take them with me. Uncle Walter had high blood pressure. So we made up our minds to bar the house and take the whole family, what was left of them, and go—Aunt Lil too.

When we got to Goose Bay I decided I would try and get a job with the Americans because McNamara would be pullin' out soon, and the Americans were lookin' for civilian workers. They were just buildin' up the Base, what we calls the American side now. So we went there and had no sweat gettin' a job. Everything was fine, we all got jobs.

We lived at Otter Creek but we knew we couldn't stay there very long because they wanted it for storage tanks for airplane gas and things like that. We would have to get a place to stay. We moved ashore into one house because there was too many of us in a small boat—three families of us, you see. We had picked up another family at Makkovik. That made it a family of Perraults, one of Saunderses and us Broomfields. The Perraults had a house that they had lived in the winter before, so they were all set. After we were there for so long and it seemed as though we weren't goin' to move, the Air Force was gettin' impatient. One night they sent down a couple of men, a couple of officers, from the RCAF, to find out what we were doin' there and when we were goin' to move. We said we couldn't move unless we had a place to move to.

After these two men from the RCAF came, we begin to get worried, so we started to ask a few questions of the Americans, like when they were goin' to find us a place to stay and where. The Americans were gettin' worried because we told them if we couldn't find a place to stay, we would have to pack up and move back while we could get back in boat. That made them a little more worried so they started lookin' around for us. Finally we went off with a carpenter foreman in a little jeep with some engineers from the American side. We had to find a place outside a five-mile circle because the five-mile circle was reserved for Base use. They decided on the place that is now Happy Valley. We spent that evening just clearin' off land and so on. They gave us ten days off.

Then we went back to Otter Creek and took our families in two boats. We had some lumber and things the Americans gave us at the dock, so we went and loaded what we could take on the boats. The three families of us moved over and put up our tents. The next day we went and got the rest of the lumber and so on. The place was a little creek sort of place, all willows and trees. I cut down five trees before I got either one to fall, that's how thick they were together. So, anyway, we lived in tents there. The Americans sent down a carpenter to help us lay the foundations of our houses. They were there about five days. In the ten days we had off we got most of the work done, and then we went back to work and worked on our houses at night and on Sundays. We didn't have to work on the Base on Sundays. Everything was done by kerosene lanterns, just little old storm lanterns. Uncle Walter had died in the Air Force hospital, and I took over his family to look after. Anyway we were the first three families in Happy Valley: Gil Saunders, Thorwald Perrault and myself, John Broomfield.

September 26th, 1943 was the day we moved to what is now Happy Valley. Through the winter, comin' on towards spring, more families began to move in from different places: North West River, Mulligan, Rigolet, Cartwright, Table Bay and so on. The first winter though there were six families: Mr. Saunders, Mr. Perrault, myself, Mr. Bob Davis, Mr. Frank Martin, and Mr. Byron Chaulk. That made up Happy Valley the first winter.

The first name they had for Happy Valley was "Refuge Cove," because we had such a hard time tryin' to find a place to stay. I remember Ken Rector, the carpenter foreman, havin' a sign made and put on the bank where we could read it, Refuge Cove. Later on in the winter some of the American airmen used to come down when they had a day off. Some of them young fellers was just drafted into the service and was feelin' a bit lonely, so they walked down to get a cup of tea from some of our women. They got a warm welcome. They had such good times they started callin' the place "Happy Valley," a place they could go for happiness and get away from the Base. That's how Happy Valley really got its name in the first place. Now Happy Valley has over six thousand people—a great difference.

We walked two miles and then a truck would pick us up and take us the rest of the way to work, and at night she would take us back as far as she could, and we'd walk the two miles back home. That's what we had to do when we were buildin' our houses. On November 1st I moved into my house. It was only a little house, 10' x 18', but boy, that felt like a hotel after livin' in a tent for so many months. We all moved into our houses about the same time, one perhaps a little earlier than the others.

Most of those early people to Goose Bay got pretty good jobs. 'Tis nobody down to what we calls...well, there got to be labourers, I know, and 'tis no disgrace to be a labourer, but it's only natural to try and get a trade so you can get higher pay. Most of us got jobs where we weren't labourers anymore. Some are mechanics, some are heavy equipment operators, some are carpenters and so on. Surprisin'. I don't know how it happened, but it seems like people from Labrador, north and south, have been able to work up pretty fast. Perhaps it's on account of the way we lived, jack-of-all-trades. When you wanted something done on the coast, you couldn't run and get a tradesman, you had to do it whether it be a mechanic, doctor, wood-chopper or whatever it was, you had to do it yourself. If you wanted something made, you went to work and made it yourself. I think that gave us a big boost.

When I went to work on the American side I tried for a job in the carpenters' shop, but I couldn't get any. I took a job as labourer for a while. I needed a job with a family of orphans to bring up. Then one of the carpenters went on leave so I went to work with the carpenters for a month—I was still on labourers' pay. When the carpenter came back, the superintendent said he wasn't goin' to put me on the labourer's job anymore.

He asked, "How would you like to go to work in the sheet metal shop for the winter?"

What I was thinkin' about was as a labourer I would be outside shovellin' snow, pilin' up lumber and things like that. With winter comin' on I thought, 'in anywhere as long as it's inside.' So I said I'd take it. He pointed out a sign with a pair of sheet-metal snips painted on it. He told me to go over there and tell the young man I was to be his helper. I went over and it was the first time I had seen this young man. He was busy with two blow torches goin', doin' some solderin' work. After he finished he turned off the torches and looked around at me.

He says, "Yes, sir, can I do something for you?"

I said, "Mr. Stoffer, the superintendent said I would be your helper from now on if you want me."

He said, "I've been askin' for this since I landed here."

"Don't get too excited about it," I said.

"Why not?" he asked.

I said, "You see all those machines? I don't even know what they are. That's a pair of tin snips; I knows what they are, but that's the only thing I knows." I didn't have a clue.

He asked, "Have you ever done any work like this before?"

I said, "No, no more than make my tent stove when I went off trappin'. That was usin' an old axe for a coal chisel and I bent the metal between two planks and cut off wire nails for rivets and so on, the hard way."

He said, "You'll learn."

After I was in there a while I found out that it was a lot like carpentry work. You use the rule and tape a lot. The only difference was that you used rivets instead of nails and instead of a saw you used the snips to cut your material. So it wasn't too hard after all. He showed me quite a lot about it and then I made up my mind to see if I couldn't get somewhere with it so I sent out for a home correspondence course, took lessons and got myself a trade.

I was there two years with that foreman and after he left he recommended me for foreman. After I was workin' there for twelve years I found I was gettin' nervous. Well, I suppose I can't take responsibility like some people. How it really started, I went to the hospital for a check-up and the doctor told me that I was just nervous. He advised me to take a year off, so I decided I would try something on my own. I went to Happy Valley and got a few machines and started on my own. I said I'd go back on the Base after the year was up, but I found I could make a livin' at it. You know, it's wonderful to be on your own and be your own boss, so I didn't bother to go back. I'm still workin' at my sheet-metal shop in Happy Valley.

To be truthful about it, I'm in Happy Valley because I got to be there, but I still feels like this—Big Bay—is my home. I haven't got too many years and I'll be a pensioner, and if things go like they're goin'—my health is good and I'm still active—I'll come back here to live. I likes the fisherman life and I likes freedom....

— John A. Broomfield
[9.3:5]

FIRST WHEN I COME TO Goose Bay to work, we were living in the barracks. There was a group of us from all over Labrador, some of us only kids. I was barely sixteen, and we were often homesick and lonely. The only worthwhile entertainment that I could see was this fellow from north, Uncle Johnny Broomfield. He had an autoharp, and every evening he'd sing songs and tell us stories. He used to sing the alphabet song, the one that starts 'A is for anchor.' I've tried so hard to remember what the songs were, but I can't. I was so taken up with the whole thing—he sort of kept us alive. Dad was working down here too, and he thought some lot of Uncle Johnny. For him to get there in time for Uncle Johnny's songs was the end of a perfect day. This went on all through the year. He talked about the church, about friends and everything. He was a real human being.

After I left McNamara I lost track of John for a number of years. They were living down in Happy Valley when I met up with him again. I went to work in the paint shop on the Base and Uncle Johnny was foreman in the sheet-metal shop. There was a little hole in the wall between the two shops and we used to talk back and forth through it. Uncle Johnny always made it a point to talk to us every morning—he never missed a day. He'd say 'Hello" or tell us a funny little story through this hole, and always once a week, maybe more, I'd get an invitation to come to the Valley. Johnny had some seal meat, or a duck, or some fish... "Something from home," he'd always say. This is how I got to know him well and to know the family, Ebert and all those. He was so good, better than most parents I have ever seen.

Later on, after I grew up, I watched him work in the community as a leader, not only in the church but in everything. Maybe we would get a call from the American side saying they had a building for the community for a Boy's Club or something. John would go to whatever source he could, maybe the Hudson's Bay Company, for a truck. He always told us that we should do some good for others every day, and he'd talk a group of us into going to work with him. I remember one time he got enough of us together to saw an old building apart and bring it down. I believe now 'twas used as a school. Anyway, after a while the crew dwindled away. It got right down to only Johnny and Hayward Mercer, I think. That was John, always out to help others....

— Charles Pardy
[9.3:20]

THE HISTORY OF HAPPY VALLEY begins in 1943.

First, I would like you to close your eyes and try to imagine that there was nothing but trees everywhere—not a house of any description. There were birch, spruce, fir, and willow trees, and moss covering the ground....

The men came first and cut down enough trees to make tent space. It was midnight when they arrived, having come from Otter Creek by motorboat and getting stuck on the sand bar. Eventually we arrive, and when we left the boat we had to pull ourselves up over the bank by the trees and willows. There we found three tents pitched—so life began in Happy Valley. Our baggage and belongings were stacked on the bank and covered with tarpaulins.

During the weeks that followed, everyone was busy with the building of houses... The sound of hammers could be heard quite late at night. The work was done by kerosene or gas lamps or lanterns. After three weeks the houses were about ready for the families. True, they were not large [10' x 18']. A good deal of material was provided by the Americans, and it was quite common to see large packing cases being towed across the creek. Stoves were made from oil drums, and our little homes were warm, though not completely finished.

Our water had to be carried up over the bank by the bucket-full. As it was not always quite pure and fresh, the doctors on the Base informed us that all the water must be boiled. When the creek froze over, we had to go out with an ice chisel and make a hole from which to dip the water.

Our provisions, oil, and gas, had to be bought at North West River, our nearest shopping place. As the men were only able to get off for a short while, we had to think ahead and purchase enough to last for a few months. During the open water season the men could travel by motor boat. In the winter they often went in one of the trucks which was hauling gravel from North West River. It was an all-day job and sometimes meant staying overnight and walking the greater part of the twenty-five miles from North West River to our home.

As months passed more houses were built here, there and everywhere, all shapes and sizes. The place was called Refuge Cove. Medical care was given by the American and Canadian doctors, and we had much to thank them for. Epidemics, of course, broke out as time went on but all were cared for. When the population became too large, Dr. Paddon from North West River took over despite the difficulties of transportation. However, most of us survived all the troubles and trials of the pioneering days and now as we look back we wonder how we did.

As the population increased there was a need for a school. I commenced this work in our home, where as many as fifteen children squeezed in to try to learn a little bit of history, geography, arithmetic, spelling, Bible lessons, and other things. Visiting people from the Base realized that a school building was needed. Here the RCAF came to our aid and a building was donated. Before it could be brought down, a road had to be made. The RCAF asked some of the men to mark trees and cut a path so that the bulldozer would be able to cut the road through. This was done in 1946. A little later the building for school and church was hauled down. There was much work to be done on it but the men gave up work on their own houses and made the school ready for use. This building served the purpose for a number of years. The first teacher was Mr. Ralph Penny, who came to take charge in March after having taught at Mud Lake during the winter.

Church services were conducted on Sunday evening by the Chaplain and Padre from the Canadian and American bases. For special Sundays, transportation was often sent down to take anybody who wished to attend services on the Base. Both the Anglican minister from Cartwright and Reverend Burry from North West River made occasional visits.

1947 brought an increase in the population which in turn brought problems, difficult to overcome. The RCAF suggested that a committee be formed to act between our community and the Base authorities. This was known as the Liaison Committee. With their help and representatives from the Base, many obstacles were overcome with regard to school problems, and many cases of sickness were attended to which otherwise might have proved fatal.

It was during this year that the Hudson's Bay Company decided to open a store which would be more convenient for people to obtain provisions than having to go all the way to North West River. The RCAF once again came to our assistance and gave us a building which was reconstructed and opened by the HBC. This was used for about three years. It is now the RCAF Dental Clinic. The distance from the store to the Valley is about six miles, a long walk when carrying a load of groceries and other household supplies. The HBC provided a van, although it was not sufficient for all the supplies purchased. Often we waited until the workmen's truck came along and squeezed ourselves and provisions in with the men. Later, the Company had a larger truck for the purpose. Being an open vehicle, it was not always a warm ride, and our vegetables sometimes got frozen.

During the winter months it was felt that there should be a resident minister as the population was steadily increasing. There were three major denominations to be cared for: Anglicans, United Church and Moravians. The Chaplains and Padres on the Base were not in a position to undertake the religious work of the Community. The authorities on the Base were consulted and after several meetings and discussions had taken place, it was decided to apply for a minister who would be a non-denominational minister-in-charge. With the assistance of the American and Canadian clergy, a letter was written asking for the help of some interested person. In due course, an answer was received from Paster McKinney in which he offered his services as resident minister for Happy Valley. This was brought up before all interested persons and it was decided that he be asked to take up residence in Happy Valley. In the summer of 1948, Reverend McKinney became the first resident minister. For five years he and his family did much good work in the community. Two of his daughters were teachers in our school. As time went on, each denomination felt that it would like to have its own church and minister, especially since Reverend McKinney was not authorized to baptize babies or marry young couples. These had to be performed when the minister of the particular denomination paid a visit to the Valley....

By the year 1949 the number of children of school age were unable to attend the school previously mentioned. The RCAF was again approached and they very kindly gave another building. This was hauled down and reconstructed by voluntary labour. The three-room school was named The North Star School by one of the principals, Miss Betty Decker. As in the first school building, the classrooms had to be heated with firewood. Stoves were made from oil drums that had to be cut down and stove pipes were attached. Obtaining sufficient firewood to heat the rooms was quite a problem. Fathers of children attending the school were asked to bring firewood. As time went on the men found it very difficult to go off cutting wood, hauling it to their homes and sawing and splitting it in proper lengths for the stoves. Naturally, they had to do this for their own homes, consequently, very few could find the extra time to supply the school with wood. There were still other buildings in the making that called for free labour after their day's or night's work on the RCAF and American bases. Some men were working on night shifts and needed sleep during the day. After much thought and consideration it was decided that the children attending the school should each bring a chunk of wood when they came. Those who were living here at the time will probably recall having to remind their children to take their wood as well as their books to school. Some brought very small pieces and some brought very dry wood, which of course did not hold a fire for any length of time. Often it meant sitting in a cold room with coats and parkas on until a really warm fire was burning and perhaps doing some exercises to get warmed up. You can imagine that it would be quite difficult to seat fifty children around a stove made from a drum so that each child could feel the warmth. That is what we tried to do in order to carry on school.

Desks and chairs were a headache. Again, fathers were asked to make desks and chairs for their children. In the meantime, it meant improvising. This was done by using such things as a door, a sheet of wallboard or tintest, and a very large and cumbersome blackboard. These were supported on trestles used by workmen for making low scaffolds. Benches were used as seats, but most of the children had to kneel. This was rather hard on the knees as the so-called tables were too high for them to sit and do their work. Some tables and chairs were not too strongly constructed, and now and again something would collapse, much to the amusement of the whole class. However, the upper grades—from two to eleven—were more fortunate and most had proper desks and chairs.

Around this time the wood problem became more serious. It was decided to discontinue using wood and use fuel oil instead. This meant that the stoves had to be changed and the oil purchased from the Imperial Oil Company on the Base. Much more expensive, but more satisfactory in order to carry out school work. Two of the male teachers worked in their spare time and made a hook-up system for the flow of oil from the big tanks. Thus, another difficult problem was overcome.

— Alice Perrault
[1.4:21]

I WAS ABOUT SIXTEEN YEARS old when we built the *Western Bride*. Every inch of timber that went into her Uncle Far and me sawed it with the pit saw. Uncle Far was used to sawin' because he sawed with Father. We was two years building the *Western Bride*. Father, of course, he was a pretty good carpenter and a strong, able-bodied man, much bigger than me. I guess I turned after my mother—small—but I got a lot of guts. Anyway, we built the *Western Bride* right there in Paradise River, and we put everything into her, all kinds of works. Father ordered the nails, of course, because you couldn't buy nails for big boats like that around here then. You'd have to send to St. John's, Newfoundland for that. She was fifteen tons.

When we got her finished, we took her out across the grass, just by hand, and launched her. When we pushed her into the water we didn't have any whiskey to baptize her, only a dipper of water to heave across her bow, so being the youngest builder, I took the can of water and, as she dipped her rear end in the water, I hove the water around her bow. Father took this hammer and tacked her nameplates on each side of her, the "*Western Bride*." I think Father got the name from a book. He was very curious and he looked through things and saw all kinds of names, and I think that's where he found the name. Probably it was the name of some other kind of schooner that was built long years ago but, right then at that time, there was nare other boat in any community around such as Cartwright, Pack's Harbour or up around Newfoundland, that we could find, that was called *Western Bride*. So Father decided that was a good name and that's what she went by. That was about 1936.

So that was all right, we put her in the water and we anchored her in the river off from where we live now. The old house was probably a little way back from this one we're in now. That was in June, early part of June. We had a small motor boat at that time, five or six horse-power or something like that, and 'twas the same as with the rest of the schooners, we used to sail along and when 'twould get calm you'd have to haul the motor boat up by the side and tow the *Western Bride* into a harbour. We used to move from here, Paradise River, over to our summer place at Calloway's Cove with everything aboard, right from buckets to the dogs and their tubs, I guess, and the hens. The only thing was that you couldn't have the hens too close to the dogs because they'd bite their heads off.

The very first day we sailed to Calloway's Cove in the *Western Bride*, that very same evening poor Father took a piece of plank that come off the deck and sat down after supper and made a pork board for Grandmother Learning. He carved his initials and the year he built the boat in it, and it's still hung up in our house at Calloway's Cove. I could show it to you tonight if we was there. That's one of Dad's handicraft work, a pork board that he made for Grandmother. We still uses that for cuttin' up our pork [salt pork].

After we left Calloway's Cove, that first summer, we sailed to Dumplin and fished there for part of the summer. The codfish got scarce so we hoisted up our sails and went down to Indian Islands, Aunt Emmeline's home. I think Aunt Emmeline would remember that. We fished there probably up to the middle of September, sailed back to Pack's Harbour, discharged our load of fish, went back to Dumplin and picked up our luggage and sailed back to Paradise River again in October.

I remember comin' up Dumplin Run the evening of October 25th, I believe it was. It was blowin' a gale of wind and the water was very rough. Father went below for a cup of tea just after we left Dumplin Harbour, give the wheel over to my brother Forward, I guess. We was sailin' along. Good breeze. I was pretty idle at that time. I went up in the spar, right up and I sat down on the crosstree, crossbar, in the riggin', away up about thirty feet. I put me arms around the mast and clung on. She listed on that side and then she'd fall back on the other side, back and forth in the sea. By and by the Old Feller, of course, he looked out of the cabin and when he saw me he bawled, "Get the hell down out of that. You'll tumble overboard."

I didn't pay no attention at all. That's the kind of guy I was. I stayed there until he done eatin' his lunch. Finally he come out and grumbled at me and, of course, I come down. So we come on—didn't call to Cartwright that time I don't believe— straight through Main Tickle and straight on to Paradise River. When we got to Paradise we anchored. Everything aboard again: dogs, hens, berries, fish and everything else. Yes, that was a fine little boat, no doubt about it.

We shifted from Dumplin to Goose Bay in the *Western Bride*, sailed down in the fall, in September. We got to Goose Bay the 22nd of September. That was when I was in my early twenties, I suppose. I wasn't my own boss then, I had to go by Father's orders. Work was pretty scarce around the Labrador then, particularly here in Sandwich Bay. Fish and salmon was hard to get at that time and the cost of living was pretty high, same as it is today, costly. There was good work at Goose Bay, and Father was in his health and strength at that time and he was 'Skipper' certainly, so 'twas like the old saying says, 'Father's word went before mine.'

We sailed down that fall in September, got into Goose Bay the 22nd of September. We didn't get right into Goose Bay with the boat; anchored out somewhere down around Sandy Point, or somewhere or other. Father was quite used to the names of places 'cause he travelled there quite a bit with Dr. Paddon. We anchored and went on in to Goose Bay in motor boat, went in to a creek, there in the Valley. It was a very, very narrow place at that time. There was a big bank there with trees as thick as they could stow together. When we got up over the bank there was a man standin' there, Uncle Roy McLean, and he invited us in for the night. I didn't know what to make of the Valley, 'twas all strange, the people was strangers. There was one house away down in the woods one way and another down the other way. I didn't know where I was goin' to end up. If there was a way of gettin' out of the Valley that night, I'd have been the first one to leave. I'd have put my foot on a plank and got out of it. But there was no choice, I was there and I couldn't get out of it. Transportation, at that time, was very hard to find. You had to sail all the way from Goose Bay to Cartwright and there wasn't very many motor boats on the road, so when you got in there you was tagged. 'Twas either make up your mind to stay or get out first chance. Father had a large family so he figured on stayin' a few years, so that included all of us; we all had to stay there certainly.

We straightened away for three or four days and, of course, Father wanted to get work for everybody right away—myself, Uncle Far and all of us. We finally got a little building from Jim Learning, which was his storehouse, I guess; very small, no bedrooms. Poor old Buck Michelin was there and he had a little house (I was still young, not married) so Buck said, "Come over along with me, boy. You can live with me, stay 'long with me and give your father more room."

I was glad of the chance—great chance to get a girlfriend, see. So over I goes and I stayed there with Uncle Buck for about four or five years I guess.

Goin' back to the work now: some days after, we went to work, we went down to the dock where most of the labourers were cuttin' sticks to build a platform for the tractor to come ashore on. I went down and Uncle Ike Rich, from down the Rigolet area and a much older man than I was, and we was there and we saw this 'thing' comin' down through the bushes and we got frightened, you know; this great big thing comin' along, trees goin' flyin', sticks gettin' broke off. We begin to run away because we thought we was goin' to be trampled over.

Uncle Ike said, "What in the devil is this comin' along in the willows?"

I said, "I don't know what it is but I'm not takin' no chance. I'm gettin' the hell out of here." So I took off.

The poor old man said, "Don't be silly, boy, that thing is not goin' to hurt you. There's a man operatin' that."

"What? A man operatin' the like of that!"

He said, "He's not goin' to run into us."

I said, "My goodness, so much trees fallin' down in front, he won't even see us. We should get out of the way anyway."

We runned out on the sand. I'll never forget that.

I was workin', oh, probably six years, and I put away a few dollars and I decided I was able to take over a wife, so this is what I done, I got married. I built my own home and settled down for some twenty-odd years.

I worked in Goose Bay for thirty-two and a half years. I worked with the Americans for thirty years and with the Department of Public Works for two and a half years. I enjoyed workin' with the Americans. They were very, very fine people to work for, but I felt like a dog on a chain. You had to get up early in the morning and get out and look for transportation to the job. If you had a bus run you had to pay your twenty-five cents or fifty cents to get up and another to get back. Eventually I got a truck of my own. But, still and all, you could just go to the job and back, and that's all you could get out of it. It's much the same as a road around here. You can only go to the end and then come back again. You had to be on the job at a certain time and if you wasn't there at that certain time you had a schooner-load of paperwork to fill out. But this is the way the Air Force works, and if you're workin' for them and they're payin' you to work, then you must work, and if you lose a day, well, you got to suffer for it. In other words, you got to explain why you were absent. And I was never used to this kind of thing, although my record was excellent and I got no complaints against the people I worked for, anymore than I just wasn't used to being tied down this long. I was more or less took with the free life. So I figured I put in a pretty good share of time and I only had a small family. I was reared up with a family of fifteen and we never starved to death around the Sandwich Bay area, so I decided to come back to Paradise River.

When I put in my notice that I was goin' to quit my job, there was a lot of questions asked me: "Why are you quittin'?" "What are you goin' to live on?" and so on. This probably sounds silly, to wonder what I was goin' to live on. I didn't see anybody starve on the Labrador where I come from yet.

My foreman, Mr. Dick Quinn, said, "Boy, you shouldn't go back to Paradise River, Mr. Learning. You'll be starved to death."

"Boy," I said, "I'm not much of a man, but if I starves to death by goin' back to Paradise River, somebody here in Goose Bay is goin' to be awful god-dammed hungry."

He laughed, you know.

I was back home about four years before I went back to Goose Bay and when I did go back, one of the first people I laid eyes on was Dick Quinn. He come over and shook hands with me.

"It doesn't look like you're starved to death," he said. "You looks fine."

I said, "Yes, I feels a lot better than when I left here, Dick."

Calloway's Cove has been in the Learning family perhaps ninety odd years, I'd say—that's including my uncles and one thing and another before me. My Uncle Albert Learning took it over from an old man by the name of Calloway, many years ago. It gradually came down through to my father and then me and my brother Forward, and I suppose someday, when we fades away, our sons will take it. My father died on November 6th, 1966. I believe it was 1966. I fished there on and off over the years, about twenty-eight years probably. I'd come up from Goose Bay and do my salmon fishery for a month each summer, which was a vacation. I always took my thirty or thirty-five days and come back to my real spot of salmon fishery, which can't be beat in a Labrador man's mind and courage. You were born and reared on that and I still looks for that. I'm still in the same position now as I was when I was ten years of age as regards to lookin' for salmon and fish. You can't beat the old free country no matter what it is. I was like a bird in a cage at Goose Bay, sufferin' more than anything else because my mind wasn't there, it was back in Calloway's Cove.

The day I got back to Paradise River, September 15, 1968, I was like a dog let off a chain. You can imagine a dog chained on all summer with the collar wrapped tightly around his neck; the minute you unclip him he's gone wild, the same as a wild animal. Well, I was much the same way. Now I'm back from Goose Bay and I'm my own boss again.

— Samson Learning
[10.1:28]

I FIRST STARTED TO TRAP back in the early thirties. 'Twasn't like these days, 'twas the hard way. You took your old sled with about a month or two and a half or three months' stock of food and you'd drag it behind you with your snowshoes on, over hills, through woods or whatever it might be. We never took dogs in the woods. That's the way we did it in Eagle River. If you had to go through the woods and over hills with dogs, you'd only have to haul extra loads—dogs' feed. Perhaps the goin' would be so rough that you'd probably end up haulin' the dogs too, so 'twas better not to bother wit' the dogs.

I started trappin' by meself when I was fifteen. Me and Uncle Steve Brown and Clarence used to go in perhaps about a hundred miles, then we'd branch off and go our own ways. Then perhaps we wouldn't see no one for a couple of months. We'd leave Separation Point when there was enough ice to travel on, 'cause you couldn't travel on Eagle River in canoe. We'd go to the headwaters of Eagle River—Park Lake and Owl Brook. I used to go up against the mountains, in back of the Mealy Mountains. We wouldn't get back for Christmas because we'd be too late startin' off, waitin' for the ice to make. We'd get back around the end of January.

I believe I had one Christmas home from the time I was fifteen until 1935. We went in on water that year, left home in September. We portaged over a hundred miles. 'Twas all portage you might call it, carryin' two canoes, carryin' three months' stock of food. Two and a half barrels of flour, I believe it was, and all the other stuff accordin' to three months' stock of food. We had to make sure we had plenty; didn't want to run short. We left home the twentieth of September and we got back the twenty-third of December.

One time I cut meself. I was all by meself, nobody else for miles around. I was choppin' ice, settin' traps, and 'twas kind of mild, you know. Me axe handle was covered in ice. I picked up a tree top to brush off the tent. I made a chop but I missed the darn brush I chopped at, and the axe come down on the back of me hand. I cut a couple of veins. Well, I had a mess of blood that night!

I had to start campin' wit' one hand, and wherever I went there was a stream of blood pourin' out. I had to set the tent, cut wood and cut it up with one hand. Some bad startin' off like that, after used to usin' two all your life.

When I got in the tent I had everything covered in blood—tent, stove and everything else. I had no flummy-dum cooked for me supper. I was hungry, starvin' to death. I mixed an old flummy. I think 'twas half water and half blood and flour mixed together. I had blood all over the stove and, when I got the fire goin', the blood started roastin'. That smelled some good, like some kind of good meat—made me hungrier than ever.

After I got me tent up, I got in and tried to get the blood slowed down and get it to stop. I had it slowed down pretty good then I reached around to get something to put on it. I suppose I must have moved me hand or something...well, it looked like a piece of red wool goin' down. It was spurtin' blood ag'in. I said, "To hell wit' that." I had an old pipe wit' me, so I lit 'en up and stuck me hand out and let 'en run. I had a darn good smoke. Then I got at 'en ag'in and slowed it down very good. Then I got some dry flour and dabbed it on and put a partridge crop over that, outside. Then I wrapped strips of flour bag around right tight and lashed it wit' bankline. In the morning around four o'clock I got up and, right where my vein was, 'twas like a bullet hole. That's where the blood was pourin' out like a fountain. The main vein was chopped. In the morning the flesh was puffed out in the hole and it never bleed nothing after, nothing worthwhile. I lost blood enough that time that it made quite a difference.

I had to go across a range of mountains, haulin' me sled. Me legs used to get shaky, I lost enough blood to get weak. I started off almost straight across…. Three days later I met Roy Brown.

I was goin' across a darn good old portage, and the darn sled hooked into a darn tree. I had me hand up in a sling. I was real mad. I made a wicked pluck and the haulin' line broke and went 'smack' across me sore hand. I think I said a few bad words then and there.

When I met Roy, the first thing he noticed was blood on me snowshoes. He didn't notice me hand in the sling. He bawled, "How many?" He thought I killed a lot of caribou. Poor Roy, didn't know what to think.

After the first night it wasn't too bad. I could work a lot better then with one hand than I can now with two. If I had to set a tent now, it'd take me from daylight in the morning 'till dark in the evening.

There wasn't many girls around them times. You'd go in the bush and be gone maybe two and a half or three months. When you come out the first girl you saw looked awful good no matter how bad lookin' she was.

The war broke out in 1939 and 'twas like everything else, 'twas a job that had to be done. Three of us left Cartwright in September 1940: me, Frank Hefler and Howard Martin.

War broke out in September 1939 but the way it was in Labrador, then, you had to wait for the magistrate, in the summer, to sign on. He only come once in the summer and he never come 'till August after the war broke out. When he come we went aboard to sign on, and then we had to wait for a call from St. John's before we could go. 'Twas September before we got the call. Oh, we knew all about the war; heard about it on the radio. The magistrate wasn't recruitin' people, but he was takin' your name if you wanted to volunteer. In St. John's, when they had a draft made up, they'd send you overseas. There was one hundred and seventy-five went over altogether from Newfoundland, six from Labrador. There was three men from Cartwright and three from Battle Harbour.

After two years from this side, you could leave to come home, but I never made it for five years…. After I come back from overseas I worked at Goose Bay for fourteen and a half years, but that wasn't much of a life for me. 'Tis all right for a man that got a family. He had to do it. But just a guy's self, if he can make a livin' like we fellers is used to in Labrador, trappin' and fishin', that's all right. Well, it didn't really matter if he made a livin' or not, if you was single, you was only starvin' yourself. You wasn't starvin' no woman and children.

I worked on the American Base fourteen and a half years. I started workin' in 1946. There was quite a bunch of us come down from Sandwich Bay that time. We only got odd jobs when we got there first, but in the spring things opened up a bit and we all got jobs.

I was workin' as an electrical linesman. There'd be days when there'd be nothing to do. Eight hours with nothing to do seemed like a week. You'd be wishin' you were down the bay fishin', summertime, or up in the river huntin', wintertime. But you couldn't leave, had to be on the job just walkin' around the shop day after day. That was worse than five years of war, a lot. In the last of it I said, "What in the hell am I doin' here anyway, wastin' what few years of my life I got left in a place like this when I don't have to?" So I decided to quit. I give them a month's notice on the first of June. That was 1962.

They wanted to know why I was quittin'. I told them there was only two things worth livin' for as far as I was concerned, women and freedom. I wasn't gettin' nare woman so I was goin' to have freedom.

I started trappin' up in Churchill River in 1962. When you're trappin' there's always something to look forward to. You're off to your traps all day, then in the night you're thinkin' about where you're goin' tomorrow, where you might set a trap and all that. You're thinkin' and figurin' until you went to sleep. You were always thinkin' and figurin'.

I kept at trappin' 'till a few years ago when me legs started to give out. I couldn't walk anymore any good, and 'twas gettin' worse all the time. Now I'm down here and I can't get up there at all. It's not so good now, time is long. One thing that's left to look forward to is the kids comin' down on weekends, to my cabin. Only for the kids comin' to see me, life wouldn't be worth livin' at all.

— Harold Brown
[6.3:4]

Somewhere beyond those distant hills is where I long to be.
The rivers and the lonely lakes are calling out to me.
They're saying, 'Come back home old man, back here where you belong,
'Cause time for you is running out, and you've been gone so long.

^So take me to the country, just the way it used to be,
To once more ride her rivers and sleep beneath the trees.
Let me watch the morning sun spread out across the land,
And if I only live one day, I'll die a happy man.

When I was such a younger man I led a trapper's life.
The country was my living; the country was my life.
The country was my comfort, my companion and my home.
Of all the years I've travelled there, I never felt alone.

So take me to the country, just the way it used to be,
To once more ride her rivers and sleep beneath the trees.
Let me watch the morning sun spread out across the land,
And if I only live one day, I'll die a happy man.

I know my days are numbered, but I have few regrets.
I'm too old to be dreaming but not to old to wish.
If I could have my way to do what's on my mind,
I'd trade away tomorrow for a ticket back in time.

Please take me to the country, just the way it used to be,
To once more ride her rivers and sleep beneath the trees.
And let me watch the morning sun spread out across the land,
And if I only live one day, I'll die a happy man.

Harry Martin
Song for Henry Mesher[1]

[9.3:31]

EPILOGUE

In August 1995, exactly nineteen years after Anne disappeared from the side of a mountain over Ramah Bay and became part of the terrible beauty of this land, I returned to Labrador expecting the worst. I had heard that in the six years since my last visit the moratorium on cod and salmon had all but shut down the coastal villages. Embittered fishermen now believed that in accepting government cheques for their presently useless fishing licenses they had relinquished both their children's patrimony and their centuries-old way of life. If and when the fishery resumed, Labradorians might be unable to participate. I had also observed with dismay that the gravel road across Nitassinan to Quebec had become the "Trans-Labrador Highway" on regional maps—implying an interstate through what had been one of the hemisphere's last great roadless areas. And I knew that Happy Valley-Goose Bay, already collecting refugees from places grown complicated and stressful, was flooding with newcomers eager to capitalize on the mining boom. I supposed the Labradorians would be hard to find, a minority even in Happy Valley, and all traces of them days would have vanished. But none of this was entirely true.

The plane from Newfoundland tobogganed across a bed of clouds until, nearing Goose, it dropped into the rain zone over the western highlands of the Mealy Mountains. Below us the angular, riffled courses of the Kenamu, Kenamish, and Traverspine rivers were etched in a landscape perhaps less frequented by man than it has been for centuries. We landed on wet tarmac just as a sweet Labrador sunset flooded the shallow gap between earth and overcast, transfiguring the suddenly enraptured world—firred hillsides, squat airport buildings, tethered bush planes—in golden light. At the still-tiny airport Doris Saunders, editor of *Them Days Magazine*, wove my welcome into loose strands of banter with friends and relatives in the room. It had been many years since we met, and while we had corresponded throughout the evolution of this book, neither would have recognized the other but for recent photos I had seen of her.

As Doris drove me down to her home in the Valley I could see that the village had indeed grown, but new neighborhoods were peripheral to old, and the original settlement looked much as it always had, though far less raw. Houses were tidier, many with new vinyl siding, and there were lawns and gardens where for so long the sandy soil, pounded into a hardpan by dogs and children, had defied cultivation. Some of the otherwise undistinguished homes of the town founders still gazed out toward the river from their original plots along the bank. Many had been expanded or upgraded by the founders' grown children, and the rosy Labrador birches left standing when the land was cleared fifty years ago had stretched their satiny limbs up over the yards and become regal.

All through town, new houses and old held Labradorians. Amused that I would think them lost, Doris pointed them out one after another: Goudie, Blake, Tuglavina, Trimm, Voisey, White, Mesher, Pottle, Williams, Pye, Rumbolt, Shiwak, Snook, Kippenhuck, Chubbs, Winters, Lane, O'Brien, O'Dell, Broomfield, Nitsman, Penny, Pike, Spearing, Sheppard, Wolfrey, Yetman, Rendell, Ponniuk, McLean, Lyall, Chaulk, Manak, Adams, Gear, Hamel, Martin, Flowers, Oliver, Rich, Keefe, Pardy, Michelin, Davis, Montague, Mugford, Ikey, Toomashie, Palliser, Jacques, Learning, Lethbridge, Coombs, Saunders, Curl, Decker, Dyson, Mitchell, Earle, Tooktoshina, Edmunds, Bird, Heard, Holwell, Perrault, Fequet, Andersen, Ford, and on and on. They were all there. Most of the newcomers from the Island and Outside lived in subdivisions on the high plateau near the airfields rather than in Happy Valley.

Doris stopped often as we did errands, chatting to people through the rolled-down window of her intrepid pick-up, named "Susan" after her eighteenth-century Inuit Ancestor. Uncle Bob Davis, now nearly eighty, was building another last boat under the birches in his back yard. He had installed brass portholes salvaged from the Smithsonian's dear lamented research vessel *Tunuyak*, on which my family and the close-knit group of colleagues who worked with my husband had adventured among the enchanted archipelagos of Labrador for so many years. We drove past the Paddon Memorial Home where Doris interviewed Flora Baikie and many of the other old timers before they passed away. She said they were contented there, those frontier men and women so good at making the best of things, comfortable and happy to be cared for and occasionally remembered.

Joe Goudie had replaced his mother Elizabeth's old home on Hamilton River Road with a modern gabled house like those he admired 'Outside' when representing Labrador in the Newfoundland government. Gone the woodstove where Aunt Liz baked us redberry cakes and trappers' bread in the early 1970s, and the TV corner where late in life this celebrated "woman of Labrador" had become addicted to her soaps. In his modern kitchen Joe prepared for us a tasty meal of arctic char, the only prime Labrador fish then excluded from the moratorium. In fact, he said, the northern outports were actively trying to develop new markets for char and to keep abreast of the shifting demand for other kinds of marine resources. At present it was shrimp, crabs, scallops, sea urchins, and certain deep-water fish previously considered worthless. Federal Aboriginal development funds helped capitalize these expensive ventures, enabling Native cooperatives to obtain the large modern vessels required for offshore harvesting and processing. Southern Labradorians, denied Aboriginal status, were trying to do the same on their own. The communities were hanging on, as they always had. Life has never been easy on the coast.

After dinner Joe brought out a bottle of Chicoutai, a cloudberry liqueur made by the Innu of Quebec. It was superior to the Scandinavian Laponica and suggested yet another way that Labradorians could participate in an environmentally benign form of local resource use. There are actually quite a few such options, from specialty foods to eco-tourism, all potentially marketable at top dollar because they are rare and unique. Like Uncle Johnny Broomfield, many Labradorians are entrepreneurial by inclination. The computer, Internet, and fax machine are helping them transcend the ice-bound shipping lanes and torpid postal systems that have for so long contributed to the country's commercial isolation. Ironically, it is technology that could become the ultimate salvation of Labrador's environment and culture. Successful entrepreneurs generally bring a number of employees up with them. From this perspective, Labrador's future did not seem quite so bleak.

Another day Doris and two of her childhood pals from Cartwright took me on a pilgrimage to Muskrat Falls, twenty-five miles up the Trans-Labrador Highway. While it is true that this track is now more or less open year-round and supports land transport of goods from Quebec—with a consequent decline in the cost of living for Labradorians—I must confess I was relieved to find it decidedly primitive, its gravel surface pitted with bone-jarring potholes and gullies. Sections still wash out in heavy rains, just as they did in the early 1970s when it was built for summer access to the Churchill Falls dam and Premier Smallwood's failed logging venture, scars of which are finally beginning to heal. Berry bushes and fireweed have covered the clear-cut hillsides, young spruce are coming up among the birch and alder saplings, and glacial sand no longer flushes into the Grand River with every rain.

The pick-up lurched down to Muskrat Falls on a newer side road that cuts across bogs and boreal woodlands that once represented a good day's bushwhacking. During the early years when our expeditions began in Goose Bay, we came here to relieve the tedium of protracted last minute preparations and delays. For me it was always an eagerly awaited return to the 'real Labrador,' wild Labrador, long since dispelled from Happy Valley and the sterile, overheated U.S. Air Force facilities in which we lodged on the Base. In the open forest between the road and falls we had camped on soft meadows of caribou moss and romped in sandy blow-outs delicately inscribed with the passings of mice and, sometimes, the ominous tracks of wolf, bear, and moose. We had chased ptarmigan through birch groves and reveled in the tart explosions of flavour from redberries miraculously overlooked by resident creatures through the long winter. The first year we went Josh was just walking, Ben four, our friend Anne a formidable fourteen swooping ungainly and grinning down hillsides, hair flying through birches and sunlight like ravens—but in those days, we were all new in this magical world together. We read Tolkien aloud in the evenings.

After an eye-straining day in *Them Days* genealogical files, I was whisked away by Doris to see the sunset from North West River. A bridge has replaced the rickety red cable car which used to provide access to the old Hudson's Bay Company trading post and Grenfell Mission buildings on the Settler side, when it wasn't broken. Automobiles have changed the character of the village, to be sure, but its charm and tranquillity remain intact. Thanks to the fact that residents can now commute to Goose Bay, it has assumed some of the characteristics of a bedroom community, including a touch here and there of affluence. In the cemetery at the crossing on the hill, Ambrose Brooks himself presides over a congregation of descendants—Blakes, Goudies, Michelins, Baikies, Montagues—resting now under a plump quilt of mosses and ground shrubs. We watched the sun go down from Sunday Hill Park, a pretty little sanctuary which citizens of the town had made for its 250th anniversary. It was just one of several new recreation areas around western Lake Melville that served as focal points for community gatherings like the annual regatta and canoe races the day before my arrival.

Down in the spruce grove on the point, Uncle Roland Baikie welcomed us for tea and stories around his kitchen table. Later that week, Doris and her granddaughter Heather treated me to a blustery night in a cabin on his property. It was wired for electricity, but we preferred to cook on the woodstove by the light of a kerosene lamp and pretend. For all the easy comfort so close at hand, the outlaw wind roaring in from Lake Melville was no less awesome in the night than it has ever been; the anguished moon, her ebony mane entangled with stars, is no less blinding in its clarity; and it is not to be regretted that lonely pensioners can admire their country's glorious tantrums from the safety of kitchens heated at the flip of a switch.

But what of the changes ahead? Can they be absorbed so easily? How much longer before the acid haze from refineries tarnishes even this bright moon? Two years, three, maybe four? How long before even Labrador's ancient cranky gods will be driven from this, their final refuge, by yellow machines plowing through the virgin land, tearing its fragile, berried skin, splintering its delicate bones, its primeval silence, its exquisite solitude and balance. What then would remain of the "labrador" in Labrador? And what will it mean for Heather?

She was six-going-on-seven then, a bright, engaging child. Although her blue eyes and golden hair belie the Aboriginal blood in her veins, she is Labradorian to the core—sensible but sensitive, unfailingly generous, direct, wise, and private. Like many of her forbears, she loves to read. By the time she left elementary school she would be computer literate as well. In all likelihood she will attend university outside Labrador, perhaps in Nova Scotia, where some of the young people today find they encounter less prejudice than in Newfoundland. As adults, Heather and her contemporaries will be thoroughly prepared to move about with confidence in the outside world. This was not the case for their parents. Those who made the break often returned, unhappy with the money-driven pace of life and the dislocation from their community. That may not be true much longer. If Labrador cannot compete with the opportunities available beyond its borders—or if the land loses its magic and the community its Labradorian coherence—Heather's may be the first generation to leave for good.

Economic opportunity and environmental preservation: to many in Labrador these seem unreconcilable alternatives. It has been a long time since America and Lower Canada stood at that crossroads. Oh we still fight to preserve our wilderness areas, but these are but remnants of something already lost, compounds circumscribed by highways, laced with old mines and logging roads, infiltrated by toxic haze from distant cities, and crowded with their neon gore-tex refugees. None is large enough to dispel the awareness that it is now part of man's world. We suffer its wildness to exist for our pleasure, but only to the extent that it is economically convenient.

When we last stood at this juncture, whether it was the shores of what would become New England and Quebec or the feet of the unbreached Rockies, we did not have a choice. We did not know that we could so thoroughly conquer wilderness that it would come to have intrinsic value. Nor could we imagine that the industrial and technological environment we would replace it with could subjugate us in turn and rob us of a vital part of our soul, so that to save ourselves we would have to scramble to preserve the last vestiges of land where one could still sense the pulse of the universe. We did not know a lot of things then that we know now. Indeed, we know enough now—about economics, about the true costs of major extractive and industrial projects in marginal environments, about the long-term benefits of small-scale sustainable enterprises, about the consequences of disrupting the intricate relationships that sustain ecosystems, about making conscious choices—to do better this time. But will we, will they?

Now as ever, Labrador's future is not in its own hands but in those of outsiders whose primary goal is exploitation, whether for noble or selfish ends. They are unlikely to recognize the value of a place that remains one of the last on earth where one can still experience the planet as it was on the afternoon of the Seventh Day, before mankind began to remake it. It will come down to this: What is the immediate dollar value of primeval silence, of a landscape in which man can rediscover what he really is, of wilderness for its own sake?

I saw little evidence of the mining activity in Happy Valley during the summer of '95, although advertisements in *The Labradorian* and *Voisey's Bay News*, a propaganda sheet for the mining industry, clamored for attention: "buy your mining supplies at my store," and "try the miners' special dinner at my restaurant." The local Chamber of Commerce had gone all out to recast traditional businesses into what it hoped would be competitive mining-support industries. But so far, little of the action was reaching Happy Valley or its would-be mining services. Exploration teams wanted only to get in and out of the field as quickly as possible, which in Labrador has never been easy. Activity was therefore concentrated at the airfields and adjacent hotels, where prospectors frustrated by the shortage of available transportation or bad flying weather paced the floors and swilled beer. Many found more expeditious ways into the bush through Labrador City or flew their own helicopters in from Outside, bypassing Happy Valley-Goose Bay altogether.

Nain was the real center of mining activity. There, I was told, helicopters clattered across the sky from dawn to dark, and groups of strangers dominated the village paths. Strangers in the store, strangers peeking into the old Moravian church, strangers making deals with local leaders in the back rooms of community buildings. The packs of children who usually adopt visitors right away hardly took notice any more, while the Hebronemiut elders stood aside of the pathways, confounded, as the big strangers passed. Confounded seemed to be the operative word for the whole village. Anxiety about the pace of change was deadlocked with hopes for a better future. It was obvious to all that the town—indeed the country—desperately needed a new revenue base and jobs. While the Innu opposed any mining activity until their land claims were resolved, the Inuit were initially conflicted. They, too, are attached to their land and freedom, but they are as pragmatic as the southern Settlers, from whom they differ only in location. Through much of the summer of '95, they kept their silence as the rest of Labrador waited for them to decide if it was good, or bad, this thing that was happening to the country.

The only information to reach Happy Valley-Goose Bay and US and Canadian media during this period came from PR agents for the mining companies. They reported that the exploration camps were models of environmental correctness, that pending Native land claims would be respected, that Labradorians were being consulted and their concerns promptly addressed, and that a majority welcomed mining in their land and the prospect of employment and higher standards of living. The companies made a point of hiring local labourers at the exploration sites. As a result, there was little overt opposition—no watch-dog groups, no citizens' councils, no open town meetings, no letters to the editors, and no investigative reporting on Voisey's Bay while I was there. Privately, however, individuals were beginning to voice not only dismay but a paralyzing, unshakable, and certainly self-fulfilling conviction that there was nothing anyone could do to stop the mining even if they wanted to. It is too big, some said; the Native leaders have all been bought off and, in the end, who wouldn't be, because when the deck is stacked against you, you've got to take care of 'number one.'

Meanwhile, Newfoundland was leasing out claims in Labrador at a rate of over ten thousand a day. By June, a fifth of the country lay under a grid of intersecting boundaries, some of them literally cut through the bush; by September there was hardly an acre left to let, and the provincial government had made tens of millions of dollars in fees. Prospectors flooded in to complete reconnaissance work. Although exploration generally involves drilling and other kinds of invasive activity, environmental concerns and Native rights were shoved aside in the rush. Diamond Fields Resources, which had staked out most of the prime mineral sites in Labrador prior to announcement of its discovery, seems indeed to have conducted work in a responsible way, undoubtedly to counter founder Robert Friedlander's criminal environmental reputation, but few others followed suit.

Autumn brought new insults to the northern communities in the form of "no trespassing" signs on the local berry grounds. Residents removed them—naturally—along with the stakes that mark these remote mining claims. It is a typically Labradorian form of resistance, a statement of fact simple as the interloping Settler's trap left disarmed and hanging from a tree in Nitassinan. Initial reports filtering in from the environmental impact studies were also helping consolidate public opinion. To most everyone's surprise, archaeological teams hired by Diamond Fields found important aboriginal remains on the principal Voisey's Bay claim and in the vicinity of planned roadways. Legally, these cannot be disturbed until they have been excavated or preserved, and local Aboriginal groups are the ones who determine their disposition.

By September residents of Nain and Davis Inlet were beginning to speak out against the rapid pace of exploration. As Inuit leaders discovered how insignificant was their role in the decision-making process, disillusionment eroded the trust so painstakingly cultivated by Diamond Fields during the summer. The promise of employment and a brighter economic future had begun to dim as well. An August issue of the *Globe and Mail* projected that even extensive mining in Labrador would generate fewer than a thousand jobs—far less if smelting were done elsewhere in Canada—and most of these would go to experienced mining and construction workers from outside the province. A few Labradorians might obtain positions as cooks and labourers, and there would be some modest economic spin-offs in Nain, Happy Valley, and the western iron-mining towns of Wabush-Labrador City. But it was becoming clear that mining would not replace the fishery in terms of buoying the entire population. It would be no panacea for unemployment, and the social and environmental price tag would be enormous. One way or another, within fifty years it would all be finished. The exhausted mines would close, miners would leave. Labrador would be left on the trash heap of industrial greed, her vast expanses of virgin land violated, possibly littered with ghost towns, crumbling roadways and port facilities, abandoned refineries, mountains of waste rock, toxin-leaching residues, dead ponds and streams. Then would Labrador, so long a secret Eden, at last deserve her reputation as "the land God gave to Cain."

As October leaned towards November, opposition building in the northern settlements began to resonate across the country. Citizens' commissions formed—women's groups, Aboriginal groups, and Settlers gathered to debate their country's future. People began speaking out through the media, and Innu, Inuit, and many of the Settlers were saying with one voice, "We have a right to demand that mining activity cease until the land claims and environmental impact studies are complete and we are guaranteed a say in decisions regarding our land and our lives."

For a brief moment in the fall of 1995—the first in their history, and possibly the last, because they are not immune from divide-and-conquer tactics—the people of Labrador acknowledged their commonalties and stood together on behalf of the country they share and love, each in its own way. For the Innu and Inuit, attachment to the land is spiritual, beyond words. They have passed it on in carvings, dance, song, and stichery. For the Settlers it is unabashedly sentimental. They too have passed it on in needlework, song, and art, but also in words, in poetry. These expressions of love have accumulated generation after generation into a culture. The ties thus created are profound and enduring, even among those who have moved away, even among the increasingly village-bound younger generation whose lives are circumscribed more by the TV and computer screen than a trapline or windswept barren. 'Them days,' as I found on my visit, is not entirely a way of life or a time gone by. It is also a state of mind. As such it lives on in the people, nourished by the enduring wildness of the land. It has been as central to the Settler psyche as to the Aboriginal, and it may be their strongest weapon against the legions of avarice now massing on the horizons. Since 1995, while plunging nickel prices have temporarily postponed development of Voisey's Bay, bulldozers have begun clearing land for the massive and as yet unfunded hydroelectric projects on the Grand River just above Happy Valley, and surveyors are staking out the first miles of a roadway that is eventually to stretch from the Straits all the way across southern Nitassinan to Goose Bay, facilitating access for lumber giants like Abitibi Price.

While searching a college anthology for a half-remembered poem after my return home in 1995, I stumbled on one of Carl Sandburg's tributes to the common man, "The People Will Live On." Penned nearly a century ago, its inexplicable allusion to "labrador" and steel lends it an uncanny prescience. It concludes:

"The people know the salt of the sea
and the strength of the winds
lashing the corners of the earth.

The people take the earth
as a tomb of rest and a cradle of hope.
Who else speaks for the Family of Man?
They are in tune and step
with constellations of universal law.

The people is a polychrome,
a spectrum and a prism
held in a moving monolith,
a console organ of changing themes,
a clavilux of colour poems
wherein the sea offers fog
and the fog moves off in rain
and the labrador sunset shortens
to a nocturne of clear stars
serene over the shot spray
of northern lights.
The steel mill sky is alive.
The fire breaks white and zigzag
shot on a gun-metal gloaming.
Man is a long time coming.
Man will yet win.
Brother may yet line up with brother:

This old anvil laughs at many broken hammers.
There are men who can't be bought.
The fireborn are at home in fire.
The stars make no noise.
You can't hinder the wind from blowing.
Time is a great teacher.
Who can live without hope?
In the darkness with a great bundle of grief
the people march.
In the night, and overhead a shovel of stars for
keeps, the people march:
Where to? What next?"

In my mind, I always return to the hilltop. The day is warm, a 'T-shirt day,' no
flies. I have wandered all morning from bakeapple meadows to slopes where blueberries festooning the outcrops grow especially sweet over the sun-warmed rock.

With no particular destination I have followed the paths of least resistance toward the most beckoning greenswards and ridgelines, scouting out terraces where ancient people staked a tent or flaked tools for the day's hunt. I have savoured the varied flavours of clear water from a dozen streams, and plunged into pools so cold they snatch your breath away and leave you clean and sparkling to the depths of your soul. I have let the sun dry me as I walked barefoot over soft mosses toward the highest hill, certain I was the only person to visit this place in maybe a hundred years, maybe ever. Clothed again I wade through the tuckamore thickets that guard the slopes, using my hands to help pull free of gripping branches until I gain the firmer tundra and the loping bare rock of the summit.

I sit on a boulder once laid gently down by the dying glacier. Next to me is a tall pile of flat stones encrusted with lichens. The *inuksuit*—stone men—are so old no one, not even the elders, have stories of their origins or know who made them and why. Around me is the island, the places I have walked and those that I will keep in mind to explore another day. Around the island is the sea, and in the sea more islands. Icebergs, blazing white and turquoise in the deep blue day, drift slowly through the archipelago and over the horizon where they loom in the density of the earth's curve like hats, like castles, clearer in detail than those close at hand. Behind me the islands merge with the mainland in a mass of undulating blues streaked with blue-white scribbles of perpetual snow. I can see so far in the crystalline air that I imagine the thin gray line to the northeast is the loom of Greenland. And all around, stillness, the whisper of blood in my ears. A bee speeds from the vanishing point before me and on into the vanishing point behind. A soft explosive sound announces the passing of a whale. I find it, far out among the islands, but its exhalations sound as close as the cove below. So much space, and everything in order. Everything works as it should, with no muss and bluster.

Another sound emerges from the shadowy hems of distant islands. Nowadays it is apt to be the drone of a speedboat, but in my early visits to the hilltop it was the soft, syncopated *puttitaputittaput-taput* of a trapboat making its way from net to net or threading the islands toward the village with the week's catch. It is a sound that belongs to the landscape as intimately as that of the whale or the taffeta rustle of the inquisitive raven drifting over my shoulder.

These are the people of Labrador. They have lived here not as masters of the land but as co-habitants with the fox and whale. They followed the retreating glacier north and west. They made the *inuksuit* on the high places and flaked the stone tools I find on old beach ridges. Their skulls stare at the passing seasons from dark recesses of clefts in the rock. They have walked this island alone, spear or gun in hand, gamebag slung on their back, many times, over and over. They know it in the sinister grip of fog, the terrifying rage of storms, and the ruthless indifference of death—as well as the splendor of a day like mine. They too have climbed the hill.

We all find it eventually. It is in our diaries, we Outsiders, always for us an epiphany, a long, slow exhalation of all the soul's clutter and grime and a deep infusion of pure calm, of clarity, of understanding too plain for words, of peace. Once you have been there, it is with you forever, reinforced with each visitation. For the people of this place, it is the landscape of their character, as much a part of them as the water they drink and the air they breathe. When it no longer exists, when men overpower the land and divide the vastness of its wilderness into token parks, parcels, reserves between mine pits and roadways, power lines and ports, "them days" will at last come to an end, and we will all have lost our way back home.

GLOSSARY

Aboriginal: Pertaining to a specific indigenous group or individual.
aboriginal: Generic term for indigenous people.
amautik: Woman's parka (anorak) with big hood for baby.
angakkuk: (n) (pl. angakkut) shaman; (v) to Conjure.
babiche: Strips of animal hide used for lacing and webbing.
bakeapple: Cloudberry *[Rubus chamaemorus]*.
balk: (n) Roughcut timber beams.
ballicaters: Ice shelves and barricades that form or raft up along the shoreline, from barricados.
bangbelly: Cake, pancake, or pudding made with any ingredients at hand, originally flour, baking soda, pork or seal fat, molasses, and sometimes blueberries.
barge: Large boat on which the catch of a schooner fleet could be processed.
bark: (v) Preserve rope and cloth by soaking in liquid cutch.
bawn: Smooth shore rocks where codfish were laid out to dry; can also mean grassy meadow around house or settlement.
bedlamer: Young harp seal.
berth: Fishing or sealing spot traditionally used by a family or crew. Inshore berths had "shore-fasts," usually a stick driven into a cleft in the rocks to which one end of the net was attached.
bight: Shallow cove.
birding: Waterfowl and seabird hunting.
blackberry: Crowberry *[Empetrum nigrum]*.
blueberries: 1) Sugar whorts *[Vaccinium augustifolium]*; 2) Ground whorts, whortleberry, or bilberry *[V. uliginosum]*; and 3) Tobacco whorts, possibly huckleberries.
brewis: Hardbread cooked to mush with salt cod.
brin: Burlap or sack-cloth.
buddy: Unnamed person in story.
camp: (n) Tent.
canvas: Heavy canvas or linoleum floor covering; sail.
capelin: Small sardine-like fish pursued by cod, seals, and whales.
chain drug: Chain or rope and chain to throw over komatik runners as brake.
cod trap: A large fishnet set in a square trap configuration with a leading wall to intercept and corral schools of migrating codfish.
collar: Mooring.
company: Group of birds or animals.
cossack: Outer pullover hooded coat, or dickie.
crackerberry: Bunchberry *[Cornus canadensis]*.
cracky: Small mongrel dog kept as pet; originally Innu dogs.
cronnicks: Large driftwood.

cuddy: Small enclosed storage cubby in bow or stern of an open boat.

cuff: Load.

cuffs: Mittens.

cullage: Inferior grade of fish or salmon.

cutch tar: A liquid made from steeped conifer bark and cones, solidified into blocks ("kootch") for storage and transport. It was used to soak ropes, nets, and sails to protect them from effects of salt water.

dappers & grounders: Fish hooks weighted for surface or bottom fishing.

dickie: Hooded cotton duck outer shell for anorak.

dodge: To stroll, saunter, or follow stealthily.

dogberry: Northern mountain ash [*Pyrus decora*].

duffel: Wool felt used for inner lining of anorak and skin boots.

fit out: Outfit.

flakes: Wood frame platforms for drying codfish.

full: (v) To weave the webbing in a snowshoe.

seal frame: Chain of seal nets strung together from a shorefast.

gaff: Hook.

game leg: Lame leg.

gasher: Small fishing boat.

gathering: Boil or abcess, "rising."

glover's needle: A large, flat-ended needle for canvas and other heavy fabric.

grapnels: Multi-pronged, light anchor good for holding small boats and fish nets on rocky bottoms.

greenhorn: Novice.

handy: Nearby.

harp seal: A migratory seal of the North Atlantic and Arctic oceans; *Pagophilus groenlandicus*, also called saddleback.

idle: Fun-loving, mischievous.

Innu: Montagnais (southern or mountaineer) & Naskapi (barren ground) branches of the Algonkian people; in Labrador, may refer to *métis* who have traditionally identified themselves with and lived the Innu culture.

Inuit: Canadian Eskimos; in Labrador also refers to Euro-Inuit families who have traditionally or recently identified themselves with Inuit culture or, in the latter case, qualify for membership in the Labrador Inuit Association by virtue of their geographic location.

Inuk: Inuit person.

inukshuk: (pl. inuksuit) Rock cairn made to look like man, usually as landmarks but also as caribou-driving aides. On Baffin Is. and northern Ungava, some are known to have special spiritual significance.

jannies: Mummers.

jannying: Mummering.

jar: Local name for the ringed seal, *Pusahispida* or *Phocahispida*, a common nonmigratory earless seal of north Polar seas.

jent: Jaunt.

jigger: Unbaited lead codfish snagging hook molded in shape of codfish

"jug": (v) Jigged.

junk: Chunk, as of wood.

kablunak: (Quallunaak) White person.

komatik: Long sled for pulling loads behind dogteams or skidoos.

kudlik: Soapstone lamp made by early Inuit.

landwash: Tideline.

limbin': Removing branches.

liveyer: This West-of-England term for people 'who live here' usually refers in Labrador specifically to Settlers of coastal areas whose main orientation was the cod fishery.

lofting: Tintest or particalboard sheets used as interior covering for walls and ceilings.

longliner: Motorized fishing boat of up to 60 feet for the mid-shore fishing zone.

lop: Short, choppy waves.

lun: Lee, or sheltered side of land.

marl off: (v) Stroll or meander.

mat: Hooked rug.

météo: Innu shaman.

Métis: Elsewhere refers to Indian-European half-breeds. In Labrador it is the politically preferred and virtually synonymous term for Settler and indicates inhabitants of mixed Euro-Aboriginal blood who are ineligible for membership in the LIA by virtue of their birthplace and residence.

"mind to": Trouble or remember to.

mukashan: Innu ceremonial deer-meat feast.

nare: Not any.

Native: see Aboriginal. As used by Labrador Settlers, might refer to members of mixed families with aboriginal lineage on the male side. Newfoundlanders referred to all Labradorians with aboriginal blood as "Natives."

native: Considered indigenous to a place.

"no price": Worthless.

path: Trapline or trapping grounds by custom "owned" by a specific trapper and passed on to the youngest child or person of choice.

paunch: (v) To gut a game animal.

pease: (v) Seep through.

peel: (n) Salmon (usually immature) weighing less than five lbs..

"poor old": Now deceased.

puncheon: Wooden cask or barrel of 44-140 gallons.

puncheon tub: Half a puncheon used as a tub.

punt: Small wooden rowboat.

quarred ice: Ice flooded with water.

quintal: 112 lbs. weight, used to measure dried codfish.

race: (n) Generation.

rackets: Snowshoes, racquettes.

rattle: Waterfall, rapid, or narrow sea passage swept by strong currents and therefore often unfrozen in winter.

ravelled: Unravelled.

redberry: Locally also 'partridgeberry,' mountain cranberry *[Vaccinium vitis-idaea]*.

reeve: (v) To unravel; to pass a rope through a hole.

risin': (n) 1) Abcess or boil; 2) Horizontal strip of wood supporting seats and thwarts in small boats; 3) Batch of yeast bread dough.

rooms: Fishing station.

row: Fight, ruckus.

run: (n) Narrow strait or passage between islands; tickle; reach.

scravel: Scurry, scramble.

scrunchion: The crispy fried-out remains of rendered fat.

seal frame: The shape in which seal nets were set out in the water.

seine: Deep net drawn or thrown around a school of fish and pursed up like a bag.

Settler: Here usually refers to the mixed-race (métis) inhabitants of Labrador who have historically identified themselves with their European forebears.

shallops: Large, partly decked fishing vessel rigged with lug sails.

shareman: Person working on "shares."

shares: Portion of the catch.

shift: (v) Change clothing or location.

silipak: Dickie, wind parka.

sish ice: Thin layer of new ice, or fine, granular ice floating on surface of sea.

slew: (v) To turn around.

slink: (n) Lean, white-fleshed spring salmon returning to the sea after a winter in the lakes.

slob: Slushy ice.

square-flipper: Bearded seal, a large migratory seal of the North Atlantic *[Erignatus barbatus]*.

squat: (v) To squash, flatten.

stage: Elevated platform for landing and processing fish.

stagehead: Wharf end of the stage where boats pull up and unload fish.

stem: (v) To go against the current.

stem: (n) Bow of boat.

stick: Limbed tree.

stog: (v) To stuff.

stoggy: Wet wood; anything stiff, sluggish, or sticky.

stollard: Stalwart.

stroud: Heavy cotton fabric; winding sheet or shroud.

stunned: Witless, naive.

sud line: Strong grade of line used to attach fish hooks to trawl line and for other purposes.

taluk: Portable hunting screen.

tap: (v) To sew heavy outer soles on skin boots.

thole pins: Wood-peg oar locks.

tail: (v) To set traps on a trap line or path.

tickle: (n) Narrow, hazardous boat passage.

tilt: (v) Small hut or shelter, usually of unpeeled logs.

a "time": Communal party or celebration with food, drink, dancing, and other entertainments.

tintest: Particle wallboard.

token: Spirit, apparition, ghost.

"to once": As soon as possible.

Torngat: One of the chief spirit's of the Inuit.

truckyin': Trading.

tuckamores: Scrubby brush and shrubs.

turn: Load of wood.

ulu: Semi-circular Inuit knife commonly called a "woman's knife."

umiavik: Umiak or large open skin boat.

"Uncle/Aunt": Familiar term of respect and affection selectively bestowed on community elders by people who know them.

waders: High rubber boots, hip boots.

water pups: Blisters and sores on hands and wrists of cold-seas fishermen.

wooding: Cutting trees for firewood.

work: Handiwork, craft item made for sale.

yarnin': Telling tall tales, or yarns.

ENDNOTES

PREFACE

1. Anyone interested in reading further can obtain a subscription to Them Days at P.O. Box 18, Station B, Happy Valley, Labrador, Canada A0P 1E0, or e-mailing at: themdays@can-com.net. Some back issues are available. If you wish to support their work, consider enclosing a contribution. They operate on a shoestring.
2. This term for the Innu language seems to be a fairly recent construct. It is often simply called "Innu language" by those who work with the Innu.
3. Them Days staff has made editorial omissions in transcribing tapes of rambling interviews, and has edited some narratives at the request of narrators embarrassed to appear incorrect in print.
4. Title of photo-essay on Newfoundland and Labrador by Yva Momatiuk and John Eastcott, Camden House Publishing, 1988.

CHAPTER 1: THE LAND GOD GAVE TO CAIN

1. See Glossary for ethnic definitions.
2. Labradorite is a semi-precious triclinic feldspar with iridescent oil-like colors that shift in relation to the angle of the viewer. Found almost exclusively in Labrador, it is used for jewelry and, more recently, mined and exported to Italy as architectural facing stone.
3. Labrador's much diminished fishery now ships crabs, some salmon, char, turbot, shrimp, and scallops to Newfoundland and Montreal (subject to annually changing government subsidies and moratoriums).
4. The herd actually begins its migration from the area south and west of Ungava Bay and its legendary source in the Torngat Range.
5. A document dated 1752 [Privy Council Records III, No. 198, p. 884], indicates that people then subscribed to Hakluyt's view that Venetians Nicholas and Antonio Zeni visited Labrador in 1309, and that Norman and Basque fishing vessels had also preceded the Cabots to Labrador.
6. Gosling (p. 196) refers to the discovery of an enormous cache of long-decayed whalebone buried on a bed of tiles on Eskimo Island near Henley Harbour. This would probably have been of Basque, rather than Viking origin, as the author of the citation proposes.
7. Courtemanche, on visiting Hamilton Inlet in 1702, refers to remnants of existing European establishments which he attributes to French traders previously active in the area.
8. Gosling, p. 130.
9. Although forbidden to reside on the coast after 1763, Brouague's successors continued operating between Bradore Bay and St. Modeste until 1795, presumably from temporary or illegal shore stations (Kennedy, p. 21).
10. An anonymous memoir, "Concerning Labrador," written in 1715 apparently by a priest (possibly Pretre Laire) after exploring Hamilton Inlet from one of the stations in the

Straits, espoused the view that the Inuit had been misjudged and, if treated fairly, could cooperate in development of a profitable seal fishery and trade in their territory. This visionary document proposes a comprehensive and enlightened exploitation of Labrador that may have inspired George Cartwright, who adopted this kindly approach to the native people. The document is reprinted in Gosling, p. 135-47 and Privy Council Records Vol. 7, p. 3696.

[11.] "Narrative of Voyage by Sieur Louis Fornel to Baye des Esquimaux, 16 May to 27 Aug. 1743." from Archives de la Marine, Paris. in Provincial Archives of Newfoundland, Privy Council Records No. 1277:3280-3303.

[12.] see P. Charest, "Les Inuit du Labrador Canadien au milieu du siécle dernier et leurs descendants de la Basse Côte Nord." *Études Inuit Studies*, 22:1, 1998, p. 5ff.

[13.] The 1752 attempt to establish a Moravian base in Labrador resulted in the supposed murder of Bro. Jean Christian Erhardt and his shore party near Hopedale. As no member of the party spoke Inuktitut, it is likely the Inuit misunderstood the purpose of their visit. In 1763, the year Canada came under British rule, Bros. Jens Haven and Christian Drachardt received approval from the Mission board to make a second attempt. On voyages to the coast in 1764 and '65, the Brethren befriended groups of Inuit, with whom they were able to communicate in Greenlandic Inuktitut. On the second voyage they assisted Governor Palliser in negotiating a peace agreement with the Inuit which was, with one notable exception, thereafter observed by Inuit and British alike. These promising encounters encouraged the Brethren to submit a formal proposal to the British government for full title to land in Labrador. British trade authorities were reluctant to grant full and exclusive rights but did so finally in 1769 when it occurred to them that this would free new enterprises in the south, such as Cartwright's, from visits by the troublesome Inuit. A grant for 100,000 acres in the "vicinity of Esquimaux Bay" was awarded in 1769. In 1770 the Moravians selected a site for their mission near Nuneingoak in what they mistakenly thought was Esquimaux Bay. The following year fourteen missionaries, including three couples, returned to erect the Nain mission house and—placing themselves in the hands of God—took up residence behind its protective palisade.

[14.] The island of Newfoundland was officially ceded to Britain in 1713 and was thenceforth a British colony overseen by an appointed governor.

[15.] It is Governor Palliser (whose eagerness to shape the destiny of Labrador seems often to distort the accuracy of his reports) who recounts the story of Inuit raids. A neighboring merchant adds that in 1766-67 at two separate outposts some of Darby's men turned on and killed a fellow servant. Darby himself eventually returned to Europe, where he won recognition for his role in some of England's military campaigns, but retained ties with Labrador at least through 1772 when he petitioned the Board of Trade for compensation owed by one Lieut. Samuel Davis, who had usurped his fishing post.

[16.] Kennedy, p. 28.

[17.] This date is given in *Alluring Labrador*, p. 24. Gosling, p. 384, claims Cartwright sold out in 1793. He himself claimed his posts were usurped by John Noble, who later purchased them in partnership with one of the Hunts and held them through the war years, after which they were purchased by Philip Beard.

18. Jackson, p. 26ff.

19. According to Anick (1976) Pozer possessed "large and extensive premises with fishing and hunting establishments in Esquimaux Bay for fifty years and upward" until his death in 1823. His trade was with the Innu. After his death the North West River Post passed on to Claude Denechau, then Flavian Dufresne, then in 1828 to Jean Olivier Brunet. William Lampson got it from Brunet and sold it to Nathanial Jones of Quebec in 1832. In 1835 it was purchased by David Ramsey Stewart of Boston, who sold it to the Hudson's Bay Company later that year. Privy Council Records suggest the posts at North West River and Rigolet were unoccupied from the 1750s until 1784, when Pierre Marcoux first came to the bay, and that Pozer purchased them from his partner Dumontier's widow in 1815.

20. Makko is the Inuktitut word for "two," as well as the name Hopedale Inuit called Marcoux, according to the Moravian Periodical Accounts. Since Makkovik Bay has two lobes, the derivation is subject to debate.

21. Cartwright, George. *A Journal of Transactions and Events During Residence of Nearly Sixteen Years on the Coast of Labrador*, vols. I-III. London: Newark, 1792.

22. Kennedy, p. 14.

23. Jackson, p. 15.

24. Rev. Thomas Hickson's count from his visit in 1824, cited in Tanner, p. 466.

25. Reported by Rev. George Hutchinson in SPG Missionary Reports, 'E' Series, 1864-65, from the Public Archives of Newfoundland and Labrador. See also, Rev. U.Z. Rule, *Reminiscences of My Life*, 1927, St. John's, NF.

26. Brothers Kohlmeister and Kmoch made an epic voyage around Killinek and into Ungava Bay in 1811, marking positions on the George and Koksoak Rivers for future Moravian stations aimed at serving the wild Inuit of the Ungava and north Labrador peninsulas. The project was eventually abandoned due to HBC claims that Ungava Bay was within their charter lands. The expedition is described in Kohlmeister and Kmoch's journals, published in London, 1814.

27. One Perrault, a sealer from the Gulf Coast of Quebec, (possibly Jacques Perrault l'ainé [1718-1775] or his decendant) signed a 1770 petition urging the Lords of Trade to return jurisdiction of the Labrador coast as far as Hamilton Inlet to Quebec [Privy Council Records III, No. 264, p. 1049]. Antoni Perrault allegedly came to Labrador with HBC. Since many of the independent Canadian planters retreated to the Kings Posts when dispossessed of their properties east of Mingan, and HBC took over the Kings Posts early in the British period, it is conceivable that this is the same family.

28. Lieutenant Roger Curtis called the village Arvertok on maps resulting from his surveys for Captain Cook in the 1760s. It appears as Arviktok on later Moravian maps.

29. Their destination was usually said to be Chateau, in which case it was probably Noble & Pinson's post, but some also visited Cartwright's post in Sandwich Bay and Slade's at Battle Harbour.

30. Missionaries assigned to the stations were required to take a basic course in medicine, and many went to heroic lengths to relieve the suffering of their flock. As the collection of archaic medical instruments in the Hopedale museum attests, some attempted more radical forms of treatment and surgery. It is hard to imagine these instruments could have

been used to good effect in any but the most expert hands, and puzzling that such standard practices as inoculation were routinely denied the vulnerable and endangered race of Labrador Inuit.

31. The Montagnais hunted seals on a regular seasonal basis, but the Naskapi are said to have disliked the meat and may not have pursued them actively in the past.

32. Armitage (p. 40) gives this date. Gosling (p. 443) says the episode happened in 1857 at Fort Nascopie, Esquimaux Bay District. It is possible the policy was enforced more than once.

33. See Mailhot (1997) for a comprehensive analysis of Innu kinship and territorial customs.

34. Zimmerly, p.63.

35. This date is from Journals of the Legislative Assembly, Provincial Archives 2701. *Alluring Labrador* cites 1867 as the date a mission opened in North West River.

36. Dr. Grenfell's description of his encounter with the Pallisers, as told by Gosling (1910), p.455: "While some families contrive to maintain themselves in a rough plenty, the greater number are always in the depths of poverty. The margin between these two conditions is slight and easily broken down. An accident or illness, a bad fishery, or an unsuccessful furring season, plunges an independent family into direst poverty, from which they cannot extricate themselves unaided. Only last summer Dr. Grenfell found a family living on an island in Hamilton Inlet in an absolutely destitute condition. The mother was of Scotch descent, the father a half-breed Eskimo, and there were five or six children. They were half clad and had no provisions; they had neither gun, nor axe, nor fishing gear; yet the children seemed to be in fairly good condition. 'What do you have to eat?' asked Grenfell of one of the children, and received the unexpected and laconic reply, `Berries, zur.' It is in such cases as this that Grenfell acts the part of Providence. Several of the children were taken to the head-quarters of the Mission at St. Anthony, and the family helped to make another start in life. Without his assistance they would certainly have starved…

These Settlers are so few in number and live so far apart, that they can afford each other but little mutual support. It is, however, a beautiful trait in their characters that they are always ready to share their scanty supplies with anyone who is worse off.

The medical needs of this population were formerly supplied by a doctor who travelled up and down the coast on the mail steamer, making fortnightly trips during the summer months. This was naturally very ineffectual, and if people got seriously ill they just died.

When accidents occurred, there was no one to bind the wound or set the limb. Terrible stories are told of the sufferings endured. As an instance, some years ago a little girl crawled out of a hut on a bitterly cold day, and was found by her father with both feet terribly frozen. Mortification set in, and the father saw that the child must die unless her feet were cut off. Laying the poor little creature down, he put her feet across a block of wood and chopped them off with his axe. Grenfell found her still alive when he went down in the spring, and succeeded in restoring her to health. She was afterwards adopted by a charitable lady in the United States, and is now a strong and useful member of society."

CHAPTER 2: THE STRAITS

1. "Excerpt from a letter written by Warrick Smith to J. R. Smallwood, St. John's, 17 March 1943." Held by the Centre of Newfoundland Studies, Memorial University of Newfoundland, along with a copy of the Map of Newfoundland, 1616, by Captain John Mason. [Map #94, Association of Canadian Map Libraries and Archives.]
2. Laurier Turgeon, 1995 (unpublished mss.).
3. Tanner, p. 577.
4. Gordon Handcock in Mannion, 1986, p.18.
5. Thornton in Mannion, 1986. p. 169
6. Thornton's (1986) research indicates 22 Englishmen, five Newfoundland girls (all quickly married off to Settlers), and eight Newfoundland families (most related to the girls) arrived in the area between 1830 and 1850. Most of the Newfoundlanders, she found, were from Carbonear and settled in East St. Modeste, Carrol's Cove, and Red Bay. Oral history seems to differ from these findings in some respects.
7. Thornton's findings for 1850-80: People from Trinity Bay settled West St. Modeste; Brigus and St. John's families went to Forteau; Bell Island people went to L'anse au Loup and L'anse au Diable; and the folks from Portugal Cove clustered at Pinware and West St. Modeste. Twenty-one more Englishmen came at this time, nearly all from the Isle of Jersey. With them came seven "Frenchmen.."
8. Population estimates are included only to provide a rough idea of the scope of these communities as they were derived from a 1980 publication (*Alluring Labrador*) and are no longer current.
9. Patricia Thornton's work, cited above, gives important insights and detail. However, without names for the Settlers she enumerates by period, origin, and destination, it is impossible to cross-reference her findings, obtained from Newfoundland records, with the oral histories and other records on Labrador.
10. Orangemen's Day, commemorating English King William of Orange's victory over the Irish at the Battle of Aughrim.

CHAPTER 3: NORTH OF CHATEAU

1. The Sixth Voyage 1786.
2. This Inuit family does not seem to have originated in the Battle Harbour area, but rather to have been part of the main Ivuktoke-Nain clan. Nor did Cartwright encounter any resident Inuit near Charles River, indicating that the Putlavamiut had either disappeared by then or had only resided there on a seasonal or temporary basis.
3. Some believe the corpses were disinterred by grave robbers, perhaps even by Phippard, rather than left unburied. They remained on the surface through the 19th century, as noted by several travellers.
4. Slade & Company Ledgers, Box 23, in the Public Archives of Newfoundland and Labrador. MG 460.
5. Kennedy, p. 37
6. Jackson, p. 17

7. At Rigolet in the late 1960s these were called "short-rubber" dances, and they were held at the end of the fishing season, when the hipboots were no longer needed and could be rolled down. I do not know if the term was used elsewhere.

8. Tanner, 745.

9. Tanner, 744.

10. Tanner, 743.

11. John Abbott, "Report on Labrador" to G.F. Grimes, Minister of Marine & Fisheries, 1923. *Them Days*, 16.1:3.

CHAPTER 4: PARADISE

1. Peyton was called "the Daniel Boone of N.B.B." in Slade's ledgers for 1783, having earned a swashbuckling but even then somewhat unsavoury reputation as wild Indian hunter for his genocidal campaigns against the last of the Beothuks in 1781.

2. Reichel's map, "Labrador [Showing Settlement in the Central Coastal Region]." published 1872 from trips made in 1857 by Br. Elsner and 1870 by Br. O'Hara.

3. He sent an advance crew to winter there in 1774.

4. Gosling (1910), p. 398, citing Gov. Thomas Cochrane's letter of instructions to Capt. William Patterson, Judge of the Court of Civil Jurisdiction at Labrador, 1826.

5. Anick, p. 642, citing Chappell, Edward. *Reise nach Neufundland und der sudlichen Kuste von Labrador*. Jena, 1819.

6. *Them Days*, 17.4:32.

7. Quite possibly, the prosperous Hunt Company had its origins with the Charles and/or John Hunt who were trading with Slade's at Battle Harbour as early as 1783.

8. Tanner, p. 745.

9. Geo. Cartwright. *Journals...* (1792), vol. I, p. 88.

10. Probably the grandson of the original William Phippard, first to settle in Ivuktoke. He had a summer station at Sand Hill Cove. Progenitor Phippard had a son in Ivuktoke as of 1824. Phippards eventually gravitated to the Batteau area.

11. A major gale in 1885 is described in the *St. John's Evening Telegram*, October 26, 1885. The October 30 edition published a list of vessels lost or damaged and lives lost [11.1:13].

12. Williams claims to have come in 1828 on a petition he signed as "planter of Esquimaux Bay" in 1835. This petition, one for merchants and planters of Esquimaux Bay, another for those of Sandwich Bay, is a helpful indicator of residents just prior to the arrival of the Hudson'a Bay Company. It is found in the Provincial Archives of Canada, MG11, CO 194/94, p. 333, 328. The list of planters and merchants is published in Anick, p. 644.

13. The "indians" referred to are Cartwright's Inuit companions and household servants Cattook (female age 26), Tweegock (female age 18), Tweegock's three and a half-year-old daughter Phyllis, and Jack (age 17), who is possibly the "Captain Jack" or the "Young Jack" trading with Slade's in 1798. Curiously, Fornel encountered an Inuit "Captain Jack" in one of the bays of the Atlantic Shore on his voyage to Ivuktoke in 1743. This fellow and his crew had a sailing vessel with which they seem to have been trading with the French on the south shore and Gulf. They spoke a pidgeon French and seemed quite territorial

about their bay and trading monopolies. This suggests a family tradition for Cartwright's Inuit friends that predates his tenure on the coast by at least a generation.

14. "Monday, June 26, 1786: With assistance of Noble & Pinson's people, I had a flagstaff set up on the top of the hill, at the back of the house, which henceforth I shall distinguish by the name of Flagstaff Hill." Geo. Cartwright. *Journals*...[12.1:42].

15. Thus "Dove Brook"

16. Geo. Cartwright. *Journals*...(1792), vol. II.

17. Evidently a room at back of house for classes and services by visiting clergy and teachers.

CHAPTER 5: TORNGAT

1. The lesser *torngat* (singular *torngak*) are the helping spirits, benevolent or malign, of *angakkut*. According to Brs. Kohnmeister and Kmoch (1811), the great *Torngak* associated with creation in Labrador governs the movements of caribou from his lair in a mountain cave near Killinek and is often depicted as a huge white bear. Anthropologist J. Garth Taylor suggests that the traditionally benevolent *Tuurngaatsuk* (rendered in early Moravian spellings as variations on *Torngasuk*) is equated with both *Torngak* and Moon Man, brother of Sun Woman and provider of fish and sea mammal, if not all game, for Inuit who abide by his taboos ["Deconstructing deities: *Tuurngatsuak* and *Tuurngaatsuk* in Labrador Inuit religion," *Etudes/Inuit/Studies*, 1997, 21 (1-2): 141-158]. His abode on the moon is an important destination for *angakkut* as well as the most desirable resting place for *inua*, or spirit, of the deceased Inuit. After a century of relentless demonization by the Moravian missionaries, both greater and lesser *torngat* survived in the Inuit stories mainly as irrational instruments of human or supernatural vengeance requiring more or less constant appeasement, rather than as agents of a para-rational system of mores and rules governing Inuit behavior and affording them with some sense of control over their social and natural environment.

2. Labrador's acidic soils tend to destroy organic remains. Except in rare locations on the Torngat coast where permafrost has resisted periodic thaws, it is therefore unusual to find remnants of carved bone, clothing, wood implements, and basketry that undoubtedly comprised much of the material culture of inhabitants.

3. Gov. Hugh Palliser in a Dispatch to the Earl of Halifax, Sept. 11, 1765. (Privy Council Records, Vol. 7, p. 3299), quoted in Brice-Bennett (1981), p. 9.

4. These attitudes were reported by the Bro. Jens Haven (1771), Bro. Layritz (1773), Bro. Crantz (1820), George Cartwright (1773) and others. See Gosling p. 165, CBB p. 9, Davey, p. 162-3, Crantz, p. 293.

5. Carol Brice-Bennett, *Two Opinions: Inuit and Moravian Missionaries in Labrador, 1804-1860,* 1981, p. 89. This unpublished thesis and Kleivan's *The Eskimos of Northeast Labrador*, 1966, contributed to the analysis in this chapter. Histories of the Moravians in Labrador are also recounted in Gosling (1910), Tanner (1947), Davey (1905), Peacock (*Them Days*, 1.3:3), and Hutton (1920), among others.

6. Ibid. p.308.

7. The Hudson's Bay Company established posts in Rigolet and North West River in the 1830s, buying out the competition in that region within a few years. In 1837 they bought out D.

R. Stewart in Kaipokok Bay, 20 miles from Hopedale, and in 1857 opened a post at Davis Inlet, between Hopedale and Nain. On the north coast, HBC posts were opened an Nachvak in 1868 and Saglek in 1870 in direct competition with Mission operations.

8. See Carol Brice-Bennett (1981) describing the "Report of the Visitation of the Mission in Labrador by Br. L. T. Reichel, in the Summer of 1861," from Moravian Periodical Accounts 24:263-77.

9. Tanner p. 548, based on the opinion of Lucien Turner (1894), p. 159.

10. It was probably Haley's Comet.

CHAPTER 6: THE MORAVIAN COAST

1. The missionaries who opened Hopedale station initially wished to include the Innu among their converts but abandoned the idea upon discovering that not only were the Innu reluctant to come near Inuit villages, most were already Catholic.

2. This was a radical departure from established policy, agreed to by church officials on the condition that subsequent transfer of the property to another party be subject to approval by the Mission [Brice-Bennett, p. 445].

3. Brice-Bennett, p. 450.

4. Kleivan, p. 63.

5. Crantz, quoted in Packard, p. 253.

6. Davey, 1905. p. 249.

7. Brice-Bennett, p. 39.

8. Ibid.

9. Hy Lucy signed the 1835 petition as "planter" in Esquimaux Bay district since 1825.

10. Englishmen Moses Brown and Jonathan Cole wintered with Slade's at Battle Harbour in 1808 and 1809; in 1832 Cole was "company agent" at Battle Harbour. Brown signed the Esquimaux Bay petition in 1835. A Cole later appears in Kaipokok as HBC manager, and "E. Cole" is living in Kaipokok Bay near the post in 1872. A literate half-breed Cole is at Roger's Harbour with Sam Broomfield in the 1880s. He has a brother at Strawberry Harbour. Thomas Cole married Susannah Williams of Tub Harbour in 1860 and moved to Newfoundland.

11. Moravian Inuit did not use last names until the 1890s, decades after their un-converted cousins to the south, who were gradually Europeanizing even without intermarriage. Hopedale was the first station to encourage the Inuit to adopt surnames. Nain and Okak followed. The congregants were free to pick their own names. When asked why he chose the Inuktitut word for 'green,' a member of the Nain congregation explained, "as in spring the fresh green of the trees burst forth from the buds, so it is my desire that a new life, wholly devoted to the Lord, should spring forth out of my former life of sin." The missionaries were pleased. [see *Them Days*, 17.3:34 ff.]

12. A Mr. Thomas had trading posts at Cape Charles in 1779 [Kennedy, p. 37] and later at Tub Harbour. William, John, Isaac, and Andrew Thomas figure in Slade's records. William was listed as "planter" in 1784. In 1811 John is in partnership with George Dempster and William Broomfield at Hawkes Bay.

13. Reed was born in 1806, half-breed son of William Reed who summered in Battle Harbour and traded at the northern outposts as agent for Slade's. Local legend claims William Sr. and Jr. were murdered by a Hopedale Inuit named Paulo. Family legends of the Brooks clan in Ivuktoke say they drowned off Cape Harrison with Junior's bride, Elizabeth Brooks.

14. See *Them Days*, 7.4:9.

15. Charles Anstey appears in Slade Company records as early as 1774 as "status unknown." He owed the company £89. Mrs. Anstey did laundry for the company in 1787, and Mark is listed as "servant" in 1790.

16. Privy Council Records III, No. 264, p. 1049.

17. See Randy Ames in Carol Brice-Bennett, ed., 1977, p. 207.

18. *Them Days* 5.2:7 (1848 cited in 11.4:42).

19. See *Them Days* 5.2:32 for genealogical charts.

20. She is identified as Mary Broomfield by Caroline Jacques in *Them Days* 8.2:9, who says Mary's mother was Inuit, her father (presumably Broomfield) drowned when she was small, and that her marriage with S. J. Thomas occurred in 1830.

21. Henriksen, p. 15.

22. Killinek itself closed in 1979, its residents transferred to Ft. Chimo in Ungava Bay.

23. Charles McNeill, Jr. and John and Ernest Lyall built stages there in 1885.

24. In 1893 Eliot Corwen transcribed his notes from a voyage to the Labrador coast with the magistrate. He tells of investigating the suspected hemlock murders of "old Benjamin" and Tom Brown's wives, and of Tom Brown's twelve-year-old daughter. Asa Benjamin, 12, was also taken with symptoms, and his father, fearing for the safety of his family, sent the rest of them to Hopedale. Brown had reportedly murdered his first wife and baby, and so abused his second that she died. This was his third wife, and already he talked of taking a fourth. He was greatly feared by the winter settlers, and Corwen hazarded the opinion that someone would soon shoot him to be rid of the threat. [Corwen, 1893. pp. 76-7, 82-3]

25. Torsten Andersen [Kverna] married Mary Thomas, whose mother, Mary Broomfield, was half Inuit. He did not wish his family to know this, or his children to marry anyone with Native blood.

26. Pomiuk, the little lame boy whose story is the subject of a book by W. B. Forbush, Boston, 1903.

CHAPTER 7: GRANDE BAIE DES ESQUIMAUX

1. The names Sheshatshiu and its locative Sheshatshit derive from the Innu/Cree name for the Grand River/Lake Melville system, Kessessasskiou, or "great outlet." The Labrador Innu were once know as the "people of Kessessasskiou" by the Cree and Gulf Innu. At least the western part of the Lake was central to their territory (Mailhot, 1997). Recent archaeological finds suggest that Innu occupation of the current village predates the arrival of European traders.

2. Maritime Archaic Indians were first to occupy this area. Sites dating back to 7000 BP having been found in Groswater Bay. After their abrupt departure ca. 3500 BP, a succession

of Indian cultures made brief appearances in the bay. During the short tenure of the Dorset people (2800-2400 BP), the area appears to have been shared. The first major Indian group to take hold in central Labrador since the Maritime Archaic period is called Point Revenge culture and may be ancestral to the modern Innu. They enjoyed unlimited access to the shores of Lake Melville and Groswater Bay until the arrival of the Ivuktoke Inuit ca. 500 BP.

3. R. Jordan in *Them Days*, 2.1.24.

4. Tanner (1947) p. 466.

5. Demographic information sporadically collected by visitors and government agencies throughout the 19th century are not given much credence today as most were neither systematic nor complete.

6. The practice of taking Labrador Inuit to Europe, Africa, and America for exhibition occurred through the 19th century in spite of Moravian and government attempts at intervention. Most of the Native participants were horribly exploited and died of disease and maltreatment. Those who went to Chicago in 1893 were ultimately never paid and left to find their way home, many carrying diseases to the coastal communities. The lame boy, Pomiuk, who remained in the U.S. and was commemorated in a book by that name, was a member of the Ivuktoke party.

7. The Pallisers are descendants of Mikak (see Moravian Coast chapter) and probably borrowed the name from Newfoundland's first governor.

8. Dr. Paddon changed the name from Serkoak to Shiwak because he thought it was easier to pronounce [Zimmerly (1975):187]. The biography of John Shiwak of Rigolet, killed in action in World War I, has been published in *Canadian Magazine* (see Lacey Amy, "An Eskimo Patriot," CM, Vol. 51, No. 3, [1918]: 212-218.).

9. In 1860 visitor Charles Hallock described the Inuk nick-named "Ike the Mormon," because he had five wives, as the most traditional of the southern Inuit. The Ikeys may be descendants. (Zimmerly [1975], p. 112).

10. An Adams, storekeeper at Rigolet in the mid-1800s, is listed as European by Reichel and is likely the origin of the Inuit family name, whether by blood or association.

11. Tanner (1947), p. 509.

12. Hallock encountered the Inuk Shokalough on his visit to Hamilton Inlet in 1860. He had a 60-ton schooner of his own manufacture, crewed by Inuit and used for the business of the HBC at Rigolet (see Zimmerly [1975], p. 111).

13. The Lucy's progenitor is probably the Hy Lucey who signed the 1835 petition as "planter," in the bay since 1825, or the Peter Lucy of unknown origin whose name was given to a brook on the south shore of Lake Melville and who may have operated a small trading post at its mouth in the 18th century.

14. "Tuktusna" on Reichel's 1872 map, "Tooktooshner" in Chimmo (1869), p.19. They are said locally to have come from Baffin Is.

15. Unattributed paper on Mesher Family history provided by Doris Saunders, editor of *Them Days*.

16. Zimmerly, p.103.

17. Br. Elsner, cited in Zimmerly, p. 63. Methodists made sporadic attempts to establish a base in central Labrador for their circuit preachers, beginning with the visit in 1822 of a Rev. Johnson, who was discouraged by the proprietary Moravians from pursuing this goal. Rev. Thomas Hickson followed in 1824, preaching in Ivuktoke until 1826. Rev. Ellidge, in Snooks Cove in 1826-27, terminated the effort as fruitless. Other accounts [W.H.A. Davies (1843), p. 91] claim the Inuit were receptive to the preachers but the whites tormented them and seduced the Inuit away. Some of these Inuit later came to Hopedale and were baptized by the Moravians.

18. Anglican Bishop Feild, visiting the coast (probably south of Ivuktoke) in 1848, found that while most Settlers called themselves C of E, few could read or had any religious instruction. The Moravians also report that most Settlers in their area also called themselves C of E. Although well established in southern Labrador, the Anglican Church was not active in central Labrador in the 19th century.

19. There are apparently two Oliver families in Labrador, both initiated by a "Tom." The other was called "HBC Tom Oliver" in 1850. One of these families may have been related to the Thomas Oliver on Slade's 18th century Battle Harbour ledgers.

20. Newfoundland held a surrogate court for the Labrador coast as far north as Ivuktoke from 1811 to 1824. Cases were heard on shipboard. Verdicts and punishments might not be given until the following summer. In Judge Pinsent's time, the boat also carried mail, medicines and books for the Settler families. Circuit courts visited the coasts 1826-34, and 1863-74, abandoned each time for lack of cases and resumed at the insistence of coastal merchants to justify taxation and duties.

21. With the commencement of annual steamer service from Newfoundland to Hamilton Inlet and Hopedale in 1878 came the first regular mail service and transportation along the coast. A medical student on board provided some care for the fishermen.

22. While churches and church schools were established in seven southern communities between 1849 and 1860, there were none north of Francis Harbour on the Atlantic Shore before the twentieth century. The Methodists sent circuit teachers to families in Sandwich Bay and Hamilton Inlet from 1889 until the 1920s. The first boarding school available to central Labrador families was opened by the Moravians at Makkovik in 1897 (Ben-Dor says 1919). Rev. Gordon's Muddy Bay School in Sandwich Bay boarded children from Ivuktoke from 1919 until 1928. Until education became compulsory in 1949, children rarely attended for long periods of time as they were needed by their families. It is said that the Inuit remained the best educated group in Labrador until the 1960s.

CHAPTER 8: NITASSINAN

[1.] Mailhot, 1997.

[2.] See Mailhot (1997) p. 166 ff. for a good synopsis of Innu philosophy and its role in current political positions.

[3.] Hind, p. 97.

[4.] Armitage, p. 14.

[5.] Hind, Vol.II, p. 10.

[6.] Mailhot, p. 62 ff.

[7.] Armitage, p.56.

[8.] Hind, Vol. I, p. 84 ff.

[9.] Armitage, p. 37.

[10.] Hind, p. 343.

[11.] Armitage, p. 52.

[12.] Armitage, p. 56.

[13.] Peter Martin Associates Limited of Toronto.

[14.] Viking Penguin, 1988.

[15.] Horwood, Harold. New York: Doubleday Books, 1972.

[16.] Mina Hubbard's successful attempt to make the trip her husband had lost his life attempting several years earlier in the legendary Wallace-Hubbard Expedition.

[17.] Mersai Michelin came alone from Trois Rivieres. Joseph was born in Labrador in 1845.

[1.] Copyrighted. Reprinted with permission of Harry Martin.

CHAPTER 9: THE JOURNEY TO GOOSE

[1.] Copyrighted. Reprinted with permission of Harry Martin.

BIBLIOGRAPHY

Ames, Randy. "Land Use in the Postville Region," *Our Footsteps Are Everywhere*. Labrador Inuit Association, 1977 (article).

——"Land Use in the Rigolet Area," *Our Footsteps Are Everywhere*. Labrador Inuit Association, 1977 (article).

Andersen, Joan. *Makkovik: 100 Years Plus*. St. John's: published by Joan Andersen in cooperation with Robinson-Blackmore Printing and Publishing, 1996 (book).

Anick, Norman. "The Fur Trade in Eastern Canada Until 1870," vol. 1, Unpublished Document No. 207. Ottawa: Parks Canada, Department of Indian and Northern Affairs, 1976 (article)

Armitage, Peter. *The Innu (The Montagnais-Naskapi)*. New York: Chelsea House Publishers, Indians of North America Series, ed. Frank W. Porter III, 1990 (book).

Baikie, Margaret. *Labrador Memories: Reflections at Mulligan*, Happy Valley, NF: Them Days Inc., (undated, booklet).

Baikie, Leslie. "Up and Down the Bay," Halifax, NS: Unpublished summary and compilation of records on the history of Esquimaux Bay in the 19th century, 1989. Them Days Archive, 270 BAI.

Ben-Dor, Shmuel. *Makkovik: Eskimos and Settlers in a Labrador Community, a Contrastive Study in Adaptation*. Institute of Social and Economic Studies # 4. St. John's: Memorial University of Newfoundland, 1966 (book).

Bernard, Sir Francis. "Account of the Coast of Labrador," [16 February 1761]. *Collections of the Massachusetts Historical Society for the Year 1792*, vol. 1, 233-237.

Biggar, H.P. *Early Trading Companies of New France*. Toronto, 1901. Facsimile edition. Clifton, NJ: Augustus Kelly, 1972 (book).

Borlase, Tim. *Labrador Studies: The Labrador Inuit*. Happy Valley, NF: Labrador East Integrated School Board, 1993 (book).

——*Labrador Studies: The Labrador Settlers, Métis and Kablunangajuit*. Happy Valley, NF: Labrador East Integrated School Board, 1994 (book).

Brice-Bennett, Carol. "Two Opinions: Inuit and Missionaries in Labrador, 1804-1860." St. John's: Memorial University of Newfoundland, 1981 (MA thesis).

——, ed. *Our Footsteps Are Everywhere: Inuit Land Use and Occupancy in Labrador*. Labrador Inuit Association, 1977 (book).

Brody, Hugh. "Permanence and Change Among Inuit and Settlers of Labrador," *Our Footsteps Are Everywhere*. Labrador Inuit Association, 1977 (article).

Browne, P.W. *Where the Fishers Go: the Story of Labrador*. New York: Cochrane Publishing, 1909 (book).

Buckle, Francis. *The Anglican Church in Labrador, 1848-1998*. The Archdeaconry of Labrador, 1998 (book).

Campbell, Lydia. "Sketches of Labrador Life" [*The Evening Herald*, St. John's, Dec. 3, 4, 5, 6, 7, 10, 12, 13, 18, 20, 24, #1894, Feb. 6, 1895], reprinted by Them Days Inc., 1984 (booklet).

Cartwright, George. *A Journal of Transactions and Events During a Residence of Nearly Sixteen Years on the Coast of Labrador.* Three Volumes. Newark: Allin and Ridge, 1792; facsimile edition, Ann Arbor: University Microfilms International, 1981 (books)

"Census for the Labrador Coast, 1863-64," *Them Days Magazine,* 16.2:50 (article)

Charest, Paul. "Les Inuit du Labrador canadien au milieu du siecle dernier et leurs descendants de la Basse-Cote-Nord." *Etudes Inuit Studies,* vol. 22, no. 1 (1998): 5-35.

Chimmo, W. "A Visit to the Northeast Coast of Labrador during the Autumn of 1867 by H.M.S. Gannett." *Journal of the Royal Geographic Society,* London. vol. 38 (1868): 258.

Curtis, Lt. Roger. "Particulars of the Country of Labrador, extracted from the Papers of Lieutenant Roger Curtis, of His Majesty's Sloop the Otter, with a Plane-Chart of the Coast" [1774]. Communicated by the Honourable Daines Barrington. Them Days Archive, File P.L. 153 (excerpt from unidentified book).

Davey, Rev. J.W. *The Fall of Torngak: or, the Moravian Mission on the Coast of Labrador.* London: S.W. Partridge & Company and Moravian Mission Agency, 1905 (book).

Davies, W.H.A. "Notes on Esquimaux Bay and the Surrounding Country." Literary and Historical Society of Quebec. *Transactions,* vol. 4, no. 1 (Feb. 1843): 70-94 (report).

———. "Notes on Ungava Bay." Literary and Historical Society of Quebec. *Transactions,* vol. 4, no. 2 (March 1854): 128ff. (report).

Elsner, Leo. "Br. Elsner's Report of a Journey from Hopedale to Northwest River, Esquimaux Bay, in April 1857." *Moravian Periodical Accounts,* vol. 22, no. 239, 441-51. [TD Archive File 30/8:66], (report).

Elton, C.S. *Voles, mice and lemmings: Problems in population dynamics.* Oxford: Clarendon Press, 1942 (book).

Erlandson, Erland. "Chimo Correspondence," in Davies, K.G. ed. *Northern Quebec and Labrador Journals and Correspondence: 1819-35.* London: The Hudson's Bay Record Society, 1963.

Finlayson, Nicholas. "Journals, 1830," in Davies, K.G. ed. *Northern Quebec and Labrador Journals and Correspondence: 1819-35.* London: The Hudson's Bay Record Society, 1963.

Fitzhugh, William. *Environmental Archaeology and Cultural Systems in Hamilton Inlet, Labrador.* Smithsonian Contributions to Anthropology, no. 16. Washington: Smithsonian Institution Press, 1972 (book).

Gosling, W.G. *Labrador: Its Discovery, Exploration, and Development.* Toronto: Mussen Books; London: Alston Rivers Ltd., 1910 (book).

Goudie, Elizabeth. *Woman of Labrador.* Toronto: Peter Martin Associates Limited, 1973 (book).

Hallock, Charles. "Three Months in Labrador," *Harper's New Monthly Magazine,* vol. 22, no. 81 (1861): 577-579, 743-765 (article).

Handcock, Gordon. "English Migrations to Newfoundland," in Mannion, John J. *The Peopling of Newfoundland: Social and Economic Papers # 8.* Institute of Social and Economic

Studies No. 8, Memorial University of Newfoundland, St. John's. 1977. Reprinted University of Toronto Press, 1986.

Hansen, Marcus Lee. *The Atlantic Migration, 1607-1860.* Cambridge: Harvard University Press, 1940 (book).

Harris, Tim, ed. *Popular Culture in England, c. 1500-1850.* New York: St. Martin's Press, 1995.

Harrisse, Henry. *Découverte et évolution Cartographique de Terre-Neuve et des Pays Circonvoisins, 1497 - 1501 - 1769: Essais de Géographie Historique et Documentaire.* London: Henry Stevens, Son & Stiles, 1900 (book)

Henriksen, George. *Hunters in the Barrens.* Institute of Social and Economic Research, Memorial University of Newfoundland. St. John's: Social and Economic Studies 12, 1973 (book).

Hickson, Rev. T. "1820 Journal," in Arminius Young, *One Hundred Years in the Wilds of Labrador,* London: Arthur H. Stockwell, Ltd., 1931. Copy in Them Days Archive, File 37/2.

Hind, Henry Youle. *Explorations in the Interior of the Labrador Peninsula: The Country of the Montagnais and Nasquapee Indians.* Vols. 1 & 2. London: Longman, Green, Longman, Roberts, and Green, 1863 (book).

Hutton, S.K. *Among the Eskimos of Labrador.* Seeley, Service & Co., 1920 (book)

Jackson, Lawrence. *Bounty of a Barren Coast: Resource Harvest and Settlement in Southern Labrador — Phase One.* Labrador Institute of Northern Studies, Memorial University of Newfoundland, St. John's, 1982 (book).

Kennedy, John C. *People of the Bays and Headlands.* Toronto: University of Toronto Press, 1995 (book).

Kleivan, Helge. *The Eskimos of Northeast Labrador.* Oslo: Norsk Polarinstitutt, 1966 (book).

Kohlmeister, Benjamin and George Kmoch. *Journal of a Voyage from Okkak on the Coast of Labrador to Ungava Bay Westward of Cape Chudleigh; undertaken to explore the Coast, and visit the Esquimaux in that unknown Region.* London. 1814 (book).

Kurlansky, Mark. *Cod, a Biography of the Fish that Changed the World.* New York: Walker and Company, 1997 (book).

Labrador Institute of Northern Studies. "Understanding a Provincial Historical Resource: a Preliminary Historical Survey of Battle Harbour," Memorial University of Newfoundland, Happy Valley-Goose Bay, NF, 1990 (paper).

Le Huenen, Joseph. "The Role of the Basque, Breton, and Norman Cod Fishermen..." *Arctic,* vol. 37, no. 4, December 1984 (article).

Low, A.P. "Report on Explorations in the Labrador Peninsula Along the East Main, Koksuak, Hamilton, Manicougan and Portions of Other Rivers in 1892-93-94-95." *Geological Survey of Canada, Annual Reports,* (New Series), vol. 8, part L, 1896 (report).

Lysaght, Averil M. *Joseph Banks in Newfoundland and Labrador, 1766: His Diary, Manuscripts and Collections.* Berkeley: University of California Press, 1971 (book).

Mailhot, José. *The People of Sheshatshit; in the Land of the Innu.* translated by Axel Harvey, Institute of Social and Economic Research, Memorial University of Newfoundland. St. John's: Social and Economic Studies 58, 1997 (book).

McLean, John. *Notes of a Twenty Five Years' Service in the Hudson's Bay Territory.* Originally in two volumes by Richard Bentley, New Burlington Street, London. 1849. Facsimile edition by Greenwood Press, Publishers, New York, 1968 (book).

Mesher, Dorothy, *Kuujjuaq: Memories and Musings.* Unica Publishing Company Ltd., 1995 (book).

Moravian Periodical Accounts and related documents (English translations). Them Days Archive, Files 30/8:1 (1834), 2 (1836), #3 (1839), 5(1840), 6-8 (1841), 24 (Index), 35 (Hopedale 1852-3), 53 (1878), 54 (1790-95), 55 (1797), 56 (1801), 57 (1805-9), 58 (1810-12), 59 (1813-17), 60 (1818-20), 65 (1830-33), 66 (Elsner's Journey), 69 (1869-79), 79, 80 (Journeys and topical reports), 81 (1895 "Labrador"), 83 (1896-7 "Makkovik Settlers"); 30/16:1 (1771-80 Nain diary in questionable translation, including information on Inuit behavior, travels, Mikak, European traders in vicinity), 2 (1791-1808 excerpts from Nain diary in questionable translation, including information on Mikak and naming of Inuit); 30/17 (transcripts selected by Lawrence M. Lande, 32 pp.); 30/20 (letter from O'Hara re. inhabitants of coastal Labrador, 1871, 2pp.).

Packard, A.S. *The Labrador Coast: A Journal of Two Summer Cruises to That Region.* New York: N. D. C. Hodges. 1891.

Paine, Robert, ed. *The White Arctic.* Institute of Social and Economic Research, Memorial University of Newfoundland. St. John's: Social and Economic Studies 7, 1977 (book).

Peacock, Rev. F.W. "The Moravian Church in Labrador," *Them Days Magazine,* 1.3:3, 1975, (article excerpted from book).

Plaice, Evelyn. *The Native Game.* Institute of Social and Economic Research, Memorial University of Newfoundland. St. John's: Social and Economic Studies 40, 1987 (book).

Poole, C. J. *Catucto: Battle Harbour, Labrador, 1832-1822.* St. Anthony, NF: Bebb Publishing Ltd., 1996 (book).

Privy Council (Great Britain) Judicial Committee. *In the matter of the boundary between the Dominion of Canada and the colony of Newfoundland in the Labrador Peninsula, between the Dominion of Canada of the one part and the colony of Newfoundland of the other part....* 12 volumes. W. Clowes and Sons, Ltd. London, 1927.

——Vol. III, No. 198, p. 884 ff. Report of Lords of Trade on Petition of Merchants, 1752.

——No. 199, p. 195. General Murray's Report [on newly acquired British lands in E. Canada], 1762.

——No. 215, p. 935 ff. Remarks of Governor Palliser, 1765.

——No. 217, p. 940. Commission of Sir Thomas Adams, Bart. of HMS Niger, 1765.

——No. 222, p. 946. Gov. Palliser's dispatch regarding meeting and treaty with Inuit, 1765.

——No. 224, 225, 227, p. 949 ff. Gov. Palliser's accounts to Lords of Trade regarding Canadian and Newfoundland merchants on the Labrador, 1765.

——No. 230, p. 963 ff. Lords of Trade to King George III regarding Moravians, 1765; p. 968, Names of Quebec merchants with grants in Labrador east of R. St. John. (see also No. 244, p. 993, 998).

——No. 248, p. 1005, 1014, 1015, 1024-26. Gov. Palliser on merchants and fisheries on Labrador coast, his efforts to destroy seal fishery in favour of British cod fishery, 1967.

——No. 260, p. 1032. Gov. Palliser's account of Inuit raid on Nicholas Darby's station at Charles River, 1767.

——No. 264, p. 1049. Petition of Quebec sealers (including one Perrault) regarding return of Labrador Coast to Quebec jurisdiction, 1770.

——No. 268, p. 1059 ff. George Cartwright on difficulties encountered in Labrador, case for year-round posts, description of dealings with Inuit (including Mikak), 1773.

——No. 280, 281, p. 1089-90. Roger Curtis's account of Native bands in Labrador, 1773.

——No. 295, p.#1142. John Cartwright compares advantages of seal over cod fishery on coastal Labrador, 1773-74.

——No. 299, p. 1151 ff. George Cartwright on merchant activity on the coast, and history of Noble & Pinson and its rivalry with him, 1774.

——No. 305, p.#1160. George Cartwright tells of Coghlan's efforts to dispossess him of posts in Sandwich Bay, 1775.

——No. 310, p. 1166. Summary of the Case of Nicholas Darby in Labrador, including refs. to Lymburner & Grant at Bradore, and story of Lt. Samuel Davis, 1777.

——No. 319, p.1182. Third-hand reference to two Englishmen left in Esquimaux Bay "[he actually ended up in the Makkovik Kaipokok area] in great distress" (Phippard & Nooks, 1778) and to arrival of two Canadians (Marcoux & Marchand) in 1785-86, 1788.

——No. 322, p. 1185. Chief Justice Reeves reports on abuse of servants by merchants on coast of Labrador, 1792.

——No. 324, p. 1189. Capt. Crofton reports on Inuit working at sealing posts in Bradore, downsizing of Noble & Pinson operations, decrease of Inuit visiting Temple Bay since 1795, alludes to Marcoux's post "70 leagues N. of Temple Bay" as main one trading with Inuit, 1798.

——No. 327, p. 1194. Report on Americans in Labrador fishing and trading with Natives and British merchants, black-market trade in fish, 1807.

——No. 337, p. 1208 ff. Petition of Philip Beard & Company with history of his operation in Sandwich Bay, including purchase from Noble & Hunt, and problems with Nova Scotian squatter, McPherson. Alludes to Americans and wheat embargoes during War of 1812, 1818.

——No. 343, p.#1222 ff. Capt. William Martin's report of trip to Lake Melville. Reports Canadians dominate salmon fishery and deal in furs with Innu, while cod fishery is mainly pursued by American firms "which have numerous summer stations on the islands." Supply of Labrador "settlements" remains a problem after the war due to confusing jurisdiction and laws. Concern about starvation, 1821.

——No. 354, p. 1232. Size and origin of cod and seal fishery on coast of Labrador, 1825.

——Vol. VIII, No. 370, p. 1251 ff. Gov. Palliser recounts atrocities committed by New England colonists and Newfoundlanders on Labrador Natives. Credits Lymburner as source of information, names perpetrators and their vessels, 1766.

——No. 392, p. 1269 ff. History of Jeremiah Coghlan of Fogo, including his dispatch of Charles Hellinss to Esquimaux Bay in 1776 or '77, and the story of John Peaton's [Peyton] maverick operation and involvement with William Phippard and John Nooks the year before they were abandoned in Esquimaux Bay, 1777.

——No. 433, p. 1317 ff. Account of the voyage of the Moravian missionaries and negotiation of treaty with Inuit, 1765

——No. 434, p. 1321. Order granting land to Moravians, 1769.

——No. 445, p. 1333. Reference to southern Inuit flocking to Moravians in north, 1771-3.

——No. 453, p. 1340. Moravian Mission manuscript from Canadian Archives, report from Nain in which Inuit refer to themselves as Carolit and the Innu as Adlat.

——No. 466, p.1354 ff. Extracts from *Moravian Periodical Accounts*, Nain, in which Inuit describe clan warfare and murders in Saglek and Killinek, 1790. Page 1355ff., Hopedale: statement of intent to convert "Red Indians" as well as Inuit, and of difficulties with both groups.

——No. 469, p. 1362. Gov. Palliser's orders to surrogates regarding treatment of servants at the Labrador stations, 1766.

——No. 470, p. 1364. Report of murders within Nicholas Darby's crew in 1766 and 1767, and possibly 1765.

——No. 485, p.#1380. More information on Philip Beard's problems with Nova Scotian firm of Coudert & Jennings, 1820.

——No. 1301, 3381-90. Statement, 25 August 1789, of Marcoux re. Plante vs. Marcoux.

——No. 1062, p. 2472 ff. Historical Sketch; Section I—Governmental and Commercial Relations with the Labrador Indians.

——No. 1276-7, p. 3277-3303. Application for concession in and Journal of voyage to Baye des Esquimaux by Sieur Louis Fornel.

——No. 1419-20, p. 3691-3715. Anonymous Memoire, 1715, Concerning Labrador, plus Supplement to, 1717.

Provincial Archives of Newfoundland and Labrador. "Slade & Co.: Fogo, Twillingate and Labrador," PANL, F.A. 67, MG 460 (unpublished paper).

——"Slade & Co. Records," PANL, MG 460 #23, 34, MG 244, Reel 1-3 (ledger books and microfilms).

Public Archives of Canada. "The humble petition of the Merchants, Planters and others residing in Esquimaux Bay on the Coast of Labrador..." [and ditto] "...residing in Sandwich Bay on the Coast of Labrador..." (16 September 1835), with correspondence between Gov. Prescott of NF and Lord Glenelg, 24 May 1836 and 29 June 1836 respectively. PAC MG11, CO 194/94, p. 333, 328 [see also Anick, p. 644].

Reichel, Levin T. "Labrador [Showing Settlement in the Central Coastal Region]", [from trips made by Br. Leo Elsner in 1857 and updated by Br. James O'Hara in 1870], 1872, facsimile map No. 135, ACMI facsimile map series, Ottawa: Association of Canadian Map Libraries and Archives, 1989 (map).

Rompkey, Ronald, ed. *Labrador Odyssey: The Journal and Photographs of Eliot Curwen on the Second Voyage of Wilfred Grenfell, 1893*. Montreal: McGill-Queens University Press, 1996 (book).

Saunders, Doris. *Alluring Labrador*. Them Days Inc., 1980 (book).

Schwartz, Fred. "Land Use in the Makkovik Region," *Our Footsteps Are Everywhere*, Labrador Inuit Association, 1977 (article).

Slade & Company's Battle Harbour Diary, 1831-32, in *Them Days Magazine*, 6.2,3,4. (articles)

Tanner, Väinö. *Outlines of the Geography, Life and Customs of Newfoundland-Labrador*. Acta Geographica 8, No. 1 & 2. Originally published by Oy. Tilgmann Ad., Helsinki. 1944. Translation published by Cambridge University Press, London, 1947 (book).

Taylor, J. Garth. "The Two Worlds of Mikak," Part I, *The Beaver*, Winter 1983: 4-13; Part II, *The Beaver*, Spring 1984: 18-25 (articles).

Thornton, Patricia. "The Democratic & Mercantile Bases of Initial Permanent Settlement in the Strait of Belle Isle." (1977), in Mannion, John J. *The Peopling of Newfoundland: Social and Economic Papers # 8*. Institute of Social and Economic Studies No. 8, Memorial University of Newfoundland, St. John's. 1977. Reprinted University of Toronto Press, 1986.

Turgeon, Laurier. "Chronological Refinement of Basque Whaling Stations in the Gulf and Estuary of the Saint-Lawrence from the 16th to the 18th Centuries," 1995 (unpublished paper).

Wadden, Marie. *Nitassinan, the Innu Struggle to Reclaim Their Homeland*. Vancouver/Toronto: Douglas and McIntyre, 1992 (book).

Williamson, Tony. *From Sina to Sikujaluk: Our Footprint*. Labrador Inuit Association, 1997 (published report).

Young, Arminius. *A Methodist Missionary in Labrador*. S. and A. Young, Toronto, 1916 (book).

Zimmerly, David. *Cain's Land Revisited: Cultural Change in Central Labrador, 1775-1972*. Institute of Social and Economic Research, Memorial University of Newfoundland. St. John's: Social and Economic Studies 16, 1975 (book).

INDEX & CONCORDANCE

italic pages are from narrative sections

354, 361
settlement, 314, 315-317, 319
HBC in, 311, 312, 316-319, 319-321, *326-342*
International Grenfell Assn. in, 323-324, 467
merchants, 26, 27, 32, 313, 315-317, *326-340*, 466n
occupations, 318, 320, *330-331, 333, 334, 335, 336, 337, 340-341*
Settlers, 314, 315, 316, 317, *351, 359-360*, 467n
social infrastructure and conditions, 318, 319-320, 321, 323, *336*, 467
social life and customs, 321, 323, *335-336, 337-338, 345-346, 363-364, 366-367*
Baikie family, 317, 321, 322, 323, *325, 349, 363, 365, 366, 367, 396, 425*, 449, 451
Baine Johnston and Company, 104, *114, 118*
Baker Lake, NWT, *271*
Baldwin, Br., *273*
Bally Hale, Ireland, 62
Banks, Sir Joseph, 138
Banque Union of Jersey (collapse of in 1873), 61, 140
Barbel, Marie-Anne (Mme. Louis Fornel), 27
Barber [Barbour] family, 62, *66, 67*
Barbour family (Inuit), *236, 237, 238, 239, 265, 392*
Barney family, 62, *66, 67, 74, 81, 88, 92, 93, 98, 99*
Barney, Stan, *424*
Bartlett, Capt. Bob, *82, 83, 289*
Bartlett, Capt. William, 257, 259, *289, 305*
Basques, 23, 24, 56, 138, 464n
Batteau, 32, *114, 119, 164, 423*
Batten, John, *129*
Battle Harbour, 27, 30, 31, 35, 36, 46, 58, *81*, 102, 103-104, 108, 109, 110, *112, 113*,

114, 115-120, 320, *336, 445*
Bay of Islands (Moravian Coast), 254
Bay of Islands, NF, *81*
Bay Roberts, NF, *115, 117, 303, 412*
Bayne & Brymer, 29
Bazil, Louis, 26
Beals family, *71*
Beard [Baird], Philip & Company, 31, 139, 140
Belben family, 62
Belbin family, *81*
Beliveau, Jean, 315
Bell family, 61, *66, 79*
Bell Island, NF, 62
Belle Isle, 58, 102
Benjamin family (Inuit), *233, 315*
Ben's Cove, 259, *292, 295, 296, 303*
Beothuk Indians, 22, 137, 249, *462*
Berries, *184-186, 191*
Best family, 58, 315, 316
Best, Robert (Emery & Best), 58, 59, 315
Big Bay [Jack Lane's Bay], 254, 255, 256, *280, 282, 283, 284, 286, 301*, 392, *429, 430, 431, 435*
Big Brook [Michael's River], *427*
Big Hill, *396*
Big Island (Atlantic Shore), *114*
Big Island (Hamilton Inlet), *348*
Big Island [Tunungayualuk], *278*
Big Lake, *416*
Big Neck, *308*
Bird family, *154, 160, 167, 169, 179*, 254, 316, *339, 424, 426*, 449
Bird, Joseph & Son [Thomas], 31, 59, 60, 62, 104, 254, 315, 316, 317
Birdseye, Clarence, *112, 113*, 142
Black Bear Bay, 105, *130*
Black Bird Bay, *126*
Black Head, *149, 165, 179*
Black Head Run, *149*
Black Island (Groswater Bay),

Little Bay, *286*
Little Lake, 312
Liverpool, England, 31, 259, *282*
Liveyers, 4, 40, 51, 55, 63, 104, 105, 106, 107-110, *154*
Livingston College, London, *286*
Lobstick Lake, 377, *396, 402, 405, 416*
Lockwood School, *132*
Loder, Millicent Blake, *173*
Lodge Bay, 104, 105
Logging and sawmilling, 44, 50, 108, 109, 137, 260, 262, 263, *340-341*, 450, 452
London, England, 48, *357*
Long Beach Point, *81*
Long Point (Straits), *71, 73*
Long Point (Sandwich Bay), *153*
Long Pond (Straits), *96*
Lookout Lake, *416*
Louie's Rapid (Grand River), *403*
Lowe family, *72*
Lower Island Cove, *305*
Lowlands (Lake Melville), *359, 425*
Lucas, Lieutenant Francis, 28, 30, 197
Lucy family, 253, *305, 306-308*, 314
Luddy's Brook, *148*
Lundberg, Br. & Sr. John Eugene, *285*
Luscombe family, 103
Lyall family, *229*, 257, 263, *274, 290, 295, 296, 305*, 317, *340, 359*, 449
Lymburner & Grant, 32, 57, 315
Lymburner, John & Adam, 32

–M–

MacCarthy, Father, *70*
MacDonald family, *160*
Macmillan, Cdr. Donald, 263, *284, 381, 392*
MacRae, R.D., *149, 154, 186, 187*
Magaruse [Marcuse?], 102
Mail & transport services, *70, 81, 88, 89, 92, 112, 141, 164, 227, 237, 239, 333, 336, 392, 474n*
Main Tickle, 136, *426, 440*

Makkovik, 32, 49, 50, 51, *123, 124, 125*, 142, 197, 202, 241, 249, 251, 252, 257, 258, 259, *292, 293, 294, 295, 296, 297-306, 307*, 315, *336, 387, 426, 427, 428, 430, 431, 432*
Makkovik Bay, *428*
Makkovik Bight, 258
Malta, *286*
Manak family, 253, *282, 284*, 449
Manetuasuk, *227*
Mangroves, Charlie, *116-118*
Manstock, Cyril, *89*
Maraval, 113
March, Bishop John, *71*
Marchand, Louis, 253
Marconi, *116, 119, 419*
Marcoux, Pierre, 31, 32, 63, 102, 252-253, 315
Marie Lake, *398*
Maritime Archaic Indian culture, 21, 57, 196, 472n
Markuse family, 253
Marsal, Sieur Antoine, 26, 29, 101, 105
Martin family (Sandwich Bay), ix, 103, *112, 130, 132, 160, 167, 176, 179, 188, 192, 211, 382, 414, 423, 426, 433, 445, 447*, 449
Martin family, Inuit, *212, 239, 240, 241, 242, 267, 277*
Martin, Bishop & Sr., *225, 231, 273*
Martle Pond, *127*
Mason, Capt. John (mapmaker), 56
Maunders of St. John's, *274*
McDonald family, 62, *71, 112, 147, 148, 153, 188*
McKenzie family, 317, *354*, 371
McKinney, Paster, *438*
McLean family, 317, *334, 340, 341, 402, 441*, 449
McNamara Construction Co., *420, 428, 430, 431, 432, 435*

Ungava Bay, 37, 38, 42, 43, 44, 45, 199, 249, 269, 312, 371
Ungava Peninsula, 317, 369
United States Air Force [USAF], *421,* 450
Unknown Lake. *See* Ossokmanuan Lake
Upatik, *269, 270, 382*
Upper Island Cove, *305*

–V–

Vallies Bight, *335, 341, 348, 427*
Venison Islands, 46
Venison Tickle, 104
Victoria Act (1851), 374
Viking(s), 21, 22, 135, 464n
Voisey family, 140, 256, 257, 261, 263, *267-269, 276, 339,* 449
Voisey's [Tasiujatsuak] Bay ["Emish"], 22, 202, 250, 256, 259, 260, 264, *267, 269, 275, 276,* 376, *388-389, 414, 416,* 453, 454, 455

–W–

Wage labour, 50, 51, 108, *164-165,* 321, 323, 375, *421-422*
Waghorne, Rev. Arthur C., 322
Wakefield, Dr., *271*
Waldmann, Br. S., *226*
Wales, Welsh, *151, 152,* 251, *300*
Walker, Johnny, *301*
Wallace, Dillon, 48, 378
Ward, Br. Arthur, *226*
Wars, European (effect on Labrador), 26, 30, 31, 32, 35, 59, 60, 61, *66,* 136, 139, 253, 315, 322, *350*
War of Independence, American, 31, 34
Waterford, Ireland, 31, 140
Watts family, *273, 327, 428*
Webb family, 258, 263, *270, 271*
Webbek Harbour, 51, 316
Webber family, *133, 419*
Weddings, 38, *70, 155-156, 301, 349,* 357-358, 366

Welfare/Dole/Relief, 44, 51, 52, *96, 115-120, 166,* 262, *265, 375, 386-387, 388,* 394
Wells, Ray, *121*
West Bay, *124,* 135, 136, *155,* 312, 316, 318, 319
West Country, England, 29, 31, 39, 40, 104
West St. Modeste, 26, 47, 63, *71, 88,* 394
Wester Island (Turnaviks), *305*
Western Bride, 439-441
Western Tickle, *158*
Weymouth, George, 23
White Bear Islands, *148*
White Bear River, 141, *168, 178, 179, 181, 183. 191, 192*
White family, 258, *278, 280,* 449
White Point, *120*
Whittle, John and "Sarah," 103, 314, 315, *351, 352, 365*
Wild Bight, *92*
Williams family, 136, *151, 155, 162, 169, 306,* 316, *395, 425, 426,* 449
Williamson, Tony, xii
Willihatus, *227*
Winters family, 104, *182, 183,* 268, 276, *292, 294, 306,* 449
Wolfrey family, 103, *292, 334, 337,* 449
Wolfrey's Cove, *346, 427*
Wolfrey's Point, *366*
Woman of Labrador, 323, 378
World War(s), 51, *117, 165,* 237, 247, 274, *280,* 328, *420, 421,* 430, 445
World's Fair, *306-307, 314, 357, 473n*
Wrixson, John, 32, 135, 136
Wunderstrands, 134

–X Y Z–

Yetman [Yeatman] family, 104, 449
Young, Rev. Arminius, 141, 319, *358*
Zoar, 256, *265, 274-278*

Table of Narrators